Acting on Words

S0-AZA-582

An Integrated Reader, Rhetoric, and Handbook

David Brundage *Athabasca University*

Michael Lahey *University of Alberta*

PEARSON

Prentice
Hall

Toronto

National Library of Canada Cataloguing in Publication

Brundage, David
   Acting on words : an integrated reader, rhetoric, and handbook /
David Brundage, Michael Lahey.

Includes index.
ISBN 0-13-120093-3

   1. College readers. 2. Exposition (Rhetoric) I. Lahey, Michael, 1954- II. Title.

PE1408.B78 2003   808'.0427   C2003-904611-7

Copyright © 2004 Pearson Education Canada Inc., Toronto, Ontario
All Rights Reserved. This publication is protected by copyright, and permission should be obtained
from the publisher prior to any prohibited reproduction, storage in a retrieval system, or transmission
in any form or by any means, electronic, mechanical, photocopying, recording, or likewise. For information regarding permission, write to the Permissions Department.

ISBN 0-13-120093-3

Vice-President, Editorial Director: Michael J. Young
Acquisitions Editor: Marianne Minaker
Marketing Manager: Toivo Pajo
Senior Developmental Editor: Martina Van de Velde
Production Editor: Charlotte Morrison-Reed
Copy Editor: Kathleen Richards
Production Coordinator: Patricia Ciardullo
Page Layout: Carolyn E. Sebestyen
Art Director: Mary Opper
Cover and Interior Design: Anthony Leung
Cover Image: Photonica

1 2 3 4 5   08 07 06 05 04

Printed and bound in Canada.

For Professors Faith Guildenhuys, Tom Henighan, Robert Lovejoy, Robin MacDonald and the entire English Faculty of Carleton University, 1969 to 1975. Their commitment to student-centred teaching predated the term.
David Brundage

For Rosemary and Catherine Lahey, "whose lights burn clear."
Michael Lahey

Brief Contents

Table of Contents

PART 2 THE RHETORIC 257

Preface

TO THE INSTRUCTOR

As teachers, we all know that students have many different learning styles. We also know that each of us has his or her own approach to teaching writing, in many cases tempered by years of practice. In one complete package, this book offers you the full support you need to enhance your personal approach to first-year composition. We have developed the readings, rhetorical instruction, and usage guidelines through careful consultation with a wide range of Canadian college and university instructors. Our aim is to provide engaging, clear, accurate, and complete information that serves rather than dictates your methods.

We have also designed the text as a resource to be explored from various angles. Some instructors might choose to begin with readings and summaries, others with oral presentations and personal writing, others with the basics of writing and grammar review, and still others with critical thinking and debate. Whatever the entry point and path you wish to follow, you will find frequent cross-references connecting you and your students to other relevant elements. This interconnected structure allows you to emphasize your selected sections with the support they need.

Our Instructor's Manual offers further useful support, in the form of classroom activities, recommended audio-visual supplements, summaries of reading selections, overhead transparency masters of step-by-step procedures, and suggested answers to exercises and activities. Our examples throughout the textbook are plentiful and sometimes surprising, while our ESL support is particularly thorough. A website specially dedicated to this text can be found at <www.pearsoned.ca/brundage/>. As well, the English 255 Introductory Composition website through Athabasca University, at <www.athabascau.ca/courses/engl/255/>, provides further resources and examples, under "Supplementary Resources." These two sites will be updated periodically with new student writing and peer editing as well as other support for your consideration.

In all parts of the text, we have tried to maintain a lively tone—both nurturing and challenging—while cultivating the reader's skills and awareness in developing sound writing and critical thinking. Our hopes will be fulfilled if you find this book helps you deliver some of your best teaching.

TO THE STUDENT

Over many years of working with student writers, we have found many who believe they cannot write well and who do not enjoy writing. Usually this obstructive belief dissolves as they realize that they *can* write well and, furthermore, that writing well can be very useful as well as fun.

In this book we try to help you prove to yourself—and to your instructors—that you *can* write well, and we try to make the experience as meaningful and as manageable as possible. For those of you who already enjoy and excel at writing, we offer detailed advice to help you stretch yourself further.

The ability to write and communicate effectively contributes a great deal to academic and all-round success. This book is based on years of guiding Canadian students to that fulfillment. If you perform your part—explore the practice activities, ask questions, look for answers, apply the various models and strategies presented for each type of writing—we assure you that the success of so many past students who have followed our methods will be yours as well.

Using Our Basic System

Each time you receive an essay assignment, select your topic and ask yourself "Why am I writing this essay?" The answer is not simply "Because my instructor wants it." The deeper question to answer is "What type of writing am I to practise in this assignment?" Am I being asked to communicate personally or more analytically? Am I being asked to explain something or to argue something? The answer to this question—which we could also phrase as "What is my purpose?"—links you automatically to established guidelines for the sort of writing that best serves that purpose. Always begin your response to any assignment by deciding what type of writing is needed, then going to the relevant reference guidelines in the *Rhetoric* and the appropriate prose models in the *Reader* that will help you structure that type of writing. It is as simple as that. We explain those prose guidelines and prose models clearly; we make them as easy to locate and apply as possible.

A second question you will want to answer is "Who is my audience?" A precise response to this question takes you immediately to examples of tone and style suitable for that selected group of readers. Again, we identify and illustrate a useful range of tones, along with the verbal and stylistic building blocks that construct those tones.

This book, then, is a repository of key rhetorical guidelines to be accessed *according to your own insight into what you need*. The table of contents represents your Help menu. To use it effectively, always remember to answer the two preliminary questions: "What is my purpose in this writing?" and "To whom am I writing?"

Both the *Reader* and the *Rhetoric* are organized to lead you quickly to the information and examples you need for your identified purpose and audience. Checklists of steps to a successful essay, summary, and research paper consolidate much of the advice onto single-page reminders. Another list, "Twelve Logical Fallacies" (also in Chapter 7, "Argumentation"), helps you to identify and solve basic errors of reasoning in your essays.

The *Reader*

You have probably heard that careful writers tend to be careful readers. This rule of thumb owes to the fact that you learn various approaches that serve your own writing needs from what you read. To inspire and guide your writing, we provide a variety of interesting short readings with comments, questions, and guidelines to help you gain those useful tools from every page. We have selected these readings with your interests in mind, and with care so that you can develop the range of skills you need to succeed in your academic and career challenges. We balance writing by academics and professionals throughout the *Reader* (and the *Rhetoric* that follows it) with writing by students like you. We set a standard that is challenging yet within reach!

The *Rhetoric*

The *Rhetoric* strives to discuss in detail every type of writing you are expected to produce at college or university. Fortunately, it is not intended as something you must consume from start to finish. Rather it is a set of definitions, tips, debates, and guidelines designed for informed reference. The primary meaning of the word "rhetoric" is simply "the art of language." Unfortunately it has taken on a secondary modern meaning as well, of empty, long-winded, self-serving prose. We use the word in its first sense, laying out steps in understanding and applying the art of language. Following these steps judiciously, you will find they help make your essay writing more efficient and more powerful.

The Research Paper

A major section of the *Rhetoric*, "The Research Paper" (Chapter 11), gives you the detailed step-by-step guidance you need to plan, research, and write effective papers that draw on a number of sources. We include advice on how to document sources using either MLA or APA styles. We also provide up-to-date tips and cautions regarding Internet research.

Oral Presentations

Research suggests that much more than half of today's important business communication is spoken. The rhetorical training you derive from this book in combination with your English course will serve you in various oral contexts. To help you to connect rhetorical guidelines to public speaking fully, we include a major section on oral presentations. Many of us fear these, so we acknowledge this concern and offer ways to overcome presentation anxiety. A learned facility in spoken presentations will contribute tremendously to your self-confidence in both your academic and career prospects. Please refer to our section on "Oral Presentations," Chapter 14.

The *Handbook*

We have developed our *Handbook* in simple, clear language to help you understand the main principles of grammar and to address common problems and frequently asked questions. We integrate all the parts of this text, so you will find the help you need with grammar, punctuation, and sentence structure presented clearly and consistently throughout. Our concentrated instruction in Section 3 of the *Handbook*, "Fifteen Common Errors" helps you and your instructor concentrate on a manageable number of problems. Take care of just these 15 potential problems, and you will be well on your way to correct, even professional, writing!

Extra Language Support

If English is not your first language, you may welcome the additional language support for eight of the selections in the *Reader*. See the Appendix to the *Reader*, "Language Support for Eight Selected Readings." For each of these readings, we offer pre-reading vocabulary, idioms and expressions, references, and language pointers particular to that reading. Though designed to lessen the confusions that English poses for second-language learners, this support should be useful to all readers.

For additional help with various aspects of English usage for second-language learners and support for seven other readings, see "If English Is Not Your First Language" and "Language Support for Selected Readings" under "Supplementary Resources" on the Athabasca University website for English 255 Introductory Composition <**www.athabascau.ca/courses/engl/255/**>. You may see the Pearson site for this same material and also for additional support for readings in this text at <**www.pearsoned.ca/brundage/**>.

ACKNOWLEDGMENTS

Many talented and dedicated people have contributed their time and efforts to *Acting on Words*. We would like to thank Professor Rebecca Cameron for parts of "The Research Paper" and "Directional Process"; Tasha Ausman for "Essays in Exams" and support sections on "Writing and Revising a Scientific Paper" and "Writing a Case Analysis"; Veronica Baig for all the ESL support elements both in the book and online; and Joyce Miller for "The Oral Presentation" and a supplementary support section online, "Writing a Film Review."

Lisa Cameron, Robbie Chernish, and the Athabasca University Centre for Language and Literature contributed significantly to our extensive searches for readings. Editor John Ollerenshaw, Athabasca University, reviewed Chapter 12, "Documentation." Reference librarians Ione Hooper of the University of Alberta and Pat Wauters of Lethbridge Public Library provided valuable assistance with research. Theresa Daniels, Shamim Datoo, Carolyn Preshing, and their administrative colleagues with the Department of English at the University of Alberta gave generously of their time in the preparation of the manuscript. Tasha Ausman tracked down a number of copyright holders. Joyce Miller worked extensively on permissions. Shari Mitchell contributed manuscript assistance. We wish to express our deepest thanks to all for these services.

In addition, we wish to thank Marian Allen, co-author of *Forms of Writing*, for having pioneered approaches and standards of great value to this book. Similar recognition is owing to writing course designer and coordinator John Thompson. We thank the fine tutorial staff of Athabasca University's English 255 Introductory Composition as well; their numerous suggestions have made a significant contribution. Peter Roccia, program chair in the MacEwan School of Communications, provided valuable strategies and direction at the outset. Kelly Torrance made this work possible with essential support and understanding in the formative stages. Aquisitions Editor Marianne Minaker enabled the next step to reality; she and the entire team at Pearson Education have been a pleasure to work with.

On a personal note, we thank the following instructors for their support, guidance, and inspiration, past and present: Professors Lynn Penrod and Mark Simpson of the University of Alberta; Professors Stanley Cowan, John Fraser, Bruce Greenfield, Ron Huebert, and Victoria Rosenberg of Dalhousie University; and Professors Ann J. Abadie, Donald Kartiganer, and Jay Watson of the Center for Southern Culture, University of Mississippi.

It will be clear from some of the readings in this text that we have been readers and admirers of *Reader's Choice* by Kim Flachman, Michael Flachman, and Alexandra MacLennan. Finally, we are greatly indebted to our many reviewers, who offered good advice and suggestions at various stages of the manuscript's development.

Part 1 THE READER

INTRODUCTION

THE READINGS in *Acting on Words* have been chosen to demonstrate different styles and methods of writing. Our selections pursue a wide range of evocative, expository, and persuasive aims and represent narrative, descriptive, analytical, and argumentative structures. The pieces range from personal and informal to academic and formal. The tone of Section 1, "Self and Other," is primarily exploratory and personal; that of Section 2, "Knowledge and Ideas," more formally analytical; and that of Section 3, "Tomorrow and Tomorrow," decidedly persuasive. While each section demonstrates a wide variety of related tones and strategies, the basic distinction between sections underscores our three featured writing categories: personal, exposition, and persuasion. If the essay you are working on is personal, study some selections from Section 1 of the *Reader* and find those with approaches that might be adapted to your purpose. Look at appropriate essays in Section 2 for ideas on how to structure expository or analytical essays, and look at Section 3 for examples of argumentation.

In our selection of readings, we have also attempted to reflect your potential interests as a post-secondary student. The first section of the *Reader* starts with topics or concerns of the self, then moves on to relations between the self and larger social identifications, such as family and nation. The second section deals with many of these same issues of self and relationship to society, but from a broader analytical perspective. This section addresses the world of formal knowledge and ideas. The third section, which again engages the same basic topics, invites you to ponder and debate these issues with an eye to the future, whether you see that future as dangerous or promising, apocalyptic or utopian.

Introductions to the three sections help to provide context and focus for the specific topics represented. In addition, each reading has a short introduction providing background on its author, audience, and subject. At the end of each selection, a brief list of sources, "For Further Reading," suggests specific articles, books, websites, or other information related to the subject. Questions are also provided in "For Further Thinking," to stimulate discussion and writing. These questions serve a number of

purposes: they help you focus on important ideas in the reading, they invite critical response to methods and strategies, and they suggest types of research to consider in order to examine the topic more deeply. Finally, after each reading, questions called "Looking Back and Ahead" suggest links to other sections of the *Reader* and to your interests and activities.

The selections in the *Reader* represent a wide range of authors: poets and short-story writers as well as scholars, journalists, and essayists. A generous number are student writers offering experiences, styles, and approaches that may parallel your own. Numerous professional authors, including many Canadians of varied regions and heritages, also offer their perspectives on issues of importance to today's society. A strong sampling of scholarly writers is included, as are well-known incisive thinkers, such as Margaret Atwood, Mordecai Richler, and Pierre Trudeau. Classic authors have been remembered, too, illustrating some of the fine writing expertise from which subsequent generations have drawn. Within this collection of different voices, we believe you will find much to admire, question, emulate, and rebut.

To help you benefit from these selections to the fullest, read Chapter 8, "The Summary," in the *Rhetoric*. This chapter describes the importance of active reading, with detailed guidance in how to write a summary. You will probably be asked to write at least one summary as part of your writing assignments, but it is also a good idea to write a brief summary of any selection that particularly interests you or that has been selected for class discussion. Check with your instructor and classmates to see how successfully you are capturing the main intents, strategies, and ideas of the different selections. One of the best ways to become a stronger reader and thinker is to learn how to write a successful summary. For help with reading the short stories, see the section on literary analysis in the *Rhetoric*.

If writing may be likened to breathing out, then reading is breathing in. All good writers realize it is not possible to do one without the other. We hope our selections help to make reading as valuable as it can be, by claiming your personal interest as well as furthering your personal, academic, and civic growth.

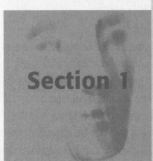

THE
READER

Section 1 Self and Other

According to Johnny Moses, a Nootka storyteller raised on the west coast of Vancouver Island, when people ask why there is no word for *I* or *me* in his language, he tells them that the grandmothers say it's "because the ego is so big it doesn't need a name." The word *ego*, for *self*, was made famous through the writings of Austrian psychologist Sigmund Freud (1856–1939). Freud characterized the ego as that part of the self which moderates between the sometimes unruly, disruptive forces of self-interest—the id—and those of broader social awareness and even repressive self-censure—the superego. In this section of the *Reader*, we present selections that explore the personal sense of self in relation to others: both other individuals and larger group identifications. Under this broad topic, our selections deal with relationships to landscape and place; to appearance, physical and sexual identity; to friends, lovers, and family; to community and region; and to history, culture, and nation.

Most of us have at least one location that we experience as private and special. In many cases, we may have had a special place tracing back to childhood, a place rich in nurturing associations and private reflection. Much of who we are today could be uncovered and understood in our feelings for that childhood refuge, the early sense of space. In her essay "White Breast Flats," Peigan author Emma Lee Warrior describes a number of such places in her own life, all bound within the community where she grew up. Like Pierre Trudeau in his essay "The Ascetic in a Canoe," Warrior speaks from a strong first person perspective and explores an individual closeness to nature. Unlike Trudeau, however, she focuses on evoking her subject rather than on building an explicit argument about it. After you have read Warrior's essay, the "Looking Back and Ahead" section invites you to read Trudeau's. The comparison will likely invite specific questions on how and why "White Breast Flats" impresses an audience as fundamentally evocative rather than as argumentative. Perhaps this comparison will also point out that, in its own way, evocation, too, is persuasive; that is, it offers the implicit statement of a defined self, persuading us of the reality of the author's topic, concern, and point of view or thesis. (You may wish to review Chapter 3, "Thesis Statements" in the *Rhetoric*, as well as Chapter 5, "The Personal Essay.")

How we appear to ourselves and to others is surely an issue of intense concern. In Section 1, several essays offering different perspectives on the matter of personal appearance raise a number of questions. Are the issues different for males or females? How do culture and generation shape the self? Through the concern with identity and self-presentation, the selections in this part of the *Reader* introduce broad questions of one's sex, race, and class. From a rhetorical standpoint, you may wish to consider how these essays, though essentially personal like Warrior's, use other rhetorical organizations as well to pursue their main concerns.

Appearance and personal identity lead to our next main focus in Section 1, family and generations. What sets generations apart? What holds them together? How many shapes are there for the family unit? Through a variety of evocative, implicit, personal approaches, selections in this part of the *Reader* raise these sorts of questions and invite considered responses. Finally, "Self and Other" presents personal expressions of national or broader civic identification. In contrast to selections in Section 3 of the *Reader*, which offer formally developed definitions and arguments on topics of nationhood, the selections in Section 1 are presented more as seeds than as wholly elaborated statements of belief.

In many ways the essays in Section 1, from sense of personal place to sense of nationhood, all connect to the process of keeping a journal that we address in the first part of the *Rhetoric*. In college or university, you will likely be expected to produce analytical and persuasive writing typical of Section 2 and Section 3 of the *Reader* rather than the type of writing featured in Section 1. However, keeping a journal will develop your skills to write on topics from a personal standpoint before developing a more formal and academic tone and rhetorical approach. You may also wish to consider that, as a lifelong communicator, you will encounter personal moments apart from formal studies, civic and business activities, when you wish to employ a strong form of evocation. We think you will find that the essays in this section provide excellent and enjoyable models of personal reflection and response.

Philip Kevin Paul A Wsa'nec' Indian (b. 1971), Paul received a degree in writing and English from Camosun College and the University of Victoria. He has written a report for the Institute of Ocean Sciences on correlations between place names in Saanich, British Columbia, and scientific research. He says that writing is not central in his life, but he uses it to express what *is* central.[1]

---

[1] Daniel David Moses, and Terry Goldie, eds., *An Anthology of Canadian Native Literature in English*, 2nd ed. (Toronto: Oxford University Press, 1998) 514.

Belly Button

My mother was careful
about what she ate
when it was my turn

inside her. It was already me
5   well before she had problems
getting up out of chairs.
Already me before I had elbows
to poke her with,
her hand on her tight skin
10   waiting for my next move.

It was my presence in her,
my nearly unstoppable growing,
that made her breasts tender,
her tailbone sore,
15   made her hungry
and ill. So many times

she has spelled out the odds
I was up against.
Her joke about my arrival,
20   the pill in my tiny fist.

When I was old enough to be
curious, I asked her
about the small round hole in my tummy.

She said, *That's your belly button,*
25   *it used to be your mouth.*

Emma Lee Warrior Emma Lee Warrior (b. 1941) grew up on the Peigan Reserve in southern Alberta, where she attended a boarding school with rules and restrictions she found oppressive. In *An Anthology of Canadian Native Literature*, edited by Daniel David Moses and Terry Goldie, she comments that this repression spurred her toward writing. Warrior has published stories and poems in a number of journals, including *Canadian Fiction Magazine*. One of her best-known stories, "Compatriots," looks ironically at the desire of some White people to immerse themselves in romantic notions of Aboriginal life.

Warrior obtained a Master of Arts degree from the University of Washington, and although she has continued to live in the state of Washington, she remains closely connected to her home community: "[t]hat landscape is within me." The following personal essay demonstrates the depth of that connection. "White Breast Flats" was first published in *A Gathering of Spirit: Writing and Art by North American Indian Women*, edited by Beth Brant (Sinister Wisdom Books, 1984; reprint Ann Arbor, MI: Firebrand Books, 2001).

For more support regarding English as a Second Language, visit the website for Athabasca University's English 255 Introductory Composition course at <www.athabascau.ca/courses/engl/255/>. See "If English Is Not Your First Language" and "Language Support for Selected Readings."

White Breast Flats

1   As one grows older, and the past recedes swiftly as a bird, wings extended in the wind, there are people and places whose contours, caught through the clouds of memory, take on the dimensions of myth. For me, one such place is White Breast Flats on the Peigan Reserve in southwest Alberta where the plains give way to the foothills, the Rockies loom near, and the great obelisk Chief Mountain stands powerfully at the entrance to northern Montana. White Breast Flats is a name known only to a few. My grandfather, Otohkostskaksin (Yellow Dust), was the one who told me that name, and recently, when I read the name in a book, I felt a special joy. Seeing it in print, so many years and miles later, seemed to establish the place as fact, and it opened again for me the pages of that precious time in my past.

2   White Breast Flats was occupied solely by my grandparents, and on occasion by my mother. It was located on the first bottomland north of the Old Man River on the west end of the reserve, and the land that rose behind it—the valley wall I suppose you could call it—reached its highest point there, a half-mile from bottom to top, two miles in span. That valley wall was laced with a maze of foot-trails, and there were bushes aplenty of saskatoon, whiteberries, gooseberries, chokecherries, and bullberries. There were also wild turnips and cactus berries there. All of these berries gave nourishment to my sister, to my brother, and to me as we played or just wandered through.

3   The bottomland stretched from the base of the hill towards the river for a mile and a half at its farthest point and a quarter of a mile at its closest. The one-roomed log house my grandparents lived in was situated about a half a mile from the hill and about two hundred feet from the river. The Old Man has probably eaten away the spot where the house stood, for the bank crept a little closer each year. The trees were

of several varieties, but other than the willows, cottonwoods, chokecherry, saskatoon, and pussywillows, I am still unable to name the trees that made up the forest. Where there were no trees, the grasses grew wild and rampant, and I can still see fields of yellow and white sweet clover and the ever-present and venomous purple thistles which stabbed at us with their thorns every chance they got.

4   We were brought up to fear bears; and although I never saw a bear while I was growing up, I was always on the lookout for the one which I was sure was waiting for me to relax my guard. The most fearsome thing I ever saw was a snake. I was afraid of water; and the river bank we clambered down to reach the green, swirling currents was dotted with holes which I thought were the homes of deadly and poisonous snakes. My sisters were both strong swimmers and enjoyed swimming across the river, but I would churn inwardly with fear as I watched them splash and drift away, bantering and yelling with abandon. And there I would be, standing first on one dirt-caked rock with a dried-up water spider stuck to it, and moving to another, sometimes walking in the water up to my knees very cautiously and carefully, for the rocks were slippery. Sometimes a fish would awake and swim off suddenly, making my heart jump and my throat constrict with a scream I held in. The river was a malevolent thing to me, never friendly. I watched warily for the mythical water-being which I was convinced lived somewhere in the greenest, deepest part. It had to. Otherwise, where did all the foam come from which flecked the river's surface; it had to be the water-being's spittle.

5   One particular day, I was standing on the river's edge again, watching my two sisters, whom I resented and admired for their fearlessness, when I slipped and fell into the water. It was in the evening and the sun's last rays had turned the river into a golden, glinting, and somehow not so perilous place. I imagined that the water below the surface where the water-being lived was illuminated. In a matter of minutes the warmth of the day was exchanged for the coolness of the evening. My skin was prickled with goosebumps from the chill, and I decided to put on my cotton dress until the two mermaids left the water. I picked up my dress and almost died with fright! A big snake slithered out of my dress. I screamed, and my mother, who had been washing and rinsing clothes some distance away, came running, and I got to ride her piggyback all the way home. I even had her throw my dress in the river, something I always remember, for we were very poor and could ill afford to throw clothing away.

6   There were plants that my grandmother would collect for her medicinal and everyday purposes. She would hang mint to dry in bunches from a line tied across the length of the room, close to the ceiling. I loved the smell of it, and although I didn't care for mint tea then, I do now. It's not only the taste that I enjoy; it's the remembering of moments of my childhood. Every so often I happen upon a cup of wild mint tea, and the bitterness of it, if the tea is made too strong, brings me back to my mother's house when I was probably five or six years old and deathly ill—or so I remember, because my grandmother was summoned. She was a medicine woman and had in her possession all kinds of herbs and

roots with which she brought back to health anyone who was ailing. She came into the house on a cold, winter day, bundled up with shawls and blankets. The snowy wind whipped the log house until chinks of the limestone plaster were peeled off and swept away in the storm. My mother kept plugging up the cracks with rags to keep the snow from being blasted inside. The wet snow that stuck to my grandmother's wraps hissed as it hit the stove. She carried a flour sack, and from this she took out a bag that was made from fawn hide, spotted and with the little hooves on it. Inside the bag she had wrapped still other small bundles, and she took out something greasy and rubbed it on my chest. On top of that she placed a layer of dried leaves. Ritually she spat on these, and covered the leaves with a hot cloth. She gave me a drink of an awful-tasting brew, and I wouldn't have drunk it if she hadn't been the one to give it to me. She then chanted holy songs, her voice a little frail and weak at first but gaining strength and fullness until the sound was a soothing prayer. She had a sacred rattle made from rawhide and painted with red ochre; this she shook in time with the cadence of her voice. She closed her eyes as she sang, and as I watched her I saw that she had painted her face with the red ochre, and the hair that framed her face was tinted with it. After her song, she prayed that my health be restored and I be blessed with a long and happy life. From the little buckskin bag rubbed with the sacred red ochre, she took some paint that had the consistency of uncooked pastry but which became oily when rubbed in her hand. This she rubbed on my face and then she left, leaving some brew and plants for my mother to administer to me. She also left an orange in plain sight that I could have when I was well enough. Oranges during the Second World War were rare, and not seen unless at a feast.

7   Sometimes I can detect the smell of sweetgrass when there is none around. I've grown to know that it is only my grandparents coming to visit me. Sweetgrass—an appropriate name for a special plant. Sweetgrass is the incense the old Indians used to honor the Creator, and the burning of it was a daily occurrence in my grandparents' home. Each morning my grandfather would get up and make the fire in the stove and as soon as the warmth made getting up comfortable, my grandmother would rise and they would pray together. He would burn incense to greet the Creator, to give thanks for life and health of family and friends, and to ask for guidance in living the day, as well as for help in some special need. Then they shared a song between them and a smoke on their pipe from chunk tobacco.

8   A quarter of a mile east of the house and just where the woods began was a spring. This was where my grandfather got our drinking water. He used a wooden stoneboat to haul it. The stoneboat was constructed of two logs at the bottom; they were the runners, smooth and heavy. On top of them were wide planks of board, bolted onto the logs. The planks were so old, I used to sit and scratch them with my fingernails and a papery, powdery substance would come off the wood. Grandfather would hitch up the team, and we children tagged along, jumping on and off the stoneboat with our dogs barking happily behind us until we reached the spring. He tied the team to a tree above the spring and carried two pails to

bring water back to the old metal-girded wooden barrel. He would make twenty or thirty trips until the barrel was full, and then he would put a canvas cover over it and tie the cover on with a rope. Once the water was brought home, my grandmother would have a drink of it first, then set about to making a pot of tea.

9   A slow-moving stream which leaked off the river and eased by the spring was a refrigerator for butter, meat, and the seasonal garden vegetables. The vegetables came from my grandfather's garden at the base of the hill. Everything grew in abundance there: carrots, rhubarb, turnips, onion, radishes, lettuce, potatoes, and sugarbeets. It was neat and ordered, with its straight rows and well-tended mounds of earth. It was fascinating to watch the steam rising from the garden after my grandfather watered it or after a rainfall or shower. I thought a mysterious creature, perhaps a cousin of the water-being, inhabited the earth, and the steam was its breath just as the flecks of foam in the river were the water-being's spittle. I never hung around the garden alone.

10   The stream that adjoined the spring was the home of a thousand minnows. We would catch some in a jar and take them home, and although we fed them flies and bread, they always died. Long-legged water spiders glided silently around the stream and the little frogs of grey, green, or brown jumped noiselessly, even when they landed in the water. Only our big, clumsy dogs would ruin the silent stream with their panting, lolling tongues as they splashed in, sitting right in the water to have a drink. Then they would shake their wet bodies mightily until it seemed as though it was raining. Our shouts of anger and surprise would usually result in their jumping on us with friendly licks and muddy paws. Surprisingly, of all the dogs we had (it seemed they were all shaggy) the only one I remember is Pete. Pete, the short-haired hound with long legs, a tail like a whip, and shiny ears, one of which would sometimes get stuck inside out or underside up, was blacker than the deepest badger-hole we dared peep into, and he had white, laughing teeth and a rosy, wet tongue.

11   There was a faded, creaking ghost house on top of the hill. It had two stories and no windows or doors, just openings from which whitemen ghosts watched passersby. It used to belong to a white man I knew only as Inopikini, which means Long Nose. We would go to the ghost house in broad daylight, always in the protective company of my mother and grandmother. The wind was always blowing through the house, flapping wallpaper, rattling floorboards, shingles, and window-casings. It was a wonderful, mysterious, scary place to go poking around in. It had lots of rooms, small ones and big ones. There were old curly shoes, clothing of all kinds, pieces of furniture, bits of toys, stray dishes, cracked cups without handles, and faded pictures still in their frames. We never took anything, because then Inopikini would haunt us until we returned what we had taken, or else, if he was a real mean ghost, he would twist our faces.

12   There was a trapdoor in one room which we never dared to open because we were sure something stayed down there, but we would stomp across it, each one stomping harder than the last but always with mother or grandmother in the

room. After we verbally challenged the ghosts who had the guts to come out and meet us face to face, we would climax our visit by scaring only ourselves and stampede off in hysterical screams, our bodies prickling and our eyes wild with fear, not daring to look back lest we see Inopikini hot on our trail.

13   I always expected to see a tall, emaciated man with hair all over his skin and blood around his nostrils and perhaps little horns growing out of his head. He was always garbed, in my imagination, in the cracked, curly boots he left in his house and his body covered with the rags scattered about through the rooms.

14   Summer reminds me of my grandmother mashing cherries in her tipi, which was erected as soon as it was warm enough to sleep outside. My old grandmother used to herd us up the hill to dig for turnips and pick berries for some upcoming feast, but those were the times we wished berries didn't grow. It was always a hot day when we yearned to be down by the spring and we quarreled amongst ourselves and sneaked away.

15   On hot summer days when I wearied of playing or had nothing to do, I would go ask my grandmother to check my head because it was itchy. She would put aside whatever she was doing and check my head, all the while telling me stories until I fell asleep. Sometimes when I didn't fall asleep soon enough for her, she would tell me to erase a cloud by rubbing my hands together and concentrating on that cloud. I demolished many a cloud. My grandmother was a tireless old woman who never rested. She was always busy beading, fixing deerskins, fixing berries (drying, mashing, sorting), repairing clothing, cooking, sweeping, washing clothes and minding us kids. She would gather wood on a big piece of canvas and carry it home on her back or drag it behind her. Then she would sit at the woodpile and chop wood with her hatchet, which she also used for butchering the deer my grandfather killed.

16   I haven't been to White Breast Flats for a long time now, too long. The log house and outer buildings have long been dismantled and carried away for firewood, and the paths and roads are overcome by weeds. Only the descendants of the magpies, gophers, rabbits, and frogs have reclaimed their ancestral grounds. Perhaps a rusted wagon-wheel or a skeletal hay-mower tells a hanging eagle that people once lived here. White Breast Flats will not happen again; it only lives in the longings and hearts of Ippisuwahs, Piiksi Kiipipi Pahtskikaikana, and Itsinakaki, the grandchildren whose voices once rang clear and echoed through its secret places.

For Further Thinking

1. Personal writing tends to follow a more spontaneous, casual, and informal structure than academic writing. Can you discern a clear pattern to the structure of "White Breast Flats"?

2. Is Warrior's pattern of organization suited to her meaning? Explain.

3. Explain whether this essay is more fundamentally narrative, descriptive, or reflective. These three terms are defined in Chapter 5 of the *Rhetoric*.

4. Describe the tone or tones of this essay. What meanings do these suggest?

Looking Back and Ahead

1. As a memoir, Warrior's essay has strong connections to five other selections in this section of the *Reader*: "Brownie," "Franken-Frogs and the Mushroom Bear," "The King and I," "The Hockey Sweater," and "A Midwife in Rankin Inlet." After reading all of these, describe what you consider the central qualities of this form of writing.

2. As non-fiction, "White Breast Flats" nevertheless shares characteristics with fiction. What elements does it have in common with the two short stories in this section, "The Summer My Grandmother Was Supposed to Die" and "Thanks for the Ride"?

3. Compare and contrast the portraits of grandmothers in "White Breast Flats," "The Summer My Grandmother Was Supposed to Die," and "Thanks for the Ride." What reasons might you give for the notable differences?

4. Read "The Ascetic in a Canoe" by Pierre Elliott Trudeau in Section 3 of this *Reader*. What similarities and differences do you find between his attitude to nature and that of Warrior in "White Breast Flats"? What rhetorical differences occur in the two essays?

5. Contrast the different approaches to describing a Native community used by Emma Lee Warrior in "White Breast Flats" and Gisela Becker in "A Midwife in Rankin Inlet." Do you feel both writers have made good choices? Explain.

For Further Reading

"Aboriginal Issues." Department of English, Carleton University. April 2003 <http://schoolnet2.carleton.ca/english/ext/aboriginal/issues/lit-imag.html>. This site offers activities, resources, and issues related to the major figures of Native oral literature—characters such as Coyote, Glooscap, and Nanabush.

American Native Press Archives. April 2003 <http://www.anpa.ualr.edu>. This is one of the world's largest repositories of Native thought.

Johnson, Alexandra. *Leaving a Trace: On Keeping a Journal: The Art of Transforming a Life into Stories*. Boston: Little, Brown and Co., 2001.

————. *The Hidden Writer: Diaries and the Creative Life*. New York: Doubleday, 1997. Her writing has appeared in *The New Yorker*, the *New York Times Book Review*, and *The Nation*, among other American publications. She teaches the memoir at Wellesley College and the Harvard Extension School.

King, Thomas, ed. *All My Relations: An Anthology of Contemporary Canadian Native Fiction*. Toronto: McClelland & Stewart, 1990. The introduction, by Cherokee author Thomas King, surveys a wide range of different writing by Native authors and considers the difficulties of defining this body of literature.

Moses, Daniel David, and Terry Goldie, eds. *An Anthology of Canadian Native Literature in English*. 2nd ed. Toronto: Oxford University Press, 1998. The editors have assembled an impressive range of authors and genres. "Compatriots" by Emma Lee Warrior is available in this collection.

Roger Fouts This brief memoir describes how Fouts' pet dog sacrificed her life to save his brother. Fouts went on to earn a Ph.D. and to perform groundbreaking research into communication with chimpanzees. Continuing Jane Goodall's resistance to the traditional approach, which views animals as completely detached from humans, Fouts developed a 30-year friendship with Washoe, the chimp at the heart of his book *Next of Kin*. In that book, Fouts chooses first-person voice, in keeping with his belief that animal research must embrace a personal aspect. His approach invites debate concerning the decision to communicate scientific research and analysis in a popular, personal style. "Brownie" has been excerpted from *Next of Kin*.

Brownie

1 My closest animal companion was our dog, Brownie. Feisty and fiercely loyal, Brownie was a fixture of our household. She needed us and we needed her. In addition to guarding the house, she baby-sat the youngest kids in the fields during the harvest season.

2 One day I saw Brownie do something that shaped my view of animals forever. She saved my brother's life. It happened during cucumber-picking season when I was four years old. The whole family—my parents, six brothers, and one sister—had been out in the field all day working. Brownie had been watching over me and my nine-year-old brother, Ed, whenever he got tired of picking. By the time the sun was going down our Chevy flatbed was piled high with boxes of cucumbers. It was time to head home for dinner. Ed wanted to ride back on our older brother's bicycle, a big thing that he could barely control. My parents said OK and Ed headed out on the bike, chaperoned by Brownie. Twenty minutes later, the rest of us clambered onto the truck and left the field with my twenty-year-old brother, Bob, driving.

3 It was the dry season, six months or so since the last rain, and the dirt road was blanketed with four or five inches of chalky dust. As the truck drove along the well-worn tire ruts in the road, it kicked up a huge cloud of dust that covered us on all sides, making it impossible to see more than two feet ahead or behind. After going along for a while, we suddenly heard Brownie barking very loudly and very persistently. We looked down and we could just make her out next to the front fender. She was sniping at the right front tire. This was very strange behavior. Brownie had come to the fields hundreds of times and had never once barked at the truck. But now she was practically attacking it. My brother Bob thought this was odd but didn't give Brownie much thought as he plowed ahead even as her barking became more frenzied. Then, without further warning, Brownie dove in front of the truck's front tire. I heard her shriek, and I felt a thump as we drove over her body. Bob hit the brakes, and we all got out. Brownie was dead. And right there in front of the truck, not ten feet away, was Ed, stuck on his bike in the deep tire rut, unable to escape. Another two seconds and we would have run him down.

4 Brownie's death was devastating to all of us. I had seen animals die before, but this one was my nearest and dearest friend. My parents tried to explain that

Brownie had only done what either of them would have done for us. No one doubted for a second that Brownie had sacrificed her own life to save my brother's. She saw a dangerous situation unfolding, and she did what she had to do to protect the boy she had been baby-sitting for so many years. Had she not acted, the course of our family's life would have been very different.

For Further Thinking

1. "No one doubted for a second that Brownie had sacrificed her own life to save my brother's." Is this view of a dog's behaviour consistent with your own experiences and observations?

2. By telling this personal story in a book on chimpanzee behaviour, Fouts signals his personal relationship to his work. Do you feel this personal writing style in an academic work compromises the author's objectivity? Why or why not?

3. Is this memoir fundamentally narrative, descriptive, or reflective? These terms are described in Chapter 5 of the *Rhetoric*.

4. Review our discussion of thesis statements in Chapter 3 of the *Rhetoric*. Do you feel this personal essay has an explicit or implicit thesis statement? Explain.

Looking Back and Ahead

1. As a memoir, Fouts's essay has strong connections to five other selections in this section: "White Breast Flats," "Franken-Frogs and the Mushroom Bear," "The King and I," "The Hockey Sweater," and "A Midwife in Rankin Inlet." If you have not already done so, describe what you consider the central qualities of this form of writing.

2. Read John Markoff's "The Doomsday Machines" (p. 135). Do you think Roger Fouts would take some of the concerns in this article seriously?

3. Read Brenda Platt's "Global Warming and Population" (p. 113). In that essay, Platt uses the detached style Fouts has chosen not to use in his book on Washoe the chimpanzee. Is it an oversimplification to suggest that more use of the personal style in scientific writing might help guard against the dangers described in "The Doomsday Machines"?

For Further Reading

Burns, Bill. *Raising Susan: A Man, a Woman, and a Golden Eagle*. Toronto: Stoddart, 1999. Bill Burns is a creative writing teacher and publisher of the poetry journal *Quarter Moon Quarterly*. A native of Winnipeg, he spent 17 years as an editor at the CBC. He now lives in Cloverdale, B.C.

Goodall, Jane. *Through a Window: My Thirty Years with the Chimpanzees of Gombe*. Boston: Houghton Mifflin, 1990, especially pages 14–15. Goodall describes how, in 1960, it was "not permissible . . . to talk about an animal's mind." She discusses the effects this belief had on language.

Johnson, Alexandra. *Leaving a Trace: On Keeping a Journal: The Art of Transforming a Life into Stories*. Boston: Little, Brown and Co., 2001.

————. *The Hidden Writer: Diaries and the Creative Life*. New York: Doubleday, 1997.

Pifer, Linda, Kinya Shimizu, and Ralph Pifer. "Public Attitudes toward Animal Research: Some International Comparisons." Chicago Academy of Sciences, Sauk Valley Community College. April 2003 <http://www.psyeta.org/sa/sa2.2/pifer.html>.

Randour, Mary Lou. *Animal Grace: Entering a Spiritual Relationship with Our Fellow Creatures*. Novato, CA: New World Library, 2000. Program director of Psychologists for the Ethical Treatment of Animals (PSYETA), Randour builds on Gary Kowalski's *The Souls of Animals* and Susan McElroy's *Animals as Teachers and Healers*.

Sheldrake, Rupert. *Dogs That Know When Their Owners Are Coming Home and Other Unexplained Powers of Animals*. New York: Three Rivers Press, 1999. Sheldrake, an ethologist, offers numerous case examples suggesting that animals use unexplained psychic abilities to enable their bonds with humans.

Mordecai Richler Born and bred in a Montreal Jewish "ghetto," Mordecai Richler is widely considered that rarest of Canadian novelists, the satirist. Satire uses irony (representing or stating the opposite of what the author truly believes) to attack aspects of human nature and behaviour. For example, *The Apprenticeship of Duddy Kravitz* (1959) portrays a young man so obsessed with owning land that he makes greater and greater moral compromises, even to the point of marketing a deadly pharmaceutical.

Having rejected the conventional side of his religious background, Richler incensed members of the Jewish community through his unflattering portraits of Jewish characters. He also enraged many Quebec nationalists through repeated attacks on a perceived racist bias in their history and current ideology. What many of Richler's "victims" fail to realize is that his ultimate target is not any one group but rather the whole of contemporary North American society.

For more support regarding English as a Second Language, visit the website for Athabasca University's ESL Writing Skills program at <www.athabascau.ca/courses/engl/255/>. See "If English Is Not Your First Language" and "Language Support for Selected Readings."

The Summer My Grandmother Was Supposed to Die

1 Dr. Katzman discovered the gangrene on one of his monthly visits. "She won't last a month," he said.

2 He said the same the second month, the third and the fourth, and now she lay dying in the heat of the back bedroom.

3 "God in heaven," my mother said, "what's she holding on for?"

4 The summer my grandmother was supposed to die we did not chip in with the Greenbaums to take a cottage in the Laurentians. My grandmother, already bedridden for seven years, could not be moved again. The doctor came twice a week. The only thing was to stay in the city and wait for her to die or, as my mother

said, pass away. It was a hot summer, her bedroom was just behind the kitchen, and when we sat down to eat we could smell her. The dressings on my grandmother's left leg had to be changed several times a day and, according to Dr. Katzman, any day might be her last in this world. "It's in the hands of the Almighty," he said.

5   "It won't be long now," my father said, "and she'll be better off, if you know what I mean?"

6   A nurse came every day from the Royal Victorian Order. She arrived punctually at noon and at five to twelve I'd join the rest of the boys under the outside staircase to peek up her dress as she climbed to our second-storey flat. Miss Bailey favoured absolutely beguiling pink panties, edged with lace, and that was better than waiting under the stairs for Cousin Bessie, for instance, who wore enormous cotton bloomers, rain or shine.

7   I was sent out to play as often as possible, because my mother felt it was not good for me to see somebody dying. Usually, I would just roam the scorched streets. There was Duddy, Gas sometimes, Hershey, Stan, Arty and me.

8   "Before your grandmaw kicks off," Duddy said, "she's going to roll her eyes and gurgle. That's what they call the death-rattle."

9   "Aw, you know everything. *Putz*."

10   "I read it, you jerk," Duddy said, whacking me one, "in Perry Mason."

11   Home again I would usually find my mother sour and spent. Sometimes she wept.

12   "She's dying by inches," she said to my father one stifling night, "and none of them ever come to see her. Oh, such children," she added, going on to curse them vehemently in Yiddish.

13   "They're not behaving right. It's certainly not according to Hoyle," my father said.

14   Dr. Katzman continued to be astonished. "It must be will-power alone that keeps her going," he said. "That, and your excellent care."

15   "It's not my mother any more in the back room, Doctor. It's an animal. I want her to die."

16   "Hush. You don't mean it. You're tired." Dr. Katzman dug into his black bag and produced pills for her to take. "Your wife's a remarkable woman," he told my father.

17   "You don't so say," my father replied, embarrassed.

18   "A born nurse."

19   My sister and I used to lie awake talking about our grandmother. "After she dies," I said, "her hair will go on growing for another twenty-four hours."

20   "Says who?"

21   "Duddy Kravitz. Do you think Uncle Lou will come from New York for the funeral?"

22   "I suppose so."

23   "Boy, that means another fiver for me. Even more for you."

24   "You shouldn't say things like that or her ghost will come back to haunt you."

25   "Well, I'll be able to go to her funeral anyway. I'm not too young any more."

26   I was only six years old when my grandfather died, and so I wasn't allowed to go to his funeral.

27   I have one imperishable memory of my grandfather. Once he called me into his study, set me down on his lap, and made a drawing of a horse for me. On the horse he drew a rider. While I watched and giggled he gave the rider a beard and the fur-trimmed round hat of a rabbi, a *straimel*, just like he wore.

28   My grandfather had been a Zaddik, one of the Righteous, and I've been assured that to study Talmud with him had been an illuminating experience. I wasn't allowed to go to his funeral, but years later I was shown the telegrams of condolence that had come from Eire and Poland and even Japan. My grandfather had written many books: a translation of the Book of Splendour (the Zohar) into modern Hebrew, some twenty years work, and lots of slender volumes of sermons, hasidic tales, and rabbinical commentaries. His books had been published in Warsaw and later in New York.

29   "At the funeral," my mother said, "they had to have six motorcycle policemen to control the crowds. It was such a heat that twelve women fainted—and I'm *not* counting Mrs. Waxman from upstairs. With her, you know, *anything* to fall into a man's arms. Even Pinsky's. And did I tell you that there was even a French Canadian priest there?"

30   "Aw, you're kidding me."

31   "The priest was some *knacker*. A bishop maybe. He used to study with the *zeyda*. The *zeyda* was a real personality, you know. Spiritual and worldly-wise at the same time. Such personalities they don't make any more. Today rabbis and peanuts come in the same size."

32   But, according to my father, the *zeyda* (his father-in-law) hadn't been as celebrated as all that. "There are things I could say," he told me. "There was another side to him."

33   My grandfather had sprung from generations and generations of rabbis, his youngest son was a rabbi, but none of his grandchildren would be one. My Cousin Jerry was already a militant socialist. I once heard him say, "When the men at the kosher bakeries went out on strike the *zeyda* spoke up against them on the streets and in the *shuls*. It was of no consequence to him that the men were grossly underpaid. His superstitious followers had to have bread. Grandpappy," Jerry said, "was a prize reactionary."

34   A week after my grandfather died my grandmother suffered a stroke. Her right side was completely paralysed. She couldn't speak. At first it's true, she could manage a coherent word or two and move her right hand enough to write her name in Hebrew. Her name was Malka. But her condition soon began to deteriorate.

35   My grandmother had six children and seven step-children, for my grandfather had been married before. His first wife had died in the old country. Two years later he had married my grandmother, the only daughter of the most affluent man in the *shtetl*, and their marriage had been a singularly happy one. My

grandmother had been a beautiful girl. She had also been a shrewd, resource-ful, and patient wife. Qualities, I fear, indispensable to life with a Zaddik. For the synagogue paid my grandfather no stipulated salary and much of the money he picked up here and there he had habitually distributed among rabbinical students, needy immigrants and widows. A vice, for such it was to his impe-cunious family, which made him as unreliable a provider as a drinker. To carry the analogy further, my grandmother had to make hurried, surreptitious trips to the pawnbroker with her jewellery. Not all of it to be redeemed, either. But her children had been looked after. The youngest, her favourite, was a rabbi in Boston, the oldest was the actor-manager of a Yiddish theatre in New York, and another was a lawyer. One daughter lived in Montreal, two in Toronto. My mother was the youngest daughter and when my grandmother had her stroke there was a family conclave and it was decided that my mother would take care of her. This was my father's fault. All the other husbands spoke up—they protested hotly that their wives had too much work—they could never manage it—but my father detested quarrels and so he was silent. And my grandmother came to stay with us.

36   Her bedroom, the back bedroom, had actually been promised to me for my seventh birthday, but now I had to go on sharing a room with my sister. So nat-urally I was resentful when each morning before I left for school my mother in-sisted that I go in and kiss my grandmother goodbye.

37   "Bouyo-bouyo," was the only sound my grandmother could make.

38   During those first hopeful months—"Twenty years ago who would have thought there'd be a cure for diabetes?" my father asked. "Where there's life, you know."—my grandmother would smile and try to speak, her eyes charged with effort; and I wondered if she knew that I was waiting for her room.

39   Even later there were times when she pressed my hand urgently to her bosom with her surprisingly strong left arm. But as her illness dragged on and on she became a condition in the house, something beyond hope or reproach, like the leaky ice-box, there was less recognition and more ritual in those kisses. I came to dread her room. A clutter of sticky medicine bottles and the cracked toilet chair beside the bed; glazed but imploring eyes and a feeble smile, the wet smack of her crooked lips against my cheeks. I flinched from her touch. And after two years, I protested to my mother, "What's the use of telling her I'm going here or I'm going there? She doesn't even recognize me any more."

40   "Don't be fresh. She's your grandmother."

41   My uncle who was in the theatre in New York sent money regularly to help support my grandmother and, for the first few months, so did the other children. But once the initial and sustaining excitement had passed the children seldom came to our house any more. Anxious weekly visits—"And how is she today, poor lamb?"—quickly dwindled to a dutiful monthly looking in, then a semi-annual visit, and these always on the way to somewhere.

42   When the children did come my mother was severe with them. "I have to lift her on that chair three times a day maybe. And what makes you think I always catch her in time? Sometimes I have to change her linen twice a day. That's a job I'd like to see your wife do," she said to my uncle, the rabbi.

43   "We could send her to the Old People's Home."

44   "Now there's an idea," my father said.

45   "Not so long as I'm alive." My mother shot my father a scalding look. "Say something, Sam."

46   "Quarrelling will get us nowhere. It only creates bad feelings."

47   Meanwhile, Dr. Katzman came once a month. "It's astonishing," he would say each time. "She's as strong as a horse."

48   "Some life for a person," my father said. "She can't speak—she doesn't recognize anybody—what is there for her?"

49   The doctor was a cultivated man; he spoke often for women's clubs, sometimes on Yiddish literature and other times, his rubicund face hot with menace, the voice taking on a doomsday tone, on the cancer threat. "Who are we to judge?" he asked.

50   Every evening, during the first few months of my grandmother's illness, my mother would read her a story by Sholem Aleichem. "Tonight she smiled," my mother would report defiantly. "She understood. I can tell."

51   Bright afternoons my mother would lift the old lady into a wheelchair and put her out in the sun and once a week she gave her a manicure. Somebody always had to stay in the house in case my grandmother called. Often, during the night, she would begin to wail unaccountably and my mother would get up and rock her mother in her arms for hours. But in the fourth year of my grandmother's illness the strain began to tell. Besides looking after my grandmother, my mother had to keep house for a husband and two children. She became scornful of my father and began to find fault with my sister and me. My father started to spend his evenings playing pinochle at Tansky's Cigar & Soda. Weekends he took me to visit his brothers and sisters. Wherever my father went people had little snippets of advice for him.

52   "Sam, you might as well be a bachelor. One of the other children should take the old lady for a while. You're just going to have to put your foot down for once."

53   "Yeah, in your face maybe."

54   My Cousin Libby, who was at McGill, said, "This could have a very damaging effect on the development of your children. These are their formative years, Uncle Samuel, and the omnipresence of death in the house . . . ."

55   "What you need is a boy friend," my father said. *"And how."*

56   After supper my mother took to falling asleep in her chair, even in the middle of Lux Radio Theatre. One minute she would be sewing a patch in my breeches or making a list of girls to call for a bingo party, proceeds for the Talmud Torah, and the next she would be snoring. Then, inevitably, there came the

morning she just couldn't get out of bed and Dr. Katzman had to come round a week before his regular visit. "Well, well, this won't do, will it?"

57   Dr. Katzman led my father into the kitchen. "Your wife's got a gallstone condition," he said.

58   My grandmother's children met again, this time without my mother, and decided to put the old lady in the Jewish Old People's Home on Esplanade Street. While my mother slept an ambulance came to take my grandmother away.

59   "It's for the best," Dr. Katzman said, but my father was in the back room when my grandmother held on tenaciously to the bedpost, not wanting to be moved by the two men in white.

60   "Easy does it, granny," the younger man said.

61   Afterwards my father did not go in to see my mother. He went out for a walk.

62   When my mother got out of bed two weeks later her cheeks had regained their normal pinkish hue; for the first time in months, she actually joked with me. She became increasingly curious about how I was doing in school and whether or not I shined my shoes regularly. She began to cook special dishes for my father again and resumed old friendships with girls on the parochial school board. Not only did my father's temper improve, but he stopped going to Tansky's every night and began to come home early from work. But my grandmother's name was seldom mentioned. Until one evening, after I'd had a fight with my sister, I said, "Why can't I move into the back bedroom now?"

63   My father glared at me. "Big-mouth."

64   "It's empty, isn't it?"

65   The next afternoon my mother put on her best dress and coat and new spring hat.

66   "Don't go looking for trouble," my father said.

67   "It's been a month. Maybe they're not treating her right."

68   "They're experts."

69   "Did you think I was never going to visit her? I'm not inhuman, you know."

70   "Alright, go." But after she had gone my father stood by the window and said, "I was born lucky, and that's it."

71   I sat on the outside stoop watching the cars go by. My father waited on the balcony above, cracking peanuts. It was six o'clock, maybe later, when the ambulance slowed down and rocked to a stop right in front of our house. "I knew it," my father said. "I was born with all the luck."

72   My mother got out first, her eyes red and swollen, and hurried upstairs to make my grandmother's bed.

73   "You'll get sick again," my father said.

74   "I'm sorry, Sam, but what could I do? From the moment she saw me she cried and cried. It was terrible."

75   "They're recognized experts there. They know how to take care of her better than you do."

76   "Experts? Expert murderers you mean. She's got bedsores, Sam. Those dirty little Irish nurses they don't change her linen often enough, they hate her. She must have lost twenty pounds in there."

77   "Another month and you'll be flat on your back again. I'll write you a guarantee, if you want."

78   My father became a regular at Tansky's again and, once more, I had to go in and kiss my grandmother in the morning. Amazingly, she had begun to look like a man. Little hairs had sprouted on her chin, she had grown a spiky grey moustache, and she was practically bald.

79   Yet again my uncles and aunts sent five dollar bills, though erratically, to help pay for my grandmother's support. Elderly people, former followers of my grandfather, came to inquire about the old lady's health. They sat in the back bedroom with her, leaning on their canes, talking to themselves and rocking to and fro. "The Holy Shakers," my father called them. I avoided the seamed, shrunken old men because they always wanted to pinch my cheeks or trick me with a dash of snuff and laugh when I sneezed. When the visit with grandmother was over the old people would unfailingly sit in the kitchen with my mother for another hour, watching her make *lokshen*, slurping lemon tea out of a saucer. They would recall the sayings and books and charitable deeds of the late Zaddik.

80   "At the funeral," my mother never wearied of telling them, "they had to have six motorcycle policemen to control the crowds."

81   In the next two years there was no significant change in my grandmother's condition, though fatigue, ill-temper, and even morbidity enveloped my mother again. She fought with her brothers and sisters and once, after a particularly bitter quarrel, I found her sitting with her head in her hands. "If, God forbid, I had a stroke," she said, "would you send me to the Old People's Home?"

82   "Of course not."

83   "I hope that never in my life do I have to count on my children for anything."

84 The seventh summer of my grandmother's illness she was supposed to die and we did not know from day to day when it would happen. I was often sent out to eat at an aunt's or at my other grandmother's house. I was hardly ever at home. In those days they let boys into the left-field bleachers of Delormier Downs free during the week and Duddy, Gas sometimes, Hershey, Stan, Arty and me spent many an afternoon at the ball park. The Montreal Royals, kingpin of the Dodger farm system, had a marvellous club at the time. There was Jackie Robinson, Roy Campanella, Lou Ortiz, Red Durrett, Honest John Gabbard, and Kermit Kitman. Kitman was our hero. It used to give us a charge to watch that crafty little Jew, one of ours, running around out there with all those tall dumb southern crackers. "Hey, Kitman," we would yell, "Hey, shmo-head, if your father knew you played ball on *shabus*—" Kitman, alas, was all field and no hit. He never made the majors.

"There goes Kermit Kitman," we would holler, after he had gone down swinging again, "the first Jewish strike-out king of the International League." This we promptly followed up by bellowing choice imprecations in Yiddish.

85   It was after one of these games, on a Friday afternoon, that I came home to find a crowd gathered in front of our house.

86   "That's the grandson," somebody said.

87   A knot of old people stood staring at our house from across the street. A taxi pulled up and my aunt hurried out, hiding her face in her hands.

88   "After so many years," a woman said.

89   "And probably next year they'll discover a cure. Isn't that always the case?"

90   The flat was clotted. Uncles and aunts from my father's side of the family, strangers, Dr. Katzman, neighbours, were all milling around and talking in hushed voices. My father was in the kitchen, getting out the apricot brandy. "Your grandmother's dead," he said.

91   "Where's Maw?"

92   "In the bedroom with . . . You'd better not go in."

93   "I want to see her."

94   My mother wore a black shawl and glared down at a knot of handkerchief clutched in a fist that had been cracked by washing soda. "Don't come in here," she said.

95   Several bearded round-shouldered men in shiny black coats surrounded the bed. I couldn't see my grandmother.

96   "Your grandmother's dead."

97   "Daddy told me."

98   "Go wash your face and comb your hair."

99   "Yes."

100   "You'll have to get your own supper."

101   "Sure."

102   "One minute. The *baba* left some jewellery. The necklace is for Rifka and the ring is for your wife."

103   "Who's getting married?"

104   "Better go and wash your face. Remember behind the ears, please."

105   Telegrams were sent, the obligatory long distance calls were made, and all through the evening relatives and neighbours and old followers of the Zaddik poured into the house. Finally, the man from the funeral parlour arrived.

106   "There goes the only Jewish businessman in town," Segal said, "who wishes all his customers were German."

107   "This is no time for jokes."

108   "Listen, life goes on."

109   My Cousin Jerry had begun to affect a cigarette holder. "Soon the religious mumbo-jumbo starts," he said to me.

110   "Wha'?"

111   "Everybody is going to be sickeningly sentimental."

112   The next day was the sabbath and so, according to law, my grandmother couldn't be buried until Sunday. She would have to lie on the floor all night. Two grizzly women in white came to move and wash the body and a professional mourner arrived to sit up and pray for her. "I don't trust his face," my mother said. "He'll fall asleep."

113   "He won't fall asleep."

114   "You watch him, Sam."

115   "A fat lot of good prayers will do her now. Alright! Okay! I'll watch him."

116   My father was in a fury with Segal.

117   "The way he goes after the apricot brandy you'd think he never saw a bottle in his life before."

118   Rifka and I were sent to bed, but we couldn't sleep. My aunt was sobbing over the body in the living room; there was the old man praying, coughing and spitting into his handkerchief whenever he woke; and the hushed voices and whimpering from the kitchen, where my father and mother sat. Rifka allowed me a few drags off her cigarette.

119   "Well, *pisherke*, this is our last night together. Tomorrow you can take over the back room."

120   "Are you crazy?"

121   "You always wanted it for yourself, didn't you?"

122   "She died in there, but."

123   "So?"

124   "I couldn't sleep in there now."

125   "Good night and happy dreams."

126   "Hey, let's talk some more."

127   "Did you know," Rifka said, "that when they hang a man the last thing that happens is that he has an orgasm?"

128   "A wha'?"

129   "Skip it. I forgot you were still in kindergarten."

130   "Kiss my Royal Canadian—"

131   "At the funeral, they're going to open the coffin and throw dirt in her face. It's supposed to be earth from Eretz. They open it and you're going to have to look."

132   "Says you."

133   A little while after the lights had been turned out Rifka approached my bed, her head covered with a sheet and her arms raised high. "Bouyo-bouyo. Who's that sleeping in my bed? Woo-woo."

134   My uncle who was in the theatre and my aunt from Toronto came to the funeral. My uncle, the rabbi, was there too.

135   "As long as she was alive," my mother said, "he couldn't even send her five dollars a month. I don't want him in the house, Sam. I can't bear the sight of him."

136   "You're upset," Dr. Katzman said, "and you don't know what you're saying."

137   "Maybe you'd better give her a sedative," the rabbi said.

138   "Sam will you speak up for once, please."

139   Flushed, eyes heated, my father stepped up to the rabbi. "I'll tell you this straight to your face, Israel," he said. "You've gone down in my estimation."

140   The rabbi smiled a little.

141   "Year by year," my father continued, his face burning a brighter red, "your stock has gone down with me."

142   My mother began to weep and she was led unwillingly to a bed. While my father tried his utmost to comfort her, as he muttered consoling things, Dr. Katzman plunged a needle into her arm. "There we are," he said.

143   I went to sit on the stoop outside with Duddy. My uncle, the rabbi, and Dr. Katzman stepped into the sun to light cigarettes.

144   "I know exactly how you feel," Dr. Katzman said. "There's been a death in the family and the world seems indifferent to your loss. Your heart is broken and yet it's a splendid summer day . . . a day made for love and laughter . . . and that must seem very cruel to you."

145   The rabbi nodded; he sighed.

146   "Actually," Dr. Katzman said, "it's remarkable that she held out for so long."

147   "Remarkable?" the rabbi said. "It's written that if a man has been married twice he will spend as much time with his first wife in heaven as he did on earth. My father, may he rest in peace, was married to his first wife for seven years and my mother, may she rest in peace, has managed to keep alive for seven years. Today in heaven she will be able to join my father, may he rest in peace."

148   Dr. Katzman shook his head. "It's amazing," he said. He told my uncle that he was writing a book based on his experiences as a healer. "The mysteries of the human heart."

149   "Yes."

150   "Astonishing."

151   My father hurried outside. "Dr. Katzman, please. It's my wife. Maybe the injection wasn't strong enough. She just doesn't stop crying. It's like a tap. Can you come in, please?"

152   "Excuse me," Dr. Katzman said to my uncle.

153   "Of course." My uncle turned to Duddy and me. "Well, boys," he said, "what would you like to be when you grow up?"

For Further Thinking

1. Identify a fundamental irony in the plot of this story.

2. Are there symbolic overtones to the final scene of the story, which begins when the boy steps outside onto the stoop in the sun? Include possible symbolic meanings of what the doctor and the rabbi say.

3. The National Film Board's production of this short story, by Caroline Leaf, chooses to omit the rabbi's closing explanation of why the grandmother took seven years to die. How would you interpret the significance of the rabbi's explanation, and do you feel it should have been omitted in the film version?

4. As precisely as you can, describe the point of view used in this story. How does it affect our interpretation?

5. Identify some of the one-line jokes that occur, mostly in dialogue. What is the overall effect of this element of humour?

Looking Back and Ahead

1. Contrast the portraits of grandparents in this story to those in Emma Lee Warrior's "White Breast Flats" (p. 6). How do the different characterizations contribute to different moods and the authors' underlying outlooks on life?

2. Contrast Richler's portrait of the narrator's grandmother and Alice Munro's portrait of Lois's grandmother in "Thanks for the Ride" (p. 62). What differences in moods and underlying attitudes to life emerge from this comparison?

3. Roch Carrier's fictional memoir "The Hockey Sweater" is also set in the province of Quebec, in a similar time period to that suggested in Richler's story (post-war 1940s or early 1950s). What do these two pieces of writing have in common? In what significant ways are they different?

For Further Reading

Leaf, Caroline, dir. "*The Street*" (short animated film). In *Leonard Maltin's Animation Favourites from the National Film Board of Canada*. National Film Board, 1995. The short story represented by Leaf is the same one as "The Summer My Grandmother Was Supposed to Die."

Richler, Mordecai. *The Street: Short Stories*. Toronto: McClelland and Stewart, 1969. The story we have reprinted is the second in the collection. Other editors sometimes give this short story the same title as the collection.

————. *Barney's Version*. Toronto: Knopf Canada, 1997. Richler's consummate final work of fiction incorporates, deepens, and polishes his lifelong themes and devices.

————. *Oh Canada! Oh Quebec!* Toronto: Penguin, 1992. Of all Richler's non-fiction, this book is perhaps his most controversial, outraging Quebec nationalists, most if not all of whom refused to read it.

Schmid, Vernon R.J., compiler. "Well-Known People Who Happen to Be Canadian." Online. Maintained by John Terning. April 2003 <**http://schwinger.harvard.edu/ ~terning/bios/Richler.html**>.

National Library of Canada. April 2003 <**http://www.nlc-bnc.ca**>. Click on "search" for information on Richler.

Leanna Rutherford An estimated 10 million people in the United States have an eating disorder.[2] Given the similarities between that society and ours, we can expect the problem to be similarly entrenched north of the border. Researchers suggest, in fact, that in "developed" countries, one in every 200 young women is affected. Anorexia nervosa, one of several types of eating disorder, is now considered the third most common chronic illness among the younger female population; while such estimates are hard to give, some observers believe that upwards of 20 percent of those identified with the condition die within 20 years of onset.[3] Furthermore, the problem seems to be occurring at increasingly early ages, with sufferers as young as eleven. Canadian Leanna Rutherford's personal account therefore speaks to a serious problem, one that is extremely difficult to overcome, one with unavoidable socio-cultural implications. This article appeared in *Canadian Living Magazine*, 1998.

[2] Andrea Gordon, "Eating Disorder: Anorexia Nervosa," *Hospital Practice* 36. 2 (2001): 36.

[3] See <http:/eatingdisorders.about.com/library/weekly/aa110200a.htm?terms=eating+disorders>.

An Anorexic's Recovery

1   It was March 1995. I was 17 and in my graduating year of high school when I decided that I wanted to lose weight—10 pounds, maybe 15, certainly not more than 20. I was five eight and 155 pounds. I wanted to impress the boys in university and I thought being thin would help. So I went on a diet.

2   People with eating disorders do not wake up one morning and say to themselves, "I am not going to eat any more" or "I think I will start bingeing and purging." Nobody called me fat or told me life would be perfect if I lost 50 pounds. I can't pinpoint one event that directly led to my disorder. I just needed something to depend on, something to think about and to put all my effort into. I just happened to find dieting at the wrong time. It was comforting to take a break from the changes and worries in my life to concentrate on what I was, or wasn't, going to eat that day. It was also nice to pat myself on the back every time I resisted eating.

3   By June graduation I was down to 130 pounds. I was satisfied but afraid I might regain weight, so I kept dieting. When I entered Bishop's University in Lennoxville, Que., that fall, I weighed 120 pounds. I had heard about the Frosh 15, the 15 pounds on average that university students supposedly gain in first year. I decided that I, dieter extraordinaire, would not become part of that statistic.

4   When I went home to Halifax at Thanksgiving, I weighed myself for the first time in a month and a half. I weighed 115 pounds. I can remember standing on the bathroom scale and saying aloud to myself, "This is a problem. I have got to stop losing weight."

5   But I had lost perspective on what "normal eating" was. I thought that if I ate one piece of pizza or one cookie, I would immediately put on 10 pounds and continue to gain uncontrollably.

6   I returned to school, determined to maintain a weight of at least 112 pounds. I bought a scale and promised myself I would gain five pounds. I increased my daily food intake by one apple and one glass of skim milk.

7   But I weighed myself obsessively—several times a day—to be sure I didn't gain more than five pounds. Within a week I stopped eating the extra food and cut back my intake even further.

8   This is when my mental distortion began. Although I had a scale and knew that 112 pounds at five eight was very thin, I would look in the mirror and see fat everywhere. In reality, though, it was not that any of my body parts were large, but simply out of proportion. My hips looked big because my waist was so thin. My thighs appeared huge to me in comparison to my buttocks and calves. My bones had begun to stick out. I could count every rib and vertebra. But it happened so slowly that I accepted it as normal.

9   My friends eventually begged me to start eating more. But it was too late. I had lost touch with reality. My weight was the only thing that mattered.

10   At Christmas I returned home to a horrified family. I wasn't just thin, I was emaciated. But aside from my looks, I still seemed to have it all together. I was an honours student when I entered university and had an 82 percent average after my first semester. I had made lots of friends and had balanced my social and academic obligations. Except for the state of my health, I was a success story.

11   When I went back to university in January, my life dissolved both emotionally and physically. I cried at least twice a day, although never in public. I couldn't get up for class. I couldn't even walk up the stairs without sitting down to take a rest. Every single moment was a fight between me and every cell in my body—cells that were begging me to give in and nourish them.

12   I yearned to confide in someone but I was convinced that getting help meant getting fat. I carried on in silence.

13   I knew that I could not continue living that way but I saw no alternative. Losing the anorexia nervosa felt like losing everything. I was convinced that it was all I had—my only support, my only true friend.

14   One day in early March, my roommate came home from class to find me curled up, crying and talking about suicide. She walked over and handed me the number for the National Eating Disorder Information Centre Support Line and said, "I'm going to give you 48 hours to phone them. If you don't, then I will." It was a moment for which I will be eternally grateful. She had nagged me in the past about getting help but she had gone easy on me, hoping I would find the help myself. Now she was forceful. She refused to watch me die.

15   I called the support line and said quite simply, "I have a problem. I need help." The counsellor asked me a few questions about my situation and gave me some telephone numbers to call. The closest resource centre was an hour and a half away by car and I had no way to get there.

16   As far as I was concerned, I had made the effort and the medical world had failed me. My roommate did not give up. She told me to go to the medical clinic on campus and again gave me an ultimatum: either I would go myself, or she would go for me. I was not as easily persuaded as I had been before. I made excuses for myself, pretending I'd done all I could.

17   She kept her word. Three days later I was summoned to the doctor's office and asked if I had "lost control." How to answer that question? If I told the doctor I could handle it, maybe she would leave me alone. Only, I knew I had no control. I knew I needed help. And deep down a voice was begging me not to kill myself. So I answered, "No, I don't have control. I can't stop."

18   For the next two and a half months I hated everyone, including friends and family. I was in the hospital and was physically forced to gain weight. I knew I wanted to get better but I didn't believe that that was the doctors' intent. I thought they were my enemies, ruining my life and making me "fat."

19   Legally, anorexia is a mental illness. If you are mentally incapable of eating normally, you can be committed to a hospital and forcibly nourished through the use of restraints and tubal feeding. That may sound extreme, but remember, it is a life or death situation.

20   When I was finally admitted to a voluntary program, I promptly checked myself out. My parents were livid. They kept saying that it was the stupidest thing I had ever done. I told them I was in control again and in fact I believed that I was. I didn't think I needed an in-patient clinic to help me eat. That was the anorexia speaking. It was still very much alive inside my brain.

21   My parents tried everything they could. They begged, made deals, threatened to take away privileges, but finally they gave in. They were my parents, they loved me and ultimately they couldn't bring themselves to refuse to allow me to come home. They did, however, come up with the idea of making me sign a contract. If I lost weight again, or made any decisions they deemed irrational, I would be recommitted to the hospital immediately.

22   With this horrific threat over my head, I went home. It took nine weeks to find an available therapist experienced in counselling patients with eating disorders.

23   Once out of the hospital, I lost all the weight I had gained there and more. Even while seeing my therapist, I managed to drag myself down to a deathly 90 pounds. I hid my weight by wearing baggy clothes and avoiding being weighed.

24   But I finally found the strength to initiate my own battle. The doctors could talk to me, even force-feed me, but until I found my own reasons to be healthy, no one could do more than keep me alive. I had missed a year of university. It took 10 months of boredom, loneliness and tears to realize that anorexia and life are incompatible, that I couldn't weigh 90 pounds and be happy. That is when I began my struggle toward normal eating.

25   Recovery is a long process. I still see both my psychologist and nutritionist monthly and I have 10 more pounds to gain to reach the goal weight I determined with my nutritionist. I'm in my third year of a degree in neuroscience at Dalhousie University in Halifax.

26   Now there is more to my day than what I eat and how much I weigh. I can finally look at a plate of food and see substance and nutrients instead of the

number of calories and grams of fat. I can go out to dinner and to parties without being scared by the prospect of unexpected food. And a few months ago, I threw out my bathroom scale.

For Further Thinking

1. What causes of her disorder does Rutherford identify or imply in her account? How would you best describe the relation between these causes? What, in your opinion, is the main cause of an eating disorder?

2. What effects does Rutherford present? Does she devote more attention to effects than to causes? Do you feel her story is representative of the problem in general?

3. What do you think helped Rutherford recover from her disorder? What, in general, do you believe can and should be done to help those who suffer from eating disorders?

4. Do you think that writing about her disorder has helped Rutherford deal with the experience? Explain.

Looking Back and Ahead

1. What do researchers identify as common psychological causes of eating disorders? You might wish to consult some of the websites listed below for answers. Is Lois in Alice Munro's short story "Thanks for the Ride" representative, in some ways, of these psychological conditions? Explain.

2. Read Susan McClelland's "The Lure of the Body Image" (p. 83). It used to be commonly assumed that the obsession with appearance was distinctly female. What do you think is the role of one's sex in obsessions related to appearance?

3. Do today's young women have more alternatives and opportunities than their grandmothers and great-grandmothers, and should they therefore be held more responsible for their problems and behaviour? Or are today's young women just as vulnerable to external forces beyond reasonable control?

4. Read Sarah Schmidt's "College Girl to Call Girl" (p. 104). What thematic differences and similarities might be shown between that report on middle-class prostitution and the topic of female eating disorders?

For Further Reading

"Eating Disorders." April 2003 <http://eatingdisorders.about.com/library/weekly/>. This site offers numerous links to a wide range of issues related to eating disorders and resources: cultural considerations, ways to help, mental issues, over-exercise, personal stories, symptoms, treatments, frequently asked questions, and facts versus common misconceptions.

Gordon, Andrea. "Eating Disorder: Anorexia Nervosa." *Hospital Practice* 36. 2 (2001): 36.

Hornbacher, Marya. "Wasted: A Memoir of Anorexia and Bulimia." *Canadian Medical Association Journal* 161. 5 (7 September 1999): 551.

Sargent, Judy Tam. *The Long Road Back: A Survivor's Guide to Anorexia*. Georgetown, ON: North Star, 1999.

Yager, Joel, ed. *Eating Disorders Review*. Albuquerque: University of New Mexico. A bi-monthly newsletter of clinical information for professionals working with patients with eating disorders.

Young, Adena. "Battling Anorexia: The Story of Karen Carpenter." April 2003 <http://atdpweb.soe.berkeley.edu/quest/Mind&Body/Carpenter.html>. "Sad but true, the death of Karen Carpenter in 1983 opened the eyes of the world to this life-threatening disease."

Corinne Wasylewich In the following account, Wasylewich, a "thirty-something wife, mother, nurse, and runner" living in Lethbridge, Alberta, illustrates one approach to keeping a personal-progress journal. While preparing for the 42.2-km Calgary Stampede Marathon, she recorded her activities and progress (along with the reactions of family, friends, and co-workers) during six months of training. Quoting John Bingham, Wasylewich concludes, "The miracle isn't that I finished. The miracle is that I had the courage to start." In precise detail, her journal, an English course assignment, lays out the daily crystallization of that courage.

See our comments in Chapter 2 of the *Rhetoric* (under "Combinations of Types") for further discussion of how this sample of writing combines more than one rhetorical strategy and might be considered personal, expositional, and—in its inspirational effect—even persuasive.

Marathon Journal

1   I have never thought another person would read any of my personal journals. I hope this will not be as painful to read as it was occasionally to write. While preparing for the Calgary Stampede Marathon, I kept track of my progress. The following are excerpts from that journal.

2   Four days of the week were designated running days, Sunday was usually the day for long runs. Two days were set aside for cross training. That left me with one sacred day a week to rest and carbo-load (in other words, pig out). The theory behind running every other day is to give the big muscle groups in the legs a chance to rest and recover. Cross training usually consists of an exercise to strengthen the upper body. Endurance activities tend to exhaust the major muscles used, and the body relies on accessory muscles to "help out."

3   (XT denotes cross training. Km. is my abbreviation for kilometre.)

January 5, 1998

4   My first day of marathon training. I bought my winter running tights. I told the staff at Runners' Soul I plan to "run Calgary" in July. They responded with polite, yet skeptical smiles. I swam 1.5 Km. Swimming felt good for my shoulders.

January 6

5   Ran 8 Km. in 46:40. I ran through the coulees. There was a bit of snow on the north facing slopes. It was –15C. I ran slowly and walked down the hills. I need to get my knees accustomed to the torture that is yet to come.

January 9

6   7.5 Km. 51:40. I ran home from work. There was a lot of snow on the trail and a west wind trying to stop me. –20C. It felt as if I could go forever today, even though the snow made my legs work too hard. Everyone from work who drove by offered me a ride. They looked so cold in their frosty cars. I was warm all over.

January 11

7   10 Km. 58:00. I had to run on the treadmill because it was –50C. I felt like a hamster. It may be this cold for my marathon; I really wanted to run outside!

January 15

8   XT. Super-sets for my arms, it didn't feel so super. Pumping iron until my muscles are exhausted is not easy. I can hardly hold my pen to write in this journal.

January 20

9   8 Km. 54:00. I ran around Chalmers Street. There was a delicate, sparkly snow falling. I had nowhere specific to go and nothing on my mind. This was a very tranquil, meditative run.

January 25

10   14.5 Km. 1:55:25. I ran down and around the river bottom. It was a sunny day, no wind, just a dusting of snow left. Christian and Dee came with me. My legs were so wobbly at the end I could hardly stand up.

January 27

11   6.5 Km. 40:00. I ran out to Charlie Brown's farm. What have I done to myself? My toenails hurt so much from Sunday's run I could hardly put my shoes on. My quads were really tired and heavy. Because of all these troubles, it was a slow run.

February 1

12   16 Km. 1:48:00. We followed the same route as last Sunday, only a little further. There was a chilly north wind today. Christian and Dee came along again. They both said this is as far as they will go with me, regardless of how many lattes I buy after. The ache in my legs actually felt good today.

February 6

13   8.5 Km. 53:00. I ran to the Penny Coffee House from home. It was a windy and cool day, but at least there was no snow to fight. My legs felt wooden and I was very tired. I had to pee in the bushes—how humiliating!

February 8

14   16 Km. 1:44:00. Today I ran out on the bald, windswept prairie. I had to fight with a farmer's dog. My toenails are bruised and swollen. I was introspective today. I know I will run 42.2 Km. even if I have to go through more pain to get there.

February 12

15   XT. I worked a very stressful, exhausting twelve-hour shift in the Emergency Room. My colleagues are asking why my toenails are purple. I told them it's contagious. They think I'm strange.

March 1

16   21 Km. 2:25:30. I ran an "inner-city tour." It was sunny and +4C. I am glad I read that after an hour of exercise the body needs some electrolyte replacement; otherwise I couldn't have choked down the power bar I had to eat. My neighbours watched with great curiosity when I hosed my legs down with ice-cold water. It felt so good.

March 13

17   XT. Well, not really. I had good intentions to weight train, but was so tired I fell asleep at 7:30!

March 28

18   30.5 Km. 3:39:00. Dad figured this route for me. I don't think he likes me. The wind howled and my toenail fell off. Cows were staring at me, laughing. Every muscle in my body ached. There was no joy in this run. Why am I doing this?

April 4

19   Road Race. I ran 10 miles today in 1:30:00. Paul ran it with me. He really pushed me for the last mile because my legs were cramping. I swallowed the first bug of the season. It was good protein.

April 14

20   7.5 Km. 44:00. I ran to the University and around the lake. Spring is on the way; I saw the first yellow-headed blackbird. I stumbled on both my ankles, and my knees were hurting. I'm sure it was the new shoes I bought. I think the staff at Runners' Soul are starting to believe that I will do a marathon on my own.

May 24

21   38.6 Km. 4:36:00. Paul and I ran the back roads from Claresholm to Stavely Provincial Park. We saw a lot of gophers and some bunnies. (They're better company than the cows.) Paul did well for the first three hours, and then he started to com-

plain. He stopped grumbling when I told him I would run ahead and get the van. Ha. Now I know what chaffing is. My legs were tired but they felt strong. I have only one more long run until—MARATHON.

June 25

22   4 Km. 20:00. I pushed the kids in the stroller. I had to bribe them with sugar. My knees feel good. We just ran around the neighbourhood and we saw a snake. No harm done.

July 3

23   5 Km. 25:00. I ran the "usual route" above the coulees. It was a hot and humid day—rare for us. Two days left. Every muscle, tendon, and joint was singing in harmony. I am ready.

July 5

24   MARATHON! 42.2 Km., 26.2 miles, and I ran it all! It took me four hours and thirty-two minutes. I did it! My legs were numb for the last five Km. Everyone was there to cheer for me. My family, my friends, and even some colleagues! It felt so good. I ran slowly for the first three hours, then I pushed it. I passed so many people; I had no idea I am a relatively competitive person. They gave me a medal at the end! My kids think I won the Calgary Stampede Marathon. I ate two cheeseburgers, large fries, beans and ribs, and a huge piece of cheesecake. I didn't do too badly for a lacto-vegetarian. There is a quote I remember reading: "The miracle isn't that I finished. The miracle is that I had the courage to start" (John Bingham, *The Penguin Chronicles*).

25   Since I ran "my" marathon, the staff at Runners' Soul put my name on the marathon wall, and four of my friends and two of my colleagues have joined running clubs. I would like to think that my enthusiasm and joy for running was and continues to be contagious.

For Further Thinking

1. How would you describe the tone of this journal? What elements contribute to that tone?

2. Is the tone effective or not? Explain.

3. In what ways does this journal combine types, or modes, of writing? After framing your answer, see Chapter 2 of the *Rhetoric* for our ideas on how the modes combine in this piece.

4. How valuable is a personal-progress journal to accomplishing goals, and if it is helpful, explain why.

Looking Back and Ahead

1. Discuss possible similarities between "Marathon Journal" and Michel Tremblay's "The King and I" (p. 37).

2. Discuss possible connections between "Marathon Journal" and the previous selection, Leanna Rutherford's "An Anorexic's Recovery."

3. One of the websites listed at the end of the previous reading deals with concerns about possible over-exercise. Where is the line, do you think, between maintaining fitness and becoming obsessive?

For Further Reading

British Broadcasting Corporation. Education Department. Online <http://www.bbc.co.uk/education/work/life/selfdevelopment.shtml>. This site offers short personal stories about various aspects of work life. It provides excellent examples of life writing by a broad range of people. A 10-step guide to self-development provides a strategy for adding direction and purpose in your life.

Johnson, Alexandra. *Leaving a Trace: On Keeping a Journal: The Art of Transforming a Life into Stories.* Boston: Little, Brown and Co., 2001.

Journal of Sport & Exercise Psychology 20. 1 (March 1988).

Thomas LaBrie This essay, by a transplanted Cajun oil and gas industry employee, now living in East Java, Indonesia, is a memoir of "foolish youth," a coming-of-age story. The story was posted on the Athabasca University English 255 peer-editing Web board, delighting fellow students and instructors alike.

Tom and his friend Marvin embark on a night of "froggin'"—Cajun for catching bullfrogs by hand. They enliven the enterprise with a little "pop rouge"—Cajun for mushroom juice diluted with strawberry soda. Tom encounters a frog with fangs, Marvin runs from a bear, which turns out to be a possum, and the author concludes with some ruminations on the "haphazard way we fling ourselves into adventure without thought to the dangers or consequences of our actions."

Franken-Frogs and the Mushroom Bear

1   Ah, the lessons we learn from youth. Sometimes we run across the memories of these lessons long after we have experienced them and more often, forgotten them. This is one I will always remember.

2   On a hot, boring summer day in 1976, I received a phone call from my good friend, Marvin. Marvin wanted to know if I would accompany him on a froggin' expedition later that night. Since it was pretty boring at that moment, I agreed. Marvin spent most of his time huntin', fishin', froggin' or shrimpin': anything that had to do with the outdoors, that's where Marvin was. Marvin was a veritable encyclopedia on about just about every type of animal to be found in the woods in and around Acadiana.

3   That evening I went over to Marvin's house, actually his Mom's house, but he insisted we call it his, to meet him so we could set out to go froggin'. Marvin

said he had something special lined up for our froggin' trip tonight. He pulled out a quart jar with some red liquid in it that looked a lot like Marvel Mystery Oil. It turned out to be a batch of mushroom juice, diluted with strawberry soda, or "pop rouge" as it is known to Cajuns. We both had a pretty wild streak in those younger days, and had been known to sip mushroom tea occasionally. I was a little hesitant about mixing froggin' with mushrooms. Marvin said he had tested this batch for potency and had given it a "mild" rating. He figured we would get a mild buzz, which would make the froggin' interesting. We each drank about a fourth of the quart while we sat outside on the gate of his pickup, before we set out to do our froggin'. Froggin', which is Cajun terminology for catching bullfrogs, can be done with a gig or by hand. Using a gig is referred to as giggin', but no real Cajun would be caught giggin'. Froggin' is done with bare hands. This means that you have to reach down and grab that critter with your bare hand, while your partner is shining the light in his eyes. Now froggin' can be done alone, but there's not much fun in it alone. There is no one there to witness you wet your pants when you come up with that water moccasin instead of the frog. It also takes a lot more skill because you have to shine the light and catch the frog at the same time. It's not that easy. Partners are also very helpful when you are going to frog a canal. Each partner gets on one bank and shines the light for the other one across the bank, directing him to the frogs, which he usually can't see because they tend to hug the banks, which are full of brush or overhangs. He also can't see that big moccasin sitting next to the frog!

4   Marvin and I had decided to do our froggin' on the bit canal. The canal is about 35 feet wide and 7 feet deep. It is full of water during rice planting season, but empties when the pumps are turned off around June or July, once the rice-harvesting season gets underway. The canal had about a foot of water in it, which was good from a froggin' aspect. We parked the truck and trekked up the canal levee. There we decided who was going to get the good bank (the one we were on) and who would get the bad bank (the one on the other side). Marvin got the good side.

5   The mushroom was definitely working. Shining my headlight around to spot frogs on Marvin's side was spellbinding. The hot muggy night had just a bit of mist in it, which made the lamp beam more defined, more otherworldly, sort of like a *Star Wars* light sabre. Marvin apparently was fascinated with his headlight, too. We must have been there for a good 10 minutes transfixed by the light show before one of us decided we better get back to the business of the frogs.

6   After nabbing a few frogs, I swear I heard voices coming from that sack. I ventured a quick peek into the sack and let out a yelp when my light came across the face of a demon frog! Wide sinister lips gleamed out at me, with a huge set of alligator-like teeth between them. Franken-Frogs! Sack closed! "What was that?" Marvin asked. "Nothing, nothing at all," I replied. I was very careful to keep the sack a safe distant from my body for fear of encountering those teeth!

7   We came to a small area where the canal crossed through a swamp. There was a small pond down at the bottom of the levee on Marvin's side. Marvin decided he would go down and frog the small pond and I would wait for him. I was sitting on the levee with my headlight switched off, marvelling at the wonderful show the stars were putting on overhead, totally oblivious to the rest of the universe.

8   Suddenly there came a blood-curdling scream from the other side of the levee. I jumped up and looked in the direction that I had last seen Marvin heading. I could see his headlight beam cutting through the night sky like the spotlights at a Hollywood premiere in fast-forward mode. There was this continuous, high-pitched shriek coming from Marvin's side of the levee. It sounded like he was trying to say something, but it was drowned out by that shriek. Marvin burst over the top of the levee with a leap that would have made Carl Lewis look like an amateur. He cleared the levee and crossed the canal over to my side in the blink of an eye, hardly getting his boots wet in the process. He scrambled up the levee on my side of the canal with one great leap and landed a few yards from me, still screaming at the top of his lungs. I was amazed, scared, confused, and hallucinating, all at the same time. In all that uproar I had neglected to switch on my headlight. Marvin was standing about 3 yards from me, but didn't know where I was. I switched it on and the beam caught him right in the eyes, which was enough to set him into full flight along the canal levee. I had no idea what he was screaming about and was not about to stay there and find out what it was. I proceeded to high-tail it behind Marvin. He ran out of steam about half a mile down the levee. I could see his headlight beam in the distance, cutting through the night air. When I finally caught up with him, I was too tired from the run to do anything other than stand there, bent over at the waist, trying to suck in oxygen. Marvin's face had a look of horror on it that I will never forget. Looked to me like he had seen the Devil. I got him to calm down a bit and asked him what the hell happened on the other side of the levee. "A bbb,bbbb, bbbeeearrr!!!" he stammered. "Biggest one I have ever seen, 15 feet tall, with big bloody fangs and evil, glowing red eyes!" he went on.

9   A bear! An evil bear, no less! Wow, right here in Morse, Louisiana. What the hell were we going to do? My head was spinning. Probably from the run and the mushrooms. We discussed going back to town and reporting to the sheriff, then we contemplated going to town and getting all of our buddies, tracking it down and shooting it. Maybe we would need some silver bullets, if it was a truly evil bear. Then a thought struck me. A bear? Evil bear? Here in Morse? I looked at Marvin, sitting there heaving, drenched in sweat, terror etched on his face. "Marvin, was that a grizzly bear, a brown bear, a gummy bear or a Marvin-on-mushrooms bear?" I asked. Marvin looked up at me with a puzzled look on his face. Slowly it began to sink in and he burst out laughing like a madman, and so did I. Bears, in Morse? Not very likely. We must have laughed non-stop for 15 minutes. We went back over to where Marvin long-jumped

across the canal. We easily traced his flight path through a stand of small reed grass. Marvin sure does travel straight when in full terror mode! At the beginning of the broken-reed trail was Marvin's sack of frogs, right where he dropped it. Just then he shined his headlight towards a small group of trees about 10 yards from the edge of the small pond. Up about 15 feet off the ground sprang forth a set of red, menacing eyes. We both jumped back a little. A closer look turned up a possum bedding down for the night. He hissed at us, showing us all *his* teeth. Marvin's mushroom bear. We busted out in a fit of laughter again that lasted for 10 minutes. Our sides hurt so much we decided to call it a night.

10   This particular adventure marked a turning point in my life. In the months that followed the mushroom-bear incident, I found myself reliving it over in my mind. Of course I could not help but laugh at the silliness of the whole thing, but there was something buried in the experience that I could not put my finger on. After a few more replays, it occurred to me that maybe it was not the experience itself, rather the haphazard way that we flung ourselves head-long into the adventure, without any thought as to the dangers or consequences of our actions. Much of it can be attributed to the zealousness of youth. However, I resolved to be just a little more careful, a little more thoughtful, a little more aware in the future. That lesson has guided me well to this day.

For Further Thinking

1. Have you had an experience that parallels the one LaBrie describes in this essay? What is the nature and importance of such experience?

2. Is this essay primarily narrative, descriptive, or reflective (using these terms as described in Chapter 5 of the *Rhetoric*)?

3. How would you characterize the tone of this essay? Give examples of how this tone is created.

4. How important are the Cajun expressions in this article?

5. Certain mushrooms can be deadly. Should the author have said more about mushrooms in Morse, Louisiana?

Looking Back and Ahead

1. As a memoir, LaBrie's essay has strong connections to five other selections in this section, "White Breast Flats," "Brownie," "The King and I," "The Hockey Sweater," and "A Midwife in Rankin Inlet." If you have not already done so, describe what you consider the central qualities of this form of writing.

2. Essays such as Mark Radford's "Different Worlds" (p. 43), Susan M. Keaveney's "When MTV Goes CEO" (p. 99), and Anita Lahey's "The Genome Generation" (p. 132) emphasize differences between generations. While reading LaBrie's essay, were you more conscious of generational distinction or universality?

3. How does LaBrie's behaviour compare to that of the girls in "White Breast Flats" (p. 6)? Do boys and girls come of age in significantly different ways? Explain.

For Further Reading

Johnson, Alexandra. *Leaving a Trace: On Keeping a Journal: The Art of Transforming a Life into Stories*. Boston: Little, Brown and Co., 2001.

State of Louisiana. April 2003 <http://www.state.la.us/index.htm>. This site briefly explains the history of the Cajuns in New Orleans, beginning with the expulsion of the Acadians from Lower Canada during the French and Indian War (1765–1763). The site also provides information and services for visitors to the State of Louisiana, with links to other sites.

Michel Tremblay   In this wry memoir, one of Quebec's most renowned writers describes how, on his fourteenth birthday, he gained the courage to bluff his way into an R-rated film, *The King and I*.

Best known for his plays, Tremblay had to wait three years before anyone would produce his landmark drama *Les Belles-Soeurs* (*The Sisters-in-Law*, 1965). Its use of *joual* (informal, everyday French, sometimes regarded as debased) and accurate depictions of east-end working-class society was not deemed appropriate for literature. Many critics have also said that Tremblay is too pre-occupied with Quebec concerns; however, his wide popularity outside the province suggests that focusing on what he knows and cares about has only enhanced his appeal. "The King and I" comes from *Bambi and Me*, a collection of 12 autobiographical narratives, each centred around a film.

The King and I

1   On the day I turned fourteen, June 26, 1956, I decided that from now on I was going to go to movies with the adults, even though I didn't meet the age requirement. I'd had enough of animated cartoons, lives of saints, edifying melodramas or Heidi coming down from her mountain to take care of a little cripple in town. I wanted to see Susan Hayward in her strapless gowns, Lana Turner in her fuzzy sweaters, Marilyn Monroe lying in her Niagara Falls. At the time I wasn't very interested in French films, I saw too many on television, and I was getting sick of Fernandel's faces, Georges Guétary's quavery voice and the tralala of Suzy Delair.

2   At the Palace theatre they were advertising a musical comedy entitled *The King and I* which I'd never heard of but which immediately grabbed my attention: in the ad in *La Presse*, a beautiful woman wearing a wide satin gown was dancing in the arms of what appeared to be a half-naked Indo-Chinese man. That was all I needed to make up my mind and I set out with pounding heart to mount an assault on a movie theatre that had the reputation of being invincible if you were under sixteen.

3   I hadn't yet made the mistake of my brother Bernard who'd drawn on a moustache once to get into the Passe-Temps with our aunt Robertine, only to be met with the cashier's laughter. She'd regretted her action as a matter of fact when my father's sister decided to come to her nephew's defense with her sten-

torian voice and her flowery language. On Mont-Royal Street people were still talk-ing about it. No, I was dressed simply: blue pants, short-sleeved white shirt, red V-neck, my Pat Boone shoes. I probably looked like a cartoon version of a real little gentleman.

4 From my window on the St. Catherine Street tramway I could see the ad for the film, the same one but in colour, and my courage failed me. If besides ask-ing me my age, the cashier demanded some ID . . . if she called the police . . . if I landed in jail because I'd wanted to see a film that, in the end, was really too "adult" for me. . . . I stayed on for a few stops and got off at Ogilvy's. It was barely ten-thirty a.m. (the first showing was at eleven) and I was already sweat-ing. I walked back as far as Eaton's, across the street from the Palace, and stood on tiptoe to try and see what the cashier looked like. . . . Impossible, needless to say. I crossed the street, avoiding the cars and streetcars that were coming in tight ranks in both directions.

5 She didn't look particularly easy-going. I pretended to be checking out the photos—which were very beautiful actually, glossy and sharp and made you want to see the damn film even more—while I kept glancing furtively towards the glass cage. The cashier was old, fat, serious, and she handed out the tickets like some rare and precious manna, gesturing broadly and staring hard at the cus-tomer. She wasn't there to enjoy herself and she let you know it.

6 Did that mean I was sentenced to another two years of Heidi and her goat and her fat neighbour?

7 Deciding I'd been standing there too long, the cashier took a coin and started rapping it against her glass cage, gesturing to me to move on. I must have looked like a depraved child who stands around in front of dirty pictures, so I took off, my shoulders hunched and my tail between my legs.

8 It was a quarter to eleven and my birthday was already ruined.

9 I needed consolation.

10 I darted into Eaton's and headed straight for the record department on the fifth floor.

11 At that time you could buy classical recordings on the Remington and Plymouth labels for the huge sum of ninety-nine cents. They all sounded equally bad and had probably been recorded in studios the size of match-boxes, but I made do with them because I didn't know anything else, my budget being, to say the least, lim-ited. I already owned a fairly impressive collection, basics like the inevitable suites from *Carmen* or *Peer Gynt* and excerpts from *Swan Lake,* but also some works that were less obvious for a neophyte of fourteen—Bruch's violin concerto, for in-stance, or Stravinsky's *Pulcinella*. I also had Mozart's *Cosi* sung by second-rate German singers with flowery names like Elsie Plümaacher, whose Italian sounded hilarious. But I didn't mind, I was learning, I liked everything, I thought it was all sublime, I cried like a calf over Saint-Saëns' ballet music for *Samson and Delilah* as much as over the first chorus of Bach's *St. John Passion*.

12   I was going then to work off my frustration and for another twenty-four cents, buy a fine classical recording that would bring me dozens and dozens of hours of listening instead of the hypothetical pleasure of watching the lady in the long dress dance with the half-bare-naked Siamese man. Obviously I'd decided that *The King and I* wasn't worth risking jail for and that, in any event, it would probably bore me to death.

13   Eaton's record department had listening booths for customers where I'd already spent quite a lot of time choosing among three or four records, often unable to make up my mind; I was known there and the salesladies liked me because I was probably their only teenage customer who bought something besides the records of Patti Page or Gale Storm.

14   That morning though I was out of luck, there was a new girl at the cash register whom I seemed to be disturbing, so much did she look as if she wanted to be somewhere else.

15   And our conversation got off to a very bad start.

16   "Could you open this record for me please, I'd like to listen to it." She looked at me as if I were a dog turd on a velvet cushion.

17   "Sorry, I don't speak French."

18   I knew it was store policy for people to speak English but there was no way that girl was an Anglo, absolutely no way! The accent, the face, the hairdo, the clothes, the gum—it was all straight from the Plateau Mont-Royal or the Faubourg à mélasse. She was a carbon copy of my cousin Lise who worked next door at Kresge's, who used to tell us how people would order a cheese sandwich in English and she'd bring them a ham sandwich in French . . . and that most of all, nobody was going to make her speak English if she didn't feel like it! Except that the Eaton's salesgirl had decided to play the game.

19   She wasn't much older than I was, she was a long way from twenty in any event, and I decided to stand up to her.

20   "Don't make me laugh, you're as French as I am. . . . Anyway, I don't want a conversation, I just want you to open this record. . . ."

21   She raised her eyebrows in circumflex accents and shook her head. And in her best English accent came out with an "I beg your pardon," that emerged from her lips like the most elegant *joual*.

22   I couldn't help laughing.

23   "Look, make a little effort, okay, I know you aren't English so why keep trying?"

24   The salesgirl leaned across the counter towards me.

25   "What the hell do you want, you little creep, you want me to lose my job?"

26   She glanced furtively to her right and pretended she was busy at the cash register.

27   Near the escalators, some manager or other was watching us suspiciously, not even bothering to hide his dismal performance as an underpaid spy out to catch *in flagrante delicto* two francophones who were communicating in their lan-

guage. I got the picture in an instant: the constant humiliations, the harassment, the small and pitiful capitulations. I felt sorry for her. And for me.

28   "Okay, pretend I talked English to you. He didn't hear us."

29   I felt like an asshole. So did she.

30   She ripped the cellophane off the record sleeve and held it out with an extremely stupid look on her face.

31   "Think you're smart, eh? Just wait till you're in my shoes!"

32   As I headed for the listening booth I came across the record of *The King and I* in the place of honour on the display racks. I picked it up, looked at it from every angle. It looked fantastic!

33   Of course I wanted to listen to it. On my way back to the cash register to have it opened, I noticed the spy who'd come to stand next to the salesgirl, smiling ferociously as he watched me come back. They weren't going to make me speak English with them! When I got to the counter I showed the salesgirl the record, totally ignoring the manager, I tore the cellophane myself with my thumb the way I'd seen her do with the other record, then I turned my back on them.

34   It was a very small victory, a victory by omission rather than a genuine active resistance, but I was still very proud of myself.

35   Unlikely as it may sound, what follows is absolutely true.

36   I don't remember anything about the classical record, all I know is that it didn't interest me and I didn't spend much time with it.

37   I put *The King and I* on the turntable, hoping the music would be worthy of the album cover. The opening was pleasant enough in the Oriental-American style of the fifties, but it didn't really grab me and I nearly put the record back in its envelope. Then came the first song, "I Whistle a Happy Tune." The words leaped out at me like a message that Anna, the English school-mistress who had just arrived in Siam to teach the king's children, was sending out to me personally across time, a record, a film, a song, and I was blown away:

38   "Whenever I feel afraid
I hold my head erect
And whistle a happy tune
So no one will suspect
I'm afraid."

39   The song was addressed to me personally! The secret was in its off-hand manner. If I wanted to get inside that theatre I had to be the opposite of the beaten dog who goes and hides in the corner so he'll be forgotten before he even gets scolded for doing something wrong! I had to be so off-hand the cashier would feel she had to let me in even though she could see I wasn't sixteen yet. Most of all, she mustn't know I was terrified of her. I shouldn't have run away, I should have faced up to her—holding my head erect.

40   I sped back to return the two records, telling the salesgirl in a superior tone: "They're boring!" and ran to the theatre without stopping.

41   The dragon was still at her post; there was no one going inside because the film had started ages ago. The cashier was listlessly leafing through a magazine while she waited for the next wave of customers who wouldn't turn up for an hour at least. I gathered up the small amount of courage I still had despite my wobbly legs, the sweat running down my back, my rapidly pounding heart and the lump in my throat and I managed to arrive at the ticket booth whistling, just like on the record. It wasn't very loud, but you could hear it. I don't know if you could really call it casual, but I hoped it would give the illusion. Bravely, I dropped my seventy-five cents in front of her, looking her straight in the eye. "Please God, don't let her recognize me! Don't let her create a scandal so I have to defend myself in English, I can't speak it well enough and I don't want to be laughed at on top of everything else!" Inwardly I was the Krakatoa about to erupt, but outwardly I wanted to give the impression I was someone for whom going to the movies was nothing out of the ordinary, a critic maybe, yes, why not, a rather blasé critic who's stuck with seeing this film he doesn't really want to see and he's going now, just before noon, so he won't ruin an entire day. Someone who couldn't care less if they let him in or not, because this film, really. . . . She probably didn't look at me or else she admired my nerve enough to disregard her rules and her convictions, but the fact remains that I ended up holding a ticket without having hell open up at my feet or lightning strike my slender little body. It was almost too easy, I hesitated for a fraction of a second before walking away from the cashier.

42   I had a ticket for *The King and I* two years early!

43   I'll always remember the state of euphoria I was in as I climbed the thickly-carpeted stairs. I looked at myself in the huge mirror that ran along the banister on both sides, multiplying my reflection infinitely. . . . Though I looked like a little bum! A little bum in his Sunday best who wants access to something he's unworthy of. . . . How could I deceive anybody? I was still whistling but my mouth was frozen, I felt as if never again would I be able to relax the muscles in my lips.

44   The ticket-taker didn't even look at me and I went down into the theatre deep in a Nirvana whose intensity measured 8.5 on the Richter scale.

45   It was a wall-to-wall screen, Cinemascope in all its splendor, and a Siamese ballet as revised by Rogers and Hammerstein was unfurling its extravagance while Rita Moreno intoned: "Run, little Eva, run!" I raced to the most anonymous seat, the one where nobody ever sits because it gives you a headache, and let myself be swallowed up for two and a half hours by the faintly sickening but oh so reassuring syrup of the colours, the music, the dances, the songs, the sets, the stunning dresses worn by Deborah Kerr (who would be the great idol of my teenage years, at least till the arrival of Shirley MacLaine in *Some Came Running*), and the seductive outfits worn by Yul Brynner.

46   I was thrilled, moved, and I swore that from now on I was going to movies "for adults" at least once a week. No more silly kids' stuff for me; starting now, the global production of movies, at least whatever made it to Montreal, was mine. I was an adult.

For Further Thinking

1. Do you, like Tremblay, have memories of an incident that publicly marked your passage into adulthood? How does your experience resemble his? How does it differ?

2. Comment on how the memoir combines psychological and political obstacles.

3. Describe the structure of this memoir. Is it simply rambling and episodic, or does each new event play into the underlying concern? Explain.

4. How would you describe the mood and tone of this essay? Give examples of elements that contribute to this effect.

5. Talking about *Bambi and Me* with David Homel of *Books in Canada* magazine, Tremblay said, "Each chapter was like a step forward for the character, a discovery of fear, of sexuality, of art. . . ." Is this true of "The King and I"? If so, explain how.

Looking Back and Ahead

1. Tremblay remembers when French was considered inferior to English, when even French employees in the "posh" English-owned stores had to pretend their preferred language was English. How much does this history influence the attitude described by François Hébert in "Je Me Souviens" (p. 54)?

2. As a memoir, Tremblay's essay has strong connections to five other selections in this section, "White Breast Flats," "Brownie," "Franken-Frogs and the Mushroom Bear," "The Hockey Sweater," and "A Midwife in Rankin Inlet." If you have not already done so, describe what you find to be the central qualities of this form of writing. How does each writer's sense of self differ from the other essayists?

For Further Reading

Johnson, Alexandra. *Leaving a Trace: On Keeping a Journal: The Art of Transforming a Life into Stories*. Boston: Little, Brown and Co., 2001.

Jutra, Claude, dir. *Mon Oncle Antoine* (film). National Film Board, 1971. Set in a small Quebec town, this film conveys an idea of the oppression felt by many Francophones in a social and economic system dominated by the English and abetted by the powerful church.

"Michel Tremblay." The Canadian Theatre Encyclopedia. April 2003 <http://www.canadiantheatre. com/t/tremblaym.html>. This site offers a wide range of information on Tremblay.

Tremblay, Michel. *Bambi and Me*. Trans. Shelia Fischman. Toronto: Talon Books, 1998. (Originally pub. 1990 by Leméac as *Les vues animées*.) This work of 12 autobiographical narratives, each centred on a particular film, contains the essay "The King and I."

————. *The Fat Woman Next Door Is Pregnant*. Trans. Sheila Fischman. Toronto: Talon Books, 1981. The first in the tetralogy *Chroniques du plateau Mont-Royal*, this novel powerfully conveys Tremblay's vision of life in working-class rue Fabre.

————. *Therese and Pierrette and the Little Hanging Angel*. Trans. Sheila Fischman. Toronto: Talon Books, 1984. Continuing Tremblay's saga of his working-class neighbourhood, this novel focuses on three schoolgirls.

Mark Radford It is often observed that in the past 150 years, society has changed more radically and rapidly than ever before in recorded history. Those of us in our forties or fifties recall the days before television, never mind home computers; in some cases, our parents recall the first motor car to have appeared on the streets of their small town. Certainly with the advent of Internet, the past 15 years have seen a great deal of social change driven by technology. More change is likely to occur in the next 10 or 20 years of your lifetime than has occurred in all of ours. While it may be argued that apparent trends sometimes take unexpected turns, for now the rate of technical and social revolution seems to be constantly accelerating. The following essay reflects on this context of rapidly changing society, with attention to the major differences it produces between the generations.

A married father of three children who manages a Calgary high-tech company while pursuing his bachelor's degree part time, Mark Radford wrote this essay mostly as a tribute to his father.

Different Worlds

1   The world is changing rapidly. When I think about the way my father grew up, compared to the way I grew up and the way my son is growing up now, I'm amazed by the differences. Changes are all around us everyday, some seemingly significant and others not, but it isn't until you consciously compare certain things over a number of years that the significance is truly revealed. The differences between my childhood and my son's are not as fundamental as the differences between my father's and mine, but they are still significant.

2   My father was born in 1925 near Napanee, Ontario. He was seven years old in 1932, the height of the Great Depression. Imagine what life was like for a seven-year-old boy with three older sisters and no father, during the worst economic times in the history of this country. They lived in an old house without electricity or plumbing. He shared the one bedroom with his sisters. His favourite sister was the one who would go with him to the outhouse at night because he was too scared to go on his own (inside plumbing was for rich people). The wood-burning stove was used for cooking as well as heating the house. Horses were more common than cars on the dirt roads and the only way for him to get anywhere, including the three miles to school, was to walk.

3   My father told me about his childhood, how there were days when his mother wouldn't let him go to school because she didn't have any food to give him for lunch. On those days he went looking for work or food. He would put a

handful of corn he'd obtained from some neighbour's farm in a pile and wait for three or four pigeons to gather. Then he'd shoot them all with one shot from an old shotgun he had. Pigeon sandwiches were a treat! He didn't have adequate food or clothing, so he grew up hungry and cold. He spent his free time fishing and hunting for food. He learned to swim on his own, by watching his older sisters. For fun, he and his friends would go swimming in the Napanee River or Lake Ontario. They would cause mischief for entertainment, such as knocking over people's outhouses or spearing pickerel out of season in the small streams, where the big fish came to spawn. He worked cutting and stacking wood. He made one dollar for a full cord of wood (four feet by four feet by eight feet long). If he worked hard, he could make a dollar in a twelve-hour workday. School came second when compared to survival. My father made it as far as grade seven, and learned basic math, reading and writing skills, before he left home, at age twelve, to get a job. He went to live and work on a farm, but the owner was mean-spirited and worked my father very hard. When he was fifteen years old, he lied about his age and joined the Navy. Life in basic training was the best he'd experienced so far. For the first time in his life, he had warm clothes, good boots and three square meals each day. Then he went into active duty in World War II. He was a gunner on a corvette (a small gunship) escorting supply ships across the North Atlantic in the 1940s. It took three men to operate one gun, two to unload, reload, and turn the gun on the horizontal and vertical axis. The third man aimed and fired. My father was the third man. He was sixteen years old and terrified of dying. That's how my father grew up.

4   I was born in 1960 and grew up in a Toronto, Ontario, suburb. I was the fifth of seven children. My brother and I shared one of the five bedrooms in the house. There were two bathrooms, a recreation room (which we called the TV room because that's where the colour television was), and a big backyard with apple trees. The house was centrally heated with an oil-burning furnace. There was a stone fireplace in the living room, but it was only used on special occasions such as Thanksgiving or Christmas. We had two telephones, one in the kitchen and one in my parents' bedroom. The paved driveway ran the length of the property to the two-car garage at the back. The neighbourhood streets were paved and we played in the ditches that ran alongside them. My father, a supervisor for a painting company, had a company pickup truck. My mother, a stay-at-home mom, drove a station wagon.

5   When I was seven years old, my parents bought a cottage lot on a beautiful lake in cottage country, three hours' drive north of Toronto. I spent most weekends and all my summer holidays there. My grandmother taught me how to swim by tying a rope to my life jacket and walking along the edge of the boat dock. As a twelve-year-old, I had to work every morning around the cottage. I moved dirt with a wheelbarrow, raked leaves or cut grass and shrubs. In the city, I helped my father do yard work and in the winter, shovel snow. My afternoons and evenings were free time.

6   As a teenager at the cottage, I had a best friend next door. We used our dads' motorboats to go fishing, exploring, chasing seagulls or racing each other across the lake and back. We had motorized mini-bikes, to ride wildly up and down the dirt roads. We collected pop bottles alongside the road and cashed them in at the local gas station. We played on the same baseball team. We went swimming in the lake several times each day. We made tree forts, fought pea-gun wars, played lawn darts, Frisbee, and badminton. We made bows and arrows from tree branches and used them to hunt frogs. On rainy days we played chess, made crafts, or read books. In the winter my brother and I shovelled the snow off a large section of the frozen lake and flooded it with buckets of water, to make a skating rink. The whole family played hockey, crack-the-whip, and other skating games. We had two snowmobiles and spent virtually all our days outside. At night we played cards and other family games at the kitchen table, or read books by the fire.

7   In the city, we played hide-and-seek, tag, and other outdoor children's games. My brother and I built a go-cart and raced it up and down the driveway against other neighbourhood go-carts. When it grew dark, we went inside to watch television for a little while before bedtime. In the winter we played hockey in the driveway after school, until our mother called us in for dinner. After gorging myself at dinner, including vegetables grown in our own garden, prepared on the electric stove, I went to work on my homework. I learned touch-typing in junior high school, so I could type my school assignments on our manual typewriter at home. I researched them in the school library and graduated from high school with honours. I walked or rode my bike almost everywhere I went, including the one mile each way to school.

8   When I turned sixteen, I started working during my summer vacations. As a painter's helper, I earned ten dollars per hour. I bought my first stereo that summer, and dozens of LP records. On dates with my girlfriend, I drove a car my sister and I shared.

9   That's how I grew up. My son was born in 1986 and he has a younger brother and sister. He lives in a house in a suburban area of Calgary. He has his own bedroom, as do his siblings. There are four bathrooms for five people to use, a family room and a den. The backyard he rarely plays in is one-fiftieth the size of the one I grew up playing in. The house is centrally heated with natural gas. The gas fireplace, which is used everyday during the winter, turns on by the flick of a wall switch. He calls his friends on any one of the seven telephones in the house, or emails them. The driveway is cement and the garage is attached to the house. Like most other streets, his is paved and has curbs and sidewalks. His father drives a minivan and his stay-at-home mom drives a station wagon.

10   He takes swimming and skating lessons at a recreation centre, karate lessons at a private studio, and attends Boy Scouts. He helps with household chores and volunteers at the swimming pool and ski hill. My son takes drum lessons and practises on his drum set in the basement. The instructor comes to

the house once each week. My son spends his summer vacations at day camps, amusement parks, watching television, and hanging out in the neighbour-hood. He eats better meals than I did, mainly because we now know what's nu-tritious and what isn't. However, all the food is bought at the grocery store (who has time for a garden?). I badger him to go outside to play, but he resists. His main leisure activities stem from playing video and computer games or watching video movies on any one of the three colour televisions with video-cassette recorders in the house. He can touch-type on the computer keyboard and complains when he has to take turns doing his homework on it because we have only one—he wants his own. Some homework assignments in his junior high school classes must be typed on a computer and he surfs the Internet for information to complete them. His writing is barely legible, but no one cares because everything is printed from the computer. Handwriting does-n't seem to be an important or valuable skill, to him or his teachers. He rarely walks anywhere and rides a bus the one mile to school because it's too far to walk, or considered not safe to do so. For his thirteenth birthday, my son re-ceived a new stereo for his bedroom. Now he buys compact discs, or borrows mine. This is how he's growing up.

11   The world has changed and continues to change at an ever-increasing pace. Although my father, my son, and I grew up in the same country, we grew up in different worlds.

For Further Thinking

1. From listening to parents, grandparents, or other elders, what details of life before your birth most interest, surprise, or disturb you?

2. Would you agree that the first decades of your life were significantly different from those of your parents? If so, in what respects?

3. What do you like best and least in your generation's way of life? What do you think you would have liked best and least in the way of life of your parents' generation, and of your grandparents' generation?

4. Considering life today in comparison to life when your grandparents were growing up, do you think things are getting worse or better? Explain.

5. Prepare a diagram or outline of the various comparisons within Radford's essay. For assis-tance, you may wish to refer to "Comparison-Contrast" in Chapter 6 of our *Rhetoric*. Identify any passages where Radford establishes a comparison within a comparison. Observe any other rhetorical structures.

Looking Back and Ahead

1. Michel Tremblay in "The King and I" refers to a childhood of poverty in the 1950s, while Radford's father was establishing a comfortable home in suburban Toronto. Do you

agree that while some members of society have been getting richer over the last few decades, many have been getting poorer?

2. Does Radford's son fit into the generation defined by Susan Keaveney in her essay "When MTV Goes CEO" (p. 99)? If not, define the characteristics of a post-X generation.

3. Compare Radford's survey of three generations to Pat Deiter-McArthur's survey in "Saskatchewan's Indian People—Five Generations" (p. 87).

For Further Reading

Coupland, Douglas. *Generation X: Tales for an Accelerated Culture*. New York: St. Martin's, 1991. With this first novel, Coupland—who hails from Vancouver—gave currency to the term designating those born between 1965 and 1975 or so.

Dunn-Cane, Kathleen, Joan L. Gonzalez, and Hildegarde P. Stewart. "Managing the New Generation." *AORN Journal* 69. 5 (May 1999): 930. The authors define three generations of health-care workers—the Silent Generation (1925–1942), the Boomers (1946–1964), and the Xers (1965–1975)—and the management style most suited to each.

Finley, Michelle. "New Generation Gap: Hackers." April 2003 <http://www.wired.com/news/politics/0,1283,34617,00.html>. The author points out that internet vandalism is usually attributed to "kids." She argues that this may be a form of intergenerational snobbery between "old hackers" who went online before 1991 and those who came after the advent of the World Wide Web.

"Generation Gap." ThinkQuest. April 2003 <http://library.thinkquest.org/23440/?qskip=1>. This site contains information and contributions from members of the five generations alive today.

University of Pittsburgh. Intergenerational programs. April 2003 <http://www.pitt.edu/~gti/>. This website links you to more information on resources, movements, programs, and American public policy on healing the divisions between young and old.

Wellner, Alison Stein. "Make Love, Not Art?" *Forecast* 21. 3 (March 2001): 1. Baby boomers are often characterized as creative and interested in the arts, but have they turned away from the values they were supposed to embody?

Nicole Lombard A South African whose mother tongue is Afrikaans, Nicole Lombard was living and studying in Manitoba when she wrote this English assignment about the special challenges of adapting to English as spoken in Canada.

She refers to two other essays in her discussion. One, by James Baldwin, an Afro-American writer, argues that Black English should be respected as a language in its own right rather than seen as a mere dialect (or a variation of a base language). In the other essay Lombard cites, American poet Adrienne Rich describes her experience as a teacher in a New York City "open admissions" program. (Both essays are listed under "For Further Reading.")

Speaking South African English in Canada

1   I have often wondered why the software on my computer has only an American English and a British English spell-check and only an American English thesaurus. What about South African English, Canadian English, and all the other English-speaking countries?

2   It is common knowledge that all the English-speaking countries speak a version of the English language that is unique to that country. I believe that the reason for this is that "people evolve a language in order to describe and thus control their circumstances or in order to describe a situation they cannot articulate" (Baldwin 139). Each country has developed a language that was influenced by its own history and circumstances. This explains why South African English is so different from the English spoken in England and all the other English-speaking countries: even though all the versions of English spoken in the English speaking countries originated from British English, "they each have very different realities to articulate, or control" (Baldwin 139).

3   The English language in South Africa has always had a lot of influence from other languages. First it was influenced by Dutch and French, then by Afrikaans and then by all the black languages spoken in South Africa. At present South Africa has 11 official languages, which sounds like a lot, but luckily we don't have to speak or even understand them all. To be totally honest, I can't even name them all. The largest percentage of people in South Africa speak Zulu as a first language, the second largest percentage speak Afrikaans, with English competing with Sotho and Xhosa for third place. English is the first choice as a second language and it is also the business language of South Africa. With all these influences, it is no surprise that South Africans find it hard to understand the English spoken in England, the United States, Canada, Australia, and New Zealand.

4   Some time ago I read a very short article in *Time* magazine in which the writer mentioned an English dictionary that gives you the different words used to describe the same thing (or more or less the same thing) in all the different versions of English. Since we have been in Canada, we have experienced a lot of problems with the different words used in Canadian English and such a dictionary would be a great help. To illustrate our problem, I give a few examples of the different words for that same thing: we wear our "costumes" to the beach; to make lasagna we use "mince" and not hamburger; we eat "biltong," "koeksisters" and "wors," we sit outside on our "stoep," and we drive a "bakkie" and not a truck. I have many times during conversations with Canadians seen puzzled looks on their faces, caused by some strange word that I used. Most of the time I don't even have an idea which word caused the problem.

5   The way we pronounce words also causes great confusion. Unfortunately for us, we live in F5 in a complex of townhouses. The letter *f* has caused numerous problems so far, because the way we say *f* sounds similar to how

Canadians say *a* (although we don't think they sound similar at all). I have been practising to pronounce the *f* like a Canadian, but I think that I need a lot more practice before I will be understood. I sometimes think it will be easier just to move to A5.

6 Although the fact that we speak South African English creates a problem when we communicate with Canadians, it is not our only problem. On page 139 in "If Black English Isn't a Language, Then Tell Me, What Is?" James Baldwin says, "Language, incontestably, reveals the speaker." The problem that we have is that English is our second language. It is the language that we use to speak to strangers and do business. Even our English speaking co-citizens in South Africa could understand Afrikaans well enough so that we could express ourselves clearly. The problem is that if a person cannot express him- or herself clearly, people often think of such a person as dumb or slow. This has happened with the Blacks in South Africa who couldn't understand English or Afrikaans. According to Adrienne Rich in "Teaching Language In Open Admissions" (151), it has also happened in America that non-English-speaking people have been regarded as dumb.

7 I have come to accept that while I live in Canada language will always be a problem. Although we all speak a common language, I speak South African English and I will never be able to have a conversation without hoping that I am not misunderstood.

Works Cited

Baldwin, James. "If Black English Isn't a Language, Then Tell Me, What Is?" *English 255 Writing Skills Reader*. Athabasca, AB: Athabasca University, 1988. 139–42.

Rich, Adrienne. "Teaching Language in Open Admissions." *English 255 Writing Skills Reader*. Athabasca, AB: Athabasca University, 1988. 143–60.

For Further Thinking

1. Have you encountered difficulty understanding and being understood by other speakers of English? What accounted for the difficulty? Compare your experience to Lombard's.

2. How many different words can you think of to name the same thing? Can you trace your sample words to different countries, regions, or social groups? Explain.

3. The state of California once had 50 of North America's 250 Native languages; 20 of those 50 languages died last century and all the rest are in danger of imminent extinction. What is your opinion of the arguments for and against English as the common global language?

4. As well as containing elements of personal narrative, Lombard's essay uses a number of other rhetorical strategies. Identify some of these, and provide examples. (See Chapter 6 of the *Rhetoric* if you are uncertain what other patterns of organization to look for.)

Looking Back and Ahead

1. Read Michel Tremblay's "The King and I" (p. 37). What tensions and ironies do you find in that essay on the subject of English dominating the globe?
2. Do you know people from other regions of Canada whose English sounds as foreign to you as Nicole Lombard's might sound? Read Diane Mooney's "Newfoundlandese, if You Please" (p. 109) for some interesting detail on how Old World speech, modified by regional history, remains a vibrant part of the Canadian tapestry.
3. Daphne Read's essay "A Story to Pass On" (p. 216) alludes to the close bonds between language, culture, and a sense of security. Record your feelings when you hear a familiar word, such as "river." In contrast, how do you feel hearing the object named in a foreign language? How does multilingualism affect your reaction?
4. Is one of the contemporary varieties of English an international code of consumerism? See Howard Richler's "The Seven Deadly Sins Are 'In' and Proud of It" (p. 224) for his opinion on this question.
5. George Orwell's "Politics and the English Language" (p. 227) remains one of the most important essays on the impact of language. What seems to be Orwell's attitude toward a diversity of Englishes? Where do you stand on this issue?

For Further Reading

Baldwin, James. "If Black English Isn't a Language, Then Tell Me What Is?" *The Price of the Ticket: Collected Nonfiction, 1948–1985.* New York: St. Martin's, 1985. 650–52. Online. April 2003.

Ballantyne, Elizabeth, Richard Dionne, and Evan Jones, eds. *Canadian Thesaurus.* Markham, ON: Fitzhenry and Whiteside, 2001. April 2003 <http://www.fitzhenry.ca/thesaurus.htm>. Twelve years in the making, this work emphasizes distinctly Canadian choices and provides synonyms for 13 000 entries.

Falk, Lillian, and Margaret Harry. *The English Language in Nova Scotia: Essays on Past and Present Developments in English Across the Province.* Lockeport, NS: Roseway, 1999.

Grady, Wayne. *Chasing the Chinook: On the Trail of Canadian Words and Culture.* Toronto: Viking, 1998. In 41 informal, discursive essays, Grady ponders the origins and significance of distinctly Canadian words such as "Acadia" and "joual."

Heller, Louis G., Alexander Humez, and Malcah Dror, eds. *The Private Lives of English Words.* Tarrytown, NY: Wynwood, 1991. The authors tell the stories behind more than 400 words and expressions, taking us to distant times, places, and people.

Hoffman, Eva. *Lost in Translation: A Life in a New Language.* New York: E.P. Dutton, 1989. Polish immigrant Hoffman discusses her problems with living in Vancouver with a new language: "the signifier has become severed from the signified" (p. 106).

Labov, William. "The Organization of Dialect Diversity in North America." Phonological Atlas of North America, home page. Paper presented to ICSLP4, the Fourth International Conference on Spoken Language Processing, Philadelphia, PA, Oct. 6, 1996. April 2003 <http://www.ling.upenn.edu/phono_atlas/ICSLP4.html>.

McCrum, Robert, William Cran, and Robert MacNeil, eds. *The Story of English*. London: Faber, 1986. This book is based on a series of videotapes by the BBC. The tapes are available from most public libraries.

Rich, Adrienne. "Teaching Language in Open Admissions." *The Uses of Literature*. Ed. Monroe Engel. Cambridge, MA: Harvard University Press, 1973. April 2003 < http://astro.temple.edu/~sparkss/richopenadmissions.htm>.

Roch Carrier One of Quebec's foremost writers, Roch Carrier (b. 1937) has achieved success in a remarkable range of forms: novels, short stories, children's fiction, plays, screenplays, and poetry. He sets much of his fiction in rural Quebec and characteristically deals with fears of the English, with hypocrisy, and with ironic reversal. Like Michel Tremblay, Carrier is widely read in North America as well as abroad. He has served as executive director of the Canada Council for the Arts and is currently National Librarian of Canada.

The following story accurately reflects 1950s Quebec. One man, Maurice "Rocket" Richard (1921–2000), number 9 of the Montreal Canadiens, symbolized the pride and aspirations of French-speaking Quebecers. In March 1955, Clarence Campbell, president of the National Hockey League, suspended Richard for striking a referee; his decision provoked the "Rocket Richard Riot," identified by some historians as the beginning of Quebec's nationalist movement.

See the Appendix at the end of the *Reader*, Part I (p. 240), for more support for this reading. This support may particularly benefit you if English is not your first language.

The Hockey Sweater

1   The winters of my childhood were long, long seasons. We lived in three places— the school, the church and the skating-rink—but our real life was on the skating-rink. Real battles were won on the skating-rink. Real strength appeared on the skating-rink. The real leaders showed themselves on the skating-rink. School was a sort of punishment. Parents always want to punish children and school is their most natural way of punishing us. However, school was also a quiet place where we could prepare for the next hockey game, lay out our next strategies. As for church, we found there the tranquility of God: there we forgot school and dreamed about the next hockey game. Through our daydreams it might happen that we would recite a prayer: we would ask God to help us play as well as Maurice Richard.

2   We all wore the same uniform as he, the red, white and blue uniform of the Montreal Canadiens, the best hockey team in the world; we all combed our hair in the same style as Maurice Richard, and to keep it in place we used a sort of glue—a great deal of glue. We laced our skates like Maurice Richard, we taped our sticks like Maurice Richard. We cut all his pictures out of the papers. Truly, we knew everything about him.

3   On the ice, when the referee blew his whistle the two teams would rush at the puck; we were five Maurice Richards taking it away from five other Maurice

Richards; we were ten players, all of us wearing with the same blazing enthusiasm the uniform of the Montreal Canadiens. On our backs, we all wore the famous number 9.

4　One day, my Montreal Canadiens sweater had become too small; then it got torn and had holes in it. My mother said: "If you wear that old sweater people are going to think we're poor!" Then she did what she did whenever we needed new clothes. She started to leaf through the catalogue the Eaton company sent us in the mail every year. My mother was proud. She didn't want to buy our clothes at the general store; the only things that were good enough for us were the latest styles from Eaton's catalogue. My mother didn't like the order forms included with the catalogue; they were written in English and she didn't understand a word of it. To order my hockey sweater, she did as she usually did; she took out her writing paper and wrote in her gentle schoolteacher's hand: "Cher Monsieur Eaton, Would you be kind enough to send me a Canadiens' sweater for my son who is ten years old and a little too tall for his age and Docteur Robitaille thinks he's a little too thin? I'm sending you three dollars and please send me what's left if there's anything left. I hope your wrapping will be better than last time."

5　Monsieur Eaton was quick to answer my mother's letter. Two weeks later we received the sweater. That day I had one of the greatest disappointments of my life! I would even say that on that day I experienced a very great sorrow. Instead of the red, white and blue Montreal Canadiens sweater, Monsieur Eaton had sent us a blue and white sweater with a maple leaf on the front—the sweater of the Toronto Maple Leafs. I'd always worn the red, white and blue Montreal Canadiens sweater; all my friends wore the red, white and blue sweater; never had anyone in my village ever worn the Toronto sweater, never had we even seen a Toronto Maple Leafs sweater. Besides, the Toronto team was regularly trounced by the triumphant Canadiens. With tears in my eyes, I found the strength to say:

6　"I'll never wear that uniform."

7　"My boy, first you're going to try it on! If you make up your mind about things before you try, my boy, you won't go very far in this life."

8　My mother had pulled the blue and white Toronto Maple Leafs sweater over my shoulders and already my arms were inside the sleeves. She pulled the sweater down and carefully smoothed all the creases in the abominable maple leaf on which, right in the middle of my chest, were written the words "Toronto Maple Leafs." I wept.

9　"I'll never wear it."

10　"Why not? This sweater fits you . . . like a glove."

11　"Maurice Richard would never put it on his back."

12　"You aren't Maurice Richard. Anyway, it isn't what's on your back that counts, it's what you've got inside your head."

13　"You'll never put it in my head to wear a Toronto Maple Leafs sweater."

14　My mother sighed in despair and explained to me:

15   "If you don't keep this sweater which fits you perfectly I'll have to write to Monsieur Eaton and explain that you don't want to wear the Toronto sweater. Monsieur Eaton's an *Anglais*; he'll be insulted because he likes the Maple Leafs. And if he's insulted do you think he'll be in a hurry to answer us? Spring will be here and you won't have played a single game, just because you didn't want to wear that perfectly nice blue sweater."

16   So I was obliged to wear the Maple Leafs sweater. When I arrived on the rink, all the Maurice Richards in red, white and blue came up, one by one, to take a look. When the referee blew his whistle I went to take my usual position. The captain came and warned me I'd be better to stay on the forward line. A few minutes later the second line was called; I jumped onto the ice. The Maple Leafs sweater weighed on my shoulders like a mountain. The captain came and told me to wait; he'd need me later, on defense. By the third period I still hadn't played; one of the defensemen was hit in the nose with a stick and it was bleeding. I jumped on the ice: my moment had come! The referee blew his whistle; he gave me a penalty. He claimed I'd jumped on the ice when there were already five players. That was too much! It was unfair! It was persecution! It was because of my blue sweater! I struck my stick against the ice so hard it broke. Relieved, I bent down to pick up the debris. As I straightened up I saw the young vicar, on skates, before me.

17   "My child," he said, "just because you're wearing a new Toronto Maple Leafs sweater unlike the others, it doesn't mean you're going to make the laws around here. A proper young man doesn't lose his temper. Now take off your skates and go to the church and ask God to forgive you."

18   Wearing my Maple Leafs sweater I went to the church, where I prayed to God; I asked him to send, as quickly as possible, moths that would eat up my Toronto Maple Leafs sweater.

For Further Thinking

1. Make an outline of the narrative structure of this story. Does it have specific parts and connections between the parts? How do these work? After you have given some thought to these questions, see our analysis of this story in Chapter 5 of the *Rhetoric*.

2. What would you state as the theme of this story?

3. Although the story deals with barriers between French and English, hockey is often said to be "in the blood of all Canadians," a force of unification beyond the power of politicians and business leaders. What do you think of this perception?

4. What are your own connections with the narrator of the story? Is his childhood significantly different from yours? Explain.

5. Discuss the commingling of hockey and religion in this story.

Looking Back and Ahead

1. Compare the narrative voice of this memoir-like story to that of Mordecai Richler's short story "The Summer My Grandmother Was Supposed to Die" (p. 14). What are the similarities and differences?
2. Do you think Roch Carrier, like François Hébert, author of the next selection, would vote "yes" to Quebec independence? Explain your answer.
3. Compare the young narrator of this fictional memoir to the young Michel Tremblay of "The King and I" (p. 37). What are the important similarities and differences?
4. Although "The Hockey Sweater" is fiction, it has strong connections to five non-fiction memoirs in this section, "White Breast Flats," "Brownie," "Franken-Frogs and the Mushroom Bear," "The King and I," and "A Midwife in Rankin Inlet." If you have not already done so, describe what you consider the central qualities of these two forms of writing.

For Further Reading

Blaise, Clark. "I'm Dreaming of Rocket Richard." *Tribal Justice*. Toronto: Doubleday, 1974. Like the story by Carrier, Blaise's "I'm Dreaming of Rocket Richard" deals, in part, with cultural implications surrounding the man who often claimed that he "was just a hockey player."

Carrier, Roch. *La Guerre, Yes Sir!* Trans. Sheila Fischman. Toronto: Anansi, 1970.

—————. *The Hockey Sweater and Other Stories*. Trans. Sheila Fischman. Toronto: Anansi, 1979. The original collection, aimed at young readers, is *Les Enfants du bonhomme dans la lune* (Children of the Man in the Moon).

Cohen, Sheldon, prod. *The Sweater* (animated film). National Film Board, 1980. This version follows the story very closely. Cohen's animation is delightful, as is the narration by Roch Carrier.

Dryden, Ken. *The Game*. Toronto: Macmillan, 1999. Considered the best hockey book ever written as well as among the 100 best Canadian books of the twentieth century, *The Game* offers a thought-provoking look at a life in the sport.

"Maurice Richard." April 2003 <http://www.spelten.com/MauriceRichard/>. See this site for extensive information on the Montreal Canadiens as well and their place in Quebec history.

François Hébert From *Saturday Night*, June 24, 2000, this memoir asserts the author's support for Quebec sovereignty. Quebec's official motto "Je Me Souviens" means "I remember." For Francophone Quebecers (Québécois) in particular, this has come to refer to their commitment never to forget their history, rights, and culture. Having lost legal possession of their territory in 1763, Quebec Francophones hold fast to their identity through language, art, institutions, and historical perspective.

Feeling outvoted on core issues, many Francophone Quebecers find political sovereignty an appealing idea. Furthermore, many French-speaking intellectuals believe the only way to resist the forces of Americanization is to gain greater control over political and economic policies. But St. Jean Baptiste Day, the setting for this article, has meanings and roots beyond secular nationalism. For more information about St. Jean Baptiste Day, see the entry for this reading in the Appendix at the end of the *Reader*.

See the Appendix, Part I (p. 241), for more support for this reading. It may particularly benefit you if English is not your first language.

Je Me Souviens

1   When I was a child in Montreal, there were fewer public festivities—jazz, film, or otherwise—and fewer demonstrations. There were more Stanley Cup parades, before hockey was played for Americans and for money, but the two big annual events, year in, year out, were the Santa Claus parade and *la Fête Nationale*: Saint Jean Baptiste Day. These celebrations were pagan and cosmological, linked to the movement of the earth around the sun; December and June are now merely months, just words in our timetables. Santa Claus, as everyone knows, has long been kidnapped by Amex, Visa, and Mastercard, who make him sing and play bit parts in department stores. *La Saint-Jean* has also evolved.

2   In the beginning it was a summer-solstice celebration, but by the time it was brought to New France by the earliest settlers it had been appropriated by the Church. When Quebec City's population was barely 200 souls, Jesuit records portray *la Saint-Jean* as a pious and dour procession. Understandable, then, that the celebration has all but disappeared into history in France; understandable, too, that it took the hanging of Lower Canada's *patriotes* for the celebration to catch on as a proto-nationalist event in Quebec.

3   God still existed here then. We did not have a country of our own, but we did have religion and a language. We still don't have a country of our own and we don't have much religion anymore, but we cling to our language—and to our *Fête Nationale* to confirm what we know we are. Like St. Patrick's Day, it is ethnic and fun with plenty of beer; like Canada Day, it has a somewhat obligatory, civic side. And, of course, there's the political aspect, which has changed over the years—conservative in the fifties, rather violent in the sixties, showbizzy in the seventies. Then there were the referendums, but that is another story, not yet history.

4   In the country, people used to build a big bonfire and sing old French songs till late at night, as if to make June 24 go on forever. Even the mosquitoes joined the party, refusing to bite us; and the stars nodded as they blinked through the smoke and sparks. I wasn't part of those bucolic celebrations, because I lived in Montreal, where by the 1950s we were being bombarded with American hits. I can still hear the "lidl-dabl-dooya" of the commercials for Brylcreem, which helped me style an Elvis 'do,' "so that all the gals would love me."

5   In those days, *la Saint-Jean* was above all a parade with floats celebrating, say, Shipshaw's new aluminum plant or gorgeous Holstein cows. The apotheosis was

the child Jean Baptiste on the final float, his blond curls making him a mystic lamb. He had a touching, rather pathetic look, not unlike that of Jean Charest before his trip to the barber.

6   The religious orders had their say regarding plans for *la Saint-Jean*, particularly the music lovers among them who directed all the choirs and brass bands that came from the four corners of Quebec. They came from other provinces, too, because French Canada existed in those days, thanks to the devotion of the *curés*, and the brothers who taught us, and the sisters who looked after us. But when their network was dismantled by the Quiet Revolution and secularization, it led to the first Quebec secession—from francophones in the rest of Canada.

7   I enjoyed watching the regiments of cadets from distant parishes march by; I thrilled to the military marches, to the drums and the brass, to the light and to the colours of the Vatican and Quebec flying side by side. Watching them, time would run backwards in my heart and I'd be transported to the Plains of Abraham to save Montcalm. Destiny turns, we win the battle, and send the English packing. Then I fly off to settle some scores with the redcoats responsible for the ethnic cleansing of Grand-Pré: the Acadians applaud as if I were David bringing down Goliath or Superman, or Maurice Richard outsmarting Johnny Bower ten times in five minutes. Finally I take back Maine, Detroit, Pittsburgh, and Louisiana.

8   Later, in the 1970s, there would be the performances on the grass on Mount Royal (and grass in our nostrils), with songs by Robert Charlebois and others blessed with the gift of bringing people together to express a common cause. And dancing on Rue Saint-Denis to Gilles Vigneault's *Tam Ti Delam* and the incantatory poems of Raoul Duguay. As things heated up, everyone needed a cold beer. Handily, Molson's had by then adopted the two-nations thesis: in Quebec the beer was called Laurentide; elsewhere, Canadian.

9   There is a contradiction in celebrating the existence of a country that does not exist, so there was a certain agitation in Quebec at *la Saint-Jean*. One does not move easily from a satisfied religious and national celebration to the cultural and political demonstration of a dissatisfaction. As the independence movement gained momentum, the crowd threw bottles at Prime Minister Trudeau, who had come to scoff at the nationalists on one June 24. More recently, William Johnson, leader of Alliance Quebec, strolled alongside bearers of blue and white flags—and got a cream pie in the face, enabling him to prove what he wanted to prove, namely that Quebec nationalists are very mean people.

10   Now that the times have become athletic and environmental, *la Saint-Jean* has turned into a march, with the whole family in sneakers, sporting grins and toting bottled water, proceeding from the centre of town to the Olympic Stadium, everyone waving little flags like blue and white flames, with newcomers from Haiti, Vietnam, Latin America enthusiastically encouraged to join in. It's an effort to make the parade less ethnic by making it more ethnic. Or vice versa.

11   But there are a thousand ways to celebrate. Car horns, tam-tams, face-painting, spaghetti suppers, games for the kiddies, picnics in the park, confetti, low-cut necklines . . .

12   As for me, I display my flag on my balcony, above the geraniums, between June 15 and July 2. On July 1, I spare a thought for the French writer Louis-Ferdinand Céline—it's the anniversary of his death. And I kid my federalist neighbour, a guy by the name of Bourgeois. I've got nothing against the colour red as far as geraniums are concerned; but on a flag I prefer blue. It's inscribed on my DNA, I guess.

For Further Thinking

1. René Lévesque, said one former American ambassador, would have been hanged in the United States for treason. What is your opinion of Canada's official toleration of the separatist forces?

2. How many of Hébert's historical references are familiar to you? Do Canadian schools provide a complete and balanced consideration of our history? Elaborate.

3. Have you ever attended La Fête Nationale (St. Jean Baptiste Day)? What is your opinion of this celebration?

4. What do you think should be done to address the ongoing possibility of Quebec separation?

5. What rhetorical techniques does Hébert use in this essay? To what extent is it personal, and to what extent expository? (See Chapters 5 and 6 in the *Rhetoric*.)

Looking Back and Ahead

1. Among the heroics Hébert imagines himself performing to make amends for past losses is a re-enactment of the exploits of Maurice Richard. Compare this essay with Roch Carrier's "The Hockey Sweater." Discuss similarities and possible differences between the blending of politics and hockey in these two essays.

2. Consider similarities and differences between "Je Me Souviens" and Emma Lee Warrior's "White Breast Flats" (p. 6).

3. Consider similarities and differences between "Je Me Souviens" and Michel Tremblay's "The King and I" (p. 37). Do you think both authors would stand on the same side in a referendum on Quebec sovereignty? Explain.

4. Read Pat Deiter-McArthur's "Saskatchewan's Indian People—Five Generations" (p. 87) and Habeeb Salloum's "The Other Canadians and Canada's Future" (p. 200). How do they relate to aspirations of Quebec?

For Further Reading

The Canadian Encyclopedia. April 2003 < http://www.thecanadianencyclopedia.com/index.cfm>. Covers the history of the French in Canada and North America, referendums and plebiscites in world and Canadian history, the Quebec referendums of 1980 and 1995, and Francophone-Anglophone relations in Canada.

Dubois, René-Daniel. April 2003 <http://www.couch.ca/history/1998/Dubois.html>. The Montreal playwright shares his acerbic thoughts on old-style Canadian nationalists.

Lamont, Lansing. *Breakup: The Coming End of Canada and the Stakes for America.* New York: Norton, 1994.

Mathews, Georges. *The Quiet Resolution: Quebec's Challenge to Canada.* Trans. Dominique Clift. Toronto: Summerhill Press, 1990.

The Unity Archive: Essays and Papers. April 2003 <http://www.uni.ca/archive1.html>. This pro-federalist site contains an excellent collection of essays that support both sides of the debate, including one written by Lucien Bouchard, former federal cabinet minister and former premier of Quebec, when he was an undergraduate student.

Pamela Swanigan How do you define a Canadian? What does it mean to be a citizen of this country? Answers often consider cultural pluralism, social security, and "niceness," as well as naïveté, provincial mediocrity, and hypocrisy—depending on whom you ask. In any case, it could probably be said with some fairness that few people on this planet have a harder time putting their sense of national identity into words. Born and raised in the United States, half Black, half White, Pamela Swanigan, an expatriate American and former professional sports writer, offers her views on what makes Canadians distinct. Her article appeared in *Saturday Night* magazine, January 27, 2001.

I Am Half-Canadian

1   In times of deep national self-reflection, and even on the other two days of the year, I tend to think there's nothing wrong with being Canadian that being an ex-American wouldn't fix. We expat Americans are probably the happiest Canadians around, taking Air Canada convolutions and hospital waiting lists as minor burbles of an admirable system. Some of this is probably indoctrination—our upbringing inclines us to be patriotic—but more of it, I think, is inoculation, particularly against that great pox of the Canadian psyche, the so-called identity crisis.

2   Not that we don't experience Canadian society as amorphous and callow, like everyone else; just that we can see these qualities are only a "crisis" in the same way that Vancouver is part of the Pacific Northwest—which is to say, strictly by American reference points. Conventional wisdom holds that the U.S. attained its cohesive culture by leaping into the nation-forging crucible of war at every opportunity, whereas Canada, having chosen a more peaceable route, remains (to use Robert Fulford's words) "an art object, an abstraction—a piece of fiction, perhaps."

3   Philosophical footsy-playing aside, what ex-Americans know that other Canadians do not is that America has historically used a less, shall we say, traditional method to maintain its self-definition. America treats identity as a zero-sum proposition: you can be this, but only if you're not that. Canadians may worry that we sketchily define ourselves by what we are not, but Americans suffer the opposite problem: everyone's forced to pick one definition and stick to it. As such, Americans have become the most highly summarized people on the planet; if this makes their national fabric a tightly woven one, it also makes it one of a largely synthetic fibre.

4   Take, for instance, a typical American employment form, such as the one I recently received from a college in California. "Federal and state mandates require that we compile summary data on the gender and ethnicity of the applicants," it declares, before assuring you that although it is about to elicit personal information from you, nobody will ever use any of it for any purpose that could remotely affect your life. It then offers six choices of what it calls "ethnic background" (a category that wanders happily between skin colour, continental origin, language, and state residency) and exhorts, "Please check only one." You may be black, white, Hispanic, Asian, Hawaiian, or American/Alaskan Indian. Or again, you may not, in which case you're out of luck. (By contrast, the Canadian census form allows you to check as many boxes as you like.)

5   Americans are required to pigeonhole themselves in this manner at every turn: on college applications, insurance forms, medical forms, military forms, and in many states used to have to do so on their driver's licences. As cultural conception goes, it's about as organic as a Kraft Singles slice.

6   Nor is this fixation a recent contrivance: America has taken a (literally) black-and-white view of identity from the day it was born. Marriage or propagation between blacks and whites was outlawed in nearly every state during the antebellum years, and in almost half of them it remained a crime until 1967. (Fortunately for my black father, my white mother, and my sister and I, California was not one of them, though my mother was disowned and our house in Oakland was torched.) The "one-drop" rule, which states that any person of traceable African ancestry is legally black, had become law nationwide by the 1850s, and variations of it still exist throughout the country. To this day, as sociologist F. James Davis writes, "'racially mixed' is not an accepted racial category in the United States for a child who has any black ancestry at all. One is either white or black." (I tried saying I was "both" once, in an NBA locker room at the beginning of my sports-writing career, and set off a debate that ended with Michael Jordan saying gravely, "You want to know what you are Pam? You are 'other.'")

7   Though racial identity is the big bugaboo in the U.S., nationality has been fashioned into a similar kind of straitjacket. Canadian brain-drainees may be surprised to find that their new government used to forbid, and still does not recognize, dual citizenship, and that indeed, their new American compatriots regard

anything beyond a passing fondness for one's origins as vaguely seditious. My American-born stepfather got some insight into U.S. attitudes about national identity last summer, on a family trip to San Francisco, when U.S. customs officials hauled him into an interrogation room at the Vancouver Airport and searched his luggage. "Is it because I'm a known socialist?" he asked hopefully. (At the time, he held a minor post in the provincial NDP cabinet and was eager for any sop to his ego.) The customs officials growled back, "How did you lose your American status?" When he told them that he had voluntarily relinquished it in order to become a Canadian citizen, they searched him thoroughly. And then they sent his luggage to San Luis Obispo.

8   Granted, the crenellations of the boxed-in American national psyche can be fascinating; I myself used to find them the most mysterious and seductive questions of identity in the world. (This was before we had both the Tories *and* the Alliance.) But envy-prone Canadians might also want to note that to many ex-Americans, living in Canada is like getting out of jail, and that perhaps if there is a crisis, it is only the natural crisis of freedom. I can't speak for central Canada, with its 350-year-old Euro-colonial foundation, but here in Vancouver almost everybody has some major ambiguity or conflict or multiplicity of heritage; we swim around in our fluid identities like Alice in her pool of tears, battling and occasionally appreciating our aggregate citizenships and the expansive versions of our selves. It's unsettling and often distressing, yes; West Coast Canadian culture is uncongenial and unsophisticated, true; and no one who has lived here for very long could fail to notice the indecisiveness about identity that, especially among young white males, amounts to an epidemic. But to American-Canadians, who know something about the most proximate alternative, this is exactly the way it should be.

For Further Thinking

1. What do you think of Swanigan's conclusion that "to many ex-Americans, living in Canada is like getting out of jail, and that perhaps if there is a crisis, it is only the natural crisis of freedom"? Ill at ease with this free-fall state of identity, Clark Blaise believes that "unstable identities are 'preying' at the moment on Canada."[4]

2. Make a list of the various points that Swanigan treats through comparison-contrast (the section entitled "Comparison-Contrast" in Chapter 6 of the *Rhetoric* can help).

3. Swanigan refers to a comment made to her by American basketball superstar Michael Jordan. Is she simply name-dropping or does Jordan's presence have a significant bearing on her thesis? Explain.

4. Swanigan admits that she cannot speak for the central eastern regions of Canada, that her assessment of Canadianism applies mainly to Vancouver. Do you think her conclusion, if valid, can be stretched to apply across the country?

5. Does Canadian immigration policy and practice treat members of all races equally? You may need to do some research to shape and defend your opinion. You may also wish to interview people.

Looking Back and Ahead

1. Swanigan's family home in Oakland was "torched" because her White mother married a Black man. Read Dorothy Williams' essay "The Quebec Experience: Slavery 1628–1834" (p. 90) for another side to consider in measuring Canada's racial tolerance.
2. Pursuing issues raised in the previous question, read Pat Deiter-McArthur's "Saskatchewan's Indian People—Five Generations" (p. 87). Do you feel this article raises valid challenges to the conclusions Swanigan suggests?
3. Swanigan suggests that the group of Canadians most insecure in their identity is young White males. What do you think of this opinion? If you feel there is some truth to it, how does this observation tie in to the thesis of Susan McClelland's "The Lure of the Body Image" (p. 83)?
4. Bharati Mukherjee (see "The Tenant," p. 164) left Canada disgusted with the racism she felt here. In contrast, she prefers the United States. After her story we list other sources where you can pursue her views on this topic. Compare her opinion to Swanigan's. How do you explain and perhaps reconcile these two opposite claims?

For Further Reading

Clarke, George Elliott. "The Career of Black English: A Literary Sketch." In *The English Language in Nova Scotia*. Eds. Lilian Falk and Margaret Harry. Lockeport, NS: Roseway, 1999.

Edwards, John. "Reactions to Three Types of Speech Sample from Rural Black and White Children." In *The English Language in Nova Scotia*. Eds. Lilian Falk and Margaret Harry. Lockeport, NS: Roseway, 1999.

Hoff, Joan Whitman. "Crisis of Canadian Identity as Explored Through Canadian Philosophy." Online. Lock Haven University, Pennsylvania. < **http://www.lhup.edu/ library/InternationalReview/canadian.htm**>.

Huggan, Graham, and Winifred Siemerling. "U.S./Canadian Writers' Perspectives on the Multiculturalism Debate: A Round-Table Discussion at Harvard University." *Canadian Literature*, 164 (Spring 2000), pp. 82–111. Panel addresses were made by Clark Blaise, Nicole Brossard, George Elliott Clarke, and Paul Yee. American Geeta Patel then responded.

Jacobs, Selwyn, dir. *The Road Taken* (film). National Film Board, 1996. Online at < **http:// cmm.nfb.ca/E/titleinfo/index**>. Filmmaker Selwyn Jacobs has produced a number of independent and NFB films on the history of Blacks in Canada.

Kelly, Jennifer. *Under the Gaze: Learning to Be Black in White Society*. Halifax: Fernwood, 1998, pp. 26–57. A history of Black experience in Canada, with attention to public polices affecting Blacks.

---

[4] Clark Blaise, in "U.S./Canadian Writers' Perspectives on the Multiculturalism Debate," *Canadian Literature* 164 (Spring 2000): 88.

Alice Munro On the prowl for two young women and a good time, two out-of-town young men cruise into Mission Creek, Ontario, population 1 700, described by a fly-speckled sign in Pop's Café as follows: "Gateway to the Bruce. We love our children." George, the aggressive older cousin, matches Dick with Lois, a girl of few but choice words. A much older Dick—later in time—narrates the account of his own voyage to sexual experience with the more knowing Lois and his observations of her.

Alice Munro was born in Wingham, Ontario, in 1931 and has remained emotionally close to her place of birth. Much of her fiction concerns the social restrictions experienced by characters in a rural world reflecting her own. "Thanks for the Ride" first appeared in *The Tamarack Review* and was later collected in *Dance of the Happy Shades* in 1968. Munro has been twice awarded the Governor General's Award for fiction, is the first Canadian to have received the Canada-Australia Literary Prize, and recently received the U.S. National Book Critics Circle fiction prize for the short-story collection *The Love of a Good Woman*. She is widely regarded as one of Canada's finest writers and among the world's best short-story writers.

See the Appendix at the end of the *Reader*, Part I (p. 245), for more support for this reading. This support may particularly benefit you if English is not your first language.

Thanks for the Ride

1   My cousin George and I were sitting in a restaurant called Pop's Cafe in a little town close to the Lake. It was getting dark in there, and they had not turned the lights on, but you could still read the signs plastered against the mirror between the fly-speckled and slightly yellowed cutouts of strawberry sundaes and tomato sandwiches.

2   "Don't ask for information," George read. "If we knew anything we wouldn't be here" and "If you've got nothing to do, you picked a hell of a good place to do it in." George always read everything out loud—posters, billboards, Burma-Shave signs, "Mission Creek. Population 1700. Gateway to the Bruce. We love our children."

3   I was wondering whose sense of humour provided us with the signs. I thought it would be the man behind the cash register. Pop? Chewing on a match, looking out at the street, not watching for anything except for somebody to trip over a crack in the sidewalk or have a blowout or make a fool of himself in some way that Pop, rooted behind the cash register, huge and cynical and incurious, was never likely to do. Maybe not even that; maybe just by walking up and down, driving up and down, going places, the rest of the world proved its absurdity. You see that judgment on the faces of people looking out of windows, sitting on front steps in some little towns; so deeply, deeply uncaring they are, as if they had sources of disillusionment which they would keep, with some satisfaction, in the dark.

4   There was only the one waitress, a pudgy girl who leaned over the counter and scraped at the polish on her fingernails. When she had flaked most of the polish off her thumbnail she put the thumb against her teeth and rubbed the nail back and forth absorbedly. We asked her what her name was and she didn't answer.

Two or three minutes later the thumb came out of her mouth and she said, inspecting it: "That's for me to know and you to find out."

5   "All right," George said. "Okay if I call you Mickey?"

6   "I don't care."

7   "Because you remind me of Mickey Rooney," George said. "Hey, where's everybody go in this town? Where's everybody go?" Mickey had turned her back and begun to drain out the coffee. It looked as if she didn't mean to talk any more, so George got a little jumpy, as he did when he was threatened with having to be quiet or be by himself. "Hey, aren't there any girls in this town?" he said almost plaintively. "Aren't there any girls or dances or anything? We're strangers in town," he said. "Don't you want to help us out?"

8   "Dance hall down on the beach closed up Labour Day," Mickey said coldly.

9   "There any other dance halls?"

10   "There's a dance tonight out at Wilson's *school*," Mickey said.

11   "That old-time? No, no, I don't go for that old-time. *All-a-man left* and that, used to have that down in the basement of the church. Yeah, *ever'body swing—* I don't go for that. Inna basement of the *church*," George said, obscurely angered. "You don't remember that," he said to me. "Too young."

12   I was just out of high-school at this time, and George had been working for three years in the Men's Shoes in a downtown department store, so there was that difference. But we had never bothered with each other back in the city. We were together now because we had met unexpectedly in a strange place and because I had a little money, while George was broke. Also I had my father's car, and George was in one of his periods between cars, which made him always a little touchy and dissatisfied. But he would have to rearrange these facts a bit, they made him uneasy. I could feel him manufacturing a sufficiency of good feeling, old-pal feeling, and dressing me up as Old Dick, good kid, real character—which did not matter one way or the other, though I did not think, looking at his tender blond piggish handsomeness, the nudity of his pink mouth, and the surprised, angry creases that frequent puzzlement was beginning to put into his forehead, that I would be able to work up an Old George.

13   I had driven up to the Lake to bring my mother home from a beach resort for women, a place where they had fruit juice and cottage cheese for reducing, and early-morning swims in the Lake, and some religion, apparently, for there was a little chapel attached. My aunt, George's mother, was staying there at the same time, and George arrived about an hour or so after I did, not to take his mother home, but to get some money out of her. He did not get along well with his father, and he did not make much money working in the shoe department, so he was very often broke. His mother said he could have a loan if he would stay over and go to church with her the next day. George said he would. Then George and I got away and drove half a mile along the lake to this little town neither of us had seen before, which George said would be full of bootleggers and girls.

14   It was a town of unpaved, wide, sandy streets and bare yards. Only the hardy things like red and yellow nasturtiums, or a lilac bush with brown curled leaves, grew out of that cracked earth. The houses were set wide apart, with their own pumps and sheds and privies out behind; most of them were built of wood and painted green or grey or yellow. The trees that grew there were big willows or poplars, their fine leaves greyed with the dust. There were no trees along the main street, but spaces of tall grass and dandelions and blowing thistles—open country between the store buildings. The town hall was surprisingly large, with a great bell in a tower, the red brick rather glaring in the midst of the town's walls of faded, pale-painted wood. The sign beside the door said that it was a memorial to the soldiers who had died in the First World War. We had a drink out of the fountain in front.

15   We drove up and down the main street for a while, with George saying: "What a dump! Jesus, what a dump!" and "Hey, look at that! Aw, not so good either." The people on the street went home to supper, the shadows of the store buildings lay solid across the street, and we went into Pop's.

16   "Hey," George said, "is there any other restaurant in this town? Did you see any other restaurant?"

17   "No," I said.

18   "Any other town I ever been," George said, "pigs hangin' out the windows, practically hangin' off the trees. Not here. Jesus! I guess it's late in the season," he said.

19   "You want to go to a show?"

20   The door opened. A girl came in, walked up and sat on a stool, with most of her skirt bunched up underneath her. She had a long somnolent face, no bust, frizzy fair; she was pale, almost ugly, but she had that inexplicable aura of sexuality. George brightened, though not a great deal. "Never mind," he said. "This'll do. This'll do in a pinch, eh? In a pinch."

21   He went to the end of the counter and sat down beside her and started to talk. In about five minutes they came back to me, the girl drinking a bottle of orange pop.

22   "This is Adelaide," George said. "Adelaide, Adeline—Sweet Adeline. I'm going to call her Sweet A, Sweet A."

23   Adelaide sucked at her straw, paying not much attention.

24   "She hasn't got a date," George said. "You haven't got a date have you, honey?"

25   Adelaide shook her head very slightly.

26   "Doesn't hear half what you say to her," George said. "Adelaide, Sweet A, have you got any friends? Have you got any nice, young little girl friend to go out with Dickie? You and me and her and Dickie?"

27   "Depends," said Adelaide. "Where do you want to go?"

28   "Anywhere you say. Go for a drive. Drive up to Owen Sound, maybe."

29   "You got a car?"

30   "Yeah, yeah, we got a car. C'mon, you must have some nice little friend for Dickie." He put his arm around this girl, spreading his fingers over her blouse. "C'mon out and I'll show you the car."

31   Adelaide said: "I know one girl might come. The guy she goes around with, he's engaged, and his girl came up and she's staying at his place up the beach, his mother and dad's place, and—"

32   "Well that is certainly int-er-esting," George said. "What's her name? Come on, let's go round and get her. You want to sit around drinking pop all night?"

33   "I'm finished," Adelaide said. "She might not come. I don't know."

34   "Why not? Her mother not let her out nights?"

35   "Oh, she can do what she likes," said Adelaide. "Only there's times she don't want to. I don't know."

36   We went out and got into the car, George and Adelaide in the back. On the main street about a block from the cafe we passed a thin, fair-haired girl in slacks and Adelaide cried: "Hey stop! That's her! That's Lois!"

37   I pulled in and George stuck his head out of the window, whistling. Adelaide yelled and the girl came unhesitatingly, unhurriedly to the car. She smiled, rather coldly and politely, when Adelaide explained to her. All the time George kept saying: "Hurry up, come on, get in! We can talk in the car." The girl smiled, did not really look at any of us, and in a few moments, to my surprise, she opened the door and slid into the car.

38   "I don't have anything to do," she said. "My boy friend's away."

39   "That so?" said George, and I saw Adelaide, in the rear-vision mirror, make a cross warning face. Lois did not seem to have heard him.

40   "We better drive around to my house," she said. "I was just going down to get some Cokes, that's why I only have my slacks on. We better drive around to my house and I'll put on something else."

41   "Where are we going to go," she said, "so I know what to put on?"

42   I said: "Where do you want to go?"

43   "Okay, okay," George said. "First things first. We gotta get a bottle, then we'll decide. You know where to get one?" Adelaide and Lois both said yes, and then Lois said to me: "You can come in the house and wait while I change, if you want to." I glanced in the rear mirror and thought that there was probably some agreement she had with Adelaide.

44   Lois's house had an old couch on the porch and some rugs hanging down over the railing. She walked ahead of me across the yard. She had her long pale hair tied at the back of her neck; her skin was dustily freckled, but not tanned; even her eyes were light-coloured. She was cold and narrow and pale. There was derision, and also great gravity, about her mouth. I thought she was about my age or a little older.

45   She opened the front door and said in a clear, stilted voice: "I would like you to meet my family."

46   The little front room had linoleum on the floor and flowered paper curtains at the windows. There was a glossy chesterfield with a Niagara Falls and a To

Mother cushion on it, and there was a little black stove with a screen around it for summer, and a big vase of paper apple blossoms. A tall, frail woman came into the room drying her hands on a dishtowel, which she flung into a chair. Her mouth was full of blue-white china teeth, the long cords trembled in her neck. I said how-do-you-do to her, embarrassed by Lois's announcement, so suddenly and purposefully conventional. I wondered if she had any misconceptions about this date, engineered by George for such specific purposes. I did not think so. Her face had no innocence in it that I could see; it was knowledgeable, calm, and hostile. She might have done it, then, to mock me, to make me into this caricature of The Date, the boy who grins and shuffles in the front hall and waits to be presented to the nice girl's family. But that was a little far-fetched. Why should she want to embarrass me when she had agreed to go out with me without even looking into my face? Why should she care enough?

47   Lois's mother and I sat down on the chesterfield. She began to make conversation, giving this the Date interpretation. I noticed the smell in the house, the smell of stale small rooms, bedclothes, frying, washing, and medicated ointments. And dirt, though it did not look dirty. Lois's mother said: "That's a nice car you got out front. Is that your car?"

48   "My father's."

49   "Isn't that lovely! Your father has such a nice car. I always think it's lovely for people to have things. I've got no time for these people that's just eaten up with malice 'n envy. I say it's lovely. I bet your mother, every time she wants anything, she just goes down to the store and buys it—new coat, bedspread, pots and pans. What does you father do? Is he a lawyer or doctor or something like that?"

50   "He's a chartered accountant."

51   "Oh. That's in an office, is it?"

52   "Yes."

53   "My brother, Lois's uncle, he's in the office of the CPR in London. He's quite high up there, I understand."

54   She began to tell me about how Lois's father had been killed in an accident at the mill. I noticed an old woman, the grandmother probably, standing in the doorway of the room. She was not thin like the others, but as soft and shapeless as a collapsed pudding, pale brown spots melting together on her face and arms, bristles of hairs in the moisture around her mouth. Some of the smell of the house seemed to come from her. It was a smell of hidden decay, such as there is when some obscure little animal has died under the verandah. The smell, the slovenly, confiding voice—something about this life I had not known, something about these people. I thought: my mother, George's mother, they are innocent. Even George, George is innocent. But these others are born sly and sad and knowing.

55   I did not hear much about Lois's father except that his head was cut off.

56   "Clean off, imagine, and rolled on the floor! Couldn't open the coffin. It was June, the hot weather. And everybody in town just stripped their gardens,

stripped them for the funeral. Stripped their spirea bushes and peenies and climbin' clemantis. I guess it was the worst accident ever took place in this town.

57   "Lois had a nice boy friend this summer," she said. "Used to take her out and sometimes stay here overnight when his folks weren't up at the cottage and he didn't feel like passin' his time there all alone. He'd bring the kids candy and even me he'd bring presents. That china elephant up there, you can plant flowers in it, he brought me that. He fixed the radio for me and I never had to take it into the shop. Do your folks have a summer cottage up here?"

58   I said no, and Lois came in, wearing a dress of yellow-green stuff—stiff and shiny like Christmas wrappings—high-heeled shoes, rhinestones, and a lot of dark powder over her freckles. Her mother was excited.

59   "You like that dress?" she said. "She went all the way to London and bought that dress, didn't get it anywhere round here!"

60   We had to pass by the old woman as we went out. She looked at us with sudden recognition, a steadying of her pale, jellied eyes. Her mouth trembled open, she stuck her face out at me.

61   "You can do what you like with my gran'daughter," she said in her old, strong voice, the rough voice of a country woman. "But you be careful. And you know what I mean!"

62   Lois's mother pushed the old woman behind her, smiling tightly, eyebrows lifted, skin straining over her temples. "Never mind," she mouthed at me, grimacing distractedly. "Never mind. Second childhood." The smile stayed on her face, the skin pulled back from it. She seemed to be listening all the time to a perpetual din and racket in her head. She grabbed my hand as I followed Lois out. "Lois is a nice girl," she whispered. "You have a nice time, don't let her mope!" There was a quick, grotesque, and, I suppose, originally flirtatious, flickering of brows and lids. "'Night!"

63   Lois walked stiffly ahead of me, rustling her papery skirt. I said: "Did you want to go to a dance or something?"

64   "No," she said. "I don't care."

65   "Well you got all dressed up—"

66   "I always get dressed up on Saturday night," Lois said, her voice floating back to me, low and scornful. Then she began to laugh, and I had a glimpse of her mother in her, that jaggedness and hysteria. "Oh, my God!" she whispered. I knew she meant what had happened in the house, and I laughed too, not knowing what else to do. So we went back to the car laughing as if we were friends, but we were not.

67   We drove out of town to a farmhouse where a woman sold us a whisky bottle full of muddy-looking home-made liquor, something George and I had never had before. Adelaide had said that this woman would probably let us use her front room, but it turned out that she would not, and that was because of Lois. When the woman peered up at me from under the man's cap she had on her head and

said to Lois, "Change's as good as a rest, eh?" Lois did not answer, kept a cold face. Then later the woman said that if we were so stuck-up tonight her front room wouldn't be good enough for us and we better go back to the bush. All the way back down the lane Adelaide kept saying: "Some people can't take a joke, can they? Yeah, stuck-up is right—" until I passed her the bottle to keep her quiet. I saw George did not mind, thinking this had taken her mind off driving to Owen Sound.

68   We parked at the end of the lane and sat in the car drinking. George and Adelaide drank more than we did. They did not talk, just reached for the bottle and passed it back. This stuff was different from anything I had tasted before; it was heavy and sickening in my stomach. There was no other effect, and I began to have the depressing feeling that I was not going to get drunk. Each time Lois handed the bottle back to me she said "Thank you" in a mannerly and subtly contemptuous way. I put my arm around her, not much wanting to. I was wondering what was the matter. This girl lay against my arm, scornful, acquiescent, angry, inarticulate and out-of-reach. I wanted to talk to her then more than to touch her, and that was out of the question; talk was not so little a thing to her as touching. Meanwhile I was aware that I should be beyond this, beyond the first stage and well into the second (for I had a knowledge, though it was not very comprehensive, of the orderly progression of stages, the ritual of back- and front-seat seduction). Almost I wished I was with Adelaide.

69   "Do you want to go for a walk?" I said.

70   "That's the first bright idea you've had all night," George told me from the back seat. "Don't hurry," he said as we got out. He and Adelaide were muffled and laughing together. "Don't hurry back!"

71   Lois and I walked along a wagon track close to the bush. The fields were moonlit, chilly and blowing. Now I felt vengeful, and I said softly, "I had quite a talk with your mother."

72   "I can imagine," said Lois.

73   "She told me about that guy you went out with last summer."

74   "This summer."

75   "It's last summer now. He was engaged or something, wasn't he?"

76   "Yes."

77   I was not going to let her go. "Did he like you better?" I said. "Was that it? Did he like you better?"

78   "No, I wouldn't say he liked me," Lois said. I thought, by some thickening of the sarcasm in her voice, that she was beginning to be drunk. "He liked Momma and the kids okay but he didn't like me. *Like me,*" she said, "What's that?"

79   "Well, he went out with you—"

80   "He just went around with me for the summer. That's what those guys from up the beach always do. They come down here to the dances and get a girl to go around with. For the summer. They always do.

81   "How I know he didn't *like* me," she said, "he said I was always bitching. You have to act grateful to those guys, you know, or they say you're bitching."

82   I was a little startled at having loosed all this. I said: "Did you like him?"

83   "Oh, sure! I should, shouldn't I? I should just get down on my knees and thank him. That's what my mother does. He brings her a cheap old spotted elephant—"

84   "Was this guy the first?" I said.

85   "The first steady. Is that what you mean?"

86   It wasn't. "How old are you?"

87   She considered. "I'm almost seventeen. I can pass for eighteen or nineteen. I can pass in a beer parlour. I did once."

88   "What grade are you in at school?"

89   She looked at me, rather amazed. "Did you think I still went to school? I quit that two years ago. I've got a job at the glove-works in town."

90   "That must have been against the law. When you quit."

91   "Oh, you can get a permit if your father's dead or something."

92   "What do you do at the glove-works?" I said.

93   "Oh, I run a machine. It's like a sewing machine. I'll be getting on piecework soon. You make more money."

94   "Do you like it?"

95   "Oh, I wouldn't say I loved it. It's a job—you ask a lot of questions," she said.

96   "Do you mind?"

97   "I don't have to answer you," she said, her voice flat and small again. "Only if I like." She picked up her skirt and spread it out in her hands. "I've got burrs on my skirt," she said. She bent over, pulling them one by one. "I've got burrs on my dress," she said. "It's my good dress. Will they leave a mark? If I pull them all—slowly—I won't pull any threads."

98   "You shouldn't have worn that dress," I said. "What'd you wear that dress for?"

99   She shook the skirt, tossing a burr loose. "I don't know," she said. She held it out, the stiff, shining stuff, with faintly drunken satisfaction. "I wanted to show you guys!" she said, with a sudden small explosion of viciousness. The drunken, nose-thumbing, toe-twirling satisfaction could not now be mistaken as she stood there foolishly, tauntingly, with her skirt spread out. "I've got an imitation cashmere sweater at home. It cost me twelve dollars," she said. "I've got a fur coat I'm paying on, paying on for next winter. I've got a fur coat—"

100   "That's nice," I said. "I think it's lovely for people to have things."

101   She dropped the skirt and struck the flat of her hand on my face. This was a relief to me, to both of us. We felt a fight had been building in us all along. We faced each other as warily as we could, considering we were both a little drunk, she tensing to slap me again and I to grab her or slap her back. We would have it out, what we had against each other. But the moment of this keenness passed. We let out our breath; we had not moved in time. And the next moment, not

bothering to shake off our enmity, nor thinking how the one thing could give way to the other, we kissed. It was the first time, for me, that a kiss was accomplished without premeditation, or hesitancy, or over-haste, or the usual vague ensuing disappointment. And laughing shakily against me, she began to talk again, going back to the earlier part of our conversation as if nothing had come between.

102   "Isn't it funny?" she said. "You know, all winter all the girls do is talk about last summer, talk and talk about those guys, and I bet you those guys have forgotten even what their names were—"

103   But I did not want to talk any more, having discovered another force in her that lay side by side with her hostility, that was, in fact, just as enveloping and impersonal. After a while I whispered: "Isn't there some place we can go?"

104   And she answered: "There's a barn in the next field."

105   She knew the countryside; she had been there before.

106   We drove back into town after midnight. George and Adelaide were asleep in the back seat. I did not think Lois was asleep, though she kept her eyes closed and did not say anything. I had read somewhere about *Omne animal,* and I was going to tell her, but then I thought she would not know Latin words and would think I was being—oh, pretentious and superior. Afterwards I wished that I had told her. She would have known what it meant.

107   Afterwards the lassitude of the body, and the cold; the separation. To brush away the bits of hay and tidy ourselves with heavy unconnected movements, to come out of the barn and find the moon gone down, but the flat stubble fields still there, and the poplar trees, and the stars. To find our same selves, chilled and shaken, who had gone that headlong journey and were here still. To go back to the car and find the others sprawled asleep. That is what it is: *triste. Triste est.*

108   *That headlong journey.* Was it like that because it was the first time, because I was a little, strangely drunk? No. It was because of Lois. There are some people who can go only a little way with the act of love, and some others who can go very far, who can make a greater surrender, like the mystics. And Lois, this mystic of love, sat now on the far side of the car-seat, looking cold and rumpled, and utterly closed up in herself. All the things I wanted to say to her went clattering emptily through my head. *Come and see you again —Remember—Love—* I could not say any of these things. They would not seem even half-true across the space that had come between us. I thought: I will say something to her before the next tree, the next telephone pole. But I did not. I only drove faster, too fast, making the town come nearer.

109   The street lights bloomed out of the dark trees ahead; there were stirrings in the back seat.

110   "What time is it?" George said.

111   "Twenty past twelve."

112   "We musta finished that bottle. I don't feel so good. Oh, Christ, I don't feel so good. How do you feel?"

113   "Fine."

114   "Fine, eh? Feel like you finished your education tonight, eh? That how you feel? Is yours asleep? Mine is."

115   "I am not," said Adelaide drowsily. "Where's my belt? George—oh. Now where's my other shoe? It's early for Saturday night, isn't it? We could go and get something to eat."

116   "I don't feel like food," George said. "I gotta get some sleep. Gotta get up early tomorrow and go to church with my mother."

117   "Yeah, I know," said Adelaide, disbelieving, though not too ill-humoured. "You could've anyways bought me a hamburger!"

118   I had driven around to Lois's house. Lois did not open her eyes until the car stopped.

119   She sat still a moment, and then pressed her hands down over the skirt of her dress, flattening it out. She did not look at me. I moved to kiss her, but she seemed to draw slightly away, and I felt that there had after all been something fraudulent and theatrical about this final gesture. She was not like that.

120   George said to Adelaide: "Where do you live? You live near here?"

121   "Yeah. Half a block down."

122   "Okay. How be you get out here too? We gotta get home sometime tonight."

123   He kissed her and both the girls got out.

124   I started the car. We began to pull away, George settling down on the back seat to sleep. And then we heard the female voice calling after us, the loud, crude, female voice, abusive and forlorn:

125   "Thanks for the ride!"

126   It was not Adelaide calling; it was Lois.

For Further Thinking

1. Define the story's point of view as precisely as you can. How does this point of view contribute to the mood and theme of the story?

2. Find a section of the story in which Munro uses comparison-contrast to reveal the characters of Dick and George. What characteristics emerge from this passage of comparison?

3. The French writer Émile Zola (1840–1902) propounded a theory of "naturalism." Subjects are to be observed by the writer as if by a scientist observing specimens in a laboratory. Human will is not free but rather governed by external forces. To what extent does Munro's story fit into the realm of naturalism?

Looking Back and Ahead

1. In tone, how does "Thanks for the Ride" compare with Mordecai Richler's story "The Summer My Grandmother Was Supposed to Die" (p. 14)? What other similarities and/or differences do you find in these two stories?

2. Read Robertson Davies' essay "The Pleasures of Love" (p. 177). Discuss his view of love in that essay in reference to the view Munro's characters appear to have. How does the attitude Davies expresses compare to the attitude implied by Munro in "Thanks for the Ride"?

3. Read David Suzuki's essay "The Right Stuff" (p. 181). One argument against teaching sex education in junior high or high school is that it promotes sexual promiscuity among youth. What contribution to this debate does "Thanks for the Ride" suggest?

4. How are class and sexuality tangled up as sources of identity and of power in the story?

For Further Reading

Biography and works of Alice Munro. April 2003 < http://www.bedfordstmartins.com/literature/bedlit/authors_depth/munro.htm>.

"Bruce County." Human Resources Development Canada. April 2003 < http://www.brucecounty.on.ca>. An overview of Bruce County, where this story is set.

Ellis, Julia, Jan Small-McGinley, and Lucy De Fabrizio. *Caring for Kids in Communities: Using Mentorship, Peer Support, and Student Leadership Programs in Schools*. New York: Peter Lang Publishing, 2001. A community resource for program planning and leadership development in youth, this material provides examples of common problems and solutions.

Keegan, Alex. "Alice Munro: The Short Answer." April 2003 < http://www.eclectica.org/v2n5/keegan_munro.html>. A forum for responses to Keegan's analysis.

Munro, Sheila. *Lives of Mothers and Daughters: Growing Up with Alice Munro*. Toronto: McClelland & Stewart, 2001. Munro's eldest daughter provides a sympathetic yet critical memoir of life with a famous writer.

Ross, Catherine Sheldrick. *Alice Munro: A Double Life*. Toronto: ECW Press, 1992.

Gisela Becker Gisela Becker, a registered midwife, has travelled widely throughout her career. Originally from Germany, she has worked extensively in northern Canadian communities, serving Inuit and other Native people. A strong advocate of midwifery, she now resides in Fort Smith in the Northwest Territories. This essay was a university paper.

In her essay, Becker remembers a painful experience, a baby stillborn to one of her clients. She mentions that the Birthing Centre with its midwives receives strong community support and respect, because midwifery has been a traditional part of Inuit life and because most Inuit women have many babies. In this way, Becker found a natural cultural tie with her clients. In our mainstream society, in contrast, midwifery remains a marginalized vocation. In July 2000, for example, when Alberta reluctantly allowed midwives to practise in hospitals, only Ontario and British Columbia had this provision. In some cases of midwives entering into regular hospitals, there have been reports of tensions between them and the other hospital staff whose more detached, empirical approach to their work conflicts with the midwives' approach.

A Midwife in Rankin Inlet

1   I had already been working for almost one year in Rankin Inlet in the Birthing Centre as a midwife. Rankin Inlet is a community at the Hudson's Bay coast in the Keewatin Region, now part of Nunavut. Most people in Rankin Inlet are Inuit, native Canadians also known as Eskimos. The Inuit do not like to be called Eskimos, because, so I was told, the name is discriminating and means "those who eat raw fish," while the term Inuit means "the people."

2   As long as the Inuit remember, they lived in a world of ice and snow, constantly concerned with finding enough food to survive, following the Caribou herds, always moving from one place to the next, building their igloos and tents wherever needed and never leaving anything behind. Then about 40 years ago the Canadian Government forced the Inuit to settle down by introducing general schooling and southern health care to the people. It was only then that the settlement of Rankin Inlet developed and Inuit have been living in the community since 1960.

3   The Birthing Centre in Rankin Inlet has been a direct result of Inuit lobbying to have births to take place on Inuit land. Women did not want to leave their homes, children and husbands to go to Winnipeg, Edmonton, or Montreal to give birth and to be away from home for weeks.

4   Midwifery had been traditionally an important part of Inuit life also because Inuit families are large and the women have many babies. There has been nothing more beautiful than listening to the old midwives' stories from the times before southern health care took over in the north.

5   The Birthing Centre with its midwives has been enjoying a great deal of community support and respect.

6   The Health Centre was packed with people that needed to be seen by the nurses and midwives that particular morning I still remember so well. Young mothers carrying their babies on their back in the *amauti*, a traditional piece of clothing, waiting patiently for their infants to be seen, elders in their fur coats, their faces dark and wrinkled from hard lives out on the land, waiting to be seen by a nurse. Young pregnant teenagers chatting to each other waiting for their prenatal appointments with the midwives. One woman caught my attention: She was sitting in the corner of the waiting area, almost removed from everything around her. When I looked into her eyes I knew instantly that something was wrong. We had known each other for months. She was about to have her second baby and I had been her midwife throughout this pregnancy. Annie [her name has been changed by the author] was a healthy young woman and I had been looking forward to the birth. As she entered my office I could sense the despair in this usually smiling and happy woman.

7   I tried to put her at ease, smiled at her, and asked, "What can I do for you today, Annie?" It took a moment before she pulled herself together to answer me. Finally I heard her say: "I have not felt my baby moving for over a day now!" Her sad eyes met mine.

8   For a moment I was in shock and speechless myself. A little while later I heard myself say, "Let me examine you and see if we find the baby's heart rate. It sometimes happens that women do not feel their babies move for a while." Yet something told me that Annie knew intuitively that her baby had died inside her.

9   She nodded and lay down on the table. I palpated her abdomen to locate the baby. "It should be an easy task now to find the baby's pulse, if it was there," I thought to myself. I could not find it and I kept searching for it for a while not wanting to allow the truth to be said. I turned the fetal monitor off and helped Annie into a sitting position.

10   Our eyes met again. Instead of saying something to her, my eyes filled with tears in sorrow and pain for her. It was then that she broke down herself and sobbed in my arms. A while later we were able to talk about the death of her baby and we called her husband and family to come to meet us in the Health Centre.

11   What Annie did not know was that this was the very first time this had happened to me as a midwife! I had been fifteen years a midwife, I had supported colleagues through hard times like this, and I had participated in workshops about loss and grieving, but it suddenly hit me hard: I had not been prepared for the death of a baby. Are we ever? I was devastated. As a midwife you are constantly concerned about the well-being of your clients and their babies. You want the best and safest outcome for them but also the most natural way, if possible.

12   A few hours after Annie had seen me she went into labour. Her partner was with her, her mom, and her mother-in-law. I will never forget the silence in the birthing room: no listening to the baby's heart rate, no questions if it was a boy or a girl, no joyful expectations. Annie gave birth like most other Inuit women: stoically, with no expression of pain. A while later a little boy was born with no signs of life. He looked perfect, as if he were asleep, and I wondered again why he had to die. I wrapped him in a blanket and gave him to his mother. As Annie took him she asked me, "Is there nothing you can do to make him live?" This was one of the most heartbreaking moments in my life. I could only gently remind her that he had died.

13   After everybody had said goodbye to this little boy I took him to a separate room and examined him. I took a photograph of him and got his footprint. Something to give to the parents later. As I looked at him, my midwife partner and friend was watching me and said, "Gisela, there is absolutely nothing you could have done differently. You have provided good care for her and you are an excellent midwife. I have been through this myself and it is very hard."

14   Very late that night I locked the Health Centre as I was the last person to leave. Walking home, I saw the most beautiful northern lights in the sky. An Inuit elder had told me once, "Never talk when you see northern lights. They are the souls of our grandmothers and grandfathers. They will always be with us."

15   Later that week I opened the local newspaper and found the following announcement:

16   "God looked around his garden
And found an empty space;
He put his arms around him
And lifted him to rest;
God's garden must be beautiful,
He only takes the best.

17   Born and taken on . . .

18   Our special thanks to Gisela at the Rankin Inlet Birthing Centre for her compassion and caring and to our family and friends for their love, support and understanding."

For Further Thinking

1. Have you had an experience similar to Becker's, of living and perhaps working in a culture quite different from the dominant one where you grew up? What did you gain from this experience?

2. Becker and her patient Annie communicate with each other without speaking. Is the rapport between them similar to or different from the rapport you believe is typical between doctors and patients? Explain.

3. Midwives in Canada have long found themselves struggling for greater respect and understanding. They believe that a number of unexamined falsehoods about birth and midwifery are used to deny their care to a full spectrum of women. Do you agree?

4. In your opinion, what should the father's role be throughout the pregnancy of the mother of his baby? What should be his role during the baby's birth?

Looking Back and Ahead

1. As an advocate of midwifery, Becker risks offering critics a story they might use to associate her profession with failure. Why do you think she chose to tell this particular story, and is there any similarity between her purpose and that of Roger Fouts in "Brownie" (p. 12)?

2. In "The Doomsday Machines" (p. 135), John Markoff reports on a number of dramatic concerns about abuses of science. Obstetrics is not mentioned in the inventory. Should it be? Are our standard hospital births unnatural to the point of concern?

3. As you read Becker's essay, did you, at some point, find yourself contemplating media images of substance abuse and suicide? How does this coverage compare to the views presented by Becker, by Emma Lee Warrior in "White Breast Flats" (p. 6), and by Pat Deiter-McArthur's "Saskatchewan's Indian People—Five Generations" (p. 87)?

For Further Reading

Banks, Maggie. *Home Birth Bound: Mending the Broken Weave*. Hamilton, NZ: Birthspirit Books, 2000.

————. *Breech Birth Woman-Wise*. Hamilton, NZ: Birthspirit Books, 1998.

Canadian Association of Midwives. <http://www.canadianmidwives.org>. The national professional association of individual midwives across Canada and their professional associations. History of midwifery, the midwifery model of care, contact information, and links to newsletters and position papers.

Canadian Medical Association Journal 163. 1. Canadian Medical Association. April 2003 <http://www.cmaj.ca/>. Click on "Back Issues" to find the report of the decision permitting midwives access to hospitals in Alberta.

Ehrenreich, Barbara, and Deirdre English. *Witches, Midwives, and Nurses: A History of Women Healers*. New York: Feminist Press, 1973.

Gedalof, Robin. *Paper Stays Put: A Collection of Inuit Writing*. Edmonton: Hurtig, n.d.

gentlebirth.org. April 2003. <http://www.gentlebirth.org/archives/brtrauma.html>. A wealth of information on birthing, parenting, midwifery, pregnancy, and more.

Goer, Henci, and Don Creevy. *Obstetrics Myths versus Research Realities*. New York: Bergin and Garvey, 1995.

Midwifery Today. <http://www.MidwiferyToday.com>. Begun in 1986 as a print magazine in Eugene, Oregon, this advocacy organization has now added a quarterly print newsletter and weekly email newsletter.

Midwives Alliance of North America. April 2003 <http://www.mana.org/>. Numerous links to information related to midwifery, including an excellent list of books on birthing for clinical and general readers.

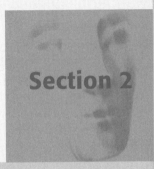

THE
READER

Section 2 Knowledge and
Ideas

In his study of William Shakespeare (1564–1616), biographer Park Honan argues that the greatly celebrated Renaissance poet was deeply concerned with "a fracturing of the medieval unity and a loss of a faith that once bound together Western Europe."[5] Canadian novelist Mordecai Richler (1931–2001) expressed exactly the same concern by putting his struggles as a writer into context: namely, the problem of having to define his own moral standards, his own authority, in a world where values, beliefs, and faiths now vary drastically from person to person. This challenge is expressed in the introductory poem of this section, "Dover Beach" by Matthew Arnold (1822–1888). In it the poet laments the loss of universal faith; science has undermined the literal truth of religion without substituting clear, absolute answers. The poet's only touchstone of meaning becomes that of personal relations. Echoing this sentiment some 100 years later, American songwriter Paul Simon wrote, "I stand alone without beliefs; / The only truth I know is you." Few would argue with this assessment of the modern human condition. Never has humanity had such wide and easy access to so much information, yet how much of it is important, and how are we to determine that importance? Perhaps the more we learn, the harder it is to feel certain about anything; the more we must struggle to select, process, and understand.

This section of the *Reader* will not restore absolute "objective" truth. However, it will demonstrate common ways that people of many different beliefs working in many different fields go about organizing information.

This section concentrates particularly on samples of writing produced by writers whose goal is to focus not on themselves as participants in observation, evaluation, and communication, but rather on a body of information. In many cases, the writing contains some degree of disinterested analysis of the same information. The first thing you may notice is that the point of view used in nearly all selections in this part of the *Reader* is that of a third person. While third person does not arguably create real objectivity or impartiality, it does deflect attention away from the writer and onto his or her subject. Though there has been considerable challenge to this approach over the past 40 years in academic circles, third person remains the approved point of view for a great deal of scholarly writing, especially in scientific and technical areas. An important part of your training as a scholar in your chosen field will be to master third person voice and suitably detached tones and levels of language.

Readings in Section 2, like those in Section 1, deal with issues of identity, generational, social, and cultural experience, as well as people's relations to nationhood and learning. From a rhetorical standpoint, however, "Knowledge and Ideas" demonstrates various methods that you will find described in Chapter 6 of the *Rhetoric*. As in Section 1, supplementary readings are listed after the selections, along with questions for further thinking and for comparisons to other essays in the *Reader*.

---

[5] Park Honan, *Shakespeare: A Life* (Oxford: Oxford University Press, 1999) 344.

Matthew Arnold The editors of the *Harbrace Anthology of Poetry*[6] state that Matthew Arnold is "frequently referred to as the poet of alienation." He is, they say, "preoccupied with the isolation of the individual and the difficulty of knowing the self." Though very much a Victorian (1822–1888), and a believer in progress of institutions and culture, Arnold was also sensitive to the shortcomings of his age. He longed for a time (perhaps imaginary) when fundamental questions of being seemed easier to answer. The son of a headmaster, he was educated at Oxford, stayed on as a professor of poetry for 10 years, then served as an inspector of schools. His critical works, such as *Culture and Anarchy* (1869), which deals with the need to balance the individual and his or her social group, are generally more widely respected today than his poetry. Yet several poems, including "Stanzas from the Grande Chartreuse" (1855) and "Dover Beach" (1867), remain classics of his time.

---

[6] Jon C. Stott, Raymond Jones, and Rick Bowers, *The Harbrace Anthology of Poetry* (Toronto: Harcourt, 1994).

Dover Beach

The sea is calm to-night.
The tide is full, the moon lies fair,
Upon the straits; —on the French coast the light
Gleams and is gone; the cliffs of England stand,
5   Glimmering and vast, out in the tranquil bay.
Come to the window, sweet is the night-air!
Only, from the long line of spray
Where the sea meets the moon-blanch'd land,
Listen! you hear the grating roar
10 Of pebbles which the waves draw back, and fling,
At their return, up the high strand,
Begin, and cease, and then again begin,
With tremulous cadence slow, and bring
The eternal note of sadness in.

15 Sophocles long ago
Heard it on the Ægean, and it brought
Into his mind the turbid ebb and flow
Of human misery, we
Find also in the sound a thought,
20 Hearing it by this distant northern sea.

The Sea of Faith
Was once, too, at the full, and round earth's shore
Lay like the folds of a bright girdle furl'd.
But now I only hear
25 Its melancholy, long, withdrawing roar,

Retreating, to the breath
Of the night-wind, down the vast edges drear
And naked shingles of the world.

Ah, love, let us be true
30   To one another! for the world, which seems
To lie before us like a land of dreams,
So various, so beautiful, so new,
Hath really neither joy, nor love, nor light,
Nor certitude, nor peace, nor help for pain;
35   And we are here as on a darkling plain
Swept with confused alarms of struggle and flight,
Where ignorant armies clash by night.

Jane Farrow   In this article from *Saturday Night,* December 1999/January 2000, the writer suggests that a new genre of writing has emerged in Canadian popular music, thanks to the wave of young women songwriters and singers such as Sarah McLachlan and Alanis Morissette. Farrow sees connections to Pauline Johnson, Margaret Laurence, and various other literary writers, arguing that women's writing has "transformed Canadian literature by dwelling on the mysterious interior lives of housewives, daughters, and retirees." In the 1960s, she contends, Joni Mitchell "imported" this impulse into the lyrics of pop music, making it "more emotional and personal than ever before." In the transition, women's writing is joining men's in an "expression of cultural democratization." The author implies that self-indulgence, in some cases, outweighs literary value, but if boys can "grunt and thrash and call it music, then girls can sob, sigh . . . and collect royalties, too."

Diary Rock

1   Somewhere, right now, there's a teenager lying on her bedroom floor, writing furiously in her diary. She's peeved at her best friend, thinks the new boy in class is crush material, and is scheming up a way to wear her mother's cashmere to school on Friday. It's a familiar scenario, but where her mother might have hidden such confessions under her mattress, today's teen queen is more likely to plunk them out on a guitar or piano and see if she can swing a record deal.

2   Only in the last decade has the girl-with-guitar singing achingly personal lyrics become as common as the boy band thrashing cover tunes in the garage. It's a cultural shift that has a lot to do with two women, both Canadians: Sarah McLachlan and Alanis Morissette.

3   McLachlan's Lilith Fair tour, a New Age "celebration of women in music," pulled in $50 million in ticket sales in its first two years. This mass marketing of self-affirming female culture flows directly from the smash success of Morissette's

confessional 1995 album *Jagged Little Pill*: 28 million copies, the highest-selling female solo album ever.

4   Morissette and McLachlan have plumbed the depths of personal loneliness and insecurity; they have gushed, sobbed, suffered, and raged their way to the top. Of course, plenty of women have sung the sour-relationship blues, but Alanis translated the raw urgency and unapologetic vengefulness of diary writing into lyrics, famously asking her ex-boyfriend whether his new girlfriend is "perverted like me." The poetry isn't exactly Byron, but it did encourage young women to view their diaries as art, rather than mere emotional catharsis.

5   Perhaps the propensity for journal writing is in our cultural genes. Canadian women writers have always tended towards introspection. Back in the 1800s, Susanna Moodie and Catharine Parr Traill wrote personal narratives of survival on the Canadian frontier. Their creativity was often fuelled by the rage and impotence they felt at being isolated, exhausted, cold, and chronically rejected by snooty Upper Canadian publishers.

6   And then there was the turn-of-the-century performance poet Pauline Johnson. In buckskins and a bear-claw necklace, Johnson would invoke her three-eighths Mohawk roots and belt out her revenge fantasies against inattentive lovers and traitorous white men.

7   This high-intensity sharing is carried on, each in her own way, by Margaret Laurence, Alice Munro, Gabrielle Roy, Marie-Claire Blais, Margaret Atwood, and Mavis Gallant. These women's books transformed Canadian literature by dwelling on the mysterious interior lives of housewives, daughters, and retirees.

8   In the sixties, Joni Mitchell imported this impulse into the world of rock, making it more emotional and personal than ever before.

9   Today's diary-divas—McLachlan, Morissette, and dozens of other lesser knowns—have created their own legacy in pop music by building on a preexisting one in Canadian literature. Their music appeals to listeners because it provides an island of authenticity in a sea of derivative macho braggadocio. Most crucially, they've shown the world that women don't have to mimic male rock swagger or sing lyrics someone else wrote to get people to listen to them.

10   Like punk before it, diary-rock is an expression of cultural democratization. It asserts that if boys can grunt and thrash and call it music, then girls can sob, sigh, and share their unedited exorcisms—and collect royalties too.

For Further Thinking

1. Farrow refers to young women seeing their diaries as potential art rather than simply emotional catharsis. What do you think is necessary, if anything, to make these two terms mutually inclusive?

2. What do you think is gained by basing a song, poem, or story on diaries and journals rather than trying to shape it independently of such source material?

3. What appears to be Farrow's attitude to her subject? Define her tone as precisely as you can. What do you think of her term "diary-divas"?

4. Farrow claims that Joni Mitchell imported the consciousness of novelists and poets into rock. Can you suggest other rock performers (female or male) who have drawn upon literary models? (Hint: Sometimes rock musicians downplay literary influence because it doesn't sound cool.)

5. How many other female rock writers can you name aside from Sarah McLachlan and Alanis Morrissette? Perhaps offer an analysis of their images, techniques, and themes.

Looking Back and Ahead

1. Our next selection, Susan McClelland's "The Lure of Body Image," deals with a form of what Farrow calls "macho braggadocio." In popular music, this braggadocio often emerges as physical threats and insults to women and authority figures. Do you agree with former rock star Grace Slick (formerly of Jefferson Airplane) that Eminem is a worthy creative artist, or is he sadly behind McLachlan and Morissette on the progressive continuum of popular art?

2. The media often like to play on a perceived battle of the sexes. Clearly this theme is believed to help sales and ratings. Are female and male pop artists actually that different from each other or pursuing such conflicting goals? Read Kim Pittaway's essay "Crystal Balls" (p. 160) for her view of the battle-of-the-sexes approach.

3. See Leanna Rutherford's "An Anorexic's Recovery" (p. 25). At the end of that essay we list a website about singer Karen Carpenter, whose beautiful voice, talent, and fame could not overcome her anorexia. Will the new generation of female talents help to remove problems of oppression, often expressed as low self-esteem and eating disorders? The signs may not be entirely positive. See also Paula Chin, "Anne Murray and Daughter," *People Weekly*, 52, No. 18 (Nov. 8, 1999), pp. 128–32, 134.

For Further Reading

Ockerbloom, Mary Mark, ed. "A Celebration of Women Writers: Writers from Canada." Online. Digital Library. April 2003. <http://digital.library.upenn.edu/women/_generate/CANADA.html>. Links to Canadian women writers, including all those mentioned by Jane Farrow, are available at this site.

Enright, Robert. "Words and Pictures: the Arts of Joni Mitchell." *Border Crossings* 20. 1 (Feb. 2001): 18–31.

"Sue Foley: Singer, Songwriter, and Guitarist." *Contemporary Canadian Biographies* (Jan.– Feb. 2001). April 2003 <http://www.antones.com/artists/s_foley.html>.

"Canada's Early Women Writers: A Biographical Database." Online. Ed. Carole Gerson. Department of English, Simon Fraser University. Electronic Document Centre, Simon Fraser University Library. April 2003 <http://edocs.lib.sfu.ca/>. This database covers up to 1940.

Manning, Kara. "Various Artists: R-E-S-P-E-C-T: A Century of Women in Music." April 2003 <http://www.rhino.com/features/liners/75815lin.html>. Why did it take nearly 100 years for women to get equal time on the radio, on the charts, and, for that matter, in the public consciousness?

Susan McClelland This article, from *Maclean's*, February 22, 1999, examines extreme measures some men are taking to achieve the "beefcake look." Example and interview, statistical reports on steroid use, and cause-effect analysis are combined to assemble various explanations for why men feel compelled to look muscular. McClelland also considers consequences and suggests alternatives.

The Lure of the Body Image

1   The year Ralph Heighton of Pictou, N.S., turned 30, he decided to lose some weight. At five-foot-nine, pushing 210 lbs., Heighton says when he stood in front of the mirror, he knew something wasn't working. He joined the YMCA in the nearby town of New Glasgow, started taking nightly walks and altered his diet, cutting out the late-night pizzas and pitas with spiced beef, onions and sauce. Now, at 34, Heighton fluctuates around the 185-lb. mark and has converted one of the three bedrooms in his new two-storey home into a gym, complete with weights and a tattered heavy bag bound by duct tape. Heighton, a wildlife technician with Nova Scotia's Department of Fisheries, says he has achieved his goal of feeling better. Though still single, he says bashfully that he thinks he has never looked as good—which was one of his key reasons for getting in shape. "The magazines sort of force this body image on you of what it means to be a physically fit person," says Heighton. "Whether we want to admit it or not, this image is what we want to look like."

2   The idealized male body image nowadays is beefy and muscled, as epitomized in the Calvin Klein underwear advertisements showcasing the bulging pecs and rippling abdomen of Antonio Sabato Jr. And like Heighton, hundreds of thousands of men in Canada are flocking to gyms and health clubs in the quest to look buffed and toned. There are signs, however, that some men are taking the image to extremes. Statistics on steroid use show an alarming number of male teenagers across the country are using the substance illegally simply to put on muscle. Men are increasingly being diagnosed with eating disorders. And plastic surgeons report a general increase in men seeking their services to improve their appearance. "This is an early warning," said New York City author Michelangelo Signorile, whose book *Life Outside* chronicles the history of body image among homosexual men. "This 'cult of masculinity' isn't just in gay culture as so many like to believe. It envelops the entire culture. It is an obsessive devotion to an ideal."

3   Although worshipping the body is hardly new, the emphasis on the beefcake look has evolved gradually in North America over the past 100 years. Both Signorile and Brian Pronger, a philosopher in the Faculty of Physical Education at the University of Toronto, say that many men, straight and gay, adopted a more masculine appearance after the Oscar Wilde trials in the 1890s associated effeminate behaviour with homosexuality in the popular mind. Pronger

and Signorile also say that women's suffrage and, later, the modern feminist movement caused men to covet a larger appearance as a means of defending men's status. "As women take up more space in traditionally masculine places," says Pronger, "some men feel compelled to take up more in order to maintain their position."

4   It takes a lot of sweating and spending to achieve a hard-body look. According to a 1995 report published by the Canadian Fitness and Lifestyle Research Institute, men spend more than twice as much as women in all categories related to fitness, including clothing, exercise equipment, membership fees and instruction. Brad Whitehead, who works for one of the largest distributors of creatine, a controversial supplement that increases the energy capacity in muscles, says sales have increased 130 per cent since 1997.

5   Calvin Klein and other underwear merchants are not alone in using men with buffed bodies to sell products. Other advertisers include Coca-Cola, Nike and Marlboro, which has introduced a bulkier version of its original "Marlboro Man." As well, magazine stands now offer dozens of titles devoted to health, fitness and muscle, tantalizing readers with snappy headlines like "Great abs in eight weeks." Their pages are adorned with ads featuring big, bulky men selling muscle-building supplements.

6   One of the sad consequences of the push towards a hyper-masculine image is that it can rarely be obtained without the use of potentially harmful drugs. A 1993 study conducted for the Canadian Centre for Ethics in Sport concluded that four per cent of males aged 11 to 18—as many as 83,000 young Canadians—used anabolic steroids in 1992 and 1993. In the study, which involved 16,169 high-school and elementary students, one in five reported that they knew someone who was taking anabolic steroids. Among the reasons given for their use, nearly half said it was to change their physical appearance. That contrasted starkly with previously held notions that steroids were used mostly to increase athletic performance, says Paul Melia, the Centre's director of education. "The reality for most of these young men, even if they do get on a regimen of weight training, is that they are not going to look like these picture boys," said Melia. "And sustaining that look is a full-time job."

7   In a downtown Toronto gym, Mike, a 32-year-old former bodybuilder and weight lifter and a longtime user of anabolic steroids, says as many as four out of five of the 18- to 25-year-old men using the facility are on the illegal drugs. When he started using steroids 16 years ago, Mike says, he was part of an elite group of men who took them for competitive reasons. "Today it is for the body image," he says. "And these kids stack—they add steroid upon steroid, thinking they are going to get a certain look. They take this stuff, go out to night clubs, get drunk and mix everything together. It's all for image."

8   Mike says one result of working out seriously can be that, no matter how big their muscles get, men start thinking they are still not big enough. It is a phenomenon disturbingly similar to cases of eating disorders among women who be-

lieve they are too big, no matter how thin they get. Maintaining a hard body takes not only a regimen of heavy workouts, but also a dedication to eating right and at times dieting to avoid gaining fat, says Mike. And psychologists across the country say one result of those self-imposed pressures is an increased incidence of eating disorders among men. According to Dr. Howard Steiger, a clinical psychologist and director of the eating disorder program at Douglas Hospital in Montreal, surveys have shown that five to 10 per cent of eating disorder sufferers are men. He says most people with eating disorders have unstable self-esteem. He also says there are increasing sociocultural pressures on men to connect their self-esteem to body image. While there are no new national figures, specialists in many centres say that bulimia nervosa, characterized by binge eating and vomiting, is on the rise in men. "What you find," says Steiger, "are people who diet too much, who condition too much, and what you are doing is setting up this pressure of hunger—a constant state of undernutrition that eventually leads to bulimic-type eating patterns."

9   In addition to steroid use and erratic eating behaviour, John Semple, secretary treasurer of the Canadian Society of Plastic Surgeons, says he believes men are increasingly having plastic surgery to alter their body image. Dr. Bill Papanastasiou, a plastic surgeon in Montreal, estimates that only 10 per cent of his patients were male when he opened his practice 13 years ago. Today, it is as high as 15 to 20 per cent. In Halifax, plastic surgeon Dr. Kenneth Wilson says one of the most common surgeries he does for men is liposuction. For Nathan Estep, a 27-year-old from Detroit who spent $1,800 in Pontiac, Mich., in 1997 to have liposuction done on his waistline, the surgery has transformed his life. Since he was 10, Estep was a constant dieter, at times bulimic, and for many years tried to control his weight using diet drugs including Dexedrine, ephedrine and laxatives. Today, Estep says he can walk proudly, with his shirt off and with no hint of any fat from his childhood returning. "I was a fat kid— I had fat in the wrong places." he says. "The first thing I did after the liposuction was go to the beach, take my shirt off and eat a pint of Häagen-Dazs. I feel like a new man."

10   According to Pronger, who has been studying the philosophy of physical fitness for five years, a person with a hard, fit body considers it a signal of discipline and a capacity for hard work. "When you see somebody who is overweight," he says, "often the response is how did they let themselves get like that." The mistaken presumption, he adds, is that the person doesn't have the discipline to be a productive citizen. One of the solutions, says Pronger, is to teach children to look at body images in the same critical way they are told to consider art and literature—to be able to recognize what has merit. "If we were doing the same with physical education, people could learn to have a different reaction to these extreme body images," he says. "They would say, 'Hey, I don't want to be part of this pressure to fall in love with a highly commercialized image.'"

For Further Thinking

1. Do you think McClelland's article overstates the problem of steroid abuse among boys and men? Explain.

2. Critics such as Jean Kilbourne, author of *Deadly Persuasion* (1999) and her film series *Killing Us Softly* (1979–2000), have pointed out how advertising presents distorted images of women, stressing two myths: the sex goddess or the perfect homemaker. The *Maclean's* article states, "One of the sad consequences of the push towards a hyper-masculine image is that it can rarely be obtained." Is the unrealistic portrayal of men in advertising as damaging as the portrayal of women?

3. How effectively do you feel the article has used studies and statistics?

4. What do you think of McClelland's suggested alternatives and solutions?

Looking Back and Ahead

1. McClelland quotes Dr. Howard Steiger as saying that 5 to 10 percent of those suffering eating disorders are men, and there is widespread professional opinion that bulimia nervosa is on the rise in men. See Leanna Rutherford's "An Anorexic's Recovery" (p. 25) for more information on eating disorders.

2. McClelland's article ends with reference to the dangers of falling in love "with a highly commercialized image." What possible connection can you find between this article and George Orwell's "Politics and the English Language" (p. 227)?

3. Read Plato's "Allegory of the Cave" (p. 119). Where in his model of reality would Plato likely assign the images of "beefcake" men and "cheesecake" women that we see in magazines as well as on televisions and our computer screens?

For Further Reading

Farrell, Warren. *The Myth of Male Power*. New York: Simon & Schuster, 1993. Farrell argues that, far from being powerful, man is the disposable sex.

Kilbourne, Jean. *Deadly Persuasion: Why Girls and Women Must Fight the Addictive Power of Advertising*. New York: Free Press, 1999. Jean Kilbourne is best known for her *Killing Us Softly* film series, which examines the effects of the media on women's self image. In this book, she analyzes the way advertising creates and then feeds an addictive mentality.

Media Awareness Network. April 2003 <**http://www.media-awareness.ca/eng/med/class/ teamedia/special5.htm**>. The goal of this site is to develop critical thinking skills in young people. Media Awareness hosts six links to Special K ads. Take a look at these ads and decide what influence the media has on our minds.

Media Literary Online Project. Gary Ferrington, director. College of Education, University of Oregon, Eugene. April 2003 <**http://interact.uoregon.edu/MediaLit/HomePage**>.

Rempel, Byron. "Men's Body Image: The Brad Pitt Syndrome." April 2003 <**http://canoe. talksurgery.com/consumer/new/**>. The author considers the effects of the media on men's body image, and concludes that the pressure to succeed is still the greatest pressure on men.

Stanford University. April 2003 <http://www.stanford.edu/>. Search for the keywords "performance-enhancing drugs" for a number of articles on this site.

Pat Deiter-McArthur (Day Woman) In clear, concise prose, Deiter-McArthur uses classification and description to characterize the five generations of Saskatchewan's Natives from the treaty-signers to today. This piece of written history by a Native writer represents a new cultural form, as traditional Native history has been handed down orally, by designated storytellers. This fact, and the desire of the invading Europeans to appropriate lands and re-place Native cultures with their own, meant that little attention was paid to Native history in books until recently, and Native authors on Native history could not be found. That situation changed in Canada in 1992 with the publication of *Canada's First Nations* by Métis historian Olive Dickason, Canada's first history of its Native peoples by a Native. It is an even-handed look at all of the participants.

In the following essay, Deiter-McArthur mainly reports the historical facts as she knows them, and leaves the interpretation to us.

The Vision Quest

I am an Indian and a member of the Fifth Generation.

I have choice, strength, and freedom.

I have an obligation to my Treaty-Signers,
and others who knew no freedom,
5   and to my future—to be the
best I can be.

What I dream, I am. The fulfillment of
my dream is my Vision Quest.

Saskatchewan's Indian People—Five Generations

1   It has been about five generations since Saskatchewan Indian people have had sig-nificant contact with European settlers. The First Generation strongly influenced by Europeans were the treaty-signers. The key characteristic of this generation was their ability to have some input into their future. They retained their tribal cul-tures but realized that they had to negotiate with the Europeans for the better-ment of future generations. They did not give up their language or religion or the

political structures of nationhood. They were perceived by government as an "alien" nation to be dealt with by treaty.

2   The Second Generation (1867–1910) of Indian people was the object of legal oppression by the government. This generation lived under the absolute rule of an Indian agent, a government employee. Through the Indian Act, this generation was denied their religion, political rights, and freedom to travel off their reserves. A pass and permit system was strictly adhered to on the prairies; every Indian person required a pass to leave the reserve and a permit to sell any agricultural produce. All children were required to attend residential schools run by the churches. The goals of their schools were, first, to make Christians out of their students and to rid them of their pagan lifestyles and, second, to provide a vocational education.

3   Tuberculosis was a major killer of Indian people during this time and contributed to decimating their population in Saskatchewan to a low of five thousand in 1910. This generation was treated as wards and aliens of Canada.

4   The laws which served to oppress the second generation were in place until the early 1950s. The Third Generation (1910–1945) was greatly affected by these laws and schooling. This generation can be described as the lost generation. These people were psychologically oppressed. They rejected their Indianness but found that because of the laws for treaty Indians they could not enjoy the privileges accorded to whites. This third generation was our grandfathers' generation. Many Indians at this time could speak their language but would not because of shame of their Indianness. They were still required by law to send their children to residential schools, to send their sick to Indian hospitals, and to abide by the Indian agent. They rarely had a sense of control over their own lives. This generation was considered wards of the government and denied citizenship.

5   Our fathers' time, the Fourth Generation since treaty-signing, can be best described as the generation of an Indian rebirth. This generation (1945–1980) is characterized by a movement of growing awareness—awareness that being Indian is okay and that Indian people from all tribes are united through their aboriginality, historical development, and special status.

6   This generation saw the rise of Indian and Native organizations across Canada, the return of traditional ceremonies, and an acknowledgement of the need to retain traditional languages and cultural ways.

7   Indian people of this generation were given the right to vote in 1960. The pass and permit system was abandoned in the late 1930s. In 1956, Indian children could attend either residential schools or the local public schools. However, the effects of this generation being raised within an institution and their parents being raised in the same way had a severe impact on these individuals. The residential school not only taught them to suppress their language but also to suppress their feelings and sense of individualism. The continued attack on Indian languages by residential schools left this generation with an ability only to understand their language, but many were not sufficiently fluent to call their Native language their first language.

8   During the sixties, there was a rise in Indian urbanization, a trend that continues today. This generation also contributed to an Indian baby boom that is estimated to be eight to ten years behind the non-Indian baby boomers. The federal and provincial vote allowed Indian people to legally consume alcohol. Alcoholism, suicides, and violent deaths were on the rise for this generation.

9   This was a period of experimentation by both the Indian communities and the government. Unfortunately, neither side was ready for each other. The intended government goal of assimilation was besieged with problems of racism, poverty, maladjustment, and cultural shock.

10   Today's Indian people are part of the Fifth Generation. The fifth generation is faced with choices: assimilation, integration, or separation. Indian people are now able to intermarry or assimilate with non-Indian without the loss of their Indian status. Indian leaders across Canada are seeking a separate and constitutionally recognized Indian government. Indian government is to provide its own services within Indian reserves. Integration allows Indian people to retain a sense of their cultural background while working and living within the larger society.

11   The fifth generation people are the first children since treaty-signing to be raised by their parents. Many of this fifth generation are not able to understand a Native language. Their first and only language is English. This generation is generally comfortable about their Indianness without strong prejudicial feelings to others. However, this generation is challenged to retain the meaning of Indian identity for their children.

For Further Thinking

1. Is the history reported in this article new information for you, or do you feel it has already been covered in previous school curricula? Have you had direct experience of Native history?

2. If you have direct knowledge of Native cultures, do you think they have elements that would benefit our wider society? If so, explain.

3. Comment on Deiter-McArthur's basic methods of exposition in this essay.

4. Do you feel, in some instances, that forms of propaganda hinder the treatment of Native issues? Explain your opinion.

Looking Back and Ahead

1. Deiter-McArthur concludes her survey with the suggestion that although the fifth generation (today's young adults) is the first since treaty-signing to be raised by their parents, nevertheless their loss of Indian language may make it difficult to retain their Indian identity. How does this point apply to Habeeb Salloum's essay "The Other Canadians and Canada's Future" (p. 200)?

2. After reading "Saskatchewan's Indian People—Five Generations," how do you interpret Pierre Trudeau's reference to "the greatness of those who founded" this land in "The Ascetic in a Canoe"(p. 156)?

For Further Reading

Aboriginal Rights Coalition of British Columbia. April 2003. <http://arcbc.tripod.com/> The site explains that legal action to secure Native right to lands in the province was touched off largely by the federal government's 1969 White Paper.

Bringhurst, Robert. *A Story as Sharp as a Knife: The Classical Haida Mythtellers and Their World*. Vancouver: Douglas & McIntyre. Bringhurst translates and studies oral stories of classical Haida literature, in his judgement, "one of the world's great mythologies."

Campbell, Maria. *Halfbreed*. Toronto: McClelland and Stewart, 1973. This autobiography, the inspiration for innumerable Native authors, describes the Saskatchewan Métis.

————, trans. *Stories of the Road Allowance People*. Penticton, BC: Theytus, 1995. Combined with original artwork, this book presents a number of traditional stories from the Saskatchewan Métis.

Dickason, Olive. *Canada's First Nations: A History of Founding Peoples from Earliest Times*. Toronto: McClelland & Stewart, 1992.

Dorothy Williams Born and raised in the Little Burgundy community of Montreal, Dorothy Williams was in her final year at Concordia University when the Quebec Human Rights Commission approached her to write an internal document on the mobility of Blacks in Montreal. After three years of research, the resulting document was published by Les Éditions Yvon Blais in 1989. The version in our *Reader* was abridged by the editors of *Boundaries of Identity*, an anthology of works on Canadian culture. This paper not only will surprise you by disclosing an unfamiliar part of Canadian history, but will provide an example of academic research serving a well-defined purpose.

The editors of *Boundaries of Identity* have formatted this essay according to a house style of documentation rather than MLA or APA. A list of works cited has not been included at the end. Contrast this style of documentation to the MLA or APA systems, which we recommend for your research papers. See Chapter 12.

See the Appendix at the end of Section 3 of the *Reader*, Part I (p. 248), for more support for this reading. This support may particularly benefit you if English is not your first language.

The Quebec Experience: Slavery 1628–1834

1   In 1606, Samuel de Champlain reached Canada. It was on this third trip that Matthew da Costa, a Black man, accompanied Champlain. He was chosen by Champlain because of his linguistic ability—he knew the language of the Acadian Micmacs. This was obviously not da Costa's first trip to Canada,[1] but this was the first record of a Black man in Canada.[2]

2   The subsequent history of Black immigration to Canada was one of enslavement. African slavery began slowly in New France from 1628 onward.[3] Oliver Lejeune was the first slave to be imported. He came from the island of Madagascar.[4] Though this was the beginning of the institution of slavery, it was not till 1685 with the introduction of the "Code Noir" that it attained some legal status.[5] The status of slaves was regulated by this code, which though never officially proclaimed, was used as a customary law in New France for slave ownership.

3   May 1, 1689, is considered the official birth date of African slavery in Canada. On that day Louis XIV, King of France, "reluctantly" gave permission to his subjects of New France to import African slaves. After 1689 the practice of slave owning by the French merchant class and clergy became common.

4   No exact census of the slave population in Quebec can be found, though local records revealed 3,604 separate slaves by 1759; of these 1,132 were Negroes.[6] Most of the African slaves were domestic servants who lived in or near Montreal, where 52.3 percent of the known total lived. In fact, unlike the American colonies, the majority of slaves in Quebec (77.2%) resided in towns.

5   The slave owners' mentality and religious attitudes in New France were said to have differed greatly from those of British colonies to the south. Those Canadian historians that have even chosen to mention slavery in Canada often describe a romantic, or an idealized, slave regime in New France.[7]

6   The very nature of Roman Catholicism and its doctrine, "which held that the spiritual nature of the slave transcended this temporary status and that to give a man his freedom was to please God" (Winks, 1971: 12), supposedly created a "tolerant benevolence" and more humane laws in New France. Thus, even though the Church in New France tended to soften the effects of slavery, this religious justification allowed it to condone the institution—even when slaves were tortured and killed.[8]

7   One recorded example is that of Marie Joseph Angélique, who in her bid for freedom destroyed almost half of Montreal by fire in 1734. Forty-six buildings including the convent, the church, and the hospital were consumed (*Silent Minority*, n.d.: 12).

8   Yet despite this incendiary disaster there is no mention of this event in the recent literature on the story of Montreal. Is this because Montreal's early historians believed that the destruction of about half of the city had no impact on its social and economic development? Could it be that the actions of a recalcitrant slave were not worth noting? Angélique's hideous punishment is a testament to the fact that Montreal's citizens felt otherwise.

9   On the day of her execution, Angélique was first tortured until she confessed her crime. Then she was driven through the streets in the scavenger's wagon. . . . A burning torch had been placed in her hand. At the main door of the parish church in Place d'Armes she was made to kneel . . . and her hand was cut off. Then, once again, she was placed in the scavenger's wagon and taken to the place of public execution and hanged. After her body was burnt at the stake, her ashes were scattered in the wind.[9]

10   "Slavery is slavery in whatever form it takes."[10] The veracity of this statement was underscored in New France. Those enslaved were not content. Many tried to escape—some repeatedly. Slave owners fought back in the courts and in the Church to protect their right to own human property. The strongest deterrent against escape, the Code Noir, though not always enforced in the colony, gives an indication of the colonists' supposedly benign view of slavery:

11   Si le Noir s'évade, on lui coupe les oreilles et on le marque au fer rouge d'une fleur de lys à l'épaule; s'il récidive, on lui coupe les jarrets. S'il ose recommencer une troisième fois, c'est la mort. (Marcil, 1981: 75) [If a Black tries to escape, we cut off his ears and we brand a fleur de lys on his shoulder with a hot iron; if he repeats the crime, we cut the hamstrings on the back of his legs. If he dares to try a third time, the penalty is death.]

12   In reality, the "benevolence" exhibited by slave owners in New France towards their African slaves was due to economic and social factors rather than any humanistic tendency. Panis, or Indian slaves, were a cheap source of labour for agricultural and hard manual work, whereas the African represented a superior type of slave labour in the towns and cities. African slaves were to be found in the houses of government officials, or of wealthy merchants and seigneurs.

13   Not only were the expensive African slaves used as "labour saving devices" (Winks, 1971), but they were also considered valuable property that functioned as symbols of social status amongst the elite. Considering their domestic work status, their high price, and the degree of difficulty in obtaining them, most African slaves were "benevolently" treated simply because longevity of service was desired.

14   Official slavery survived in New France for seventy-one years, and only briefly during this time did conditions favour the potential growth of slavery. Between 1663 and 1704, in an expanding New France, slave labour might have been used to considerable advantage; but slavery was not given full legal support until 1709, well after the colony had developed its mercantilist base. And after 1713, when New France fell into decline, the institution declined with it.

15   The decline of slavery in New France can be understood as an economic development. The chief reason slavery gained little hold in New France arose from the fact that the economy was almost exclusively based on the fur trade. Unlike the mass-production gang labour economies to the south, free entrepreneurial labour was far more advantageous for the beaver trade in the north. As long as the colony was so dependent on the fur trade, there was little demand for either domestic servants or manual labourers. The decline in slavery, like the treatment of slaves, was not due to a particularly humane French regime, but rather, it was a circumstance of geography and political economy.

16   However, not all Blacks in the colony were slaves. Manumission was practiced and encouraged by the clergy. Freed Black men were entrepreneurs, such

as fur traders and fishermen. Many also had valuable and prestigious roles as mediators between the Indians and the French.[11] Trudel (1960) estimates that in 1759, just prior to the defeat of New France, 962 households had slaves. Though the economic structure had placed relatively little importance on the acquisition of slaves, slavery was part of the accepted social order in New France.

Revival: 1760

17   With the Conquest and the introduction of British laws and institutions into Lower Canada, slavery grew in importance and obtained greater legal status. African slavery, which was a dying institution under the French, was revived in two stages: under the British, slavery continued for another seventy-four years.

18   First, General Amherst in September 1760 officially agreed to the requests of the conquered French that both the Black and Indian slaves would remain enslaved. This policy was supported by the British government.[12]

19   Secondly, during and after the War of Independence of 1776–88, Loyalists, Black and White, slave and free, streamed into Canada. Twelve percent of the registered forty-two thousand United Empire Loyalists that entered Canada were of African descent. However, most of the free Black loyalists went to the Maritimes.

20   Seven thousand white Loyalists came to Lower Canada. Many brought "their more valuable slaves with them as they hastily fled the United States" (Walker, 1980). In spite of this influx, more French citizens (97%) continued to own slaves than the English in Lower Canada.[13] Those Loyalists who had entered Canada without slaves considered slavery a symbol of the "republicanism" they had just fled. Later on, many of these Loyalists became staunch abolitionists.

21   Approximately three hundred new slaves were brought into Lower Canada by Loyalists. Although it is not possible to establish a figure for the exact number of slaves brought into Montreal, the number living there increased substantially (Barrolo, 1976). Negro slaves virtually supplanted Panis slaves in Montreal. Also, because many of the slaves came from larger plantations where they had been trained to do specific jobs, the variety of work done by Blacks in Montreal's labour market was greatly expanded. Free Blacks and slaves were sawyers, carpenters, blacksmiths, and candlemakers. In the early days of Montreal, Blacks held important roles in the city's economy.

22   However, unlike the Maritimes and Upper Canada, the majority of the Blacks that entered Quebec were slaves (Winks, 1971). The reasons for this were twofold. First, this was probably due to the unavailability of fertile land in southern Quebec. Other than the slaves of Loyalists, free Blacks could not settle in Quebec as easily as in the less densely populated regions of Canada, for much of the cultivated land was already held through the seigneurial system and was meted out through family and kinship ties.

23   Secondly, the center of colonial economic power in Canada resided in Lower Canada. Here, the new colonial administrators favoured the expansion of slavery in order to alter the mercantilist base of production. The British in Europe were

in the forefront of the capitalist mode of economy. The previous experience of the British showed that a slave economy increased the chances of capitalist production, while at the same time it extended the notion of private property which was essential to the development of capitalism.

24   From the correspondence of military governor General James Murray, it was apparent that the British administrators stationed in the Canadas were anxious to develop such an attitude in Quebec. In 1763, he wrote to a colleague in New York: "Without servants nothing can be done and (French) Canadians will work for nobody but themselves. . . . Black slaves are certainly the only people to be depended upon.[14]

25   Subsequent British laws attempted to confirm and strengthen the rights of White property owners. For example: "In legislation passed to encourage immigration to British North America, one article specifically allowed the importation of 'Negroes,' household furniture, utensils of husbandry or clothing. The same law discouraged the immigration of free Blacks" (Warner 1983: 4; Case 1977: 9).

26   The entrenching of such a political attitude led to more hardship for the "human chattel" in the colonies. This was felt throughout the North American colonies, so much so that slaves in the Canadian provinces under British rule increased their efforts to escape. A southbound underground railroad was established, and between 1788 and 1792 slaves held in Canada fled to the slave-free northern states under the Americans (Thomson, 1979). Contrary to popular belief, the first underground railroad between the U.S. and Canada existed to free slaves held on Canadian territory (Walker, 1980).

Abolition 1789–1834

27   The actual fight to abolish slavery in Quebec began in 1789 when the Chief Justice, Sir James Monk of the Court of King's Bench, released two slaves on a two-hundred-year-old technicality, and went on to say that therefore "slavery did not exist in the province" (Winks, 1971: 100). This dictum was upheld through court decisions in subsequent years by other judges. These decisions led to "fear among slave-owners in Montreal that the courts could no longer be counted on to regard their slaves as chattels. The value of slaves deteriorated," and slaves escaped more and more frequently.[15] As the owners lost their legal right to purchase and sell human property, the right to own such property became tenuous.

28   Moreover, about 1790, the press headed by A. Brown and J. Nelson, owner-editors of the *Quebec-Gazette,* spearheaded the attack on the institution of slavery in the province. That same year Joseph Papineau, on behalf of the citizens of Montreal, presented a petition to provincial authorities to abolish slavery. Though nothing was done immediately, in 1801 and 1803 two abolitionist bills were presented in the provincial legislature (Israel, 1928: 65). Both bills were defeated, but the simple tabling of the bills kept the abolition issue alive in Lower Canada.

29   Elsewhere, abolitionist forces met with greater success. In Upper Canada, Lieutenant Governor Simcoe guided an anti-slavery bill through the Upper Canada legislature. This bill "encouraged slaves to escape into the free areas of the Northwest territories of the U.S. and into Vermont and New York" (Bartolo, 1976). This combination of judicial and legislative intervention and media influence created an anti-slavery attitude. By 1820 this attitude helped to effectively end "legal" slavery in Quebec.[16]

30   For 125 years, a total of 5,400 people had been enslaved in the province: one thousand of whom were of African descent (Trudel, 1960). On August 1, 1834, when the Imperial Act freed nearly eight hundred thousand slaves in the British colonies, there were "probably fewer than half a hundred" left in all of British North America (Winks, 1971: 111).

Conclusion

31   Canada was not created for the equality of all its citizens. As a colony, its existence was maintained for the wealth of its owners, and as a nation it continues to maintain this goal. Class and race, like language and religion, are issues sometimes used by different elite groups at different times to keep people divided; such divisions maintain the status quo. Still, human beings are very adaptable. One can learn another language, change religion or win a lottery. For the vast majority of people there is "chance" or opportunity to move up or down the vertical ladder.

32   But race is a very different issue from these other three categories mentioned above. The reason is socio-cultural. There is a prevailing belief among the general populace that Blacks are Canada's newest immigrants. This assumption remains despite the historical proof to the contrary. There has been an obvious and systematic obfuscation of the historical Black presence in this country.

33   Systemic historical racism (one that does not acknowledge the existence of Blacks) is a two-sided issue. Against Blacks it maintains the illusion that they are foreigners to this soil, while it clearly sets up the assumption that Canada was, and is, a White country. One consequence of these lies is the day-to-day struggle for acceptance by Blacks, and the "polite" racism of tolerant Canadians.

34   When a White individual sees a Black person, he or she sees first and foremost that the individual is Black. A Black man is a "no good" man. No, it does not matter whether he speaks Bantu, Creole or French. It matters not whether he lives in a hovel or the finest home in Westmount. It does not even matter whether his ancestry in this country goes back to 1825 or even 1659. Generation after generation, his Blackness is a visible sign of his difference from all that is "Canadian."

35   It is this social reality that continues to dictate, consciously or unconsciously, much of the social interaction for Blacks in Quebec.

36   Today, Montreal's Black population is a multi-cultural, multi-lingual community consisting of Blacks from Africa, Europe, Canada (further divided between the Maritime Blacks and the rest), the Caribbean, and Latin America. On the whole, though Black Quebecers prefer certain neighbourhoods (anglophone

Blacks in the west and francophone Blacks in the east), residency has not been prescribed solely by linguistic convention. The presence of great socio-economic diversity within Montreal's Black population has also fuelled Black mobility. This pattern is evident within all class groupings, even amongst the disadvantaged and working classes in the inner-city whose mobility aspirations mirror those of the middle and upper classes in the off-island and metropolitan suburbs.

37   Notwithstanding the above elements—which played a role in the dispersal of the community—there were other counterbalancing factors conducive to the formation of residential clusters. Foremost, we see that the historical pattern of Black mobility in Montreal was clearly influenced by the racist response of Montreal's property owners to the Black householder. For though Blacks came to Montreal with many different national, cultural and socio-economic frameworks, all too quickly these immigrants came to realize that their unique social and national identities mattered little in a society that put a much greater emphasis on their racial characteristics than on their socio-economic status.

38   It was not long ago in Montreal that Blacks in their search for housing were often confronted with signs that read, "No niggers, dogs or Jews allowed." Today signs like this may not be the fashion, but in many instances they have only been replaced with more subtle ways and means of denying access.

Notes

1. Historians speculate that da Costa had previously visited as a crew member of Portuguese vessels that had fished off Newfoundland. See "Silent Minority" (n.d.); L. Bertley (1977), *Canada and Its People of African Descent* (Pierrefonds: Bilongo Pub.); E. Thornhill (1982: 2), "Race and Class in Canada: The Case of Blacks in Quebec" (Seminar paper, Montreal), arguing that Matthew served in the Poutrincourt-Champlain expedition of 1606. J. Bertley (1982: 7) in "The Role of the Community in Educating Blacks in Montreal from 1910 to 1940 with Special Reference to Reverend Dr. Charles Humphrey Este," M.A. Thesis (Montreal: McGill University), reports that Matthew settled at the Port Royal Habitation on the bank of the Annapolis River in Nova Scotia, where he died and was buried.

2. According to Bertley (1977: 11–13) and J. Bertley (1982: 7), there is early documented proof that Africans *discovered* the "New World" in the 14th century, thus predating Columbus. See *The Montreal Star* (1975, 9 April) "Ancient Stones Bear Witness: Libyans Visited Quebec in 500 B.C., Archeologist Says."

3. Other accounts such as R. Winks (1971), *The Blacks in Canada: A History* (Montreal: McGill-Queen's University Press), refer to earlier dates: 1501 in Newfoundland by Gaspar Corte Real, and 1608 in Acadia by Sieur Du Gua de Monts; both were slave owners of Indians and Africans. See: n.a., "Black Days in the North: Sad Roots" in *Canadian Heritage* (1979, December).

4. C. Marcil (1981), "Les communautés noires au Québec" in *Éducation Québec* (vol. II, no. 6), says Lejeune was from Guinea rather than from Madagascar. Both places are cited as possible in "Silent Minority."

5. "The Code was designed to protect owners from slaves' violence and escape," as cited in Colin Thomson (1979: 17), *Blacks in Deep Snow: Black Pioneers in Canada* (Toronto: J.M. Dent & Sons Ltd.).

6. According to Winks (1971: 9), no exact census of the slave population in Quebec can be found. See Paul Dejean (1978: 95), *Les Haïtiens au Québec* (Montréal: Les Presses de l'Université du

Québec). See also: Dr. G. Hill (1983), "Black History in Early Ontario," paper presented to Fairweather Lecture Series, University of Ottawa.

7. F.X. Garneau, in *Histoire du Canada Français depuis sa Découverte,* claimed that "the peculiar institution never sullied the skies of Canada." And T. Watson Smith, in *The Slave in Canada,* mentioned that the prominent Canadian historians in 1889 had neglected "this sombre and unattractive chapter." Not much in Canadian historiography has changed since then. A sampling of contemporary college and university textbooks still confirms that the deliberate obfuscation of slavery within Canadian history continues. See: W.L. Morton (1963), *The Kingdom of Canada;* E. McInnis (1969), *Canada: A Political and Social History;* R.C. Harris and J. Warkenton (1974), *Canada Before Confederation.* This attitude at the national level contrasts with the writing of Montreal's earliest historians, many of whom have included the slave chronology in their texts. See: Teril, *A Chronology of Montreal and of Canada, A.D. 1752.* Hector Berthelet, *Montréal le Bon Vieux Temps;* Atherton, Montreal, 1535–1914.

8. For an account of this and other punitive measures taken against slaves, see: "Negro Slavery in Montreal" (n.d.); M. Trudel (1960), *L'esclavage au Canada Français: histoire et conditions de l'esclavage* (Québec: Presses de l'Université Laval); Wilfred Israel (1928: 66–67), "Montreal Negro Community," M.A. Thesis (Montreal: McGill University); L. Bertley (1976), "Slavery" in *Focus Umoja Montreal,* no. 16; Bertley (1977); Thomson (1979); D. Williams (1983), "The Black Presence in Montreal: A Multi-Cultural Community"; L. Warner (1983), "Profile of the English-Speaking Black Community in Quebec" (Montréal: Comité d'implantation du plan d'action à l'intention des communautés culturelles); "Silent Minority" (n.d.); Marcil (1981).

9. For an account of the role of the Church in her death, see Thornhill (1982: 3).

10. Case (1977: 10). Other historians have ignored this fact. With one breath they describe Canadian slavery as benevolent. "The evidence, on the whole, would indicate that the conditions of slaves were not hard." *Negro Slavery* (n.d.). "As a rule, it appears that the slaves were not badly treated . . ." Bartolo (1976: n.p.) "Blacks in Canada: 1608 to Now" in *A Key to Canada,* Part II (Toronto: National Black Coalition of Canada). "Black slaves in Canada had it easier than their cousins in the States and the West Indies" (Heritage, 1979: 43). One of the more recent perspectives found in *Quebec Women: A History,* The Clio Collective (1987: 97), published by The Women's Press (Toronto), even goes so far as to present a picture of Black slaves as being uneducable and therefore responsible for their harsh treatment. The writers, while acknowledging that "the death rate amongst these slaves was high," go on to explain that it was because "adapting to white society was difficult." Thus, they conclude, slaves "did not always make ideal servants, even if they did not have to be paid for their work."

11. For a discussion of the varied occupations of free Blacks in the colony, see *Silent Minority* (n.d.: 5–8); Winks (1971); Marcil (1981).

12. After the Conquest, colonial officials "sent instructions to promote the establishment of 'plantations' in Canada," similar to those of the South (*Negro Slavery,* n.d.). While this plantation system was not instituted, these official edicts served to clarify and re-establish the right of slave-owning in the colony.

13. See Bartolo (1976: n.p.). For a list of prominent slave owners see: J. Walker (1980: 12), *A History of Blacks in Canada: A Study Guide for Teachers and Students* (Hull: Minister of State); Bertley (1977); "Negro Slavery"; Marcil (1981); Winks (1971); Thornhill (1982); W.R. Riddell (1919), "The Slave in Upper Canada" in *The Journal of Negro History,* ed. G. Woodson (Lancaster: The Association for the Study of Negro Life and History, Inc.) vol. II.

14. Ida Greaves (1930: 11), "The Negro in Canada," *Economic Studies,* No. 16 (Montreal: McGill University).

15. Israel (1928: 65). Chief Justice Osgoode in 1803 decided in Montreal that "slavery was incompatible with the laws of the country."

16. Israel (1928: 64). In fact, this eradication would seem to have occurred even earlier. The last slave had the distinction of being overthrown by judicial interference. See also: Borthwick (1891), *History of Montreal;* Greaves (1930); "Negro Slavery"; Marcil (1981).

For Further Thinking

1. Canadians may sometimes feel superior to Americans because, supposedly, we did not participate in slavery. Has Williams uncovered an aspect of Canadian history that is generally suppressed?

2. Marie Joseph Angélique's destruction of half of Montreal by fire cannot be found in the vast majority of books about that city. What is your opinion of this omission? What historical evidence can you track down about this incident?

3. What rhetorical structures do you find in this essay? Review Chapter 6 of the *Rhetoric* if you are uncertain what sorts of organizational patterns to look for.

4. Williams concludes, as does Native rights advocate David Joyce in his paper "A Basic Philosophical Response to the Infamous White Paper Position," that Canada "was not created for the equality of all its citizens. As a colony, its existence was maintained for the wealth of its owners and as a nation it continues to maintain this goal." What is your opinion of this conclusion?

5. Determine the line between exposition and argumentation in this essay.

6. Evaluate Williams' treatment of sources. Why does she provide some page references but not others? Can you identify places where more background may be needed?

Looking Back and Ahead

1. Read Pamela Swanigan's "I Am Half-Canadian" (p. 58). Do you think Swanigan would share Williams' indictment of Canada as racist? If you think the two writers would not agree, suggest possible reasons for their differences of opinion.

2. Bharati Mukherjee left Canada, disgusted with the racism she felt here, for the United States. At the end of her short story, "The Tenant" (p. 164), we list other sources where you can pursue her views on this topic.

3. Have you, your family, or friends experienced racism in Canada?

For Further Reading

Bertley, L. *Canada and Its People of African Descent*. Pierrefonds, PQ: Bilongo, 1977.

Bramble, Linda, and D. Revell. *Black Fugitive Slaves in Early Canada*. St. Catharines, ON: Vanwell, 1988.

Clarke, George Elliott. "The Career of Black English: A Literary Sketch." *The English Language in Nova Scotia*. Eds. Lilian Falk and Margaret Harry. Lockeport, NS: Roseway, 1999.

Edwards, John. "Reactions to Three Types of Speech Sample from Rural Black and White Children." *The English Language in Nova Scotia*. Eds. Lilian Falk and Margaret Harry. Lockeport, NS: Roseway, 1999.

Gale, Lorena. *Angélique*. Toronto: Playwrights Canada Press, 1999. Gale's play takes up the ordeal of Marie Joseph Angélique, the slave woman who, in her bid for freedom, destroyed almost half of Montreal.

Hill, Daniel G. "Black History in Early Toronto." Paper presented to the Black History Conference, University of Toronto, 1978. April 2003 <http://collections.ic.gc.ca/magic/mt40.html>. This site discusses the slavery of Africans and the Pawnee First Nations in

the Niagara region of Upper Canada and includes historical ads for the return of runaway slaves.

Hornby, Jim. *Black Islanders: Prince Edward Island's Historical Black Community*.
Charlottetown: Institute of Island Studies, 1991.

Jacobs, Selwyn, dir. *The Road Taken* (film). National Film Board, 1996. Filmmaker Selwyn
Jacobs has produced a number of independent and NFB films on the history of Blacks
in Canada. Also online. April 2003. See <**http://cmm.nfb.ca/E/titleinfo/
index.epl?id=33259&recherche=simple&coll=onf**>.

Kelly, Jennifer. *Under the Gaze: Learning to Be Black in White Society*. Halifax: Fernwood, 1998.

Pollock, Irwin. "Jewish Slave Owners . . . in Quebec." *Canadian Jewish Outlook* 22. 6 (June
1984): 6–7.

"Slavery." Society for the Protection and Preservation of Black Culture in Nova Scotia. April
2003 <**http://www.bccns.com/history_slavery.html**> This site documents the history
of slavery in Canada from a royal mandate issued by Louis XIV in 1689 to its abolition
in 1834.

Walker, J.A. *History of Blacks in Canada: A Study Guide for Teachers and Students*. Hull:
Minister of State, 1980.

Winks, R. *The Blacks in Canada: A History*. Montreal: McGill-Queen's University Press, 1971.

Susan M. Keaveney In the following article from *Marketing Management* magazine, Fall 1997,
Susan Keaveney provides a broad definition of Generation Xers, under headings such as "latchkey kids,"
"techno-babes," "life-balancers," and "free agents." She concludes with a number of questions about
how members of this generation will behave by the middle of the millennium. The article invites
comparisons to the novel *Generation X* by Vancouverite Douglas Coupland.

Associate professor of marketing at the University of Colorado, Keaveney teaches marketing
management, international marketing, and services marketing for the graduate School of Business and
Executive MBA programs. She has also worked in retail, financial services, and health care. With
Philip R. Cateora she wrote *Marketing: An International Perspective,* and she has been active in the
"internationalization" of business schools.

Keaveney's article does not state a precise time span for Generation X, but implies that the
term covers those growing up in the 1970s and 1980s. Others have defined Generation X more
narrowly as those born between 1965 and 1975.[7] Would you call yourself a Generation Xer,
and if not, what is your relationship to that generation? Are you aware of approaching the following
article with any assumptions about the characteristics of this group?

---

[7] See Kathleen Dunn-Cane, Joan L. Gonzalez, and Hildegarde P. Stewart, "Managing the New Generation,"
AORN Journal 69. 5 (May 1999): 930.

When MTV Goes CEO

1   What happens when the "unmanageables" become managers?

2   "Who will take the helm?" is one question that will keep CEOs awake at
night in the next millennium. Most wonder what corporate culture in services

firms will look like when the 40 million Gen Xers in the work force—now twenty- and thirty-something employees—take over as managers.

3   Much has been written about Gen X employees, most of it negative. Early studies accused them of being arrogant, uncommitted, unmanageable slackers—disrespectful of authority, scornful of paying dues—tattooed and pierced youths who "just don't care." Recent interpretations, however, offer some new and somewhat different insights.

Arrogance or Independence?

4   Gen Xers have been characterized as the "latchkey kids" of the '70s and '80s; often left on their own by divorced and/or working parents, these young people became adept at handling things on their own and in their own ways. Many became self-motivating, self-sufficient, and creative problem-solvers. Their independence, which baby-boom managers sometimes interpret as arrogance, may also reflect a need to feel trusted to get a job done.

5   As employees, Gen Xers enjoy freedom to manage their own schedules. They don't watch a clock and don't want their managers to do so. Whether work is done from nine-to-five or noon-to-eight—at home, in the office, or over lattes—is irrelevant to this group because Gen Xers are results-oriented. They seek guidance, inspiration, and vision from their managers but otherwise prefer to be left alone between goal-setting and deliverables.

6   Many Gen Xers excel at developing innovative solutions, but need clear, firm deadlines to set boundaries on their creative freedom. They have been known to bristle under micromanagement but flourish with coaching and feedback.

Techno-Babes

7   Gen X grew up with rapidly changing technology and the availability of massive amounts of information. Many developed skills at parallel processing or sorting large amounts of information quickly (which is sometimes interpreted as a short attention span). Most are skilled at understanding and using technologies, adapt quickly to new platforms, and are practiced at learning through technological media. They value visual as well as verbal communication.

8   Gen X employees excel in a technologically advanced environment. They demand state-of-the-art capabilities, such as telecommuting, teleconferencing, and electronic mail, in order to work efficiently and effectively. To baby-boom managers this may seem to be a preference for impersonal means of communicating, living, and working, but Gen Xers do not see it that way; for example, they have modified electronic language and symbolism to express emotions such as surprise, anger, and pleasure.

Get a Life

9   Gen X employees don't live to work, they work to live. They place a high value on prototypical family values that they feel they missed. Having observed their parents trade personal lives for "the good of the company," this group wants balance in

their lives, demanding time for work, play, family, friends, and spirituality. Gen X employees are skeptical of forgoing the needs of today for a later, uncertain payoff.

10   When on the job market, Gen Xers will openly ask life-balance questions. This can be a turnoff for unprepared interviewers used to classic baby-boomer scripts featuring such lines as "How can I best contribute to the company?" and "My greatest weakness is that I work too hard."

11   In contrast, Gen Xers want to know "What can you do to help me balance work, life, and family?" They expect companies to understand and respect their needs as individuals with important personal lives. This focus on "getting a life" causes some to label them as slackers. Viewed from another perspective, however, Gen Xers could be seen as balanced individuals who can set priorities within time limits.

Just Do It

12   Gen X grew up with scandals in politics (Watergate, Whitewatergate), literature (The Education of Little Tree), journalism (Janet Cooke), business (Ivan Boesky, Michael Milliken), entertainment (Milli Vanilli), professional sports (Pete Rose, Tonya Harding), and religion (Jim and Tammy Bakker). It's not surprising that they're cynical about authority, irreverent about hierarchy, hate bureaucracy, loathe hidden agendas, and disdain politicking. They demand honesty and clarity, and respect substance over style.

13   Gen X employees tend to focus on the big picture, to emphasize outcomes over process or protocol. They respect clear, unambiguous communication— whether good news or bad. Gen Xers prefer tangible rewards over soft words. Cash incentives, concert tickets, computer equipment, or sports outings go farther with this group than "attaboys," plaques, or promises of future rewards.

Free Agents

14   Growing up in a period of corporate downsizing and right-sizing fostered Gen X beliefs that the future depends on their resumes rather than loyalty to any one company. Not surprisingly, Gen X employees seek challenging projects that help them develop a portfolio of skills.

15   What might appear to a baby-boom manager as job-hopping can be interpreted as a Gen Xer's pattern of skills acquisition. Similarly, a refusal to just "do time" in an organization, often interpreted as disloyalty and a lack of commitment, may come from an intolerance for busywork and wasted time.

16   Gen Xers will thrive in learning organizations where they can embrace creative challenges and acquire new skills. Smaller companies and work units will be valued for the opportunities they provide for Gen X employees to apply their diverse array of skills and, thereby, prove their individual merit.

17   Managers who enact their roles as teachers and facilitators rather than "bosses" will get the most from their Gen X employees. Training is valued by this group but should be immediately relevant; the best training seems to be

self-directed or tied to self-improvement, personal development, and skills-building.

18   Some baby-boom managers hope that the differences between themselves and their Gen X employees will fade away as less-conforming behaviors are abandoned with age and experience. But what if the wished-for assimilation into corporate culture—as presently defined by baby-boomers—doesn't occur? Or, what if, more likely, the assimilation is less than complete? What vestiges of Gen X's culture will be maintained? What will be absorbed, what will fade away?

Unmanageable or Entrepreneurial?

19   As a group, Gen X was not predicted to become "the establishment," yet the establishment will claim them nevertheless. Having rebelled against standard business hours and micromanagement, they might find it difficult to make such demands of their subordinates. Having disdained bosses, they might be uncomfortable being bosses themselves; having shunned hierarchy and titles, they may find their own managerial monikers awkward to bear.

20   Their emphasis on independence, combined with technological expertise, suggests that Gen X managers will support continued growth in telecommuting. This trend could put particular stresses on services firms that require contact personnel on-site to service customers. However, the creative problem-solving excellence of Gen X managers, combined with their technological prowess, will support new approaches to the issue of front-line service coverage.

21   Their life-balance beliefs suggest that Gen X managers will support family-friendly corporate policies. Firms will experience a continued drive toward flexible work schedules and reduced hours that benefit both Gen Xers (who strive for balance throughout their careers) and baby boomers (who put off "life" until their career dues were paid). Firms will manage differences in needs for employee benefits with cafeteria plans that allow Gen Xers to select benefits that support early family concerns (insurance, child care) and allow baby boomers to focus on 401ks [U.S.] and retirement plans.

22   Gen Xers' "just do it" attitudes and impatience with corporate cultures that seem to support style over substance indicate that Gen X managers will support a more casual workplace. Expect "dress-down Fridays" to expand to encompass the entire workweek, with formal business attire required on an as-needed basis such as in the presence of customers. (Gen Xers will respect social niceties when they agree that there's a good reason.)

23   Some "free-agent" Gen Xers will ultimately be unable or unwilling to make the transition to corporate manager. As Scott Adams' Dilbert cartoons make painfully clear, many Gen Xers fear ending up in dead-end support jobs, especially when they see the road to the top clogged with baby-boom managers. We are likely to see many choose an alternative lifestyle by becoming entrepreneurs. Indeed, the U.S. Bureau of Labor Statistics reports that 80% of Americans starting their own businesses today are between ages 18 and 34. The trend may di-

lute corporate pools of promotable junior managers but provide a needed infrastructure for corporate outsourcing.

Culture Clash or Diversity?

24 Other Labor Bureau Statistics show that in the next decade one in three workers will be over age 55. This has tremendous implications for a burgeoning culture clash between Baby Boomers and Gen Xers within corporations.

25   Facing the issue squarely and approaching Gen X workplace issues as issues of cultural diversity are necessary to get the most from the two groups of managers. Firms must understand, respect, and respond to the needs of each group. Lines of communication must be opened and maintained. For example, mentoring programs that pair the institutional memory and experience of baby boomers with the technological prowess and creativity of Gen Xers can help to foster mutual respect between the two groups.

The Vision Thing

26 Before mid-millennium, Gen Xers will be the CEOs of the future. This is a time when Gen X's visionary qualities will be most valued by firms. Will their anger with pollution, devastation of natural resources, and waste inspire them to responsible environmental stewardship? Will their disgust with corruption and scandal stimulate ethical corporate leadership? Will their experiences as the forgotten generation motivate them to create supportive corporate cultures? Will their experiences as a marginal group help them to envision, and sponsor, corporate cultural diversity? Only time will tell.

For Further Thinking

1. If you are not sure about the meaning of the term micromanagement, talk about it with classmates or otherwise do some research. Decide whether you agree with Keaveney that many Generation Xers dislike micromanagement, and whether you share their attitude.

2. Do you know of other cultures that particularly value visual as well as verbal communication in learning? With the visual emphasis in today's computer age, is it possible that cultures based on written alphabets are learning a new appreciation for oral traditions?

3. What predictions concerning Generation Xers does Keaveney make in the section titled "Unmanageable or Entrepreneurial?"? Do you agree with some or all of these forecasts? Explain your opinions.

4. What answer would you give to Keaveney's questions in "The Vision Thing"? Will Generation Xers hold true to their principles on the environment, resources, corporate ethics, and multicultural tolerance? How could they enact these beliefs by shaping a better future from within the existing corporate system?

5. Does Keaveney's article have an explicit thesis statement? How would you express the thesis of this essay?

Looking Back and Ahead

1. Read Mark Radford's essay "Different Worlds" (p. 43). Does his personal observation of three generations illustrate or contradict the points Keaveney makes?
2. Choose two or three essays from the *Reader* that are of particular interest to you. Then, using Keaveney's description of Generation Xers, say what you think would be their attitude to issues or concerns raised in the essays you have chosen.
3. Does Generation X's so-called visual emphasis when communicating overrule their interest in issues raised by Howard Richler in "The Seven Deadly Sins Are 'In' and Proud of It" (p. 224) and George Orwell in "Politics and the English Language" (p. 227)? Explain.

For Further Reading

Coupland, Douglas. *Generation X: Tales for an Accelerated Culture.* New York: St. Martin's, 1991.

Dunn-Cane, Kathleen, Joan L. Gonzalez, and Hildegarde P. Stewart. "Managing the New Generation." *AORN Journal* 69. 5 (May 1999): 930. The authors define three generations of health-care workers: the Silent Generation (1925–1942), the Boomers (1946–1964), and the Xers (1965–1975).

"Susan Keaveney." University of Colorado. April 2003 <http://www.cuddenver.edu/index.htm>. For a profile of Susan Keaveney follow the links to the Business School Faculty to Marketing.

University of Pittsburgh. Intergenerational Programs. April 2003 <http://www.pitt.edu/~gti/>. This website contains links to more information on resources, movements, programs, and American public policy dedicated to healing divisions between young and old.

Wellner, Alison Stein. "Make Love, Not Art?" *Forecast* 21. 3 (March 2001): 1. Baby boomers are often characterized as creative and interested in the arts, but have they turned away from the values they were supposed to embody?

Sarah Schmidt Observing that tuition fees have risen on average by 126 percent over the last nine years, far more rapidly than inflation or the minimum wage, Schmidt finds "a growing number of middle class women" who are turning to that oldest of professions to make it through their school years. Combining interviews with statistical research, Schmidt describes students working in all forms of Canada's off-street prostitution trade, which now accounts for 80 percent of the country's sex trade. Consulting a number of sources, including police detectives, escort service managers, sociologists, and other researchers, she ends by asking whether this practice is unavoidable, as some of her subjects claim.

College Girl to Call Girl

1 Stacy is dealing with all the typical end-of-term pressures of university: term-paper angst, exam anxiety, career stress. And by day, she is indeed a typical, perhaps model student, working at her co-op job placement and visiting the library at York University in Toronto to prepare for a career in advertising.

2 But at around eight, most evenings, Stacy heads out to pay the bills.

3 And this 25-year old, from an upper-middle-class Oakville, Ont., home, doesn't serve up coffee at Starbucks. Though she grew up much like any suburban child of a chartered accountant and a homemaker—bedtime stories, piano lessons, cottage weekends, trips to Disneyland—Stacy now goes out on "calls," as many as six times a night, condoms in hand, to pleasure clients as a prostitute.

4 Most men expect intercourse. A few are satisfied with oral sex. The odd one—either "really drunk or really lonely," she says—just wants to talk. But she doesn't call herself a hooker, and she doesn't wear high heels, fishnet stockings or short skirts. As a student "escort," Stacy dresses like any college girl going out to the movies or a bar. That's the way the men like it.

5 For a growing number of middle-class youths graduating this spring, prostitution isn't seen as a shameful trap, but as a means of making it through the lean student years on the way to a respectable career. Escorts like Stacy are dispatched by agencies to upscale hotel rooms, private homes and even offices. She may turn tricks, but in her own mind she is far away from the streets and alleys and whores desperate for $20 for a fix. She serves mostly professionals, who can afford the house call.

6 "You're looking at a very different kind of situation in the year 2000. Most people don't know what prostitution looks like. People have no clue," says sex-trade researcher John Lowman, a professor of criminology at Simon Fraser University in Vancouver. "What we have is a class-based system of prostitution. Just like you have a hierarchy of food services, you have a hierarchy of sex services."

7 Over the last nine years, tuition fees in Canada have risen on average by 126 per cent, far more rapidly than inflation and the minimum wage. About half of the student population graduates with an average debt load of $25,000, up from $8,000 in 1990.

8 Off-street prostitution has experienced a similar explosion, and many Canadian cities have cashed in by charging annual licensing fees to "massage parlours," "escort agencies" and "encounter counsellors." Researchers estimate that off-street prostitution now comprises approximately 80 percent of Canada's sex trade. And students work in every part of it, from phone sex and stripping up to turning tricks. Ads in weekly newspapers promote "College Cuties," "Adorable Students," "University Girls," and "Hot College Hard Bodies."

9 Fifteen years ago, such ads were unheard of. This year alone, escort ads in the *Montreal Mirror*, for example, have increased by 50 per cent. Since 1995,

they've increased five-fold in Victoria's *Monday Magazine*. Even NBC's new megahit, *The West Wing,* has featured a subplot about a Washington, D.C., law student who doubles as a high-priced call girl.

10   For her part, Stacy stumbled into the business three years ago. She knew someone else who was doing it. She was ineligible for student loans because she had defaulted on a previous one, and her stepfather did not want to pitch in. "There's no way a $7-an-hour job is going to pay my rent and tuition. It's not possible."

11   Escort work is far more lucrative: Stacy scores $170 for a one-hour call, $130 for a half-hour (the agency keeps $80 and $70 in each case). On the other hand, it's also a lot more demanding than steaming up a latte while wearing a funny hat.

12   "I remember the first time, I felt sick," recalls Stacy. And it has not gotten much easier with time. "It's not something I want to be doing. I hate it."

13   "People think, 'Students? Not students!'" says sociologist Cecilia Benoit. "They think of sex workers as marginal women, women who are down and out. It ain't like that."

14   The University of Victoria professor, in partnership with the Prostitution Empowerment and Education Society of Victoria, is undertaking a study on the health conditions of the city's off-street sex-trade workers. Findings so far show that some come from troubled backgrounds, but many don't, and their control over working conditions also varies. The danger of assault or murder is certainly lower than it is for street prostitutes.

15   Stacy's boyfriend knows how she pays her bills. "He doesn't like it, but he doesn't make me feel bad about it." Otherwise, she doesn't discuss it with family or friends.

16   Still, Detective Bert O'Hara of the Sexual Exploitation Squad of the Toronto Police Services observes that off-street sex work has "become more socially acceptable." In the past, it occurred in cheap motels; now, it's in private homes and commercial establishments. When Det. O'Hara and his colleagues take a peek inside, they find a range of participants: housewives earning extra cash, students covering their bills, single moms making grocery money.

17   Police continue to focus on the more visible, and cheaper, blue-collar street prostitution, Lowman says, while "men with money can buy sex with impunity." And at this end of the sex trade, both sides get to pretend they're just having a normal social interaction, at least to a degree.

18   Louis, manager of a Montreal escort service, knows students sell well to a particular class of men. His Baby Boomers' Playground serves up "young female students for your utmost fantasy," according to the ad. It's a perfect match: The clients, middle-aged professionals, prefer to mix sex with intelligent talk, not just idle chatter, Louis says.

19   Harvard grad Bennett Singer came to the same conclusion when he investigated the sex industry to research a novel he co-authored about his alma mater.

The Student Body, to be released in paperback next month, is based on a real-life prostitution scandal that rocked the prestigious Brown College in 1986. "They enjoy an intelligent conversation with a young, refined person with an active mind," says Singer, executive editor of *Time Magazine*'s education program.

20 Anna, the daughter of a businesswoman and an academic, was recruited a few years ago to pursue graduate work at one of Canada's leading research institutions, but a financial and personal crisis led her to work as a "high-end call girl." Her clients' educations matched her own.

21 And you can see why they would fall for Anna's quick wit, wholesome face, welcoming eyes and a warm smile. As an escort, she dressed business-casual, "so we could get past the front desk." Her first client, "a virgin who didn't want to be a virgin anymore," made it easier for her to break into the business.

22 "I still felt cold, though," she says, and she never got over that feeling. She just "put on a happy face," even on the night she had seven calls. "I was in total shock. That night was a bit stunning."

23 Still, she says she actually met one man, a broker, whom under different circumstances she would have dated. "My God, you're like a girlfriend," Anna remembers him saying. Unlike most, he "needed a full connection. He was so nice."

24 University of Toronto student and former escort Alicia Maund has heard similar coping strategies from Toronto's sex-trade workers. "They say, 'He's a banker. It's at the King Eddie [a high-class hotel], so it's okay.'"

25 Stacy is a case in point. "To me, there's a difference," she says. "It's not prostitution. I realize in essence everybody's doing the same thing, but I portray myself with a level of respect." That doesn't mean she's all that fond of her regulars, though. "They like to think we have something. I just fake it. I don't want these people to know me. I don't want to be friends with them."

26 Carolyn Bennett shakes her head at Stacy's rationalizations. "Whatever way you look at it, it's prostitution. You still get paid for sex," says the outreach worker for the Halifax-based Stepping Stone Association, a drop-in centre for street prostitutes.

27 John, a general-studies college student and former sex worker in Vancouver, agrees completely. "It's a cop-out," he says. "I don't mind being called a hustler." Before he started hustling, minimum-wage work was "killing my spirit," he says, and his parents, a nurse and labourer, couldn't really help out. He was saddled with a growing student loan when his girlfriend, also a student, introduced him to the idea of escort work.

28 "It really freaked me out initially. It was unimaginable for me. It seemed horrible, but I was totally desperate for money."

29 John has floated in and out of the massage business since 1996. There, the rules were clear: the rub-down always includes a hand job, but nothing else. But he had more flexibility as an independent. On outcalls, "I charged what I could get away with," he says, which sometimes exceeded $150 an hour.

[Handwritten margin notes, left side:]

John-> raised in traditional suburban values <- like enjoys it because he feels its powerful to have someone fantasize about him

he's debating whether to do it again or not $# $

-> stigma is in the how long you stay in the business ① hurts them the longer you stay, ② running into previous clients after you stop. -> its just a job nothing more.

just a means to an end -> to get to what she really wants in life.

30   Though he was raised with "traditional values" in the suburbs, John, like many young, educated sex workers, is also a bit of an adventurist. "To have someone project a fantasy onto you, for the purposes of the hour, to see you as the fantasy, that's powerful. I think there's something that draws me in."

31   Nonetheless, at first he didn't tell anyone. "I didn't want to deal with them trying to comfort me, or seeing me differently." Today, most of his friends know, but not his parents. "It would kill my mom. It would kill them both." They're still wrestling with his bisexuality, he says, though he feels like his father should understand. "He's done the worst jobs."

32   John is facing a more immediate decision, though. He's been out of the business for a while, but a friend at the University of British Columbia has a regular client that would like to add John to the equation. "I have to figure that out for myself and my partner. But I could sure use the money."

33   His caution makes sense. For many students, it seems, the real stigma in sex work is tied to how long you do it. Anna only lasted six weeks—her parents intervened when they found out, and gave her "total freedom, total choice and support." She still sounds a bit stunned by the experience. "It was a very healthy choice in a bizarre situation. Had I stayed longer, it would have hurt me," says Anna, now a high-tech professional.

34   Another reason to get out quickly is to minimize the risk of running into former clients in later life. Anna says she would pretend not to recognize them. "People don't deal with the issue well." But she also wishes people would "get over their hang-ups," she says. "It's just a job."

35   Maybe so, but Stacy would rather land that advertising job after graduation and put this kind of work behind her for good. "I don't want to be doing this," she says. "I want to do something for myself. I know I'm an intelligent person."

For Further Thinking

1. Is Schmidt shaping a story simply to fulfil a perceived reader demand for sex and drama, or has there truly been a significant increase in the number of university students turning to off-street prostitution to pay the bills?

2. Review our section on "Example" in Chapter 6 of the *Rhetoric*. Does "College Girl to Call Girl" use this kind of organizational approach efficiently? Explain.

3. What is your opinion of Schmidt's implication that the students she spoke with reveal self-delusion, as well as a form of snobbery?

4. What is your opinion of Schmidt's research on this article? Is there any point she could or should have pursued more thoroughly?

5. In response to those who look down on prostitutes, certain writers and social critics maintain that the most common form of prostitution is marriage. Morley Callaghan developed this theme in the novel *Such Is My Beloved*, for instance. What does this claim mean, and is there any truth to it?

Looking Back and Ahead

1. According to Susan Keaveney's chronology ("When MTV Goes CEO" p. 99), Stacy, 25, is a Generation Xer. Can her way of paying the bills be reconciled with Keaveney's characteristics of Generation X? Explain.
2. Describe Lois's attitude toward sex in Alice Munro's "Thanks for the Ride" (p. 62). Compare her attitude to that of Stacy. Are their attitudes more similar than different? Consider possible reasons for their attitudes.
3. Read George Orwell's essay "Politics and the English Language" (p. 227). When discussing and conducting business, university sex-trade workers apparently use a different sort of language from those "on the street." Could this educated language promote self-delusion? Give examples.

For Further Reading

Campbell, Maria. *Halfbreed*. Toronto: McClelland and Stewart, 1973. For part of her early life, Campbell fought a vicious circle of prostitution and heroin addiction.

"Fucking (with Theory) for Money: Toward an Interrogation of Escort Prostitution." *Postmodern Culture*, 2. May 1992. Online. April 2003 <**http://muse.jhu.edu/ journals/postmodern_culture/v002/2.3extavasia.html**>. This article is a feminist deconstruction of the dynamics between the escort, the client, and the agency. It must be accessed through libraries that subscribe to the journal.

Lau, Evelyn. *Runaway: Diary of a Street Kid*. Toronto: HarperCollins, 1989. Lau describes her life of prostitution, at first glance one very different from that described by Schmidt.

"Realm of Shade.com." Online. April 2003 <**http://www.realm-ofshade.com/meretrix/ links/general.shtml**>. This site, which is organized and maintained by an organization of sex trade workers, lists academic essays on controversial issues related to this business. It displays an evident bias, however, toward accepting the sex trade while seeking to reform it.

Stewart, Darren. "Tuition Doubled in Past Ten Years." Online. e.Peak News, Simon Fraser University's independent student newspaper. April 2003 <**http://www.peak.sfu.ca/ the-peak/2000-3/issue2/ne-tuition.html**>. In this article, the Ottawa bureau chief for Canadian University Press provides statistical information on tuition fees in Canadian degree-granting institutions. He considers finance and cost trends at various universities, as well as the viewpoints of university presidents.

Diane Mooney Canada's youngest province, which entered Confederation in 1949, Newfoundland is this country's oldest point of European contact. The population resides mainly on the island of Newfoundland, principally on the Avalon Peninsula. By contrast, Labrador, on the mainland, is sparsely populated. Rated well below Canada's other regions on the United Nations "quality of life" scale, Newfoundland risks sliding even further behind as politicians in the richer provinces pressure Ottawa to reduce or discontinue federal equalization payments from rich to poor.

In the following essay, marine biology student Diane Mooney takes us on a tour of major linguistic regions, combining classification-division, spatial process, and descriptive process to celebrate the range of cultures and languages in her home province. A trained environmental technician, Mooney grew up along the rugged shores of Newfoundland. She calls herself "an avid tourist of the island . . . where there is always a new culture and dialect to discover." If you have never visited Newfoundland, talk to some of your classmates who have been there, to prepare you for reading this essay.

For more support regarding English as a Second Language, visit the website for Athabasca University's English 255 Introductory Composition course at <www.athabascau.ca/courses/engl/255/>. See "If English Is Not Your First Language" and "Language Support for Selected Readings.".

Newfoundlandese, if You Please

1   I learned recently that people who visit Newfoundland become fascinated with our unique dialect. If they travel to different areas of the island, they quickly realize that every little nook and cranny, of which there are many, has its own specific sound. Not too long ago I travelled to the Port au Port peninsula on the province's West Coast. Here, the inhabitants are French descendants and speak with an odd accent, Newfoundland French, I guess. Being from an Irish settlement on the East Coast, I had difficulty understanding their speech as they did mine. All the different descendants in Newfoundland play a major role in our dialect. It seems as though our ancestors, who came from many different areas, never quite lost their own speech: they all just adapted to the lives they settled into. There were many settlements all along the coast and inland across the island, all with a different adaptation of English. As Baldwin says in his essay "If Black English Isn't a Language, Then Tell Me, What Is?" "people evolve a language." He was referring to the African Americans of the United States. The same can be said for the Irish, English, British, and French of Newfoundland. The difference is that they didn't just evolve into one, they evolved into one with many different variations.

2   Starting with the Avalon Peninsula of the East Coast of Newfoundland, with which I am most familiar, it is easy to tell who first settled in what area simply by their speech. The Southern Shore of the island is Irish, and to this day you can hear an Irish accent in their voices. People on the Southern Shore refer to their fathers as "daa." Whether this is an Irish thing or just a Southern Shore thing, you won't hear it anywhere else in the province. You may look even deeper into each individual community. Some are all Catholics and came from one area of Ireland with their own dialect; others are all Anglican coming from a different area of Ireland with another dialect. However, there are very few Anglicans on the Southern Shore; the Catholics drove out most.

3   Not too far away in the Trinity-Conception area, again they are mainly Irish—Anglican Irish. The dialect here can be quite difficult to understand. A number of areas drop their "h's" and this is one of them. For example, "I'm goin'

'ome to clean me 'ouse de once." Translation: "I am going home to clean my house now." "De once" means it is going to be done immediately—at once. To a visitor from outside the province or even to someone from within the province this can also be very difficult to understand, especially with the speed of Newfoundland speech. All Newfoundlanders talk fast; this is just a given.

4   Moving off the Avalon into Central Newfoundland we have moved out of the fishing communities into logging and mining towns, mainly fishermen who moved inland in winter to hunt and log when they couldn't fish settled in these areas. The settlements there today are pretty mixed with dialects coming from all over. One area in particular always uses "we" and "I" when making references to themselves instead of "us" and "we." For example, "Be careful or they'll come after we or I." Translation: "Be careful or they will come after us." Again something that can be very confusing and interesting to the non-native.

5   Most of Newfoundland believes that the West Coast of the island is trying to sound like mainlanders. They say "eh" a lot and have a slight twang in their speech. In reality though, it probably goes back to when the French settled, which is still so strong on the Port au Port peninsula.

6   The Northern Peninsula, which is very large and stretched out but not heavily populated, seems to be in a world of its own. Some communities drop their "h's" while others add extra "h's." For example, "First you put your happles in the hoven and you bake 'em on 'igh." Translation: "First you put your apples in the oven and you bake them on high." Some others on the tip of the Northern Peninsula, which is so close to Quebec, have a tendency to slip into some French dialect as well.

7   Taking in only major sections of the province, any tourist can see clearly that Newfoundland has many different descendants and therefore many different dialects. As Baldwin suggests, when so many different languages are put together, they have to come up with a way to communicate that everyone can understand. Because Newfoundland is so spread out, a language evolved and each little cove and inlet adapted its own version.

For Further Thinking

1. What other island could be said to offer a different dialect for every new "nook and cranny"? How is this of relevance to Mooney's focus on variety?

2. Would you say that you speak English fast or slow? Is your accent difficult for others? How have your ancestry and region shaped your style of English?

3. Is there a common Canadian English—truly distinct from the language of the United Kingdom, Commonwealth countries, and United States—or does our country simply have pockets of regional speech?

4. In your own words, express Mooney's thesis as completely and precisely as you can.

5. From what you know of Newfoundland—and you could always add to that knowledge with a little further research—how important do you think its forms of English have been to its cultural life?

Looking Back and Ahead

1. Compare Mooney's essay and Nicole Lombard's "Speaking South African English in Canada" (p. 47). Would Lombard's difficulties be heightened or lessened in Newfoundland?
2. Read George Orwell's "Politics and the English Language" (p. 227). Would he approve of the French dialect that Mooney finds included on the Northern Peninsula? What do you think of his opinion on this matter?
3. On the whole, do you think the types of English that Mooney describes particularly lend themselves to the political abuses described by Orwell? Why or why not?
4. Read Susan Keaveney's characterization of Generation Xers, "When MTV Goes CEO" (p. 99). Do you imagine the generational features that Keaveney describes are more or less prominent in Newfoundland's young adults than in those of Colorado, where Keaveney lives? Do you think the world is headed toward a global culture where the distinctions of a Newfoundland will have all but disappeared?

For Further Reading

Baldwin, James. "If Black English Isn't a Language, Then Tell Me, What Is? *The Price of the Ticket: Collected Nonfiction 1948–1985*. New York: St. Martin's, 1985. 650–52.

Carter, Peter, dir. *The Rowdyman* (film). Written by Gordon Pinsent. National Film Board, 1972. Script in Bowie, Douglas, and Tom Shoebridge, eds. *Best Canadian Screenplays*. Kingston, ON: Quarry Books, 1992. Focusing on a hard-drinking, womanizing rogue, this film treats the setting—Newfoundland—as a major presence.

Memorial University Department of Folklore. April 2003 <http://www.mun.ca/folklore/>.

Newfoundland folklore, language, and literature. The Memorial University Archive. April 2003 <http://www.mun.ca/folklore/munfla.html>. Work is proceeding toward a published compilation.

Shebib, Don, dir. *Goin' Down the Road* (film). Written by William Fruet. Phoenix Film, Inc., 1970. Script in Bowie, Douglas, and Tom Shoebridge, eds. *Best Canadian Screenplays*. Kingston, ON: Quarry Books, 1992. A landmark 1970s film about two drifters who leave the Atlantic region—in this case, Nova Scotia—in pursuit of legendary Toronto. The film is now available in the Séville Pictures DVD Signature Collection.

Story, G.M., W.J. Kirwin, and J.D.A. Widowson. *Dictionary of Newfoundland English*, 2nd ed. Toronto: University of Toronto Press, 1999. April 2003 <http://www.heritage.nf.ca/dictionary/default.html>.

Brenda Platt For more than a decade, widely divergent opinions have been heard from different quarters on global warming. But in 1997, supported by a commissioned study, 38 countries signed the Kyoto Accord, agreeing to reduce carbon emissions. According to the study, "greenhouse gases" (produced by burning oil, gas, and coal) have significantly contributed to the warming of our planet. The following paper by Brenda Platt examines the possible influence of population on global warming and evaluates different strategies for dealing with the problem.

This technical paper gives us some of the background needed to appreciate the debate over connections between population and the trend toward global warming. Platt completed her paper before the United States began calling the Kyoto Accord into question. As you prepare to read this essay, consider how you define the word "science." What relationships and obligations do you consider part of the scientist's role?

Global Warming and Population

1   The relationship between population and the sustainability of local environments has been a subject for discussion for several centuries: philosophers in ancient China fretted about the need to shift the masses to underpopulated areas; Plato said that cities with more than 5 040 landholders were too large; in a 1798 essay Thomas Malthus concluded that the increasing population in England would eventually lead to society's collapse. More recently, however, discussions have broadened to include the relationship between population and global environmental change. This presentation will address the latter relationship by examining global warming. It will attempt to answer two questions stemming from these discussions. Does population growth contribute to global warming? Should population control be a central strategy in stabilizing global environmental change? In order to answer these questions it is necessary to introduce key concepts, explore some ways in which population can cause global environmental change, and clarify some of the opposing positions in the debate.

2   Global warming is the increase in the mean average temperature of the earth's atmosphere. It occurs when the so-called greenhouse gases (carbon dioxide, methane, nitrous oxide, tropospheric ozone) absorb infrared radiation from the planet's surface that would otherwise escape into space. This absorbed radiation is converted to heat and the atmosphere becomes warmer. The predicted consequences include a decline in agricultural productivity, desertification, changes in forestation patterns, more and stronger storms, and flooding of low-lying coastal regions.

3   Some resources, such as food, grow linearly. Linear growth occurs when a quantity increases by a fixed amount during each time interval (e.g., 1, 2, 3, 4). Fossil fuels, such as coal and petroleum, do not replenish themselves in a period of time that is humanly meaningful; thus, they are considered to be non-renewable resources. Human population grows exponentially. Exponential growth occurs when a quantity increases by a constant percentage of the whole

in a constant time period (e.g., 1, 2, 4, 8). In 1850 there were 1 billion people, today there are 6.5 billion, and there may well be 16 billion people on earth by the year 2050.

4   The theory of demographic transition proposes that economic development leads to lower death rates, which causes a population boom. However, economic and social changes that follow from this development will eventually lead to lower birth rates. The so-called less developed countries of the Third World have thus far not experienced this transition as did the developed world. Population growth in these countries accounts for about 90% of current global growth.

5   Carrying capacity is the total number of humans that the earth and its resources can support. As the number of people on this planet increases, there is a similar increase in the demand for resources. There is some concern that the increased demand for resources will outstrip the supply, and considerable effort has been spent in determining the earth's carrying capacity. Overshoot is growth beyond the carrying capacity.

6   This increased demand for resources is the link in the relationship between population and global warming. Consider, for example, the impact of the increased demand for food on greenhouse gas emissions. Flooding rice paddies and raising cattle release methane by providing large areas of warm, anaerobic environment that are rich in organic matter. After biochemical changes, part of the nitrogen applied as fertilizer to fields is released into the atmosphere as nitrous oxide. Carbon dioxide is produced by machinery, such as tractors and trucks, used in agricultural production. Nitrous oxide and carbon dioxide are released where tropical forests are burned on a massive scale to clear land for ranching or slash and burn agriculture. It is estimated that deforestation accounts for 15–30% of annual global carbon dioxide emissions. Furthermore, the destruction of forests is a loss of a major carbon dioxide sink; that is, a mechanism for the absorption and sequestration of atmospheric carbon dioxide. Consider also the increased demand for energy for cooking and heating, building supplies, industrial products and mobility, and the relationship between population and global warming becomes evident.

7   One can conclude that population growth does contribute to global warming. Should population control, therefore, be a central strategy in stabilizing global environmental change? For many years finding the answer to this question has been widely debated and the subject of several popular books. The answer remains far from definitive. One extreme of the debate argues that the "root cause of most environmental damage is excessive growth in human population"; the other extreme maintains that "more [population] is better."

8   According to Paul Ehrlich, author of best-selling books such as *The Population Bomb* and *The Population Explosion*, population control is the only answer. Tragedy is inevitable and neither technology nor social adjustments will be effective. For the United States, Ehrlich advocates taxes and other economic disincentives.

His most radical proposals, however, are targeted at the rapidly expanding populations of the less developed countries. Ehrlich's proposals for these countries include triage (food aid only to nations with aggressive population-control policies and demonstrable ability to achieve food self-sufficiency) as well as sterilization—whether voluntary or coerced.

9   Ehrlich's views and proposals have been criticized on ethical and human rights grounds. Religious groups oppose artificial contraception and abortion; human rights organizations brand them as racist for targeting the poor and marginalized; and women's rights organizations contend that reproductive choices can ultimately be made only by the individual woman, and not administered through population programmes likely developed and managed by privileged males.

10   Julian Simon, a conservative economist, sits at the other extreme of the debate. He is author of several books, include *The Ultimate Resource* and *Theory of Population and Economic Growth*. He believes that more people and more wealth have correlated with more, not less, resources and a cleaner environment. He reasons that larger human populations will continue to adapt and develop new technologies which will provide the solutions to any environmental problems that may emerge, as they have in the past. Population size and growth, he points out, bring an increase in the world's stock of knowledge; and the more they grow, the faster will be the progress of civilization. He supports his argument by saying that resources are more available today than before, not more scarce, as indicated by their falling prices. For Simon, the problem is not too many people, but a failure (in some parts of the world) in the functioning of markets that allow these adaptations and technological developments to occur.

11   Criticism of Simon's view is two-pronged. First, many technological solutions have proven to be unsustainable in the long term; the so-called Green Revolution is a prime example. Second, market prices of environmental resources often do not reflect their true social value. His arguments, like Ehrlich's, have lost much of their validity.

12   The views of Ehrlich and Simon represent the polar opposites in the population control debate. One extreme is overly catastrophic while the other is too cornucopian. Neither perspective is particularly helpful in engendering change. Obviously, people and the environment are closely intertwined. This relationship, however, is not static. Furthermore, there are other factors that contribute to global warming and must be considered. These contributing factors include overconsumption, faulty technological choices and inappropriate government policies.

13   **Overconsumption** describes the use of resources by a group in a society or a society as a whole that is out of proportion to its numbers. Analogous to this is the inequitable distribution of wealth on the planet. While the industrialized nations comprise only 25% of the world's population, they consume approximately 75% of the world's resources. For example, it has been pointed out that the production of a [western] meat-based diet requires more resources—land, water and energy—than a vegetarian diet typically consumed in developing countries. In

the last 40 years, the rate of per capita energy and material consumption has increased faster than human population. Exponentially increasing consumption is as harmful as any exponential increase in population.

14   **Faulty technological choices** are also a contributing factor to global warming. For example, most of the energy used in the world today is derived from the oxidation, or burning, of fossil fuels, which releases approximately six billion tons of carbon dioxide—a greenhouse gas—into the atmosphere each year. There are several alternative sources of energy that do not release greenhouse gases or cause other environmental damage; for example, wind power, solar photovoltaic generation of electricity, solar hydrogen, and geothermal energy. In less developed countries, the choice is not available simply because the technology is not available. In developed countries, the technology is available or can easily be made available. However, industries perceive it in their best interest to maintain the status quo. Thus, choices are often made to maximize profit rather than minimize the impact to the environment.

15   **Inappropriate government policies** on energy facilitate this in a number of ways. Government funding for research and development of alternative energy sources is inadequate or non-existent. Generous tax incentives and subsidies have been granted to fossil-fuel industries despite the fact that these industries encourage the emission of greenhouse gases. From 1994 to 1995, for example, government subsidies for an offshore oil project (Hibernia) in Canada amounted to $249.5 million. Inappropriate government policies in less developed countries encourage exploitation of tropical forests, subsequently increasing greenhouse gas emissions and reducing carbon dioxide sinks. These policies are driven by severe economic pressures afflicting debt-burdened countries. For example, governments grant timber concessions for low fees and reduce income or export taxes to national and foreign-owned businesses. Policies formulated with political or development goals in mind also exploit tropical forests by encouraging mass transmigration to or "colonization" of previously sparsely inhabited regions.

16   For many years the dominant view has been that **population growth** is creating a global environmental crisis. The dominant strategy in tackling this crisis, therefore, has been to control population growth, particularly in the less developed countries. According to Asoka Bandarage, this view and strategy has been manufactured and supported by a few powerful actors such as the United Nations Fund for Population Activities, the United States State Department and the Pew Charitable Trust's Global Initiative. In her book, *Women, Population and Global Crisis,* she claims that these actors have "created a powerful cult of population control."

17   This strategy is flawed in three main aspects. First, the term "population control" implies coercion. All individuals, groups or nations seeking to humanely and effectively avert a global environmental crisis should drop this strategy forthwith. Coercive practices often defeat their own aims. The process of reducing birth rates in India suffered a severe setback after protests over a forced sterilization policy. It is now recognized that smaller families and slower population growth depend not on "control" but on free choice.

18   Second, this strategy offers a simple, narrow and fragmented solution to a very complex problem. All factors (population, overconsumption, technology, inappropriate policies) create the problem. A more reasonable strategy, given the magnitude and seriousness of the problem, must be holistic: that is, it must tackle all contributing factors. To date, there has been negligible effort to develop and implement initiatives that would eliminate or ameliorate harmful practices and behaviour. As no single cause is dominant, it is impracticable to assume that treating only one of the factors might be sufficient.

19   Third, the overriding objective of lowering the birth rate undermines the quality of the health and well-being of society in general, and women in particular. At the International Conference on Population and Development held in Cairo in 1994, 179 countries approved a World Population Plan of Action. This plan aimed at keeping global population below 9.8 billion by the year 2050. The prejudice against health care is evident in the relative expenditures first proposed in this Plan: $10.2 billion for family-planning programmes, $1.2 billion for broader reproductive-health services. The latter was raised to $5 billion following pressure from women's groups. However, it remains apparent that broader health needs, such as access to primary health care and reducing infant and maternal mortality, are not being met. Many of the contraceptive technologies used in these family-planning programmes are administered in health systems that are ill equipped to distribute them safely or ethically. Furthermore, the plan pays scant attention to women's education and skills training, gender equality, poverty alleviation, access to resources and credit, etc.

20   In conclusion, therefore, population control should not be a strategy in protecting the global environment. Family-planning programs should be undertaken with the central goal of empowering women to make rational choices for themselves and their families. They should not, however, be considered the *central* strategy in protecting the global environment.

Works Consulted in Addition to Required Course Readings

Bandarage, Asoka. *Women, Population and Global Crisis: A Political Economic Analysis*. London: Zed Books, 1997.

French, Hilary F. "Forging a New Global Partnership to Save the Earth" (1995). *Taking Sides: Clashing Views on Controversial Environmental Issues*. Connecticut: Dushkin/ McGraw-Hill, 1997.

Harrison, Paul. "Sex and the Single Planet: Need, Greed, and Earthly Limits" (1994). *Taking Sides: Clashing Views on Controversial Environmental Issues*. Connecticut: Dushkin/McGraw-Hill, 1997.

Hartmann, Betsy. "Population Fictions: The Malthusians Are Back in Town" (1994). *Taking Sides: Clashing Views on Controversial Environmental Issues*. Connecticut: Dushkin/McGraw-Hill, 1997.

Lindahl-Kiessling, Kerstin, and Hans Landberg (eds.). *Population, Economic Development and the Environment: The Making of Our Common Future*. New York: Oxford University Press, 1994.

Paehlke, Robert C. *Environmentalism and the Future of Progressive Politics*. New Haven: Yale University Press, 1989.

Simon, Julian. "More People, Greater Wealth, More Resources, Healthier Environment" (1994). *Taking Sides: Clashing Views on Controversial Environmental Issues*. Connecticut: Dushkin/McGraw-Hill, 1997.

For Further Thinking

1. Do you agree with Platt's opinion of the two diametrically opposed views on population control (Ehrlich versus Simon)?

2. Alberta native k.d. lang, a vegetarian, has been criticized by the province's powerful beef lobby for letting down the province with her appearance on anti-meat television advertisements. Why do beef producers feel threatened enough to stand up for their industry, while expecting lang and other vegetarians to "keep a low profile"?

3. Examine the use of cause/effect organization in this essay. (See "Cause-Effect" in Chapter 6 of the *Rhetoric* about this rhetorical pattern.)

4. The 1997 United Nations Kyoto Accord on controlling carbon emissions commits the signatories to cutting emission of "greenhouse gases" (produced by burning oil, gas, and coal) by 5.2 percent by 2010. In March 2001, newly inaugurated U.S. President George W. Bush described global warming as a fabricated fear. Should Platt have looked at a wider range of opinion when stating the predicted consequences of global warming?

5. At an inaugural meeting of 34 international energy ministers of the environment in Montreal, only the United States and Canada refused to sign a document to support meeting the Kyoto goals. Was this refusal in keeping with Canada's international image?

Looking Back and Ahead

1. Given the wide range of views Platt has summarized in this and other essays, does John Markoff's article "The Doomsday Machines" (p. 135) seem too one-sided? Contrast the different styles and approaches of Platt's essay and Markoff's.

2. What similarities and differences do you find in this essay and Anita Lahey's "The Genome Generation" (p. 132)?

For Further Reading

Abasi, S.A., P. Krishnakumari, and F.I. Khan. *Hot Topics: Everyday Environmental Concerns*. New Delhi, New York: Oxford University Press, 1999.

Drake, Frances. *Global Warming: The Science of Climate Change*. London, New York: Oxford University Press, 2000.

Epstein, Paul R. "Is Global Warming Harmful to Health?" *Scientific American*, 2000. April 2003 <http://www.sciam.com/2000/0800issue/0800epstein.html>. Computer models suggest that many diseases will proliferate as the earth's atmosphere heats up. Are we beginning to see these predictions come to pass now?

News report describing European dissatisfaction with President George W. Bush's U.S policy reversal on the Kyoto Accord. BBC News Online. April 2003 <**http://www. climateark.org/articles/2001/1st/eubackky.htm**>.

Philander, George S. *Is the Temperature Rising? The Uncertain Science of Global Warming*. Princeton, NJ: Princeton University Press, 1998.

The Science and Environment Policy Project (SEPP). April 2003 <**http://www.sepp.org/ pressrel/petition.html**>. SEPP is a group of American scientists and businesspeople opposed to the 1997 Kyoto agreement on reducing levels of carbon emissions.

Seitz, Frederick. "A Major Deception on 'Global Warming.'" *Wall Street Journal* 12 June 1996. President emeritus of Rockefeller University and past president of the U.S. National Academy of Sciences, Seitz maintains that fears of global warming are grounded on "shaky science."

Plato   Plato, the Greek philosopher and poet (approximately 428 B.C.–348 B.C.), wrote his *Dialogues* 2300 years ago. Probably no other single work has had as much historic impact—shaping the thought of the ancient world, the Middle Ages, the Renaissance, and contemporary times. Regarding the teacher as "a gardener who aids his plants, but is unable to do for them what they must do for themselves,"[8] Plato adopted the dialectical method: the gardener of his *Dialogues*— named after Plato's own teacher, the philosopher Socrates—asks his pupils leading questions with the intent of guiding them to insights they can then experience on their own. To further this pursuit of knowledge, Plato, in 386 B.C., founded the Academy,[9] not far from Athens; it endured for 900 years, longer than any other educational institution.

Plato held to the existence of a realm of timeless truth or being—an intellectual world containing the intelligible forms and system of all that we experience, as well as the potential for a great deal of good that we can enact. Teaching and learning, therefore, consist in drawing out a pre-existing or inherent knowledge rather than in pouring knowledge from one container (the teacher) into the other (the pupil). In the following dialogue, Socrates instructs Glaucon "in a figure[10] how far our nature is enlightened or unenlightened." He describes human beings chained in an underground cave, watching shadows on the wall. Socrates then goes on, allegorically, to describe their ascent to the good, and the importance of that ascent to the state.

---

[8] Edith Hamilton and Huntington Cairns. *Plato: The Collected Dialogues*, Princeton: Princeton University Press, 1961.

[9] The word comes from the name of the man reputed to have revealed to the brothers of Helen of Troy the place where she was hidden after Theseus kidnapped her. Academus lived in the country not far from Athens, on an estate filled with olive trees, adorned with statues, and watered by the river Cephissus. This property, known as Akademeia, was where Plato met with his students. The word passed through Latin and entered English in the fifteenth century meaning the grove where Plato taught. By the next century, the term was extended to mean any place of higher learning. By the seventeenth century, the word also meant a group devoted to promoting learning or to the pursuit of arts and sciences. See Luis G. Heller, Alexander Humez, and Malcah Dror, *The Private Lives of Words* (Tarrytown, NY: Wynwood, 1991).

[10] Metaphor, conceit, or analogy—all of which, when extended and formally structured, with explicit connections, become allegory.

Allegory of the Cave (from *The Republic*, Book VII)

1   And now, I [Socrates] said, let me show in a figure how far our nature is enlightened or unenlightened:—Behold! human beings housed in an underground cave, which has a long entrance open towards the light and as wide as the interior of the cave; here they have been from their childhood, and have their legs and necks chained, so that they cannot move and can only see before them, being prevented by the chains from turning round their heads. Above and behind them a fire is blazing at a distance, and between the fire and the prisoners there is a raised way; and you will see, if you look, a low wall built along the way, like the screen which marionette players have in front of them, over which they show the puppets.

2   I [Glaucon] see.

3   And do you see, I said, men passing along the wall carrying all sorts of vessels, and statues and figures of animals made of wood and stone and various materials, which appear over the wall? While carrying their burdens, some of them, as you would expect, are talking, others silent.

4   You have shown me a strange image, and they are strange prisoners.

5   Like ourselves, I replied; for in the first place do you think they have seen anything of themselves, and of one another, except the shadows which the fire throws on the opposite wall of the cave?

6   How could they do so, he asked, if throughout their lives they were never allowed to move their heads?

7   And of the objects which are being carried in like manner they would only see the shadows?

8   Yes, he said.

9   And if they were able to converse with one another, would they not suppose that the things they saw were the real things?

10   Very true.

11   And suppose further that the prison had an echo which came from the other side, would they not be sure to fancy when one of the passers-by spoke that the voice which they heard came from the passing shadow?

12   No question, he replied.

13   To them, I said, the truth would be literally nothing but the shadows of the images.

14   That is certain.

15   And now look again, and see in what manner they would be released from their bonds, and cured of their error, whether the process would naturally be as follows. At first, when any of them is liberated and compelled suddenly to stand up and turn his neck round and walk and look towards the light, he will suffer sharp pains; the glare will distress him, and he will be unable to see the realities of which in his former state he had seen the shadows; and then conceive someone saying to him that what he saw before was an illusion, but that now, when he

is approaching nearer to being and his eye is turned towards more real existence, he has a clearer vision,—what will be his reply? And you may further imagine that his instructor is pointing to the objects as they pass and requiring him to name them,—will he not be perplexed? Will he not fancy that the shadows which he formerly saw are truer than the objects which are now shown to him?

16   Far truer.

17   And if he is compelled to look straight at the light, will he not have a pain in his eyes which will make him turn away to take refuge in the objects of vision which he can see, and which he will conceive to be in reality clearer than the things which are now being shown to him?

18   True, he said.

19   And suppose once more, that he is reluctantly dragged up that steep and rugged ascent, and held fast until he is forced into the presence of the sun himself, is he not likely to be pained and irritated? When he approaches the light his eyes will be dazzled, and he will not be able to see anything at all of what are now called realities.

20   Not all in a moment, he said.

21   He will require to grow accustomed to the sight of the upper world. And first he will see the shadows best, next the reflections of men and other objects in the water, and then the objects themselves; and, when he turned to the heavenly bodies and the heaven itself, he would find it easier to gaze upon the light of the moon and the stars at night than to see the sun or the light of the sun by day?

22   Certainly.

23   Last of all he will be able to see the sun, not turning aside to the illusory reflections of him in the water, but gazing directly at him in his own proper place, and contemplating him as he is.

24   Certainly.

25   He will then proceed to argue that this is he who gives the seasons and the years, and is the guardian of all that is in the visible world, and in a certain way the cause of all things which he and his fellows have been accustomed to behold?

26   Clearly, he said, he would arrive at this conclusion after what he had seen.

27   And when he remembered his old habitation, and the wisdom of the cave and his fellow-prisoners, do you not suppose that he would felicitate himself on the change, and pity them?

28   Certainly, he would.

29   And if they were in the habit of conferring honours among themselves on those who were quickest to observe the passing shadows and to remark which of them went before and which followed after and which were together, and who were best able from these observations to divine the future, do you think that he would be eager for such honours and glories, or envy those who attained honour and sovereignty among those men? Would he not say with Homer,

"Better to be a serf, labouring for a landless master,"

and to endure anything, rather than to think as they do and live after their manner?

30   Yes, he said, I think that he would consent to suffer anything rather than live in this miserable manner.

31   Imagine once more, I said, such a one coming down suddenly out of the sunlight, and being replaced in his old seat; would he not be certain to have his eyes full of darkness?

32   To be sure, he said.

33   And if there were a contest, and he had to compete in measuring the shadows with the prisoners who had never moved out of the cave, while his sight was still weak, and before his eyes had become steady (and the time which would be needed to acquire this new habit of sight might be very considerable), would he not make himself ridiculous? Men would say of him that he had returned from the place above with his eyes ruined; and that it was better not even to think of ascending; and if anyone tried to loose another and lead him up to the light, let them only catch the offender, and they would put him to death.

34   No question, he said.

35   This entire allegory, I said, you may now append, dear Glaucon, to the previous argument; the prison-house is the world of sight, the light of the fire is the power of the sun, and you will not misapprehend me if you interpret the journey upwards to be the ascent of the soul into the intellectual world according to my surmise, which, at your desire, I have expressed—whether rightly or wrongly God knows. But, whether true or false, my opinion is that in the world of knowledge the Idea of good appears last of all, and is seen only with an effort; although, when seen, it is inferred to be the universal author of all things beautiful and right, parent of light and of the lord of light in the visible world, and the immediate and supreme source of reason and truth in the intellectual; and that this is the power upon which he who would act rationally either in public or private life must have his eye fixed.

36   I agree, he said, as far as I am able to understand you.

37   Moreover, I said, you must agree once more, and not wonder that those who attain to this vision are unwilling to take any part in human affairs; for their souls are ever hastening into the upper world where they desire to dwell; which desire of theirs is very natural, if our allegory may be trusted.

38   Yes, very natural.

39   And is there anything surprising in one who passes from divine contemplations to the evil state of man, appearing grotesque and ridiculous; if, while his eyes are blinking and before he has become accustomed to the surrounding darkness, he is compelled to fight in courts of law, or in other places, about the images or the shadows of images of justice, and must strive against some rival about opinions of these things which are entertained by men who have never yet seen the true justice?

40   Anything but surprising, he replied.

41   Anyone who has common sense will remember that the bewilderments of the eyes are of two kinds and arise from two causes, either from coming out of the light or from going into the light, and, judging that the soul may be affected in the same way, will not give way to foolish laughter when he sees anyone whose vision is perplexed and weak; he will first ask whether that soul of man has come out of the brighter life and is unable to see because, unaccustomed to the dark, or having turned from darkness to the day, is dazzled by excess of light. And he will count the one happy in his condition and state of being, and he will pity the other; or, if he have a mind to laugh at the soul which comes from below into the light, this laughter will not be quite so laughable as that which greets the soul which returns from above out of the light into the cave.

42   That, he said, is a very just distinction.

43   But then, if I am right, certain professors of education must be wrong when they say that they can put a knowledge into the soul which was not there before, like sight into blind eyes.

44   They undoubtedly say this, he replied.

45   Whereas our argument shows that the power and capacity of learning exists in the soul already; and that just as if it were not possible to turn the eye from darkness to light without the whole body, so too the instrument of knowledge can only by the movement of the whole soul be turned from the world of becoming to that of being, and learn by degrees to endure the sight of being, and of the brightest and best of being, or in other words, of the good.

46   Very true.

47   And must there not be some art which will show how the conversion can be effected in the easiest and quickest manner; an art which will not implant the faculty of sight, for that exists already, but will set it straight when it has been turned in the wrong direction, and is looking away from the truth?

48   Yes, he said, such an art may be presumed.

49   And whereas the other so-called virtues of the soul seem to be akin to bodily qualities, for even when they are not originally innate they can be implanted later by habit and exercise, the virtue of wisdom more than anything else contains a divine element which never loses its power, and by this conversion is rendered useful and profitable; or, by conversion of another sort, hurtful and useless. Did you never observe the narrow intelligence flashing from the keen eye of a clever rogue—how eager he is, how clearly his paltry soul sees the way to this end; he is the reverse of blind, but his keen eyesight is forced into the service of evil, and if he is mischievous in proportion to his cleverness?

50   Very true, he said.

51   But what if such natures had been gradually stripped, beginning in childhood, of the leaden weights which sink them in the sea of Becoming, and

which, fastened upon the soul through gluttonous indulgence in eating and other such pleasures, forcibly turn its vision downwards—if, I say, they had been released from these impediments and turned in the opposite direction, the very same faculty in them would have seen the truth as keenly as they see what their eyes are turned to now.

52 Very likely.

53 Yes, I said; and there is another thing which is likely, or rather a necessary inference from what has preceded, that neither the uneducated and uninformed of the truth, nor yet those who are suffered to prolong their education without end, will be able ministers of State; not the former, because they have no single aim of duty which is the rule of all their actions, private as well as public; nor the latter, because they will not act at all except upon compulsion, fancying that they are already dwelling apart in the islands of the blest.

54 Very true, he replied.

55 Then, I said, the business of us who are the founders of the State will be to compel the best minds to attain that knowledge which we have already shown to be the greatest of all, namely, the vision of the good; they must make the ascent which we have described; but when they have ascended and seen enough we must not allow them to do as they do now.

56 What do you mean?

57 They are permitted to remain in the upper world, refusing to descend again among the prisoners in the cave, and partake of their labours and honours, whether they are worth having or not.

58 But is not this unjust? he said; ought we to give them a worse life, when they might have a better?

59 You have again forgotten, my friend, I said, the intention of our law, which does not aim at making any one class in the State happy above the rest; it seeks rather to spread happiness over the whole State, and to hold the citizens together by persuasion and necessity, making each share with others any benefit which he can confer upon the State; and the law aims at producing such citizens, not that they may be left to please themselves, but that they may serve in binding the State together.

60 True, he said, I had forgotten.

For Further Thinking

1. What do you think of Socrates' contemplation of the prisoners conferring honours on each other according to who is quickest to see and categorize the passing shadows?

2. Through a diagram or notes, try to account for some of the comparisons suggested by this dialogue.

3. If, as Socrates says, the light of the fire stands for the power of the sun, then what does the sun represent?

Looking Back and Ahead

1. What do you think Socrates, as characterized by Plato, would think about the value of pursuing a beefcake look (see Susan McClelland's "The Lure of the Body Image," p. 83)? Explain your answer.
2. Pierre Elliott Trudeau, who was trained in Jesuit schools, with emphasis on scholastic reasoning, was a great admirer of Plato. Does Trudeau's essay "The Ascetic in a Canoe" (p. 156) have any stylistic similarities to "Allegory of the Cave"? Explain.
3. Mordecai Richler, described in our introduction as primarily a satirist ("The Summer My Grandmother Was Supposed to Die," p. 14), would likely agree with Plato's Socrates that the "state of man" is "grotesque and ridiculous." Does this suggest that writers of satire are, in fact, frustrated Idealists who feel they have glimpsed Plato's idea of the good, and now must compare it to the usual state of human affairs?

For Further Reading

Anthony F. Beavers, gen. ed. "Exploring Ancient World Cultures." Online course supplement. Department of Philosophy and Religion, University of Evansville, Indiana. April 2003 <http://eawc.evansville.edu/grpage.htm.> Well worth a visit, this award-winning site contains "maps" to Plato's *Dialogues*, a biography, a discussion of Plato's significance, a history of interpretation, and new hypotheses and links to his works.

"Greek history." ThinkQuest. April 2003 <http://library.thinkquest.org/10805/timeline.html>. The site created by a group of students at Gretna High School, Virginia, includes maps, time-lines, and sources.

Kraut, Richard, ed. *The Cambridge Companion to Plato.* Cambridge: Cambridge University Press, 1992.

"Plato." Online library. Questia.com. April 2003 <http://www.questia.com>. More than 14 000 scholarly titles on Plato selected by academics and librarians. Access a complete book or article online.

Plato, *The Dialogues of Plato*, 2 volumes. Trans. B.M.A. Jowett. New York: Random House, 1937.

Rowe, C. J. *Plato.* New York: St. Martin's Press, 1984.

Carl Jung Psychology—the study of the human mind—was not regarded as its own discipline until the early twentieth century. Austrian therapist Sigmund Freud (1856–1939) is generally recognized as the "father of modern psychology" and psychoanalysis. In 1906 Freud met a Swiss explorer in the new field, Carl Jung (1875–1961), and served as this young man's mentor for about seven years. Major differences between the two emerged, however, when Jung defended his belief in psychic realities and metaphysical subjects, which Freud rejected.

Jung's idea of the collective unconscious—a reservoir of cultural memories, dreams and myths—led him to explore comparative religions, alchemy, the *I Ching*, and astrology.[11] He cast horoscopes of his patients, hoping to use the insights of astrology in combination with his own psychotherapeutic ideas; he also made a statistical study of the relations between the horo-scopes of marriage partners, described in his work *Synchronicity: An Acausal Connecting Principle* (1955). Jung's ideas on personality are the basis of today's widely used Myers-Briggs Type Indicator, and his form of psychotherapy has influenced a wide range of artists and writers, including Canadian writer Robertson Davies (1913–1995). Perhaps see "The Pleasures of Love," p. 177.

[11] Colin Wilson. *The Occult* (London: Hodder & Stoughton, 1971), p. 324.

[12] See paragraph 14 on page 129. This adjective derives from the name René Descartes (1596–1650). Sometimes considered the "father" of modern philosophy, the French mathematician attempted to make philosophy "sci-entific," in keeping with the empirical values of his time. His system emphasized doubt, skepticism, and a de-nial of feelings. For an interesting critical interpretation of Descartes' influence on today's world, see Albert Borgman, *Crossing the Postmodern Divide* (Chicago: University of Chicago Press, 1992).

On Synchronicity

1   It might seem appropriate to begin my exposition by defining the concept with which it deals. But I would rather approach the subject the other way and first give you a brief description of the facts which the concept of synchronicity is intended to cover. As its etymology shows, this term has something to do with time or, to be more accurate, with a kind of simultaneity. Instead of simultaneity we could also use the concept of a *meaningful coincidence* of two or more events, where something other than the probability of chance is involved. A statistical—that is, a probable—concurrence of events, such as the "duplication of cases" found in hospitals, falls within the category of chance. Groupings of this kind can consist of any number of terms and still remain within the framework of the probable and rationally possible. Thus, for instance, someone chances to notice the number on his street-car ticket. On arriving home he receives a telephone call during which the same number is mentioned. In the evening he buys a theatre ticket that again has the same number. The three events form a chance grouping that, although not likely to occur often, nevertheless lies well within the framework of probability owing to the frequency of each of its terms. I would like to recount from my own ex-perience the following chance grouping, made up of no fewer than six terms:

2   On April 1, 1949, I made a note in the morning of an inscription contain-ing a figure that was half man and half fish. There was fish for lunch. Somebody mentioned the custom of making an "April fish" of someone. In the afternoon, a former patient of mine, whom I had not seen for months, showed me some im-pressive pictures of fish. In the evening, I was shown a piece of embroidery with sea monsters and fishes in it. The next morning, I saw a former patient, who was visiting me for the first time in ten years. She had dreamed of a large fish the night before. A few months later, when I was using this series for a larger work and had just finished writing it down, I walked over to a spot by the lake in front of the house, where I had already been several times that morning. This time a fish a foot long lay on the sea-wall. Since no one else was present, I have no idea how the fish could have got there.

3   When coincidences pile up in this way one cannot help being impressed by them—for the greater the number of terms in such a series, or the more unusual its character, the more improbable it becomes. For reasons that I have mentioned elsewhere and will not discuss now, I assume that this was a chance grouping. It must be admitted, though, that it is more improbable than a mere duplication.

4   In the above-mentioned case of the street-car ticket, I said that the observer "chanced" to notice the number and retain it in his memory, which ordinarily he would never have done. This formed the basis for the series of chance events, but I do not know what caused him to notice the number. It seems to me that in judging such a series a factor of uncertainty enters in at this point and requires attention. I have observed something similar in other cases, without, however, being able to draw any reliable conclusions. But it is sometimes difficult to avoid the impression that there is a sort of foreknowledge of the coming series of events. This feeling becomes irresistible when, as so frequently happens, one thinks one is about to meet an old friend in the street, only to find to one's disappointment that it is a stranger. On turning the next corner one then runs into him in person. Cases of this kind occur in every conceivable form and by no means infrequently, but after the first momentary astonishment they are as a rule quickly forgotten.

5   Now, the more the foreseen details of an event pile up, the more definite is the impression of an existing foreknowledge, and the more improbable does chance become. I remember the story of a student friend whose father had promised him a trip to Spain if he passed his final examinations satisfactorily. My friend thereupon dreamed that he was walking through a Spanish city. The street led to a square, where there was a Gothic cathedral. He then turned right, around a corner, into another street. There he was met by an elegant carriage drawn by two cream-coloured horses. Then he woke up. He told us about the dream as we were sitting around a table drinking beer. Shortly afterward, having successfully passed his examinations, he went to Spain, and there, in one of the streets, he recognized the city of his dream. He found the square and the cathedral, which exactly corresponded to the dream-image. He wanted to go straight to the cathedral, but then remembered that in the dream he had turned right, at the corner, into another street. He was curious to find out whether his dream would be corroborated further. Hardly had he turned the corner when he saw in reality the carriage with the two cream-coloured horses.

6   The *sentiment du déja-vu* is based, as I have found in a number of cases, on a foreknowledge in dreams, but we saw that this foreknowledge can also occur in the waking state. In such cases mere chance becomes highly improbable because the coincidence is known in advance. It thus loses its chance character not only psychologically and subjectively, but objectively too, since the accumulation of details that coincide immeasurably increases the improbability of chance as a determining factor. (For correct precognitions of death, Dariex and

Flammarion have computed probabilities ranging from 1 in 4,000,000 to 1 in 8,000,000). So in these cases it would be incongruous to speak of "chance" happenings. It is rather a question of meaningful coincidences. Usually they are explained by precognition—in other words, foreknowledge. People also talk of clairvoyance, telepathy, etc., without, however, being able to explain what these faculties consist of or what means of transmission they use in order to render events distant in space and time accessible to our perception. All these ideas are mere names; they are not scientific concepts which could be taken as statements of principle, for no one has yet succeeded in constructing a causal bridge between the elements making up a meaningful coincidence.

7   Great credit is due to J.B. Rhine for having established a reliable basis for work in the vast field of these phenomena by his experiments in extrasensory perception, or ESP. He used a pack of 25 cards divided into 5 groups of 5, each with its special sign (star, square, circle, cross, two wavy lines). The experiment was carried out as follows. In each series of experiments the pack is laid out 800 times, in such a way that the subject cannot see the cards. He is then asked to guess the cards as they are turned up. The probability of a correct answer is 1 in 5. The result, computed from very high figures, showed an average of 6.5 hits. The probability of chance deviation of 1.5 amounts to only 1 in 250,000. Some individuals scored more than twice the probable number of hits. On one occasion all 25 cards were guessed correctly, which gives a probability of 1 in 298,023,223,876,953,125. The spatial distance between experimenter and subject was increased from a few yards to about 4,000 miles, with no effect on the result.

8   A second type of experiment consisted in asking the subject to guess a series of cards that was still to be laid out in the near or more distant future. The time factor was increased from a few minutes to two weeks. The result of these experiments showed a probability of 1 in 400,000.

9   In a third type of experiment, the subject had to try to influence the fall of mechanically thrown dice by wishing for a certain number. The results of this so-called psychokinetic (PK) experiment were the more positive the more dice were used at a time.

10   The result of the spatial experiment proves with tolerable certainty that the psyche can, to some extent, eliminate the space factor. The time experiment proves that the time factor (at any rate, in the dimension of the future) can become psychically relative. The experiment with dice proves that moving bodies, too, can be influenced psychically—a result that could have been predicted from the psychic relativity of space and time.

11   The energy postulate shows itself to be inapplicable to the Rhine experiments, and thus rules out all ideas about the transmission of force. Equally, the law of causality does not hold—a fact that I pointed out thirty years ago. For we cannot conceive how a future event could bring about an event in the present. Since for the time being there is no possibility whatever of a causal expla-

nation, we must assume provisionally that improbable accidents of an acausal nature—that is, meaningful coincidences—have entered the picture.

12   In considering these remarkable results we must take into account a fact discovered by Rhine, namely that in each series of experiments the first attempts yielded a better result than the later ones. The falling off in the number of hits scored was connected with the mood of the subject. An initial mood of faith and optimism makes for good results. Scepticism and resistance have the opposite effect: that is, they create an unfavourable disposition. As the energic, and hence also the causal, approach to these experiments has shown itself to be inapplicable, it follows that the affective factor has the significance simply of a *condition* which makes it possible for the phenomenon to occur, though it need not. According to Rhine's results, we may nevertheless expect 6.5 hits instead of only 5. But it cannot be predicted in advance when the hit will come. Could we do so, we would be dealing with a law, and this would contradict the entire nature of the phenomenon. It has, as said, the improbable character of a "lucky" hit or accident that occurs with a more than merely probable frequency and is as a rule dependent on a certain state of affectivity.

13   This observation has been thoroughly confirmed, and it suggests that the psychic factor which modifies or even eliminates the principles underlying the physicist's picture of the world is connected with the affective state of the subject. Although the phenomenology of the ESP and PK experiments could be considerably enriched by further experiments of the kind described above, deeper investigation of its bases will have to concern itself with the nature of the affectivity involved. I have therefore directed my attention to certain observations and experiences which, I can fairly say, have forced themselves upon me during the course of my long medical practice. They have to do with spontaneous, meaningful coincidences of so high a degree of improbability as to appear flatly unbelievable. I shall therefore describe to you only one case of this kind, simply to give an example characteristic of a whole category of phenomena. It makes no difference whether you refuse to believe this particular case or whether you dispose of it with an *ad hoc* explanation. I could tell you a great many such stories, which are in principle no more surprising or incredible than the irrefutable results arrived at by Rhine, and you would soon see that almost every case calls for its own explanation. But the causal explanation, the only possible one from the standpoint of natural science, breaks down owing to the psychic relativization of space and time, which together form the indispensable premises for the cause-and-effect relationship.

14   My example concerns a young woman patient who, in spite of efforts made on both sides, proved to be psychologically inaccessible. The difficulty lay in the fact that she always knew better about everything. Her excellent education had provided her with a weapon ideally suited to this purpose, namely a highly polished Cartesian[12] rationalism with an impeccably "geometrical" idea of reality. After several fruitless attempts to sweeten her rationalism with a somewhat more

human understanding, I had to confine myself to the hope that something unexpected and irrational would turn up, something that would burst the intellectual retort into which she had sealed herself. Well, I was sitting opposite her one day, with my back to the window, listening to her flow of rhetoric. She had had an impressive dream the night before, in which someone had given her a golden scarab—a costly piece of jewellery. While she was still telling me this dream, I heard something behind me gently tapping on the window. I turned round and saw that it was a fairly large flying insect that was knocking against the window-pane from outside in the obvious effort to get into the dark room. This seemed to me very strange. I opened the window immediately and caught the insect in the air as it flew in. It was a scarabaeid beetle, or common rose-chafer (*Cetonia aurata*), whose golden-green colour most nearly resembles that of a golden scarab. I handed the beetle to my patient with the words, "Here is your scarab." This experience punctured the desired hole in her rationalism and broke the ice of her intellectual resistance. The treatment could now be continued with satisfactory results.

15   This story is meant only as a paradigm of the innumerable cases of meaningful coincidence that have been observed not only by me but by many others and recorded in large collections.

For Further Thinking

1. In Chapter 6 of the *Rhetoric*, "Definition" is discussed last. This is because the act of defining a complex concept may call upon any of the other patterns of writing we discuss. How many other expository patterns can you find in Jung's passage?

2. Have you ever been thinking of a friend you haven't spoken to in a long time, only to find out that he or she has just left or will soon leave you a message? Have you had dreams or insights about the future that were proven true? What is your opinion of psychic experiences in general? What is your opinion of the "scarab" experience reported by Jung?

3. Jung suggests that the "psychic factor . . . modifies or even eliminates the physicist's picture of the world." Have the recent discoveries of quantum mechanics altered this picture sufficiently to reconcile the "psychic factor" and the "physicist's picture"?

4. Do you think Jung's misgiving about universities' excluding certain subjects is a valid concern, even today?

5. Do you think an acceptance of psychic reality is culturally determined to some extent? Explain.

Looking Back and Ahead

1. Could Jung's idea of the collective unconscious and psychic apprehension be reconciled, in any way, with Plato's notion of a realm of Eternal Ideas (see the "Allegory of the Cave," p. 119)?

2. Emma Lee Warrior refers to the spirits of her grandparents visiting her in "White Breast Flats" (p. 6). What do you think Sigmund Freud might have thought of this belief? How do you think Jung might have responded. Perhaps conduct some brief research on both thinkers before offering your response.

3. What might Jung say about the unspoken communication passing between the midwife and her patient in "A Midwife in Rankin Inlet" (p. 72)?

4. Read John Markoff's "The Doomsday Machines" (p. 135). It is sometimes said that whereas the East concentrates on inner reality and being, the West most values exterior action and time (rapid change). Has the West listened too little to the Jungs of the world, paid too little attention to inner reality while pursuing external systems without the necessary inner resources to handle them?

5. Read Robertson Davies' essay "The Pleasures of Love" (p. 177). In what ways and for what reasons can you imagine Davies embracing the values and beliefs of Jung?

For Further Reading

Boeree, C. George. "Personality Theories: Carl Jung, 1875–1961." April 2003 <http://www.ship.edu/~cgboeree/jung.html>. Dr. Boeree's site is a comprehensive introduction to Jung's biography and his significance, with links and an annotated bibliography of books on Jung.

Campbell, Joseph, ed. *The Portable Jung*. Trans. R.F.C. Hull. New York: Viking, 1971. A world leader in the study of comparative religion and mythology, Campbell himself was a major pioneer in new thought.

"Carl Jung." Online library. Questia.com. April 2003 <http://www.questia.com>. Access to the complete texts for more than 2500 titles on Jung.

Davies, Robertson. *The Manticore*. New York: Viking, 1972. Davies' admiration of Carl Jung is reflected in his Deptford Trilogy, particularly in this, the second novel of the trilogy.

Ebon, Martin, ed. *The Signet Handbook of Parapsychology*. New York: New American Library, 1978. Ebon provides a thorough historical overview of the subject, then organizes articles according to their cross-disciplinary connections.

Hauke, Christopher, and Ian McAlister. *Jung and Film: Post-Jungian Takes on the Moving Image*. New York: Brunner-Routledge, 2001. An analyst and a lecturer in psychoanalytical studies examine movies and their place in our psychological development.

Sharp, Daryl. "Jung Page." Online. Jungian Lexicon. Ed. Donald Williams, Boulder, Colorado. April 2003 <http://www.cgjungpage.org/jpintro.html>. This article is a good introduction to Jungian psychology by a Jungian analyst. This site offers numerous links to professional and academic organizations.

Sheldrake, Rupert. *Dogs That Know When Their Owners Are Coming Home and Other Unexplained Powers of Animals*. New York: Three Rivers Press, 1999.

Wolman, Benjamin B. *Handbook of Parapsychology*. New York: Van Nostrand, 1977. Wolman covers research methods, perception and communication, and parapsychology applied within a variety of areas such as healing and survival of bodily death. The work of J.B. Rhine of Duke University, American pioneer in the field, is described and examined.

Anita Lahey Using the example of Evan Steeg, CEO of Kingston, Ontario-based Molecular Mining Corporation, and the Human Genome Project, Lahey presents the new field of "bioinformatics." She goes on to identify other larger firms, all involved, like Molecular Mining, in using advanced software to find meaningful patterns in biological data. Through this software capability, researchers are hoping to sift through thousands of possibilities to isolate promising combinations, without the need for actual laboratory activity. Five recent Queen's University grads make up Steeg's software team. "The discipline is so new," he says, "there simply aren't a lot of people who can do the work."

In preparing to read this article, consider your own attitude to computers. Members of the baby boom and previous generations sometimes object that using a computer to do formerly hands-on functions, including one's calculating, spelling, grammar revision, etc., encourages a flabby mind and sometimes sloppy and derivative work. What would you reply to this opinion?

The Genome Generation

1   Medical scientists, move over. Tomorrow's new drugs will come from math whizzes like Evan Steeg.

2   "I'm going to be a geek here. I love this stuff," warns Evan Steeg, clicking furiously at his laptop. Using a PowerPoint flowchart of human genes, Steeg, co-founder, president and CEO of Kingston, Ont.-based Molecular Mining Corp., explains how his company's data mining software can do with biological data what mathematics has done with stock data for years: find meaningful patterns. "You have eight stocks," Steeg begins, hands flapping. "Whenever these three stock prices go down, these five go up. You have something valuable you can exploit. The same is true biomedically." The difference is in the byproduct: a client of Steeg's would use data mining to find, for example, the right gene at which to target a drug.

3   Say "genes" and a lot of people think microscopes. But Steeg wants nothing to do with "messy lab applications." He is a mathematician and computer scientist—training that is suddenly very well suited to tackling the mysteries of genetics. So well suited, in fact, that this past spring, Steeg was handed US$2 million from venture capital firms SR One Ltd. (an arm of pharma giant SmithKline Beecham) and Cardinal Health Partners of Princeton, NJ. The deal immediately pegged Molecular Mining as one of the more promising entries in the infant sector of bioinformatics: roughly defined, the use of computer science to analyze biochemical data. Steeg, a New York native and University of Toronto PhD who did postdoctoral work at Queen's University, won't be making new drugs. But the pharmaceutical giants he's courting as clients will be. Experts predict those companies will spend up to US$1 billion on bioinformatics research by 2002.

4   Credit this surge to the whopping three gigabytes of data coming out of the Human Genome Project—a 13-year effort that's almost finished cataloguing the three-billion-part sequencing of human DNA, including a "map" of the estimated 100,000 genes it contains.[13] Couple that with computing advances that

allow pharmaceutical companies to work with millions of potential drug compounds simultaneously, and you've got data-gobbling neurobiologists and biochemists who need digesting help—fast. Enter the genome miners.

5   Steeg's company is neither the first nor the biggest. Spotfire Inc. of Cambridge, Mass., and Silicon Genetics of San Carlos, Calif., both have well-established software offerings. And Germany's Lion Bioscience AG recently penned an agreement with Bayer AG that could ultimately be worth up to $100 million, including royalties. But with its proprietary algorithms and five PhD founders—including three Queen's professors and the director of the machine learning project at the US National Library of Medicine, all pioneers in bioinformatics—Molecular Mining may be one of the brainiest contenders. "There are very few companies working in this field who are applying thoroughbred computer science to the data of biotechnology," says Barbara Dalton, the vice-president at SR One who signed Steeg's deal. "Most offer canned, standard software products, as opposed to a partner who will help you maximize the value of your data." That higher level of science—and personalized service—is what the sector needs, says Roland Somogyi, director of neurobiology for Incyte Pharmaceuticals in Palo Alto, Calif. "Molecular Mining wants to work its way into the problems of a particular client. That's very important."

6   While Molecular Mining has yet to land a client or even launch a product, several potential customers have supplied it with confidential databases on which to test its software. That code uses what Steeg describes as a "horror show" of algorithms designed to, for example, sift through the reactions of 50,000 genes to dozens of different drug compounds, and isolate the few drug and gene combinations that show a promising response. "When you're looking for brute-force, complex relationships, you need very efficient algorithms," says Somogyi. "That's one of the most important components they have to offer."

7   Steeg, a youthful 38 with thick brown hair and a tree-trunk build, still has his challenges. Among them: incorporating attractive visualization into his software and surviving the often long process of securing the right type of data set from a potential client. What he also has, though, is firsthand experience in his clients' world (he's worked for Dupont) and first pick of Queen's grads (five make up his software team). The latter is a real ace, as the discipline is so new there simply aren't a lot of people who can do the work. "It's not like we've just come from Bay Street," says Steeg. "You have to understand enough about chemistry or biology to know which assumptions you can make."

---

[13] The Human Genome Project was completed in April 2003 and identifies the approximately 30,000 genes in human DNA.

For Further Thinking

1. What is your enthusiasm level for computers? Could you imagine pursuing a field like bioinformatics? What are the special challenges of this work?

2. What sorts of rhetorical patterns are used in this article? (Refer to Chapter 6 of the *Rhetoric* for the typical rhetorical structures.)

3. Does Lahey's article have a clear thesis? In your own words, what is her thesis?

4. Does Lahey commit any oversimplifications or other logical fallacies in this report? (See "Logical Fallacies" in Chapter 7 of the *Rhetoric*.) Is her tone neutral, objective?

5. Identify an analogy used by Lahey to clarify a main idea. How effective is this analogy? (See "Comparison-Contrast" in Chapter 6 of the *Rhetoric* for more discussion of analogies.)

Looking Back and Ahead

1. Lahey's use of the word "generation" in her title—supported by what she goes on to describe—strongly suggests that anyone older than 40 or so has missed the current state of the art in computer expertise and applications. See Susan Keaveney's "When MTV Goes CEO" (p. 99). What are the connections between that essay and "The Genome Generation"?

2. Read John Markoff's "The Doomsday Machines" (p. 135). Is it fair to say that where his essay is strongly pessimistic about the future of science, Lahey's is strongly optimistic?

3. Compare and contrast the tone and style of Lahey's article to those of Jane Farrow's "Diary Rock" (p. 80).

For Further Reading

"Books on Bioinformatics." April 2003 <http://cui.unige.ch/~bioinfo/biobook.html>. This is a list of books available on the subject.

"Human Genome Project Information." April 2003 <http://www.ornl.gov/hgmis>. This site features information about genome programs of the U.S. Department of Energy's Office of Science, including its Human Genome Project.

"Introduction to Bioinformatics." April 2003 <http://bioinformatics.weizmann.ac.il/cards/>. This academic website of the Weizmann Institute of Science defines bioinformatics and offers information about the functions of all human genes.

National Human Genome Research Institute (NHGRI). April 2003 <http://www.nhgri.nih.gov/index.html>. The site provides information into the biochemical process of mapping DNA and chromosomes and contains current projects and progress on many genome-related matters.

"Virtual Frog Dissection Kit." Hosted by the Distributed Systems Department, Computing Sciences, at the Ernest Orlando Lawrence Berkeley National Laboratory for the U.S. Department of Energy's Office of Science. April 2003 <http://www-itg.lbl.gov/>. Through this page visitors can link to the popular Interactive Frog Dissection Kit, part of the Whole Frog Project. Use your computer to dissect a virtual frog and examine its parts. No mess!

John Markoff In Mary Shelley's famous novel of 1818, young Victor Frankenstein loses his mother to death; consumed by grief, he vows to overcome this nemesis of mankind. Applying the new scientific force of his age—electricity—he succeeds in charging life into a Creature assembled from body parts stolen from graves and charnel houses. The story switches to the Creature's point of view, and we realize that this lonely, unnamed being longs for love and acceptance. He is the ultimate outcast of literature—and the tragic outcome of his story is, of course, inevitable. For those uneasy with the direction of scientific research and invention, the story is a powerful metaphor of reckless application.

In the following magazine article, John Markoff provides further fuel for those on the doom side of the debate over science. His sources, referred to as a "representation of serious scientists," illustrate a willingness, perhaps an increasing willingness, on the part of those in science to open their own field to serious critical, ethical scrutiny. After the scientific concerns of the twentieth century, it seems that many in today's world are heeding the warning of works such as *Frankenstein*.

See the Appendix at the end of the *Reader*, Part I (p. 250), for more support for this reading. This support may particularly benefit you if English is not your first language.

The Doomsday Machines

1   In the space of three short decades, the computer chip industry has come to resemble the Sorcerer's Apprentice.

2   The exponential growth in computing power has produced stunning advances in a range of sciences and engineering fields ranging from decoding the human genome to the design of machines that can outplay the best human chess player.

3   And that in turn has led to exuberant predictions of a dawning of vast new Information Age utopias.

4   Sentient intelligent machines are as close as three decades away, many industry leaders believe; smart materials that can repair themselves and genetically coded immortality may also be just around the corner.

5   Given the hype and relentless optimism, perhaps it's not surprising that serious scientists and researchers have begun to explore darker, less inviting visions of the future.

6   This month an unlikely new doomsday prophet has emerged.

7   In an essay in *Wired* magazine, a popular forum for high-technology boosterism, Bill Joy, the chief scientist at Sun Microsystems, warns that the human species may be on the verge of collective suicide.

8   "The 21st-century technologies—genetics, nanotechnology and robotics—are so powerful that they can spawn whole new classes of accidents and abuses," he writes.

9   Joy is hardly a Luddite, but his gloomy pronouncements fit squarely into a long tradition of apocalyptic warnings about technology run amok, dating back to ancient Greeks, and voiced more recently in a millennial laundry list of threats, including nuclear winters, global warming, ozone depletion, marauding comets, the dispersion of deadly biological toxins by the Japanese Aum Shinrikyo cult in Tokyo subways, as well as the spectre of Y2K calamities sending civilization back to smoky caves.

10   As harrowing as all those threats may have appeared, for Joy and others the worst is yet to come.

11   The new danger, they argue, is self-replication, the technique at the heart of both modern biotechnology and the relatively new field of "material sciences" (the creation of advanced materials such as new ceramics or liquid crystal displays), which has the capacity for both tremendous good as well as destruction. The fears fall in three broad areas.

Robotics

12   The science fiction writer Isaac Asimov once described a world in which advanced machines, even if their intelligence vastly exceeded that of humans, could be programmed so they would never intentionally take any action that would harm people.

13   Now a number of writers and scientists are suggesting a more ominous, Darwinian scenario in which super-intelligent machines might evolve along with, and ultimately compete with, human society.

14   Consider a future world in which robots operate with microprocessors a million times more powerful than today's.

15   Hans Moravec, a robotics scientist at Carnegie Mellon University, conjures images in his writings of totally automated factories and networks that will emerge as soon as 2020.

16   These robotic systems will be able to program themselves and compete vigorously with humans for resources, perhaps creating self-sufficient artificially intelligent economies that could squeeze humans out of existence. (Think about a factory that decides to create an army of Robocops.)

17   Another computer scientist, Vemor Vinge, says machine intelligence will awaken sometime between 2005 and 2030, a date he calls "the singularity."

18   Vinge argues that this evolutionary watershed might accelerate progress well beyond human control.

19   Others suggest that the Internet may someday reach a critical mass of interconnections that at the least might exhibit some kind of chaotic behaviour, perhaps even some kind of sentience. The problem, of course, is that such a system might be intelligent but not rational, thrashing around like a newborn baby—turning off power systems or launching missiles at random.

Nanotechnology

20   Nanotechnology refers to mechanical engineering on a molecular scale. The holy grail for nanotechnologists [is] sub-microscopic chemical or mechanical machines called assemblers that can reproduce and repair themselves.

21   There are already many industrial examples of micro-assemblers. For example, Polymerase Chain Reaction, the exponential amplification of DNA fragments, has become a standard tool of biotechnologists.

22   And recently IBM researchers described a process that permits chemical assemblers to self-assemble tiny magnetic particles into a perfectly aligned array of dots, each composed of several thousand atoms, for future disk drives.

23   Joy believes that within several decades, similar advances will lead to incredibly low-cost solar power, vastly more powerful computers and cures for everything from cancer to the common cold.

24   But here's the catch: in the wrong hands, or perhaps accidentally, nanotechnology could open a Pandora's Box.

25   This nightmare has long been the stuff of science fiction. Readers of Kurt Vonnegut's 1963 novel *Cat's Cradle* may remember "ice-nine," the final creation of the story's scientist, Felix Hoenikker.

26   Ice-nine was solid at room temperature. In other words, the molecules of H_2O in ice-nine had "discovered" a way to stack up to form a crystalline solid at temperatures where other molecules of H_2O were still in a liquid phase.

27   This contagious modification ultimately freezes the world's oceans. For several decades now, however, nonfictional scientists have been toying with the different ways that H_2O molecules can stack together.

28   And in real life, it might be possible to create tough omnivorous bacteria that could out-compete real bacteria. Spread by the wind, like blowing pollen, they could be designed to replicate swiftly and reduce life on earth to dust in a matter of days, according to Eric Drexler, one of the nation's principal advocates for nanotechnology. (Drexler advocates the construction of a series of high technology "shields" to ward off these kinds of threats.)

Genetic Engineering

29   While both robots and nanotechnological weapons are at least a generation away, genetic weapons are not. Joy and other scientists have begun to warn of near-term terrorist threats based on genetically engineered biological weapons.

30   "Much of the talk about information-based weapons is baloney," said Edward Feigenbaum, the former chief scientist of the U.S. Air Force.

31   "But biological terrorism is real and the government is beginning to take steps to defend against it."

32   Some scientists are worried both about the spectre of genetic experiments accidentally escaping into the population and also what Joy calls a "white plague" (a reference to another science fiction novel, by Frank Herbert)—genetically engineered bioweapons that could be targeted on a specific region or race.

33   It doesn't end there—there are even more exotic technological threats.

34   Last year a brief media frenzy broke out over speculation that the Brookhaven National Laboratory's Relativistic Heavy Ion Collider could create an artificial black hole that would devour the earth in a matter of minutes.

35   Scientists insisted that such fears were unfounded, yet as Armageddon scenarios go, it was a doozy. Earlier this month several physicists filed suit in federal court to stop the experiment.

36   Of course, it could be that Joy is wrong. After all, it is possible to take comfort in the thought that despite several thousand years of predictions of impending doom, the human species is, by and large, thriving. Still, it is a bit unsettling.

37   Perhaps Mark Twain put it best: "I'm all for progress. It's change I can't stand."

For Further Thinking

1. Consider your own personal experiences with the effects of science, technology, and medicine. Have they been good, bad, or a mixture of both?
2. What rhetorical patterns predominate in Markoff's article? (See Chapter 6 of the *Rhetoric*, "Patterns (Methods) of Exposition" for a discussion of structures.) Should we have catalogued this article, as we have, in this section of the *Reader*, as exposition?
3. What would the science students and teachers you know say about this article by Markoff?
4. How would you describe the tone of this article?
5. Do you think science will bring a good or bad future, or some variation? Explain and illustrate with an example for each point.
6. In paragraph 9, Markoff refers to the "spectre of Y2K calamities." How did you feel about Y2K in 1999? How do you feel about it now?

Looking Back and Ahead

1. Read George Orwell's essay "Politics and the English Language" (p. 227). Rhetorically, how similar is that essay to Markoff's? Consider both structure and purpose.
2. What organizational and stylistic differences can you find between Markoff's essay and Brenda Platt's "Global Warming and Population" (p. 113)?
3. Many North American Native elders envision a harsh future of environmental malaise if the current order continues. Are there congruencies of vision between Markoff's essay and Emma Lee Warrior's "White Breast Flats" (p. 6)?
4. According to the Web site of the Science and Environmental Policy Project (SEPP), more than 15 000 reputable scientists have signed a petition dismissing the findings of the scientists whose report to the United Nations led to the Kyoto Accord (1997). What do you imagine these anti-Kyoto scientists would think of Markoff's essay?

For Further Reading

BBC news report describing European dissatisfaction with President George W. Bush's U.S.A. policy reversal on the Kyoto Accord. Online. April 2003 <http://www.climateark.org/articles/2001/1st/eubackky.htm>.

Branagh, Kenneth, dir. *Mary Shelley's Frankenstein* (film), 1995. Directed by the celebrated Shakespearian actor and filmmaker, this version claims to rescue the story from Hollywood and return it to Shelley's original intentions.

Epstein, Paul R. "Is Global Warming Harmful to Health?" Online. *Scientific American*, 2000. April 2003 <http://www.sciam.com/2000/0800issue/0800epstein.html>.Computer models suggest that many diseases will proliferate as the earth's atmosphere heats up. Are we beginning to see these predictions come to pass now?

Orwell, George. *Nineteen Eighty-Four*. 1949. London: Penguin Books, 1954. In this cautionary fable, science and technology act as servants of a ruthless, dictatorial political order.

The Science and Environment Policy Project (SEPP) petition regarding Kyoto Accord. Online. April 2003 <http://www.sepp.org/pressrel/petition.html>. SEPP is a group of American scientists and businesspeople opposed to the 1997 Kyoto agreement on reducing levels of carbon emissions.

Seitz, Frederick. "A Major Deception on 'Global Warming.'" *Wall Street Journal*, June 12, 1996. A president emeritus of Rockefeller University and past president of the U.S. National Academy of Sciences, Seitz maintains that fears of global warming are grounded on "shaky science."

Shelley, Mary. *Frankenstein*. 1818 text. Ed. Marilyn Butler. Oxford: Oxford University Press, 1993. There was a second, quite altered edition in 1831, but Butler argues that Shelley, under pressures from her publishers, softened her social criticisms.

Brian D. Johnson Atom Egoyan's 1997 feature film *The Sweet Hereafter*, shown at the Cannes Film Festival in France, won the Grand Prix, the International Critics' Prize, and the Ecumenical Jury Prize. Egoyan was nominated for Best Director at the Academy Awards, rare recognition for a non-American. He represents a Canadian talent pool that includes such diverse artists as directors Denys Arcand, Anne Wheeler, and David Cronenberg. The National Film Board has won 10 Academy Awards; Canadian animation rates among the most highly respected in the world. Since the early days when Canadian Mary Pickford became a huge star in Hollywood, Canadian actors have been achieving great success across the border.

Yet at home, Canadian films generate just 2 percent of box office receipts; one in 20 films seen in Canada is Canadian, a ratio of .05. For all the peculiarly Canadian disincentives, however, some filmmakers remain in Canada to face the likelihood of being ignored and/or financially ruined should they manage to finish their next pictures. One who has avoided that fate so far, and remained in Toronto despite attractive offers from Hollywood, is Atom Egoyan. In the following article from *Maclean's*, September 13, 1999, Brian Johnson interviews Egoyan at length, then relates his character to his films and finds "a person of immense contradiction."

Atom's Journey

1   Lunch with Atom Egoyan. He arrives late, on the run in a day of interviews. This is Toronto, his home town, but he might as well be on tour. His personal publicist hovers close by; a driver waits at the curb outside the restaurant. Affable and full of energy, Egoyan takes a seat in the corner booth, a dark wood enclosure with

a thick curtain that can be drawn for privacy. Should it be open or closed? "Closed," Egoyan suggests. The curtain is drawn and suddenly the booth feels strangely private, like a sleeper compartment on a train. It is the kind of place where secrets could be revealed, with the awkward intimacy that you would expect to find . . . in an Atom Egoyan film. The only question is, how to catch the waiter's eye?

2   It is the sort of dilemma Egoyan can appreciate. He has built a career out of creating coolly hermetic worlds on film, dramas that are ripe with understated menace and employ none of the usual tricks to catch the eye of the audience. His latest movie, *Felicia's Journey*—which opens the Toronto International Film Festival (Sept. 9 to 18) this week—tells the eerie story of a gentle serial killer (Bob Hoskins) closing in on an Irish girl (Elaine Cassidy) adrift in the industrial barrens of England. There is not a single scene of violence, but there is an overwhelming sense of violation.

3   Egoyan's films are all about violations of innocence and trust. And, as he eventually reveals over lunch, the theme is rooted in a trauma from his own teenage years that he has been reluctant to discuss until now. "It was a really primal adolescent experience," he says. "The way in which people can camouflage things is absolutely vital to my experience of growing up."

4   Born in Cairo of Armenian parents, Egoyan immigrated to Victoria with his family at the age of 3. Now 39, he is the most accomplished Canadian director of his generation. With eight features to his credit, he has received two Oscar nominations, five Genies, four prizes from Cannes, five honorary degrees and a French knighthood. He lives in Toronto with his Armenian wife, Beirut-born Arsinée Khanjian, and their five-year-old son, Arshile. Khanjian, who has appeared in all his films, is now a rising star in her own right. And their creative marriage has become the quintessential Canadian immigrant success story, an artful romance of two outsiders working their way from the margins to the heart of the cultural elite.

5   The name Atom Egoyan, meanwhile has become synonymous with the peculiar identity of Canadian cinema, which has acquired a reputation for introversion and sexual pathology. But despite his reputation for chilly abstraction, there is a deeply personal sense of compassion that runs through all of Egoyan's films, a fixation on the secrets and lies buried at the core of the nuclear family. From *Family Viewing* (1987) to *The Sweet Hereafter* (1997), Egoyan returns again and again to tales of bereft parents and lost children, stories in which sexuality keeps striking uncomfortably close to home.

6   Anyone looking at Egoyan's recent movies cannot help but notice a disturbing pattern. In 1994's *Exotica*, a father mourns the violent death of his daughter by ritually doting on a young stripper costumed as a schoolgirl. In *The Sweet Hereafter*, a father carries on an incestuous affair with his adolescent daughter. And now in *Felicia's Journey*, a pregnant teenager slides into the clutches of a paternal predator. Three movies. Three stories of father figures obsessed with teenage

girls. It is one thing for a director to keep coming back to the same themes—Catholic redemption for Martin Scorsese, technological mutation for David Cronenberg—but the pattern in Egoyan's work is so specific, so personal and ultimately so creepy, it raises the question: What is at the bottom of it?

7   The obsession goes back to an experience Egoyan had as a teenager growing up in Victoria, which he has finally agreed to talk about. "There was a young woman," he says, "whom I adored from a very young age, and who was inaccessible to me for the longest time. Later on, it was revealed that there was an abusive relationship with her father. All the clues were there. But it wasn't a society at that point that could read them or respond to them, and I felt kind of helpless about it. So rather than address it, I went into denial over it, like everybody else."

8   The father's behaviour left Egoyan with a distressing lesson in life and art. "I suppose the thing that confused it more than anything," he says, "is that he himself was an artist, and it was so obvious what was going on, from the work he was doing and presenting publicly and the way he was behaving. But no one could actually talk about it. There was this incredible shroud of secrecy. And I was completely, madly in love with her. From about 13 to 18. And it wasn't until the last year when it became more . . ." Egoyan pauses. "I feel weird about it, because it's her story," he says. "The pain that she went through was a lot more than mine. I was an observer."

9   Egoyan never talked to the father about the incest, but ended up in awkward negotiations with him about the terms of his own romantic intentions. "When the father realized I was serious about her," he says, "I had to make promises to him which I ultimately couldn't keep—in terms of keeping my relationship with his daughter platonic. It was a very strange time, because I was living a double life." Complicating things even further is the fact that, for the girl, the incest had an element of romantic delusion. "And that's what *The Sweet Hereafter* explored," explains Egoyan. "What is the experience of incest on the victim when it's not the obvious exercise of violent power, but this blurring of love?"

10   Egoyan says that he himself had an "ideal upbringing." His parents, Joseph and Shushan, who met at art school in Egypt, are both painters. His mother, now 65, recently mounted her first solo exhibition in Victoria. And when Atom was 10, he remembers going to the provincial museum for a show of his father's work called *Birds*—"which was a very attractive title to the population of Victoria, until they realized these were canvases of dead birds. My father would suspend dead birds around the house. It was a little bit gothic."

11   His parents, who supported their art by running a small furniture store, "gave me great work models as to what an artist does," adds Egoyan, who worked in the store from a young age. "I became very aware of the mechanics of operating a small business. That gave me a very practical sense of how to manage a production, and how to be modest. And I became very aware of the making of art, and the appreciation of art. I was around it all the time. A lot of my father's

friends were artists. And my sister [Eve Egoyan] is a concert pianist doing very unusual music."

12   But as an Armenian child trying to assimilate, Atom endured a degree of culture shock. He did not speak English when he first went to school. "I remember very clearly episodes where my parents had to explain to the teacher, 'If he says this it mean he has to go to the bathroom, and if he says that, it means he's hungry.' I remember saying to a teacher in Armenian, 'I'm hungry,' and then being shown to the bathroom."

13   Egoyan developed a love for the absurd at an early age, crafting teenage plays in the spirit of Ionesco, Beckett and Pinter, then short films as an undergraduate at the University of Toronto. By the time he made his first feature, *Next of Kin* (1984), at the age of 23, he says he had become "really aware of the fact that identity is possibly a construct."

14   Much of Egoyan's work dwells on blurred identity, a Canadian "construct" if ever there was one. In *Next of Kin*—which opens with a shot taken from a camera on an airport baggage carousel—a young man joins an Armenian family in Toronto by pretending to be a long-lost son. In *Family Viewing,* a young man learns that his father is erasing the family's home videos by shooting sex scenes with his new wife. A series of shadowy father figures began to emerge in Egoyan's films—the seductive insurance man in *The Adjuster,* the grieving accountant in *Exotica,* the manipulative lawyer in *The Sweet Hereafter.* But none is as dark as Hilditch, the mild-mannered monster played by Hoskins in *Felicia's Journey.*

15   Based on the 1994 novel by Irish author William Trevor, it is a spare drama that brings two characters together with quiet, claustrophobic intensity. Felicia is a naïve 17-year-old from rural Ireland who has come to the English city of Birmingham searching for Johnny, the lover who has left her pregnant. Lost, alone and unable to find him, she is befriended by Hilditch, a quiet catering manager who has made a macabre pastime of collecting and disposing of homeless girls.

16   Living alone in the gloomy house where he grew up, Hilditch seems locked in a time warp. He spends his nights preparing elaborate meals while watching black-and-white videos of a 1950s cooking show hosted by his dead mother. Played by Khanjian, she is a comically flamboyant character with a French accent who cruelly exploits her son (Hilditch as a chubby boy) on camera. Hilditch's video archive also includes tapes of his victims, recorded with a camera hidden in his Morris Minor. Egoyan has been developing the idea of fetishized video artifacts ever since *Family Viewing.* And by grafting it onto Trevor's novel, along with the burlesque horror of the cooking show, he has placed a surreal signature on an essentially realistic drama.

17   Repression builds in *Felicia's Journey* with the claustrophobic weight of English weather. Cutting between past and present, Egoyan shifts from Ireland's green fields to Britain's bleak industrial landscape, and from the sharp intolerance of Felicia's Irish-Catholic father to the insidious comfort of her English bene-

factor. The movie is an underhanded thriller, bereft of catharsis. And as Egoyan slowly tightens the noose of suspense (which turns out to be a slipknot), the stalking, predatory camera seems more sympathetic to the killer than to his prey. "The camera betrays the feelings of the person behind it at all moments," Egoyan explains. "I was far more fascinated in Hilditch than in Felicia. The story of a young woman looking for the father of her child is not as interesting to me, dramatically, as this monster who is responsible for evils beyond description, yet doesn't seem aware of it."

18   Egoyan's empathy for Hilditch popped into alarming focus during the filming. Hoskins fell sick on the day he was to improvise the videotaped scenes of the victims talking to Hilditch in his car. So Egoyan played the killer's role, which is largely off-camera. "I put on his gloves, I put on his coat, and I had to go through a serial rejection of each of these women in a car," the director recalls. Hilditch's side of the dialogue does not appear in the film "but when you see him grab one of the women, it's my arm," says Egoyan. "What I realized in the process is that so much of my job is about trying to seduce people. The darkest side of what we do as directors is make people do something they wouldn't do otherwise—and what is Hilditch if not a director?"

For Further Thinking

1. Is Egoyan's theme of incest compassionate for victims or sensationalistic? Explain through analysis of one or two Egoyan films in which this motif occurs.

2. What do you think Egoyan means when he says "identity is possibly a construct"?

3. Is Johnson correct to say that blurred identity is a particularly "Canadian construct"?

4. There are several parallels between *Felicia's Journey* and *The Silence of the Lambs*. Compare and contrast these two films. Do they reflect marked differences between Canadian, British, and American values? Do they expose some essential contradictions and complexities in Canadians and their relationship to the United States? If so, in what ways?

5. As a writer, does Egoyan reap any possible artistic benefit from feeling somewhat of a stranger at home? Explain.

Looking Back and Ahead

1. Are there any similarities between the world of *The Sweet Hereafter* and that of Alice Munro's "Thanks for the Ride" (p. 62)? Explain.
2. Read our section on critical analysis in Chapter 10 of the *Rhetoric*. What is the balance of expository to critical writing in Johnson's article? Identify sections where one form or the other predominates.
3. Read "I Am Half-Canadian" by Pamela Swanigan (p. 58). Do you think she would agree that Canadian identity is possibly a construct, and that blurred identity is a particularly Canadian construct?

4. Read our section on "Writing a Film Review." (You can find this on the website accompanying this text at <www.pearsoned.ca/brundage/> or at the Eglish 255 website available through Athabasca University, at <www.athabascau.ca/courses/engl/255/>, which provides further resources and examples, under "Supplementary Resources.") Then try your hand at reviewing a film, maybe a Canadian one. Some suggestions? *Goin' Down the Road*, director Don Shebib; *Last Night*, director Don McKellar; *My American Cousin*, director Sandy Wilson; *Jesus of Montreal*, director Denys Arcand; *Dance Me Outside*, director Bruce McDonald; *Le Confessional,* director Robert Lepage (if you pick *Le Confessional*, see also Alfred Hitchcock's *Notorious*, 1946).

For Further Reading

Bass, Ellen, and Laura Davis. *The Courage to Heal: A Guide for Women Survivors of Child Sexual Abuse*. New York: Harper & Row, 1988.

Bowie, Douglas, and Tom Shoebridge. *Best Canadian Screenplays*. Kingston, ON: Quarry Books, 1994. Contains *Goin' Down the Road*, *Mon Oncle Antoine*, *The Grey Fox*, *My American Cousin*, *Jesus of Montreal*.

Davis, Laura. *Allies in Healing: When the Person You Love Was Sexually Abused as a Child*. New York: Harper Perennial, 1991.

Dorland, Michael. "So Close to the State(s): The Emergence of Canadian Feature Film Policy." University of Toronto, Toronto, 1998. April 2003 <http://www.nottingham.ac.uk/film/journal/bookrev/so_close.htm>. Includes information on Canadian films.

"Fine Line Films presents *The Sweet Hereafter* by Atom Egoyan." April 2003 <http://www.finelinefeatures.com/sweet/>. Official website of the film with information on the story, film notes, cast, videos, shop, and Atom Egoyan.

Fraser, Sylvia. *My Father's House: Memoir of Incest and of Healing*. New York: Harper & Row, 1987. In Canada, Fraser's book opened up public discussion of this previously taboo subject.

National policies and programs for Canadian film. Administered by Department of Canadian Heritage. April 2003 <http://www.pch.gc.ca>. Select "Arts and Culture," then "Film."

"Nell Shipman." April 2003 <http://www.utoronto.ca/shipman/>. About the Canadian film pioneer.

The Sweet Hereafter. Screenplay. April 2003 <http://www.finelinefeatures.com/sweet/cmp/sweethereafter.txt>.

"Writing a Film Review" under "Supplementary Resources," English 255 Introductory Composition cover page <www.athabascau.ca/courses/engl/255/> or the *Acting on Words* website at <www.pearsoned.ca/brundage/>.

Wayne C. Booth Born in 1921 in American Fork, Utah, Wayne C. Booth received his Ph.D. in literature from the University of Chicago in 1950. He went on to become a distinguished professor of English, serving as president of the Modern Languages Association in 1982. His major published work, *The Company We Keep: An Ethics of Fiction* (1988), examines in depth and detail his long-standing concern with the relationship of writer and reader. Now retired, Booth is working on a rhetoric of religious discourse.

Booth's essay "The Rhetorical Stance" uses various structures, notably comparison-contrast and cause-effect, to define his idea of the ideal "stance" or relationship to take with one's reader.

See the Appendix at the end of the *Reader*, Part I (p. 252), for more support for this reading. This support may particularly benefit you if English is not your first language.

The Rhetorical Stance

1   Last fall I had an advanced graduate student, bright, energetic, well-informed, whose papers were almost unreadable. He managed to be pretentious, dull, and disorganized in his paper on *Emma*, and pretentious, dull, and disorganized on *Madame Bovary*. On *The Golden Bowl* he was all these and obscure as well. Then one day, toward the end of the term, he cornered me after class and said, "You know, I think you were all wrong about Robbe-Grillet's *Jealousy* today." We didn't have time to discuss his objections, so I suggested that he write me a note about them. Five hours later I found in my faculty box a four-page polemic, unpretentious, stimulating, organized, convincing. Here was a man who had himself taught freshman composition for several years and who was incapable of committing any of the more obvious errors that we think of as characteristic of bad writing. Yet he could not write a decent sentence, paragraph, or paper until his rhetorical problem was solved—until, that is, he had found a definition of his audience, his argument, and his own proper tone of voice.

2   When I think back over the experiences which have had any effect on my own writing, I find the great good fortune of a splendid freshman course, taught by a man who believed in what he was doing, but I also find a collection of other experiences quite unconnected with a specific writing course. I remember the professor of psychology who penciled one word after a peculiarly vacuous paper of mine: *Bull.* I remember the day when P.A. Christensen talked with me about my Chaucer paper and made me understand that my failure to use effective transitions was not simply a technical fault but a fundamental block between him and my meaning. His off-the-cuff pronouncement that I should *never* let myself write a sentence that was not in some way *explicitly* attached to preceding and following sentences meant far more to me at that moment, when I had something I wanted to say, than it could have meant as part of a pattern of such rules offered in a writing course. Similarly, I can remember the devastating lessons about my bad writing that Ronald Crane could teach with a simple question mark on a graduate seminar paper, or a penciled "Evidence for this?" or "Why this section here?" or "Everybody says so. Is it true?"

3   Such experiences are not, I like to think, simply the result of my being a late bloomer. At least I find my colleagues saying such things as "I didn't learn to write until I became a newspaper reporter" or "The most important training in writing I had was doing a dissertation under old Blank." Sometimes they go on to say that the freshman course was useless: sometimes they say that

it was an indispensable preparation for the later experience. The diversity of such replies is so great as to suggest that before we try to reorganize the freshman course, with or without explicit confrontations with rhetorical categories, we ought to look for whatever there is in common among our experiences, both of good writing and of good writing instruction. Whatever we discover in such an enterprise ought to be useful to us at any level of our teaching. It will not, presumably, decide once and for all what should be the content of the freshman course, if there should be such a course. But it might serve as a guideline for the development of widely different programs suited to the widely differing institutions in which we work.

4   The common ingredient that I find in all of the writing I admire—excluding for now novels, plays, and poems—is something that I shall reluctantly call the rhetorical stance, a stance which depends on discovering and maintaining a proper balance among three elements: the available arguments about the subject itself; the interests and peculiarities of the audience; and the voice, the implied character, of the speaker. I should like to suggest that it is this balance, this rhetorical stance, difficult as it is to describe, that is our main goal as teachers of rhetoric. Our ideal graduate will strike this balance automatically in any writing that he considers finished. Though he may never come to the point of finding the balance easily, he will know that it is what makes the difference between effective communication and mere wasted effort.

5   What I mean by the true rhetorician's stance can perhaps best be seen by contrasting it with three corruptions, unbalanced stances often assumed by people who think they are practicing the arts of persuasion.

6   The first I'll call the **pedant's stance**: it consists of ignoring or underplaying the personal relationship of speaker and audience and depending entirely on statements about a subject—leaving out, that is, the notion of a job to be done for a particular audience. It is a virtue, of course, to respect the bare truth of one's subject, and there may even be some subjects which in their very nature define an audience and a rhetorical purpose so that adequacy to the subject can be the whole art of presentation. For example, an article on "The Relation of the Ontological and Teleological Proofs," in a recent *Journal of Religion,* requires a minimum of adaptation of argument to audience. But most subjects do not in themselves imply in any necessary way a purpose and an audience and hence a speaker's tone. The writer who assumes that it is enough merely to write an exposition of what he happens to know on the subject will produce the kind of essay that soils our scholarly journals, written not for readers but for bibliographies.

7   In my first year of teaching I taught a whole unit on "exposition" without ever suggesting, so far as I can remember, that the students ask themselves what their expositions were *for*. So they wrote expositions like this one—I've saved it, to teach me toleration of my colleagues: the title is: "Family relations in More's *Utopia*." "In this theme I would like to discuss some of the relationships

with the family which Thomas More elaborates and sets forth in his book, *Utopia.* The first thing that I would like to discuss about family relations is that overpopulation, according to More, is a just cause of war." And so on. Can you hear that student sneering at me, in this opening? What he is saying is something like "you ask for a meaningless paper, I give you a meaningless paper." He knows that he has no audience except me. He knows that I don't want to read his summary of family relations in *Utopia,* and he knows that I know that he therefore has no rhetorical purpose. Because he has not been led to see a question which he considers worth answering, or an audience that could possibly care one way or the other, the paper is worse than no paper at all, even though it has no grammatical or spelling errors and is organized right down the line, one, two, three.

8   An extreme case, you may say. Most of us would never allow ourselves that kind of empty fencing. Perhaps. But if some carefree foundation is willing to finance a statistical study, I'm willing to wager a month's salary that we'd find at least half of the suggested topics in our freshman texts as pointless as mine was. And we'd find a good deal more than half of the discussions, of grammar, punctuation, spelling, and style totally divorced from any notion that rhetorical purpose to some degree controls all such matters. We can offer objective descriptions of levels of usage from now until graduation, but unless the student discovers a desire to say something to somebody and learns to control his diction for a purpose, we've gained very little. I once gave an assignment asking students to describe the same classroom in three different statements, one for each level of usage. They were obedient, but the only ones who got anything from the assignment were those who intuitively imported the rhetorical instructions I had overlooked—such purposes as "Make fun of your scholarly surroundings by describing this classroom in extremely elevated style" or "Imagine a kid from the slums accidentally trapped in these surroundings and forced to write a description of this room." A little thought might have shown me how to give the whole assignment some human point, and therefore some educative value.

9   A complete and pedantic divorce of writing from human purposes is revealed in a recent publication of the Educational Testing Service, called "Factors in Judgments of Writing Ability." In order to isolate those factors which affect differences in grading standards, ETS set six groups of readers—businessmen, writers and editors, lawyers, and teachers of English, social science, and natural science—to reading the same batch of papers. Then ETS did a hundred-page "factor analysis" of the amount of agreement and disagreement, and of the elements which different kinds of graders emphasized. The authors of the report express a certain amount of shock at the discovery that the median correlation was only .31 and that 94% of the papers received either 7, 8 or 9 of the 9 possible grades.

10   But what *could* they have expected? In the first place, the students were given no purpose and no audience when the topics were assigned. And then

all these editors and businessmen and academics were asked to judge the papers in a complete vacuum, using only whatever intuitive standards they cared to use. I'm surprised that there was any correlation at all. Lacking instructions, some of the students undoubtedly wrote polemical essays, suitable for the popular press; others no doubt imagined an audience, say, of *Reader's Digest* readers; and others wrote with the English teachers as implied audience. An occasional student with real philosophical bent would no doubt do a careful analysis of the pros and cons of the topic assigned. This would be graded low, of course, by the magazine editors, even though they would have graded it high if asked to judge it as a speculative contribution to the analysis of the problem. Similarly, a creative student who has been getting As for his personal essays would write an amusing, colorful piece, graded "F" by all the social scientists present, though they would have graded it high if asked to judge it for what it was.

11   One might as well assemble a group of citizens to judge students' capacity to throw balls, say, without telling the students or the graders whether altitude, speed, accuracy, or form was to be judged. The judges would be drawn from football coaches, jai alai experts, lawyers, and English teachers, and asked to apply whatever standards they intuitively apply to ball throwing. Then we could express astonishment that the judgments did not correlate very well, and we could do a factor analysis to discover, lo and behold, that some graders concentrated on altitude, some on speed, some on accuracy, some on form—and the English teachers were simply confused.

12   One effective way to combat the pedantic stance is to arrange for weekly confrontations of groups of students over their own papers. We have done far too little experimenting with arrangements for providing a genuine audience in this way. Short of such developments, it remains true that a good teacher can convince his students that he is a true audience, if his comments on the papers show that some part of dialogue is taking place. As Jacques Barzun says in *Teacher in America*, students should be made to feel that unless they have said something to someone, they have failed; to bore the teacher is a worse form of failure than to anger him. From this point of view we can see that the charts of grading symbols that mar even the best freshman texts are not the innocent time savers that we pretend. Plausible as it may seem to arrange for more corrections with less time, they inevitably reduce the student's sense of purpose in writing. When he sees innumerable W13s and P19s in the margin, he cannot possibly feel that the art of persuasion is as important to his instructor as when he reads personal comments, however few.

13   The first perversion, then, springs from ignoring the audience or over-reliance on the "pure" subject, whatever that could be. The second, which might be called the **advertiser's stance**, comes from *under*valuing the subject and overvaluing pure effect: how to win friends and influence people.

14   Some of our best freshman texts—Sheridan Baker's *The Practical Stylist*, for example—allow themselves on occasion to suggest that to be controversial or argumentative, to stir up an audience, is an end in itself. Sharpen the controversial edge, one of them says, and the clear implication is that one should do so even if the truth of the subject is honed off in the process. This perversion is probably in the long run a more serious threat in our society than the danger of ignoring the audience. In the time of audience-reaction meters and pre-tested plays and novels, it is not easy to convince students of the old Platonic truth that good persuasion is honest persuasion, or even of the old Aristotelian truth that the good rhetorician must be master of his subject, no matter how dishonest he may decide ultimately to be. Having told them that good writers always to some degree accommodate their arguments to the audience, [a teacher must] explain the difference between justified accommodation—say changing *point one* to the final position—and the kind of accommodation that fills our popular magazines, in which the very substance of what is said is accommodated to some preconception of what will sell.

15   At a dinner about a month ago I sat between the wife of a famous civil rights lawyer and an advertising consultant. "I saw the article on your book yesterday in the Daily News," she said to me, "but I didn't even finish it. The title of your book scared me off. Why did you ever choose such a terrible title? Nobody would buy a book with a title like that." The man on my right, whom I'll call Mr. Kinches, overhearing my feeble reply, plunged into a conversation with her, over my torn and bleeding body. "Now with my *last* book," he said, "I listed 20 possible titles and then tested them out on 400 businessmen. The one I chose was voted for by 90 percent of the businessmen." "That's what I was just saying to Mr. Booth," she said. "A book title ought to grab you, and *rhetoric* is not going to grab anybody." "Right," he said. "My *last* book sold 50,000 copies already; I don't know how this one will do, but I polled 200 businessmen on the table of contents, and . . ."

16   At one point I did manage to ask him whether the title he chose really fit the book. "Not quite as well as one or two of the others," he admitted, "but that doesn't matter, you know. If the book is designed right, so that the first chapter pulls them in, and you *keep* 'em in, who's going to gripe about a little inaccuracy in the title?"

17   Well, rhetoric is the art of persuading, not the art of seeming to persuade by giving everything away at the start. It presupposes that one has a purpose concerning a subject which itself cannot be fundamentally modified by the desire to persuade. If Edmund Burke had decided that he could win more votes in Parliament by choosing the other side—as he most certainly could have done—we would hardly hail this party-switch as a master stroke of rhetoric. If Churchill had offered the British "peace in our time," with some laughs thrown in, because opinion polls had shown that more Britishers were "grabbed" by these than by blood, sweat, and tears, we could hardly call his decision a sign of rhetorical skill.

18   One could easily discover other perversions of the rhetorician's balance—most obviously what might be called the **entertainer's stance**—the willingness to sacrifice substance to personality and charm. I admire Walker Gibson's efforts to startle us out of dry pedantry, but I know from experience that his exhortations to find and develop the speaker's voice can lead to empty colorfulness. A student once said to me, complaining about a high school teacher, "I soon learned that all I had to do to get an A was imitate Thurber."

19   But perhaps this is more than enough about the perversions. Balance itself is always harder to describe than the clumsy poses that result when it is destroyed. But we all experience the balance whenever we find an author who succeeds in changing our minds. He can do so only if he knows more about the subject than we do, and if he then engages us in the process of thinking—and feeling—it through. What makes the rhetoric of Milton and Burke and Churchill great is that each presents us with the spectacle of a man passionately involved in thinking an important question through, in the company of an audience. Though each of them did everything in his power to make his point persuasive, including a pervasive use of emotional appeals that have been falsely scorned by many a freshman composition text, none would have allowed himself the advertiser's stance; none would have polled the audience in advance to discover which position would get the votes. Nor is the highly individual personality that springs out at us from their speeches and essays present for the sake of selling itself. The rhetorical balance among speaker, audience, and argument is with all three men habitual, as we see if we look at their nonpolitical writings. Burke's work on the Sublime and Beautiful is a relatively unimpassioned philosophical treatise, but one finds there again a delicate balance: though the implied author of this work is a far different person, far less obtrusive, far more objective, than the man who later cried *sursum corda* to the British Parliament, he permeates with his philosophical personality his philosophical work. And though the signs of his awareness of his audience are far more subdued, they are still here: every effort is made to involve the *proper* audience, the audience of philosophical minds, in a fundamentally interesting inquiry, and to lead them through to the end. In short, because he was a man engaged with men in the effort to solve a human problem, one could never call what he wrote dull, however difficult or abstruse.

20   Now obviously the habit of seeking this balance is not the only thing we have to teach under the heading of rhetoric. But I think that everything worth teaching under that heading finds its justification finally in that balance. Much of what is now considered irrelevant or dull can, in fact, be brought to life when teachers and students know what they are seeking. Churchill reports that the most valuable training he ever received in rhetoric was in the diagramming of sentences. Think of it! Yet the diagramming of a sentence, regardless of the grammatical system, can be a live subject as soon as one

asks not simply "How is this sentence put together?" but rather "Why is it put together in this way?" or "Could the rhetorical balance and hence the desired persuasion be better achieved by writing it differently?"

21   As a nation we are reputed to write very badly. As a nation, I would say, we are more inclined to the perversions of rhetoric than to the rhetorical balance. Regardless of what we do about this or that course in the curriculum, our mandate would seem to be, then, to lead more of our students than we now do to care about and practice the true arts of persuasion.

For Further Thinking

1. What does Booth achieve with the opening anecdote?
2. Where do you feel Booth first states his thesis?
3. What rhetorical method of elaboration is anticipated in the paragraph following his thesis statement?
4. Prepare a diagram or outline of this essay in which you break it into main sections. How do we recognize transitions between sections?
5. From your own experience as a writer, do you think Booth's definition makes sense? Explain.

Looking Back and Ahead

1. Can you find essays, or portions of essays, in the *Reader* that illustrate degrees of the pedant's stance, the advertiser's stance, and the entertainer's stance? You might wish to range beyond the *Reader* as well to look for other examples.
2. Are there two or three selections in the *Reader* that you would hold up as fine examples of a rhetorical stance achieved as Booth defines it? Explain your choices.

For Further Reading

"Wayne C. Booth." The Literature, Arts, and Medicine Database. Produced and maintained by the Hippocrates Project, New York University School of Medicine. April 2003 <http://endeavor.med.nyu.edu/lit-med/lit-med-db/webdocs/webdescrips/booth1355-des-.html>. For information on the critic's major work *The Company We Keep: An Ethics of Fiction* (1988).

Burton, Professor Gideon O. "The Forest of Rhetoric." Brigham Young University. April 2003 <http://rhetoric.byu.edu/>. An award-winning online guide to the terms, patterns, and purposes of rhetoric as it has been taught and practised for the past 2000 years. It also contains an excellent references list.

European Schoolnet. April 2003 <http://eun.org/eun.org2/>. How schools in Sweden approach the teaching of rhetoric as a holistic method for developing civic awareness locally and globally. Search for "teaching civics."

Hawk, Byron. List of journals in rhetoric and composition. George Mason University. April 2003 <http://mason.gmu.edu/~bhawk/journals/links.html>. This site links you to recent and past ideas about rhetorical learning.

Online Writers Lab (OWL). Purdue University. April 2003 <http://rc.english.purdue.edu/teaching.html>. One of the most popular and respected online resources for help with essay writing. Select "Writing Lab."

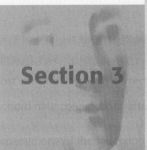

Section 3

Tomorrow and Tomorrow

As a post-secondary student, you are vitally engaged in preparing for your future—most obviously, for your career, but surely no less for your role as a person and citizen. Some of us, young and old, would agree that today's younger generation, on the whole, has encountered different challenges and complexities than those who graduated in the 1960s and 70s, though today's adolescents have been spared race riots, segregation, Vietnam, police spying on Canadian campuses, Watergate, and the FLQ October Crisis. Certainly it is often felt that tomorrow's problems loom as enormous. A Southam News feature of February 2001 consulted a panel of philosophers, ethicists, and religious studies professors for their views of the most pressing issues facing humanity in the next 10 years. The panel identified major concerns related to the environment, computers, genetic engineering, nuclear arms, and nationalism, along with rising social dilemmas—an increasing gap between rich and poor, immoderate work patterns, and a perceived increase in callousness. They all pointed, as well, to an issue we discussed in our introduction to Section 2 of this *Reader*, colliding values and beliefs: "With globalism and immigration bringing cultures closer together, whose ethical system will we follow?"[14]

A number of such concerns were raised by writers in the previous section of the *Reader*, but in this section, which deals again with the main topics we have visited in Sections 1 and 2, you will find writers using language specifically to weigh choices, to assert their own values, and in some cases to propose solutions. Rhetorically, the following selections relate to the aims and methods discussed under Argumentation and Persuasion, so it would be a good idea to review that part of the *Rhetoric* in conjunction with Section 3 of the *Reader*. In Section 3, you will find a number of articles pursuing opposed or significantly divergent tacks. For example, euthanasia is justified in one essay, rejected in the next. Again, you will not find simple or incontestable answers—but you will, most likely, come to appreciate the importance of argumentative skills in preparing for a future of complexity and challenge. Argumentation also encourages tolerance and moderation toward views you may ultimately oppose. It encourages fair-mindedness: that is, you are urged to consider other ways of looking at issues, and to respect those ways, before settling on your own. In a society of varied beliefs, this attitude of tolerance is very important, but equally important is the skill to validate your own views amidst a cluster of contradictory outlooks. And if those views are to be put into effective operation, it is crucial that you express them clearly, thoroughly, and convincingly. The word "argumentation" may seem to connote conflict and opposition, but may be more usefully conceived as a technique toward reconciliation. Public debate helps identify various worthwhile ideas, from which, with effort, consensus may eventually be achieved. For all the divisions and tensions within Canada, our country was founded and has survived—in the face of numerous obstacles—as the result of key agreements attained through public debate. Your careful consideration of the divergent opinions expressed in the following section may well lead you to formulate new thoughts and insights based on a synthesis of various different positions.

Crucial to your use of argumentation is an awareness of the major role of language itself in reinforcing our assumptions. To signal this importance, we have placed two selections on language at the end of the section. The final essay, by George Orwell, challenges us to consider the intimate relationship between language, thinking, and social well-being. Accepting Orwell's thesis on the power of language to shape reality, economist David Smith has questioned excess use of military metaphors in argumentation. "Suppose instead of thinking about argument in terms of war," he says, "we were to think of argument as a pleasing, graceful dance."[15] We may take heart that for all the challenges ahead, there is no shortage of creative will to use language knowingly and wisely. We hope you grow pleasantly surprised to find that a heightened appreciation of language and its effects contributes to all spheres of your own life.

[14] Douglas Todd, "Our Top 10 Moral Issues," *Edmonton Journal* 11 February 2001, E5.

[15] David Smith, "Burying the Hatchet in Language," *Peace Magazine* August 1977, reproduced in *Reader's Choice*, 3rd Can. ed. Eds. Kim Flachmann, Michael Flachmann, and Alexandra MacLennan (Scarborough: Prentice Hall, 2000) 540–44.

William Butler Yeats Born and raised in Dublin (1865–1939), William Butler Yeats based many of his poems on Irish legends and folklore as well as on classical mythology. Like Carl Jung, Yeats studied and respected metaphysical subjects that, ironically, now would be called New Age. He held to a common folk belief that history unfolds in 2000-year cycles. The Classical Age was marked by the union of the god Zeus in the form of a swan and a human being, Leda. The Christian Age, ending the Classical, began with the union of the Holy Spirit as a dove and the Virgin Mary. According to this timetable, the Christian Age is already over—but presumably, in Yeats's vision, a 2000-year order of new life is on its way. Some dismiss Yeats's ideas as those of a crank, though few would deny the power and skill of his poetry. In fact, most critics rank him as among the very finest poets of the twentieth century. And for some, his visions and metaphysical insights are equally profound. Many writers have drawn from this poem for their own novels, poems, and essays.

The Second Coming

Turning and turning in the widening gyre
The falcon cannot hear the falconer;
Things fall apart; the centre cannot hold;
Mere anarchy is loosed upon the world,
5   The blood-dimmed tide is loosed, and everywhere
The ceremony of innocence is drowned;
The best lack all conviction, while the worst
Are full of passionate intensity.

Surely some revelation is at hand;
10 Surely the Second Coming is at hand.
The Second Coming! Hardly are those words out
When a vast image out of *Spiritus Mundi*
Troubles my sight; somewhere in sands of the desert
A shape with lion body and the head of a man,
15 A gaze blank and pitiless as the sun,
Is moving its slow thighs, while all about it
Reel shadows of the indignant desert birds.
The darkness drops again; but now I know
That twenty centuries of stony sleep
20 Were vexed to nightmare by a rocking cradle,
And what rough beast, its hour come round at last,
Slouches towards Bethlehem to be born?

Pierre Elliott Trudeau In 1969, Beatle John Lennon met the newly elected Canadian Prime Minister and declared, "If all politicians were like Pierre Trudeau there would be world peace." Trudeau was that rarest of politicians—one who could stand beside the world's biggest rock star and appear every bit as charismatic. Ironically, he did not have political career aspirations, joining the Liberal Party only at the appeal of incumbent leader Lester Pearson, who was looking to build a team of French Canadians. From there Trudeau somehow slipped into leadership of the party, then—on the promise of a "Just Society"—ascended to 24 Sussex Drive.

Champion of a unified, strongly centralized Canada, Trudeau was known as a man of intellect and reason over emotion—but he had the power to inspire great passions. He delivered one of his most inspirational speeches in 1980, six days before the first Quebec referendum on separating from Canada, when he defended a national bicultural heritage against Premier René Lévesque's suggestion that only full-blood Francophones are Quebecers. However, a year earlier, losing the election of 1979, Trudeau appeared finished in politics, but six months later returned with a majority government. Altogether, he served as prime minister for 15 years, one of the longest serving heads of state in the Western world.

In his memoirs Trudeau wrote, "A lot of people want to go back to the basics sometimes, to find their bearings. For me, a good way to do that is to get into nature by a canoe." His relationship with nature, though, had a haunting finale. The one event he did not appear ready to endure was the loss of his son Michel, swept by an avalanche into Kokanee Lake near Nelson, British Columbia. A year later Trudeau was hospitalized with pneumonia; he died on September 28, 2000, at age 81. Many believe the son's death hastened his own.

See the Appendix at the end of the *Reader*, Part I (p. 253), for more support for this reading. This support may particularly benefit you if English is not your first language.

The Ascetic[1] in a Canoe

1   I would not know how to instil a taste for adventure in those who have not acquired it. (Anyway, who can ever prove the necessity for the gypsy life?) And yet there are people who suddenly tear themselves away from their comfortable existence and, using the energy of their bodies as an example to their brains, apply themselves to the discovery of unsuspected pleasures and places.

2   I would like to point out to these people a type of labour from which they are certain to profit: an expedition by canoe.

3   I do not just mean "canoeing." Not that I wish to disparage that pastime, which is worth more than many another. But, looked at closely, there is perhaps only a difference of money between the canoeists of Lafontaine Park and those who dare to cross a lake, make a portage, spend a night in a tent and return exhausted, always in the care of a fatherly guide—a brief interlude momentarily interrupting the normal course of digestion.

4   A canoeing expedition, which demands much more than that, is also much more rewarding.

5   It involves a starting rather than a parting. Although it assumes the breaking of ties, its purpose is not to destroy the past, but to lay a foundation for the future. From now on, every living act will be built on this step, which will serve as a base long after the return of the expedition . . . and until the next one.

6   What is essential at the beginning is the resolve to reach the saturation point. Ideally, the trip should end only when the members are making no further progress within themselves. They should not be fooled, though, by a period of boredom, weariness or disgust; that is not the end, but the last obstacle before it. Let saturation be serene!

7   So you must paddle for days, or weeks, or perhaps months on end. My friends and I were obliged, on pain of death, to do more than a thousand miles by canoe, from Montreal to Hudson Bay. But let no one be deterred by a short-age of time. A more intense pace can compensate for a shorter trip.

8   What sets a canoeing expedition apart is that it purifies you more rapidly and inescapably than any other. Travel a thousand miles by train and you are a brute; pedal five hundred on a bicycle and you remain basically a bourgeois; paddle a hundred in a canoe and you are already a child of nature.

9   For it is a condition of such a trip that you entrust yourself, stripped of your worldly goods, to nature. Canoe and paddle, blanket and knife, salt pork and flour, fishing rod and rifle; that is about the extent of your wealth. To remove all the useless material baggage from a man's heritage is, at the same time, to free his mind from petty preoccupations, calculations and memories.

10   On the other hand, what fabulous and undeveloped mines are to be found in nature, friendship and oneself! The paddler has no choice but to draw every-thing from them. Later, forgetting that this habit was adopted under duress, he will be astonished to find so many resources within himself.

11   Nevertheless, he will have returned a more ardent believer from a time when religion, like everything else, became simple. The impossibility of scandal creates a new morality, and prayer becomes a friendly chiding of the divinity, who has again become part of our everyday affairs. (My friend Guy Viau could say about our adventure, "We got along very well with God, who is a damn good sport. Only once did we threaten to break off diplomatic relations if he continued to rain on us. But we were joking. We would never have done so, and well he knew it. So he continued to rain on us.")

12   The canoe is also a school of friendship. You learn that your best friend is not a rifle, but someone who shares a night's sleep with you after ten hours of pad-dling at the other end of a canoe. Let's say that you have to be lined upon a rapid and it's your turn to stay in the canoe and guide it. You watch your friend stumbling over logs, sliding on rocks, sticking in gumbo, tearing the skin on his legs and drinking water for which he does not thirst, yet never letting go of the rope; meanwhile, safely in the middle of the cataract, you spray your hauler with a stream of derision. When this same man has also fed you exactly half his catch, and has made a double portage because of your injury, you can boast of having a friend for life, and one who knows you well.

13   How does the trip affect your personality? Allow me to make a fine distinc-tion, and I would say that you return not so much a man who reasons more, but a more reasonable man. For, throughout this time, your mind has learned to

exercise itself in the working conditions which nature intended. Its primordial role has been to sustain the body in a struggle against a powerful universe. A good camper knows that it is more important to be ingenious than to be a genius. And conversely, the body, by demonstrating the true meaning of sensual pleasure, has been of service to the mind. You feel the beauty of animal pleasure when you draw a deep breath of rich morning air right through your body, which has been carried by the cold night, curled up like an unborn child. How can you describe the feeling which wells up in the heart and stomach as the canoe finally rides up on the shore of the campsite after a long day of plunging your paddle into rain-swept waters? Purely physical is the joy which the fire spreads through the palms of your hands and the soles of your feet while your chattering mouth belches the poisonous cold. The pleasurable torpor of such a moment is perhaps not too different from what the mystics of the East are seeking. At least it has allowed me to taste what one respected gentleman used to call the joys of hard living.

14   Make no mistake, these joys are exclusively physical. They have nothing to do with the satisfaction of the mind when it imposes unwelcome work on the body, a satisfaction, moreover, which is often mixed with pride, and which the body never fails to avenge. During a very long and exhausting portage, I have sometimes felt my reason defeated, and shamefully fleeing, while my legs and shoulders carried bravely on. The mumbled verses which marked the rhythm of my steps at the beginning had become brutal grunts of "uh! uh! uh!" There was nothing aesthetic in that animal search for the bright clearing which always marks the end of a portage.

15   I do not want you to think that the mind is subjected to a healthy discipline merely by worrying about simplistic problems. I only wish to remind you of that principle of logic which states that valid conclusions do not generally follow from false premises. Now, in a canoe, where these premises are based on nature in its original state (rather than on books, ideas and habits of uncertain value), the mind conforms to that higher wisdom which we call natural philosophy; later, that healthy methodology and acquired humility will be useful in confronting mystical and spiritual questions.

16   I know a man whose school could never teach him patriotism, but who acquired that virtue when he felt in his bones the vastness of his land, and the greatness of those who founded it.

Notes

1. *Ascetic:* In the early Christian church, one who renounced social life and comfort for solitude, self-mortification, and religious devotion. One who leads a very austere and self-denying life (*Funk and Wagnall's Standard Dictionary*).

For Further Thinking

1. The film *Black Robe*, based on the novel by Brian Moore, presents an ascetic priest who practises true self-flagellation, renounces the flesh, embodies austerity. Trudeau loved expensive clothes and fancy sports cars. He was used to money, the good life of Upper Outremont, Montreal. His famous red rose in the buttonhole was hardly a symbol of denial. So how seriously should we take his self-depiction as an ascetic?

2. Have you had any experience of canoeing or perhaps of canoe-tripping? If so, do you share Trudeau's sense of its value? Explain. Does Trudeau commit logical fallacies?

3. Does this essay contain an acceptable balance of support for its points? Explain.

4. Trudeau, like Wayne Booth (p. 144), uses "he," "him," and "a man," presumably as inclusive of men and woman. Despite their generation, does such narrowness hurt their claims?

Looking Back and Ahead

1. Educated in Jesuit schools, Trudeau received a classical education increasingly rare in Canada. Along with Catholic theology, he was steeped in rhetoric, debate, and ideas—such as those of Plato. Read "Allegory of the Cave" (p. 119). Is Trudeau's essay stylistically akin to Plato's in any important sense? Explain.

2. Refer to Wayne C. Booth's essay "The Rhetorical Stance" (p. 144). Trudeau was 24 when he wrote this essay. Does his "stance" pass the Booth test, or is there something a little faulty about it somewhere? Explain.

3. Refer to Emma Lee Warrior's "White Breast Flats" (p. 6). Contrast her relationship with nature with Trudeau's, or at least with the one Trudeau represents here as his (the ascetic). What do you think she would say to his way of experiencing nature?

4. Contrast the style of this essay to that of Trudeau's *Memoirs*, written when he was 74. What are the notable differences? Which do you prefer and why?

For Further Reading

Christiano, Kevin J. *Pierre Elliott Trudeau: Reason Before Passion*. Toronto: ECW, 1994.

Cohen, Andrew, and J.L. Granatstein, eds. *Trudeau's Shadow: The Life and Legacy of Pierre Elliott Trudeau*. Toronto: Random House, 1998. See in particular the essay "A Child of Nature" in which James Raffan explores Trudeau's canoe identity: "For some the image was a cynically shallow and clichéd attention-grabber; for others the [paddling] may have signified something more . . ."

Johnson, Pauline. "The Song My Paddle Sings." Online text. Digital Library, University of Toronto. April 2003 <http://eir.library.utoronto.ca/rpo/display/poem1096.html>. This poem by E. Pauline Johnson was a cornerstone of the nineteenth-century myth of the Canadian wilds.

Maclean's. "Trudeau: Special Commemorative Edition." October 2000.

Ockerbloom, Mary Mark, editor. "Celebration of Women Writers Project." In collaboration with the On-line Books Page, University of Pennsylvania. See "Pauline Johnson" for links to information about her. April 2003 <http://digital.library.upenn.edu/women/>.

O'Malley, Martin. "One of Our Best and Brightest: Pierre Elliott Trudeau Indepth." April 2003 <http://cbc.ca/news/indepth/trudeau/>. CBC's *Indepth* features a documentary on the life of Trudeau. With a chronology of Trudeau's life, audio and video clips, tributes, photos, archives, headlines, and goodbyes, this site gives a stellar impression of Canada's most influential leader.

Trudeau, Pierre Elliott. *Against the Current: Selected Writings, 1939–1996.* Ed. Gérard Pelletier. Toronto: McClelland & Stewart, 1996.

——————. *Memoirs.* Toronto: McClelland & Stewart, 1993.

Kim Pittaway Responding to anthropologist Helen Fisher's book *The First Sex: The Natural Talents of Women and How They Are Changing the World*, Pittaway expresses dissatisfaction with the author's thesis. She feels that Fisher is really saying, "The future belongs to women! Let's honour our foremothers and kick some testosterone butt." Fisher emphasizes that men's and women's brains have developed differently, with women superior at synthesis or "web thinking," skills demanded by the future. Pittaway argues that the next generation of women has moved beyond a confrontational battle-of-the-sexes approach, which she says "takes us backward instead of forward, to a place where we can only conceive of winning if someone else loses. Our foremothers didn't work to get a place at the table so that they could make the boys eat in the kitchen." Pittaway's essay represents a form of persuasive analysis. In preparing to read this selection, you might wish to review our discussion of "Critical Analysis" in Chapter 10 of the *Rhetoric*.

For more support for this reading, visit the website for Athabasca University's introductory composition course at <**www.athabascau.ca/courses/engl/255/**>. Under "Supplementary Resources," see " If English Is Not Your First Language" and "Language Support for Selected Readings."

Crystal Balls

1   It was close to midnight on a New Brunswick New Year's Eve. The eve of a new decade, 1979. An Oscar Peterson LP spun on the turntable, but no one could hear it: the room was filled with laughter, cigarette smoke and the clink of glasses and plates piled high with Mom's lasagna. Then Dad posed the question: not the usual "What are your resolutions?"—too boring—but "What will your life be like in 2000?" I don't remember a single word uttered by any of my parents' guests because I was too busy trying to figure out what I was going to say. Finally, my turn came—and Dad skipped right over me. It was my mom who noticed me giving him the evil teenage eye. "Tom, Tom, wait a minute—you missed Kim," she said. And so I made my predictions: in the year 2000, I'd be 35 (more than twice my age at the time and inconceivably distant to my 15-year-old brain). I wouldn't be living in Moncton—I'd be someplace big, maybe Halifax. I'd be a journalist or a movie director. And I'd be married with kids.

2   Halifax lost out to Toronto. The only movie directing I do is when I pause the VCR to replenish the chip bowl, and the husband and kids . . . . [L]et's just say news reports on efforts to extend ovarian viability catch my eye and my no-blind-dates rule has been rescinded. I got "journalist" and "35" right though.

3   Twenty years later, we're heading into the most-hyped New Year's Eve ever. And the question "Where will we be?" is echoing in my head.

4   What does the future hold for Canadian women? Peering into the new millennium, I'm tempted to be a "woman first" cheerleader. Part of me wants to shout "The future belongs to women! Let's honour our foremothers and kick some testosterone butt."

5   I wouldn't be alone, either. In her new book *The First Sex: The Natural Talents of Women and How They Are Changing the World,* anthropologist Helen Fisher argues that the future does indeed belong to women: that men's and women's brains have developed differently; that we are better at "synthesis" or "web thinking"—gathering facts and insights from a wide range of sources and experiences—while men are stuck with one-step-at-a-time linear thinking and a more limited view. Basically, this means women can listen to the radio traffic report, feed the cat and make breakfast all at the same time, while the guys tend to do one thing at a time. Try asking a man a question while he's reading the newspaper, says Fisher, and you'll get a firsthand demonstration of one-track brains. Women also have better language and people skills and more acute senses, and all of that means tomorrow is ours for the asking.

6   I couldn't get past the first chapter of Fisher's book. The fact is, I don't want the future to belong to women. That sort of ownership bothers me. For one thing, it sounds too much like the flip side of the lines used to keep women in their place in the past. "Women make excellent workers when they have their jobs cut out for them, but . . . they lack initiative in finding work themselves," said a bulletin issued in 1943 to male supervisors in the transportation industry. "Be tactful when issuing instructions or in making criticisms. Women can't shrug off harsh words the way men do," it continued. I have the reprint pinned to my bulletin board as a reminder of how far we've come. (I harbour a special affection for management tip No. 3: "General experience indicates that 'husky' girls—those who are just a little on the heavy side—are more even-tempered and efficient than their underweight sisters.") I'm sure the women in my family—and probably yours too—heard a variation on those lines.

7   I think of my mother and grandmothers as trailblazers, though I'm sure they'd never have described themselves that way. Catherine Gillis, my mother's mother, studied at Halifax's Mount Saint Vincent University and worked with my grandfather in every business he ever ran. Edna Pittaway, my father's mother, was a working mom long before the phrase was coined: she worked in a fac-

tory soldering knick-knacks. My mother, Marie, just retired after 40 years as a nurse and a teacher, two stereotypical pursuits—but not so stereotypically, she brought home a paycheque that always equalled my dad's.

8   My grandmothers saw the working world change from a time when women were hired only because the men were off fighting a war to an age when their granddaughters (my sister and me and our cousins) could pick and choose from a world of options. In my mother's lifetime, the advances can be seen in the slogans used to fight for change: "Equal pay for work of equal value." "Freedom of choice," "No means no"—phrases that defined then-revolutionary ways of thinking about what it means to be female.

9   But I'm not ready to add "The future belongs to women" to the list. It offers a limited view of what the possibilities really are and takes us backward instead of forward, to a place where we can only conceive of winning if someone else loses. Our foremothers didn't work to get a place at the table so that they could make the boys eat in the kitchen.

10   The possibilities of the future are so much broader than a women-first focus allows. As I look into the future, I'm taking my cue from a friend who calls me on it every time I start a sentence with a gender-based generalization, such as "Men always . . ." or "Women tend to. . .".

11   She's in her 20s, and while the gap in our ages is small, it's big enough that her view of the world is different from the one I grew up with. She, like many women her age, doesn't define her world in gender terms.

12   Sure, she sees the differences, but she's more likely to chock them up to individual rather than gender attributes. She doesn't seem to feel the need to fight to be heard—perhaps because she's grown up entitled to speak.

13   She's aware that rich white guys still make up the lion's share of the world's business and political leaders. She knows that paycheques aren't genderless. But she's figured out that the next stage of the battle of the sexes, to use that quaintest of terms, isn't about winning and losing, top and bottom; it's about being who you were meant to be in a world that celebrates each individual's unique gifts. After all, who wants to be on top all of the time?

14 This New Year's Eve, after I've checked my supply of spring water, batteries, canned food and cash, I'll pose a question to my co-celebrants: "What will your life be like in 2020?" Sure, 2020 is only a baby step into the new millennium, but predictions are tricky and I'm reluctant to push past the 20-year frontier. There will be laughter, the clinking of glasses and even the stray whiff of cigarette smoke coming from the porch, as we take our turns peering into the future. And I promise not to skip over my dad when it's his turn to speak.

15   What will my life be like in 2020? I think I might be in Halifax. Directing a movie. And getting ready for the birth of my first child. Where will you be?

For Further Thinking

1. Can you point to an era or a culture where equality existed or exists between the sexes? Will the patriarchy, if it gives way entirely, will be replaced by a matriarchy?

2. Is Pittaway devising her own form of political correctness; that is, if women *are* demonstrably better than men at certain key functions, should we deny this evidence only because it offends our notions of equality or hopes for the status quo future?

3. What is your attitude to the so-called battle of the sexes? Do you feel your attitude on this topic differs significantly from that of your parents, friends, and/or your children?

4. Are differences in behaviour and abilities between the sexes a matter of nature or nurture? Explain your view.

5. Has feminism accomplished its goals, as Pittaway suggests? Are we ready for a society that is "gender blind"?

Looking Back and Ahead

1. Is Lois's experience in Alice Munro's "Thanks for the Ride" (p. 62) specific to young women of her time and place only? If sexism explains part of Lois's problem, has the matter been resolved?

2. How does Pittaway's conception of time compare or contrast to that of other authors in our *Reader*? Is the future better, worse, or static?

For Further Reading

Cary, Sylvia. "The Big Bash." *Men's Fitness* 14. 10 (Oct. 1, 1998) 78. This article looks at the potential harm that may come from male-bashing jokes.

Farrell, Warren. "Santee, Columbine . . .: Why Boys Are the Way They Are." Vekline, managed by Kathryn and William Van Vechten. April 2003 <http://www.consciousloving.com>. The author argues that boys are raised to consider themselves disposable for the good of society, and the unforeseen effects that belief can have. To find Farrell's essay, search under "Relationship Articles."

Fisher, Helen. *The First Sex: The Natural Talents of Women and How They Are Changing the World*. New York: Random House, 1999.

Newitz, Annalee. "Myth of the Million Man March." *Bad Subjects: Political Education for Everyday Life* 23 (Dec. 1995). April 2003 <http://eserver.org/bs/>. Founded in 1992 at the University of California at Berkeley, *Bad Subjects* is a nonprofit collective that promotes political debate and works toward changing people's thinking at the grassroots level. This article in the organization's magazine examines how various social movements, including men's and women's, create power switches, without challenging the underlying assumption of hierarchical power.

Sommers, Christina Hoff. *Who Stole Feminism? How Women Have Betrayed Women*. New York: Simon and Schuster, 1994. Sommers' book argues that "gender" feminists (those who regard men as enemies) have co-opted the feminist movement from the original feminists who wanted profound and lasting equality.

Reviews of *Who Stole Feminism?* by Christina Hoff Sommers:

Favourable:

Wood, Garth. "Review: *Who Stole Feminism: How Women Have Betrayed Women.*" 21 June
    1994. April 2003 <http://www.menweb.org/throop/books/sommers/
    gwood-sommers.html>.

A shorter version of this online review also appeared in the magazine *Balance: The
    Inclusive Vision of Gender Equality*. Online magazine. July 1994. Kate Orman, editor.
    May 2003 <http://www.geocities.com/Athens/Forum/8305/index.html>.

Unfavourable:

Flanders, Laura. "The 'Stolen Feminism' Hoax: Anti-Feminist Attack Based on Error-Filled
    Anecdotes." Online. Fairness and Accuracy in Reporting. April 2003
    <http://www.fair.org/extra/9409/stolen-feminism-hoax.html>. This article appears
    on the website of FAIR (Fairness and Accuracy in Reporting), a U.S. national media-
    watch group.

Bharati Mukherjee Bharati Mukherjee was born in Calcutta, India, in 1940 to a wealthy family. At eight years of age, she moved to England with her family for nearly four years, and has travelled extensively since then. Mukherjee holds a B.A. from the University of Calcutta, an M.A. from the University of Baroda, an M.F.A. in Creative Writing and a Ph.D., both from the University of Iowa. She has been a literature professor in both Canada and the United States and a prominent commentator on post-colonial studies.

In "The Tenant," Mukherjee continues to explore her central themes of the individual's search for personal and cultural identity in a multicultural international society. Maya, like many of Mukherjee's characters, struggles with the complexities of migration, heritage, and cultural alienation in the United States. Mukherjee, who lived in Canada for a brief period, has always maintained that she found the United States less racist than Canada. Mukherjee now describes herself as an "American" and resists the notion of a "hyphenated identity." Many of her views on cultural identity are considered both progressive and regressive, but almost always controversial.

"The Tenant" is from Mukherjee's story collection *The Middleman and Other Stories* (1988), which won the National Book Critics Circle Award.

The Tenant

1   Maya Sanyal has been in Cedar Falls, Iowa, less than two weeks. She's come, books and clothes and one armchair rattling in the smallest truck that U-Haul would rent her, from New Jersey. Before that she was in North Carolina. Before that, Calcutta, India. Every place has something to give. She is sitting at the kitchen table with Fran drinking bourbon for the first time in her life. Fran Johnson found her the furnished apartment and helped her settle in. Now she's brought a bottle of bourbon which gives her the right to stay and talk for a bit. She's breaking up with someone named Vern, a pharmacist. Vern's father is also

a pharmacist and owns a drugstore. Maya has seen Vern's father on TV twice already. The first time was on the local news when he spoke out against the selling of painkillers like Advil and Nuprin in supermarkets and gas stations. In the matter of painkillers, Maya is a universalist. The other time he was in a barbershop quartet. Vern gets along all right with his father. He likes the pharmacy business, as business goes, but he wants to go back to graduate school and learn to make films. Maya is drinking her first bourbon tonight because Vern left today for San Francisco State.

2   "I understand totally," Fran says. She teaches Utopian Fiction and a course in Women's Studies and worked hard to get Maya hired. Maya has a Ph.D. in Comparative Literature and will introduce writers like R.K. Narayan and Chinua Achebe to three sections of sophomores at the University of Northern Iowa. "A person has to leave home. Try out his wings."

3   Fran has to use the bathroom. "I don't feel abandoned." She pushes her chair away from the table. "Anyway it was a sex thing totally. We were good together. It'd be different if I'd loved him."

4   Maya tries to remember what's in the refrigerator. They need food. She hasn't been to the supermarket in over a week. She doesn't have a car yet and so she relies on a corner store—a longish walk—for milk, cereal, and frozen dinners. Someday these exigencies will show up as bad skin and collapsed muscle tone. No folly is ever lost. Maya pictures history as a net, the kind of safety net travelling trapeze artists of her childhood fell into when they were inattentive, or clumsy. Going to circuses in Calcutta with her father is what she remembers vividly. It is a banal memory, for her father, the owner of a steel company, is a complicated man.

5   Fran is out in the kitchen long enough for Maya to worry. They need food. Her mother believed in food. What is love, anger, inner peace, etc., her mother used to say, but the brain's biochemistry. Maya doesn't want to get into that, but she is glad she has enough stuff in the refrigerator to make an omelette. She realizes Indian women are supposed to be inventive with food, whip up exotic delights to tickle an American's palate, and she knows she should be meeting Fran's generosity and candor with some sort of bizarre and effortless countermove. If there's an exotic spice store in Cedar Falls or in neighboring Waterloo, she hasn't found it. She's looked in the phone book for common Indian names, especially Bengali, but hasn't yet struck up culinary intimacies. That will come— it always does. There's a six-pack in the fridge that her landlord, Ted Suminski, had put in because she'd be thirsty after unpacking. She was thirsty, but she doesn't drink beer. She probably should have asked him to come up and drink the beer. Except for Fran she hasn't had anyone over. Fran is more friendly and helpful than anyone Maya has known in the States since she came to North Carolina ten years ago, at nineteen. Fran is a Swede, and she is tall, with blue eyes. Her hair, however, is a dull, darkish brown.

6   "I don't think I can handle anything that heavy-duty," Fran says when she comes back to the room. She means the omelette. "I have to go home in any

case." She lives with her mother and her aunt, two women in their mid-seventies, in a drafty farmhouse. The farmhouse now has a computer store catty-corner from it. Maya's been to the farm. She's been shown photographs of the way the corner used to be. If land values ever rebound, Fran will be worth millions.

7   Before Fran leaves she says, "Has Rab Chatterji called you yet?"

8   "No." She remembers the name, a good, reliable Bengali name, from the first night's study of the phone book. Dr. Rabindra Chatterji teaches Physics.

9   "He called the English office just before I left." She takes car keys out of her pocketbook. She reknots her scarf. "I bet Indian men are more sensitive than Americans. Rab's a Brahmin, that's what people say."

10   A Chatterji has to be a Bengali Brahmin—last names give ancestral secrets away—but Brahminness seems to mean more to Fran than it does to Maya. She was born in 1954, six full years after India became independent. Her India was Nehru's India: a charged, progressive place.

11   "All Indian men are wife beaters," Maya says. She means it and doesn't mean it. "That's why I married an American." Fran knows about the divorce, but nothing else. Fran is on the Hiring, Tenure, and Reappointment Committee.

12   Maya sees Fran down the stairs and to the car which is parked in the back in the spot reserved for Maya's car, if she had owned one. It will take her several months to save enough to buy one. She always pays cash, never borrows. She tells herself she's still recovering from the U-Haul drive halfway across the country. Ted Suminski is in his kitchen watching the women. Maya waves to him because waving to him, acknowledging him in that way, makes him seem less creepy. He seems to live alone though a sign, THE SUMINSKIS, hangs from a metal horse's head in the front yard. Maya hasn't seen Mrs. Suminski. She hasn't seen any children either. Ted always looks lonely. When she comes back from campus, he's nearly always in the back, throwing darts or shooting baskets.

13   "What's he like?" Fran gestures with her head as she starts up her car. "You hear these stories."

14   Maya doesn't want to know the stories. She has signed a year's lease. She doesn't want complications. "He's all right. I keep out of his way."

15   "You know what I'm thinking? Of all the people in Cedar Falls, you're the one who could understand Vern best. His wanting to try out his wings, run away, stuff like that."

16   "Not really." Maya is not being modest. Fran is being impulsively democratic, lumping her wayward lover and Indian friend together as headstrong adventurers. For Fran, a utopian and feminist, borders don't count. Maya's taken some big risks, made a break with her parents' way. She's done things a woman from Ballygunge Park Road doesn't do, even in fantasies. She's not yet shared stories with Fran, apart from the divorce. She's told her nothing of men she picks up, the reputation she'd gained, before Cedar Falls, for "indiscretions." She has a job, equity, three friends she can count on for emergencies. She is an American citizen. But.

17   Fran's Brahmin calls her two nights later. On the phone he presents himself as Dr. Chatterji, not Rabindra or Rab. An old-fashioned Indian, she assumes. Her father still calls his closest friend, "Colonel." Dr. Chatterji asks her to tea on Sunday. She means to say no but hears herself saying, "Sunday? Fiveish? I'm not doing anything special this Sunday."

18   Outside, Ted Suminski is throwing darts into his garage door. The door has painted-on rings: orange, purple, pink. The bull's-eye is gray. He has to be fifty at least. He is a big, thick, lonely man about whom people tell stories. Maya pulls the phone cord as far as it'll go so she can look down more directly on her landlord's large, bald head. He has his back to her as he lines up a dart. He's in black running shoes, red shorts, he's naked to the waist. He hunches his right shoulder, he pulls the arm back; a big, lonely man shouldn't have so much grace. The dart is ready to cut through the September evening. But Ted Suminski doesn't let go. He swings on worn rubber soles, catches her eye in the window (she has to have imagined this), takes aim at her shadow. Could she have imagined the noise of the dart's metal tip on her windowpane?

19   Dr. Chatterji is still on the phone. "You are not having any mode of transportation, is that right?"

20   Ted Suminski has lost interest in her. Perhaps it isn't interest, at all; perhaps it's aggression. "I don't drive," she lies, knowing it sounds less shameful than not owning a car. She has said this so often she can get in the right degree of apology and Asian upper-class helplessness. "It's an awful nuisance."

21   "Not to worry, please." Then, "It is a great honor to be meeting Dr. Sanyal's daughter. In Calcutta business circles he is a legend."

22   On Sunday she is ready by four-thirty. She doesn't know what the afternoon holds; there are surely no places for "high tea"—a colonial tradition—in Cedar Falls, Iowa. If he takes her back to his place, it will mean he has invited other guests. From his voice she can tell Dr. Chatterji likes to do things correctly. She has dressed herself in a peach-colored nylon georgette sari, jade drop-earrings and a necklace. The color is good on dark skin. She is not pretty, but she does her best. Working at it is a part of self-respect. In the mid-seventies, when American women felt rather strongly about such things, Maya had been in trouble with her women's group at Duke. She was too feminine. She had tried to explain the world she came out of. Her grandmother had been married off at the age of five in a village now in Bangladesh. Her great-aunt had been burned to death over a dowry problem. She herself had been trained to speak softly, arrange flowers, sing, be pliant. If she were to seduce Ted Suminski, she thinks as she waits in the front yard for Dr. Chatterji, it would be minor heroism. She has broken with the past. But.

23   Dr. Chatterji drives up for her at about five ten. He is a hesitant driver. The car stalls, jumps ahead, finally slams to a stop. Maya has to tell him to back off a foot or so; it's hard to leap over two sacks of pruned branches in a sari. Ted Suminski is an obsessive pruner and gardener.

24   "My sincerest apologies, Mrs. Sanyal," Dr. Chatterji says. He leans across the wide front seat of his noisy, very old, very used car and unlocks the door for her. "I am late. But then, I am sure you're remembering that Indian Standard Time is not at all the same as time in the States." He laughs. He could be nervous—she often had that effect on Indian men. Or he could just be chatty. "These Americans are all the time rushing and rushing but where it gets them?" He moves his head laterally once, twice. It's the gesture made famous by Peter Sellers. When Peter Sellers did it, it had seemed hilarious. Now it suggests that Maya and Dr. Chatterji have three thousand years plus civilization, sophistication, moral virtue, over people born on this continent. Like her, Dr. Chatterji is a naturalized American.

25   "Call me Maya," she says. She fusses with the seat belt. She does it because she needs time to look him over. He seems quite harmless. She takes in the prominent teeth, the eyebrows that run together. He's in a blue shirt and a beige cardigan with the K-Mart logo that buttons tightly over the waist. It's hard to guess his age because he has dyed his hair and his moustache. Late thirties, early forties. Older than she had expected. "Not Mrs. Sanyal."

26   This isn't time to tell about ex-husbands. She doesn't know where John is these days. He should have kept up at least. John had come into her life as a graduate student at Duke, and she, mistaking the brief breathlessness of sex for love, had married him. They had stayed together two years, maybe a little less. The pain that John had inflicted all those years ago by leaving her had subsided into a cozy feeling of loss. This isn't the time, but then she doesn't want to be a legend's daughter all evening. She's not necessarily on Dr. Chatterji's side is what she wants to get across early; she's not against America and Americans. She makes the story—of marriage outside the Brahminic pale, the divorce—quick, dull. Her unsentimentality seems to shock him. His stomach sags inside the cardigan.

27   "We've each had our several griefs," the physicist says. "We're each required to pay our karmic debts."

28   "Where are we headed?"

29   "Mrs. Chatterji has made some Indian snacks. She is waiting to meet you because she is knowing your cousin-sister who studied in Scottish Church College. My home is okay, no?"

30   Fran would get a kick out of this. Maya has slept with married men, with nameless men, with men little more than boys, but never with an Indian man. Never.

31   The Chatterjis live in a small blue house on a gravelly street. There are at least five or six other houses on the street; the same size but in different colors and with different front yard treatments. More houses are going up. This is the cutting edge of suburbia.

32   Mrs. Chatterji stands in the driveway. She is throwing a large plastic ball to a child. The child looks about four, and is Korean or Cambodian. The child is not

hers because she tells it, "Chung-Hee, ta-ta, bye-bye. Now I play with guest," as Maya gets out of the car.

33   Maya hasn't seen this part of town. The early September light softens the construction pits. In that light the houses too close together, the stout woman in a striped cotton sari, the child hugging a pink ball, the two plastic lawn chairs by a tender young tree, the sheets and saris on the clothesline in the back, all seem miraculously incandescent.

34   "Go home now, Chung-Hee. I am busy." Mrs. Chatteji points the child home-ward, then turns to Maya, who has folded her hands in traditional Bengali greet-ing. "It is an honor. We feel very privileged." She leads Maya indoors to a front room that smells of moisture and paint.

35   In her new, deliquescent mood, Maya allows herself to be backed into the best armchair—a low-backed, boxy Goodwill item draped over with a Rajasthani bedspread—and asks after the cousin Mrs. Chatterji knows. She doesn't want to let go of Mrs. Chatterji. She doesn't want husband and wife to get into whis-pered conferences about their guest's misadventures in America, as they make tea in the kitchen.

36   The coffee table is already laid with platters of mutton croquettes, fish chops, onion pakoras, ghugni with puris, samosas, chutneys. Mrs. Chatterji has gone to too much trouble. Maya counts four kinds of sweetmeats in Corning casseroles on an end table. She looks into a see-through lid; spongy, white dumplings float in rosewater syrup. Planets contained, mysteries made visible.

37   "What are you waiting for, Santana?" Dr. Chatterji becomes imperious, though not unaffectionate. He pulls a dining chair up close to the coffee table. "Make some tea." He speaks in Bengali to his wife, in English to Maya. To Maya he says, grandly, "We are having real Indian Green Label Lipton. A nephew is bringing it just one month back."

38   His wife ignores him. "The kettle's already on," she says. She wants to know about the Sanyal family. Is it true her great-grandfather was a member of the Star Chamber in England?

39   Nothing in Calcutta is ever lost. Just as her story is known to Bengalis all over America, so are the scandals of her family, the grandfather hauled up for tax evasion, the aunt who left her husband to act in films. This woman brings up the Star Chamber, the glories of the Sanyal family, her father's philanthropies, but it's a way of saying, *I know the dirt.*

40   The bedrooms are upstairs. In one of those bedrooms an unseen, tormented presence—Maya pictures it as a clumsy ghost that strains to shake off the body's shell—drops things on the floor. The things are heavy and they make the front room's chandelier shake. Light bulbs, shaped like tiny candle flames, flicker. The Chatterjis have said nothing about children. There are no tricycles in the hallway, no small sandals behind the doors. Maya is too polite to ask about the noise, and the Chatterjis don't explain. They talk just a little louder. They flip the embroidered cover off the stereo. What would Maya like to hear? Hemanta

Kumar? Manna Dey? Oh, that young chap, Manna Dey! What sincerity, what tenderness he can convey!

41 Upstairs the ghost doesn't hear the music of nostalgia. The ghost throws and thumps. The ghost makes its own vehement music. Maya hears in its voice madness, self-hate.

42 Finally the water in the kettle comes to a boil. The whistle cuts through all fantasy and pretense. Dr. Chatterji says, "I'll see to it," and rushes out of the room. But he doesn't go to the kitchen. He shouts up the stairwell. "Poltoo, kindly stop this nonsense straightaway! We're having a brilliant and cultured lady-guest and you're creating earthquakes?" The kettle is hysterical.

43 Mrs. Chatterji wipes her face. The face that had seemed plump and cheery at the start of the evening now is flabby. "My sister's boy," the woman says.

44 So this is the nephew who has brought with him the cartons of Green Label tea, one of which will be given to Maya.

45 Mrs. Chatterji speaks to Maya in English as though only the alien language can keep emotions in check. "Such an intelligent boy! His father is government servant. Very highly placed."

46 Maya is meant to visualize a smart, clean-cut young man from south Calcutta, but all she can see is a crazy, thwarted, lost graduate student. Intelligence, proper family guarantee nothing. Even Brahmins can do self-destructive things, feel unsavory urges. Maya herself had been an excellent student.

47 "He was First Class First in B.Sc. from Presidency College," the woman says. "Now he's getting Master's in Ag. Science at Iowa State."

48 The kitchen is silent. Dr. Chatterji comes back into the room with a tray. The teapot is under a tea cozy, a Kashmiri one embroidered with the usual chinar leaves, loops, and chains. "*Her* nephew," he says. The dyed hair and dyed moustache are no longer signs of a man wishing to fight the odds. He is a vain man, anxious to cut losses. "Very unfortunate business."

49 The nephew's story comes out slowly, over fish chops and mutton croquettes. He is in love with a student from Ghana.

50 "Everything was A-Okay until the Christmas break. Grades, assistantship for next semester, everything."

51 "I blame the college. The office for foreign students arranged a Christmas party. And now, *baapre baap!* Our poor Poltoo wants to marry a Negro Muslim."

52 Maya is known for her nasty, ironic one-liners. It has taken her friends weeks to overlook her malicious, un-American pleasure in others' misfortunes. Maya would like to finish Dr. Chatterji off quickly. He is pompous; he is reactionary; he wants to live and work in America but give back nothing except taxes. The confused world of the immigrant—the lostness that Maya and Poltoo feel—that's what Dr. Chatterji wants to avoid. She hates him. But.

53 Dr. Chatterji's horror is real. A good Brahmin boy in Iowa is in love with an African Muslim. It shouldn't be a big deal. But the more she watches the

physicist, the more she realizes that "Brahmin" isn't a caste; it's a metaphor. You break one small rule, and the constellation collapses. She thinks suddenly that John Cheever—she is teaching him as a "world writer" in her classes, cheek-by-jowl with Africans and West Indians—would have understood Dr. Chatterji's dread. Cheever had been on her mind, ever since the late afternoon light slanted over Mrs. Chatterji's drying saris. She remembers now how full of a soft, Cheeverian light Durham had been the summer she had slept with John Hadwen; and how after that, her tidy graduate-student world became monstrous, lawless. All men became John Hadwen; John became all men. Outwardly, she retained her poise, her Brahminical breeding. She treated her crisis as a literary event; she lost her moral sense, her judgment, her power to distinguish. Her parents had behaved magnanimously. They had cabled from Calcutta: WHAT'S DONE IS DONE. WE ARE CONFIDENT YOU WILL HANDLE NEW SITUATIONS WELL. ALL LOVE. But she knows more than do her parents. Love is anarchy.

54   Poltoo is Mrs. Chatterji's favorite nephew. She looks as though it is her fault that the Sunday has turned unpleasant. She stacks the empty platters methodically. To Maya she says, "It is the goddess who pulls the strings. We are puppets. I know the goddess will fix it. Poltoo will not marry that African woman." Then she goes to the coat closet in the hall and staggers back with a harmonium, the kind sold in music stores in Calcutta, and sets it down on the carpeted floor. "We're nothing but puppets," she says again. She sits at Maya's feet, her pudgy hands on the harmonium's shiny, black bellows. She sings, beautifully, in a virgin's high voice, "Come, goddess, come, muse, come to us hapless peoples' rescue."

55   Maya is astonished. She has taken singing lessons at Dakshini Academy in Calcutta. She plays the sitar and the tanpur, well enough to please Bengalis, to astonish Americans. But stout Mrs. Chatterji is a devotee, talking to God.

56   A little after eight, Dr. Chatterji drops her off. It's been an odd evening and they are both subdued.

57   "I want to say one thing," he says. He stops her from undoing her seat belt. The plastic sacks of pruned branches are still at the corner.

58   "You don't have to get out," she says.

59   "Please. Give me one more minute of your time."

60   "Sure."

61   "Maya is my favorite name."

62   She says nothing. She turns away from him without making her embarrassment obvious.

63   "Truly speaking, it is my favorite. You are sometimes lonely, no? But you are lucky. Divorced women can date, they can go to bars and discos. They can see mens, many mens. But inside marriage there is so much loneliness." A groan, low, horrible, comes out of him.

64   She turns back toward him, to unlatch the seat belt and run out of the car. She sees that Dr. Chatterji's pants are unzipped. One hand works hard under his Jockey shorts; the other rests, limp, penitential, on the steering wheel.

65   "Dr. Chatterji—*really!*" she cries.

66   The next day, Monday, instead of getting a ride home with Fran—Fran says she *likes* to give rides, she needs the chance to talk, and she won't share gas expenses, absolutely not—Maya goes to the periodicals room of the library. There are newspapers from everywhere, even from Madagascar and New Caledonia. She thinks of the periodicals room as an asylum for homesick aliens. There are two aliens already in the room, both Orientals, both absorbed in the politics and gossip of their far-off homes.

67   She goes straight to the newspapers from India. She bunches her raincoat like a bolster to make herself more comfortable. There's so much to catch up on. A village headman, a known Congress-Indira party worker, has been shot at by scooter-riding snipers. An Indian pugilist has won an international medal—in Nepal. A child drawing well water—the reporter calls the child "a neo-Buddhist, a convert from the now-outlawed untouchable caste"—has been stoned. An editorial explains that the story about stoning is not a story about caste but about failed idealism; a story about promises of green fields and clean, potable water broken, a story about bribes paid and wells not dug. But no, thinks Maya, it's about caste.

68   Out here, in the heartland of the new world, the India of serious newspapers unsettles. Maya longs again to feel what she had felt in the Chatterjis' living room: virtues made physical. It is a familiar feeling, a longing. Had a suitable man presented himself in the reading room at that instant, she would have seduced him. She goes on to the stack of *India Abroads*, reads through matrimonial columns, and steals an issue to take home.

69   Indian men want Indian brides. Married Indian men want Indian mistresses. All over America, "Handsome, tall, fair" engineers, doctors, data processors—the new pioneers—cry their eerie love calls.

70   Maya runs a finger down the first column; her fingertip, dark with newsprint, stops at random.

71   Hello! Hi! Yes, you *are* the one I'm looking for. You are the new emancipated Indo-American woman. You have a zest for life. You are at ease in USA and yet your ethics are rooted in Indian tradition. The man of your dreams has come. Yours truly is handsome, ear-nose-throat specialist, well-settled in Connecticut. Age is 41 but never married, physically fit, sportsmanly, and strong. I adore idealism, poetry, beauty. I abhor smugness, passivity, caste system. Write with recent photo. Better still, call!!!

72   Maya calls. Hullo, hullo, hullo! She hears immigrant lovers cry in crowded shopping malls. Yes, you are at ease in both worlds, you are the one. She feels she has a fair chance.

73   A man answers. "Ashoke Mehta speaking."

74   She speaks quickly into the bright-red mouthpiece of her telephone. He will be in Chicago, in transit, passing through O'Hare. United counter, Saturday, two p.m. As easy as that.

75   "Good," Ashoke Mehta says. "For these encounters I, too, prefer a neutral zone."

76   On Saturday at exactly two o'clock the man of Maya's dreams floats toward her as lovers used to in shampoo commercials. The United counter is a loud, harassed place but passengers and piled-up luggage fall away from him. Full-cheeked and fleshy-lipped, he is handsome. He hasn't lied. He is serene, assured, a Hindu god touching down in Illinois.

77   She can't move. She feels ugly and unworthy. Her adult life no longer seems miraculously rebellious; it is grim, it is perverse. She has accomplished nothing. She has changed her citizenship but she hasn't broken through into the light, the vigor, the *hustle* of the New World. She is stuck in dead space.

78   "Hullo, hullo!" Their fingers touch.

79   Oh, the excitement! Ashoke Mehta's palm feels so right in the small of her back. Hullo, hullo, hullo, He pushes her out of the reach of anti-Khomeini Iranians, Hare Krishnas, American Fascists, men with fierce wants, and guides her to an empty gate. They have less than an hour.

80   "What would you like, Maya?"

81   She knows he can read her mind, she knows her thoughts are open to him. *You,* she's almost giddy with the thought, with simple desire. "From the snack bar," he says as though to clarify. "I'm afraid I'm starved."

82   Below them, where the light is strong and hurtful, a Boeing is being serviced. "Nothing," she says.

83   He leans forward. She can feel the nap of his scarf—she recognizes the Cambridge colors—she can smell the wool of his Icelandic sweater. She runs her hand along the scarf, then against the flesh of his neck. "Only the impulsive ones call," he says.

84   The immigrant courtship proceeds. It's easy, he's good with facts. He knows how to come across to a stranger who may end up a lover, a spouse. He makes over a hundred thousand. He owns a house in Hartford, and two income properties in Newark. He plays the market but he's cautious. He's good at badminton but plays handball to keep in shape. He watches all the sports on television. Last August he visited Copenhagen, Helsinki and Leningrad. Once upon a time he collected stamps but now he doesn't have hobbies, except for reading. He counts himself an intellectual, he spends too much on books. Ludlum, Forsyth, MacInnes; other names she doesn't catch. She suppresses a smile, she's told him only she's a graduate student. He's not without his vices. He's a spender, not a saver. He's a sensualist: good food—all foods, but easy on the Indian—good wine. Some temptations he doesn't try to resist.

85   And I, she wants to ask, do I tempt?

86 "Now tell me about yourself, Maya." He makes it easy for her. "Have you ever been in love?"

87 "No."

88 "But many have loved you, I can see that." He says it not unkindly. It is the fate of women like her, and men like him. Their karmic duty, to be loved. It is expected, not judged. She feels he can see them all, the sad parade of need and demand. This isn't the time to reveal all.

89 And so the courtship enters a second phase.

90 When she gets back to Cedar Falls, Ted Suminski is standing on the front porch. It's late at night, chilly. He is wearing a down vest. She's never seen him on the porch. In fact there's no chair to sit on. He looks chilled through. He's waited around a while.

91 "Hi." She has her keys ready. This isn't the night to offer the six-pack in the fridge. He looks expectant, ready to pounce.

92 "Hi." He looks like a man who might have aimed the dart at her. What has he done to his wife, his kids? Why isn't there at least a dog? "Say, I left a note upstairs."

93 The note is written in Magic Marker and thumb-tacked to her apartment door. DUE TO PERSONAL REASONS, NAMELY REMARRIAGE, I REQUEST THAT YOU VACATE MY PLACE AT THE END OF THE SEMESTER.

94 Maya takes the note down and retacks it to the kitchen wall. The whole wall is like a bulletin board, made of some new, crumbly building-material. Her kitchen, Ted Suminski had told her, was once a child's bedroom. Suminski in love: the idea stuns her. She has misread her landlord. The dart at her window speaks of no twisted fantasy. The landlord wants the tenant out.

95 She gets a glass out of the kitchen cabinet, gets out a tray of ice, pours herself a shot of Fran's bourbon. She is happy for Ted Suminski. She is. She wants to tell someone how moved she'd been by Mrs. Chatterji's singing. How she'd felt in O'Hare, even about Dr. Rab Chatterji in the car. But Fran is not the person. No one she's ever met is the person. She can't talk about the dead space she lives in. She wishes Ashoke Mehta would call. Right now.

96 Weeks pass. Then two months. She finds a new room, signs another lease. Her new landlord calls himself Fred. He has no arms, but he helps her move her things. He drives between Ted Suminski's place and his twice in his station wagon. He uses his toes the way Maya uses her fingers. He likes to do things. He pushes garbage sacks full of Maya's clothes up the stairs.

97 "It's all right to stare," Fred says. "Hell, I would."

98 That first afternoon in Fred's rooming house, they share a Chianti. Fred wants to cook her pork chops but he's a little shy about Indians and meat. Is it beef, or pork? Or any meat? She says it's okay, any meat, but not tonight. He has an ex-wife in Des Moines, two kids in Portland, Oregon. The kids are both

normal; he's the only freak in the family. But he's self-reliant. He shops in the supermarket like anyone else, he carries out the garbage, shovels the snow off the sidewalk. He needs Maya's help with one thing. Just one thing. The box of Tide is a bit too heavy to manage. Could she get him the giant size every so often and leave it in the basement?

99   The dead space need not suffocate. Over the months, Fred and she will settle into companionship. She has never slept with a man without arms. Two wounded people, he will joke during their nightly contortions. It will shock her, this assumed equivalence with a man so strikingly deficient. She knows she is strange, and lonely, but being Indian is not the same, she would have thought, as being a freak.

100   One night in spring, Fred's phone rings. "Ashoke Mehta speaking." None of this "do you remember me?" nonsense.

101   The god has tracked her down. He hasn't forgotten. "Hullo," he says, in their special way. And because she doesn't answer back, "Hullo, hullo, hullo." She is aware of Fred in the back of the room. He is lighting a cigarette with his toes.

102   "Yes," she says, "I remember."

103   "I had to take care of a problem," Ashoke Mehta says. "You know that I have my vices. That time at O'Hare I was honest with you."

104   She is breathless.

105   "Who is it, May?" asks Fred.

106   "You also have a problem," says the voice. His laugh echoes.

107   "You will come to Hartford, I know."

108   When she moves out, she tells herself, it will not be the end of Fred's world.

For Further Thinking

1. How does Maya view her social and cultural position in the United States? How does she retain her interest in and connection to India?

2. What does Maya look for in her romantic relationships? How might her private life be related to her sense of her cultural identity?

3. What is the meaning of the story's title? How might the title have other than geographical and spatial connotations?

4. How does Maya's anticipation of happiness with Ashoke contradict her earlier statements about love, personal independence, and cultural gender stereotypes? What is the significance of Maya's changed characterization at the story's end?

5. How do the different male characters influence Maya's attitudes? What presumptions do these men hold about Maya?

Looking Back and Ahead

1. How does Maya's situation compare and contrast with Pamela Swanigan's in "I Am Half-Canadian" (p. 58)?
2. Discuss Maya's situation in terms of Atom Egoyan's suggested concept of "constructed identity" (Brian D. Johnson's "Atom's Journey," p. 139).
3. Compare and contrast Maya's situation with that of Emma Lee Warrior in "White Breast Flats" (p. 6).
4. Do you think Mukherjee would agree or disagree with Habeeb Salloum's main points in "The Other Canadians and Canada's Future" (p. 200)?

For Further Reading

Alam, Fakrul. *Bharati Mukherjee*. New York: Twayne Publishers, 1996.

Brewster, Anne. "A Critique of Bharati Mukherjee's Neo-nationalism." *SPAN* (Journal of the South Pacific Association for Commonwealth Literature and Language Studies). Ed. Vijay Mishra, Vols. 34–35 (1992–1993). Brewster writes, "Generally, in Australia, discussions of what is often called 'migrant writing' draw attention to the marginality of this discourse and the ways in which it interrogates the literary canon. These discussions position 'ethnicity' as oppositional to nationalism . . ."

Morton-Mollo, Sherry. "Cultural Collisions: Dislocation, Reinvention, and Resolution in Bharati Mukherjee." *Proteus* 11. 2 (Fall 1994): 35–38.

Mukherjee, Bharati. "American Dreamer." *Mother Jones*. January–February 1997. Also online. April 2003 <http://www.mojones.com/mother_jones/JF97/mukherjee.html>. Mukherjee discusses her fascination with the promise of the United States compared to the hopelessness of Canada.

————. "Two Ways to Belong in America." *New York Times*. 22 Sept. 1996. Mukherjee contrasts her views about relating to the United States with those of her sister. Also Sawnet. Concordia University, Montreal. April 2003 <http://www.umiacs.umd.edu/users/sawweb/sawnet/books/two_ways.html>. A forum for those interested in South Asian women's issues, this website offers other information on Mukherjee as well.

Pradhan, Shilpi. "Bharati Mukherjee." Emory University. April 2003 <http://www.emory.edu/ENGLISH/Bahri/Mukherjee.html>. This website provides a short biography of Mukherjee, a summary of the themes in her writing, and a good list of online sources.

Questia.com. April 2003 <www.questia.com>. Research interracial relationships and marriage through the self-proclaimed world's largest online library.

Sengupta, C. "Asian Protagonists in Bharati Mukherjee's *The Middleman and Other Stories*." *Language Forum* 18. 1–2 (Jan.–Dec. 1992): 148–56.

"Voices from the Gaps: Women Writers of Color." A Web project of the University of Minnesota, the English Department, and the American Studies Department. April 2003 <http://voices.cla.umn.ed/authors/MUKHERJEEbharati.html>. This site provides biography, bibliography, criticism, and links.

Robertson Davies Novelist, playwright, raconteur, and essayist, Robertson Davies (1913–1995) grew up in Thamesville, Ontario, the son of a journalist. He was educated at Upper Canada College, Queen's University, and Oxford. After a spell as a professional actor, he edited *Saturday Night* magazine in Toronto and then the Peterborough *Examiner*. In 1961 he was appointed a Master at Massey College, University of Toronto, where he remained until retirement. He died at the age of 82 on December 12, 1995.

In 1971, the *Penguin Companion to English Literature*, edited in England, pronounced that Davies' "urbanity and elegance are unique in [English] Canadian fiction." But the qualities Canadian readers appreciate in his work are also those of his journalistic background—a sharp eye for the detail and spirit of small-town Ontario. His best known work remains *Fifth Business*, a finely crafted and graceful novel. Raised a Protestant, Davies nevertheless had an abiding interest in the more mysterious side of religious experience, and in explorers of the psyche like the Swiss pyschotherapist Carl Jung (1875–1961).

The Pleasures of Love

1   Let us understand one another at once: I have been asked to discuss the pleasures of love, not its epiphanies, its ecstasies, its disillusionments, its duties, its burdens or its martyrdom—and therefore the sexual aspect of it will get scant attention here. So if you have begun this piece in hope of fanning the flames of your lubricity, be warned in time.

2   Nor is it my intention to be psychological. I am heartily sick of most of the psychologizing about love that has been going on for the past six hundred years. Everybody wants to say something clever, or profound, about it, and almost everybody has done so. Only look under "Love" in any book of quotations to see how various the opinions are.

3   Alas, most of this comment is wide of the mark; love, like music and painting, resists analysis in words. It may be described, and some poets and novelists have described it movingly and well; but it does not yield to the theorist. Love is the personal experience of lovers. It must be felt directly.

4   My own opinion is that it is felt most completely in marriage, or some comparable attachment of long duration. Love takes time. What are called "love affairs" may afford a wide, and in retrospect, illuminating variety of emotions; not only fierce satisfactions and swooning delights, but the horrors of jealousy and the desperation of parting attend them; the hangover from one of these emotional riots may be long and dreadful.

5   But rarely have the pleasures of love an opportunity to manifest themselves in such riots of passion. Love affairs are for emotional sprinters; the pleasures of love are for the emotional marathoners.

6   Clearly, then, the pleasures of love are not for the very young. Romeo and Juliet are the accepted pattern of youthful passion. Our hearts go out to their

furious abandonment; we are moved to pity by their early death. We do not, unless we are of a saturnine disposition, give a thought to what might have happened if they had been spared for fifty or sixty years together.

7   Would Juliet have become a worldly nonentity, like her mother? Or would she, egged on by that intolerable old bawd, her Nurse, have planted a thicket of horns on the brow of her Romeo?

8   And he—well, so much would have depended on whether Mercutio had lived; quarrelsome, dashing and detrimental, Mercutio was a man destined to outlive his wit and spend his old age as the Club Bore. No, no; all that Verona crowd were much better off to die young and beautiful.

9   Passion, so splendid in the young, wants watching as the years wear on. Othello had it, and in middle life he married a young and beautiful girl. What happened? He believed the first scoundrel who hinted that she was unfaithful, and never once took the elementary step of asking her a direct question about the matter.

10   Passion is a noble thing; I have no use for a man or woman who lacks it; but if we seek the pleasures of love, passion should be occasional, and common sense continual.

11   Let us get away from Shakespeare. He is the wrong guide in the exploration we have begun. If we talk of the pleasures of love, the best marriage he affords is that of Macbeth and his Lady. Theirs is not the prettiest, nor the highest-hearted, nor the wittiest match in Shakespeare, but unquestionably they knew the pleasures of love.

12   "My dearest partner of greatness," writes the Thane of Cawdor to his spouse. That is the clue to their relationship. That explains why Macbeth's noblest and most desolate speech follows the news that his Queen is dead.

13   But who wants to live a modern equivalent of the life of the Macbeths—continuous scheming to reach the Executive Suite enlivened, one presumes, by an occasional Burns Nicht dinner-party, with the ghosts of discredited vice-presidents as uninvited guests.

14   The pleasures of love are certainly not for the very young, who find a bittersweet pleasure in trying to reconcile two flowering egotisms, nor yet for those who find satisfaction in "affairs." Not that I say a word against young love, or the questings of uncommitted middle-age; but these notions of love correspond to brandy, and we are concerned with something much more like wine.

15   The pleasures of love are for those who are hopelessly addicted to another living creature. The reasons for such addiction are so many that I suspect they are never the same in any two cases.

16   It includes passion but does not survive by passion; it has its whiffs of the agreeable vertigo of young love, but it is stable more often than dizzy; it is a growing, changing thing, and it is tactful enough to give the addicted parties occasional rests from strong and exhausting feeling of any kind.

17   "Perfect love sometimes does not come until the first grandchild," says a Welsh proverb. Better [by] far if perfect love does not come at all, but hovers just out of reach. Happy are those who never experience the all-dressed-up-and-no-place-to-go sensation of perfection in love. *?? what?*

18   What do we seek in love? From my own observation among a group of friends and acquaintances that includes a high proportion of happy marriages, most people are seeking a completion of themselves. Each party to the match has several qualities the other cherishes; the marriage as a whole is decidedly more than the sum of its parts.

19   Nor are these cherished qualities simply the obvious ones; the reclusive man who marries the gregarious woman, the timid woman who marries the courageous man, the idealist who marries the realist—we can all see these unions: the marriages in which tenderness meets loyalty, where generosity sweetens moroseness, where a sense of beauty eases some aridity of the spirit, are not so easy for outsiders to recognize; the parties themselves may not be fully aware of such elements in a good match.

20   Often, in choosing a mate, people are unconsciously wise and apprehend what they need to make them greater than they are.

21   Of course the original disposition of the partners to the marriage points the direction it will take. When Robert Browning married Elizabeth Barrett, the odds were strongly on the side of optimism, in spite of superficial difficulties; when Macbeth and his Lady stepped to the altar, surely some second-sighted Highlander must have shuddered. *What ???*

22   If the parties to a marriage have chosen one another unconsciously, knowing only that they will be happier united than apart, they had better set to work as soon as possible to discover why they have married, and to nourish the feeling which has drawn them together.

23   I am constantly astonished by the people, otherwise intelligent, who think that anything so complex and delicate as a marriage can be left to take care of itself. One sees them fussing about all sorts of lesser concerns, apparently unaware that side by side with them—often in the same bed—a human creature is perishing from lack of affection, of emotional malnutrition.

24   Such people are living in sin far more truly than the loving but unwedded couples whose unions they sometimes scorn. What pleasures are there in these neglected marriages? What pleasure can there be in ramshackle, jerrybuilt, uncultivated love?

25   A great part of all the pleasure of love begins, continues and sometimes ends with conversation. A real, enduring love-affair, in marriage and out of it, is an extremely exclusive club of which the entire membership is two co-equal Perpetual Presidents. *two equal partners??*

26   In French drama there used to be a character, usually a man, who was the intimate friend of husband and wife, capable of resolving quarrels and keeping the union in repair. I do not believe in such a creature anywhere except behind

couples who need the help/advice of a 3rd party are doomed!

the footlights. Lovers who need a third party to discuss matters with are in a bad way.

27   Of course there are marriages that are kept in some sort of rickety shape by a psychiatrist—occasionally by two psychiatrists. But I question if pleasure of the sort I am writing about can exist in such circumstances. The club has become too big.

he doesn't mean useless conversations but meaningful talks when necessary.

28   I do not insist on a union of chatter-boxes, but as you can see I do not believe that still waters run deep; too often I have found that still waters are foul and have mud bottoms. People who love each other should talk to each other; they should confide their real thoughts, their honest emotions, their deepest wishes. How else are they to keep their union in repair?

29   How else, indeed, are they to discover that they are growing older and enjoying it, which is a very great discovery indeed? How else are they to discover that their union is stronger and richer, not simply because they have shared experience (couples who are professionally at odds, like a Prime Minister and a Leader of the Opposition, also share experience, but they are not lovers) but because they are waxing in spirit?

30   During the last war a cruel epigram was current that Ottawa was full of brilliant men, and the women they had married when they were very young. If the brilliant men had talked more to those women, and the women had replied, the joint impression they made in middle-age might not have been so dismal. It is often asserted that sexual compatibility is the foundation of a good marriage, but this pleasure is doomed to wane, whereas a daily affectionate awareness and a ready tongue last as long as life itself.

31   It always surprises me, when Prayer Book revision is discussed, that something is not put into the marriage service along these lines—"for the mutual society, help, comfort and unrestricted conversation that one ought to have of the other, both in prosperity and adversity."

32   Am I then advocating marriages founded on talk? I can hear the puritans, who mistrust conversation as they mistrust all subtle pleasures, tutting their disapproving tuts.

33   Do I assert that the pleasures of love are no more than the pleasures of conversation? Not at all: I am saying that where the talk is good and copious, love is less likely to wither, or to get out of repair, or to be outgrown, than among the uncommunicative.

34   For, after all, even lovers live alone much more than we are ready to admit. To keep in constant, sensitive rapport with those we love most, we must open our hearts and our minds. Do this, and the rarest, most delicate pleasures of love will reveal themselves.

35   Finally, it promotes longevity. Nobody quits a club where the conversation is fascinating, revealing, amusing, various and unexpected until the last possible minute. Love may be snubbed to death: talked to death, never!

For Further Thinking

1. What do you think of the statement that love cannot be analyzed, that it "is the personal experience of lovers. It must be felt directly"?
2. "Love takes time"—is this true? With age, are people prepared to settle for less in love or, conversely, expect more?
3. Davies introduces a striking metaphoric comparison to emphasize his thesis. What is that comparison?
4. What is Davies' major recommendation for achieving the pleasure of love?
5. How would you define the style of this essay? What are its features?
6. How does an uncomfortable class consciousness shape Davies' metaphors?

Looking Back and Ahead

1. Contrast the style of this essay to that of Pamela Swanigan's "I Am Half-Canadian" (p. 58). Consider that both essays were published in the same magazine, but 40 years apart.
2. Compare the style of this essay to that of Jane Farrow's "Diary Rock" (p. 80), published in the same magazine 38 years after Davies' essay appeared.
3. How might Mordecai Richler's short story "The Summer My Grandmother Was Supposed to Die" (p. 14) be interpreted in light of Davies' thesis in this essay?

For Further Reading

Davies, Robertson, *Fifth Business*. New York: Viking, 1970.

————. *The Manticore*. New York: Viking, 1972.

————. *World of Wonders*. New York: Viking, 1975.

Kuchling, A.M. "Robertson Davies." April 2003 <http://www.amk.ca/davies/>. The author provides a biography, bibliography, interviews, reviews, photographs, quotations, memorials, and obituaries of Robertson Davies.

"Robertson Davies, 1913–1995." Part of "Well-Known People Who Happen to Be Canadian." Comp. Vernon R.J. Schmid, maintained by John Terning. Harvard University. April 2003 <http://schwinger.harvard.edu/~terning/bios/Davies.html>.

David Suzuki   The popular TV host of the *Nature of Things* and *A Planet for the Taking*, David Suzuki probably needs little introduction. Born in 1936 in Vancouver, a third-generation Japanese-Canadian (Sansei), he trained as a geneticist, joining the staff of the University of British Columbia in 1963. In 1969 he was appointed full professor of zoology. Three times consecutively (1969–1972), he was awarded the Steacie Memorial Fellowship as Canada's most outstanding research scientist.

Suzuki believes it is crucial for ordinary people to understand science, and that it is quite possible for them to do so, at least enough to participate in ethical debate. He understands the power of talking across rather than down to people, and makes exhaustive use of television, radio, and newspaper columns to pursue this vital dialogue. Suzuki's ongoing commitment to the ethics of science and to holistic approaches may be his greatest legacy in a field often characterized by self-reference.

The following article on sex education is taken from a collection called *Inventing the Future* (1990). To give the issue some historical context, consider that in 1967 Canada still had a law forbidding the dissemination of birth control information.

For more support for this reading, visit the website for Athabasca University's introductory composition course at <www.athabascau.ca/courses/engl/255/>. Under "Supplementary Resources," see "If English Is Not Your First Language" and "Language Support for Selected Readings."

The Right Stuff

David SUZUKI

1   Years ago I read a marvellous book entitled *Is There Life After High School?* In spite of the title, it was a serious comparison of human relationships at different stages in life. The study revealed that impressions formed in high school are more vivid and indelible than those formed at any other time in life. The author described how people in their seventies and eighties who had difficulty remembering most of their associates in university and at work would instantly recall most of their classmates by name while leafing through their high school yearbooks. In the analysis [by] the author, high school society is divided into two broad categories, the innies and the outies. The innies were football and basketball players and cheerleaders who set the whole social climate of the school. The outies were all the rest, the majority of the student body, most of whom lusted to be innies. I sure hope it's different today because that description fits my recollection of high school and it was awful. But I'm getting off the point.

2   Those high school memories are so intense because that is the time when puberty occurs. The enormous physiological changes that take place in response to the surge of new hormones through the body completely transform both anatomy and mind. I always feel kids lose about half their intelligence for a few years in response to that blast of hormones. Relationships change radically. Suddenly parents change from protective, loving gods to dictatorial wardens incessantly imposing restrictions and criticizing everything. A pubescent teenager perceives adults and members of their own age group with totally new eyes. It's not surprising then that attitudes to school, courses and studying also change dramatically.

3   In the early 1970s, I visited a small northern town to judge a science fair. Back then, it was a tough town with a transient population of men working in the oil fields and a high proportion of Native people. The night I arrived, I dropped in to the bar of the motel and a man came over and said, "I hear you're going to talk to the students at the high school tomorrow." When I affirmed it, he shocked me by adding, "They'll kill you. I'm the science teacher there and I can tell you that all they think about is sex, drugs and cars. They'll tear you apart."

4   Well, he really scared me. I immediately formed images of a blackboard jungle, filled with switchblades and drug-crazed hoods. The next day when I walked into that auditorium, it was with great trepidation. There were 400 teenagers in the gym, about a third of them Indians. They looked pretty normal, but I had been warned and knew they were just biding their time before turning into raving animals.

5   So I began by saying, "I'm a geneticist. I know that you're basically walking gonads, so I'm going to talk about sex." That opener caught their attention. I started with the beginning of human life by describing eggs and sperm, talked about chromosomes and the X and Y basis for sex determination and went on from there. The kids were dead silent and attentive. I talked for about an hour and then opened it up for questions. I was astounded at the range of topics we covered. We discussed drugs and chromosomes, test-tube babies, amniocentesis and cloning. The principal finally had to step in to dismiss the group an hour and a half after that.

6   Science education in high school should be designed around sex and human biology. It's a shock every time I hear that a school board has caved in to pressure and kept sex education out of schools. I am sure opponents of sex ed have no intention of providing that information to their own children. In a time of easy access to the most explicit films, videos, magazines and books, who can believe it's better to keep youngsters ignorant by denying them some accurate facts? They're going to get all kinds of anecdotal, apocryphal stuff about sex from their peer group, anyway.

7   By starting their instruction with human sexuality and reproduction, teachers will be able to go on to practically every other subject in science. It just takes a hard look from a different perspective. After all, we are not trying to train future scientists (only a small percentage of high school graduates will go on in science), yet all of them will be able to use information that science can provide for the rest of their lives. And you can bet they will remember those lessons vividly in their life after high school.

[handwritten margin note: its better to talk about it & them openly so they get the Right (truth) facts than incorrect facts from other sources.]

For Further Thinking

1. In your own words, what is the thesis of this essay? Do you agree with it? Why or why not? (See Chapter 8 of the *Rhetoric* for our suggestions on how to find the thesis of this essay and how to summarize the other main ideas.)

2. Review the discussion of "Logic and Logical Fallacies" in Chapter 7 of the *Rhetoric*. Are there any such fallacies in "The Right Stuff"? Explain.

3. In his book *Metamorphosis*, Suzuki writes, "We make a great mistake by associating the inheritance of physical characteristics with far more complex traits of human personality and behaviour" (p. 13). But in "The Right Stuff," doesn't he associate adolescent behaviour entirely with the physical characteristic of puberty and its hormones? Is he contradicting his own more complex understanding of cause-and-effect?

4. Suzuki gives his opponents little voice in "The Right Stuff." Are there strong reasons that you can think of for *not* teaching sex education in high school.

5. In paragraph 4, Suzuki notes that a third of the teenagers were Indians. How do you think he intends this comment to be taken?

Looking Back and Ahead

1. Read John Markoff's "The Doomsday Machines" (p. 135). Would Suzuki be more likely to side with or against the "informed sources" who foresee dangers in a number of scientific fields, including Suzuki's own field of genetics?

2. Would Suzuki support or contradict Habeeb Salloum's conclusions in "The Other Canadians and Canada's Future" (p. 200)?

3. Chapter 10 of the *Rhetoric* contains a sample critique of "The Right Stuff." Should the writer of that critique have acknowledged that Suzuki's "essay" is in fact an excerpt from a longer work? Is it fair to criticize Suzuki for failing to respond to potential counter-arguments?

For Further Reading

The David Suzuki Foundation Homepage. April 2003 <http://www.davidsuzuki.org>. Biographical information on the author.

Knudston, Peter, and David Suzuki. *Wisdom of the Elders*. Toronto: Stoddart, 1992. This work exemplifies Suzuki at his most holistic, pursuing congruities between the findings of pure science and the teachings of traditional oral cultures.

Makabe, Tomoko. *The Canadian Sansei*. Toronto: University of Toronto Press, 1998.

"Review of *David Suzuki Talks About AIDS*." University of Manitoba. April 2003 <http://www.umanitoba.ca/cm/cmarchive/vol16no1/suzukiaids.html>. A high school teacher discusses the book's usefulness as a teaching tool.

Suzuki, David. *Inventing the Future: Reflections on Science, Technology, and Nature*. Toronto: Stoddart, 1989.

—————. *Metamorphosis: Stages in a Life*. Toronto: Stoddart, 1987.

Suzuki, David with Eileen Thalenberg and Peter Knudtson. *David Suzuki Talks About AIDS*. Toronto: General Paperbacks, 1987.

James Downey   Past-president of the University of Waterloo, Downey refers to studies reported by Robert Putnam and his co-authors in *Making Democracy Work* (1993). The studies strongly link economic development to the quality of social organizations: "The communities which succeeded socially and economically did not become civil because they were rich, but rather became rich because they were civil." Downey goes on to note "the growing sense in Canada, and Ontario particularly, that this kind of social capital has been depleted." He observes that many people now feel a sense of disenfranchisement, but that it is too easy simply to blame government and business leaders. He argues that it would be "better and truer" if we all accepted responsibility, starting with our universities. He appeals to us to remember that "ideals should lie at the heart of the university." He calls upon university members—particularly those in the humanities and social sciences—to "lead by example" through practising engaged citizenship.

A Liberal Education Is Key to a Civil Society

1   Perhaps the most compelling argument for the value of a liberal education is that, without the application of the knowledge and values it embodies, civil society would be impossible. And without civility the quest for prosperity becomes both aimless and fruitless. If this argument is not being well advanced these days, it may be in part because the usual defenders of liberal education, humanists and social scientists, are not matching rhetoric with example in the community closest to them: the university.

2   Civility, as I am using it, is not a series of grace notes or decorative features added to social interaction. Nor is it a matter of feeling good or being nice towards each other. It is something more fundamental to the workings of successful communities and nations. In *Making Democracy Work,* Robert Putnam has described studies which strongly link economic development to the quality of social organizations in the community. Putnam made an historical analysis of a number of Italian communities and concluded that the ones which succeeded socially and economically did not become civil because they were rich, but rather became rich because they were civil. The best predictors of success, he concluded, were strong traditions of civic engagement as reflected by voter turnout, newspaper readership, and active membership in community organizations and networks that are organized horizontally not hierarchically. Putnam described these aspects of civic engagement as social capital, a type of capital that is augmented, not depleted, by use.

3   There is a growing sense in Canada, and Ontario particularly, that this kind of social capital has been depleted, the result in part of severe and often crude economic measures governments and corporations have taken to balance budgets, contain costs, and increase productivity. Economic disparities have grown, and so too has the sense of disfranchisement many feel. It is easy to be critical of government and business leaders in all this, but it would be better and truer if we all accepted greater responsibility, starting with ourselves, in universities.

4   What is true for communities in general is no less true for universities. The social capital represented by associations and networks of civic engagement is a precondition for academic development and effective governance. An institution that relies on mutual respect and assistance is simply more effective at achieving its ends than an oppositional, distrustful community. Social capital in the collegium, no less than in the community at large, is built from an investment of time and commitment by individuals—people who first make the effort to understand the issues and then take an active, citizen role in their resolution.

5   Many in the academy feel that this capital has been eroded on our campuses in recent years, although they are not agreed on the cause. Some blame it on size, some on the divided loyalties of professors, some on the increased emphasis on individual rights at the expense of collective obligations, and some on chilly climates of one sort or another. Whatever the root cause, it seems clear that mutually reinforcing corporatism and unionism have waxed while the spirit of community and civic engagement has waned. Waned too has any strong sense that universities have a role in society that transcends the simple formula of teaching, research, and service, or any sense at all that our ideals oblige us to become exemplary societies ourselves. Humanists and social scientists have been much better at social deconstruction than at reminding colleagues of the ideals that should lie at the heart of the university.

6   As it bears on the education universities provide, it should be acknowledged that no set of academic disciplines has a monopoly on the knowledge and values of which I speak. A liberal education only makes sense in a modern university and contemporary society if its concepts, principles, and ideals are built into the curricula of all undergraduate programs. Ironically, I believe that engineering and some other professional programs may be doing a better job of this than many programs in arts and social science, which assume they are liberal but in fact are quite narrowly specialized and leave students without a sufficiently broad base of skills, knowledge and outlook for a meaningful engagement as citizens. Which is to say that if we who profess ourselves to be humanists and social scientists wish to defend and promote the ideals of a liberal education in a hard-edged materialist culture, we must be prepared to lead by example, starting with our own universities—the programs we offer, the academic citizenship we practise.

For Further Thinking

1. Would you agree that when today's college students choose courses, the pressure to make prudent career choices takes precedence over personal interest in particular subjects? Must economics always take priority over personal growth and exploration for students?

2. Would you agree that on today's campuses "mutually reinforcing corporatism and unionism have waxed while the spirit of community and civic engagement has waned?" Do your instructors seem engaged or to be merely fulfilling the contractual obligations of "corporatism and unionism?"

3. Downey is concerned that many students today receive too narrow an education, that without breadth of knowledge, one's capacity as a citizen is limited. What is your response to this idea?

4. What forces do you believe are working against the sort of broad, "liberal" education experience Downey would like to see for tomorrow's learners?

5. Would Downey's essay be stronger if he were more specific? Is he naive to believe individuals ought to value (or even historically have placed) community ahead of self-interest?

Looking Back and Ahead

1. Read John Markoff's "The Doomsday Machines" (p. 135) and Brenda Platt's "Global Warming and Population" (p. 113). Is there a similarity between the situation of eroding liberal education and that of problems that could be lying in wait if certain economic and technological changes are not made? Further, is there a possible causal relationship between eroding liberal education and attitudes toward environmental disorders?

2. If Robert Putnam is correct that communities become rich because they are civil, why don't today's political and business leaders take a much stronger interest in renewing liberal education? How are long-term and short-term goals at possible odds?

3. Read "The Pleasures of Love" (p. 177). If Davies is right on how to sustain a pleasing marriage, what sort of education would most enable the effort he feels is needed?

4. Discuss a possible relationship between Downey's thesis and Roger Fouts' "Brownie" (p. 12).

For Further Reading

Adler, Mortimer. "General Education vs. Vocational Training." Online. April 2003 <http://realuofc.org/libed/adler/gevt.html>. The American philosopher points out that to the ancients, liberal education taught the skills to become human, whereas training for a specific job was the training of slaves. He argues that much of modern education is vocational, or in other words, slave training.

Connor, W.R. "Liberal Arts Education in the 21st Century." Online. April 2003 <http://www.aale.org/index_con.htm>. The author, president of the National Humanities Center, American Academy for Liberal Education, outlines the decline of liberal arts education in the United States, and then presents arguments for the necessity of this education. He argues that liberal arts education must re-emphasize civic and public duty, "the skills of freedom today."

Leonardi, Robert, Rafaella Nannetti, and Robert Putnam. *Making Democracy Work: Civic Traditions in Modern Italy*. Berkeley: University of California, 1993. An endowed chair in public policy at Harvard University, Putnam is also president of the American Political Science Association.

Putnam, Robert. *Bowling Alone: The Collapse and Revival of American Community*. New York: Simon and Schuster, 2000.

Schafer, Arthur. *Medicine, Morals, & Money*. Brandon: University of Manitoba, Centre for Professional and Applied Ethics, 1999. This chapbook refers to the attempts of Apotex, a pharmaceutical company, to suppress research results, derived by Dr. Nancy Oliveri, resulting in a scandal at Toronto's Hospital for Sick Children. Schafer argues that vested corporate interests increasingly threaten academic freedom and ethics.

Janice Procée and Gail Deagle The next two essays, both by part-time students and health care professionals, argue opposing sides of the debate on euthanasia: are there times when society should deem it acceptable to end a human life as an act of mercy?

The Canadian Criminal Code outlaws the counselling or abetting of suicide. In May 1988, the first-ever conviction was laid against a Canadian doctor, Maurice Genereux, for having assisted suicide. As an indication of the high level of emotion often triggered in this debate, the Crown lawyer childishly called Dr. Genereux the "Darth Vader of doctors." In the early 1990s, Sue Rodriguez, a woman suffering from Lou Gehrig's Disease, appealed for the right to a dignified death through a doctor's assistance. The Supreme Court denied her petition. In February 1994, she ended her life with a mixture of morphine and Seconal, administered by an unknown doctor. An MP in British Columbia, Svend Robinson, an advocate of legalized euthanasia, was at her side, but was later not charged. This case, re-told by the 1996 TV movie *The Sue Rodriguez Story*, generated considerable public attention regarding whether euthanasia is compassion or crime.

The issue intensified, gaining in complexity, with the Richard Latimer case. A northern Saskatchewan farmer, Latimer confessed to having killed his severely disabled 12-year-old daughter Tracy by carbon monoxide poisoning. There is disagreement over the degree of extended pain his daughter was suffering. Restricted by a form of cerebral palsy, Tracy did not seem to have a mental capacity beyond six months of age. She could not comprehend her situation and was far from being able to express what she would have wished. Tracy had undergone numerous medical interventions. Latimer's defence was that she would have endured endless, painful, futile operations and procedures, and that she would have suffered constant pain. Those critical of his action maintain that the girl was not in constant suffering and that he rejected the full extent of medical assistance available. In January 2001, after two trials by jury, appeals, a retrial owing to faulty procedure, and a refused request by the jury for a softened term, Latimer was sentenced to life in prison with no parole for 10 years. To some, this shows the government of Canada and the judicial system as cruel, inflexible, and far behind the Netherlands, which allows doctor-assisted euthanasia under specified conditions.

For help with the language of these two essays, visit the website for Athabasca University's ESL Writing Skills program at <**www.athabascau.ca/courses/engl/255/**>. Under "Supplementary Resources," see "If English Is Not Your First Language" and "Language Support for Selected Readings."

Janice Procée works in a busy Ontario emergency department. Her essay illustrates the use of research as well as argumentation. Note her use of APA documentation style. See Chapter 12.

The Case for Active Euthanasia

1   Active euthanasia is a complex and diverse issue. This particular form of euthanasia is the "purposeful shortening of human life through active or direct assistance" (Darbyshire 1987). Personal and ethical dilemmas have surrounded this subject for decades, even centuries. Pro-life activists, including various churches, strongly oppose any type of assistance for people wishing to end their lives. Modern medical technology has advanced to such a degree, however, that terminally ill patients are not just living longer—they are dying longer. Through personal and work experiences as a nurse, I have found myself swaying in favour of the right, within strict safeguards, to die with dignity.

2   The debate against euthanasia is heard from religious lobbyists and other pro-life organizations. The Catholic Church, for example, believes that only God has the right to determine our fate, and we are trying to "play God" (Ellis 1992). "God giveth life, and only God can take away" (Humphry 1986). The opposition groups fear that if euthanasia were legalized it would lead to widespread chaos and wrongful deaths. One dilemma is that if patients cannot express their desires, others may contravene their true wishes. Should a family member, a medical professional, or the caregiver have the final say? There is also great concern about organ donation, about patients not always receiving appropriate treatment because their organs are so desperately needed: "Transplant doctors circled like vultures around young, head-injured accident victims" (Trevelyan 1992). While these concerns may indeed be seen as legitimate, interestingly, there is no debate from pro-life groups regarding the issue of extreme measures to keep someone alive.

3   Before modern technology was introduced, people died by natural means without aid of life support systems. By allowing artificial respirators, feeding tubes, and a multitude of medications, we too are interfering with the natural death process, altering a life. Those opposed to the perceived cruelty of euthanasia should consider that to sustain a life that cannot breathe, eat, or function on its own is even more cruel. It is also a form of "playing God."

4   I work at the Royal Victoria Hospital in Barrie, Ontario, my home town. RVH serves a population of approximately 200 000 people. During the past two years that I have worked there I have been privy to many heart-wrenching situations involving patients who have determined their own demises through alternative means. This choice is never easy or without pain to others. Absolute prohibition of that choice, however, may simply intensify the pain of the choice individuals feel driven to make.

5   On one of my 12-hour shifts we had a patch call from an ambulance transporting a 67-year-old man who had sustained a self-inflicted single gunshot wound to the head. The ER trauma team prepared for the incoming patient. The paramedics arrived and were performing CPR [cardio-pulmonary resuscitation] when the team of doctors and nurses took over. The trauma team worked diligently for 30 to 40 minutes trying to sustain this gentleman's life; however, the gunshot would prove to be fatal. It was a highly charged emotional atmosphere as the family stood by and witnessed the passing of their loved one. Further investigation revealed that this man had recently been diagnosed with terminal cancer. He had chosen to take an active role in his own death. This unexpected choice had a devastating effect on the people he left behind. If given an informed choice, he might very well not have chosen such a violent means of death. For example, he could have learned more about the disease process and the length of survival and could have chosen to medicate himself until such time as he was past the point of pain management, and then been assisted by a professional during his final passing.

6   This past year I lost an aunt to terminal cancer. The cancer ravaged her body for over a year; we watched this horrible and crippling disease take away the strong vital person we knew her to be. She was routinely brought into the hospital where I work, and each time I saw less and less of the person I knew. The last few months of her life were nearly impossible for both her and the family to bear. She would lie in her bed, unable to move, gasping for air, begging God to take her. Yet she still showed other signs of clinging to life.

7   This is definitely not a black-and-white issue. Earlier I mentioned a need for safeguards. Although I agree with euthanasia as a choice for consenting adults, I do not agree with its being implemented for babies, disabled persons who are unable to express their concerns, coma victims, or other people who cannot express their wishes. A society more open to the complexities surrounding this issue, however, would allow us to have personal transition orders in place. Those of us who do not wish to see life extended by the aid of machines in cases where recovery is not possible, who do not wish to feel a burden to those around us, could make that preference known in writing. We should have a choice about our final days while we are still competent to make decisions.

References

Darbyshire, P. (1987). Whose life is it, anyway? *Nursing Times, 83*(45), 26–29.

Ellis, P. (1992). An act of love. *Nursing Times, 88*(37), 34–35.

Humphry, W. (1986). *The right to die: understanding euthanasia.* London: The Bodley Head.

Trevelyan, J. (1992). Or an admission of failure? *Nursing Times, 88*(37), 36–37.

For Further Thinking

1. What do you consider the strong points of Procée's essay?

2. Are her points organized as effectively as possible? Why or why not?

3. Are there any weak points here? Has she supported all her claims with sufficient, detailed evidence? Are there any opinions stated as facts and thus left unsupported? Has she omitted anything surrounding the debate that, by its absence, could appear as a deliberate evasion?

4. Comment on her tone. Is it firm yet inclusive and respectful of the other side? Are there any moments of excess emotion or any propaganda techniques? (See Chapter 7 for a discussion of various propaganda techniques.)

Looking Back and Ahead

1. Based purely on rhetorical effectiveness, do you consider this essay more or less effective than Gail Deagle's "Euthanasia Reconsidered," which follows?

2. Examine Procée's references and compare them to Deagle's. Do you feel either of these writers has better references? If so, why? Could you suggest additions to the references in either case?

At the time she wrote this paper, Gail Deagle was a part-time nursing student living in Grande Prairie, Alberta. Her paper illustrates the use of research as well as argumentation. See Chapter 12 for more information about APA style, which is used here.

Euthanasia Reconsidered

1 Discussions on controversial topics such as euthanasia, physician-assisted suicide, and the withdrawal or withholding of medical treatment are commonly held within our homes, workplaces, and governments. The last several decades have seen an increase in right-to-die activist movement groups across the nation. This is in part a result of many people being afraid that the tremendous advances in medical therapy available may expose them to unnecessary and extraordinary treatment, which would serve only to prolong their suffering in the face of death. Society's beliefs about end-of-life care and the right to make personal choices are changing. At one time, it was considered immoral and unethical to assist or aid a person to escape from pain and suffering of a terminal illness by means of murder or suicide. Many people now feel they have the right to choose voluntary death in the terminal stages of their illnesses when they are no longer able to cope. Our nation is under great pressure by citizens and activist groups to legalize euthanasia. I believe that the legalization of euthanasia would lead to abuse of that legislation.

2 Once legalized, euthanasia would become a commonplace method of dealing with serious and terminal illnesses. One of the reasons for this is that medical and technical advances in palliative care and pain control would be threatened with the sanctioning of euthanasia as a method for relieving pain and suffering. We would see an eventual decline in available funds and resources for palliative care. In the state of Oregon, where euthanasia has been legalized, there has been a reduction of funds allocated to those essential services required for the care of the terminally ill. The same has been found in the Netherlands, where euthanasia is also a legal option. Post-implementation studies have shown that terminally ill patients are presented with fewer options for community-based, end-of-life care. Because supportive services in the Netherlands have been reduced, people tend to seek out end-of-life options. An important point to consider is that when given options, most people will not exercise their option of euthanasia when they have adequate pain control and end-of-life care.

3 Another point to consider is that it is entirely feasible that our government may choose the least expensive route of care in dealing with the terminally ill.

Members of the International Anti-Euthanasia Task Force have addressed their fears that legalized euthanasia might be abused: "The cost effectiveness of hastened death is undeniable. The earlier a patient dies, the less costly is his or her care" (Tort, 2000, p. 115). It has been shown that in the Netherlands, medical treatment options are frequently withheld from those who require palliative treatment. They are left to seek out the services of physicians who will assist them in succumbing to an early death. In Oregon, health management organizations (HMOs) are planning to cover the cost of assisted suicide and, as stated earlier, have reduced funding available for palliative care.

4   Not only do our governments hold a significant amount of authority in determining how our health-care needs are met, but physicians possess incredible power as well. Barney Sneiderman, a professor in the Faculty of Law at the University of Manitoba, is concerned that physicians have the potential to abuse guidelines when they take on the role of judge and jury (1994, p. 102). Legalization would enhance the power of control for doctors, not the patients where the control is intended. Where there is legislation approving euthanasia, there are no guarantees to safeguard against possible abuse. The Netherlands model of euthanasia is one we should be watching closely when determining possibilities of abuse after legalization. Explicit guidelines were set up in that model, but those guidelines are not being followed in the fashion intended. There is nothing in place to protect citizens from abuse. That country has found that there has been a progression from the people for whom euthanasia was initially intended to those who are receiving it now. Initially, the terminally ill were the only recipients of physician-assisted suicide or euthanasia. There has been a rapid progression to include those who are chronically ill, those with psychological afflictions, and finally those who are unable to make or communicate decisions for themselves. There are on average 130 000 deaths per year in the Netherlands, 1000 of which a doctor actively caused or hastened without the patients' request.

5   Rather than requests for euthanasia being initiated by the patient, as the guidelines require, requests in the Netherlands most commonly come from family members of patients. Families become exhausted with caregiving, as there are few resources available for assistance. Given the option, many people choose to have their loved ones put to death instead of continuing the burden of caregiving. If euthanasia is legalized in Canada, the requests for assistance in dying should come voluntarily from individuals when they feel they can no longer cope with the burdens of the dying process. As seen in the Netherlands model, however, many will request assistance when they see themselves as burdens or nuisances. The next step is that requests for euthanasia will come from family or friends, as the patient is increasingly perceived as a a burden on them. The reduced value placed on a life in our society and reduced available resources would play a role in this progression. In 1997, the Hemlock Society issued a press release "which asked that family members and other *agents* be able

to procure court orders to kill *a demented parent, a suffering severely disable* [sic] *spouse, or a child* if their lives are *too burdensome to continue*" (italics in original) (Tort, 2000, p. 137).

6   Our society has a declining value for human life. Our abortion policy proves that we are a society that already accepts ridding ourselves of unwanted lives. Our society is one of convenience. Mothers who are inconvenienced by the prospect of giving birth to a child have an abortion. Family members inconvenienced by the duty of caring for one of their own who is terminally ill could seek euthanasia with or without the patient's knowledge or consent.

7   The disabled are wary and fearful that our country will legalize euthanasia. The apparent devaluation of human life brings fear to disabled persons that they will be killed against their will. Adolf Hitler set a mandate to "grant those who are by all human standards incurably ill a merciful death" (Tort, 2000, p. 118). The need for hospital beds during the war spurred Hitler to secretly euthanize the in- curably insane and those with advanced senility or other conditions that caused the individual to be a burden on society. Diane Coleman, founder and presi- dent of Not Dead Yet, claims that our society demonstrates significant prejudice against disabled persons, that society views the disabled as better off dead. She feels Dr. Jack Kevorkian is seen as a hero, which is the reason he has not been con- victed of his crimes (Tort, p. 134). The majority of people Kevorkian has per- formed euthanasia on are those with disabilities, not with terminal illnesses. Coleman goes on to say:

> According to Stephen Drake, Not Dead Yet's leading expert on Kevorkian, *The press have ignored his primary agenda to push for a class of human beings on which doc- tors can do live experimentation and organ harvesting. In his book,* Prescription Medicide, *he writes that assisted suicide is just a first step to achieving public accept- ance of this agenda.* In written testimony that Kevorkian submitted in his first trial, he said, *The voluntary self-elimination of individual and mortally diseased or crippled lives taken collectively can only enhance the preservation of public health and welfare. . . .* (italics in original).

8   Given the trends seen in the Netherlands and hearing testimony from those advocating legalization of euthanasia, the disabled population has just cause to feel threatened.

9   The value we place on human life, particularly that of the disabled, was ev- idenced when Mike Wallace of the television program *60 Minutes* interviewed a disabled woman on television. During the interview, he questioned her about whether she felt she was a burden to society and openly discussed the costs of her health care. Similar comments to any other minority groups would never have been tolerated.

10   Depression is a common reason for requesting assisted suicide in the Netherlands. In 1982, the Law Reform Commission in Canada defined the word "euthanasia" as "the act of ending the life of a person, from compas-

sionate motives, when he is already terminally ill or when his suffering has become unbearable" (p. 17). My concern is with the terminology "unbearable suffering." It is not specified that the person must be terminally ill *and* be suffering unbearably. Will someone challenge the legal system with charges of discrimination because euthanasia is reserved only for those people with terminal illnesses? Euthanasia is provided in the Netherlands, ambiguously enough, for people suffering mental anguish. An example is a woman distraught over the loss of her 20-year-old son four months earlier. Dutch courts ruled that mental suffering is grounds for euthanasia. It is suggested that a more appropriate treatment for depression is counselling and/or medication (Robinson, 2001, p. 4). Diagnosis of depression can be difficult, but the condition is very treatable.

11   The process of legalization of euthanasia most certainly raises moral and ethical questions and concerns for all citizens in Canada. It is important that we look at the models already in place to evaluate their effectiveness and drawbacks. There is strong evidence to suggest that the same abuse of euthanasia as occurs in the Netherlands model would inevitably occur in Canada. Intentions behind strict guidelines have not been sufficient in enforcing the Netherlands' program. Involuntary euthanasia and the killing of people with afflictions other than terminal illnesses are occurring despite guidelines to the contrary. It is irresponsible to think that Canada would not see the same issues arise. There is a natural progression from euthanasia for those who are terminally ill and make a request for assistance to the eradication of a life that does not fall within those parameters.

References

Law Reform Commission of Canada. (1983). *Report on euthanasia, aiding suicide and cessation of treatment*. Ottawa: Supply and Services Canada.

Robinson, B.A. (2001). Euthanasia and physician assisted suicide: All sides of the issues. *About Alternative Religions*. Retrieved April 25, 2001 from **wysiwyg://16/http://www.religioustolerance.org/euthanas.htm**.

Sneiderman, B., & Kaufert, J.M., (Eds.). *Euthanasia in the Netherlands: A model for Canada?* Brandon, MB: University of Manitoba. Legal Research Institute.

Torr, J.D. (Ed.) (2000). *Euthanasia opposing viewpoints*. San Diego: Greenhaven.

For Further Thinking

1. What do you consider the strong points of Deagle's essay?

2. Are her points organized as effectively as possible? Why or why not?

3. Are there any weak points here? Has she supported all claims with sufficient detailed evidence or citations? Are there any opinions stated as facts and thus left unsupported? Has she omitted anything surrounding the debate, which by its absence could appear as a deliberate evasion?

4. Comment on her tone. Is it firm yet inclusive and respectful of the other side? Are there any moments of excess emotion, any propaganda techniques? (See Chapter 7 in the *Rhetoric* for discussion of various propaganda techniques.)

Looking Back and Ahead

1. Based purely on rhetorical effectiveness, do you consider this essay more or less effective than Janice Procée's "The Case for Active Euthanasia" (the preceding essay)?
2. Examine Deagle's references and compare them to Procée's. Do you feel either of these writers has better references? If so, why? Could you suggest additions to the references in either case? See Chapters 11 and 12 for help with this question.

For Further Reading

"Citizen Impact." April 2003 <www.citizenimpact.ca>. Citizen Impact Canada is dedicated to "equipping Canadians for the effective expression of faith-based principles in the public square" and opposes euthanasia and assisted suicide.

"Compassion in Dying." April 2003 <http://www.compassionindying.org>. The Compassion in Dying Federation advocates for improved care and choice for the terminally ill.

"Euthanasia." Sprink. Maintained by "Ontario consultants on religious tolerance." April 2003 <http://www.religioustolerance.org/euthanas.htm>. One site that examines the issue from "all sides" (their term), looking at the history of the concept from 1225 A.D., the ethical aspects, and official statements by major Christian, Jewish, and Islamic religious organizations.

"Euthanasia" and "Living Wills." Euthanasia.com. April 2003 <http://www.euthanasia.com/>. Committed to the belief that "intentional killing of another person is wrong," this site provides information for research on euthanasia, physician-assisted suicide, living wills, and mercy killing. It also lists several other organizations opposed to euthanasia.

"The Euthanasia Prevention Coalition." April 2003 <http://www.epc.ca>. The EPC is a network of groups seeking to create "an effective social barrier to euthanasia and assisted suicide."

"Euthanasia World Directory." Euthanasia Research and Guidance Organization. Apri 2003 <http://www.finalexit.org/>. ERGO, a non-profit citizens' group, maintains this site, which provides information on right-to-die societies, pro-euthanasia, world organizations, literature, and links across the world. Its contributors are academics and right-to-die societies.

"Hemlock Society USA." April 2003 <http://www.hemlock.org/default.asp>. The society is a non-profit membership association of people "who support choice at end of life."

It was founded in 1980 by Derek Humphry, motivated by the experiences of his deceased wife.

Janz, Heidi. "Returned to Sender" (unpublished stageplay), 2000. Janz, a PhD candidate and lecturer at the University of Alberta, has written this play about Amanda, a teenaged girl with cerebral palsy who is poisoned by her father. Publication plans for the script are not known at this time.

"Robert Latimer." April 2003 <http://www.robertlatimer.com/>. A website by friends of Robert Latimer, set up by Jamie Bassett and maintained by Themmis Anno. Included are essays by academics and professionals, court transcripts, allegations, and rebuttals.

"Robert Latimer." Citizen Impact <http://www.citizenimpact.ca/latimer_ten_years_minimum.html>. This Christian advocacy group gives its reasons to support the conviction of Robert Latimer. Does the organization commit any logical fallacies in its case against Latimer?

Margaret Atwood In this article, commissioned in 1982 by *Mother Jones* magazine to explain why so many Canadians appear to be anti-American, Atwood suggests that Canada is to the United States as Gaul was to Rome. She appeals to her American readers to imagine what it would be like to be dominated by Mexico: 75 percent of the books they bought and 90 percent of the films they watched would be Mexican, and the profits would flow across the border to Mexico. Revolution against economic control, Atwood surmises, is one of the few home-grown American products that is definitely not for sale and export. She allows that Canadians helped this situation come into being, but the main concern, she feels, is that Americans "seem not to know that the United States is an imperial power and is behaving like one."

See the Appendix at the end of the *Reader*, Part I (p. 255), for more support for this reading. This support may particularly benefit you if English is not your first language.

Canadians: What Do They Want?

1   Last month, during a poetry reading, I tried out a short prose poem called "How to Like Men." It began by suggesting that one start with the feet. Unfortunately, the question of jackboots soon arose, and things went on from there. After the reading I had a conversation with a young man who thought I had been unfair to men. He wanted men to be liked totally, not just from the heels to the knees, and not just as individuals but as a group; and he thought it negative and inegalitarian of me to have alluded to war and rape. I pointed out that as far as any of us knew these were two activities not widely engaged in by women, but he was still upset. "We're both in this together," he protested. I admitted that this was so; but could he, maybe, see that our relative positions might be a little different.

2   This is the conversation one has with Americans, even, uh, *good* Americans, when the dinner-table conversation veers round to Canadian-American relations. "We're in this together," they like to say, especially when it comes to continental energy reserves. How do you *explain* to them, as delicately as possible,

why they are not categorically beloved? It gets like the old Lifebuoy ads: even their best friends won't tell them. And Canadians are supposed to be their best friends, right? Members of the family?

3   Well, sort of. Across the river from Michigan, so near and yet so far there I was at the age of eight, reading *their* Donald Duck comic books (originated, however, by one of *ours;* yes, Walt Disney's parents were Canadian) and coming at the end to Popsicle Pete, who promised me the earth if only I would save wrappers, but took it all away from me again with a single asterisk: Offer Good Only in the United States. Some cynical members of the world community may be forgiven for thinking that the same asterisk is there, in invisible ink, on the Constitution and the Bill of Rights.

4   But quibbles like that aside, and good will assumed, how does one go about liking Americans? Where does one begin? Or, to put it another way, why did the Canadian women lock themselves in the john during a '70s "international" feminist conference being held in Toronto? Because the American sisters were being "imperialist," that's why.

5   But then, it's always a little naive of Canadians to expect that Americans, of whatever political stamp, should stop being imperious. How can they? The fact is that the United States is an empire and Canada is to it as Gaul was to Rome.

6   It's hard to explain to Americans what it feels like to be a Canadian. Pessimists among us would say that one has to translate the experience into their own terms and that this is necessary because Americans are incapable of thinking in any other terms—and this in itself is part of the problem. (Witness all those draft dodgers who went into culture shock when they discovered to their horror that Toronto was not Syracuse.)

7   Here is a translation: Picture a Mexico with a population ten times larger than that of the United States. That would put it at about two billion. Now suppose that the official American language is Spanish, that 75 percent of the books Americans buy and 90 percent of the movies they see are Mexican, and that the profits flow across the border to Mexico. If an American does scrape it together to make a movie, the Mexicans won't let him show it in the States, because they own the distribution outlets. If anyone tries to change this ratio, not only the Mexicans but many fellow Americans cry "National chauvinism," or, even more effectively, "National socialism." After all, the American public prefers the Mexican product. It's what they're used to.

8   Retranslate and you have the current American-Canadian picture. It's changed a little recently, not only on the cultural front. For instance, Canada, some think a trifle late, is attempting to regain control of its own petroleum industry. Americans are predictably angry. They think of Canadian oil as *theirs.*

9   "What's mine is yours," they have said for years, meaning exports; "What's yours is mine" meaning ownership and profits. Canadians are supposed to do re-tail buying, no controlling, or what's an empire for? One could always refer Americans to history, particularly that of their own revolution. They objected

to the colonial situation when they themselves were a colony; but then, revolution is considered one of a very few home-grown American products that definitely are not for export.

10   Objectively, one cannot become too self-righteous about this state of affairs. Canadians owned lots of things, including their souls, before World War II. After that they sold, some say because they had put too much into financing the war, which created a capital vacuum (a position they would not have been forced into if the Americans hadn't kept out of the fighting for so long, say the sore losers). But for whatever reason, capital flowed across the border in the '50s, and Canadians, traditionally sock-under-the-mattress hoarders, were reluctant to invest in their own country. Americans did it for them and ended up with a large part of it, which they retain to this day. In every sellout there's a seller as well as a buyer, and the Canadians did a thorough job of trading their birthright for a mess.

11   That's on the capitalist end, but when you turn to the trade union side of things you find much the same story, except that the sellout happened in the '30s under the banner of the United Front. Now Canadian workers are finding that in any empire the colonial branch plants are the first to close, and what could be a truly progressive labor movement has been weakened by compromised bargains made in international union headquarters south of the border.

12   Canadians are sometimes snippy to Americans at cocktail parties. They don't like to feel owned and they don't like having been sold. But what really bothers them—and it's at this point that the United States and Rome part company—is the wide-eyed innocence with which their snippiness is greeted.

13   Innocence becomes ignorance when seen in the light of international affairs, and though ignorance is one of the spoils of conquest—the Gauls always knew more about the Romans than the Romans knew about them—the world can no longer afford America's ignorance. Its ignorance of Canada, though it makes Canadians bristle, is a minor and relatively harmless example. More dangerous is the fact that individual Americans seem not to know that the United States is an imperial power and is behaving like one. They don't want to admit that empires dominate, invade and subjugate—and live on the proceeds—or, if they do admit it, they believe in their divine right to do so. The export of divine right is much more harmful than the export of Coca-Cola, through they may turn out to be much the same thing in the end.

14   Other empires have behaved similarly (the British somewhat better, Genghis Khan decidedly worse); but they have not expected to be *liked* for it. It's the final Americanism, this passion for being liked. Alas, many Americans are indeed likable; they are often more generous, more welcoming, more enthusiastic, less picky and sardonic than Canadians, and it's not enough to say it's only because they can afford it. Some of that revolutionary spirit still remains: the optimism, the 18th-century belief in the fixability of almost anything, the conviction of the possibility of change. However, at cocktail parties and elsewhere one must be able to tell the difference between an individual and a foreign policy. Canadians

can no longer afford to think of Americans as only a spectator sport. If Reagan blows up the world, we will unfortunately be doing more than watching it on television. "No annihilation without representation" sounds good as a slogan, but if we run it up the flagpole, who's going to salute?

15   We *are* all in this together. For Canadians, the question is how to survive it. For Americans there is no question, because there does not have to be. Canada is just that vague, cold place where their uncle used to go fishing, before the lakes went dead from acid rain.

16   How do you like Americans? Individually, it's easier. Your average American is no more responsible for the state of affairs than your average man is for war and rape. Any Canadian who is so narrow-minded as to dislike Americans merely on principle is missing out on one of the good things in life. The same might be said, to women, of men. As a group, as a foreign policy, it's harder. But if you like men, you can like Americans. Cautiously. Selectively. Beginning with the feet. One at a time.

For Further Thinking

1. In her discussion, Atwood refers to the possibility that then-president Ronald Reagan might blow up the world. From today's perspective, does that suggestion, and therefore her whole article, appear exaggerated or, at best, biased? Are nuclear fears less or more real, as technology and international diplomacy become more complex?

2. Canada recently added its voice to those from Europe issuing stern objections to President George W. Bush for backing out of the 1997 Kyoto Accord as well as the non-proliferation arms agreement of the early 1970s. The United States then attacked Iraq against the will of the United Nations, likely violating international law. Could Atwood use the current Bush administration as further proof of her main point: that "the world can no longer afford America's ignorance" in its activities as an imperial power? Do you agree with Atwood (writing in 1982) that America's national self-imaging and active international presence are mere "ignorance"?

3. Do you accept Atwood's analogy of the United States to men and Canada to women in the power politics of relationships? (See our discussion of analogy under "Comparison-Contrast," Chapter 6; also see faulty analogies under "Logical Fallacies," Chapter 7.) The Canadian band The Guess Who boldly reversed this metaphor in their song "American Woman." What are the meanings and implications of these two opposed national metaphors?

4. Do you, like Atwood, know individual Americans who seem great, yet do you also object to the attitudes of the United States as a whole? Explain your view.

5. Make two columns on a sheet of paper. On one side, list the qualities you consider Canadian. On the other, list those you consider American. Now, from either side, select those traits you consider an ideal combination. Is there any way Canadians and Americans could take this list and draw the best from each other?

Looking Back and Ahead

1. How do the arguments, evidence, and politics (values) of Pamela Swanigan, author of "I Am Half-Canadian" (p. 58), compare/contrast to Atwood's opinions in this essay?

2. Based on the social and sexual politics of "Thanks for the Ride" (p. 62), what might Alice Munro think of the young man's comment to Atwood that, "we're both in this together"?

3. Compare and contrast the views and explicit (or perceived) values of Emma Lee Warrior ("White Breast Flats," p. 6), Michel Tremblay ("The King and I," p. 37), and François Hébert ("Je Me Souviens," p. 54) and how they might respond to Atwood's opinions in this essay.

4. In what possible ways do the following articles provide counter-points to Atwood's essay: "College Girl to Call Girl" by Sarah Schmidt (p. 104), "Saskatchewan's Indian People—Five Generations" by Pat Deiter-McArthur (p. 87), "The Quebec Experience: Slavery 1628–1834" by Dorothy Williams (p. 90), "The Genome Generation" by Anita Lahey (p. 132)? See Chapter 10 of the *Rhetoric*, "Critical Analysis," for a discussion of various methods of analysis and for evaluations of arguments.

For Further Reading

American Diplomacy. Online journal of the University of North Carolina. April 2003 <http://www.unc.edu/depts/diplomat/>. This site covers a wide range of topics related to U.S. foreign relations with links to other websites.

"Canada–U.S. Relations: The Road Not Taken." Hillwatch Inc. April 2003 <http://www.hillwatch.com/>. This site offers the history of how and why Canada differs from the United States. This U.S. government relations firm with offices in Boston and Ottawa offers up-to-date information on "hot issues" involving American foreign relations. Essays, including this one, are available through the link "Publications."

Russo, Robert. "Galbraith: An Expatriate Views Canada–U.S. Relations." *CANOE*, online magazine, a division of Netgraphe Inc. April 2003 <http://www.canoe.ca/CANOE2000/politics_7.html>. In an interview given at age 91, the economist John Kenneth Galbraith discusses Canada–U.S. relations from his unique perspective as Canadian-born advisor to American presidents from Franklin Roosevelt to Bill Clinton.

Thunderlake Management Inc. April 2003 <http://www.thunderlake.com/>. Thunderlake prepares trade policy studies and trade negotiations analysis. It monitors World Trade Organization publications. A message forum through this site encourages informed discussions of globalization, the North American Free Trade Agreement (NAFTA), and other trade and diplomacy issues.

Habeeb Salloum   Observing that non-French and non-British Canadians constitute 37.5 percent of the country's population, Habeeb Salloum believes these "others" are to many observers "an unknown force in Canadian society." The author summarizes the history of immigration to Canada, pointing out that before Trudeau chose the road to multiculturalism, immigrants were expected to assimilate. The more different they were from the predominant society that they found here, the more they were taunted. Those who were visibly different could not escape this fate.

In this March 1997 essay, Salloum acknowledges the usual criticisms of multiculturalism, but concludes that on the whole it has had a "beneficial and civilizing effect."

The non-Anglo population of Vancouver is now 30 percent of the whole and that of Toronto is 60 percent. Ironically, some of those most opposed to multiculturalism are themselves the descendants of immigrants, while university-educated people of British background most support the policy. Salloum concludes that multiculturalism protects self-esteem over an assimilation period of three generations, but that assimilation most definitely occurs, and that descendants of non-British immigrants become more "Anglo" than those whose ancestors came from the British Isles. Salloum is a Canadian author and freelance writer specializing in Canadian, Arab, Far Eastern, and Latin American topics.

The Other Canadians and Canada's Future

1   In Canada's province of Quebec, a majority, perhaps, of the inhabitants are convinced that they must act to protect their language and culture. A good section of these go much further, and seek an independent nation. On the other hand, in the English-speaking part of the country, especially in western Canada, the vast majority of people feel that the French, defeated in 1759 on the Plains of Abraham, have no claim to nationhood. This much publicized conflict was discussed by J.A.S. Evans in his article, "The Present State of Canada," in the September 1996 issue of *Contemporary Review*. These views are tempered by those of the remaining non-French and non-British Canadians—about 37.5 per cent of the population. These communities from many ethnic groups, who, with the French Canadians, form the majority of Canada's population, are to many observers an unknown force in Canadian society.

2   For nearly a half century, Canada has been living under the threat of Quebec separation. During this long period of tension between English—about 34.5 per cent—and French Canadians—about 28 per cent of the population—the immigrant minorities have been in a dilemma. Traditionally the overwhelming majority, even in Quebec, became integrated into "Anglo" society. (In Canada the "English" include a large number of Scots who have played a crucial role in the country's history.) However, in that province during the last few decades, this tendency to assimilate into dominant English culture has caused much friction, has raised concerns among French Canadians and has given rise to debates throughout Canada.

3   Amid these pressures, how do the Canadian minorities whose origins can be traced to countries from the four corners of the world see the Canada of the future? For an answer, one must travel back in history to the beginning of this [twentieth] century, when non-French and non-British Europeans in large numbers along with a few Asiatics begin to immigrate to Canada. In that period, assimilation of the minority ethnic groups, without regard to their desires, was the order of the day. In one or, at the most, two generations, the dominant Anglo-Saxon culture and language melted into its folds—not always happily—the vast majority of the sons and daughters of these immigrants.

4   No one in those days, when ethnic epithets and other derogatory terms were used to taunt immigrant groups, would ever visualize the multicultural

Canada of our times where all Canadians are treated equally. Peoples of all racial origins, in today's Canada, are encouraged to romanticize their ethnic history and, hence, to feel "at home." Canadian society has become, at least on the surface, a truly cultural mosaic.

5   However, in the past, it was very different. For the early immigrants and their offspring, the coercion to assimilate into the dominant society was overwhelming. This took many forms. Prejudice, discrimination, racial slurs and subordination into the dominant English culture, all had their effects on the newcomers. In the early years of this [twentieth] century, the acceptance of diversity—people who held unfamiliar customs and values—was not even in the cards.

6   Some of the ethnic groups, like the Dutch, Germans, Scandinavians and many of the Lebanese, assimilated quickly; others, like the Chinese, Greeks, those from the Baltic nations of Estonia, Latvia and Lithuania, and Ukrainians preserved their identity for several generations. However, all the racial minorities through interaction, but mainly through education, in no more than three generations, had totally melted into the governing English society or, to a much lesser extent, French culture in Quebec. In the process of assimilation, many members of the ethnic groups lost confidence in their identity, self-esteem and pride in their racial origin as they were absorbed into the dominant society. Even after receiving their citizenship and becoming new Canadians, usually because of their accents, many were labelled with the derogatory term DPs (displaced persons).

7   Others, if they remained visible like the blacks and Asiatics, were never accepted as true Canadians. One need only bring to mind the sad fate of Japanese Canadians during the Second World War: they had their property confiscated while their total population was interned. "Black Syrian! Black Syrian!" These epithets during my own school years were daily taunts. In those years, the school was a painful place for a child of non-British origin. To escape the daily verbal persecution, I, like the sons of many other immigrants of foreign origin, tried to hide my identity, making believe that my forefathers came from the British Isles.

8   All this changed when Canada's controversial Prime Minister, Pierre Trudeau, set the country on the road to "Multiculturalism within a Bilingual Framework" policy. His vision and that of the Liberal government at that time was this rule: "Canada's many ethnic and racial groups living in harmony while retaining, their cultures—a prop to the English-French nucleus of the country." The government believed that "multiculturalism" would bolster the equality of all Canadians, encourage participation of minorities in social institutions and strengthen the allegiance of ethnic groups to the communities in which they lived. "Multiculturalism" would co-exist with bilingualism as a "defining characteristic" of Canadian society.

9   Trudeau theorized that in a bilingual, multicultural Canadian nation the Anglo-Canadians would have to retire to their proper place, instead of interpreting Canadian identity in their own British terms. As a result, he assumed gen-

uine power sharing would follow. Rather than the American melting pot idea of assimilation into the dominant ethnic group, Canada would become a land of ethnic pluralism—a cultural mosaic of many peoples, forging unity from diversity.

10   In 1971, a policy of multiculturalism was officially adopted, legitimizing the self-conception of Canada as resting on pluralist foundations. Government policy thereafter encouraged one country, two languages, many cultures. Legislation became an instrument to legitimize and manage a diverse population within a state apparatus. It officially formalized a multicultural nation and Canada became the world's only official multicultural society. "Ethnic diversity," "ethnic pluralism," "multi-ethnic" and "poly-ethnic" were now acceptable phrases. In 1988, Canada' s multiracial and multi-lingual mélange was strengthened further by the passage of the Multicultural Act which emphasized "positive race relations." With its enactment, the country moved to the forefront of nations in dealing with ethno-racial diversity in a politically acceptable manner.

11   Among some of the ethnic groups, multiculturalism was accepted with great enthusiasm. In the 23 October 1978 issue of the Saskatoon *Star-Phoenix*, it was reported that at a Ukrainian fund-raising dinner in the city, one of the speakers stated: "Canada's unique characteristic and strength is multiculturalism." He went on to say: "Canadians have abandoned the futile evangelism of patriotic nationalism. Instead, every Canadian can enjoy the joy and pride of his cultural roots, recognized, respected and accepted as a worthwhile contributor to Canadian society."

12   On the other hand, "multiculturalism" has proved to be a controversial social policy. From the very beginning, some groups wanted to emphasize language; others religion; while a number zeroed in on folklore. Opinion varied among the ethnic societies as to how much ethnicity and interaction among other cultural groups were to be stressed. At the inception of multiculturalism, critics said that it was a ploy by Trudeau and the Liberal Party to control and manipulate ethnic groups and was only a vote-getting gimmick. Subsidizing the ethnic groups to teach their own languages, which multiculturalism supported, would, according to many at that time, retard the immigrants' assimilation into the English or French societies.

13   In the ensuing years, many denounced multiculturalism as counterproductive, irrelevant, unworkable and an expensive frill which would impede assimilation—a guise to destroy British traditions and the English language. Some asserted that it would increase the risk of racial conflict; others described it as a cultural zoo: the zoo keeper—the government—would manipulate the inhabitants.

14   Yet, on the whole, multiculturalism, despite its critics, has had a beneficial and civilizing effect on Canada. It has shaped the country's collective identity as a generous and tolerant nation, enhancing the quality of life for all its inhabitants. It has become a system of achieving national consensus without the loss of integrity—a setup which all Canadians can buy into as equals. No country in the world has ventured as far as Canada into the field of ethnic interaction.

15   Contributing an inclusive sense of common citizenship, official multicul-turalism, harnessing the power of the over ten million Canadians who are nei-ther English nor French has defused mounting Quebec pressure on federalism; blunted American influences on Canadian cultural space; enhanced the country's cultural richness; and, with the demise of Anglo-conformity, filled the void in the Canadian cultural identity. Without doubt, it has elevated Canada to the ranks of progressive countries in the judicious management of ethnic relations.

16   By the encouragement of self-confidence, self-worth and a feeling of pride in their ethnic origin, multiculturalism has helped the immigrants succeed in their social and economic life and has made them feel at home. There is no bet-ter indication of how self-image determines the future of the country than when I visited the northern Alberta Arab community of Lac La Biche in the late summer of 1996. "I love it here! In this town we prospered and here we have established our roots." Khalil Abughoush, owner of the IGA supermarket in Lac La Biche, was full of enthusiasm when talking about his small northern city. Like his fellow countrymen—20 per cent of the town's 3,000 inhabitants are of Arab-Lebanese origin—he had come to seek his fortune in this northern Alberta resort. In Canada's multicultural society, Abughoush, like the majority of im-migrants and their descendants, felt at home. As he prospered he felt no coercion to fit in, no pressure to leave his culture behind. There is no question that "multiculturalism" has succeeded, to a great extent, in making Canada's new-comers feel at home, with the exception of many of the visible minorities. For the latter, multiculturalism has been only of marginal benefit. It has failed to combat racism and discriminatory practices. Even though today one of the major priorities of multiculturalism is the elimination of racism, unofficially, the dominant Anglo and French societies continue to see visible minorities as dif-ferent, not equal, and an unstable factor in Canadian society. These visible mi-norities at present constitute 6.3 per cent of the population—expected to rise to 10 percent by the year 2000. In the large urban centres, they have become an important segment of the population. The non-Anglo population of Vancouver is 30 per cent and that of Toronto 60 per cent—20 per cent of which are visible minorities.

17   Even more forgotten by multiculturalism are Canada's "First Nations Peoples." Even though there is a widespread consensus that the country's Indigenous Peoples have been treated unfairly, they remain as the bottom stratum in Canadian society. To them, multiculturalism has brought very little benefit. In the Canada of today, for Asiatics, Africans and Aboriginals, skin colour acts as a substantial barrier to integration. The question, asked in the 2 September 1979 issue of the *Toronto Daily Star* by its columnist Richard Gwyn, persists: "How many non-whites will prove too many for the stability of Canadian society?" Even more pointedly, Stella Hryniuk, in *Twenty Years of Multiculturalism*, quotes a Canadian of French and Haitian descent as asking, "Am I a Canadian when I feel Canadian, or when others say I am a Canadian?"

18   Nevertheless, for the majority of immigrants, multiculturalism, costing the government annually a mere dollar per Canadian, has benefited the country. A good number of newcomers believe that government funding of multicultural events like dance-fests and ethnic centres will preserve their culture forever. Ethnic gatherings such as Caravan and Caribana in Toronto, Dragon Boat Races in Vancouver, Folklorama in Winnipeg and Heritage Day in Edmonton romanticize the newcomers' history and identity and offer them a feeling of belonging. Cultural community life is more visible in Canada today than in any other country.

19   However, ethnic ceremonies and dances do not change the reality that the Canadian power structure remains English and French, around which circumnavigate lesser satellite cultures. Assimilation still goes on apace, but in a more humane manner. The difference between the Canadian "mosaic" and American "melting pot" is not overwhelming—both have the same aim: assimilation. The preservation of ethnic cultures in both countries is still very dependent on new replenishment by way of immigration. Through education and intermarriage, the overwhelming majority have assimilated into mainly the English culture—by the third generation over 85 per cent. Unlike earlier in this century, they willingly melt into the host society as they ethnically dance themselves out of existence. Our family, whose members, in the main, live in western Canada, are an excellent example of this assimilation. Out of its eight members, only two married Arabs. Today, my nieces and nephews are Carletons, McWhirters and McCallums who know very little about their partially Arab origin. Their views about Canada and its future are those of the dominant Anglo society.

20   In western Canada, where non-French, non-British and non-Native origins constitute nearly half of the population, "English only" is supported by the majority of the inhabitants. The descendants of the "black Syrians" are now the most vocal opponents of multiculturalism. To them, all the new immigrants are taking away the Canadians' jobs and bringing a foreign element into Canadian society. The same view is held by many descendants of immigrants. They are multiculturalism's most vocal critics. The backlash against cultural retention comes, in the main, from assimilated members of ethnic communities. Strangely, support for cultural maintenance is strongest among university graduates of British origin.

21   The views about the future of Canada among the vast majority of these descendants of immigrant groups is more "Anglo" than those whose forefathers came from the British Isles. With the passing of the third generation, the countries of their origin are, I would say, to the majority, unknown. The legacy of their fathers to Canada are a few foods like falafel, hummus, pizzas and wonton soup. However, as they disappear, because of multiculturalism, they retain their self-esteem. Overwhelmingly, their view of Canada and its future is that of the Anglo Canadians.

For Further Thinking

1. David Suzuki, a third-generation Japanese-Canadian, makes statements in his autobiographical book *Metamorphosis* (1987) that certainly seem to support Salloum: "we children didn't understand the old culture, and didn't have the slightest interest—we were Canadians." From people you know, or perhaps your own experiences, do you think Salloum's theory is correct?

2. It is often observed that those who come to Canada see its strengths and value its beauty more highly than native-born Canadians. Is there some truth to this? Is complacency a Canadian problem?

3. What is your opinion of Canada's attitude toward immigration? What is your view on the value of new immigrants to the Canadian future?

Looking Back and Ahead

1. How does Pamela Swanigan's discussion fit with the ideas developed in this essay (see "I Am Half-Canadian," p. 58)?

2. Read "A Story to Pass On" by Daphne Read (p. 216). What special practices might be employed and considerations taken into account in a post-secondary writing class to address cultural differences and, in some cases, feelings of exclusion?

3. Read Brian D. Johnson's piece "Atom's Journey" (p. 139). How does Atom Egoyan fit into the picture that Salloum describes? Does Egoyan's notion that identity is possibly a construct accord with Salloum's ideas? What about Johnson's added idea that blurred identity is a particularly Canadian construct? Is Salloum referring at all to the same idea?

For Further Reading

Department of Canadian Heritage, Secretary of State for Multiculturalism. Online. April 2003 <http://www.pch.gc.ca/multi/index.html>.

Esses, Victoria M., and R.C. Gardner, University of Western Ontario. "Multiculturalism in Canada: Context and Current Status." Online from the *Canadian Journal of Behavioural Science*, special edition on Ethnic Relations in a Multicultural Society, 1996. April 2003 <http://www.cpa.ca/cjbsnew/1996/ful_edito.html>. This academic article is very informative.

Fleras, Augie, and Jean Lock Kunz. *Media and Minorities: Representing Diversity in a Multicultural Canada*. Toronto: Thompson Educational Publishing, 2001. Fleras teaches at the University of Waterloo, and Kunz works for the Canadian Council on Social Development.

Gunew, Sneja. "Multicultural Differences: Canada, USA, Australia." Online. Department of English, University of British Columbia. April 2003 <http://www.english.ubc.ca/~sgunew/mcmulti.htm>. The author taught at the University of Victoria, B.C.

Huggan, Graham, and Winifred Siemerling. "U.S./Canadian Writers' Perspectives on the Multiculturalism Debate: A Round-Table Discussion at Harvard University." *Canadian*

Literature 164 (Spring 2000): 82–111. Panel addresses were made by Clark Blaise, Nicole Brossard, George Elliott Clarke, and Paul Yee. American Geeta Patel then responded.

Keohane, Kieran. *Symptoms of Canada: An Essay on the Canadian Identity.* Toronto: University of Toronto Press, 1997. Keohane gives us his outsider's perspective on Canada's much debated issue of national identity, arguing that conflicting objectives have created the impasse in our search for a collective identity.

Makabe, Tomoko. *The Canadian Sansei.* Toronto: University of Toronto Press, 1998.

"Multiculturalism in Canada." News in Review, Canada Broadcasting Corporation <http://cbc.ca/insidecbc/newsinreview/April>. This site is intended for high school classes in response to a news story about Indian-born Ujjal Dosanjh, former premier of British Columbia. Besides information about Dosanjh, the site includes many interesting quotes on multiculturalism in Canada, some dating back to the 1920s.

Suzuki, David. *Metamorphosis: Stages in a Life.* Toronto: Stoddart, 1987.

Ellen Clark Why do writers write? Certainly a major reason is to say something unexpected—to startle us out of our complacency and make us see things from a new angle. Many of the selections in this *Reader*, to cite Pierre Trudeau, move "against the current." Perhaps no selection is more surprising than this one. The likelihood of a former separatist like René Daniel Dubois switching to the "No" side and scorning his compatriots for their "soft facism" seemed less likely than a Montreal Anglo's looking forward to the benefits of Quebec independence. Whether you agree with the following essay or not—written in May 2000 amidst rumours of a third call for a referendum on separation—you have to admire the author's original perspective and willingness to speak her mind. She comments that "any referendum rhetoric usually has English-speaking Quebecers worrying about their future in the province." She wanted to mitigate the typical knee-jerk rhetorical responses.

   Ellen Clark, a part-time student, works in Montreal as a full-time nurse, and might well be familiar with the hospital settings depicted by Denys Arcand in his acclaimed film *Jesus of Montreal.* The protagonist—who is seriously ill—is turned away by an unsympathetic Francophone facility. The only hospital to admit and help him is the Jewish General, with its English-speaking doctors. Arcand's application of the Biblical parable is a further reminder that across the French/English dichotomy, some artists, thinkers, and citizens do welcome the Other.

Quebec Separation: Anglophones Can Win at This Game, Too

1   The Parti Québécois held their party convention in Montreal this week. Premier Lucien Bouchard easily won the confidence vote with ninety-six percent delegate support. Mr. Bouchard has often said he will not call another referendum unless "there are winning conditions." With such overwhelming party support, Bouchard is prepared to play the referendum game again. The most publicized issues debated during the weekend convention were sovereignty, the economy, amendments

to the language law Bill 101, and access restrictions to English post-secondary education. According to Alliance Quebec President William Johnson, members of the Anglophone minority in Quebec should be quaking in their boots after hearing what the party delegates were debating.

2   I, as an Anglo, disagree and am not afraid. This is because Quebec Anglophones do not have to be fearful of the path of independence that the Parti Québécois has chosen to pursue. Anglophones and Allophones have a stake in this province and should plan for the inevitable separation. Separation does not automatically include Anglos moving out of Quebec; that move would make it too easy for the other players. It is time for Anglophones to think as Quebecers without language or cultural bias and explore what the certain separation from Canada will gain for them. There are advantages to enjoy with the advent of separation and Anglos can survive and prosper in the separate state known as Quebec. In essence, Anglos must play their part strategically in this game too and use the rules that the PQ decreed to their advantage.

3   The province is in a strong economic position. The PQ government continues to work on a long-term strategy to ensure economic, social and cultural stability at the time of separation. The unemployment rate is decreasing, businesses are moving into the province, and commercial properties have the lowest vacancy in Quebec to foreign businesses. We have huge pharmaceutical industries located on the West Island of Montreal. Aerospace and space industries have located in Laval and Dorval. The most recent coup is the announcement of the NASDAQ stock market moving into the vacated stock exchange in September. NASDAQ is just starting to build up their worldwide exchanges, so Quebec will be in on the ground floor of its growth. There is also a strong export market for hydroelectric power to the United States that will mean increased revenues with the new line being built through the Eastern Townships. Employment opportunities will be available for Anglos in the technology fields because the global industry will still function with English as the base language. Any industry that has an American head office, or that Quebec does business with, will need a quota of English-speaking employees in order to maintain communication links. The government has also been setting up the necessary financial framework to ease the separation process.

4   The infrastructure for many of the systems needed for banking is already in place with Quebec-based banking institutions such as the Caisse Populaires and Banque Nationale. The PQ government has invested in financial ventures for the last ten years, with structures in place which successfully support the economy following separation. The financial stability of the sovereign state will be secure because of the stockpiling of money over the years by the government. They have amassed huge amounts of funds from cuts to social programs and transfer of debts to municipal levels of government. They continue to build this fund by removing duplication of services and administrative levels within social programs. The merging of municipalities will also decrease administrative costs

that the government has to fund now. The government is reducing its overhead so the tax burden will be less than it is currently. While there have been many debates about the province when it becomes independent, other countries will recognize its status, because the Premier has been gathering their support.

5   There is no need to worry that Quebec will become a Third World country when it separates. This likely would have happened in 1979 if separation had occurred when the PQ first came into power. At that time, the PQ party won the election on voter emotion. The party lacked the organization, financial resources and political shrewdness to proceed with separation. In the year 2000, the situation is different. The PQ government has matured politically and has the foundation in place to set the process in motion with positive expectations. This government has rehearsed the scenario of separation endlessly and planned for any eventuality. This government has a bankroll to work with that was not there 20 years ago. At the PQ convention, Mr. Bouchard predicted there would be a surplus of $700 million year one, $1.4 billion year two and $2.1 billion year three following separation. This news is reassuring about the financial prospects. The next most popular issue of debate is the promotion of the French language.

6   Anglos and other minorities have always been concerned about the language laws of a unilingual Francophone state. One way to counteract this is through education. Education of this generation of children is one area where Anglophones and Allophones can have a tremendous advantage over Francophones and beat them at their own game. The PQ government expects everyone to learn French in school and will force immigrants to attend French-language schools from elementary to post-secondary levels. To encourage the French language, English is not taught in the French schools until grade four. English schools have already adapted the curriculum to provide French immersion programs starting in kindergarten. Rather than fighting against this law, non-Francophones should learn the French language, becoming multi-lingual with their mother tongue, French and English. They will have an advantage over unilingual Francophones if they follow this education strategy.

7   Another advantage of a bilingual education to remember is that Quebec cannot operate in a vacuum when it comes to industry. Who will international businesses hire, a multilingual person or a unilingual Francophone Québécois? In the world today, many other countries expect their children to speak three or more languages. For example, in Switzerland children graduate high school speaking all three national languages and English. The Swiss children are prepared scholastically to work at an international level without restrictions because of language barriers. On the other hand, the average Québécois does not think of the world beyond the provincial border. While the Québécois are determined to remain insular to preserve their language and culture, they neglect the larger issue of communication with the world outside. The government will not enforce Quebec language laws when it comes to a choice between the government keeping a corporation from leaving Quebec and supporting unemployed Quebecers with government social assistance.

Corporations will be able to pressure the government by threatening to leave the province if they have to adhere to strict language laws. They will play and win the game of economic hardball versus linguistic idealism.

8   The focus of this essay has been to review the usual topics of Quebec debate from a fresh perspective. Looking at the issues with the idea of using the government's own rules to survive and prosper as a Quebec Anglo has not been widely publicized until now. The focus has always been on preventing separation from happening without addressing how we manage after the fact. More people need to prepare themselves to survive the change. The alternative of walking away before the game is finished is not an option I want to see us exercise; I would rather we develop Anglo winning conditions now.

For Further Thinking

1. Some separatists accept that leaving Canada could result in a decline in living standards. They are content to make the sacrifice. Others wield studies proving, they say, that Quebec will actually gain by separation. Anti-separatists argue the opposite. What do you think of Clark's economic arguments?

2. To many outside observers, Quebec's distinctive culture is simply part of the Canadian status quo. Should Canada have agreed to acknowledge that distinctness?

3. Is Clark's metaphor of a culture and language "game" too frivolous?

Looking Back and Ahead

1. Read François Hébert's "Je Me Souviens" (p. 54) and Michel Tremblay's "The King and I" (p. 37). Would Ellen Clark and her descendants be able to feel the same in an independent Quebec as Hébert and Tremblay would? How would she establish a connection? How does Clark seem to define "culture"?

2. Read Mordecai Richler's "The Summer My Grandmother Was Supposed to Die" (p. 14). Contrast the Montreal Clark depicts with the one that the characters in Richler's short story inhabit.

For Further Reading

Hundt, Reed. *You Say You Want a Revolution: A Story of Information Age Politics.* Boston: Yale University Press, 2000. Reed puts the ongoing unity battle of Quebec and Canada into a broader, global context.

Jay, Paul, Dir. *Never-Endum Referendum* (film). National Film Board, 1997, 71 min 03 s. Jay shows Quebecers struggling with effects of the debate in their personal lives.

Lamont, Lansing. *Breakup: The Coming End of Canada and the Stakes for America.* New York: Norton, 1994.

Mathews, Georges. *The Quiet Resolution: Quebec's Challenge to Canada.* Trans. Dominique Clift. Toronto: Summerhill Press, 1990.

McDonagh, Patrick, and Janice Paskey. "Some Top Talents Are Being Lured Away, but Most Professors Are Staying Put." Online article. *The McGill Reporter* 29, No. 11, Thursday, February 27, 1997. ‹http://www.mcgill.ca/uro/Rep/r2911/move.html ›. This article discusses why some professors have left the Montreal English-language university, why others have come, and why many are staying.

Taylor, Drew Hayden. "Is Good for the French Gander." *Funny You Don't Look Like One: Observations of a Blue-Eyed Ojibway.* Rev. edn. Penticton, BC: Theytus, 1998. 134–135. "As for the Native people of the province [Quebec], it is not just a case of wanting back the land that the province says they surrendered to the government long ago. That, of course, would make them 'Indian givers.' It's simply a matter of wanting to maintain their cultural and linguistic individuality in an environment dominated by another forceful and aggressive society. Sound familiar?"

Weintraub, William, Dir. *The Rise and Fall of English Montreal* (film). National Film Board, 1993, 50 min 30 s. Between 1973 and the making of this film, some 300 000 English-speaking people left Montreal, convinced that they had no future in an increasingly politicized Quebec.

Milena Tomol   Russian immigrant and student Milena Tomol wrote the following essay in a language she says she is still learning. Her topic, life in Russia during the Communist regime, ends with a comparison to life in Canada today. What Tomol describes matches general coverage of Russia during the Cold War years; misery characterized the daily lives of many citizens. But Tomol goes on to admire how people nevertheless maintained their "rich" personalities, their curiosity, and their willingness to speak the truth. This character, she suggests, represented a wealth beyond material goods and comforts. While enduring revisionist government propaganda and surface uniformity, Russians maintained their individual spirits. During the Cold War, the West heard one such spirit in Alexander Solzhenitsyn, a writer who risked his life to depict true conditions in such searing works as *Cancer Ward* (1968) and *The Gulag Archipelago* (1973–1978). In Canada we feel fortunate and perhaps superior to have freedom of speech: we do not oppress or imprison our writers. And yet, Russian visitors to contemporary Canada have been known to object that we do not respect our writers, artists, and intellectuals. We let them speak and publish—but do we listen or follow their inspiration?

Milena Tomol was born in 1969 in a small industrial town in the heart of Russia. In 1994, she received a Bachelor's degree with distinction in chemical engineering from the Moscow Academy of Oil and Gas. She met her husband on business trips to Canada and now lives with him and her two children in Calgary, where she continues her studies by distance education.

Equal Share of Miseries

1   The inherent vice of capitalism is the unequal sharing of blessings, the inherent virtue of socialism is the equal sharing of miseries.

—Winston Churchill

2   Four years ago I bid my farewell to Russia, my homeland, and came to live in Canada. Upon my arrival, I found myself in a totally strange and unfamiliar environment. I was disoriented and confused. It felt like somebody had turned my world upside down. This left me fumbling around in search of a new foundation. I had to start my life all over again, trying to integrate myself into a new society with entirely different political and economical systems, different ideology, different culture, different language, different mentality, and different values. In other words, there was no shortage of differences to reconcile in my heart. Some were easy. Some were not.

3   The most conspicuous difference, perhaps, was the constant shortage of necessities of life in Communist Russia: food, clothing, and housing. There was no free market. Everything was distributed by the State, but it did not do a very good job of matching supply and demand. People had to wait for decades to get a place they could call home. It was a rite of passage for young people to obtain a first job, then get their names on the waiting list for an apartment and a car. Years would go by, and by the time they had families, maybe they would get a home of their own. Maybe. That was the idea, but it rarely worked that way. There were people who retired living in dormitories. It was customary for three generations of people to live in a two-bedroom apartment at the same time. As bad as it was, it was much better compared to conditions in "kommunalka," a socialist-era phenomenon, where a large apartment or house was converted into a multifamily accommodation on the "one family—one room" basis. Kitchen and bathroom had to be shared by five to eight families, each of whom had a designated day for bathing and doing laundry. Can you imagine the lively atmosphere in the kitchen on a Sunday morning? Although kommunalka was looked upon as a remnant of the wartime past, I have seen a fair number of those in my life.

4   Shopping was no picnic either. Faced with empty shelves and line-ups, people were forced to frequently scout out shops in the area and stock up on things that became available from time to time. It was a routine for my mother to run through a dozen of the local shops after a full day of work. If she was lucky to come across a "critical commodity," she used to buy it in monstrous amounts to share with friends and neighbours, who would do the same for her. At one point, food shortages were so bad that all you could find in the stores was neat rows of three-litre bottles of apple and peach juice. No wonder wives of Russian diplomats (just about the only people who could get out of the country and sample delights of the "rotting capitalist societies") were known to have mental breakdowns in Western supermarkets and department stores. They were overwhelmed by the abundance and variety of products and unable to choose. Well, seven varieties of baking powder could be quite mind-boggling even for an experienced shopper. As one Russian comedian declared after careful examination of the material blessings of Western societies, "This is communism! How come bloody capitalists got here before us?"

5   Under these circumstances, it did not matter how much money you made. What really mattered was what kind of friends you had. Connections were the quintessential currency: you get something for me, I get something for you. Here in Canada, the most prominent people are doctors, lawyers, and accountants; back home salespersons and shop assistants were the people of stature. They were the people who could get you things, tip you off if something was about to be put on the shelves that were habitually occupied by dust.

6   The shock felt by Russian people after their first shopping trips to the Western world came as no surprise because many of them were used to a coupon system of product distribution, by which every individual was entitled to a certain amount of meat, butter, sugar, etc. (whatever was in short supply) per month. These products could be purchased only with coupons dispensed by a local registry office.

7   This brings about another phenomenon of the Soviet era—registration. Absolutely everyone had to be registered at the place of residence. Without such registration one could not get a job, medical services, education, or the above-mentioned coupons. Ironically, no one could acquire the right of permanent residence without a job. In fact, it was a vicious circle that helped Big Brother to keep a watchful eye on the citizens. Under these conditions, nothing could go unnoticed; no one could move or disappear. In a very literal sense, one could run, but could not hide.

8   Given the fact that housing came from the government, people were pretty much stuck where they were born. A move to another city could come only with a job transfer or marriage. I had learned that in recent years it became possible to buy the right of permanent residence in large desirable cities like Moscow and St. Petersburg. These cities were always desirable to live in because, unlike other Russian cities and towns, they had a lot more to offer. There were restaurants, nightclubs, bars, and shops with fancy imported goods. In some respect, these cities were the showrooms of socialism for foreign visitors who, in general, were not allowed outside them, where life was different.

9   My native town, with a quarter of a million inhabitants, for example, had three restaurants, two disco clubs, and one bar. Things of this nature were perceived as decadent and superfluous in the society where the word "entertainment" had a derogatory connotation. Builders of communism did not need to be entertained—there was a plenitude of museums glorifying our revolutionary past, a multitude of exhibitions admiring our remarkably prosperous present, as well as an amplitude of art galleries celebrating our radiant future.

10   Nor did they need variety or aesthetics in architecture. Residential areas built after the Revolution looked exactly the same: endless trains of drab-looking, cookie-cutter building blocks. Even the names of the streets were the same. There were a Lenin Street and a Peace Avenue in every city. This uniformity inspired the plot of a comedy that became very popular in communist times. The dead-drunk main character is taken by mistake on a trip from Moscow to St.

Petersburg. Having slept through his flight and still only half conscious, he mumbles his Moscow address to a taxi driver who takes him to the apartment building of the same address in St. Petersburg. The building happens to look exactly the same as its counterpart in Moscow; the door lock happens to have the same key, and the apartment happens to be furnished in a similar way. As a result, our hero, absolutely oblivious of the switch, has no problem getting into bed, where he is confronted by its rightful owner, an attractive single female. In my mind, one of the reasons for the tremendous success of the movie was that such a mix-up was absolutely possible in the country where all cities were clones of one another.

11   So was everything else—cars, furniture, clothes, and even people. We were all equal (even though it was implicit that "some animals were more equal than others"). *Equal* meant *alike, same, uniform.* Everything was controlled, standardized, and censored: what we read, what we watched, what we thought. People were the "nuts and bolts" of the government machine. Individuality and creativity were discouraged (unless used to glorify the "outstanding" achievements of socialism). Mediocrity thrived. "Don't stick out and you may get by" was the motto of many.

12   And yet, beneath this miserable brainwashed uniformity there were the spirit, pride, and dignity of people with rich personalities and inquisitive minds, people who were true to themselves and not afraid to speak their minds. There were countless nights spent in the smoke-filled kitchens debating fervidly about the purpose and meaning of life. There was also the sense of brotherhood, overwhelming closeness, intimacy of minds and spirits, a feeling of connection, deep understanding, along with sincerity and selflessness.

13   People in Canada are very different in that respect. I find that they are too preoccupied with being "nice." *Nice* is a very insipid word, in my opinion. It lacks definition and character. People can be described as friendly, kind, generous, witty, intelligent, educated, etc. *Nice* does not reflect any of that. And yet it is widely used to describe people. Being nice is valued much higher than being true, honest, and open. Therefore, when people here give me a compliment I never know if they really mean it, or if they are just trying to be nice. When they agree with my opinion, I never know if they really think so, or if they just do not want to hurt my feelings. People are reluctant to say something that will show who they really are because they fear that others will not like them. Obsession with "political correctness" has reached the point where it is nothing but ridiculous. No wonder conversations about the weather are so popular. By talking about the weather people cannot offend anyone. Nor can they get to know one another really well and receive the rewards of true friendship. I see so many people in Canada who seem to "have it all" in life, but still feel lonely and unhappy. It looks to me that capitalist societies, along with the material blessings, have their own share of miseries.

For Further Thinking

1. Chart the variations of tone in this essay. Could you identify a musical effect that results?

2. Does Tomol's description of Russia more than 10 years ago match your impressions of Russia at the time? What has shaped your impression of this nation and culture?

3. How would you describe the writer's style in this essay? How much of her style, would you say, is tied to her use of English as a foreign language and to her cultural background?

4. Review our discussion of comparison in the *Rhetoric* in Chapter 7. How does Tomol use comparison as a device? Does she depart from the conventional pattern in any way?

5. Do you sympathize with the problem Tomol has with Canadian "niceness"? Do Canadians seem vague, bland, and unopinionated in order to pass as "nice"?

Looking Back and Ahead

1. What other selection in this *Reader* do you feel most resembles Tomol's essay? Explain the reasons for your choice.

2. Read George Orwell's "Politics and the English Language" (p. 227). One of the samples of bad writing he provides is taken from a Communist pamphlet. His works *Animal Farm* (1945) and *1984* (1949) clearly satirize Stalinist rule. Do you think Orwell would deplore or admire Tomol's essay? Why?

3. There is a universal belief that hardship forges character, enriching life and art. Do any other selections in the *Reader* express this view?

For Further Reading

"Marxists." Online. April 2003 <http://www.marxists.org/history/index.htm>. This page lists works by writers who participated directly in Marxist Russia.

Palat, Madhavan K., Ed. *Social Identities in Revolutionary Russia*. New York: Palgrave, 2001.

Read, Christopher. *The Making and Breaking of the Soviet System: An Interpretation*. New York: Palgrave, 2001.

"Russian history." Online. Geographia.com. InterKnowledge Corp., 1996–1997. April 2003 <http://www.geographia.com/russia/rushis01.htm>. A history of Russia on the Web.

Solzhenitsyn, Alexander. *One Day in the Life of Ivan Denisovich*. Trans. H.T. Willetts. New York: The Noonday Press, 1991.

Zickel, Raymond E., Ed. *The Soviet Union: A Country Study*. Online. Research Division, Library of Congress, 1989. April 2003 <http://memory.loc.gov/frd/cs/sutoc.html>. Funded by the American military, this site may be biased against a former Cold War enemy; nevertheless, it provides a wide spectrum of background information.

Daphne Read Daphne Read received her PhD from York University in Toronto and teaches in the Department of English at the University of Alberta. Her teaching and research interests include contemporary cultural and postcolonial studies, materialist feminism, and the politics of self-representation in fiction and non-fiction. She is currently working on projects on memory, trauma, and narrative in contemporary writing by women.

In her essay, Read examines the role of personal experience in the writing classroom, exploring concepts of "witnessing," community, autobiography, and presumptions of social and academic safety. She draws on a wide range of both scholarly and pedagogical sources to question the complex basis of the writing class as a collective. She also examines the potential for student interaction in the speaking and writing of experience. Citing the novel *Beloved* (1987) by Nobel Prize winner Toni Morrison, Read reminds us that juxtaposing stories next to each other in the classroom can produce new forms of social and narrative knowledge.

"A Story to Pass On": The Writing Class(room) as Borderland

1   It was not a story to pass on . . . .

—Toni Morrison, *Beloved*

I. Writing: The Local

2   This, too, is not a story to pass on: In Edmonton, Alberta, on November 28, 1993, Joyce Cardinal was doused with gasoline and set on fire by an unknown assailant. She died about three weeks later on December 20, 1993, in the University of Alberta Hospital. This story haunted a student who was an emergency nurse on duty when Joyce Cardinal was brought to the hospital. Through several writing courses over two years, this student tried to put the story into words; she wanted to give voice to the woman, to express solidarity with other victims of violence, to express the anguish and horror, and to find a way through it to . . . *what?* It was a story that could not be told.

3   How *does* one make sense of this story of a woman so brutally silenced?

4   One could retrace the scant narrative details available in the local newspaper and note the terrible symbolism as burning trash at midnight took the shape of a woman, and later, a Native woman, who had a severe speech impediment and left a small party to walk home alone. One could honour and mourn the creative spirit evoked in the family's vigil for the beloved: "Joyce Cardinal's family clings to a crocheted afghan, a worn piece of wool which bears her spirit while she lies swathed in bandages in a hospital bed" (Plischke). One *knows* that Cardinal's death will never be recuperated by the discovery of a letter she has written to the future. But one also knows that other voices will emerge—have emerged—"speak[ing] the words that should be spoken" (Wiebe and Johnson 329).[1] And some of these voices will emerge in the writing class(room),[2] in students' essays about personal experience where the personal and the historical are inextricably linked.

5   I begin with the death of Joyce Cardinal for many reasons. It was passed on to me by the emergency nurse, who, during the weeks of Cardinal's dying, spoke very little about the story for legal, ethical, and human reasons. Later, as she tried to write about the experience, she abstracted the pain as too much for her readers, too much to bear, finally reaching an impasse in the boundary between the particular (the awful details of Joyce Cardinal's death) and the universal (the symbolic). At one level, her writing, as I have constructed it, and my writing of this "story" raise familiar concerns about (mis)representation *and* appropriation in encounters between the Western intellectual and the Native. Are we telling just another story of Western women's encounters with the Native Other? What does it mean to tell this story, to struggle with its meanings?

6   The answer for me lies in the concept of witnessing, as described by Dori Laub, a psychiatrist, philosopher, and survivor of the Holocaust in the Second World War. In "Truth and Testimony: The Process and the Struggle," an essay born of living through the Holocaust and helping others to make sense of this historical traumatic experience, Laub identifies three processes of witnessing: "the level of being a witness to oneself within the experience, the level of being a witness to the testimonies of others, and the level of being a witness to the process of witnessing itself" (61). Although Laub is writing specifically about surviving the Holocaust, the concept of witnessing serves as a point of entry into discussions of the place of traumatic or painful experience—both personal and historical—in student writing.

7   Witnessing at all three levels can also occur in the contemporary class(room) when students write out of "the imperative need to *tell* and thus to come to *know* one's story" (Laub 63) *and* other students and teachers listen, respond, and bear witness. Thus, within Laub's framework, my student's encounter with Joyce Cardinal can be seen, not as an act of appropriation, but as an act of witnessing that could never be completed or fully understood. And I, in my capacity as teacher, became a partial witness to the process of witnessing.

8   Witnessing becomes one's way of creating a bridge across differences, a way of coming to knowledge and of promoting critical consciousness. The process of communal witnessing is, variously, a form of healing, a making visible of social injustice, and a way of coming to understand the cultural and historical determinants of individual experience. Ultimately, the process of witnessing in the class(room) is an enactment of community, however partial and temporary.

II. The Class(room): Community, Contact Zone, Borderland

9   The concept of *community* can be invoked in different ways in analyzing the class(room) as community. The class(room) can be theorized as an "invented" or "imagined community" (Anderson, Pratt), with the strengths and limitations of homogeneous communities; or the class(room) may be seen as a "contact zone," mirroring the social conflicts of a multicultural society like the United States, as Mary Louise Pratt has theorized persuasively; or, as I will argue from my ex-

perience in a Canadian location, the class(room) may be seen as a "borderland," in which community may be invented through individual struggles to articulate personal and cultural experience. *Community* in all three models embodies a utopian desire, however conflicted the reality. In its utopian mode, community connotes a "safe place," but communities—and class(rooms)—are rarely safe places for all their members.

10   In the class(room) imagined as community, teachers might express commitment to the concepts of democracy, equality, dialogue, and voice, urging everyone to participate openly and fully in a rational conversation (fundamental principles in critical pedagogy). In such an ideal space the classroom might become a "safe place." However, this assumption of safety depends on valuing the traditional split between reason and emotion, objective knowledge and subjective experience. Patricia Monture-Okanee, who is a law professor, mother, and citizen of the Mohawk Nation, reflects on what was at stake for her in feeling safe as a student:

> The overwhelming sense I had of my first few years of university education was of having finally found a place where I belonged. This is not so much a reflection of the university I attended but of where I was in my personal development. I can always remember being a "thinker." My friends have always told me I am very logical. I was well suited to the requirements of a university life. It was not until years later that I understood that this sense of belonging was a false one. My sense of belonging grew out of my status as a survivor of various incidents of abuse. In university, I did not have to feel, just think. Feelings were what I was trying to avoid. Years later I came to understand that the sense of belonging I felt was really the comfort I took in finding an environment where feelings were not essential. (11)

11   Monture-Okanee's observations, generalizable to other survivors of abuse, point to questions that feminists and borderland theorists (among others) have taken up: How does the university address the realities of such survivors? What are our responsibilities as teachers and researchers committed to social justice when we encounter students who have experienced injustice? Mary Louise Pratt, writing about teaching in the conflicted contact zone, suggests that some kinds of experience belong in the space of safe houses: "Where there are legacies of subordination, groups need places for healing and mutual recognition, safe houses in which to construct shared understandings, knowledges, claims on the world that they can then bring into the contact zone" (40). But what happens in the class(room) when there are simply individuals, not large, mutually supporting groups, who have experienced oppression?

12   Such teaching contexts may be conceived as a kind of borderland rather than contact zone, where borderland is understood in the multiple senses of Gloria Anzaldúa's *Borderlands/La Frontera*. The borderlands, Anzaldúa writes, can be physical, psychological, sexual, spiritual: "In fact, the Borderlands are

physically present wherever two or more cultures edge each other, where people of different races occupy the same territory, where under, lower, middle and upper classes touch, where the space between two individuals shrinks with intimacy" (Preface). In her inclusion of the psychological, sexual and spiritual, Anzaldúa's concept of the borderlands compels attention to the individual dimensions of experience and critical consciousness in the contact zone, borderland, or mainstream culture.

13   For Paula Gunn Allen, critical consciousness of the borderlands is best articulated by writers who cross physical and psychological borders in their everyday lives:

> The process of living on the border, of crossing and recrossing boundaries of consciousness, is most clearly delineated in work by writers who are citizens of more than one community, whose experiences and languages require that they live within worlds that are as markedly different from one another as Chinatown, Los Angeles, and Malibu. . . . (33)

14   Although Anzaldúa and Allen both begin with physical, publicly constituted borders, the "borders" in the college and university class(room) may not be as evident (apart from that between academic culture and the outside worlds of the students and teachers). But as Anzaldúa suggests, there are also private, intimate, internal borderlands which students and teachers negotiate daily and bring to their intellectual work—as writers. Though we may not live in "markedly different" worlds, I hypothesize that we all live "on the border" (however defined). Taking into account the possibility that living on the border can mean living in abusive contexts, we cannot presume that we are all *citizens* of more than one community: we are not all enfranchised within the communities we inhabit. Thus one of the challenges in the class(room) is to find ways of making different knowledges public and to produce different knowledges in the process; in other words, to transform the process of writing from an academic exercise into a meaningful process of witnessing through writing, reading, and critical thinking.

15   In an academic setting that may be more a covert borderland than an overt contact zone, the process of witnessing and community-building can take place slowly as students test the writing scene and move from careful pieces to more risk-taking exploration of their worlds. The process can also be more dramatic if, from the beginning, one or more students respond boldly to the challenge to push the limits of their writing, bringing "taboo" subjects into the class (e.g., coming out in the first essay as opposed to the last, or writing about childhood sexual abuse in the context of a first, seemingly "safe" topic) in order to clear space for further discovery. The process of community-building can also be fraught at the beginning if, in responding to an essay read aloud to the class, one student unexpectedly challenges the assumptions or stereotypes in another student's essay and shakes the class out of the "security" of decorum. However

challenging, exhausting, exhilarating this process is, the community-based view of the class(room) as borderland may also be challenged by students who, for undisclosed reasons, choose to participate only on their own terms. These challenges force a constant rethinking of teaching in the class(room).

III. Writing in the Borderlands

16   To a certain extent, articulating the borderlands in the writing class(room) is a complex process of communal storytelling which moves through texts, theory, and personal experience. "Storytelling" in this sense invokes research and critical skills as well as literary craft: it is "theorizing in narrative form" (Royster 35), autoethnography, autobiography, memoir, critique. In collective storytelling in the class(room), the borderlands move from the "outside"—the fictional, the textual, the abstract "out there"—to the "inside"—the local and particular. If the process works, if a community develops in the class(room), then a kind of communal magic can spark extraordinary intellectual activity, as when students begin to build on and respond to each other's work. But storytelling is risky in the academic setting: the combination of narrative and personal experience is subject to what Jacqueline Jones Royster calls "the power and function of deep disbelief" (34). If an audience refuses to recognize narrative as a form of theorizing, then the writer is reduced to the status of entertainer: "a storyteller, a performer" (35). Royster is referring specifically to African American writing, but the argument holds true for students and teachers in the borderland. Student "storytelling" demands the craft of skilled writers, but it also demands the acuity of skilled listeners and readers.

17   Few undergraduate students would immediately identify themselves as "writer-intellectuals," engaged in the process of collective storytelling and the production of new knowledges. One of the challenges in the class(room) is to find ways to encourage this recognition. In a full-year writing course, students experience the often astonishing growth of their peers and themselves as this process of trust and risk-taking develops. Over time they come to serve as witnesses to each other's stories, where the private becomes public (stories of growing up, abuse and violence, etc.). And they begin to write as an active, self-challenging, self-affirming community. This witnessing takes place when a student writes and then reads to the class an essay on the suicide of an intimate friend, or an essay on being the girlfriend of a man charged with the rape of another woman, or an essay on sexual abuse, on being physically different, on religious fundamentalism, homophobia and coming out—in short, when students write on being women and men in today's world. For many students who embark on the emotional journey of writing about and through their traumatic experiences, the goal is witnessing which moves beyond the class(room) to larger publics. That is, students take the tools of the writing class(room)—the emphasis on process and crafting—and adapt them to their own purposes. Their audiences, in the end, are not the class, but the larger communities to whom their experiences of trauma and healing matter most.

18   This view of teaching in the borderland emphasizes the critical importance of communal sharing and witnessing. In a haunting scene toward the end of Toni Morrison's *Beloved,* Paul D recalls Sixo's description of the Thirty-Mile Woman: "She is a friend of my mind. She gather me, man. The pieces I am, she gather them and give them back to me in all the right order" (272). In working through his own feelings for Sethe, Paul D realizes that "He wants to put his story next to hers" (273). Although Sixo and Paul D are describing intimate relationships in the context of shared oppression, their experiences can be extrapolated to the class(room). Sometimes, in the borderlands of teaching, we (the collective class) become "friends of your mind," gathering the pieces and giving them back "in all the right order." And when this happens, it is often because we put our stories next to each other, affirming our humanity and producing "noncoercive knowledge . . . in the interests of human freedom" (Said 29).[3]

Notes

This is a revised and shortened version of "Writing Trauma, History, Story: The Class(room) as Borderland" (*JAC: A Journal of Composition Theory* 18.1 [1998]: 105–21). I am indebted to numerous classes and students, who have taught me about writing and much, much more.

1.   "How *does* one make sense of this story?" I was thinking of different ways of approaching this event, suggested by the work of a number of African-American, feminist, and postcolonial writers. *"One could retrace the scant narrative details available in the local newspaper"*: neighbours reported a trash fire; horrified firefighters discovered that the "trash fire" was Joyce Cardinal, who had been set on fire by an unknown assailant. Details of her life emerged in subsequent news reports. Patricia Williams, an African-American law professor, provides an example of tracing the ways in which silenced women are represented in newspaper stories. In her essay "Mirrors and Windows," she traces the newspaper constructions of Tawana Brawley, a young African-American woman from Wappinger Falls, New York, who disappeared for four days in late November 1987 and then was found in a physically degraded state. What was her tragic story? Was she "the victim of some unspeakable crime" (169) or was she a liar? Williams' discussion of Tawana Brawley as a silenced child/woman is eloquent. *"One could honour and mourn the creative spirit evoked in the family's vigil for the beloved"*: in her essay "In Search of Our Mothers' Gardens," Alice Walker pays eloquent homage to the creativity of her foremothers, both the women damaged into madness by slavery and the women, like her mother, who expressed their creativity through their gardens. *"One* knows *that Cardinal's death will never be recuperated by the discovery of a letter she has written to the future"*: at the end of Gayatri Spivak's essay "Can the Subaltern Speak?" she tells the story of her great-aunt, who killed herself as a teenager but left a letter to be opened 50 years later in which she explained the political reasons for her death. In spite of this letter, her family continued to interpret that cause of her death as a failed romance. *But one also knows that other voices will emerge—have emerged—"speak[ing] the words that should never be spoken"*: Dori Laub writes, "One has to know one's buried truth in order to be able to live one's life" (63). And Yvonne Johnson says, "If no one ever speaks the words that should be spoken, the silence destroys you" (Wiebe and Johnson 329). Like Joyce Cardinal, Johnson had a speech impediment, a double-cleft palate, which was eventually surgically repaired, but it meant that much of her childhood was passed in silence, silence which made her even more vulnerable to abuse. Johnson is the only Native woman in Canada serving a life sentence for murder (for her role in the death of a man she believed to be a child molester). *Stolen Life: The Journey of a Cree Woman* (1998), the result of a five-year collaboration between Johnson and Rudy Wiebe, chronicles Johnson's quest to know her life. *Stolen Life*

cannot tell the story of Joyce Cardinal, but it is a letter to the present, a story not to pass on that must be passed on. In March 2001, Todd Christopher Elliott pleaded guilty to second-degree murder and received a life sentence for the murder of Joyce Cardinal. Details of the murder and the seven-year investigation are reported in articles by *Edmonton Journal* journalists Chris Purdy and David Staples.

2. In conceptualizing the space of the teaching encounter as "the class(room)," I want to suggest through the play on *class* and class*room* that the physical classroom helps to "invent" the class as community.

3. I have taken Edward Said's description of the radical imperatives of secular criticism as a description of the radical imperatives of teaching: "criticism [teaching] must think of itself as life-enhancing and constitutively opposed to every form of tyranny, domination, and abuse; its social goals are noncoercive knowledge produced in the interests of human freedom" (29).

Works Cited

Allen, Paula Gunn. "'Border' Studies: The Intersection of Gender and Color." *The Ethnic Canon: Histories, Institutions, and Interventions.* Ed. David Palumbo-Liu. Minneapolis: University of Minnesota Press, 1995. 31–47.

Anderson, Benedict. *Imagined Communities: Reflections on the Origin and Spread of Nationalism.* Rev. ed. London: Verso, 1991.

Anzaldúa, Gloria. *Borderlands/La Frontera.* San Francisco: Aunt Lute Books, 1987.

Laub, Dori. "Truth and Testimony: The Process and the Struggle." *Trauma: Explorations in Memory.* Ed. Cathy Caruth. Baltimore: Johns Hopkins University Press, 1995. 61–75.

Monture-Okanee, Patricia A. "Introduction—Surviving the Contradictions: Personal Notes on Academia." *Breaking Anonymity: The Chilly Climate for Women Faculty.* Ed. The Chilly Collective. Waterloo, ON: Wilfrid Laurier University Press, 1995. 11–28.

Morrison, Toni. *Beloved.* New York: Plume, 1988.

Plischke, Helen. "Burn Victim a 'Caring, Giving Person.'" *Edmonton Journal,* 4 Dec. 1993: B1.

Pratt, Mary Louise. "Arts of the Contact Zone." *Profession 91.* New York: MLA, 1991. 33–40.

Purdy, Chris. "Life Sentence for Killer: 'A Brutal and Barbarous Murder.'" *Edmonton Journal,* 30 Mar. 2001: A1.

Royster, Jacqueline Jones. "When the First Voice You Hear Is Not Your Own." *College Composition and Communication* 47.1 (1996). 29–40.

Said, Edward W. "Introduction: Secular Criticism." *The World, the Text, and the Critic.* Cambridge: Harvard University Press, 1983.

Spivak, Gayatri Chakravorty. "Can the Subaltern Speak?" *Marxism and the Interpretation of Culture.* Ed. Gary Nelson and Lawrence Grossberg. Urbana: University of Illinois Press, 1988. 271–313.

Staples, David. "Joyce Cardinal Murder: Years of Patient Pursuit Led the Cop to the Killer." *Edmonton Journal,* Apr. 4 2001: A1.

Walker, Alice. "In Search of Our Mothers' Gardens." *In Search of Our Mothers' Gardens.* San Diego: HBJ, 1984. 231–43.

Wiebe, Rudy, and Yvonne Johnson. *Stolen Life: The Journey of a Cree Woman.* Toronto: Knopf Canada, 1998.

Williams, Patricia J. "Mirrors and Windows." *The Alchemy of Race and Rights.* Cambridge: Harvard University Press, 1991. 166–78.

For Further Thinking

1. How does this essay argue that personal storytelling and classroom community are closely associated? How is the definition of a classroom as a "community" examined and reconsidered?

2. What, in your opinion, is the place of personal experience in the college or university classroom? How do you (and your instructor) balance the traditional classroom's demands to write formally for a grade with the sense of the writing classroom as a potential setting for personal risks and revelation?

3. Read emphasizes the deeply personal, sometimes painful, basis for a powerful writing voice. What personal influences shape your writing voice?

4. This essay combines conventionally separate forms: anecdote and argument, testimony and traditional scholarship, fiction and journalism, narrative (storytelling) theories and professional challenges. How do you respond to this combination of many knowledge forms and styles?

5. Read's essay views knowledge as a sharing within the class as a "borderland" where "Community is invented through individual struggles to articulate personal and cultural experience." How will this classroom borderland community be achieved or challenged with the continuing changes of technology, multiculturalism, and attitudes to race, class, sex, and sexual orientation?

6. Would you like to take a writing class that pursues the aims of Professor Read's "borderland class(room)"? Is there a possible risk that the desire to address students' serious personal issues could mean that writing instructors propel themselves into psychotherapeutic areas that they are not necessarily trained to handle?

Looking Back and Ahead

1. Compare the type of classroom Read proposes with the one implied in Roch Carrier's "The Hockey Sweater" (p. 51).

2. Would Pamela Swanigan ("I Am Half-Canadian," p. 58) consider Read's ideal classroom more likely to succeed in Canada or the United States? Why?

3. Read "When MTV Goes CEO" (p. 99). Does Read's proposed classroom sound like a Boomer idea, a Generation X idea, or neither? Explain.

4. Contrast the tone of Read's essay to that of Sarah Schmidt's "College Girl to Call Girl" (p. 104). What different outlooks on life and education may underlie these essays?

5. In terms of style, what other essay(s) in the *Reader* does Read's essay most resemble? Explain. What kind of writerly voice does Read create through language choice (diction), use of sources, and sentence patterns (rhythm)?

For Further Reading

DeSalvo, Louise. *Writing as a Way of Healing: How Telling Our Stories Transforms Our Lives.* New York: Harper, 1999.

Elbow, Peter, and Pat Belanoff. *A Community of Writers: A Workshop Course in Writing.* 3rd ed. Boston: McGraw-Hill, 2000.

————. *Sharing and Responding*. 3rd ed. Boston: McGraw-Hill, 2000.

Hamilton, Sharon Jean. *My Name's Not Suzy: A Life Transformed by Literacy*. Portsmouth, NH: Boynton/Cook, 1995.

Horsman, Jenny. *Too Scared to Learn: Women, Violence, and Education*. Toronto: McGilligan Books, 1999.

Laub, Dori. "Truth and Testimony: The Process and the Struggle." *Trauma: Explorations in Memory*. Ed. Cathy Caruth. Baltimore: Johns Hopkins University Press, 1995. 61–75.

Miller, Richard E. "Fault Lines in the Contact Zone." *College English* 56. 4 (1994): 389–408.

Smith, Sidonie, and Julia Watson. *Reading Autobiography: A Guide for Interpreting Life Narratives*. Minneapolis: University of Minnesota Press, 2001.

Consult also the "Works Cited" immediately following Read's essay.

Howard Richler In eighteenth-century London, the unfashionable artist and poet William Blake noted bitterly that "commerce grows on every tree." What would he say today! Studies indicate that overworked members of our society typically do not demand reduced work hours—they demand higher wages. Star athletes who 30 years ago would have earned no more than civil servants now pull in millions of dollars a year. Certain individuals in the United States and other "developed" nations have personal fortunes greater than the wealth of entire countries. The music and film industries seem to be flogging youth more than ever. Advertisers target younger and younger people, thinking of them not as developing human beings but simply as mindless consumers. Multinational corporations, exploiting cheap labour in poor countries, exert increasing influence over all institutions. Universities feel increasing pressure to treat students purely as consumers and education as a product on the shelf. As consumerism marches on—pandering to escalating levels of selfishness—many critics believe our society has become spiritually bankrupt.

Howard Richler writes a language column for the Montreal *Gazette*. In the following essay from his collection *A Bawdy Language*, he argues that with the dominance of corporatism, few words have escaped strong overtones of commerce, yet the language situation does not really disturb us since we have recently placed positive, or at least neutral, meanings on words related to all seven deadly sins. Process writing plays an important role in this essay, as Richler traces the evolution of various words from feudal times forward.

The Seven Deadly Sins Are "In" and Proud of It

1   "We *profited* from their misfortune—no, let me rephrase that, it sounds too mercantile. We *benefited*—no, that's not right—we have *gained an advantage*—no!—well, you know what I'm trying to say." A friend was relating to me a discussion she heard recently during a religious service. She said the speaker was trying to convey a sense of spiritual accomplishment but was stymied by the seemingly capitalistic nature of the verbs he employed.

2   Moneyed words are so central to our lives that any verb our hapless discussant used to communicate a sense of acquisition would have had the capitalist

taint he was trying to eschew. The words *obtain*, *earn*, and *procure* carry the same connotation. In the long history of the English language, this mercantile sense wasn't always prevalent. But with the demise of feudalism and the ability of the common man to sell his labor freely, the need for new terms to reflect the new economic realities arose.

3   Usually, when a new field of endeavor arises, a jargon comes along with it. This specialized vocabulary serves as a shibboleth to a certain group and thus helps demarcate those who should be included in the select group and those who should be excluded. This did not happen, however, with words in the economic sphere. The vocabulary of capitalism is laced with words from other domains. Words like *account*, *budget*, *business*, *company*, *consumption*, *demand*, *duty*, *income*, *interest*, *market*, *pay*, and *purchase* all existed previously and were adapted to describe the new economic system. Probably the reason a selective vocabulary didn't develop was because of the centrality of these words to everyone's existence.

4   Many of these words once had radically different meanings. For example, when you *paid* a creditor, you weren't paying him, rather you were "pacifying" him. *Purchase* originally meant "to take by force." In Old French, *un enfant de perchas* was a term for a bastard; the implication is that a bastard is the product of a rape.

5   The end of feudalism necessitated new interpretations of words. *Service* was no longer an obligation, and many of the words to describe service and servants became pejorative terms. For example, a *knave* was originally just a term for a lower-class male child, and a *lackey* was a term for a footsoldier. Conversely, words that denoted a high status, like *noble* and *gentle*, came to possess a higher moral value.

6   With the ability to sell one's labor freely, words began to take on new connotations. Originally *fortune* referred only to chance; it didn't develop its sense of "great wealth" until the end of the sixteenth century. The point is that *fortune* was no longer seen as being controlled by others but now could be controlled by an individual.

7   Some words originally had a communal rather than an individual sense. *Wealth* once had the sense of communal wellness still displayed in the word *commonwealth*. By the sixteenth century it was used to describe an abundance, but it was not until the eighteenth century that it obtained its primary association with money. *Profit* was also originally associated with a community as opposed to an individual, but the focus changed with the growing tide of capitalism. Just as the "common weal" gave way to private wealth, communal profit gave way to individual profit.

8   M.M. Poston, in *The Medieval Economy and Society*, points out that profit and economic expansion in feudal days [were] inhibited by the concept of a "just price." This price was more than an injunction against excessive profit. Since the Church was essentially a conservative institution dedicated to preserving the status quo, "[i]t linked the price system with the divinely ordained structure of society, by defining a 'just' price as that which would yield the makers of goods and their sellers sufficient income to maintain them in their respective social ranks."

9   With the movement to a more secular society, equality first became an assumption, and then an inherent right of all men. According to Raymond Williams, in *Keywords*, *equality* is first used in the fifteenth century in reference to physical quantities, and in the sixteenth century to refer to equivalence of rank. The suggestion of "freedom" is thus one that is limited to the aristocracy. It is only with the French and American Revolutions that the term acquires a universal sense.

10   The advent of capitalism led to the amelioration of many words. In feudal times, to be *free and frank* implied only that one was not bound to a master. *Generous* suggested a noble lineage and not nobility of spirit, and, according to the OED, "'liberal' was originally the distinctive epithet of those arts and sciences that were considered worthy of a free man."

11   This is not to imply that our more secular society is a morally superior one. Geoffrey Hughes, in *Words in Time,* postulates that the seven deadly sins—pride, wrath, envy, lust, gluttony, avarice, and sloth—are generally all seen, if not as virtues, then as neutral concepts. Pride is seen in a positive light, vanity has been ameliorated by terms like *vanity case*, and anger is seen as often justified. Envy and avarice are concomitant with capitalism, and lust, gluttony, and sloth are seen as facets of the "good life." No word better sums up this dramatic shift than the word *luxury*. In the fourteenth century, it had the sense of "lasciviousness" or "lust." By the seventeenth century, it had acquired a sense of habitual use of what is choice or costly, and it wasn't until the nineteenth century that it obtained its modern sense of contributing to sumptuous living.

12   But who knows? Now that the conspicuous consumption of capitalism is endangering our resource-depleted planet, perhaps one day *luxury* will regain its rapacious sense.

13   For goodness' sake, let's put the sin back in the Seven Deadlies!

For Further Thinking

1. Find one or two paragraphs that demonstrate process writing. Explain the rhetorical nature of the passage you have selected.

2. Do you think it is true that we use a type of doublespeak whereby we denude words of their original ethical and moral history? How does this process compare to the doublespeak Orwell plays with in his novel *1984* (1949)? If you haven't read that novel, we describe its concept of doublespeak under "Looking Back and Ahead," following the next selection (see p. 238).

3. What current advertisements and/or songs use formerly negative or at least ambiguous words in new, supposedly enticing ways and contexts?

Looking Back and Ahead

1. What are the connections—based on language as a subject—between Richler's essay and the following one by George Orwell?

2. Are there connections between Richler's essay and Diane Mooney's "Newfoundlandese, if You Please" (p.109)? How does "culture" exert force on language, but perhaps differently, according to both authors?

3. Is there common thematic ground between this essay and Mordecai Richler's short story "The Summer My Grandmother Was Supposed to Die" (p. 14)? Explain.

For Further Reading

"Free Trade." The Cato Institute Center for Trade Policy Studies. April 2003 ‹http://www. freetrade.org/›. The Institute supports the World Trade Organization at this site.

King, Don. W. "Narnia and the Seven Deadly Sins." April 2003 ‹http://cslewis.drzeus.net/ papers/7sins.html›. This academic paper points out how C.S. Lewis, a medievalist and author, built the seven deadly sins into his Narnia series of children's fantasies, which begins with *The Lion, the Witch, and the Wardrobe* (1950). A version of this essay first appeared in *Mythlore* 10 (Spring 1984): 14–19.

"openDemocracy." April 2003 ‹http://www.opendemocracy.net›. The openDemocracy website invites citizens to debate "the most pressing issues of our time." While disavowing any ideological position, the group does express a unifying concern that money should not be "the driving force in the world." Discussion forums deal with the complexities of today's economic, political, and social issues.

Rosenberg, Josef. "The Seven Deadly Sins of *Gilligan's Island*." Personal website. April 2003 ‹http://members.tripod.com/TTLF/gilligan.html›. Rosenberg argues that each of the characters on the TV series represents a deadly sin!

Rushman, William E. "The Seven Deadly Sins." April 2003 ‹http://www.rushman.org/ seven/›. This Catholic website defines and warns against the seven deadly sins, and contains excellent supporting information and links to the sins in classic literature.

"Top Ten Reasons to Oppose the World Trade Organization." Global Exchange. April 2003 ‹http://www.globalexchange.org/economy/rulemakers/topTenReasons.html›. Founded in 1984, Global Exchange is a non-profit research, education, and action centre.

George Orwell Born Eric Arthur Blair in Motihari, India, in 1903, George Orwell went on to a life many describe as sadly short; certainly it was a life of hardships, ill health, and grim sights. Orwell began his writing career as a voluntary tramp, experiencing firsthand the life of the homeless. It was only by the end of his life, after *Animal Farm* and *Nineteen Eighty-Four*, that he found financial success. By that time he had served in the Indian Imperial Police force in Burma (now Myanmar) for six years and fought for the Republican forces in the Spanish Civil War to liberate Spain from the Fascists. Orwell, however, had grown disillusioned with the in-fighting of the communists. *Road to Wigan Pier* (1937) and *Homage to Catalonia* (1938) expressed some of that disillusion. But his two most visionary works condemning human folly were the allegorical beast fable *Animal Farm* (1945) and the speculative nightmare *Nineteen Eighty-Four* (1949). In 1950, the year of his death, Orwell published *Shooting an Elephant and Other Essays*. This collection of non-fiction uses personal experience combined with rigorous analysis.

In one of these essays, "Politics and the English Language," Orwell argues that the English of his day is becoming vague, stale, and thoughtless, and that this condition contributes to gradual political degeneracy. His image for writing was the window, a clear pane. It doesn't attract any attention to itself; consequently, we see sharply what it focuses us to see. According to Orwell, this form of writing is the key to social and political regeneration.

Politics and the English Language

1   Most people who bother with the matter at all would admit that the English language is in a bad way, but it is generally assumed that we cannot by conscious action do anything about it. Our civilization is decadent and our language—so the argument runs—must inevitably share in the general collapse. It follows that any struggle against the abuse of language is a sentimental archaism, like preferring candles to electric light or hansom cabs to aeroplanes. Underneath this lies the half-conscious belief that language is a natural growth and not an instrument which we shape for our own purposes.

2   Now, it is clear that the decline of a language must ultimately have political and economic causes: it is not due simply to the bad influence of this or that individual writer. But an effect can become a cause, reinforcing the original cause and producing the same effect in an intensified form, and so on indefinitely. A man may take to drink because he feels himself to be a failure, and then fail all the more completely because he drinks. It is rather the same thing that is happening to the English language. It becomes ugly and inaccurate because our thoughts are foolish, but the slovenliness of our language makes it easier for us to have foolish thoughts. The point is that the process is reversible. Modern English, especially written English, is full of bad habits which spread by imitation and which can be avoided if one is willing to take the necessary trouble. If one gets rid of these habits one can think more clearly, and to think clearly is a necessary first step towards political regeneration: so that the fight against bad English is not frivolous and is not the exclusive concern of professional writers. I will come back to this presently, and I hope that by that time the meaning of what I have said here will have become clearer. Meanwhile, here are five specimens of the English language as it is now habitually written.

3   These five passages have not been picked out because they are especially bad—I could have quoted far worse if I had chosen—but because they illustrate various of the mental vices from which we now suffer. They are a little below the average, but are fairly representative samples. I number them so that I can refer back to them when necessary:

(1)   I am not, indeed, sure whether it is not true to say that the Milton who once seemed not unlike a seventeenth-century Shelley had not become, out of an

experience ever more bitter in each year, more alien [sic] to the founder of that Jesuit sect which nothing could induce him to tolerate.

—Professor Harold Laski (Essay in *Freedom of Expression*)

(2)   Above all, we cannot play ducks and drakes with a native battery of idioms which prescribes such egregious collocations of vocables as the Basic *put up with* for *tolerate* or *put at a loss* for *bewilder*.

—Professor Lancelot Hogben (*Interglossa*)

(3)   On the one side we have the free personality: by definition it is not neurotic, for it has neither conflict nor dream. Its desires, such as they are, are transparent, for they are just what institutional approval keeps in the forefront of consciousness; another institutional pattern would alter their number and intensity; there is little in them that is natural, irreducible, or culturally dangerous. But *on the other side,* the social bond itself is nothing but the mutual reflection of these self-secure integrities. Recall the definition of love. Is not this the very picture of a small academic? Where is there a place in this hall of mirrors for either personality or fraternity?

—Essay on psychology in *Politics* (New York)

(4)   All the "best people" from the gentlemen's clubs, and all the frantic fascist captains, united in common hatred of Socialism and bestial horror of the rising tide of the mass revolutionary movement, have turned to acts of provocation, to foul incendiarism, to medieval legends of poisoned wells, to legalize their own destruction of proletarian organizations, and rouse the agitated petty-bourgeoisie to chauvinistic fervour on behalf of the fight against the revolutionary way out of the crisis.

—Communist pamphlet

(5)   If a new spirit *is* to be infused into this old country, there is one thorny and contentious reform which must be tackled, and that is the humanization and galvanization of the B.B.C. Timidity here will bespeak canker and atrophy of the soul. The heart of Britain may be sound and of strong beat, for instance, but the British lion's roar at present is like that of Bottom in Shakespeare's *Midsummer Night's Dream*—as gentle as any sucking dove. A virile new Britain cannot continue indefinitely to be traduced in the eyes, or rather ears, of the world by the effete languors of Langham Place, brazenly masquerading as "standard English." When the Voice of Britain is heard at nine o'clock, better far and infinitely less ludicrous to hear aitches honestly dropped than the present priggish, inflated, inhibited, school-ma'mish arch braying of blameless bashful mewing maidens!

—Letter in *Tribune*

4   Each of these passages has faults of its own, but, quite apart from avoidable ugliness, two qualities are common to all of them. The first is staleness of imagery; the other is lack of precision. The writer either has a meaning and cannot express it, or he inadvertently says something else, or he is almost indifferent as to whether his words mean anything or not. This mixture of vagueness and sheer incompetence is the most marked characteristic of modern English prose, and especially of any kind of political writing. As soon as certain topics are raised, the concrete melts into the abstract and no one seems able to think of turns of speech that are not hackneyed: prose consists less and less of *words* chosen for the sake of their meaning, and more and more of *phrases* tacked together like the sections of a prefabricated hen-house. I list below, with notes and examples, various of the tricks by means of which the work of prose-construction is habitually dodged:

5   **Dying Metaphors.** A newly invented metaphor assists thought by evoking a visual image, while on the other hand a metaphor which is technically "dead" (e.g., *iron resolution*) has in effect reverted to being an ordinary word and can generally be used without loss of vividness. But in between these two classes there is a huge dump of worn-out metaphors which have lost all evocative power and are merely used because they save people the trouble of inventing phrases for themselves. Examples are: *Ring the changes on, take up the cudgels for, toe the line, ride roughshod over, stand shoulder to shoulder with, play into the hands of, no axe to grind, grist to the mill, fishing in troubled waters, on the order of the day, Achilles' heel, swan song, hotbed*. Many of these are used without knowledge of their meaning (what is a "rift," for instance?), and incompatible metaphors are frequently mixed, a sure sign that the writer is not interested in what he is saying. Some metaphors now current have been twisted out of their original meaning without those who use them even being aware of the fact. For example, *toe the line* is sometimes written *tow the line*. Another example is the *hammer and the anvil*, now always used with the implication that the anvil gets the worst of it. In real life it is always the anvil that breaks the hammer, never the other way about: a writer who stopped to think what he was saying would be aware of this, and would avoid perverting the original phrase.

6   **Operators *or* Verbal False Limbs.** These save the trouble of picking out appropriate verbs and nouns, and at the same time pad each sentence with extra syllables which give it an appearance of symmetry. Characteristic phrases are: *render inoperative, militate against, make contact with, be subjected to, give rise to, give grounds for, have the effect of, play a leading part (role) in, make itself felt, take effect, exhibit a tendency to, serve the purpose of, etc., etc.* The keynote is the elimination of simple verbs. Instead of being a single word, such as *break, stop, spoil, mend, kill*, a verb becomes a *phrase*, made up of a noun or adjective tacked on to some general-purpose verb such as *prove, serve, form, play, render*. In addition, the passive voice is wherever possible

used in preference to the active, and noun constructions are used instead of gerunds (*by examination of* instead of *by examining*). The range of verbs is further cut down by means of the *-ize* and *de-* formations, and the banal statements are given an appearance of profundity by means of the *not un-* formation. Simple conjunctions and prepositions are replaced by such phrases as *with respect to, having regard to, the fact that, by dint of, in view of, in the interests of, on the hypothesis that*; and the ends of sentences are saved from anticlimax by such resounding common-places as *greatly to be desired, cannot be left out of account, a development to be expected in the near future, deserving of serious consideration, brought to a satisfactory conclusion*, and so on and so forth.

7   **Pretentious Diction.** Words like *phenomenon, element, individual* (as noun), *objective, categorical, effective, virtual, basic, primary, promote, constitute, exhibit, exploit, utilize, eliminate, liquidate*, are used to dress up simple statement and give an air of scientific impartiality to biased judgments. Adjectives like *epoch-making, epic, historic, unforgettable, triumphant, age-old, inevitable, inexorable, veritable*, are used to dignify the sordid processes of international politics, while writing that aims at glorifying war usually takes on an archaic colour, its characteristic words being: *realm, throne, chariot, mailed fist, trident, sword, shield, buckler, banner, jackboot, clarion*. Foreign words and expressions such as *cul de sac, ancien régime, deus ex machina, mutatis mutandis, status quo, gleichschaltung, weltanschauung*, are used to give an air of culture and elegance. Except for the useful abbreviations *i.e., e.g.,* and *etc.*, there is no real need for any of the hundreds of foreign phrases now current in English. Bad writers, and especially scientific, political and sociological writers, are nearly always haunted by the notion that Latin or Greek words are grander than Saxon ones, and unnecessary words like *expedite, ameliorate, predict, extraneous, deracinated, clandestine, subaqueous* and hundreds of others constantly gain ground from their Anglo-Saxon opposite numbers.[1] The jargon peculiar to Marxist writing (*hyena, hangman, cannibal, petty bourgeois, these gentry, lacquey, flunkey, mad dog, White Guard*, etc.) consists largely of words and phrases translated from Russian, German or French; but the normal way of coining a new word is to use a Latin or Greek root with the appropriate affix and, where necessary, the *-ize* formation. It is often easier to make up words of this kind (*deregionalize, impermissible, extramarital, nonfragmentatory* and so forth) than to think up the English words that will cover one's meaning. The result, in general, is an increase in slovenliness and vagueness.

8   **Meaningless Words.** In certain kinds of writing, particularly in art criticism and literary criticism, it is normal to come across long passages which are almost completely lacking in meaning.[2] Words like *romantic, plastic,*

values, human, dead, sentimental, natural, vitality, as used in art criticism, are strictly meaningless, in the sense that they not only do not point to any discoverable object, but are hardly ever expected to do so by the reader. When one critic writes, "The outstanding feature of Mr. X's work is its living quality," while another writes, "The immediately striking thing about Mr. X's work is its peculiar deadness," the reader accepts this as a simple difference of opinion. If words like *black* and *white* were involved, instead of the jargon words *dead* and *living,* he would see at once that language was being used in an improper way. Many political words are similarly abused. The word *Fascism* has now no meaning except in so far as it signifies "something not desirable." The words *democracy, socialism, freedom, patriotic, realistic, justice,* have each of them several different meanings which cannot be reconciled with one another. In the case of a word like *democracy,* not only is there no agreed definition but the attempt to make one is resisted from all sides. It is almost universally felt that when we call a country democratic we are praising it: consequently the defenders of every kind of régime claim that it is a democracy, and fear that they might have to stop using the word if it were tied down to any one meaning. Words of this kind are often used in a consciously dishonest way. That is, the person who uses them has his own private definition, but allows his hearer to think he means something quite different. Statements like *Marshal Pétain was a true patriot, The Soviet Press is the freest in the world, the Catholic Church is opposed to persecution,* are almost always made with intent to deceive. Other words used in variable meanings, in most cases more or less dishonestly, are: *class, totalitarian, science, progressive, reactionary, bourgeois, equality.*

9   Now that I have made this catalogue of swindles and perversions, let me give another example of the kind of writing that they lead to. This time it must of its nature be an imaginary one. I am going to translate a passage of good English into modern English of the worst sort. Here is a well-known verse from *Ecclesiastes*:

> I returned and saw under the sun, that the race is not to the swift, nor the battle to the strong, neither yet bread to the wise, nor yet riches to men of understanding, nor yet favour to men of skill; but time and chance happeneth to them all.

10   Here it is in modern English:

> Objective consideration of contemporary phenomena compels the conclusion that success or failure in competitive activities exhibits no tendency to be commensurate with innate capacity, but that a considerable element of the unpredictable must invariably be taken into account.

11   This is a parody, but not a very gross one. Exhibit (3), above, for instance, contains several patches of the same kind of English. It will be seen that I have not

made a full translation. The beginning and ending of the sentence follow the original meaning fairly closely, but in the middle the concrete illustrations—race, battle, bread—dissolve into the vague phrase "success or failure in competitive activities." This had to be so, because no modern writer of the kind I am discussing—no one capable of using phrases like "objective consideration of contemporary phenomena"—would ever tabulate his thoughts in that precise and detailed way. The whole tendency of modern prose is away from concreteness. Now analyse these [previous] two sentences a little more closely. The first contains forty-nine words but only sixty syllables, and all its words are those of everyday life. The second contains thirty-eight words of ninety syllables: eighteen of its words are from Latin roots, and one from Greek. The first sentence contains six vivid images, and only one phrase ("time and chance") that could be called vague. The second contains not a single fresh, arresting phrase, and in spite of its ninety syllables it gives only a shortened version of the meaning contained in the first. Yet without a doubt it is the second kind of sentence that is gaining ground in modern English. I do not want to exaggerate. This kind of writing is not yet universal, and outcrops of simplicity will occur here and there in the worst-written page. Still, if you or I were told to write a few lines on the uncertainty of human fortunes, we should probably come much nearer to my imaginary sentence than to the one from *Ecclesiastes*.

12   As I have tried to show, modern writing at its worst does not consist in picking out words for the sake of their meaning and inventing images in order to make the meaning clearer. It consists in gumming together long strips of words which have already been set in order by someone else, and making the results presentable by sheer humbug. The attraction of this way of writing is that it is easy. It is easier—even quicker, once you have the habit—to say *In my opinion it is a not unjustifiable assumption that* than to say *I think*. If you use ready-made phrases, you not only don't have to hunt about for words; you also don't have to bother with the rhythms of your sentences, since these phrases are generally so arranged as to be more or less euphonious. When you are composing in a hurry—when you are dictating to a stenographer, for instance, or making a public speech—it is natural to fall into a pretentious, Latinized style. Tags like *a consideration which we should do well to bear in mind* or *a conclusion to which all of us would readily assent* will save many a sentence from coming down with a bump. By using stale metaphors, similes and idioms, you save much mental effort, at the cost of leaving your meaning vague, not only for your reader but for yourself. This is the significance of mixed metaphors. The sole aim of a metaphor is to call up a visual image. When these images clash—as in *The Fascist octopus has sung its swan song, the jackboot is thrown into the melting pot*—it can be taken as certain that the writer is not seeing a mental image of the objects he is naming; in other words he is not really thinking. Look again at the examples I gave at the beginning of this essay. Professor Laski (1) uses five negatives in fifty-three words. One of these is superfluous, making nonsense of the whole passage, and in addition there is the slip

alien for *akin,* making further nonsense, and several avoidable pieces of clumsiness which increase the general vagueness. Professor Hogben (2) plays ducks and drakes with a battery which is able to write prescriptions, and, while disapproving of the everyday phrase *put up with,* is unwilling to look *egregious* up in the dictionary and see what it means; (3), if one takes an uncharitable attitude towards it, is simply meaningless: probably one could work out its intended meaning by reading the whole of the article in which it occurs. In (4), the writer knows more or less what he wants to say, but an accumulation of stale phrases chokes him like tea leaves blocking a sink. In (5), words and meaning have almost parted company. People who write in this manner usually have a general emotional meaning—they dislike one thing and want to express solidarity with another—but they are not interested in the detail of what they are saying. A scrupulous writer, in every sentence that he writes, will ask himself at least four questions, thus: What am I trying to say? What words will express it? What image or idiom will make it clearer? Is this image fresh enough to have an effect? And he will probably ask himself two more: Could I put it more shortly? Have I said anything that is avoidably ugly? But you are not obliged to go to all this trouble. You can shirk it by simply throwing your mind open and letting the ready-made phrases come crowding in. They will construct your sentences for you—even think your thoughts for you, to a certain extent—and at need they will perform the important service of partially concealing your meaning even from yourself. It is at this point that the special connexion between politics and the debasement of language becomes clear.

13   In our time it is broadly true that political writing is bad writing. Where it is not true, it will generally be found that the writer is some kind of rebel, expressing his private opinions and not a "party line." Orthodoxy, of whatever colour, seems to demand a lifeless, imitative style. The political dialects to be found in pamphlets, leading articles, manifestos, White Papers and the speeches of under-secretaries do, of course, vary from party to party, but they are all alike in that one almost never finds in them a fresh, vivid, home-made turn of speech. When one watches some tired hack on the platform mechanically repeating the familiar phrases—*bestial atrocities, iron heel, bloodstained tyranny, free peoples of the world, stand shoulder to shoulder*—one often has a curious feeling that one is not watching a live human being but some kind of dummy: a feeling which suddenly becomes stronger at moments when the light catches the speaker's spectacles and turns them into blank discs which seem to have no eyes behind them. And this is not altogether fanciful. A speaker who uses that kind of phraseology has gone some distance towards turning himself into a machine. The appropriate noises are coming out of his larynx, but his brain is not involved as it would be if he were choosing his words for himself. If the speech he is making is one that he is accustomed to make over and over again, he may be almost unconscious of what he is saying, as one is when one utters the responses in church. And this reduced state of consciousness, if not indispensable, is at any rate favourable to political conformity.

14   In our time, political speech and writing are largely the defence of the indefensible. Things like the continuance of British rule in India, the Russian purges and deportations, the dropping of the atom bombs on Japan, can indeed be defended, but only by arguments which are too brutal for most people to face, and which do not square with the professed aims of political parties. Thus political language has to consist largely of euphemism, question-begging and sheer cloudy vagueness. Defenceless villages are bombarded from the air, the inhabitants driven out into the countryside, the cattle machine-gunned, the huts set on fire with incendiary bullets: this is called *pacification*. Millions of peasants are robbed of their farms and sent trudging along the roads with no more than they can carry: this is called *transfer of population* or *rectification of frontiers*. People are imprisoned for years without trial, or shot in the back of the neck or sent to die of scurvy in Arctic lumber camps: this is called *elimination of unreliable elements*. Such phraseology is needed if one wants to name things without calling up mental pictures of them. Consider for instance some comfortable English professor defending Russian totalitarianism. He cannot say outright, "I believe in killing off your opponents when you can get good results by doing so." Probably, therefore, he will say something like this:

> "While freely conceding that the Soviet regime exhibits certain features which the humanitarian may be inclined to deplore, we must, I think, agree that a certain curtailment of the right to political opposition is an unavoidable concomitant of transitional periods, and that the rigours which the Russian people have been called upon to undergo have been amply justified in the sphere of concrete achievement."

15   The inflated style is itself a kind of euphemism. A mass of Latin words falls upon the facts like soft snow, blurring the outlines and covering up all the details. The great enemy of clear language is insincerity. When there is a gap between one's real and one's declared aims, one turns as it were instinctively to long words and exhausted idioms, like a cuttlefish squirting out ink. In our age there is no such thing as "keeping out of politics." All issues are political issues, and politics itself is a mass of lies, evasions, folly, hatred and schizophrenia. When the general atmosphere is bad, language must suffer. I should expect to find—this is a guess which I have not sufficient knowledge to verify—that the German, Russian and Italian languages have all deteriorated in the last ten or fifteen years, as a result of dictatorship.

16   But if thought corrupts language, language can also corrupt thought. A bad usage can spread by tradition and imitation, even among people who should and do know better. The debased language that I have been discussing is in some ways very convenient. Phrases like *a not unjustifiable assumption*, *leaves much to be desired*, *would serve no good purpose*, *a consideration which we should do well to bear in mind*, are a continuous temptation, a packet of aspirins always at one's elbow. Look back through this essay, and for certain you will find that I

have again and again committed the very faults I am protesting against. By this morning's post I have received a pamphlet dealing with conditions in Germany. The author tells me that he "felt impelled" to write it. I open it at random, and here is almost the first sentence that I see: "(The Allies) have an opportunity not only of achieving a radical transformation of Germany's social and political structure in such a way as to avoid a nationalistic reaction in Germany itself, but at the same time of laying the foundations of a co-operative and unified Europe." You see, he "feels impelled" to write—feels, presumably, that he has something new to say—and yet his words, like cavalry horses answering the bugle, group themselves automatically into the familiar dreary pattern. This invasion of one's mind by ready-made phrases (*lay the foundations*, *achieve a radical transformation*) can only be prevented if one is constantly on guard against them, and every such phrase anaesthetizes a portion of one's brain.

17   I said earlier that the decadence of our language is probably curable. Those who deny this would argue, if they produced an argument at all, that language merely reflects existing social conditions, and that we cannot influence its development by any direct tinkering with words and constructions. So far as the general tone or spirit of a language goes, this may be true, but it is not true in detail. Silly words and expressions have often disappeared, not through any evolutionary process but owing to the conscious action of a minority. Two recent examples were *explore every avenue* and *leave no stone unturned*, which were killed by the jeers of a few journalists. There is a long list of flyblown metaphors which could similarly be got rid of if enough people would interest themselves in the job; and it should also be possible to laugh the *not un-* formation out of existence,[3] to reduce the amount of Latin and Greek in the average sentence, to drive out foreign phrases and strayed scientific words, and, in general, to make pretentiousness unfashionable. But all these are minor points. The defence of the English language implies more than this, and perhaps it is best to start by saying what it does *not* imply.

18   To begin with it has nothing to do with archaism, with the salvaging of obsolete words and turns of speech, or with the setting up of a "standard English" which must never be departed from. On the contrary, it is especially concerned with the scrapping of every word or idiom which has outworn its usefulness. It has nothing to do with correct grammar and syntax, which are of no importance so long as one makes one's meaning clear, or with the avoidance of Americanisms, or with having what is called a "good prose style." On the other hand it is not concerned with fake simplicity and the attempt to make written English colloquial. Nor does it even imply in every case preferring the Saxon word to the Latin one, though it does imply using the fewest and shortest words that will cover one's meaning. What is above all needed is to let the meaning choose the word, and not the other way about. In prose, the worst thing one can do with words is to surrender to them. When you think of a concrete object, you think wordlessly, and then, if you want to describe the thing you have been

visualizing you probably hunt about till you find the exact words that seem to fit it. When you think of something abstract you are more inclined to use words from the start, and unless you make a conscious effort to prevent it, the existing dialect will come rushing in and do the job for you, at the expense of blurring or even changing your meaning. Probably it is better to put off using words as long as possible and get one's meaning as clear as one can through pictures or sensations. Afterwards one can choose—not simply *accept*—the phrases that will best cover the meaning, and then switch round and decide what impression one's words are likely to make on another person. This last effort of the mind cuts out all stale or mixed images, all prefabricated phrases, needless repetitions, and humbug and vagueness generally. But one can often be in doubt about the effect of a word or a phrase, and one needs rules that one can rely on when instinct fails. I think the following rules will cover most cases:

(i) Never use a metaphor, simile or other figure of speech which you are used to seeing in print.

(ii) Never use a long word where a short one will do.

(iii) If it is possible to cut out a word, always cut it out.

(iv) Never use the passive where you can use the active.

(v) Never use a foreign phrase, a scientific word or a jargon word if you can think of an everyday English equivalent.

(vi) Break any of these rules sooner than say anything outright barbarous.

19   These rules sound elementary, and so they are, but they demand a deep change of attitude in anyone who has grown used to writing in the style now fashionable. One could keep all of them and still write bad English, but one could not write the kind of stuff that I quoted in those five specimens at the beginning of this article.

20   I have not here been considering the literary use of language, but merely language as an instrument for expressing and not for concealing or preventing thought. Stuart Chase and others have come near to claiming that all abstract words are meaningless, and have used this as a pretext for advocating a kind of political quietism. Since you don't know what Fascism is, how can you struggle against Fascism? One need not swallow such absurdities as this, but one ought to recognize that the present political chaos is connected with the decay of language, and that one can probably bring about some improvement by starting at the verbal end. If you simplify your English, you are freed from the worst follies of orthodoxy. You cannot speak any of the necessary dialects, and when you make a stupid remark its stupidity will be obvious, even to yourself. Political language—and with variations this is true of all political parties, from Conservatives to Anarchists—is designed to make lies sound truthful and murder respectable, and to give an appearance of solidity to pure wind. One cannot change this all in a moment, but one can at least change one's own habits, and from time to time one can even, if one jeers loudly

enough, send some worn-out and useless phrase—some *jackboot, Achilles' heel, hotbed, melting pot, acid test, veritable inferno* or other lump of verbal refuse—into the dustbin where it belongs.

Notes

1. An interesting illustration is the way in which the English flower names which were in use till very recently are being ousted by Greek ones, *snapdragon* becoming *antirrhinum, forget-me-not* becoming *myosotis*, etc. It is hard to see any practical reason for this change of fashion: it is probably due to an instinctive turning-away from the more homely word and a vague feeling that the Greek word is scientific.

2. Example: "Comfort's catholicity of perception and image, strangely Whitmanesque in range, almost the exact opposite in aesthetic compulsion, continues to evoke that trembling atmospheric accumulative hinting at a cruel, an inexorably serene timelessness. . . . Wrey Gardiner scores by aiming at simple bull's-eyes with precision. Only they are not so simple, and through this contented sadness runs more than the surface bitter-sweet of resignation." (*Poetry Quarterly*)

3. One can cure oneself of the *not un-* formation by memorizing this sentence: *A not unblack dog was chasing a not unsmall rabbit across a not ungreen field.*

For Further Thinking

1. Orwell's purpose seems quite clearly persuasive—to convince us that although our language is troubled, if we consider the full nature and outcome of bad language we can start to do something about it. See the description of argumentative structure and techniques in Chapter 7 of the *Rhetoric*. In what specific ways does Orwell apply principles of argumentation?

2. What other structures does he apply from the expository array? (See Chapter 6 of the *Rhetoric* for expository patterns.)

3. To appreciate fully the mood of the world when Orwell worked on this essay, do a little research on the Second World War. Talk to some people who remember that time, perhaps some who served overseas. See also the Pearson website below, *World War II and Its Aftermath*.

4. If you were to divide this essay into sections, how many would there be in the body? Is it possible to find a thesis statement toward the beginning of the essay that in fact lays out the sections to follow?

Looking Back and Ahead

1. The main character of Orwell's novel *Nineteen Eighty-Four* works for a government department that continuously falsifies records and uses the language of "doublespeak." This particular department is called the Ministry of Truth. Can you give examples in today's world of words that express a reality opposite to their denotative meaning?

2. "Parody" refers to imitation (typically an exaggeration or distortion) of something with an intent to ridicule. Orwell uses parody when he imagines what would happen if a bureaucrat tried to express a passage from the Bible. A much more gentle parody occurs in

the final scene of Roch Carrier's "The Hockey Sweater" (p. 51). Can you identify how parody functions in that instance?

3. Read "Newfoundlandese, if You Please" (p. 109). What do you think of Orwell's admonition that we exclude all "foreign" words from our English? How would that affect us in most parts of Canada, taking Montreal as just one example?

For Further Reading

Bolton, W.F. *The Language of* 1984. Oxford: Blackwell, 1984.

"George Orwell." *Encarta Encyclopedia*. Online. April 2003 <**http://encarta.msn.com/find/Concise.asp?z=1&pg=2&ti=761575966**>.

Meyers, Jeffrey. *A Reader's Guide to George Orwell*. London: Thames & Hudson, 1975.

——————. *Wintry Conscience of a Generation*. New York: Norton, 2000.

Orwell, George. *Animal Farm*. London: Secker & Warburg, 1945.

——————. *Nineteen Eighty-Four*. London: Harcourt, 1949.

——————. *Shooting an Elephant and Other Essays*. London: Harcourt, 1950.

Shelden, Michael. *Orwell: A Biography*. New York: HarperCollins, 1991. (Authorized)

Solomon, Norman. "George Orwell in 2001: Speaking from the Grave." Online. "Media Beat" (syndicated column), June 28, 2001. April 2003 <**http://fair.org/media-beat/010628.html**>. In this weekly syndicated column, the writer speculates on what Orwell would think of American policy and the media today.

Taylor, Drew Hayden. "An Indian by Any Other Name." *Funny You Don't Look Like One: Observations of a Blue-Eyed Ojibway*. Rev. edn. Penticton, B.C.: Theytus, 1998, pp. 64–66. Taylor complains "there are two dozen separate names for our people. . . . I wanna know who keeps changing all the rules."

"World War II and Its Aftermath." Online. Pearson Education. Part of an online course, "Twentieth Century Overview," with student resources. April 2003 <**http://occ.awlonline.com/bookbind/pubbooks/damrosch_awl/chapter7/medialib/238ww2.html**>. An overview of how the Second World War affected British literature and British writers, including Orwell.

Appendix
Language Support for Eight Selected Readings

The following represents special language assistance for eight selections in the *Reader*:

Roch Carrier, **"The Hockey Sweater"** (p. 51)
François Hébert, **"Je Me Souviens"** (p. 54)
Alice Munro, **"Thanks for the Ride"** (p. 62)
Dorothy Williams, **"The Quebec Experience: Slavery 1628–1834"** (p. 90)
John Markoff, **"The Doomsday Machines"** (p. 135)
Wayne C. Booth, **"The Rhetorical Stance"** (p. 144)
Pierre Elliott Trudeau, **"The Ascetic in a Canoe"** (p. 156)
Margaret Atwood, **"Canadians: What Do They Want?"** (p. 196)

We have prepared this support for students whose first language is not English, but first-language speakers of English may also find valuable help in this material.

* *Prereading Vocabulary* helps you understand potentially difficult words before you encounter them in the readings.
* *Idioms and Expressions* helps you understand the meaning of word combinations that do not make literal sense but that have special meaning when used together.
* *References* provides definitions for cultural or historical terms.
* *Language Pointers* looks at some aspect of language usage of particular prominence or interest in the reading.

You should find that this material helps you achieve a richer appreciation of the eight selected readings. These have been chosen to represent a range of fictional, personal, expository, persuasive, and research approaches.

For more support regarding English as a Second Language, visit the website for Athabasca University's English 255 Introductory Composition course at <**www.athabascau.ca/courses/engl/255/**>. See "If English Is Not Your First Language." Also see "Language Support for Selected Readings" for help with additional essays in the *Reader*.

"THE HOCKEY SWEATER" (p. 51)
Roch Carrier

Prereading Vocabulary

abominable hated, disgusting
Anglais English (French)

blazing proceeding vigorously
Cher Monsieur Dear Mr./Sir (French)
counts matters
daydreams dreamlike thoughts of the future
Docteur Doctor (French)
persecution harassment, persistently cruel treatment
strategies plans to achieve a certain goal or outcome
tranquility peace, calm, quiet
trounced beat severely
vicar a type of priest, minister, or clergyman

Language Pointers

There are some good examples of the use of the conditional construction in this article. Conditional usage is always a variation of "If event A happens, then event B will occur." There are some general verb tense rules that go along with the use of the conditional; please see "Conditional and Hypothetical Constructions" under "Supplementary Resources" at <http://www.athabascau.ca/courses/engl/255/>.

Note the following examples from this reading:

"If you wear that old sweater, people are going to think we're poor."
(Clause A—simple present; Clause B—future with "going to")

". . . please send me what's left, if there's anything left."
(Clause B [simple present] is followed by Clause A—simple present with future meaning [in this example])

"If you make up your mind about things before you try, my boy, you won't go very far in this life."
(Clause A—simple present; Clause B—simple future, negative)

"If you don't keep this sweater, which fits you perfectly, I'll have to write to Monsieur Eaton . . ."
(Clause A—simple present; Clause B—simple future)

"And if he's insulted, do you think he'll be in a hurry to answer us?"
(Clause A—simple present; Clause B—simple future)

Note: It is grammatically correct to use a comma after Clause A when Clause A is used first in a sentence.

"JE ME SOUVIENS" (p. 54)
François Hébert

Prereading Vocabulary

apotheosis elevation of human to divine rank; deification; the essence or perfect example of something
bucolic pertaining to or characteristic of shepherds or herdsmen, pastoral, rustic

cosmological relating to the universe considered as a totality of parts and phenomena subject to laws

curés French for priests

incantatory having the characteristic of intoned sounds whose tones and cadences working together have magical effects

mystic of the nature of or pertaining to spiritual mysteries and enlightenment; one who practices mysticism (direct internal communion with the divine)

Pagan one who is not a Christian, a Jew, a Moslem or a Hindu; one who worships Nature

proto- first in time or rank; chief; typical; original

solstice the time of year when the sun is at its greatest distance from the celestial equator and seems to pause before returning on its course. In the northern hemisphere the summer solstice is around June 22 and the winter solstice is around December 22.

secession the act of withdrawing from political or religious association with a certain entity

secularization to make secular, i.e., worldly as distinguished from spiritual.

showbizzy *show biz* is U.S. slang for show business. Hébert has turned the slang noun into a slang adjective by adding a typical adjectival suffix "y" (doubling the final consonant).

References

Alliance Quebec Founded in 1982, this volunteer-run organization is "committed to the preservation and enhancement of English-speaking communities and institutions within Quebec." Despite a considerable exodus of English speakers from Quebec, approximately one million remain.

Bourgeois The last name of Hébert's neighbour means a member of the middle class (from French statesman Léon Bourgeois, 1851–1925). The term is most often used disparagingly, to connote smug, self-interested character and behaviour, the opposite of a political idealist.

Brylcreem In the 1950s, the hair product Brylcreem helped define pop culture in concert with the "ducktail" style of slicked-back hair for rebellious young men. Advertising for Brylcreem used the slogan "a lidl-dabl-dooya" (a little dab will do you) as proof this product was better than "that greasy kid's stuff."

Canada Day Formerly known as Dominion Day, First of July, Confederation Day, and July the First, this annual celebration in Canada recalls July 1,1867, when the British North America Act (BNA) created the Canadian federal government and established "one Dominion under the name of Canada." The present name for this celebration was adopted in 1982 in efforts to downplay the country's colonial origins.

Louis-Ferdinand Céline (1894–1961) A French writer and doctor, Céline wrote innovative and antiheroic novels such as *Journey to the End of Night* (1932) and *Death on the Installment Plan* (1936). He is generally believed to have suffered from increasing madness in the 1940s. Accused of collaborating with the Nazis, he fled France in 1944. Declared a national disgrace in 1950, he was then pardoned and returned in 1951.

Jean Charest Born in 1958, Charest was elected to the House of Commons as the Progressive Conservative candidate for Sherbrooke in 1984. He served as Deputy Prime Minister in 1993 and held other important positions. Re-elected in 1994 and in 1997, he left federal politics and the PC Party in 1998 to become leader of the Quebec Liberals, hoping to oust the separatist PQ. In April 2003 he achieved his goal when elected premier of Quebec.

Robert Charlebois Born in 1944 in Montreal, Charlebois became a pop and rock music icon in the 1960s. Celebrated for irreverent and iconoclastic material and performances, Charlebois gave prominence to Quebec *joual* as well as to the Cajun dialect of Louisiana. In 1969, he helped establish the Rhinoceros Party, which persists today as a satirical answer to conventional Canadian politics.

David and Goliath When the Israelite David was still a shepherd boy, his father ordered him to take food to his older brothers who, with the Israelite army, were confronting an army of Philistines. A giant Philistine champion, Goliath, had been challenging Israel to send out one warrior for single combat, but none among the Israelites dared face Goliath. Confident in God, who always helped him rescue his sheep from lions and bears, David went forth with just his shepherd's sling and slew Goliath, striking him in the temple with a well-placed stone. David went on to replace Saul as King of Israel (I Samuel:17).

Raoul Duguay Born in 1939, Duguay has long held the affection of many Québécois for his distinctive and often nationalistic poetry and songs. In 1968 he co-founded L'Infonie, a 33-member music group. He is, in addition, a professor of philosophy.

ethnic cleansing of Grand-Pré Grand-Pré is a town in Nova Scotia northwest of Halifax. Its first European settlers were the French who came to be known in Atlantic Canada as the Acadians. In 1755, the British deported the Acadians, driving them to other French territories such as Louisiana. Thomas LaBrie, author of the essay "Franken-Frogs and the Mushroom Bear" (p. 33), is of Acadian ancestry.

La Fête Nationale, St. Jean Baptiste Day The celebration in Quebec of June 24 traces back to pre-Christian France, to pagan celebration of the summer solstice of light and hope. The day was later Christianized to commemorate the birth of St. John the Baptist, who became the patron saint of Quebec. In 1615, the tiny population of New France held its first mass recognizing convergence of the solstice, the birth of their patron saint, and the birth of a new country. The setting of bonfires in symbolic recognition of this hope became a June 24 custom. The day lost some of its energy with the conquest of New France, but in the nineteenth century it regained prominence as a patriotic rallying point. In 1925 the Quebec legislature declared June 24 a provincial holiday.

grass Slang for marijuana, a form of cannabis, the "soft" street drug outlawed in Canada but tolerated at various times and in various contexts. It has recently been legalized for certain medical uses and may become more generally legal in small amounts for personal use only.

hanging of Lower Canada's *patriotes* "Patriotes" was the name given after 1826 to the Parti Canadien, and to the populist movement in general in Lower Canada (Quebec). The Patriotes dominated the elected House of Assembly but were overruled by the appointed Legislative Council representing the merchant bourgeoisie, the aristocracy, and the colonial administration. Struggle for self-government in Lower Canada led to the rebellion of 1837–1838, which Britain suppressed by force and the capital punishment of 12 rebel leaders. Fifty-eight others were deported to Australia. Having crushed the rebellion, Britain passed the Act of Unification in 1840, uniting Upper and Lower Canada as one single province of Canada.

Holstein cow A type of dairy cow, the Holstein is noted for its black-and-white or red-and-white markings. It was developed in the Netherlands. Milk production was and remains an important Quebec industry.

William Johnson Born in 1931, journalist William Johnson was a former leader of Alliance Quebec. His book *Anglophobie: Made in Quebec* (1991) includes a critique of how, in his opinion, Quebec Francophone literature perpetuates vile stereotypes of Anglophones. Formerly with the *Gazette*, Johnson now writes for *The Globe and Mail*.

Maine, Detroit, Pittsburgh, and Louisiana All of these had been French possessions. By the Treaty of Paris of 1763, Spain acquired Louisiana; Britain acquired the other colonies, which the United States took over following the American Revolution (1776–1783).

Mount Royal Park The city of Montreal is often described as drawing its character from two central landmarks, the St. Lawrence River and the hill around which the city rests. The hill (or mount) is typical of the St. Lawrence River flood plain. In 1876, a park was established on Mount Royal, designed by Frederick Law Olmsted, creator of New York City's Central Park. Featuring two chalets, a pond, numerous trails, and spectacular views from various lookouts, Mount Royal Park is one of the city's most visited sites. For many years it has provided a centre for various cultural events.

New France The territory (including today's province of Quebec) that France held in North America from 1529 to 1763. For 250 years, the French were leading explorers and settlers in North America.

Plains of Abraham From 1756 to 1763, several European powers engaged in the first global conflict of recorded history, the Seven Years' War. On opposite sides of the struggle were France and England. On September 13, 1759, the crucial battle took place outside the walls of Quebec City in the fields of a farmer named Abraham. The British forces led by General James Wolfe defeated those of the French commanded by the Marquis de Montcalm. In 1763, under terms of the Treaty of Paris, almost all of New France (including Quebec) was ceded to Britain; Louisiana became a possession of Spain.

When Quebec City's population was barely 200 souls Use of "souls" in this statement is an example of synecdoche (Greek for "taking together"). Synecdoche is a literary device whereby a part of something (in this case the soul of a human) is used to signify the whole (the person). Another example is "head of cattle" to mean cattle.

The Quiet Revolution This is the period in Quebec from 1960 to 1966 following the Liberal defeat of the conservative Union Nationale party headed by Maurice Duplessis (*le Chef*). Under Jean Lesage, the Liberals instituted sweeping changes of democratization and nationalization. Lesage's motto was "Maîtres chez nous" (Masters in our own house). At the extreme end of change, the Front de Libération du Québec (FLQ) practised terrorist acts, such as bombing and kidnapping, in a desperate bid to wrench Quebec away from the rest of Canada.

Maurice Richard and Johnny Bower From the 1940s to the early 1960s, Maurice "Rocket" Richard played right wing for the Montreal Canadiens of the National Hockey League; Johnny Bower was goaltender of the archrival Toronto Maple Leafs. For the fans, more than hockey was at stake in their showdowns. You can discover whether Richard really outsmarted Bower ten times in five minutes by reading Roch Carrier's "The Hockey Sweater" (p. 51).

St. Patrick's Day March 17 recognizes St. Patrick, patron saint of Ireland, who died on that day in 461 A.D., having served as that country's second bishop. The bishop is believed to have used the three-leaf shamrock, a famous symbol of the Irish and of St. Patrick's Day, to explain the Trinity of Father, Son, and Holy Spirit. Originally a Catholic holy day, March 17, like St. Jean Baptiste Day, has evolved into a mainly secular festival. It was first celebrated in North America in Boston in 1737.

Shipshaw's new aluminum plant In the 1940s in Shipshaw, in the Saguenay–Lac Saint-Jean region northeast of Quebec City, Alcan operated a hydroelectric station that generated more hydroelectric energy than any facility in the world. The company used its energy to process primary aluminum at plants such as the one at Shipshaw. With major changes in the industry and global business, this region of Quebec has fallen from relative prosperity to hard times.

Superman In 1938, Jerry Siegel and Toronto-born artist Joe Shuster sold a new science-fiction story idea to DC Comics. For the next nine years, Shuster illustrated

Siegel's story lines about the "man of steel," sole survivor of the planet Krypton, home to an advanced race of peaceful humans. Adopting the disguise of mild-mannered reporter Clark Kent, Superman remains a mystery to the earthlings he rescues from various dangers, threats, and disasters. Reporter Lois Lane longs for Superman while looking with indifference upon her co-worker Clark Kent.

tam-tam A type of drum used in the East Indies and western Africa.

the Vatican This is the headquarters—a city unto itself—of the Pope, head of the Catholic Church. For more than 1000 years, various Popes ruled much of the Italian peninsula; in 1929 papal control was greatly reduced with the establishment of the world's smallest independent state. Within the city of Rome, this state—the Vatican—is about half of one square kilometre. The colours of the Vatican and of Quebec flew side by side because Quebec had remained primarily Catholic after the British conquest.

Gilles Vigneault Born in 1928, Vigneault became famous with songs such as "L'hiver" and "Le Rendez-vous." He epitomized the public assertion of Quebec independence.

Language Pointers

One feature of Hébert's personal voice is his use of dashes to add parenthetical information or to lend emphasis to an ending element:

> When I was a child in Montreal, there were fewer public festivities—jazz, film, or otherwise—and fewer demonstrations.

Hébert could have used commas or even parentheses to include, yet subordinate, the non-essential information between the dashes. The dashes strengthen the separation and prepare us for extra emphasis on the last point—"fewer demonstrations."

> We still don't have a country of our own and we don't have much religion anymore, but we cling to our language—and to our *Fête Nationale* to confirm what we know we are.

The effect of the dash here is to set off the last element (*Fête Nationale*) as a crucial afterword or qualification. In a sense, the dashes set up a moment of attention, like a spotlight coming after a dramatic pause. Combined with Hébert's tone of nostalgia, humour, and irony, this device contributes to a personal voice. In more formal, academic forms of writing, this use of the dash is less common.

"THANKS FOR THE RIDE" (p. 62)
Alice Munro

Prereading Vocabulary

absurdity the quality of being ridiculous
acquiescent compliant
billboards large outdoor signs or advertisements
bootleggers people selling goods (often alcohol) illegally
burrs prickly seeds

derision mockery, ridicule
fly-speckled dotted with fly excrement
fraudulent deceitful or dishonest
gravity seriousness, significance
keenness eagerness, enthusiasm
lassitude weariness, fatigue
mope be dejected, gloomy
omne animal all living beings (Latin)
plastered stuck
premeditation deliberate planning of some action
pretentious an outward, exaggerated show of importance
privies outside toilets
pudgy overweight
pumps water pumps
reducing weight loss
slovenly untidy
somnolent sleepy, drowsy
stubble the remains of grain stalks in a field after harvest
triste est it is sad (Latin)
verandah an open balcony around the edge of a building

Idioms and Expressions

all-a-man left a reference to square-dancing
bitching complaining, whining
(to be) broke to have no money
nose-thumbing to show irreverence, a lack of respect or concern
in a pinch if absolutely necessary
stuck-up snobbish, a feeling of superiority
toe-twirling foolish pride
(to be) touchy to be sensitive about something

References

Burma-Shave signs advertising billboards for that men's shaving product, with interesting sayings or adages
CPR Canadian Pacific Railway
Mickey Rooney an American movie star, the most famous child actor in America at one time

Language Pointers

Direct speech is used frequently in this short story. When people are talking, however, the language used can be quite different (not as grammatically correct, because spoken more casually), from the language as normally written. The author can use direct speech in several ways to provide atmosphere in this short story and to help develop the characters of the people involved. These methods can be confusing to non-native speakers of English. Spoken language is always idiosyncratic.

1. Words spelled the way they sound:

Linking		Missing consonant(s)		Other mispronunciation	
Inna	in a	gran'daughter	granddaughter	peenies	peonies
c'mon	come on	'night	goodnight	clemantis	clematis
gotta	got to	hangin'	hanging		
change's	change is	climbin'	climbing		
musta	must have	what'd	what did		
		where's	where does		
		ever'body	everybody		

Another example of written form being used to imitate speech is the word "int-er-esting." The hyphens are used to show that each syllable is spoken slowly and carefully and with emphasis so that this adjective becomes a sarcastic comment on the irreverent story George has interrupted. Such slow speech is meant as mockery.

2. Questions being asked but not with a question word order:

When speaking, we may sometimes ask questions, particularly yes/no questions, without using "correct" word order. English speakers do this using sentence intonation, rising on the last syllable, to indicate that a question is being asked. Note the following examples from the story; the "missing" word or words are given in parentheses:

"Okay if I call you Mickey?" (Is it . . .)
"There any other dance halls?" (Are there . . .)
"You want to go to a show?" (Do . . .)
"You got a car?" (Have . . .)
"Her mother not let her out at night?" (Doesn't . . . let . . .)
"That so?" (Is . . .)
"You like that dress?" (Do . . .)
"That how you feel?" (Is . . .)
"You live near here?" (Do . . .)

3. "Eh" as a tag:

The use of "eh" as a tag in a yes/no question is quite common in Canadian speech. Note the following examples:

"Fine, eh?"
"Feel like you finished your education tonight, eh?"
"Change's as good as a rest, eh?"

Also note that the auxiliary verb needed to construct a yes/no question is missing in the first two examples. Once again, intonation is important in identifying these sentences as questions.

4. Missing vocabulary:

In some spoken sentences, various words are "missing," and so the utterances appear to be ungrammatical. Check the following examples and note the word or words that need to be "understood":

"Dance hall down on the beach . . ." (The . . .)
"Too young." (You're . . .)
". . . not so good either." (. . . that's . . .)
"Change's as good as a rest, eh?" (A . . .)

"Doesn't hear half what you say to her." (She . . .)
"Depends." (It . . .)
"My father's." (It's . . .)
"Clean off, . . ." (It was cut . . .)
"Couldn't open the coffin." (They/We . . .)
"Used to take her out." (He . . .)

"THE QUEBEC EXPERIENCE: SLAVERY 1628–1834" (p. 90)
Dorothy Williams

Prereading Vocabulary

Act a bill that has been passed into law by a legislature
bill(s) proposed legislation
chattel personal property
fleur de lys the heraldic symbol of France
legislature an assembly of elected officials for a political area
manumission the freeing of slaves from bondage
obfuscation confusion; often deliberate obscuring of a truth
scavenger's wagon a version of a garbage truck
seigneur(s) landholder(s) in New France
status quo the current situation (Latin)
tabling the presentation of proposed legislation to a governing body
tenuous unsubstantial, weak

Idioms and Expressions

the vertical ladder a metaphor for economic condition and opportunity
on the whole generally

References

Acadia the current provinces of Nova Scotia, New Brunswick, and Prince Edward
    Island as well as southeastern Quebec and eastern Maine in the United States
American colonies those colonies governed by Britain that later formed the original
    United States
Bantu a broad language group from Africa, not a specific language
British North America the colonies of Britain in North America
Samuel de Champlain an early explorer of New France
Code Noir the legal framework governing ownership of slaves
the Conquest the loss of New France to the British in 1759
Creole the French patois (dialect) spoken in Louisiana (a southern American state)
governor the representative of the British government in the Canadas
Lower Canada the name given to New France after the Conquest
Loyalists American colonists who remained loyal to Britain
Maritimes now, the eastern provinces of Canada excluding Newfoundland and Labrador;
    historically separate colonies of Britain

Micmacs an Indian tribe that lived in Acadia

Montreal one of the early centres of settlement in New France; now the largest city in Quebec

New France the name given to the French colony in North America to 1763

New York an American state

Northwest territories an area that later became states of the United States, located to the north and west of the original colonies

off-island the core area of Montreal is an island in the St. Lawrence; newer areas are built on the mainland

Joseph Papineau a lawyer and politician in Lower Canada (1786–1871)

Quebec present-day Quebec is a province of Canada; historically, it had various names at different times (New France, Lower Canada, Canada East), and the specific land area also varied

Roman Catholicism a Christian religious denomination; the dominant church in New France

seigneurial system the feudal system of landholding that existed in New France

underground railroad a system of cooperation among anti-slavery people that helped slaves escape to freedom

United Empire Loyalists the same as "Loyalists"

Upper Canada the British colony that later became the province of Ontario

Vermont an American state

War of Independence the war in which the American colonists won their independence from Britain

Westmount an upper-class area of Montreal

Language Pointers

1. The passive voice:

   Note the use of passive voice in paragraph 9; it details the execution of Angelique. The passive is used because not only is the person or people who tortured and killed her unknown, but also because the torture and execution are emphasized. In this paragraph most of the verbs are in the simple past tense of the passive voice, with one example of the past perfect passive ("had been placed . . .").

   The passive voice is also used elsewhere in this article to provide similar emphasis to the result of some activity: "Approximately three hundred new slaves were brought into Lower Canada by Loyalists." In this case, the people performing the action are known, but are not considered as important as the result of their action.

2. Transitions and referents:

   This essay provides some very good examples of the use of transitions and referents to connect ideas between sentences and paragraphs and also to provide a flow to the writing. See paragraph 3 for an example of a referent. The first sentence starts, "May 1, 1689, is considered . . . ," and the following sentence refers to that date, "On that day . . . ." A connection is made between paragraphs 7 and 8 with the opening line of paragraph 8, "Yet despite this incendiary disaster . . . ."

3. Rhetorical questions:

   A rhetorical question is one to which an answer is not expected. Rhetorical questions can be used to provide emphasis in an argument, as in paragraph 8, where they are used to demonstrate the unimportance of Black slaves in the official historical record of Montreal.

"THE DOOMSDAY MACHINES" (p. 135)
John Markoff

Prereading Vocabulary

boosterism the activities and attitudes characteristic of "boosters"—people who promote something
darker more sinister, more threatening
dawning a beginning, the start of something new
doomsday the end of the world
hype extravagant, promotional publicity
near-term almost developed, nearly ready
utopia(s) a perfect place or situation

Idioms and Expressions

(the) catch (the) problem or difficulty
a doozy an extraordinary one of its kind
laundry list a long list
run amok behaved wildly or in a crazy way
toy(ing) with play with, imagine

References

Armageddon a disastrous conflict (from the Biblical story of the end of the world)
black hole a region of space with such dense gravity that even light cannot escape, and all matter is consumed by it
Darwinian according to Darwin's theory; the survival of the fittest
DNA deoxyribonucleic acid; the building blocks of life
holy grail a symbol of the ultimate search; something a group of people are looking for more than anything else; refers to the chalice Jesus drank from at the Last Supper
IBM International Business Machines, a multinational company
Information Age the current period in history; the previous one was the Industrial Age
Luddite during the Industrial Revolution in England, people who were afraid of new machines and broke them—after Ned Ludd, who destroyed some machines
Pandora's Box from Greek mythology, a box that held all of the various problems that afflict mankind
Robocop(s) from a futuristic movie of that title—Robocop is part human and part robot
The Sorcerer's Apprentice an animated Disney film about magic
Mark Twain pseudonym of Samuel L. Clemens, a famous nineteenth-century American novelist
Y2K the year 2000

Language Pointers

1. Newspaper style:

   Articles written in newspapers have very short paragraphs. An essay paragraph should usually have at least four sentences, but many paragraphs consist of only one sentence in newspaper articles. This style is a response to the narrow columns of print and the need to make articles easy to read. Long columns of print without a break are much more difficult to read. This newspaper sentence-paragraph construction, however, imposes an easily read structure on the material.

Compare the paragraph structure in this article to a more "normal" essay:

Normal	Newspaper Style
Paragraph 1	Paragraphs 1–4
Paragraph 2	Paragraphs 5–9
Paragraph 3	Paragraphs 10–13
Paragraph 4	Paragraphs 14–19
Paragraph 5	Paragraphs 20–23
Paragraph 6	Paragraphs 24–28
Paragraph 7	Paragraphs 29–31
Paragraph 8	Paragraphs 32–35
Paragraph 9	Paragraphs 36 and 37

Another device for making longer newspaper articles more readable is subheadings. These can also give more prereading information so readers have a better understanding of the content of a long article. Subheadings provide some added essay organization for people who may not want to read every word of an article.

2. Verb tense usage:

You will recognize a variety of verb tenses in this article. When one sentence contains a combination of tenses, that combination informs the reader about the connection between the two actions described. In the examples given here, you will see some reference to the particular contexts found within this article.

Simple Present—with a future meaning, e.g., paragraphs 4, 10, 14, and 16

Simple Present—a general statement of fact, e.g., paragraphs 20, 24, 28, 33, and 36

Simple Present—a current, repetitive situation, e.g., paragraphs 7, 8, 11, 18, 19, and 32

Simple Past—something occurred at a specified time in the past, e.g., paragraphs 12, 22, 34, and 35. Note the time clues that may be present ("recently," "last year," and "earlier this month").

Present Progressive—used to describe an ongoing situation, e.g., paragraph 13.

Present Perfect—something occurred between an unspecified time in the past and the present, e.g., paragraphs 1–3, 6, and 25. Note the time clues ("in the space of three short decades" and "this month").

Simple Present + Simple Past—a combination often used in direct speech, e.g., paragraphs 9 and 30.

Simple Present + Present Perfect—provides contrast or connection between a present situation and something that has happened as a result, e.g., paragraphs 5, 21, and 29.

Simple Present + Simple Future—shows a connection between a current situation and a possible future situation, e.g., paragraphs 15 and 17. Note that in the case of paragraph 23, "believe" is a stative verb, one not generally used in a progressive tense.

Simple Present + Present Perfect Progressive—shows a connection between a situation that is described and an ongoing situation that started at an unspecified time in the past, e.g., paragraph 27.

Simple Present + Present Perfect + Simple Past—shows a connection between a statement of fact, an event in the past and an action that resulted from it, e.g., paragraph 29.

"THE RHETORICAL STANCE" (p. 144)
Wayne C. Booth

Prereading Vocabulary

Aristotelian related to the teachings of Aristotle, the Greek philosopher (384–322 B.C.)
bent inclination, interest, and ability
bull nonsense (slang)
fencing sword play
freshman first year college or university
jai alai a fast-moving ball game originating in Spain
ontological related to metaphysical arguments about the state of being
Platonic related to the teachings of Plato, the Greek philosopher (427?–347? B.C.)
polemic argument, controversy
rhetorical concerned with writing technique or strategy for presenting a perspective
soils makes dirty, besmirches
teleological explanation of phenomena based on their possible purposes, not their causes
unpretentious without outward show or ostentation

Idioms and Expressions

Blank a generic expression for an unnamed person
cornered (someone) get (someone) in a position from which escape is impossible
late-bloomer someone who reaches a particular level of understanding or ability at a later age than his or her peers
off-the-cuff spontaneous, unrehearsed
sursum corda a cry of encouragement or exhortation (literally, "lift up your hearts"); the opening words of the Catholic mass (Latin)

References

Sheridan Baker author and former professor of English at the University of Michigan
Edmund Burke British writer and statesman (1729–1797)
Chaucer Geoffrey Chaucer (1340?–1400), poet and author of *The Canterbury Tales*
P.A. Christensen a former professor of English at Brigham Young University
Churchill Sir Winston Churchill (1874–1965), British author, statesman, and prime minister; led Great Britain in its "finest hour" to resist Nazi Germany
Ronald Crane former professor of English at the University of Chicago
Emma a novel by Jane Austen (1816)
Walker Gibson a former professor at the University of Massachusetts, author of writing and rhetoric texts
The Golden Bowl a novel by Henry James (1904)
Jealousy a novel by Alain Robbe-Grillet (*La jalousie*) (1957)
Madame Bovary a novel by Gustave Flaubert (1857)
Milton John Milton (1608–1674), English poet and essayist, best known for the epic poem *Paradise Lost*
More Sir Thomas More (1478?–1535), author of *Utopia*
Reader's Digest a popular magazine with wide, general appeal

Teacher in America a book—biographical—by Jacques Barzun (1945)

Thurber James Thurber (1894–1961), American humorous writer and artist

Utopia a novel about a perfect place and society (1516)

"peace in our time" words spoken by Neville Chamberlain, in 1939, when he was prime minister of Britain, on returning from his Munich meeting with Adolf Hitler; Chamberlain tried to accomodate or appease Hitler

Language Pointers

The use of affixes (prefixes and suffixes) is very noticeable, partly because of the level of language, very formal and intellectual, used in the essay, and also because of the manipulation of two nouns to produce adjectives.

"Platonic" is derived from Plato, the Greek philosopher, plus an adjective suffix. Similarly, "Aristotelian" is derived from Aristotle, another Greek philosopher, plus a different adjective suffix. The adjective suffixes mean "in the manner of." Note that "Platonic" has a different meaning from "platonic" (purely spiritual, not sensual) used to describe a relationship.

There are also examples of the way words change in function according to the suffixes used:

Noun (thing)	Noun (person)	Adjective
rhetoric	rhetorician	rhetorical
pedantry	pedant	pedantic
polemic	polemicist	polemical

Note that the –*ic* ending can indicate either a noun or an adjective.

A prefix, however, changes the meaning of a word, not its function. Note the negative prefixes in the following words: **un**pretentious, **dis**organized, **in**capable, **in**dispensable.

A study of word stems and affixes helps to explain the following words, but the suffix provides information about function:

automatically (auto—arising from some process or action within the object) [adverb]
pronouncement (throw forth) [noun]
pretentious, **pre**conception (before) [nouns]
confrontation (together) [noun]
ontological (being, existence) [adjective]
teleological (final, complete, perfect) [adjective]
bibliographies (pertaining to books) [noun]
controversial (against) [adjective]
obtrusive, **ob**jective (towards) [nouns]

"THE ASCETIC IN A CANOE" (p. 156)
Pierre Elliott Trudeau

Prereading Vocabulary

aesthetic relating to beauty in art or nature
ascetic a person who puts aside social life and comfort, who prefers austerity and self-denial
bourgeois middle-class person

catch amount of fish caught

chiding scolding, reprimanding

fine subtle

gumbo a type of soil, sticky mud when wet

portage the land route for transporting a boat (canoe) from one area of navigable water to another

premise an idea or concept used as the basis for an argument or conclusion

primordial first, original

rapid a part of a river where the current is very fast and the vertical drop is steep

saturation point the point at which no more of a substance (experience) can be absorbed

torpor complete or partial insensibility; stupor

Language Pointers

Parallel structures are used in a number of instances in this essay, either out of grammatical necessity, for stylistic purposes, or for both:

Paragraph 1: people who *tear themselves away from* and *apply themselves to* . . . (two- or three-part separable verbs in the simple present tense are used with a reflexive pronoun)

Paragraph 3: those who dare *to cross a lake, make a portage, spend a night in a tent and return exhausted* . . . (repeated use of the infinitive verb—although the word "to" is only required in the first instance—followed by an object)

Paragraph 4: It involves *a starting* rather than *a parting* (similar noun phrases using a gerund). its purpose is not *to destroy* the past, but *to lay* a foundation . . . (infinitive verbs used in a contrasting manner)

Paragraph 8: it purifies you more *rapidly* and *inescapably* than any other travel. (adverbs joined by a conjunction)

Travel a thousand miles by train and you are a brute; pedal five hundred on a bicycle and you remain basically a bourgeois; paddle a hundred in a canoe and you are already a child of nature. (The base form of the verb is used to introduce each idea; "you" is understood to be the subject pronoun. The verb is followed by a noun phrase including some method of transport; the conjunction "and" is used to connect the first idea to the second idea; this second idea is introduced by the pronoun "you" and verb in the simple present tense, followed by a noun phrase.)

Paragraph 9: *Canoe and paddle, blanket and knife, salt pork and flour, fishing rod and rifle* (a list of paired nouns joined by the conjunction "and")

Paragraph 12: You watch your friend *stumbling over logs, sliding on rocks, sticking in gumbo, tearing* the skin on his legs and *drinking* water . . . yet never *letting go* of the rope. (In each case, a gerund phrase is used; in the first three cases the phrase is completed with a preposition and a noun.) This same man *has* also *fed* you half his catch, and *has made* a double portage . . . (verbs in the present perfect tense in clauses joined by the conjunction "and").

Paragraph 13: spreads through *the palms of your hands and the soles of your feet* . . . (similar noun phrases joined by the conjunction "and")

"CANADIANS: WHAT DO THEY WANT?" (p. 196)
Margaret Atwood

Prereading Vocabulary

alluded referred to indirectly
annihilation complete destruction
asterisk * this symbol; a mark for special attention or notice
branch plant a subsidiary or more minor part of a company or business
bristle become irritated or upset
chauvinism in this context, glorification of one's country
divine right authority considered to be God-given
imperious domineering, arrogant
inegalitarian not believing in social and economic equality
jackboots a heavy, often military, knee-high boot (often associated with the Nazis)
john a toilet (slang)
picky choosy
quibbles minor arguments
ratio proportion or rate
sardonic scornful or derisive
scrape it together barely manage to accumulate enough money
self-righteous feeling of one's own right, correctness, superiority
snippy impertinent
spoils rewards
stamp characteristic
subjugate conquer or subdue

References

draft dodgers people who left the United States to avoid military service, particularly at the time of the Vietnam War
Gaul an ancient name for an area that approximates modern France. It became part of the Roman Empire by conquest.
Genghis Khan thirteenth-century conqueror of central Asia
Lifebuoy a brand of soap with deodorant qualities
Michigan a state of the United States that borders on Canada
Reagan Ronald Reagan, president of the United States (1981–1989)
Rome, Romans Ancient Rome and its citizens
Syracuse a city in New York State

Language Pointers

There are several examples of the use of the third person, singular generic pronoun "one" in this reading. In this usage, the pronoun "one" refers to people in general. This pronoun is not often used nowadays except in formal writing. If it is the subject of a sentence, then its associated verb must be conjugated in the same way that other third-person singular pronouns are. The following examples are from the reading:

It began by suggesting that **one start** with the feet.*
This is the conversation **one has** with Americans . . .
Pessimists among us would say that **one has** to translate the experience . . .
One could always refer Americans to history, . . . **
Objectively, **one cannot** become too self-righteous . . . **

Another generic usage is that of a plural noun without a determiner. Note the difference in meaning between "Americans" (American people in general) and "the Americans" (American people specifically), and similarly between "Canadians" and "the Canadians." Other plural nouns used in a generic manner are "men," "women," "pessimists," "members," "Canadian workers," "cocktail parties," "international affairs," "empires."

---

* In this example, there is a noun clause using the subjunctive; therefore the base form of the verb is used.

** In these examples, there is a modal term before the main verb; therefore the base form of the verb is used.

Part 2

THE RHETORIC

INTRODUCTION

THE RHETORIC aims to make your work as a student and writer as successful and rewarding as possible. The first four main sections, "Preparing," "Drafting," "Types of Writing," and "Revising," lay out guidelines to assist you every step of the way. "Preparing" offers various methods that different writers use to establish the focus and strategies they will go on to shape. The information in the next three sections has been organized to provide clear, properly illustrated guidelines to assist you with shaping and revising.

Once you have been given a writing assignment, try the preparation techniques we recommend to see which ones work best for you. Ask yourself why you are writing. Then ask how you want to influence your audience. Your answers to these questions will help you decide which type of writing is called for. Is it a personal essay that you are writing, or is it expository, analytic, or argumentative? If you aren't sure which of these four is called for in an assignment, read Chapter 2, "Reviewing the Basics" (p. 276), as well as the introductions to the personal essay, exposition, critical analysis, and argumentation. Also, consult with classmates and your instructor.

Once you know what your main purpose is, consider your intended audience. Again, your classmates and instructor should have good ideas to help you characterize the sorts of readers you are addressing and the expectations they will have. See our information on tone, voice, and level of language in Chapter 2, "Reviewing the Basics," to be sure you remember to adapt to your audience.

Then decide on a pattern, or combination of patterns, to organize your essay and develop your ideas. The patterns of narration and description are laid out in Chapter 5, "The Personal Essay." The patterns of classification-division, example, cause-effect, comparison-contrast, descriptive analysis, directive process, and definition are presented in Chapter 6, "Exposition." These nine basic patterns, however, may also be applied to fulfil the purposes of evoking scenes and moods, analyzing subjects, or arguing for or against some side of a debate. Your job is to make the best decisions concerning tone and organizational patterns that suit your purpose and audience. We have included a checklist of steps to writing an or-

ganized and detailed generic essay (at the end of Chapter 4, "Essay Structure"); this will provide a valuable guideline as you improve your drafts.

We believe the best way you can improve your writing is to become an alert reader. For that reason, Chapter 8, "The Summary," addresses the skills you need to write this special form of expository prose. Besides being a writing exercise, of course, it is a reading exercise that gives you practice in analyzing the strategies involved in composing written thoughts. The more summaries you write, the better you will appreciate the patterns and strategies used across the spectrum of writing. Chapter 10, "Critical Analysis," shows how you can use the skills of reliable summarizing to support critical evaluation.

Learning to write accurate expository essays, as well as to base your arguments and persuasive essays on current knowledge and ideas will mean developing your research skills. An important part of the following pages features instruction on research assignments, including advice on methods and problems associated with the internet. Completing the *Rhetoric* is a detailed section on oral presentations. There is a good chance that oral assignments will be woven throughout your courses, and you will likely deliver oral presentations as you proceed through your program. Once you embark on a career, written and oral communication may well prove the most important aspects of your success.

To aid your revision process, illustrated in detail under Chapter 13, "Drafting and Revising an Analytical Essay," we have included the most common weaknesses or errors in essay structure, grammar, punctuation, sentence structure, and style. Each aspect of grammar and punctuation is explained and illustrated in the *Handbook* and paragraph structure and wording are discussed in detail in the *Rhetoric*.

In the following pages, from the personal essay through exposition, summaries, evaluations, arguments, research techniques, and oral presentations, you will find what you need to put your skills into practice. This *Rhetoric* will be useful for your first-year writing assignments, and for other communication challenges that lie ahead in your academic program and in your career.

THE
RHETORIC

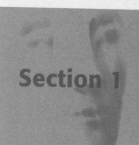

Section 1 Preparing

Chapter 1
Ways of Starting

Training for a marathon, sorting out your work space, establishing a good study routine, organizing for a long trip, or, yes, writing an essay—in every case, starting the activity will be among the hardest parts of the process. The prospect of trying to write an effective essay sometimes feels daunting, even paralyzing. Once you begin, however, your efforts can quickly lead to rewarding involvement, as you discover ideas, shape a preliminary frame for your discussion, and settle upon a clear point or collection of related points to contend and explore. Working on an essay should increasingly invigorate you as you proceed. Nevertheless, final aspects of any essay seldom come to the writer suddenly or effortlessly, but only slowly, as a process of discovery. So how does an essayist—either novice or experienced—reach that sense of readiness, that sense of sturdy content, that moment of ripeness for producing a formal, organized, analytical college paper? How does one begin?

BEGINNING WITH A TOPIC

As you explore different techniques that may ease you into your essay, you need some idea of your topic. So let's reflect a little more on the matter of a topic.

A topic is a subject: a noun, modified noun, or noun phrase, rather than a complete idea or position. "Athletics" is a topic (a noun). "Women's athletics" is a more specific topic (a noun modified by the possessive noun "women's" serving as an adjective or descriptive word). "Women's athletics in Canadian universities" is more specific still (one modified noun further narrowed by the phrase "in Canadian universities"). If we move beyond nouns or noun phrases to full sentences ("With few exceptions, women's athletics at Canadian universities remain severely underfunded"), we now have a position statement, a possible topic sentence focusing a paragraph or even a thesis sentence focusing a whole essay (see Chapters 3 and 4). That degree of commitment, or precise comment, comes about after much reflection and, usually, considerable drafting. Before reaching that stage, you may well be working with the broadest of possible topics, such as nutrition or music or athletics.

Ideally, decide to explore a topic that appeals to you in some important way, one that inspires or compels you to write about it. This will usually mean choosing a topic that you already know something about. An important value in writing is the ethos, or credibility, of the writer. Naturally someone who has completed a marathon has more ethos on the topic of training for long distance than does a non-runner. If the topic you find yourself considering, by scholarly choice or necessity, is one you do not know much about, allow yourself enough time to gain the necessary knowledge you lack, and be sure you can gain access to that knowledge through various sources (see Chapter 11, "The Research Paper").

As we know, sometimes we are asked or required to write on a topic that does not immediately interest us. In most cases, with a little patience and flexibility, we can find an interesting dimension to the topic, an angle that engages or motivates us. For example, your instructor asks you to write a personal essay, but you dislike writing about yourself. Rather than stopping there, talk with classmates and your instructor about the assignment. Find out more about the meaning of the key term "personal essay." Once you realize that your instructor requires an essay about some meaningful experience you have undergone or observed (not a revelation of private things that you wish to keep private), the topic becomes more inviting. Now you think of the first pet you owned and how it defied many stereotypical ideas about that type of pet. Your essay will be more about the pet and what you learned than about you. The topic, initially repelling, is now of strong interest.

Let's consider another example. Perhaps the assigned topic is politics. You associate politics with legislatures and national relations, matters that may not appeal to you. Your friend, however, explains that politics can refer broadly to member relations within any informal governing body, such as a family. Suddenly you are motivated. You explore the politics of the family through two or three pre-writing activities described in the following pages. These help you to discover a strong interest in the politics of sibling relationships. You then define family politics as status, struggle, and influence in the family. You analyze these values in terms of sex, age, position, personality type, and relationship to the perceived dominant family members. This leads you to think about the coping strategies that various siblings use. In conclusion, you come to some thoughts about good and bad strategies, and what your ideas mean. You then become curious to know what academic research you can find on the topic, and how that research compares to your personal inferences.

This example suggests how you can use various pre-writing strategies to help you explore and reflect on areas of personal connection; this reflection in turn furthers the important act of narrowing your topic. Consider that essay length (3 pages double-spaced, 12 pages double-spaced, etc.) also dictates how narrow your topic must be. The shorter the paper, the more care you must take to focus on a narrowed topic. In four pages, you will not be able to discuss completely your family, various strategies you have observed for coping with family politics, academic research on the topic, as well as the way your personal perceptions compare to the formal research. All of this would produce three or even four essays of at least four pages each. Your pre-writing reflections will help to provide the topic subdivisions that help you to select what feels right for your preferences, ethos, available sources, and length.

SELECTING A TOPIC FOR PRE-WRITING PRACTICE

So, before exploring any pre-writing strategy, as far as you can, choose a topic that interests you and one that you know something about. Consider the value of researching your topic and allow for the time and resources required. Be sure both time and resources are available. Think carefully about the length of the paper requested and recognize the extent to which you will need to narrow your topic. If the topic is one you care about, you will still need to explore the exact aspects of it that suit the assignment. If the topic seems uninteresting, you will need to search for some interesting aspect and ways to find out more about it. So, in the following practice activities, select one of the suggested topics for each exercise, even if none appeals to you much at first. This practice will help you discover how a seemingly dull topic can develop into an interesting possibility. In all cases, you will need to find subdivisions of the topic and consider how these could help narrow and shape your discussion. Pre-writing strategies are enjoyable and effective ways to solve these needs.

PRE-WRITING STRATEGIES

All the completed, published essays we read began as earlier forms, with only loose associations and even random points of interest in their pre-draft and early draft versions. How do these essays develop? You are probably well aware that science has come to associate the left side of our brains with logical, linear, ordered functions, and the right side with intuitive, circular, open functions. While a step-by-step logical approach to essay writing has its value and place, if you become too rigid and "logical" before your ideas are crystallized, you may end up shaping content that is not sufficiently interesting, that has not emerged from the intuitive, deeper regions of your mind (those associated with the right brain). Mordecai Richler, the award-winning novelist, worked according to a very disciplined schedule, yet while getting started he often listened to music, such as the piano improvisations of jazz musician Oscar Peterson. Various surroundings and activities may help *you* with your intuitive and creative ideas. You can employ any number of creative strategies.

In keeping with the mysteries of the right brain—that non-linear conveyer of insights—we also suggest that you not think too rigidly about writing as comprising neatly distinct stages (pre-writing, writing, revising). Consider that writing is recursive, not linear; it involves a back-and-forth motion and a multitude of tiny decisions as we move through the work. Still, we think about stages in the production of an essay because it helps us develop ways to deal with challenges that arise. At the so-called pre-writing stage, for example, you are encouraged to indulge in conceptual play. Whatever techniques you find most helpful, pre-writing is a way of talking to yourself that sets in motion some chain of associations that will eventually take shape as the essay's first draft. Here are some common strategies you can use at this pre-writing stage:

- making a collage
- freewriting
- brainstorming
- diagramming
- building a topic-sentence tree
- inkshedding
- keeping a journal

Making a Collage

Let's imagine your assignment is to analyze some aspect of Alice Munro's short story "Thanks for the Ride" (p. 62). You could begin by exploring your feelings and ideas about this story through a collage. Find images in magazines and elsewhere that express, for you, an important element of the story. For instance, what image would you choose to portray Lois's dress? How would it contrast to other images expressing her house, her previous relationships, and the town? Assemble these images onto a background, in whatever spatial relationship feels appealing and meaningful to you. A sample collage on "Thanks for the Ride" has been provided by artist Blaise MacMullin (Figure 1.1, p. 264).

   The images need not be "realistically representational"; that is, they may be abstract lines, patterns, shapes, or colours. The important thing is that these images speak to you as coming from the heart of the story. Developing this playful, intuitive, tactile relationship may help you grasp your own connections to the story from unconscious, non-verbal sources. Considering your collage, and perhaps discussing it with others, is a good transitional step from free-form communing to translating your ideas into words.

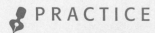

PRACTICE

Make your own collage to express your preliminary responses to one of the three other short stories in the *Reader*: "The Summer My Grandmother Was Supposed to Die" (p. 14), "The Hockey Sweater" (p. 51), or "The Tenant" (p. 164).

Freewriting

Freewriting means picking up pen or pencil (or sitting at the keyboard) and simply letting yourself go. You write whatever comes into your head, without stopping, for a designated short period. The continuous nature of freewriting allows for no hesitations in your thinking, diction, syntax, or editing: no second-guessing in any way

Figure 1.1
Sample collage
for "Thanks for
the Ride" by
Blaise MacMullin

of your thoughts in that moment. Some or even a lot of your freewriting may not even address your topic. The point is not direction or polished content here—only writing in uninterrupted motion, only unfettered thinking as highly personal expression. After all, freewriting is for you only, not for any other audience.

The following sample of freewriting comes from an essay by Peter Elbow. He notes that this is "a fairly coherent" sample; yours may be just as coherent or less so. Whatever works for you is fine.

Freewriting

I think I'll write what's on my mind, but the only thing on my mind right now is what to write for ten minutes. I've never done this before and I'm not prepared in any way—the sky is cloudy today, how's that? Now I'm afraid I won't be able to think of what to write when I get to the end of the sentence—well, here I am at the end of the sentence—here I am again, again, again, at least I am still writing—Now I ask is there some reason to be happy that I am still writing—ah, yes! Here comes the question again—What am I getting out of this? What point is there in it? It's almost obscene to always ask it but I seem to question everything that way and I was gonna say something else pertaining to that but I got so busy writing down the first part that I forgot what I was leading into. This is kind of fun oh don't stop writing—cars and trucks speeding by somewhere out the window, pens clittering across people's papers. The sky is still cloudy—is it symbolic that I should be mentioning it? Huh? I dunno. Maybe I should try colours, blue, red, dirty words—wait a minute—no can't do that, orange, yellow, arm tired, green pink violet magenta lavender red brown black green—now that I can't think of any more colours—just about done—relief? Maybe.

—Peter Elbow, "Freewriting," in *Exploring Language*, 7th ed., ed. Gary Ghoshgarian (New York: HarperCollins, 1995), 19–21.

It may help you to think of this raw prose, like making a collage or brainstorming, as a type of play. Freewriting sidesteps your inner critic, releases you from the pressures of "correct" grammar, vocabulary, and structure. As a result, you can have fun. You can enjoy the visceral experience of writing, contemplate the musical, associative, mysterious dimensions from which you may later draw ideas of potential value.

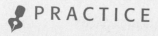 **PRACTICE**

Freewrite for one page on some of the following topics: an ideal vacation, why you do or do not vote, some good memories, a favourite song.

Brainstorming

When you brainstorm, you jot down spontaneous thoughts, feelings, associations, and notions that are evoked by your topic. As with freewriting, this activity is intuitive and open. But whereas freewriting flows continuously and inkshedding (discussed later) makes considered connections between sentences, brainstorming is more intermittent: a scattering of only possibly related points. It allows you to try out particular hunches, to let your ideas churn. Here, you still conjure rather than edit, writing down single words, phrases, or sentences. You may make lists and draw pictures to represent your conceptualizing. You may lie on the couch listening to music, asking yourself what part of your topic interests you . . . and trusting that answers will come, if you take the activity of reflection seriously. You may wish to try out your initial ideas on a friend or classmate. Some teachers and students encourage group brainstorming as a creative search in which the participants' ideas stimulate further ideas.

You may also want to try talking with only yourself rather than others. Simply put questions to yourself about your ideas. What is my sense of this? Why do I have this impression? Can I link two of my observations? If I sense some contradictions, can I account for this tension or disjunction?

The important part of brainstorming, whatever techniques you select, is to feel both stimulated and relaxed. Centuries of suddenly revealed solutions, definitions, and intuitions indicate that the results of productive brainstorming often emerge under the influence of other soothing or stimulating activities: take a bath, listen to music, clean the bathroom, write a letter, or go for a walk—just keep thinking and trying out parts of your ideas.

Brainstorming on the topic of buying a car

Graduation! Time to buy a car??? Cost/features/insurance? Really need a new one or how about second-hand? Student loan still large! → One debt after another—just normal life or becoming a consumer drone? What if . . . real life = consumer drone? Worried about all those freeway shootings in L.A.? Road rage increasing in North America? Wow! → Feel a car creates a great private space to use to and from work: music, private thoughts. But car as necessary purchase? Perhaps bus not so bad but lots of eccentric commuters who want to talk about the CIA and the X-Files. Car looking good.

PRACTICE

Brainstorm on one of the following topics: living with a difficult roommate, achieving an interesting look on $30 or less, recognizing four types of customer.

Diagramming

Diagramming draws (pun intended) on the strong link between picturing your ideas and writing about them. Once you have formed some ideas through various intuitive techniques, you visualize, explore, and develop relationships among these ideas through diagramming. The following four examples (based on Bharati Mukherjee's "The Tenant," Stewart Thompson's "Sports Salaries: No Cap Needed," Martin Simpinsky's "Ethics of Cloning," and Ruby Tuesday's "Social Concerns about the Internet") suggest how you can picture your way toward your position on a particular topic. Diagramming will help you both to develop a thesis—your specific position to be supported—and to consider counter-arguments against your thesis. In conjunction with the first example, read "The Tenant" by Bharati Mukherjee (p. 164). In conjunction with the second example, read "Sports Salaries: No Cap Needed" (p. 501).

Diagramming on the Topics of . . .

Figure 1.2
Mukherjee's "The Tenant"

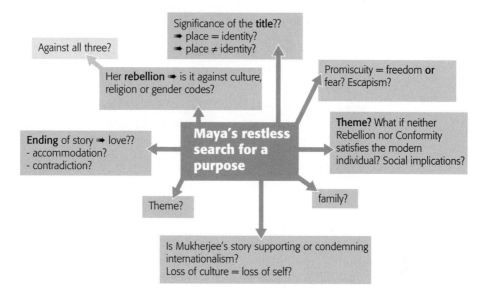

Figure 1.3
"Sports Salaries: No Cap Needed"

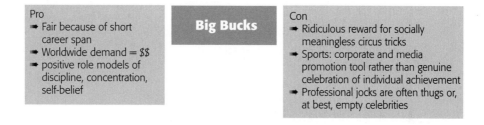

Figure 1.4
Ethics of Cloning

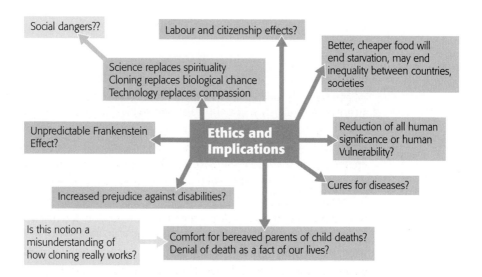

Figure 1.5
"Social Concerns about the Internet"

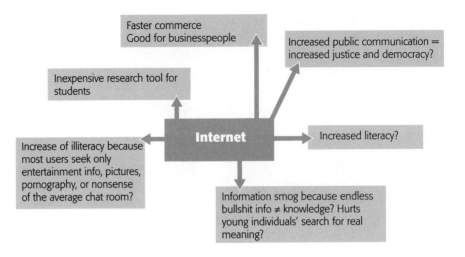

Using these examples for ideas, now try the following exercises.

PRACTICE

Diagram ideas on two or more of the following topics:

- a comparison of old-car and new-car ownership
- the benefits and/or disadvantages of home learning

- an argument for or against the Kyoto Accord
- a how-to essay sharing your enthusiasm for a favourite activity, such as pool playing

Building a Topic-Sentence Tree

Making a collage, freewriting, brainstorming, and diagramming will lead you to ideas of what you want to say on a topic. A topic-sentence tree helps you develop that sense further, to shape a tentative thesis and overall discussion. Like diagramming, a topic-sentence tree visually represents relationships, examples, assertions, and counter-points. However, it is a more advanced form of diagramming in that the statements you place in your "tree" may, with a little further consideration and re-finement, stand as topic sentences in your essay. You are still at the exploratory stage, still testing—but now with an eye to evolving fully articulated topic sentences in effective relation to the thesis (main trunk) of the whole.

See Figure 1.6 for an example of a topic-sentence tree for an essay on the film *The Blair Witch Project*.

Figure 1.6
Topic-Sentence
Tree: *The Blair
Witch Project*

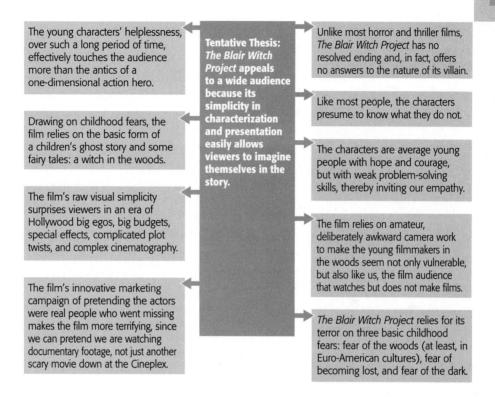

The young characters' helplessness, over such a long period of time, effectively touches the audience more than the antics of a one-dimensional action hero.

Drawing on childhood fears, the film relies on the basic form of a children's ghost story and some fairy tales: a witch in the woods.

The film's raw visual simplicity surprises viewers in an era of Hollywood big egos, big budgets, special effects, complicated plot twists, and complex cinematography.

The film's innovative marketing campaign of pretending the actors were real people who went missing makes the film more terrifying, since we can pretend we are watching documentary footage, not just another scary movie down at the Cineplex.

Tentative Thesis: *The Blair Witch Project* appeals to a wide audience because its simplicity in characterization and presentation easily allows viewers to imagine themselves in the story.

Unlike most horror and thriller films, *The Blair Witch Project* has no resolved ending and, in fact, offers no answers to the nature of its villain.

Like most people, the characters presume to know what they do not.

The characters are average young people with hope and courage, but with weak problem-solving skills, thereby inviting our empathy.

The film relies on amateur, deliberately awkward camera work to make the young filmmakers in the woods seem not only vulnerable, but also like us, the film audience that watches but does not make films.

The Blair Witch Project relies for its terror on three basic childhood fears: fear of the woods (at least, in Euro-American cultures), fear of becoming lost, and fear of the dark.

All writing is a form of re-writing, so as you develop your essay from the topic-sentence tree you will probably revise the wording of some sentences, cut certain ones and add new ones. You may wish to explore two or three versions of a topic-sentence tree for your essay.

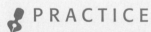 PRACTICE

Build topic-sentence trees for a potential discussion of one of the following subjects:
- a plan for improving some procedure at your college or place of work

- an analysis of a film or short story or poem
- a position for or against legalized gambling or fully legalized use of marijuana

Inkshedding

Inkshedding is really a more focused form of freewriting. Usually, you address a topic in order to express a view or analysis, and the rules of grammar apply. You take more time with your diction and syntax, and you will probably reread your piece of writing to make little adjustments. Though no grade is assigned, the instructor or your class-mates will likely read and comment on your short piece of writing, which is less likely with freewriting. Inkshedding is spontaneous writing like freewriting, but not necessarily a continuous motion activity. In some forms of inkshedding, one student can even write after another, as a chain of composition. For one inkshedding exercise, an in-structor can usually give students approximately 15 minutes to produce one-half of a page of relatively unified comment on an assigned topic. Many non-fiction prose classes and introductory English and communications classes use inkshedding as a regular writing activity that allows students quick but thorough feedback on their writing skills without undertaking the heavy writing commitment of a formal paper or in-class essay.

Here is what an inkshedding sample might look like. The exercise would focus a student's efforts on taking responsibility for a view expressed in writing. Inkshedding's spontaneous nature and short duration also encourage students to feel confident and free in their own writing voices.

Inkshedding on the topic of the Kyoto Accord

Should Canada ratify the Kyoto Accord on reducing carbon (greenhouse gas) emis-sions? I think the agreement is to reduce greenhouse gas emissions by 3.5 percent by 2012. (It was originally to be a 5 percent reduction over current levels by 2010, but it seems to me the latest stories have quoted a smaller objective and an extended time frame. This needs to be checked.) Anyway, the U.S.A., the Alberta government, Australia, and the gas and oil industries in general are opposed to the Kyoto pro-posal. These parties say they will take action to control or reduce the harmful agents in the emissions, but without guaranteeing reductions in the levels of emis-sions. This notion, they believe, will take longer than the 10 years required by Kyoto. Given increased climate and health problems, this longer wait for significant improvements may not be a good idea. Kyoto opponents say that evidence of harm is unconvincing; undeveloped countries should be made to comply with Kyoto be-fore the rest of us do; and our economies will suffer. But, on the first point, many scientists support Kyoto. On the second point, undeveloped nations don't produce nearly the levels of emissions that we do. And on the third point, economies are re-silient and too complex to be so easily assessed. Privatizing of energy in Alberta has resulted in huge cost increases for low-income consumers. That sort of "economic problem," however, does not seem to have troubled the anti-Kyoto gas and oil cartel. Opponents of Kyoto also demand a "made-by-us" approach. But almost 40 countries agreed on the Kyoto approach. How will we ever reach an agreement if every party reneges on the previous agreement and then demands to create the next one?

 PRACTICE

Produce a half-page of inkshedding on one of the fol-lowing: cellphone use, rock concert experiences, stan-dard English versus slang, non-smoking legislation, an essay of your choice from the *Reader*, violence in sports or in film, tattooing and/or body piercing, true love in the modern world, an enlightening moment.

Keeping a Journal

If you were to poll professional writers on the subject of keeping a journal, you would likely find that the vast majority either keep one or have done so at significant stages in their development. Journals are notebooks in which writers record thoughts, ideas, observations, impressions, descriptions, summaries, quotations, dreams, responses to readings, social and political events, and just about anything else of substance or fleeting impression. The journal can prove a valuable reference source, but even more importantly, the act of keeping it encourages the writer to look intently, to think seriously, to stretch awareness, and most important of all, to keep writing every day ("*jour*" is French for "day"). From this daily exercise, new inspiration and skills will flow. Spending a regular period of 20 minutes or more every day with your journal is an excellent way to discover your own thoughts and to reflect further on them. Keeping a journal is a form of meditation.

The same benefits apply if you regard yourself more as a student than a writer. The journal provides an excellent forum for thinking before and after classes. Before lectures or workshops you can write down your ideas on the approaching topic. After the class, while its content is still fresh in your mind, you can review your preliminary ideas on the topic and contrast them with what you have learned. You can raise questions and note any points that may remain unclear to you. You may amplify the examples that were given in class and test them. Dating your entries allows you to look back on the unfolding logic of your various subjects.

Journals are private. Like diaries, they represent communications with yourself, though, unlike diaries, they range far beyond straight narrative summaries of daily activities. You can summarize some degree of personal experience in your journal, but your emphasis will be on expanding your knowledge, on reflection, on exploration, on consciousness of meaning.

Remember that you are writing for yourself in order to produce private expressions that help you think through class texts or class discussions or other indirectly related issues. With an academic journal, your instructor may wish to examine your entries and may have some format requests, but otherwise entries can take whatever form works best for you. Many writing instructors find that students produce their best writing in journal entries. This may be because you feel less inhibited when writing to yourself. You can be direct, natural, and honest. These are fundamentals of good writing. So recognize the value of your journal. It can connect you with your own voice, one of the greatest breakthroughs in the growth of any writer.

Now here are three brief examples of what journal entries might look like.

Journal entry

– was given an interesting assignment in my writing class last week (finally!)

– Had to pick a news story from a recent newspaper and look for any social biases in it—in language, the photograph accompanying the article, or the headline. The teacher asked, "<u>how</u> is a meaning or interpretation created?"

– Don't know yet what exactly I'll write my analysis on, but started reading the newspaper a little bit everyday now—amazed at how the photos and headlines work as interpretation <u>before</u> I even read the news story.

– Also noticed how different newspapers treat the <u>same</u> story a little differently (The teacher asked us, "Who is the target audience of different newspapers? And for each news story?")

– Now I'll have to pick a particular story and start a rough draft of my analysis soon.

As we said, keeping a journal allows you to be more regularly productive as a writer. This makes it easier for you to write, in the same way that routine swimming, skating and stick-handling practice allow swimmers or hockey players to reach and retain their peak form. For this reason, many professional writers keep journals. Following is a sample from the journal of Canadian writer Thomas Wharton, author of two internationally acclaimed novels, *Icefields* and *Salamander*.

Sitting here, nothing by me, rock, and the flutter of the paper in the wind. The barest elements for writing.

I haven't really tried to describe the mountains themselves yet, though. How to do it without lapsing into the easy clichés about their very palpable majesty and fearfulness? Maybe try to think of them as a quantum extrapolation of the ground-up pebbles at my feet. Pick up a single rock and describe it. The cool, pitted, unpretentious, ancient, trustworthy, secretive, implacable feel of a rock in my hand. The delicate, minute surface striations and scoring etchings. Whorls of veins of colour. The globular, unplannable asymmetry that gets recreated in the vast peaks above.

Next try a boulder. Well, it's more an obelisk easily six feet taller than me. That D.H. Lawrence poem about a boy and a horse standing next to each other. The poet says they are in another world. That's what it feels like standing next to this massive rock. We are together, somehow, in another world, where no one speaks.

—Excerpt from journal of Thomas Wharton, spring 1990

Here is what Wharton says about keeping a journal and using it to work out the problem of how to describe the Rocky Mountains:

Early on, I realized that it was healthy to think of what I was doing as a kind of translation. That this place I was trying to write about had a language, so to speak, all its own, a non-verbal language. And that if I was going to go beyond mere postcard clichés about the majesty of the peaks, the pristine beauty, etc., I was going to have to try to carry across to the reader something of that non-verbal world. And that, as I carried my impressions across into words, something of that non-verbal world would be lost.

As I wrote, I kept notebooks of my thoughts, ideas, dreams, alternative story-lines, etc. I saw this series of notebooks as a kind of "dream-version" of the book I was writing, where I allowed myself to write all the immediate, unedited, silly things that might not necessarily be allowed into the novel.

And I find this dream-book fascinating to read through now because it is a raw record of process, in a way that the finished book isn't. I can see the processes of translation at work in my journals. Taking material from my own experiences and memories, from history and literature, from the sheer seductive power of words.

—Commentary by Thomas Wharton, 2002

In Wharton's novel *Icefields*, the author included a passage on pages 77–78 that drew on his previous journal entry. The character Elspeth is sipping tea while watching a distant avalanche:

> The morning after the glasshouse party she is in the chalet's front parlour, sipping hot Earl Grey tea from an eggshell china cup.
>
> From her window, she can just make out a climbing team struggling up the glacier against blowing snow. Five tiny figures huddled together, crawling slowly forward up the slope. The alpinists from Zermatt.
>
> Elspeth blows on the surface of the steaming tea, sips from it, raises her head and listens.
>
> Above the sound of the wind, she hears the distant crack and crumple of an avalanche. The thin glass in the windowframe rattles. She glances out. It takes her a moment to find the source, a slender white plume flowing down a dark seam on Mount Arcturus. The avalanche is high on the mountain and the alpinists are in no danger, but they stand motionless, watching as the cascade of snow and ice bursts over a rock ledge.
>
> So graceful and delicate from this distance, as if unconnected to the thunder echoing across the valley. At the glasshouse party, Byrne had told her there could be chunks of ice the size of train cars falling in those powdery veils.
>
> Elspeth takes another sip of tea, pleased with the bitterness of lemon.

Remember, you don't have to be writing a novel to apply the journal-writing process. Journals are the private, emotional, and analytical expressions of your impressions and developing ideas that may, in parts, make their way into your essays or exam answers or even questions and answers in class. A journal is a brainstorming form that charts a person's reflections on any number of issues.

 PRACTICE

Look in bookstores for a style of blank notebook that suits you. It should be durable, portable, yet large enough to allow fluid writing. Many writers like a notebook that lies open without pressure. Some prefer to use loose-leaf pages or whatever paper is available. Remember to date your entries and to insert them into your journal regularly and in order.

YOUR TOPIC NARROWED

Having explored a topic or topics through one or more pre-writing activities, you have now found an angle of interest and some specific points of relevance. You are now ready to move on to the next stage of more formal drafting.

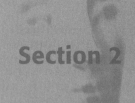

Section 2   Drafting

Chapter 2
Reviewing the Basics

Whenever and whatever you write, you want to communicate something to someone. An important step toward that goal is recognizing what type of writing is called for by the occasion, then to find, evaluate, and possibly emulate examples of the same basic type. Traditionally, these rhetorical models of non-fiction prose include narration, description, exposition, and persuasion. To assist your search for appropriate models, consider all writing as belonging to one of the three broad categories, as we consider them in this *Rhetoric*: **personal**, **expository**, and **persuasive** (which includes **argumentative**). Our explanation of these categories begins with the concept of purpose.

As a writer, you want to communicate something to someone *for a specific reason*. This purpose will determine where you place your emphasis. If you keep the big picture always in mind whenever you write, you will see three major components emerge: you the writer, your subject, and your reader. How do these three elements interact productively? Which should receive the most attention? It depends on your **purpose**.

PERSONAL WRITING

Personal writing places emphasis on the situation and perspective of the writer. For example, the primary purpose of a diary (probably the most personal form of writing) is *to evoke or express* the writer's experiences. The diary, though private, is still a

Figure 2.1
Writing Purpose

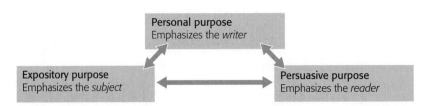

communication, in this case with oneself. Other descriptive terms for personal writing are "evocative" or "expressive," because your purpose is to evoke what a certain experience was like and to express how you felt about it. The organizational structures and techniques of **narration** and **description** almost always play a prominent role in personal writing. Narration expresses how an individual experiences the passing of a particular time frame, while description offers up the details that make your subject particular and significant.

A good first step in determining the primary purpose of a piece of writing is the pronoun test. Pronouns are words that take the place of a noun in a sentence; nouns are words naming persons, places, or things. If the work you are studying uses primarily first-person pronouns—*I*, *me*, *my/we*, *us*, *our*—then chances are its purpose is to express the writer's experiences.

Personal writing

The Health Centre was packed with people who needed to be seen by the nurses and midwives that particular morning: young mothers carrying their babies on their back in the *amauti*, a traditional piece of clothing; elders in their fur coats, their faces dark and wrinkled from hard lives out on the land; young pregnant teenagers chatting to each other. One woman caught my attention: she was sitting in a corner of the waiting area, almost removed from everything around her. When I looked into her eyes I knew instantly that something was wrong. . . .

—Gisela Becker, "A Midwife in Rankin Inlet" (p. 72)

EXPOSITORY WRITING

Writing that emphasizes the subject or message is commonly known as expository (or informative). An insurance company's damage report, for example, concentrates on the message: its primary purpose is *to inform* the reader of the facts, in careful chronological order. These facts need to be clear to a number of different readers, in and even outside the insurance company. The organizational structures of *classification-division*, *cause-effect*, *comparison-contrast*, *process analysis*, and *definition* commonly help shape expository writing.

A good first step in determining whether a piece of writing is expository is, again, the pronoun test. If the work contains primarily third-person pronouns—*he*, *she*, *it*, *they*—then chances are fairly good that the piece is intended to inform the reader about some neutral subject—more than it intends to express the writer's feelings or contentions. In academic writing, many of your instructors will tell you to use only third-person pronouns for some assignments: this choice will shift your writing into the expository sphere and highlight the results of your analysis and research. Expository writing differs from persuasive writing in that exposition generally explains rather than asserts a particular interpretation. However, some writers and instructors point out that exposition may well contain interpretations passing as neutral facts.

What about this book? We use the second-person pronoun *you* a great deal. So is our basic purpose to persuade? No, our main goal is to inform, but we are using a special form of expository writing called *directional process*. In this kind of writing we give the reader guidelines to help carry out a certain task. How-to books and a number of educational texts use this approach. Since the goal is to help the reader, this form of expository writing puts more emphasis on the reader than do other expository forms.

Exposition

Many of the scenes have obvious parallels in the New Testament. In one, an actress from the troupe appears at an audition for a TV commercial and is asked to take off her clothes—not because nudity is required in the commercial, but more because the casting director wants to exercise his power. Arriving late at the audition, Daniel, the Christ figure, shouts out to his friend to leave her clothes on, and then, when the advertising people try to have him ejected, he goes into a rage, overturning lights and cameras. It is a version, of course, of Christ and the moneylenders in the temple.

—Roger Ebert, review of the film *Jesus of Montreal* by Denys Arcand

PERSUASIVE WRITING

Persuasive writing emphasizes the reader. An advertising brochure, for example, carefully considers what its target reader desires and then attempts to show how the specific product or service satisfies the reader's desires. The purpose of this type of writing is *to influence* the reader's behaviour.

Advertising Persuasion

Enjoy Canada's first flaked-meal replacement—Vector. This product has won awards for its nutrition and marketing innovation. The flakes are a combination of whole wheat and rice and contain crunchy granola oat and soy protein clusters. Vector provides a source of vitamins A, D, E, B1, B12 and folic acid along with several minerals, dietary fibre and protein.

—Adapted from a press release

Let us consider one other important form of persuasive writing: **argumentation**. As you know, advertisers, corporate speakers, and other promotional communicators commonly omit or misrepresent facts and opinions that contradict the image or idea they wish to promote. Argumentation, however, takes pains to recognize and respect contradictory views. Its purpose is to generate action, often in form of a change of perspective, but to do so only after fairly acknowledging other choices.

Think of the familiar classroom debate as a classic example of argumentation. Students and instructors try to represent all sides of an issue, still with the goal of deciding, ultimately, on one side over others. Argumentation may be likened to a "fair trial." All the evidence should be properly considered before a verdict is made.

However, the argumentative writer promotes only one verdict. Like advertisers, argumentative writers give special attention to the listener or reader, because like the advertiser the argumentative writer seeks to shape opinion and behaviour.

Second-person pronouns (*you, your*) may signal to you that a work is persuasive (particularly if it is not an academic or legal form of persuasion). The use of these pronouns is a strategy to put special attention on you, the reader. You will find the organizational structures of *comparison-contrast* and *cause-effect* usually prominent in argumentative forms as well. Advertising usually bypasses genuine cause-effect organization of material forms while incorporating certain amounts of personal structures (narration and description) to encourage reader sympathy and identification.

Argumentation

The debate against euthanasia is heard from religious lobbyists and other pro-life organizations. The Catholic Church, for example, believes that only God has the right to determine our fate, and we are trying to "play God" (Ellis 1992). "God giveth life, and only God can take away" (Humphry 1986). The opposition groups fear that if euthanasia were legalized it would lead to widespread chaos and wrongful deaths. One dilemma is that if patients cannot express their desires, others may contravene their true wishes. Should a family member, a medical professional, or the caregiver have the final say? There is also great concern about organ donation, about patients not always receiving appropriate treatment because their organs are so desperately needed: "Transplant doctors circled like vultures around young, head-injured accident victims" (Trevelyan 1992). While these concerns may indeed be seen as legitimate, interestingly, there is no debate from pro-life groups regarding the issue of extreme measures to keep someone alive.

Before modern technology was introduced, people died by natural means without aid of life support systems. By allowing artificial respirators, feeding tubes, and a multitude of medications, we too are interfering with the natural death process, altering a life. Those opposed to the perceived cruelty of euthanasia should consider that to sustain a life that cannot breathe, eat, or function on its own is even more cruel. It is also a form of "playing God."

—Janice Procée, "The Case for Active Euthanasia" (p. 187)

Whether your specific writing purpose calls for a personal, expository, or persuasive-argumentative approach, finding and evaluating appropriate models of that approach will help you to shape your own work. In order to recognize the purpose of any piece of writing, begin with *two* main tests:

1. Check the pronouns.
2. Ask yourself whether the piece emphasizes experience (personal), information (expository), or action, including convincing the reader of a particular interpretation (persuasive).

COMBINATIONS OF TYPES

You can use the basic division we have just described to classify all forms of writing according to three categories: personal, expository, and persuasive. But beware of

PRACTICE

1. In what ways do the four preceding examples suit the category to which they have been assigned?
2. We gave the diary as one example of personal writing. Name at least three other types of personal writing.
3. We gave a report as an example of expository writing. Suggest at least three other types of expository writing.
4. We gave an advertising press release as an example of persuasive writing. Suggest at least six other types of persuasive writing, three that demonstrate the promotional forms and three that demonstrate the argumentative.
5. Notice how the *Reader* portion of this text appears in three sections, each section illustrating the purposes of personal, expository, and persuasive. Examine some selections from each section of the *Reader* and define, as precisely as you can, ways in which each selection you review illustrates the basic type it has been assigned to. (Do not select poems or short stories; the system of classification we are proposing does not apply very well to them, as we will discuss later.) Note too the ways in which aspects of your selection may *not* fit its overall classification. To understand why these deviations and overlaps may occur, see the next section, Combinatio of Types.

oversimplifications. This classification system is not absolute. Writing is far more varied, experimental, and complex than any one scheme. Most forms of writing will contain *all three* types to some degree: there will be an informative (and even persuasive) element to a diary, just as there will be an expressive and persuasive element to your next expository paper. Critical analysis (see Chapter 10) combines descriptive analysis (a form of exposition) and argumentation.

Combination of Types

Four days of the week were designated running days. Sunday was usually the day for long runs. Two days were set aside for cross training. That left me with one sacred day a week to rest and carbo-load (in other words, pig out). The theory behind running every other day is to give the big muscle groups in the legs a chance to rest and recover. Cross training usually consists of an exercise to strengthen the upper body. Endurance activities tend to exhaust the major muscles used and the body relies on accessory muscles to "help out."

January 5, 1998

My first day of marathon training. I bought my winter running tights. I told the staff at Runners' Soul I planned to "run Calgary" in July. They responded with polite yet skeptical smiles. I swam 1.5 Km. Swimming felt good for my shoulders.

January 6

Ran 8 Km. in 46:40. I ran through the coulees. There was a bit of snow on the north facing slopes. It was −15° C. I ran slowly and walked down the hills. I need to get my knees accustomed to the torture that is yet to come.

— Corinne Wasylewich, "Marathon Journal" (p. 29)

In this excerpt from her "Marathon Journal," Corinne Wasylewich uses first-person voice and certainly expresses her feelings about a personal undertaking. Her journal is, at least in part, an example of personal writing. It unfolds in report format, however, with carefully detailed notations of time, place, distance, and physical and psychological states. For much of the journal, intermixed with humour, she observes herself with a scientist's detachment. This element of impartial observation and organized recording represents expository writing. Despite her use of first person, she puts the stress on her data and observations. If you read the complete "Marathon Journal" in Section 1 of the *Reader*, you will find that in the days between January and July, Wasylewich reports on pain and doubt; there are moments when she feels ready to give up. But she perseveres, making weekly notations of how far and how fast she has run. On July 5, completing the 42.2-Km. race in four hours and 32 minutes, she wins a medal. The reading ends on an inspirational, motivational note that could very well persuade us to try drawing the utmost from ourselves, as she has done from herself. In other words, we are left with a persuasive message.

To classify a piece of writing, the determining question should be, which element is most significant? It is sometimes hard to say. Editors might well be divided on whether to classify Wasylewich's journal as personal or expository (the persuasive note, though important, is not paramount). If we imagine the three main purposes as the primary colours red, blue, and yellow, then it is reasonable to expect new and sometimes very different colours (forms) to emerge from the combinations of these primary elements. However we classify this journal, all three purposes are clearly at play within it, and to appreciate the meaning of this piece of writing, we can learn valuable lessons in where and how all three intersect and work together.

Combination of Types

In the early 1970s, I visited a small northern town to judge a science fair. Back then, it was a tough town with a transient population of men working in the oil fields and a high proportion of Native people. The night I arrived, I dropped into the bar of the motel and a man came over and said, "I hear you're going to talk to the students at the high school tomorrow." When I affirmed it, he shocked me by adding, "They'll kill you. I'm the science teacher there and I can tell you that all they think about is sex, drugs, and cars. They'll tear you apart."

Well, he really scared me. I immediately formed images of a blackboard jungle, filled with switchblades and drug-crazed hoods. The next day when I walked into that auditorium, it was with great trepidation. There were 400 teenagers in the gym, about a third of them Indians. They looked pretty normal, but I had been warned and knew they were just biding their time before turning into raving animals.

So I began by saying, "I'm a geneticist. I know you're basically walking gonads, so I'm going to talk about sex."

—David Suzuki, "The Right Stuff" (p. 181)

You may recognize, without even looking ahead to our sections on narration and description, that this excerpt uses those two personal writing approaches, especially narration. Furthermore, Suzuki writes in the first person. So, is his essay an example of personal writing? Once you read his essay in full (p. 181 of the *Reader*), you will see that in fact Suzuki uses his experiences here for larger purposes of argumentation. He goes on to tell us that the high school students listened to him with rapt interest, even when he moved on from sex to biology and a range of other scientific topics. His thesis (his central argument), drawn from this example, is that high schools should offer sex education and use it as an excellent departure point for science studies.

This combination of personal viewpoint and argumentation is quite common in the popular media. We invite you to critique the success of Suzuki's method, either now or later, in combination with further guidelines from our section on argumentation.

Combination of Types

. . . here are five specimens of the English language as it is now habitually written.

These five passages have not been picked out because they are especially bad—I could have quoted far worse if I had chosen—but because they illustrate various of the mental vices from which we now suffer. They are a little below the average, but are fairly representative samples. . . .

—George Orwell, "Politics and the English Language" (p. 227)

George Orwell goes on to provide the five passages, comprising altogether about a page of text. Since he so strongly emphasizes information (examples), does his essay belong to the category of expository writing? It does not, but rather it belongs to argumentation. Orwell's thesis (central argument) is that the English language of his day, 1946, "is full of bad habits" that aggravate sloppy thinking and thereby contribute to the "decadent" state of "our civilization." His method of argumentation is to pile on the evidence, undermining so-called reputable writers of his day and demonstrating that a sorry state of English is not only widespread, but threatening to the quality of democracy.

IMPORTANT

Classify your writing and that of others according to the emphasis you feel it places on writer, subject, or reader. This will help you focus your own work. However, as we say in our discussion of combined types, to speak of three exclusive types is to oversimplify. Look for the **dominant** purpose of any piece of writing. Do not assume when we speak of personal writing, for instance, that consideration of the writer is important to that category of writing only, or that attention to the subject is important only in informative writing. Proper consideration of writer, subject, and reader is crucial in *all* forms of writing. When we speak of the three main types that emphasize separate purposes, we distinguish between those purposes in degree relative to each other. Like painters, writers have three primary colours on their palette; in a given context they must control and blend them appropriately to express themselves effectively.

AUDIENCE

We have said that persuasive writing emphasizes the reader most, since the writer tries to sway the reader's opinions with his or her words. However, it is very important to remember that no matter what you are writing or why, you need to keep your readers in mind constantly, their presumptions and responses. If you fail to do so, you will lose them, or at least not reach them as successfully as you would like. Let's imagine you have a general purpose, which is to communicate your support for a particular cause. Pick any cause that suits you—your belief in tax relief to attract business investment, concern about poverty in the Third World, or whatever you wish. How do you communicate effectively on this subject?

You could write a letter to a potential ally, a friend. Picturing that friend will lead to a certain style and approach that suits that person. You could also agree to survey 30 homes in your neighbourhood seeking their opinions on the topic. Perhaps the local newspaper has asked you for an article on the results. Although you have your own opinion, in this case your purpose is primarily to report your findings. Your primary audience now is the newspaper editor whom you know is concerned to receive the data in a clear, organized, impartial style. If you were to develop a leaflet for the general public, based in part on your survey results but mainly intended to promote your opinion, you would have yet another audience. In this case, you must decide whether your neighbourhood seems to be for or against your opinion on the whole. How you present your argument will depend on how sympathetic or opposed to your view this group of readers is. In turn, the way you present your argument may also determine whether that audience becomes or remains sympathetic or opposed to your views. Since persuasive writing emphasizes the reader, this form demands special and, in cases, even systematic consideration of your audience.

ESSAY TOPICS

To Whom Should You Write in Your English Essays and Papers?

The obvious answer would seem to be your course instructor. But this person should not necessarily be your primary imagined audience. If your essay assignment calls for you to enter into a hypothetical writing situation, then adapt to that situation. For example, suppose you are asked to write a leaflet arguing your position on a local debate in your community. Then you would be best to consider your community as your audience. Suppose you are asked to write an essay analyzing a particular short story. The ideal audience for you to imagine in this case is probably a classmate, one who is serious, knowledgeable, and interested.

Student Drew Forsythe makes extra money for tuition fees by selling travel pieces to magazines. Here is his characterization of the magazine audience for travel writing:

You just got back from a summer holiday in Quebec City. You became fluent in the language, you kept a detailed journal of all the events, places and experiences you saw, you've got photos that look like they were lifted from the pages of *National Geographic*, and now you want to put together a story for a Quebec City publication. Forget about it. Why?

Travel writing assumes the reader is unhappy about where he or she is. This is why during the Canadian winter you won't find any travel articles chronicling a visit to the North Pole. Typically, we want to go to some remote tropical island and forget about the arctic air that blankets our country. Yet farther south and abroad, people are sold on the clean concept of snow, and lured by luminous northern lights. People in the Outback of Australia want to read about the thousands of freshwater lakes that puncture the Canadian Shield, and feel, if only for a minute, that your words have taken them there.

The anecdote David Suzuki relates in his essay "The Right Stuff" (p. 181 of the *Reader*) also exemplifies thinking from your audience's point of view.

PRACTICE

Turn to the *Reader* and examine the first page of several of the selections. Notice that the short introductions to each give background on the author and often, on the forum or publication where the piece of writing was first placed. Based on this audience information, and without looking at the article, write down what approach you think the article might follow to address its audience. Then look at the article and see if you were correct. Repeat this exercise with several other articles after reading our next section on tone.

TONE

If purpose is why you are writing and audience to whom you are writing, then tone is *how* you handle your writing. More specifically, tone is the emotional and/or ethical attitude you take to your purpose, topic, and reader. You create that tone through knowing your purpose and refining it while you consider your audience. The letter to your friend would be informal, friendly, casual, familiar. Since personal writing emphasizes the writer, your own personal presence—or voice—will be strong, adapted to the particular ideas you are expressing. You might write short sentences and paragraphs and use quirky style in your letter. In contrast to this informality, the survey report to the local newspaper editor would use standard language and punctuation. Your personal style and voice would be subordinated to predictable form, and you would pay more attention to the way you organize what you write. In the leaflet promoting your view on a particular cause, your tone would be assured and firm, but if you knew there would be resistance to your views, you would acknowledge any contrary views. Your careful organization would establish your own authority and capture interest, as you offer clear, convincing evidence for your opinion before going on to emphasize that opinion.

We have referred to diction, sentences, and paragraphs as elements that contribute to your tone. This may surprise you, since we often think of tone as primarily auditory, something we hear. When you write, however, you translate the emotion and content of your spoken voice, expressed through sound, into the same values expressed visually in marks on a page.

Editors and writers will often add **graphics** to their text, recalling that sound old cliché that a picture is worth a thousand words. Graphics support advertising, business reports, and technical essays. The colour, size, and layout of a graphic can provide important clues about the content of a piece of writing. Publishers pay careful attention to the illustrations they choose for the covers of paperback novels, for example. First those covers must grab prospective readers' attention; second, the same covers must convey a tone: the way the publisher wants would-be customers to perceive those books. Bright, flashy graphics convey a sense of energy and light-heartedness. The yellow covers of the *Computing for Dummies* books demonstrate this well. A Stephen King novel or a Gothic novel, on the other hand, will convey a darker, more sombre mood with its graphics. Even the size of type provides a clue to the character and size of the book's target audience. Large type fonts aim for a wider public audience (including perhaps children and senior citizens); smaller type fonts concentrate on a narrower, often more serious reading audience. Journalism that is frequently broken up with graphics may not be taken as seriously as journalism that relies on a written representation of facts and perspectives (the *Toronto Sun* compared to the *Manchester Guardian*, for example). Adapting graphics to purpose and audience is largely a matter of finding the most effective strategy, the suitable tone.

Although there are infinite variations of tone, there are three broad categories: informal, general, and formal:

Characteristics of Writing Tones

Elements	Informal	General	Formal
Diction	Everyday, plain, concrete, colloquial, slang, casual, contractions, shorter words	Assumes a high school education, mixes concrete and abstract, mixes shorter and longer words	Assumes a higher level of education or training, abstract, technical, jargon, longer words
Sentences	Short, simple, some fragments, some comma splices, frequent dashes	Nearly all complete, fragments very carefully controlled, somewhat longer, balances simple and combined structures, fewer dashes, and few (if any) sentence fragments or comma splices	Mostly longer and combined structures, no fragments, few dashes, no comma splices
Paragraphs	Mostly short, casual, no rigorous use of topic sentences, implied rather than explicitly stated transitions	Some longer, more fully developed, more deliberate use of topic sentences and explicit transitions within and between paragraphs	Mostly long, fully developed, consistent use of explicit transitions, complex content organized by clear patterns.

(continued)

Elements	Informal	General	Formal
Supporting details	"Warm"—anecdotes, personal descriptions, more appeal to emotion than to logic	Includes some "cooler" proofs—data, studies, logical formulations	"Cool"—empirical data and structured logical formulations, academic authorities and references
Organization (or Structure)	Casual, spontaneous, loose, lacking explicit connectors, mainly based on emotion	Deliberate, tighter, using some explicit connectors, reflecting one or more methods, blending emotion and logic, cause and effect	Highly controlled, explicitly connected throughout, tight application of patterns, mostly intellectual
Purposes	More often personal, blending of purposes but often not sustained	Some personal, expository, and argumentative, combined and somewhat controlled	Expository—often analytical, argumentative
Typical uses	Personal letters, diaries, journals, some fiction, much advertising, some newspapers	Many newspapers and magazines, business writing, many expository books and articles, fiction	Academic writing, some textbooks, scientific writing, legal documents

DICTION

Imagine you want to persuade a variety of people to re-build a rundown part of town. To a neighbour you could write, "We have to clean up this slum!" To your local politician, you might not want to be that blunt: "We need help to improve the quality of life of this once-vital area of your constituency." To a group of city planners, your tone would probably be more subdued and formal: "We need to raise the living standard in this low-income neighbourhood." All three have the same purpose, but each audience has different requirements, different presumptions, and different communication codes. You'll notice that the "slum" from the first example has become a "once-vital area" in the second, and finally a "low-income neighbourhood" in the third. All three phrases refer to the same place; the different choice of word establishes a different tone for each piece. Such word choice, or diction, is the first element of tone: the words you choose will be your reader's first clue regarding the attitude of your piece.

We could say that the three phrases given above convey different **connotations**. As opposed to "denotation"—the dictionary definition of words—"connotation" refers to the various unofficial, and no less real, meanings that gather around many words. Try exploring the dimensions of connotation through a brief exercise. Take any three "loaded" words, such as "marriage," "hunting," and "politician." Use your "gut reaction" to rate each one from plus 5 to minus 5, according to how strongly you like or dislike associations the word raises. Compare your answers with those of others in a group. You may find some interesting variations. You will most likely find strong reactions, if not to these words, then to many others you may choose for this exercise.

Certain words are highly charged, particularly for certain groups. Connotations are accumulated meanings that register the socio-political attitudes attached to these charged words. In the previous example, you can see how using different words for the same idea significantly alters the connotations of the meaning. For another example, if we speak of a "deal," we may create the sense that the transaction has a hard edge. "Arrangement," on the other hand, sounds more neutral, while "agreement" sounds positive.

You may need to treat two types of diction carefully in your writing, **colloquial language** and **jargon**. Colloquial language ("colloquial" means spoken together) comprises the informal words we use when speaking or writing to friends or colleagues. In a more formal piece directed at an audience that you do not know well, you would find your readers take you less seriously if you use such language. This impression increases if you use slang (unconventional "in" talk). When the audience expects a formal level of discussion, you should also avoid the more informal use of contractions (*can't* instead of *cannot*, etc.). Jargon refers to specialized language (professional catch phrases) used by and for a narrow audience that presumably shares a great deal of common knowledge. If you wish to reach a wider audience and the phrase seems crucial, then include a clear definition to ensure you include your reader in your discussion. If, on the other hand, you target only that specific, narrow audience, then your adding such a definition could annoy your readers because you would be telling them something you can presume they know.

Referring to the preceding table, you will notice that more informal writing tends to use short, concrete words. If you know your audience does not have formal education beyond, say, Grade 9 or 10, be careful about your choices of abstract and polysyllabic words. If your intended readers have a high level of formal education, they may feel a solid offering of short, concrete words is insufficient to convey nuances of meaning. But even with high levels of formal education, if your audience needs information in a hurry for business decisions, they will appreciate shorter, plain words. In George Orwell's "Politics and the English Language," the author advises to guard against inflated diction, since it usually obscures your meaning and makes your writing vague. Orwell recommends never using a long word where a short one will convey the same meaning, to keep our writing honest.

SENTENCES

We tend to think of long sentences as convoluted and boring, and short sentences as abrupt and simplistic. In professional writing, sentence length is more an indication of the reader's available time than it is the complexity of the writer's ideas. Short sentences imply that the reader needs the information in as short a time as possible. Magazine articles use sentences that are a little longer than those in bus advertisements, because a magazine article can usually be read at a more leisurely pace. Sentences in academic articles are even longer because the audience is expected to think hard about the information and construct a reasoned and layered response. So sentence length is often a prime indicator of what you expect your reader to do with your information. Types of sentences—from simple to various combinations—are explained and illustrated in the *Handbook* section (see p. 535).

PARAGRAPHS

Paragraphs also express tone by their length, as well as the pace at which you expect your reader to consider your writing. Tabloid newspapers prefer single-sentence paragraphs. Such writing provides information quickly, but does not encourage the reader to process the information at any complex level. In your academic writing, aim for focused, well-developed paragraphs directed by terse, explicit topic sentences, as discussed in the next chapter. A typical first-year essay employs paragraphs composed of an average five to six sentences.

ORGANIZATION

In most academic writing, you need to present your reader with a quickly identifiable structural scheme, a road map to travel through your discussion. A solid **thesis statement** in your introduction and clear **topic sentences** to head your paragraphs will form the guiding structure of your essay, the spine that holds the body together. At the least, your opening should establish the topic and perhaps the issue that the rest of the paper will develop. You will use clear connective language between structural points to help your reader follow your flow of thought. If your academic paper does not convey such purposeful organization, your reader may well decide that its tone is not sufficiently serious, nor the content sufficiently developed.

 PRACTICE

Choose any two selections from the *Reader* (for now, not a short story or a poem) and describe each according to its diction, sentence structure, paragraphs, and overall organization. Relate this information to your sense of the main purpose of the writing of each, in relation to its intended audience. Through this analysis, decide on a brief description that best suits the tone—the essayist's attitude toward his or her subject—of each selection. How are the selections essentially similar or different in tone? Explain.

VOICE

You may hear the term "voice" in discussions of tone. The idea of voice is very close to that of tone, with a useful distinction. As we have seen, tone is an overall attitude expressed by the writer toward himself or herself, the specific subject, and the audience. Your tone may well change quite radically from one piece of writing to another, while your voice will not change, or at least not very much, unless the form requires suppression of it. **Voice** may be closely identified with the character and personality of the writer, with his or her individuality. Some writers and instructors distinguish voice from style and tone as the expression of self, whereas style and tone are expressions of strategy.

Imagine the sort of voice you might expect from a seasoned oil-rig worker and the one you would expect from a career banker. At the risk of stereotyping, we might consider that the oil-rig worker and banker may vary in tone based on attitudes to the world. Both would always retain the essence of their individual voices, however, even when each person is adapting to situations in which expected formality or informality and form would vary. That part of your expression that remains in touch with the values, distinctiveness, and quirks of your own identity is your voice. This essence of you emerges in part through your social and education background, and ultimately through your personal self. Voice is one of the most difficult qualities of writing to define, yet one of the most indisputable and influential presences on the page. It subtly characterizes both the shape and the content of everything you write.

 PRACTICE

Think of one author whose writings you particularly enjoy or admire and a good number of whose works you have read. Pick two works by this writer that differ in tone. Now try to define what is consistent in the writing style and values of both works. You can choose a fiction writer or a poet, but essay writers, politicians, or newspaper columnists are also useful for this exercise. Remember, you are examining the abiding voice in one given writer (or speaker) beneath different stylistic choices and various forms.

DISTINGUISHING NON-FICTION FROM FICTION, POETRY, AND OTHER FORMS

Most of the selections in the *Reader* are formal or personal essays, journalistic or scholarly articles, or excerpts from books on specific topics: in other words, non-fiction prose. However, we have also included a number of fine and provocative short stories to represent the category of fiction; as well, each section of the *Reader* contains an introductory poem. You'll notice that in the Practice activities suggested for this chapter, we have recommended you choose non-fiction selections from the *Reader* rather than the short stories (fiction) or poems.

Literature as poetry, fiction, and drama exists in more complex forms than the genre of the essay. Although the essay itself is a literary genre, it is accessible to analysis based on personal, expository, and persuasive considerations. Fiction, poetry, drama, and other "creative" or "artistic" forms such as these certainly emphasize experience and expression, but do not always present experience the writer has directly encountered, nor present their points or themes directly. Literature often has an overwhelming emotional and even educational effect on the reader, yet the events reported may never have actually taken place. Such writing may speak in the first person, but as a person who does not actually exist; the narrator is a fictional element, a literary strategy.

This brand of writing—set apart from non-fiction (of even the highest quality) as art, as "literature"—is so diverse that no logical system of classification can capture it completely. As art, literature cannot be reduced to pre-formulated categories because art challenges such categories with its own inventions and experimentations—that is, just by being what we would call "art." Non-fiction works, no matter how personal or persuasive, fit nicely into our classification scheme, while fictional works, though related to essays in various technical ways, remain a separate category. We therefore offer a special section to assist your analysis of our selections of fiction. (See "Writing a Literary Analysis" in Chapter 10, p. 420.)

The definitions and brief discussion of the major categories of writing in the Glossary of Literary Terms at the end of this book should help clarify important generic distinctions for you, and strengthen your sense of purpose as you prepare to do your own writing for academic classes.

Chapter 3
Thesis Statements

Nothing contributes so much to the success of your essays as an effective thesis statement. The following chapter, examining this topic, will contribute significantly to improved marks in all your humanities and social science courses, provided you apply the guidelines carefully and completely.

All college and university essays attempt to go somewhere, to take their audiences on a journey over the facts, details, assertions, insights, and conclusions of the writer. In order to point your reader (and yourself) in the right direction, you need to focus your sights on the issues, interpretations, and content of your discussion.

A **thesis statement** is the one crucial sentence in an essay that focuses yourself and your readers on your chosen topic. You will be most sure of success if your thesis statement does the following:

- occurs as the last sentence of your introduction,
- expresses a strong position,
- expresses the reason(s) for this belief,
- indicates the method(s) of your essay, and
- returns in a slightly revised form as the first sentence of your conclusion.

MAKING YOUR THESIS THE LAST SENTENCE OF YOUR INTRODUCTION

You may not know where you are going until you begin to emerge from Pre-writing (see the previous section of this *Rhetoric*, Chapter 1, "Ways of Starting") and finish your first draft. In your final draft, you will want to convey the assurance that you knew your destination all along. You can create this impression if you include your thesis statement as the last sentence of your introduction. What better opportunity to announce to your reader where you are going in your essay, each step you will take to get there, and your destination?

Sample Design   Opening Paragraph of Short Essay

Xxxxxxxxxxxxxxxxxxxxxxxxxxxxxxxxxxxxxxxxxx. Xxxxxxxxxxxxxxxxxxxxxxxxxxxxxxxxx xxxxxxxxxxxxxxxxxxxxxxxxxxxxxxxxxxxxxxxxxxxxxxxxxxxxxxxxxxxxxxxxxxxxxxxxxxxxxx xxx. Xxxxxxxxxxxxxxxxxxxxxxxxxxxxxxxxxxxxxxxxxxxxxxxxxxxxxxxxxxxxxxxxxxxxxxxxx xxxxxxxxxxxxxxxxxxxxxxxxxxxxxxxxxxxxxxx. Xxxxxxxxxxxxxxxxxxxxxxxxxxxxxxxxxxxxxxxx. Xxxxxxxxxxxxxxxxxxxxxxxxxxxxxxxxxxxxxxxxxxxxxxxxxxx. Your thesis sentence goes here, concluding your introductory paragraph.

In longer essays, with introductions of more than one paragraph, the thesis statement should be the last sentence of the introduction.

Sample Design   Introduction of Longer Essay

Xxxxxxxxxxxxxxxxxxxxxxxxxxxxxxxxxxxxxxxxxxx. Xxxxxxxxxxxxxxxxxxxxxxxxxxxxxxxxxx xxxxxxxxxxxxxxxxxxxxxxxxxxxxxxxxxxxxxxxxxxxxxxxxxxxxxxxxxxxxxxxx. Xxxxxxxxxxxxxxx xxxxxxxxxxxxxxxxxxxxxxxxxxxxxxxxxxxxxxxxxxxxxxxxxxxxxxxxxxxxxxxxxxxxxxxxxxxxxx xxxxxxxxxxxxxxxxxxxxxxxxxxxxxxxxxxx. Xxxxxxxxxxxxxxxxxxxxxxxxxxxxxxxxxxxxxxxxxxx Xxxxxxxxxxxxxxxxxxxxxxxxxx. Xxxxxxxxxxxxxxxxxxxxxxxxxxxxxxxxxxxxxxxxxxxxxxxxxxx.
Xxxxxxxxxxxxxxxxxxxxxxxxxxxxxxxxxxxxxxxxxxxx. Xxxxxxxxxxxxxxxxxxxxxxxxxxxxxxxx xxxxxxxxxxxxxxxxxxxxxxxxxxxxxxxxxxxxxxxxxxxxxxxxxxxxxxxxxxxxxxxx. Xxxxxxxxxxxxxxx xxxxxxxxxxxxxxxxxxxxxxxxxxxxxxxxxxxxxxxxxxxxxxxxxxxxxxxxxxxxxxxxxxxxxxxxxxxxxx xxxxxxxxxxxxxxxxxxxxxxxxxxxxxxxxxxx. Xxxxxxxxxxxxxxxxxxxxxxxxxxxxxxxxxxxxxxxxxxxx. Xxxxxxxxxxxxxxxxxxxxxxxxxxxxxxxxxxxxxxxxxxxxxxxxxxxxxxxxxxxx. Xxxxxxxxxxxxxxx xxxxxxxxxxxxxxxxxxxxxxxxxx. Xxxxxxxxxxxxxxxxxxxxxxxxxxxxxxxxxxxxxxxxxxxx.
Xxxxxxxxxxxxxxxxxxxxxxxxxxxxxxxxxxxxxxxxxxxx. Xxxxxxxxxxxxxxxxxxxxxxxxxxxxxxxx xxxxxxxxxxxxxxxxxxxxxxxxxxxxxxxxxxxxxxxxxxxxxxxxxxxxxxxxxxxxxxxx. Xxxxxxxxxxxxxxx xxxxxxxxxxxxxxxxxxxxxxxxxx. Xxxxxxxxxxxxxxxxxxxxxxxxxxxxxxxxxxxxxxxxxxxxxxxxxxxx Xxxxxxxxxxxxxxxxxxxxxxxxxxxxxxxxxxxxx. Xxxxxxxxxxxxxxxxxxxxxxxxxxxxxxxxxxxxxxxx xxxxxxxxxxxxxxxxxxxxxxxxxxxxxxxxxxxxxxxxxxxxxxxxxxxxxxxxxxxxxxxxxxxxxxxxxxx. Your thesis sentence goes here, concluding your introduction.

Here, just before launching into the journey proper, your thesis statement clearly notifies the reader of the course you have charted. Both you and your reader should be properly oriented, secure in the direction you intend to pursue as you now begin the first leg of your exploration. Additionally, first and last items of perception tend to stand out. Providing your thesis statement at the beginning of your essay, within the **first** paragraph(s), **last** sentence, therefore helps ensure that your reader will recognize the importance of this statement as well as remember it during and after the journey. While you will not find this pattern through all the readings in the *Reader*, you will find this guideline very practical for your student papers.

 PRACTICE

Look over the following student essays.

- "Newfoundlandese, if You Please" by Diane Mooney (p. 109)
- "Different Worlds" by Mark Radford (p. 43)
- "Sports Salaries: No Cap Needed" by Stewart Thompson (Chapter 13, p. 501)

- "Sports Salaries: Enough Is Enough" by Stewart Thompson (Chapter 13, p. 504)

Does each essay place a thesis statement in the recommended opening location?

Expressing a Strong Position

The first step in constructing your thesis is to find your own opinion about the topic. You need to discover and then, in your essay, express a strong position. Remember that even an expository essay is never completely objective; it has a core of opinion. For example, on the topic of learning to play guitar, the following thesis statement might be used: "Practising one hour a day, six days of the week, is an excellent form of progress." The words "excellent" and "progress" express a strong position on the approach being recommended. Some writers and instructors might call this strong position your *controlling idea*. Every essay grows from this vital kernel.

 PRACTICE

In the student essays listed above, decide what strong position the thesis statement introduces.

How you feel about the issue under discussion will shape your presentation of facts as well as increase the reader's interest in your work. So for each assignment, select a topic that interests you. If the choices do not immediately interest you, approach one of them open-mindedly and ask questions that help you to connect personally with the subject. The more you care about your topic and the more clearly you form your own position on it, the stronger your writing on the topic will be.

Once you have selected a topic that interests you, and have explored some pre-writing activity (Chapter 1, "Ways of Starting"), write a sentence about the topic that begins, "I believe that . . ." Make sure your opinion takes a stand on an issue related to the topic. You may be choosing between two aspects, stating your view of what constitutes the main cause of something, or identifying an overall characteristic that a number of things share. Once you've done this, you will have established the first component of your thesis: a position.

✒ PRACTICE

Look at three or four articles in the expository section of the *Reader*, "Knowledge and Ideas." What strong position does each take? Can you find any selection in the *Reader* that does not take a strong position?

Including Reasons for Your Position

Next, you need to come up with reasons *why* you took this position. You don't want your thesis to be purely opinion, because then your readers can dismiss your position as only one person's opinion; someone else could feel entirely different about the subject. Without reasons, the thesis will focus on you as a person. With reasons, your thesis will focus on your ideas as a reasoned argument.

Thesis statements with reasons (direct-list)

Mordecai Richler's novels present a bitter view of humanity because even the central characters demonstrate greed, deceit, and revenge as primary values.

Alice Munro's stories demonstrate a complex view of humanity because her central characters are ordinary and flawed, her settings contain good and bad aspects, and her endings often feel unresolved.

In the above example, the reasons are those three terms that follow the word "because." This type of thesis statement contains a complete map of the essay, which will discuss each of these three reasons, one at a time in the same order as laid out in the thesis statement. We refer to this type of complete thesis statement as a **direct list**, because all the reasons for the position are listed directly. After reading a direct-list thesis statement, your audience will have no questions about the content and scope of your essay; each section of your body will deal with one of the previewed reasons, in that order.

Here are two more examples of direct-list thesis statements:

All young people should read a book a month because it promotes intellectual curiosity, a strong vocabulary, and informed opinions.

Euthanasia is valid for the terminally ill, because it allows them freedom to choose, comfort in their final hours, and peace of mind.

These direct lists provide the outline for the body of each essay. Each item in the list can be adapted to form a topic sentence that directs and shapes a paragraph at the beginning of each section. These conceptual "contact points" (the reasons listed) can guide both you and your audience through the discussion. For first-year college and university papers, the direct-list thesis statement is a good idea, since it is the most orderly and exhaustive of the various types of thesis statements: it forces you to consider everything you need to do in the essay, in clear, effective order.

How do you write your own direct-list thesis statements? One way to generate reasons for your position is to add "because" onto your "I believe" statement. This will help you come up with reasons to support your position. When developing a direct-list thesis statement, be sure your reasons are specific, as in the preceding examples. Once you have generated and stated those reasons, you will have the two major components of a strong thesis: a position on the topic *and* the support for your position.

The disadvantage of the direct list is that it sometimes leaves very little to the reader's imagination. Some writers therefore prefer their thesis statements to refer briefly to all the specific reasons for the their position without listing each of these reasons separately. Such thesis statements simply refer to all the reasons in a general way. A thesis statement of this type is referred to as a **direct box**.

Direct-box thesis statements

1. Films that address historical topics should be based on balanced views and intensive research, because sensationalized accounts treat the past as one big action movie.

2. Hamlet hesitates to kill Claudius, because as a prince he weighs political stability against personal desire.

3. Large U.S. chains, such as Chapters and Starbucks, need to be controlled, because they speed up the Americanization of Canada.

Thesis 1 provides a general reason, sensational accounts belittle the past and, from there, the body will provide specific examples and ways in which the belittling has taken place. In thesis 2, we know the essay will discuss Hamlet's struggle between his political and private life, but we do not know in what *ways* until we get to the body. Thesis 3 leaves us thinking about the speed of Americanization, but the specific instances are still left for the body. The important thing to remember is that each general reason should be directly related to the specific reasons you provide in the body; the direct box will not work if your reasons do not fit inside it.

Other writers—increasing the demand on the reader's imagination even more— may simply state their position at the beginning of their essay and leave it to the reader to find their reasons in the body. In other words, some position statements may not include any reasons, either specific or general.

After completing your "I believe because" thesis statement, you will then need to shape this sentence into third person in many cases. Expository and third-person argumentative essays are the norm for many college and university courses; for these assignments, the next step of thesis development is to translate your "I believe" state-

PRACTICE

Consider the following position statement from Pierre Elliott Trudeau's essay "Ascetic in a Canoe" (p. 156): "I would like to point out to these people a type of labour from which they are certain to profit: an expedition by canoe."

Reread the essay very carefully. Does Trudeau give specific reasons for his position?

Rewrite his position statement to work as a direct list, then as a direct box. Be sure the direct box encompasses all the specific reasons given throughout the essay.

 PRACTICE

For each of the five student essays suggested on page 293, decide whether the thesis statement conveys the writer's reasons for his or her strong position on the topic. Is the thesis statement a direct list or a direct box?

ment plus your reasons into an informational (expository) tone. To accomplish this, all you have to do is cut the words "I believe that" from the beginning of your thesis. Listen to the difference in tone created when you eliminate the personal introductory phrase from the following thesis: "I believe that governments should hire minority groups because our society is based on equality." For expository purposes, this thesis becomes "Governments should hire minority groups because our society is based on equality." The statement now carries more weight. It is no longer a personal expression of your belief, but rather an assertion that can be debated by anyone according to the facts. Both versions contain a position and a reason, but the second has signalled a reasoned and broader purpose of your message.

PRACTICE

Go back to your thesis statement versions of Trudeau's position in "The Ascetic in a Canoe." Now translate your direct-list and direct-box versions of this position into the third person.

Conveying the Method(s) You Will Use to Develop Your Discussion

There is one other thing a clear and complete thesis statement can often convey: your method. Let's take the following example: "Comparing the generation of

Canadians who lived through the Great Depression to that which came of age in the 1960s, three important differences in attitude become apparent." This statement not only conveys a strong position on the topic (the generations are significantly different) and suggests the reasons (three specific examples); it also alerts us that the discussion will proceed through the method of *comparison-contrast*. Here is another example: "Lois's character in 'Thanks for the Ride' is significantly expressed through four settings: Pop's Café, her house, the bootlegger's farmhouse, and the fields and barn." This statement alerts us that the writer will be using description, or an awareness of descriptive detail, as well as observing the effects that various details have upon our understanding of character. We can expect the writer to use verbs such as "express," "show," "indicate," "reveal," "imply," and so on, to reinforce the main purpose of the essay, asserting that setting reveals the character of Lois to us.

In the previous example, the thesis statement suggested more than one method of discussion. In some cases, your thesis statement will incontestably convey two or more rhetorical methods by which you will shape your discussion. Consider the following example: "Contrary to the common cry, Native Canadians do not receive preferential treatment; in fact, analysis of their experience with the justice system suggests they are more often the subjects of mistreatment because of cultural imperialism and misunderstanding." The opening phrase, with its use of "contrary to," signals that the essay to follow will be argumentative; its goal will be to oppose one position with a different position. The word "analysis" alerts us to expect an element of analytical writing: the writer will break a situation into component parts and examine the relationships involved. The words "subjects of" indicate the essay will devote some attention to perceived effects of a certain condition—here, cultural imperialism and misunderstanding.

 PRACTICE

For each of the five student essays suggested on page 293, decide the methods of discussion conveyed by the thesis statements.

Restating Your Thesis Toward the End of Your Essay

Restating your thesis toward the end of your essay will sum up where the journey has taken us, writer and reader, and reinforce your main message in preparation for a concluding thought or challenge. Introducing the concluding section of his essay, Trudeau writes, "Allow me to make a fine distinction, and I would say that you return not so much a man who reasons more, but a more reasonable man." In her survey of English spoken in Newfoundland, Diane Mooney writes, "Taking in only major sections of the province, it is quite easy for any tourist to see clearly that Newfoundland has many different descendants and therefore many different dialects." In both cases, the writers summarize where we have been taken—a destination that had been announced at the end of the introduction.

✍ PRACTICE

- Find exactly where Diane Mooney has placed her re-stated thesis statement.
- In the other student essays you have been examining throughout this section, does the writer re-state his or her thesis toward the conclusion? If so, identify exactly where these re-statements occur.

Using Deductive, Inductive, and Implicit Thesis Statements

Despite our advice to place your thesis at the end of your introduction, as you have already gathered, the *location* of a thesis statement may vary from essay to essay. In practice, a thesis statement may occur anywhere in the essay. In general, location of the thesis statement depends on one of three possibilities:

- deductive[16]
- inductive[17]
- implicit

In his personal reflective essay "Causes of Procrastination" (p. 303 in Chapter 4), student Willard Dudley ends his first paragraph as follows: "I review the checklist—nothing there about distractions, mounting hopelessness, and despair." Dudley's essay demonstrates **deductive thesis placement**, because his thesis comes at the beginning of his essay, in this case, as the final sentence of the opening paragraph. His thesis is essentially a direct list ("My procrastination appears caused by three problems: distractions, escalating hopelessness, and despair"). See "Classification-Division" (p. 338) in Chapter 6 for a better idea of how Dudley uses three classifications as his reasons.

For an example of **inductive thesis placement**, read "The Other Canadians and Canada's Future" by Salloum Habeeb (p. 200). Notice that his introduction comprises the first three paragraphs, and that he begins his third paragraph with the question "how do the Canadian minorities whose origins can be traced to countries over the four corners of the world see the Canada of the future?" He tells us that for the answer, we "must travel back in history." His fourth paragraph begins with in-

---

[16] The term "deductive" has a different meaning in reference to a certain form of reasoning. See "Logic" in the section on "Argumentation."

[17] The term "inductive" also has a different meaning in reference to a certain form of reasoning. See "Logic" in the section on "Argumentation." Since the terms "deductive" and "inductive" are quite commonly used in both senses, we decided to include both usages in this book. Try to keep the two distinct meanings clear. Once you understand what is meant by deductive thinking and inductive thinking, you will probably see how the terms used here refer to the placement of a topic sentence. Inductive conclusions come about *after* an experience, and inductive topic sentences come *after* the body of the paragraph.

formation about attitudes at the beginning of this century. He continues to chart the process of history, as it involved and affected minorities, then looks at various different attitudes today—all leading to a final position statement. His question in the third paragraph is a clue that he will not state a final position until sifting through all the evidence and information he considers important. Finally, in his last paragraph, he states what he believes is the answer to the question he posed at the end of his introduction. Only here, in conclusion, does he come out and state his thesis. This location—at the end of the essay—is inductive. If you decide to use inductive structure, placing your thesis at the end, it is a very good idea to focus your discussion, as Habeeb has done, with a carefully worded question by the end of your introduction. This question will alert the reader to the central issue you intend to consider and to the specific understanding you are seeking. This focus helps to keep your essay clearly structured and motivated throughout.

The last type of thesis placement (or, in a sense, non-placement) is **implicit thesis placement**. This type is the most challenging both for you and your readers. It creates an air of mystery, and so, invites your readers to participate more in your essay because they have to decipher the position you only suggest. Writing and shaping this kind of thesis statement take time and thought, so if you want your reader to consider your topic deeply, then an implied or indirect thesis will elevate your essay to a new level of sophistication. Personal essays, which tend toward informality, sometimes leave their thesis unstated. However, if an implied thesis statement takes more time for a reader to recognize, it also takes additional skill and effort for you to handle as a writer.

 PRACTICE

Inexperienced writers sometimes assume that real-life stories of danger, injury, or death are inherently dramatic and interesting. This assumption often results in narratives that are overwritten, obvious, and even manipulative. A tendency toward cliché can all too easily take over personal essays that deal with action and risk. In the following essay, West Coast student writer Tamara Pelletier places the emphasis on accurate recall, resulting in an account whose dominant impression eschews "exciting" description for a psychological point of view.

Read Tamara Pelletier's "Suspended in Time," below. In your own words, what is her thesis statement in this selection?

Sample Essay Personal Narration—Find the Thesis

Suspended in Time
Tamara Pelletier

1   I untie my apron and throw it into the laundry. I take one last look around the bakery before I lock it and leave for the weekend. I walk home even though my feet are aching. It does not seem to take as long as it usually does because I know that I do not have to return to work for two more days.

2   I grab my hastily packed bag and head for my mum's car. My little sister has her seatbelt on and is drawing in the back seat. My mum comes and sits in the driver's seat. "Do you have everything that you'll need?" she asks me. I nod and she puts the car in reverse and we back out of the driveway. She is driving me to the bus station in a city near ours so that it will not be such a long ride for me. I am excited because I am going to see a friend for the weekend.

3   We pull onto the highway and the usual banter begins about plans for the week-end along with the arguments about the radio station we listen to. We near the bus station and turn onto a main road. We go up a hill. There is a blue car two cars ahead of us that seems to be weaving a little and jolting. I think to myself, "That person is going to cause an accident."

4   A couple of seconds later the blue car brakes suddenly at the crest of the hill, to avoid hitting some ducks that are crossing the road. The car directly in front of us stops and my mum stops as well. I breathe a sigh of relief because I did not think she would make it. Just as I am about to congratulate her on not slamming into the car in front of us, I am violently thrown forward. I see a flash of white and I am suspended in time. What seems like minutes later there is the resounding echo of what must have been the thunderous sound of a crash. I open my eyes and there is broken glass all over me. My car seat is reclined. I look up and everyone else in the car is covered in glass. The hood of the car is mangled and steam is emerging from the front of the car. My little sister is screaming, she has blood on the corner of her mouth, and my mum cannot believe what has just happened. A frantic man comes to the side of the car asking if everything is OK and if he can help. He is apologizing; he must be the one who has hit us. I reach down into my purse and pull out my cellular telephone. I dial 911. I feel uncertain because I have never had to do this before. They take my name, my address, and ask me what has happened. Who is screaming? Is anyone hurt? I do not know how to answer these questions and I just ask them to send someone to help. I continue talking to the dispatcher as I get out of the car.

5   The elastic that was holding my hair in a ponytail has been knocked off by the force of my head whipping around. I begin to look in the back seat for my elastic when I notice that the car is completely demolished. We had been pushed into the car in front of us. My little sister is holding her neck and screaming, but she is walking around. Another man comes running from one of the cars that has lined up behind us and calmly says he is a volunteer firefighter and that my sister should lie down. He takes control and the ambulance and fire truck arrive. They begin to put my sister on the spine-board; they start babbling about puncture wounds and broken bones. It finally dawns on me that we have been in a very bad accident.

6   I want to walk around; I have got so much nervous energy. The ambulance attendants keep telling me to sit still, but I am shaking and I cannot see exactly what is going on from where I am sitting. I look down and see that there is blood on my

elbow. The attendant takes me to the ambulance and bandages it. I do not want it to be bandaged because it does not hurt and it has stopped bleeding. I hop out of the back of the ambulance and my sister sees that my arm has been hurt; she starts screaming all over again. Everything is moving so fast, but nothing seems to be happening. The cars are still where they were when they crashed, my sister is still on the ground screaming, and there is nothing I can do to make things change any more than they already have.

7   My mum is busy with my sister, so police officers are trying to ask me questions. I answer them as best I can through the fog that I am in. The ambulance attendants finally finish getting my sister strapped down to the spine-board and we all get into the ambulance for a ride to the emergency room. I am sitting in the front seat and we do not seem to be going fast enough to get there but too fast for comfort. The attendants start saying that my sister needs an IV but my mum (who is a nurse) is insisting that we wait until we reach the hospital.

8   When we arrive, we are rushed in through the blue swinging double doors. There is a mob of nurses and doctors who rush around and start asking questions. One of the nurses is trying to calm down my still screaming sister. They start an IV and tell her to lie still because her neck might be broken. This makes her more anxious and she gets more frantic.

9   Finally my sister calms herself down and they take her to get some X-rays. I sit in her curtained area to watch our belongings. I think she will be fine. There is a general hubbub about the ward as people are being moved around and tended. I sit quietly and watch as people walk by and listen to snippets of conversation. My situation suddenly does not seem as dire as it was just 20 minutes earlier. The ordeal is over as fast as it had begun, and the reality of what could have happened begins to set in.

Focus Questions

1. What psychological state is conveyed but never named in this essay? Give two or three descriptive details that contribute to our sense of the narrator's condition.
2. From what you know of human responses to the direct experience of traffic collisions or similar misadventures, how accurate is the portrayal in this essay? Explain.
3. Comment on the author's use of present tense. In what way does it serve the overall purpose of the essay?
4. Standard usage calls for a comma after coordinating conjunctions. (See *Handbook*, Section 2, p. 561.) For the most part, the writer disregards this rule in this essay. Is her choice justified and, if so, why?

PRACTICE

1. Read "Night Fades" by Joyce Miller (p. 333). Try to express its thesis in your own words. What kind of thesis does this essay have, in comparison to those of Mark Radford's "Different Worlds" (p. 43), Diane Mooney's "Newfoundlandese, if You Please" (p. 109), Stewart Thompson's "Sports Salaries: No Cap Needed" (p. 501) and "Sports Salaries: Enough Is Enough" (p. 504)?

2. Do you think thesis statements, in general, are more or less explicit in personal essays than in expository and persuasive essays? Explain your answer.

3. Which of the following sentences could serve as thesis statements? Which could not? Why?

   a. According to Health Canada, in 1996–1997, 20 746 male Albertans and 12 602 female Albertans died of smoking-related illnesses.

   b. Today's universities are moving further into ill-advised collaborations with private corporations, threatening scientific neutrality and pure research.

   c. The percentage of female students attending universities since 1965 has steadily risen to the point that women now outnumber men.

   d. The desire to wear a tattoo usually indicates an insecure ego.

Chapter 4
Essay Structure

To be successful, college and university papers must be well organized. As you have seen, the first step to organizing your completed draft is to write a direct-list thesis statement. The second step is to draft an outline in which the body sections match the reasons provided in your direct list. The following brief essay illustrates precise linking of direct-list reasons and body sections:

Sample Essay Direct List Thesis Matched to Body

Causes of Procrastination
Willard Dudley

1 A gentle breeze rustles the cord of my laptop. My textbook sits open, propped to the "Checklist of Steps to a Successful Essay." A page of up-to-date quotations and paraphrases lies waiting. They come from internet sources, two current books on my topic, a journal article, and even a first-hand interview. Two days of brainstorming and diagramming stare up from pages on another corner of the table. For once I have done the pre-writing activities, as recommended, completed my research, and even remembered to copy down the page numbers and bibliographic details along with my citations. There's nowhere I'd rather be for creative atmosphere than right here at my kitchen table. I should be ready to boogie. But in fact I am simply staring at the blank screen, my mind and fingers locked. I review the checklist—nothing there about distractions, mounting hopelessness, and despair.

The writer implies 3 causes of his procrastination: 1) distractions 2) mounting hopelessness 3) despair. This is his thesis statement

2 A whistle sounds: the game is about to start. I go into the living room to turn off the TV, but the kickoff returner makes it all the way to the fifty-yard line. I may as well watch the first series of plays. The team gets into the end zone, so it only follows that I watch to see how their opponents fare on the next series. I check my watch: 8:10. There's no sense starting to write till 8:30, a nice even entry point. I can have the revised draft done before midnight and still get enough sleep for early class next morning. The phone rings. It's Jill, wanting to drop in to exchange CDs. What the heck, a few minutes of visiting will do me good. Jill doesn't leave till after ten. I wait till 10:30

This paragraph focuses on 1) distractions

303

for a clean entry point, but when I sit back down to the blank screen, I keep thinking about Jill and wandering through memories of old girl-friends and places we went to-gether. A car in need of a muffler growls by. I find myself wondering what I could have done to remove the stuck oil pan in Gina's old K-Car when I look at my watch again: 10:45.

This paragraph focuses on 2) mounting hopelessness

3   Now it feels virtually hopeless. If I had started by 8 or even 8:30, I could have had the first draft just about finished and used the rest of my energy to fix those usage errors our instructor seems so fixated on. This must be what is meant by a vi-cious circle: the longer I stall the harder it is to begin. My essay is like a canoe in irons in the middle of a lake. The hardest thing about canoeing is to get started from a standstill. I've gone from floating on haphazard thoughts and diversions to brooding on the fact that it is now too late.

This paragraph foreshadows and explains 3) despair

4   Then I realize something kind of interesting. It's a little like remembering a dream halfway through the day. I realize that even when the instructor had handed us the essay assignment two weeks ago, I thought that two weeks would never be enough time. Even then I told myself it was too late. When Jill asked why I was so worried, I said it was because it would take so long doing all the pre-writing stuff, not to men-tion the research. It sounded like too many false starts and too much indecision for me. But using a collage and doing some diagramming were actually fun, and I found really good citations and did an interview all in two days. So why was I thinking there wasn't enough time? Why am I still thinking that when almost half the work has been done and the essay has to be only two and a half pages?

This paragraph focuses directly on 3) despair

5   I realize the real problem, reflected in mounting hopelessness and enshrined in despair, is that I actually believe I can't write this essay—that is, I can't write the perfect essay I imagine I should write. That's the root cause underlying the vicious circle of mounting despair: the longer I procrastinate about putting a word on the computer screen, the more I reinforce this belief. So I write whatever words come into my head to begin my first paragraph. Suddenly time expands. I am not only writing the first paragraphs of my essay, I am also reflecting on how to stop this problem from hap-pening again.

This paragraph concludes with resolutions to act upon his insight and prevent future procrastination

6   I decide that next time I tell myself to start writing by 8:00 p.m. I will stick to that, regardless of the TV or the telephone. That way I will show myself that my despair is wrong. If Jill calls to drop by, I will tell her to wait 90 minutes, till I'm done the first draft. Once I complete that draft, the rest is coasting. As I think this, I'm onto my con-cluding paragraph. It's past midnight, there still remain 40 minutes of proofing and re-vising, but I'm feeling great. I'll get up 40 minutes earlier and revise in the morning when I can take a fresh second look at what I have written. Maybe the next time I have my pre-writing and research worked out so well in advance I should show my stuff to the instructor, like some of the others have done. They seemed to be moti-vated by that, knowing they were on the right track. They also got a few tips on how

to open their particular essays. Now I'm writing my clinching words, using an appropriate aphorism. I may not yet believe that I can write the very best essays I would like to, but I no longer feel the victim of procrastination.

Using deductive organization (placing one's thesis at the beginning—Chapter 3, "Thesis Statements"), Dudley begins his essay with his explicit thesis statement. Next, since his direct list gives three reasons, he establishes conceptual links between his thesis sentence and each of his body paragraphs. He expands upon the first reason as the topic of his first body paragraph (paragraph 2). He then enlarges on the second reason in the subsequent body paragraph (3); he discusses the third reason in the paragraphs after that, (4) and (5). His final paragraph (6) states appropriate resolutions stemming from his insight. The paragraphs and the thesis are conceptually bound together throughout the essay.

Most successful academic essays achieve this same conceptual integration by proceeding from pre-writing activities toward a thesis statement and a matching outline. An outline for Dudley's essay might resemble the following:

Outline for the Essay "Causes of Procrastination"

Thesis Statement: My procrastination is caused by (1) distractions, (2) mounting hopelessness, (3) despair.

    Essay Body:
1. **Distractions**: TV, Jill, memories/associations, street noise
2. **Mounting hopelessness:** vicious circle, delay worsens the inertia
3. **Despair:** The extreme degree of hopelessness—why?
   – underlying lack of belief in self
   – acting, getting started, denies the belief

    Conclusion: Stick to schedule, get reward & encouragement for prep work

---

It is highly recommended that you prepare a direct-list thesis statement and matching outline *before* attempting to write a final draft of your essay, or any draft you regard as close to finished. This step-by-step procedure ensures your essay will have a clear position, sufficient reasons, and purposeful organization.

ORGANIZING PRINCIPLES

The outline of your body should follow a clear, effective organizing principle. Here are some common organizing principles:

- time
- space
- comparison
- features, characteristics, or aspects
- causes and/or effects

If you are telling a story or observing a step-by-step process, the principle of time or chronology will apply. "Brownie," by Roger Fouts (p. 12) is a good example of chronological organization used to tell a story. Pat Deiter-McArthur's "Saskatchewan's Indian People—Five Generations" (p. 87) also uses chronology, in this case to observe the unfolding of a historical process. Directing someone in how to make the perfect cup of coffee would be yet another case of organizing according to points in time.

If, on the other hand, you are describing a physical subject, a logical movement through space will apply. See Emma Lee Warrior's descriptive essay "White Breast Flats" (p. 6) for a good model of logical organization according to physical location. Another essay that uses space as a guiding principle is "Newfoundlandese, if You Please" (p. 109). In that essay, Diane Mooney organizes her discussion according to a logical progression through geographic regions. Comparison suggests itself as the organizing principle when you wish to place two things (or positions) side by side: for instance, to show how one exceeds the other or to distinguish an important common element between the two. You may decide to use features, characteristics, or aspects (also called points) to organize your essay. Often you may find it effective to arrange your points in order of their increasing importance or intensity, with your most important point coming last. This pattern is sometimes referred to as **climactic structure** (building to a climax). The same principle of climactic organization may be used when structuring your discussion according to a manageable number of causes or effects, as Willard Dudley's essay illustrates. More detailed information concerning structural patterns appears later in this *Rhetoric* under "Exposition" (Chapter 6).

Note on Organizational Strategies

Cultural identity is an important consideration for students and instructors to bear in mind when judging the effectiveness of organization. Deductive structure—beginning with the main claim and then expanding upon it, as Dudley has done—is by no means the only way to go about organizing your thoughts. In Middle Eastern and Russian traditions, for example, main claims are left implicit. In North America as well, traditional First Nations cultures use a non-deductive approach to organizing ideas. The Pueblo writer Leslie Marmon Silko explains this distinction when she refers to her approach as one of following patterns deriving from oral tradition: "Pueblo expression resembles something like a spider's web—with many little threads radiating from the centre, crisscrossing each other. As with the web, the structure emerges as it is made and you must simply listen and trust, as the Pueblo people do, that meaning will be made."[18] Not everyone will be comfortable with the deductive, explicit model we have given above; as Western societies become more culturally diverse, perhaps the dominant deductive norm will modify and merge with others. Habeeb Salloum would likely dispute this speculation ("The Other Canadians and Canada's Future," p. 200). In any case, consider the interplay between yourself, your purpose, and your audience when deciding on the best organizational pattern for a particular piece of writing.

INTRODUCTIONS

The introduction provides your first opportunity to inform readers of your chosen topic. The introduction also allows you to demonstrate you are serious and informed, qualified to discuss your topic with fairness and insight.

There are many types of essay introductions, but all of them do the following:

- announce the topic,
- focus the discussion, and
- limit the scope of the topic to be examined in the body of the essay.

Your commitment to clarity and organization in the introduction will go a long way to earning your audience's attention and good faith for the discussion that unfolds. A good introduction conveys your essay's first impression.

Introductions frequently take the shape of a **funnel**. The first sentence addresses the topic in broad terms: "Homelessness is an intolerable situation in a prosperous society." The second sentence begins to narrow the focus of this large topic: "Government subsidies continue to provide inadequate support for Canadian homeless people and for those on the verge of homelessness." A third and perhaps fourth sentence will continue to narrow the introduction's focus on the subject while adding particular information: "Despite the annual increase in national homelessness, politicians' recent proposals to cut taxes for social aid (and 'reward taxpayers') can only signal the continued neglect of society's most helpless citizens." Finally, you will have incrementally built your topic in your introduction to the point that your thesis statement can announce your **chief assertion** about your selected topic. The thesis statement provides your **main claim** (or controlling idea) to be established, explained, and/or argued in the essay's body paragraphs to follow. The funnel model is a helpful (and widely used) visual concept that captures the dynamic of this steady narrowing and focusing that a good introduction requires. From the first broad sentence to the specific thesis statement that you will later examine in detail, your introduction should form this mental picture:

---

[18] Leslie Marmon Silko, "Language and Literature from a Pueblo Indian Perspective," in *Critical Fictions: The Politics of Imaginative Writing*, ed. Philomena Mariani (Seattle: Bay Press, 1991) 83–93.

Figure 4.1
The Funnel
Introduction

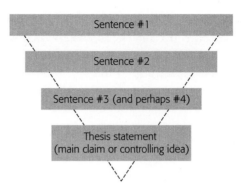

Remember that your initial introduction may be quite provisional: perhaps think of your rough copy introduction as your best intention for the present. By your final draft, you may well have changed the tone and focus of the essay and accordingly have adjusted the language of your thesis statement as well. Think of your rough copy, including your introduction, as a film you're trying to shoot: you know your chosen subject matter, but have not figured out all the best cuts and angles yet. Like most essayists, you will likely return to polish your thesis after you have completed the working version of your entire discussion.

There are several types of introductions. As an essayist you should be prepared to work confidently with all of them to allow yourself the most flexibility possible for facing different types of essays and writing situations over your student years—and after. The method that will work best for you in a given circumstance will depend on your audience and your purpose (Chapter 2, "Reviewing the Basics"), and so will require your best judgment as an evolving writer.

Six Types of Commonly Used Introductions

- The Head-on Account
- The Opening Definition
- The Gesture to Authority
- The Counter-Argument
- The Anecdote
- The Question

The Head-On Account

The **head-on account** relies on crisp declarative sentences that simply establish the topic and narrow the focus to the thesis statement. Our example of introduction-building on the topic of homelessness employs this head-on method: you declare your subject and intently press forward with clear, increasingly narrowing statements. You ask no rhetorical questions, present no provisional counter-views (alternative claims), and cite no authority beyond your own writerly voice. The head-on account sets a candid, certain, openly positioned tone for the entire essay.

We strongly recommend this no-nonsense style of introduction for your first essay in a freshman course, unless the instructor has stipulated differently in the assignment.

The Opening Definition

The **opening definition** specifies the objective meaning of a term or concept. This technique establishes your sense of fairness and of valid questioning, since you appear to be seeking some neutral middle ground with your audience. Usually the opening-definition method signals that you will carefully and reflectively add to, qualify, or refute this accepted definition in the course of your essay. This type of introduction works best with ambiguous, contested, or emotional terms and concepts, such as "community," "family," "education," "justice," "success," etc. Always use the opening-definition method sincerely, and not as a convenient way to chew up space.

The Gesture to Authority

The **gesture to authority** is a technique of establishing the importance of your topic beyond the bounds of the essay itself. This method creates initial momentum through your introduction and possibly grounds for debate in your discussion: "Lisa Bugden, a Halifax philosopher, argues that time is a slippery concept, not an empirical fact" or "A recent Canadian survey indicates that more than 65 percent of young adults disapprove of expanded military spending." By citing an authority or a published credible reference, you show that you have marshalled some pertinent facts to support your views. You should make sure, however, that your introduction integrates this reference within your own position. Make sure that outside references serve *your* own thinking. Also remember that you may cite an authority or reference to contend with that view: "The Manitoban historian Patricia Murphy hastily concludes that Louis Riel was 'an outlaw capable only of reckless decisions.' The facts and purpose of defiant uprising invite a far different interpretation, however."

The Counter-Argument

The introduction as **counter-argument** sets a debate in motion. You may cite an authority or reference as in the above example or simply state a commonly held view. This is how George Orwell begins his essay "Politics and the English Language" (p. 227):

> Most people who bother with the matter at all would admit that the English language is in a bad way, but it is generally assumed that we cannot by conscious action do anything about it.

Orwell elaborates on this typical view in his opening paragraph and then, in his second paragraph, he opposes it by asserting that "the process is reversible."

By starting with a counter-argument, you set your essay's thesis against the assertion of an authority or the commonly held view. This strategy generates a reader's interest immediately because a clearly defined debate—presumably with something important at stake—has been energetically engaged. The counter-argument introduction also confers some solid credit on you as a contentious essayist, a resolved and independent thinker, who is willing to question and redefine accepted notions. Both the opening definition and gesture to authority may adopt the counter-argument strategy of debate and contention.

The Anecdote

The **anecdote** introduction illustrates a point by way of a "language sketch": you spin a brief episode in order to tell by showing. Since this type of introduction draws upon the personal, be sure your audience will appreciate this slightly informal essay opener:

> Two of my Vancouver friends who listen almost entirely to U.S.A. music tell me that Canadian music no longer exists as a distinct cultural expression. I always quickly remind them of the Tragically Hip's continued references to Canadian history, people, places, habits, and events. I also remind them of the Guess Who's song "American Woman," a 1970s rock 'n' roll expression of the importance of Canadian cultural resistance to Americanization."

The anecdote introduction sets a slightly vulnerable, conversational tone since it strives to share between writer and reader a vivid personal experience or private observation. Some instructors may prefer that you choose the more formal, traditional approach of beginning your paper with direct exposition or analysis. There is always politics in the act of writing!

The Question

Students often overuse the **question** introduction. If you quickly reel off as many as four consecutive questions in your introduction—not necessarily in logical sequence—in the hope that some focus will magically appear on the page, you undermine the potential benefits of this strategy. Try to resist this late-night writing temptation as a strategy for your introduction.

You should usually limit your question introduction to about two carefully considered, genuine inquiries that trigger the reader's immediate interest in the forthcoming discussion. The questions should be sufficiently complex and/or significant to arouse and sustain the reader's interest: "If, as many people claim, capital punishment is legally just in extreme crimes, can anyone ensure that a system of judgment that places people on death row is itself socially just? Why, for instance, are there mostly poor people on death row?"

BODY PARAGRAPHS

The paragraphs of your body sustain your introduction's claims through carefully selected and well-organized details. In an introductory course essay, these paragraphs are usually four or five sentences long. They may be somewhat longer, but in general they are never any shorter than four or five sentences.

Topic Sentence

Each paragraph is directed by a **topic sentence**. This crucial sentence makes a concise and explicit assertion for that paragraph to expand on. Although this sentence may appear anywhere in the paragraph, it is most commonly the first sentence, and this is the location we strongly recommend for *your* topic sentences. Here is a short reflective essay by Bertrand Russell, the American philosopher and mathematician. His thesis sentence is underlined and the topic sentence of each body paragraph appears in italics. Note the close connections between the thesis and the topic sentences, and how these conceptual links are achieved largely through the careful wording of each topic sentence in relation to the thesis statement.

Sample Essay Topic Sentences Linked to Thesis

What I Have Lived For

Bertrand Russell

1   <u>Three passions, simple but overwhelmingly strong, have governed my life: the longing for love, the search for knowledge, and unbearable pity for the suffering of mankind.</u> These passions, like great winds, have blown me hither and thither, in a wayward course, over a deep ocean of anguish, reaching to the very verge of despair.

2   *I have sought love*, first because it brings ecstasy—ecstasy so great that I would often have sacrificed all the rest of life for a few hours of this joy. I have sought it, next, because it relieves loneliness—that terrible loneliness in which one shivering consciousness looks over the rim of the world into the cold unfathomable lifeless abyss. I have sought it, finally, because in the union of love I have seen, in a mystic miniature, the prefiguring vision of the heaven that saints and poets have imagined. This is what I sought, and though it might seem too good for human life, this is what—at last—I have found.

3   *With equal passion I have sought knowledge*. I have wished to understand the hearts of men. I have wished to know why the stars shine. And I have tried to apprehend the Pythagorean power by which number holds sway above the flux. A little of this, but not much, I have achieved.

4   Love and knowledge, so far as they were possible, led upward toward the heavens. *But always pity brought me back to earth.* Echoes of cries of pain reverberate in

my heart. Children in famine, victims tortured by oppression, helpless old people a hated burden to their sons, and the whole world of loneliness, poverty, and pain make a mockery of what human life should be. I long to alleviate the evil, but I cannot, and I too suffer.

5   *This has been my life*. I have found it worth living, and would gladly live it again if the chance were offered me.

Russell's first topic sentence really implies "I have sought love for three reasons." He runs his first reason into his topic sentence, which alerts the reader that at least one more reason will follow. Nevertheless, this topic sentence achieves the desired effect of focusing the paragraph on the main topic and linking it to the first reason in his thesis. His second topic sentence announces the second reason given in his thesis statement. His third topic sentence announces the third reason given in his thesis statement. This third topic sentence comes second in the paragraph, after an initial sentence summarizing the meaning of his previous two topics in a way that prepares us for the third. Here you can see that the pattern of topic sentences beginning each paragraph will naturally vary from time to time. What is the effect of these topic sentences?

Topic Sentences

The topic sentence declares a main position (claim) to be supported with appropriate detail, and it encourages unity and coherence throughout the paragraph. In the same way, a carefully drafted thesis statement announces a central position and encourages unity and coherence throughout the essay.

Supporting Details

The remaining sentences of the paragraph then provide various sorts of **supporting details** and justifications—proofs—in support of the opinion. These details or proofs may take the form of anecdotes, examples, illustrations, analogies, and other forms of logical reasoning (see Chapter 7, "Argumentation"), statistics, facts, and other data from first-hand observation or published studies (second-hand sources), and quotations or paraphrases from authorities. In an essay of literary analysis, for instance, a paragraph must do more than state a general position through its topic sentence; for example, "Lois's house in 'Thanks for the Ride' is shown as dismal and depressing." This view must then be supported by closely observed details, such as "the smell in the house, the smell of stale small rooms, bedclothes, frying, washing, and medicated ointments." A little later in the text, this smell is associated with the grandmother and likened to "a smell of hidden decay, such as there is when some obscure little animal has died under the verandah." Closely observed textual details such as these lend support to the claim in the topic sentence. Without the topic sentence, the paragraph would not be focused. Without the supporting details, the topic sentence would not be sufficiently sustained. All essay writing, in essence, is a proper balancing of claims and supports, positions and proofs. This balance results from the clarity of the topic sentences and the validity of the detailed support through the rest of the paragraph.

"Warm" and "cool" proofs provide further balance in the paragraphs of an essay. These terms refer to how personal or impersonal the supporting details appear to be. Here are three examples of proofs ranging from warm through neutral to cool. In each example, the topic sentence has been indicated in italics.

Types of supporting details (proofs), ranging from "warm" to "cool"

1. *By the encouragement of self-confidence, self-worth and a feeling of pride in their ethnic origin, multiculturalism has helped the immigrants succeed in their social and economic life and has made them feel at home.* There is no better indication of how self-image determines the future of the country than when I visited the northern Alberta Arab community of Lac La Biche in the late summer of 1996. "I love it here! In this town we prospered and here we have established our roots." Khalil Abughoush, owner of the IGA supermarket in Lac La Biche, was full of enthusiasm when talking about his small northern city. Like his fellow countrymen—20 percent of the town's 3,000 inhabitants are of Arab-Lebanese origin—he had come to seek his fortune in this northern Alberta resort. In Canada's multicultural society, Abughoush, like the majority of immigrants and their descendants, felt at home. As he prospered he felt no coercion to fit in, no pressure to leave his culture behind.

—Habeeb Salloum, "The Other Canadians and Canada's Future" (p. 200)

2. *Fundamentally, an understanding of the sacred helps us to acknowledge that there are bounds of balance, order, and harmony in the natural world which set limits to our ambitions and define the parameters of sustainable development.* In some cases Nature's limits are well understood at the rational, scientific level. As a simple example, we know that trying to graze too many sheep on a hillside will, sooner or later, be counterproductive for the sheep, the hillside, or both. More wisely, we understand that the overuse of insecticides or antibiotics leads to problems of resistance. And we are beginning to comprehend the full, awful consequences of pumping too much carbon dioxide into the Earth's atmosphere.

—HRH Charles, Prince of Wales, in the Reith lecture broadcast, May 17, 2000

3. *One of the sad consequences of the push towards a hyper-masculine image is that it can rarely be obtained without the use of potentially harmful drugs.* A 1993 study conducted for the Canadian Centre for Ethics in Sport concluded that four per cent

of males aged 11 to 18—as many as 83,000 young Canadians—used anabolic steroids in 1992 and 1993. In the study, which involved 16,169 high-school and elementary students, one in five reported that they knew someone who was taking anabolic steroids. Among the reasons given for their use, nearly half said it was to change their physical appearance. That contrasted starkly with previously held notions that steroids were used mostly to increase athletic performance, says Paul Melia, the centre's director of education. "The reality is for most of these young men, even if they do get on a regimen of weight training, they are not going to look like these picture boys," said Melia. "And sustaining that look is a full-time job."

—Susan McClelland, "The Lure of the Body Image," *Maclean's*, February 22, 1999 (p. 83)

Paragraph one uses the extended example of a particular person to help support its claim about the effects of multiculturalism. This type of support is considered "warm" because it presents information with a specific human face. An article about poverty will gain in persuasive impact if the writer portrays people struggling to survive on little income in one or two descriptive examples. On the other hand, exclusive use of individual cases can be considered unreliable and even manipulative. Our sympathies for the personalized subjects may outweigh other judgments we should make. In addition, you must be careful about drawing general conclusions from one or two specific cases, no matter how compelling they seem. Salloum could certainly not rest his thesis simply on the experience of Mr. Abughoush. But this example does draw us into the discussion; it adds "warmth."

Paragraph two uses three separate examples of activities—specific interactions between humans and nature—but without an involved person as presented in sample paragraph one. We can easily recognize the activities Prince Charles refers to, but they are presented as generalized, known facts, creating more emotional distance for us as readers than we feel when a specific case, with descriptive human detail, is used.

The data used for support in paragraph three come from a study. To determine the reliability of that study, we would need to consider the context of the study (was it biased?), and examine what procedures the researchers followed, including what statistical evaluation system they used to determine significance. Assuming these methods were sound, the study represents the most empirical (objective) of the three forms of support illustrated in these sample paragraphs. The behaviour and attitudes of people are presented again through percentages. Instead of a human face, we are presented with an abstraction representing a map of a collective situation. This approach to investigating experience and arriving at a position is considered the most scientific of the three examples above. Data from studies may be considered "cool" support in that they are detached from individuals and rendered through established logical procedures.

But remember, statistics and data may be manipulated to reach various faulty conclusions. For example, "Unemployment claims for this year exceed those of 15 years ago by 10 percent. Clearly, abuse is on the increase." This could be a **faulty comparison**, since—for one thing—the number of workers may have significantly increased over

15 years. Other factors could be involved as well. Another misuse of numbers is the following: "Salaries in our company are excellent, averaging over $70,000 per year." This could be a faulty conclusion based on the **myth of the mean**. Perhaps executives make $350,000 each, and a majority of employees earn less than $25,000. (For further discussion of abuses of evidence, proof, and argument, see Chapter 7, "Argumentation.")

Abuse of statistics and logic may have serious ethical repercussions. Consider the warning of Jonathan Swift in his classic satirical essay "A Modest Proposal" (1729).[19] In this essay, Swift adopts the voice, or "persona," of a fictional gentleman, one who would surely describe himself as logical. Marshalling facts and figures in a seemingly disinterested way, this gentleman develops a tone that is highly empirical, unbiased, and above all "civilized." His proposal, however, is that the Irish poor should sell their children as food items. So from seemingly logical recourses has sprung a monstrous idea. As you proceed through academic disciplines, remember Swift's warning that an empirical surface does not guarantee a sound, ethical conclusion. Remember that your supporting details may range from warm to cool, and where possible consider the advantages of balancing types of proofs. Remember the strengths and weaknesses of each type. The following paragraph comes from an essay by student Marylou Orchison in favour of banning smoking in public places. Notice her effective combination of warm, neutral, and cool details.

Introductory paragraph using warm and cool supporting detail

Up front, I admit it: I used to be one of the many people who indulge everyday in the pleasures of a cigarette. I would light up in public places, without any regard to the fact that over 33 000 Albertans die every year as a result of smoking-related diseases (Health Canada 1997). I was as aware as the next smoker of the arguments against public control: "My dad lived to be 104, and *he* smoked" and "I have my rights—I thought this was supposed to be a free country." I frequently used these very arguments to defend my habit. Then in 1996 my mother became seriously ill. Despite her dry hacking cough, she continued to smoke. She seemed to be suffocating. When she died, I had to face the consequences of smoking, not only for myself but for those around me.

Linking Devices (Transitional Terms)

As we have seen, through the use of explicitly worded topic sentences body paragraphs maintain conceptual links with the thesis statement in the introduction of the essay. In addition to these broad conceptual links, however, paragraphs also direct the flow of ideas through carefully chosen **linking devices**. Here is a sample paragraph by Jacqueline O'Rourke, a writing instructor, in the *English 155 Study Guide: Developing Reading and Writing Skills* (1990), showing those devices in bold.

---

[19] Described by Swift's biographer, A.L. Rowse, as "a lucid nightmare" in *Jonathan Swift: Major Prophet* (London: Thames and Hudson, 1975) 211.

✿ PRACTICE

1. Read "The Other Canadians and Canada's Future" by Habeeb Salloum (p. 200) and "The Lure of the Body Image" by Susan McClelland (p. 83). Do these articles offer sufficient proofs to convince you of their conclusions? Why or why not?

2. Choose two or three other body paragraphs from essays in the *Reader*. Identify the topic sentence of each paragraph, then the supporting details. Try to classify the details according to the forms given above. Are these details personal observations, published data, logical deductions, etc? Are they "warm" or "cool"? You might wish to compare your answers with those of fellow students,

and see whether your instructor agrees with your perceptions. Can you separate the opinions from the facts and the reasoning offered in support of those opinions?

3. Once you have separated the opinion statement (the topic sentence) from the supporting information and have done your best to classify the supporting information, identify the organizational principle the writer has used to arrange the sentences of the paragraph in relation to that topic sentence. Is the individual paragraph as carefully outlined and organized as the essay itself?

Linking devices

A home usually reflects the owner's personality. **First of all**, the furniture one chooses can tell us a lot about that person. **If one chooses** modern, colourful furniture, then we can assume that the person is a modernist, one who appreciates the present. **If one chooses** antiques, then we assume one has a sense of nostalgia for times gone by. The way one decorates the walls and floors **also** tells us a lot. **If** walls are left bare, the person may be a minimalist, **one who** prefers the simple. **If** walls are cluttered, the person may be disorganized and indecisive. **Finally, if** floors match furniture, the person may be organized and may strive to see the patterns in life. **On the other hand**, if floors are in bold contrast to walls and furniture, the person may be slightly eccentric, preferring the unpredictable and chaotic. **Therefore**, by observing someone's choice in home decoration, you can get to know that person without an actual meeting.

We can see two main types of linking devices at work in this paragraph, **transitional terms** and **repetitions**. The transitional phrases include "first of all," "on the other hand," "also," "finally," and "therefore." They reinforce a sense of logical order, reminding the reader that information is presented in a certain patterned manner. The repetition of certain key words may work as a coherence device, or the repetition may use a particular sentence pattern. In this case, the sentence pattern of dependent/independent clauses is repeated through the structure "If . . . , then . . ." As well, there is the repetition of relative clauses: "one who appreciates the present," "one who prefers the simple." In your reading of the selections in this text as well as your reading in general, pay close attention to how writers use coherence devices—transitional terms and repetitions—to glue their passages together.

Here is a partial table of **transitional terms** commonly used in connection with the organizing principles outlined earlier in this section. These terms are used within or between sentences and paragraphs.

Transitional Terms

Time:	first, next, then, later, afterwards, presently, by and by, after a while, soon, as soon as, at first
Space:	on, over, under, around, beside, by, from, next, after, across, farther, toward, at, there
Comparison:	like, unlike, in contrast, similarly, on the other hand, conversely
Features:	first, second, third (etc.), another, the last, the final, also, as well, in addition, above all, especially, indeed, more important, particularly, unquestionably
Causes/Effects:	as a result, because, consequently, so, for, therefore, thus, hence

Transitional Paragraphs

In addition to transitional words, **transitional paragraphs** (often just two or three sentences long) are sometimes used in essays to mark major shifts. Typically, such paragraphs summarize the discussion so far and preview the remaining points. As short paragraphs among longer ones, transitional paragraphs stand out as effective markers of division. This effect is lost, however, if overused.

> **Transitional paragraph**
>
> We have just seen how, in essence, Canadians may claim a certain moral superiority over Americans. This advantage pales, however, when we explore each nation on the basis of generosity.

 PRACTICE

Return to the two or three paragraphs you have already selected while working with topic sentences and forms of support. Identify all the linking devices used throughout the paragraphs. Are there any transitional paragraphs in the essays in question? Check with your classmates and your instructor to see if they agree with your observations.

Concluding Your Paragraphs

Concluding your paragraphs with an appropriate final sentence accomplishes two things:

- A concluding sentence fully articulates, or emphasizes, the main point and controlling idea of the paragraph.
- A concluding sentence looks ahead to the topic of the next paragraph.

The following paragraph from an essay by a university student, Jessica Walker, builds to a decisive concluding sentence. This paragraph comes from an essay called

"Los Niños de Nicaragua," which describes the author's trip to Managua with the non-profit organization Change for Children Association. In a previous paragraph, she has described how in certain marketplaces "projects" have been set up to offer children a place to meet and play: "Some of the projects are located in small corners of the market, blocked off from the chaos by a few boards nailed together."

Concluding paragraph (Note the final sentence)

One of the hardest things to face in the projects is the hardship in these children's lives. Most come from large families and are expected to sell goods in the market by day and then come home in the evening to help out with household chores. I met one girl who attended one of the projects for only a couple of hours in the morning because her parents wanted her to resume her sales in the market. She told me she has 10 brothers and sisters, and that after she has sold enough in the market, she must hurry home to start supper for her young brothers and sisters, clean the house, and do laundry. She seemed so much older than she really is. She drew me a colourful picture of a house with a walkway and an abundance of flowers in a front garden—a picture so similar to the ones I used to draw when I was a little girl. She lives in one of the many shacks put together with garbage-bag walls and hard-packed dirt for the floor. The home in her picture is a dream.

For the kids who live on their own in the market, life is harder still. . . . [Paragraph continues.]

Walker's terse final sentence ("The home in her picture is a dream"), summing up the details she has provided, drives home the position of her topic sentence. It also prepares us for a transition from children like this young girl to another category of children who are even more unfortunate, the homeless. This worse-off category becomes the focus of the ensuing topic sentence ("For the kids who live on their own in the market, life is harder still"). This transition also demonstrates the effect of climactic organization (building to increasingly powerful points).

Remember that paragraph conclusions, like paragraph topic sentences, frequently assist the important process of linking ideas. Now here is an example of conceptual links (between thesis and topic sentences) and linking devices (transitions, intensifiers, and repetitions) working within and between paragraphs. The thesis statement has been underlined, topic sentences are in italics, and coherence devices in bold.

Introduction to essay showing linking devices

Female action movies appear more **frequently** now since Sigourney Weaver's portrayal of the smart, tough, courageous Ripley in *Alien* and its sequel, *Aliens*. Directors realize audiences are prepared to reject the stereotype of the action movie as an **exclusively** male genre. **In particular**, let us examine how James Cameron's *Terminator II: Judgment Day*, Ridley Scott's *Thelma & Louise*, and Luc Besson's *La Femme Nikita* attempt to redefine the male action genre by depicting independent women capable of defending and asserting themselves **successfully** in moments of danger and crisis. The **significance** of this genre is its examination of everyday social presumptions about female independence, but under extreme conditions.

*These **three** films depict women using weapons capably not to endorse violence but to undermine the stereotype that only men are prepared or able to cope with danger and physical challenge.* Terminator II emphasizes the survivalist training of its central character, Sarah Connor, to show that social attitudes **alone**, not physiology, prevent women from expertise with weapons and combat skills. **Since** the film's heroine has thoroughly trained herself for a possible technical Armageddon, she has displaced the conventional need for a male to save her. The film's chief point, **beyond** all the weaponry and doomsday scenarios of its plot, is that women can perform in the **same** capacities as men, given need or opportunity.

Like Sarah Connor, *Thelma and Louise are pushed to a new social and emotional independence by the need for immediate self-defence.* **After** Thelma narrowly escapes a parking-lot rape, the two women become outlaws for killing the attempted rapist and fleeing the scene. **As** the film takes the form of the classic road movies (a male genre), the two women become **more** adept with the conventional masculine technology of guns and cars, **all the while** exposing the social restrictions **under which** women usually live **unquestioningly**. **Unfortunately**, the film's controversial ending tends to glamorize suicide as rebellion by indicating that Thelma and Louise decide that death is preferable to a compromised independence.

The thesis statement in this writing sample argues that the female action genre is important because of its examination of social presumptions about female independence. The thesis statement also asserts that everyday attitudes toward sex are dramatically exposed by the films' depiction of women in extreme ordeals and circumstances. Both topic sentences take up this position, but with narrowed focus. Topic sentence #1 forms a strong conceptual link with the thesis by identifying a common element of the films in question, the sudden need and ability of the female characters to handle firearms as capably as any male action hero. This topic sentence also makes the important distinction that the female characters' recourse to weapons is not a gratuitous aspect of a violent plot, but part of a careful undermining of a sexual stereotype. Topic sentence #2 forms links to the thesis and body paragraph #1 but continuing the analysis of how sudden jeopardy pushes the female characters of the films to self-protection and social independence. Clearly, strong conceptual links exist between thesis and topic sentences.

Within this sample, the bolded linking devices serve as transitions between statements while also effectively narrowing the scope of discussion. The transition "Like Sarah Connor" explicitly extends the discussion of the previous paragraph by setting up a comparison. The transition "unfortunately" signals that a contrast has occurred to an opinion that now opposes the previous judgment. Other terms such as "three," "alone," and "beyond" all help to narrow the focus and to intensify the controlling idea.

CONCLUSIONS

A conclusion offers you the final chance to reinforce your ideas and move your readers. This is where you want to compress your discussion into one lasting emotional or intellectual package. This package should

- reinforce main ideas
- clinch and cinch your discussion
- raise implications for further consideration

Final Sentences

Final sentences are often, therefore, aphoristic reflections on the thesis. A paper on corporate greed and environmental abuse, for example, might end with the saying of the Cree elder Lone Wolf: "Only when the last tree has died and the last river has been poisoned and the last fish has been caught will we realize we cannot eat money." In some cases, one or two final sentences of this nature will be sufficient for your conclusion.

Exhaustive Conclusions

Beginning essayists are often encouraged in their conclusions to repeat their thesis statement as well as the main points of the preceding discussion. This approach, known as the **"exhaustive" conclusion**, resembles checking off a grocery list (tell 'em what you just told 'em). The following sample exhaustive conclusion ends a paper that has examined the controversy over the Nike company's use of Third World labour to make expensive running shoes.

Exhaustive conclusion

Corporate good will cannot be measured directly on a profit sheet. The long-term benefits of the public's perception of corporate responsibility have become a fact in the modern market, however. The controversy over the continuing claims that Nike exploits Third World workers for the construction of a recreational item that promotes the health, appearance, and perhaps hollow vanity of First World joggers may impede the conscientious consumer's willingness to purchase Nike products. Nike should work more on developing a graceful long-season strategy rather than continue to grasp for the quick, questionable win, especially as young consumers become more politically aware on the global level.

Such a conclusion summarizes the essay's previous discussion. The first three sentences do not add anything new; they consolidate the content of the paper, repeating points in the same order as before, just in language slightly different from that used in the discussion itself. The final sentence may also be repeating a point made in the body, or it might be the essayist's considered recommendation not previously mentioned (in that case, a "suggestive" strategy). Whether an exhaustive or a suggestive aspect, this last sentence attempts to impress upon the reader a need for corporate change. An important part of this final sentence's rhetorical strategy is its use of a sports metaphor (the "long season" as opposed to the "questionable win") to drive home an ethical distinction. The conclusion should complete the main strategies of your paper: unity of method must be strong at this important, final point.

A weakness of the exhaustive conclusion is that it can seem predictable and tedious; it may also lull you into using too much of your earlier wording. Like a canoe, an essay should try to stay in constant motion. Even in the conclusion, where you must engage in a certain amount of backward reflection, you need to keep moving forward as well.

Suggestive Conclusions

In contrast to the exhaustive approach, the **"suggestive" conclusion** spends less time revisiting past ground and gives more attention to implications for the reader's further consideration. This strategy assumes that if your discussion has been spirited, then your main points have already been made; it simply remains to gather them briefly together for parting resonance and future consideration. The following suggestive conclusion completes an essay that has discussed three of Wayne Gretzky's contributions to the sport of hockey (as opposed to the business of hockey).

Suggestive conclusion

Gretzky's presence in hockey not only introduced more complicated and unpredictable passing strategies, intensified team play directly in front of the net, and reconceptualized the offensive player as a trickster rather than as only a power-skater and power-shooter. His curious habit of suddenly stopping behind the opposing net to survey the scene also proved to be more than a crowd-pleasing showboat gesture. Gretzky in his "office" (behind the opposing net) gave his teammates a sudden wealth of opportunities to evade defenders and position themselves for a pass in front of the net. This recurrent positioning strategy momentarily allowed Gretzky, as a lone player, to set the pace of the entire action at will. Most importantly, Gretzky in his office also demonstrated that hockey can be strategically and psychologically closer to chess than anyone before his appearance was probably willing to believe.

The conclusion's first sentence, its topic sentence, summarizes the three main points of the previous discussion. Now that the entire essay has been cinched, the writer goes on to probe further into those points, thus introducing a fourth point: that Gretzky revolutionized the game with a previously unimagined cerebral style of play. The claim that Gretzky transformed an entire sport is certainly large enough in its suggestive implications to close the whole discussion. The last sentence asserting large psychological implications to Gretzky's style of play will probably continue to resonate with the reader after she or he has finished the essay.

In most cases, your conclusions will draw upon both the exhaustive and the suggestive models. Some instructors prefer very brief conclusions of simply one or two sentences. Others may expect a full exhaustive recapitulation. Ask your instructor about his or her expectations for what a conclusion should or should not attempt.

PRACTICE

Return to the reading selections you have worked with previously in this chapter in relation to various aspects of essay structure. Identify the conclusion of each se- lection. Is the conclusion mostly exhaustive or sug- gestive? Explain. Consult classmates and your instruc- tor for comments on your perceptions.

ESSAY TOPICS

In Chapter 2, "Reviewing the Basics," we suggest that pieces of writing can usually be categorized into one of three broad types: personal, expository, or persuasive. The following topic choices also reflect this basic divi- sion. A well-rounded writer should be able to write successfully in all three categories.

Review our advice in the previous section on the direct-list thesis statement and our advice in this sec- tion on outlining your essay before writing a complete draft. This chapter also suggests ways to ensure your discussion is properly introduced, supported, con- cluded, and tied together.

Personal Essays

For any of the following personal topics, read Chapter 5 carefully, "The Personal Essay."

1. Describe a personal experience that resulted in a sig- nificant change (such as receiving a tattoo or otherwise altering your appearance; undergoing an operation; giv- ing birth; having an important dream; meeting an im- portant person; reading an important book; going on a particular trip; making a major move). Indicate why this experience was so significant. (See "Narration" (p. 327) and "Cause-Effect" (Chapter 6, p. 346); see model es- says employing these rhetorical methods.)

2. Describe a particular place that has special mean- ing for you, or describe a particular person who has played an important role in your life. (Read "Description" (p. 330); see model descriptive es- says.)

3. Discuss the most important decision you have ever made. Explain why it has been so significant. (Read "Cause-Effect" (Chapter 6, p. 346); see model cause-effect essays.)

4. Identify an important goal you are currently pur- suing or wish to pursue. Discuss this goal ac- cording to *just one* of the following five possible methods:

a) Explain the importance of this goal by stress- ing the effects that will result from it. (See "Cause-Effect" (Chapter 6, p. 346); see model cause-effect essays.)

b) Discuss three or four characteristics that will be required of you to achieve the goal. (See "Classification-Division" (Chapter 6, p. 338); see model classification essays.)

c) Describe a certain process that will be re- quired to achieve the goal. (See "Descriptive Analysis and Directional Process" (Chapter 6, p. 355); see model directional process es- says.)

d) Describe what caused you to have this par- ticular goal. (See "Cause-Effect" (Chapter 6, p. 346); see model cause-effect essays.)

e) Compare this goal to another goal you used to have. Explain why you prefer one goal to the other, or explain what is significant about each. (See "Comparison-Contrast" (Chapter 6, p. 349); see model comparison-contrast essays.)

Expository Essays

We recommend you use third person for the following expository topics (see Chapter 6, "Exposition").

5. Describe an important cultural subject. This might be a piece of clothing, an adornment, a ceremo- nial article, a building or structure, an artistic cre- ation, an oral story, a written text, or a ceremony or ritual. Demonstrate the significance of this sub- ject. (See "Description" (p. 330) and "Cause- Effect" (Chapter 6, p. 346); see model essays using these two rhetorical methods.)

6. Define what it means to be Canadian. You may wish to approach this discussion by classifying your definition according to three or four aspects. (See "Definition" (Chapter 6, p. 364) and per- haps "Classification-Division" (Chapter 6, p. 338); see model essays employing these rhetorical methods.)

7. Define the meaning of a particular ideology; for example, liberalism, feminism, environmentalism, etc. You may wish to approach this discussion by classifying your definition according to three or four aspects. (See "Definition" (Chapter 6, p. 364) and perhaps "Classification-Division" (Chapter 6, p. 338); see model essays employing these rhetorical methods.)

8. Identify and describe the ideal characteristics of a specific professional; for example, a teacher, salesperson, police officer, social worker, nurse, doctor, mechanic, academic, engineer, or hockey player. Consider listing three or four major qualities or characteristics required of the profession. (See "Classification-Division" (Chapter 6, p. 338) and perhaps "Definition" (Chapter 6, p. 364); see model essays employing these rhetorical methods.)

9. Identify the most important aspect of your heritage. Define and illustrate this aspect for those who may not be familiar with your heritage. Limited use of first person will be appropriate for this essay. (See "Definition" (Chapter 6, p. 364) as well as "Description" (p. 330); see model essays using these methods.)

10. Describe someone you regard as an important Canadian. Give at least three major achievements of this person. (See "Description" (p. 330) as well as "Classification-Division" (Chapter 6, p. 338); see model essays employing these rhetorical methods.)

11. Identify what you most like about Canada and what you most dislike about it. Elaborate sufficiently on these two sides. Weighing one against the other, what is your overall feeling about Canada? (See "Comparison-Contrast" (Chapter 6, p. 349); see model essays using this method.)

12. Describe your favourite activity in such a way as to illustrate its basics and to encourage those unfamiliar with this activity to give it a try. For this essay, you may find that second person is the best point of view, with some first person in appropriate places. (See "Descriptive Analysis and Directional Process" (Chapter 6, p. 355), and model essays using this rhetorical method.)

13. Trace the history of a particular community, group, or family over the past three generations. (See "Descriptive Analysis and Directional Process" (Chapter 6, p. 355), and model essays using this method.)

14. The novel *A Tale of Two Cities* by English writer Charles Dickens begins "It was the best of times, it was the worst of times . . ." Dickens's story is set in revolutionary France in 1789. Could the same thing be said of today: do we live in the best of times and the worst of times? Give examples to support both parts of the description, and conclude with possibilities and recommendations for our future. (See "Descriptive Analysis and Directional Process" (Chapter 6, p. 355), "Comparison-Contrast" (Chapter 6, p. 349), and "Cause-Effect" (Chapter 6, p. 346); see model essays employing these methods.)

15. Briefly describe a problem that has been affecting a particular organization, program, or operation (a sports team, an office, a committee, a company). This should be a situation you know from personal observation and/or experience. Be sure to fictionalize all names; alter details sufficiently to maintain anonymity of the group and its members. Identify the cause or causes of the problem and suggest solutions. (See "Descriptive Analysis and Directional Process" (Chapter 6, p. 355) and "Cause-Effect" (Chapter 6, p. 346); see model essays using these methods.)

Argumentation Essays

We recommend third person for these topics, though some first person may be effective in certain cases. For help with the following, see "Argumentation" (Chapter 7, p. 367), as well as model essays using an argumentative method.

16. Mary Shelley's fictional Dr. Frankenstein undertook a career in science, determined to achieve greatness. However, his drive for progress—to overcome death—resulted in misery. Is science going too far today? Develop your answer using sources such as your field of work or study, other forms of personal experience with the topic, and information you recollect from books, the media, etc. You may wish to concentrate on one particular field (medicine, genetics, information technology), and even on one particular aspect of that field. (For discussion of this topic, see "The Doomsday Machines" by John Markoff (p. 135).)

17. What are the arguments for and against legalized gambling? Which argument do you favour and why?

18. People who get tattoos are basically insecure. Respond to this opinion.

19. Should Canadian law recognize rights of the fetus? Why or why not?

20. Should Canada change its current laws on gun control? Why or why not?

✔ CHECKLIST of Steps to a Successful Essay

1. Spend at least one-quarter of your total time for this essay in pre-writing activities—experiment to find the ones that work best for you.

2. Clarify your purpose. Decide on your audience. Discover your tone.

3. If you need to research your topic, follow the recommended steps for developing research papers.

4. In the "pre-writing" phase, you may choose to write a preliminary, incomplete draft and/or begin a tentative outline and direct-list thesis.

5. Begin writing more formally. Spend at least one-half of your total time for the essay in writing at least two complete drafts.

6. Finalize a direct-list thesis and an outline of body paragraphs with good conceptual links to the thesis. Apply an appropriate principle of organization, such as climactic structure.

7. Be sure your body paragraphs contain solid supporting details and sufficient linking devices.

8. Once you have completed the first draft, revise your introduction and conclusion to improve your essay's coherence and account for any changes that might have occurred in the body.

9. Write a second complete draft, taking special care to improve clarity, coherence, and supporting details.

10. Spend at least one-quarter of the time set aside for your essay on proofreading and revising. Refer to the checklists "Fifteen Common Errors" and "Twelve Logical Fallacies" (inside front cover) to correct the most common structural, stylistic, and mechanical errors. Check your introduction and conclusion for consistency.

11. Ensure your essay has an effective title, one that conveys the topic, tone, and controlling idea of your essay.

12. Check with your instructor to be sure you follow the required format. Most essays should be double-spaced, with 1-inch margins, and printed or written on one side of the pages only. Your instructor may want you to follow a specific cover-page format as well. Any citations and references should follow prescribed MLA or APA guidelines, or whichever guidelines pertain to your academic field.

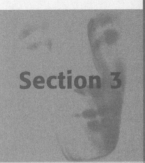

Section 3

Types of Writing

Chapter 5
The Personal Essay

Depending on your field of study, your academic assignments will likely require a *non-personal* style. So why study the personal essay? There are at least three good reasons for giving some attention to first-person voice and reflection on your life as you prepare for your career.

1. Most work on the job entails effective informal communication. The ability to speak and write purposefully in your own natural voice could prove as valuable to your employer as the ability to write a formal report. Well over half of important work-related communication is oral, and much of that is informal.

2. Mastering the personal essay takes you a step closer to becoming a well-rounded writer. Versatility counts in writing as it does in other disciplines. Musicians adept at bluegrass, rock, and country are likely to employ enriching experience and balance in each separate form as well as in blended idioms. As humans we learn and think a great deal through comparisons. To better apply *im*personal styles, we need to have some experience with personal ones.

3. The personal essay can be an excellent starting point in developing the habit of critical thinking. George Orwell's classic essay "Shooting an Elephant," for example, brings author and reader to grips with colonialism. All of the personal essays in Section One of the *Reader* contain a certain component of critical thinking. Indeed, there is an old Sufi belief that until you tell the story of your life, simply and concisely, you are not ready to progress further in knowledge and understanding. This view holds that life is holistic; the academic and personal sides of existence cannot and should not be totally severed. Accordingly, fields such as anthropology, ethology, and women's studies often use the first person as a vehicle for academic and critical expression. Vigorous debate continues over the value of employing this device. In any case, we suggest that having command of your own personal voice grounds you as a writer, connects you with yourself and the greatest degree of truth. You can then modify that natural voice to suit various different writing occasions.

PRACTICE

- List what you believe are the arguments against the use of the first person in academic writing.
- List the arguments in favour of first person as an instrument of personal accountability.

- Discuss various sides of this debate with your classmates.

DEFINING THE PERSONAL ESSAY

In the personal essay, the thesis, whether explicit or implicit, expresses a point of view on a matter of life experience important to the writer. This fact and the use of the first person places the personal essay within the expressive category outlined in Chapter 2, "Reviewing the Basics."

A wide spectrum of styles can be found in the personal essay, with moods ranging from light and humorous to profoundly solemn. The writer does not necessarily focus directly or at length on the self. A personal essay might concern something observed, with someone other than the writer as the main subject.

 PRACTICE

Arrange with two or more classmates to read at least two of the following essays from the *Reader*:

- "Brownie" by Roger Fouts (p. 12)
- "Franken-Frogs and the Mushroom Bear" by Thomas LaBrie (p. 33)
- "The King and I" by Michel Tremblay (p. 37)

- "The Hockey Sweater" by Roch Carrier (p. 51)
- "A Midwife in Rankin Inlet" by Gisela Becker (p. 72)

For each, discuss the dominant style. Identify examples of organization, paragraphing, sentence structure, and literary technique that convey voice and tone.

The personal essay has **three major impulses**:

- narration
- description
- reflection

NARRATION

Narration simply means telling a story, recounting events in chronological order. You need not be a professional novelist to benefit from the skills of a storyteller. For example, you may need these skills to begin a speech, an essay, or an article. Narrative techniques are also required in occurrence reports, though often the author uses detached third-person point of view in such cases. Regardless of the viewpoint used to tell a story, good narration relies on three characteristics:

- defining and organizing parts
- proportioning and linking parts
- expressing a sense of causality

Defining and Organizing Parts

Your story should consist of a *manageable* number of discrete sections such as expository subtopics; descriptions; summaries of stages, people, and events; or scenes of action and dialogue (reported speech enclosed within quotation marks). You need to define for yourself exactly what these parts are before you produce a final draft of your essay.

PREPARATION

Read Roch Carrier's "The Hockey Sweater" (p. 51). Define the separate sections of this fictional memoir and the types of writing techniques used in each sec- tion. What principle of organization has been used to structure these sections?

Roch Carrier has clearly conceptualized three main sections to his memoir: (1) an introductory section of background information to "set the stage"; (2) the first half of his story; and (3) the second half of his story. These broad sections can in turn be broken down into finer parts.

Part one comprises three paragraphs. The first paragraph tells, in an expository manner, about the "winters of my childhood." They were "long," and they consisted of school, church, and the skating rink. The first two places merely served the third "real" place—the rink. The rink was important above all because that was where the children became Maurice Richard. The second introductory paragraph carries on with the subject of Maurice Richard, supplying details of how the boys emulated their hero. The third paragraph narrows the subject further to describe how the boys pursued this emulation on the rink. Part one, then, works like a funnel, moving from a broad, general orientation to increasingly specific concerns. But even in paragraph three, Carrier still refers to the way things were in general, not to one particular day.

He takes us into the second part of his memoir with the opening of paragraph four: "one day." Now we enter the story proper, a story based entirely around the Toronto Maple Leafs sweater. Everything in the narration either will describe why the sweater appeared in his life or what happened as a result. First, he deals with the *whys*. In paragraph 4, he tells us that his Montreal Canadiens sweater was becoming too small and wearing out, and he summarizes the character of his mother. Much humour arises from the discord between the boy's objectives and those of his mother. All he wants is that his old Canadiens sweater last forever. She doesn't want her son to look poor, and she is too proud to buy a new sweater locally. So she orders a new one through the fashionable big department store, Eaton's.

Carrier now moves his story along by chronological cause and effect. Because his mother writes to the store, the store, in paragraph 5, replies by sending a sweater. This creates the great crisis of the memoir: Mme. Carrier, for her own practical reasons, expects her boy to wear the new sweater, even though it bears the notorious Maple Leaf. At this most intense moment, Carrier uses scene, action, and dialogue—a good way to convey crucial material. Not too much speech is recorded, so the lines of dialogue that are reported are very important. In the confrontation with her son, for example, Mme. Carrier says, "You aren't Maurice Richard." This one line resonates deeply because in its essence the story is concerned with boyhood fantasy and illusion. This scene, bringing part two of the memoir to a climax, concludes with the boy forced to wear the Maple Leafs sweater.

Part three is signalled by the transitional word "so": "So I was obliged to wear the Maple Leafs sweater. When I arrived on the rink . . ." Thus the author leads us into the final extended scene of his memoir. The boy's captain, clearly biased against the detested Toronto sweater, keeps the boy from playing. When young Carrier at last jumps onto the ice, he is penalized for too many men. He breaks his stick in frustration, and ironically the vicar assumes the boy has acted out the pride of nonconformity. The memoir ends with the amusing tag of the boy sent to church to pray for forgiveness; his actual prayer is for moths to destroy the alien sweater.

In sum, the memoir consists of a three-paragraph introduction, another long paragraph describing the decline of the Canadiens sweater, the character of the mother and her consequent decision (the inciting incident), some 10 paragraphs of action and dialogue when the Leafs sweater arrives, and a final scene of two paragraphs when the boy wears his new sweater to the rink. In each of the two major scenes, the boy's objectives are clear. In the first scene, his objective is to avoid wearing the Leafs sweater. In the second scene, his objective is to get on the ice. Focus on one main character with one clear objective is a good way to make scenes powerful. Through Carrier's control of specific scenes, we gain a touching portrait of a child's relative powerlessness before time, change, and adults.

Proportioning and Linking Parts

The charm which this memoir holds for so many readers rises in large measure through the author's craft. Carrier knows how long to spend sketching in the background, what to say, and what to leave out. He is careful not to pack in more information than three pages can contain, not to wander into tempting but digressive subplots. Whether to summarize information or to show it directly through scene and action is a major decision. Balance and variation are key principles. The writer needs to "stay ahead" of the reader—to maintain suspense, yet not to take so long propelling the story that the reader loses interest. Like all good narrative, Carrier's memoir consists of a certain amount of summary and a certain amount of direct action. Two scenes, one right after the other, are probably as much direct action as he would present before returning to further summary and exposition.

Links between the sections are simple yet essential, words such as "so," "when," and "one day." In the opening expository section, Maurice Richard ends one paragraph and, logically, becomes the main topic of the next two. Once the story proper begins, the sections are organized according to chronology, one condition occurring *as a result of* a previous action.

Expressing a Sense of Causality

We have already noted how material in "The Hockey Sweater" has been organized according to logical cause-and-effect relationships. Mme. Carrier orders a new sweater *because* the old one is worn out and *because* she cares what people think. The boy resists wearing the new sweater *because* all the boys idolize the Montreal Canadiens. He feels shame and persecution *because* his mother wins the disagreement over his wearing the sweater. He is treated unfairly by the team captain *because* of bias against the sweater, and so on. The nature of narrative plot to emphasize causes and effects compels readers to ponder the deeper meaning of the story. Why do certain things happen? What possible social, political, economic, psychological, or spiritual factors are at play? Carrier offers no explicit answers to such questions in his memoir, yet he provokes us to think beyond the issues of one boyhood to the history of Quebec and its unresolved future with English Canada.

DESCRIPTION

Description in all writing means the organized observation of significant detail. In expressive writing, this detail has two main features:

- appeal to the five senses
- service of a dominant impression

Appeal to the Five Senses

There could be many different correct answers to the following exercise. Visual images abound in Carrier's memoir. Let's take the blue-and-white Maple Leafs sweater as an appeal to sight. Sound comes in for the first time with reference to the "tranquility of God," the silence of the church. It occurs again when the referee blows his whistle. Smell and touch are both evoked, if indirectly, by the image of the hair

✒ PRACTICE

Does Carrier appeal to all five senses in his descriptions? Find five examples of language that evoke sight, sound, smell, taste, and touch.

glue. Touch enters again with the detail of the mother smoothing down the creases in the new sweater. Taste is not especially present in this memoir, though we might imagine the enjoyable taste of the blue-and-white sweater for moths, as the sweater likely contained a good portion of wool at that time. Note that all these sensuous details are precise. Student writers sometimes think that descriptive writing calls for stock, general phrases such as "a beautiful blanket of snow." But notice how such phrases are not used by Carrier or by any of the descriptive models in this book. Good description puts emphasis on the close observation of unique characteristics. Contrary to common belief, nouns and verbs matter more than adjectives and adverbs. We see this demonstrated in the following example of dominant impression.

Service of a Dominant Impression

Dominant impression refers to the central quality or characteristic created by a particular passage of description, or indeed, by an entire work. Novelists highly noted for their descriptive passages provide ample illustrations of this. Here, for example, is a passage from Charles Dickens's *The Mystery of Edwin Drood*:

> Not only is the day waning, but the year. The low sun is fiery and yet cold behind the monastery ruin, and the Virginia creeper on the Cathedral wall has showered half its deep-red leaves down on the pavement. There has been rain this afternoon, and a wintry shudder goes among the little pools on the cracked uneven flagstones, and through the giant elm trees as they shed a gust of tears. Their fallen leaves lie strewn thickly about. Some of these leaves, in a timid rush, seek sanctuary within the low arched Cathedral door; but two men coming out resist them and cast them forth again with their feet; this done, one of the two locks the door with a goodly key, and the other flits away with a folio music book.

At this point in his story, Dickens wishes to convey the suspicion of a murder. The waning of the day and season, the fallen leaves, the reds, the "uneven" flagstones, the ruined monastery, the association of one of the men with a bird (Dickens is continuing a reference to rooks—carrion birds), the rain and the cold gusts of wind that affect the "little" pools as well as the "giant" trees all contribute to a mood that is not only melancholic but, in this context, suggestive of death. One dominant impression comes through. There are no more than 15 adjectives here, to some 30 nouns. The accuracy and precision of the nouns convey much of the impression: not just a vine but a "Virginia creeper" (with a nuance of Satan creeping); not just a book but a "folio music book." The verb "flits" describes a birdlike action with no need for adjectives or adverbs.

Regarding structure, we may note how logically organized is the description. Dickens begins with a "wide angle" taking in the full scene of the cathedral, ruined monastery, and horizon. He then moves in to the creepers on the walls and follows these down, echoing the movement of the falling leaves, to the pavement. With the "shudder," he returns us to a wider awareness, encompassing the elms, yet keeps the focus downward, on the fallen leaves. The wind carries some of these leaves toward the opening door of the cathedral, thus connecting his dominant impression with the two men who emerge, one of whom, we suspect, in ironic contrast to the religious setting, is the murderer. Not all of us can animate descriptions with the magic and symbolism of Dickens, yet we can learn from such descriptions the effect of careful order, movement, and attention to specific telling detail.

What might we suggest is the dominant impression of "The Hockey Sweater"? As captured so well in the National Film Board's animated film of this memoir, the dominant impression is one of humorous conformity—all the boys dressing, acting, and thinking the same way, all aspiring to be their idol, Maurice Richard.

As you can see, description and narration are hardly separable. Rarely do we have description without some sense of story or vice versa.

REFLECTION

Similarly, we cannot read a narration or a description without sensing that through these words the writer is reflecting on some larger theme, issue, or concern. Your personal essay, however implicit its meaning, should have a thesis. When the personal essay addresses thematic ideas explicitly, the work becomes more overtly reflective. Here is the opening paragraph of student Mark Radford's personal reflection "Different Worlds":

> The world is changing rapidly. When I think about the way my father grew up, compared to the way I grew up and the way my son is growing up now, I'm amazed by the differences. Changes are all around us every day, some seemingly significant and some not, but it isn't until you consciously compare certain things over a number of years that the significance is truly revealed. The differences between my childhood and my son's are not as fundamental as the differences between my father's and mine, but they are still significant.

Radford clearly announces that he will be comparing his three subjects in order to reach a new understanding of the fundamental distinctions between their respective generations.

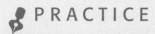 PRACTICE

Read Radford's essay (p. 43). Then review our discussion of "Comparison-Contrast" structure in Chapter 6 (p. 349) and "Comparative Analysis" in Chapter 10 (p. 417). Identify how Radford uses comparative structures to shape and propel his reflection.

Another good example of the reflective personal essay is Willard Dudley's "Causes of Procrastination" in Chapter 4 (p. 303). In that essay, we find a complete, explicit thesis statement, followed by body paragraphs telling us about each cause of his procrastination. The causes, all abstract nouns, stress ideas rather than concrete, sensuous experience. Dudley's short essay, in fact, tells us less about the details of his life and more about his inner contemplation. Because the reflective approach has a philosophical tone, the essay may seem almost *impersonal*, akin to a detached essay of analysis.

Example of a Personal Essay of Reflection

Is life getting better or worse? Everyone has his or her own answer and rationale. In the following memoir, Joyce Miller implies her view of changes that have affected rural southern Ontario over the past 40 years. A speech consultant and theatre director, Miller wrote "The Oral Presentation," Chapter 14, in this book.

Sample Essay Reflection

Night Fades
Joyce Miller

. . . and men loved darkness rather than light, because their deeds were evil. For everyone that doeth evil hateth the light, neither cometh to the light, lest his deeds be reproved.

—John 3: 29–30

1   Lying in my bedroom, I read and reread that passage. And my child's mind was troubled. Why did God say that? It seemed to me that bad things happened in the day, while the darkness was a time of mystery and delight: magical diamond stars in the velvet sky, little scurrying creatures, hectic bats, soft and silent owls.

2   That was the night to me, as I grew up in rural southern Ontario in the 1960s. The darkness gave night its purity and mystery. The darkness was essential for the safety of those who dwelt in it. Nightmares were only imaginary. Day ones were real. Was there something wrong with me for thinking that way?

3   Night was when the tooth fairy came, when mysterious gifts appeared after my dad had been to a convention or a bowling tournament. Night was when my mom would wake us up to have hoagies my dad had bought on his way home when his shift ended at 10 p.m. If you had asked me then, I would have said it was 2 a.m. In our family, we got our Christmas stockings in the blackness of Christmas Eve night. I was probably four or five the first year my brother shone a flashlight in my eyes to wake me up for my initiation into this rite. We had to be absolutely silent so as not to wake Mom and Dad, and we put on dressing gowns (the only night of the year we wore them) in order to sneak downstairs and open the candy and little gifts in our

stockings. A year came when my little sister and I waited and waited for our older sister to get back from her date and come to wake us up. Finally the sky began to lighten and we went down on our own. She and her boyfriend were asleep on the couch. She roused a little as we got our stockings and went back up to our room.

4   One Halloween night real magic happened. I slept through most of it, although I got to see the incarnation. My mom was awakened in the night by the sound of rustling and banging in my older sister's room. She assumed it was Margaret getting in from another late date and went back to sleep. In the morning she followed a trail of ashes and soot (a sure sign of magic, if you know the Christmas poem) up the stairs, down the hall, and into my sister's room. Her bed was still empty, but the room was occupied. A great horned owl stared from the headboard. It was perfectly calm (though probably muddled) as Marilyn and I were called in to see it before Dad scooped it up with a fishing net and released it. The huge wings spread, it drifted up to a tree and perched blinking before heading off in the brightness. Following the trail of clues like a family of Sherlock Holmeses, we deduced that the owl had fallen down the chimney. I have since discovered that owls often perch on chimneys for warmth. Often, they are lulled asleep by the heat and fall in. The real magic was that the grate was open and the coals were dead when our owl fell.

5   Like most country kids, when I got older I became a 4H'er. In the winter, it was dark by the time I got home from school, ate supper, and got out to feed my rabbits. The glow of the heat bulb made the winter rabbit house nearly as magical as the crystalline night. It felt warm and cozy even though it was only marginally warmer than outdoors. Steam rose from the warm water I poured out for the rabbits, who drank thirstily before it froze. A carrot apiece provided the rest of their fluid for the day.

6   One night, a tiny visitor was waiting. A little Disney-Bambi creature with a fawn-beige back, white belly, and huge eyes. Unlike mice I had seen in the rabbit house before, it did not flash away. It stood up on its little haunches and regarded me thoughtfully. My 12-year-old heart melted and the deermouse was a friend for the rest of the winter. When spring came it was light at rabbit-feeding time, and I never saw it again.

7   Each year the night was a little less black. Each year the night horizon glowed an orange grey. Each year the city moved a little closer to my home and each year I grew a little more afraid. In school I learned that southern Ontario would one day be called a "polyglot megalopolis," where the small towns chained city to city with no country in between, and the entire Great Lakes basin would be urban. On the horizon, fluorescent street lights, store lights, sign lights faded the magic velvet and the stars grew dimmer.

8   Our road, the "Seven Hills Road," was widened and the valleys filled in. Too many accidents had occurred as a result of joyriders in the hills. Mature oak trees were cut down from one side of the road to accommodate the widening. A born tree-hugger, I guess, I hugged each one, thanked it, and said goodbye before the crews moved in.

9   I began to have a recurring nightmare that the woods and fields around my house would be filled with houses. All my secret places would be filled with bulldozers, the "elephant trees" (beeches) whose elastic branches we rode like horses would be cut down, the swamp where the foxes hid would be filled in.

10   When I was 13, we moved into a little village. I staged a months-long protest against the move, but was also secretly glad, because I wouldn't have to watch the changes. When I grew up and moved into Toronto, I was happy again to be insulated from what was going on. I could grumble about Mississauga (which, by the way, was a little village when my best friend's father was born there) without needing to watch its expansion. The city had a different kind of night, a new kind of magic, and I only had to think about the "megalopolis" when I rode the Greyhound home. So I took the train instead, which still passes through picturesque farmland, though the signs of construction are becoming more obvious.

11   Now I live in Edmonton, and only get back once or twice a year for a few days' visit. Recently I drove past my childhood home. In the horse field was a house. In the woods, another house. In the field where deer grazed at dusk, a house. Across the road, where my Dad had rescued a newborn calf from the swamp, another. In neighbour Ernie's field, where I'd tasted green wheat, two more. I had awakened. It was light. I could see.

12   Yet I realize I am hypocritical. My family didn't farm (although my grandpa and uncles did). We had no reason to live in the country other than the love of it. As with these people. They are there because they want to escape the city, they love the country, they want the peace of it. And so we are destroying it.

13   And so I love the night. The bulldozers don't work then. The peace returns. And there's no more need for my nightmare.

Focus Questions

1. How is Miller's opening quotation an appropriate signal of the tone and purpose that follow?
2. What is the ratio of narration and description to reflection in this essay?
3. What is the thesis? Is it explicit or implicit?

For more sample student essays using narration, description, and reflection, visit the Introductory Composition cover page of the Athabasca University's English 255 course at <**www.athabascau.ca/courses/engl/255/**>. See "Sample Essays" under "Supplementary Resources."

ESSAY TOPICS

1. What is the most important benefit you have gained from your relationship with a particular sibling? Use examples to illustrate.
2. Describe how you have felt aided by a particular dream you have had.
3. Describe a personal trip or expedition that took an unexpected turn.
4. Reflect on the meaning of relationships, using personal examples.
5. Reflect on a significant change you have seen to your birthplace and childhood home.
6. Describe an adventure you had after agreeing to go along with a plan against your initial judgment, or when someone else went along with a plan of yours against his or her initial judgment.

Note: See the end of Chapter 4 (p. 322) for additional topics for personal essays.

Chapter 6
Exposition

Chances are that most of your writing for academic purposes will be expository. This is because at the undergraduate level, writing serves as a learning tool: you write about something in order to understand it yourself. You will also find the majority of your course textbooks are expository, that is, they inform you on some topic.

EXPOSITION DEFINED

As the word suggests, expository writing informs. Its primary purpose is to clarify a subject rather than express the voice of the writer or build an argument. Traditionally, exposition has been defined as a "neutral," "impartial," or "objective" stance, with emphasis on accurate facts and unbiased observation or an exploration of how those facts relate to each other and an overall meaning.

VARIATIONS AND MIXTURES

On the other hand, expository essays *may* use a personal approach by directly discussing the writer's relationship to the subject. Within informal forums, such as news and specialty magazines, a personal approach can help interest the reader in the subject. For instance, travel writing, sometimes viewed as its own genre, reflects a balance of personal and expository writing. The reflection "Je Me Souviens" (p. 54) is another example of combining personal and expository writing.

    Whether you explore exposition in part through the personal essay or entirely through the more traditional academic approach will be up to you and your instructor. In this chapter, we focus on the more dominant, non-personal expository essay; however, we include samples of both personal and impersonal expository writing.

FEATURES OF EXPOSITION

In Chapter 8 we provide instruction on writing the summary, an exercise in observation, accuracy, and concision. Several important features of the summary very much apply to good expository writing:

- third-person point of view
- impartial tone
- accuracy
- thorough knowledge of the topic
- conciseness
- use of your own words, aside from key technical labels
- attention to a main issue and meaningful connections

Supporting Details as Paramount

Unlike the summary, the expository essay *does* include details; it is imperative, in fact, that all important points or aspects be elaborated through appropriate details, whether data from first- and secondhand studies, statements by reputable sources, or analogies and other necessary descriptive techniques. The type of supporting detail required, and the organization of that detail, will depend on the precise nature of your essay. As with any essay, you will shape a standard opening and thesis statement, a body elaborating upon the thesis, and a conclusion.

PATTERNS (METHODS) OF EXPOSITION

Within the body you will expand on your thesis according to one or more common patterns of organization:

- classification-division
- example
- cause-effect
- comparison-contrast
- descriptive analysis and directional process
- definition

Following are brief illustrations and definitions of these six common patterns of support. Learning to recognize these patterns will improve your awareness as a reader as well as your organizational and explicative skills as a writer.

Classification-Division

There is a joke about an artist who presents his latest artwork entitled "Cow Eating Grass." When the artist turns on his computer, the screen remains blank. "Where is the grass?" asks his agent. The artist explains that the cow ate it all. "Where is the cow?" The grass was all gone, so she left. We present classification-division as the first of the expository patterns because, in a sense, it is the operating system needed to enable basic shapes and separations to appear. Things must be categorized according to their fundamental identities before we can see them, and thus think further about their relationships and meanings. Through division, we realize the possibility of deciding how to group things together.

The following partial paragraph about Canada's Aboriginal peoples at the time of European contact is taken from Olive Dickason's *Canada's First Nations*:

> These people spoke about fifty languages that have been classified into twelve families, of which six were exclusive to present-day British Columbia. By far the most widespread geographically were those within the Algonkian group, spread from the Rocky Mountains to the Atlantic and along the coast of the Arctic to Cape Fear; Cree and Inuktitut had the widest geographical ranges. This accords with Roger's hypothesis, that by the proto-historical period areas that were once glaciated (most of Canada and a portion of the northern United States) had fewer languages than areas that had been unglaciated. While Canada was completely covered with ice during the last glaciation, except for parts of the Yukon and some adjacent regions, the strip along the Pacific coast was freed very early. According to Roger's calculations, once-glaciated areas averaged eighteen languages per million square miles, and unglaciated regions 52.4 languages per million square miles (2,590,000 square kilometres) . . . . (64–66)

As you can see, the word "classified" appears in the topic sentence of this paragraph. Dickason reflects the work of linguists, specialists who study language patterns and group languages into categories according to specific shared elements versus distinctions from languages in other categories. The topic sentence identifies a division of 50 different languages, each of which can be classified into one of 12 families. Students of biology will recognize a clear parallel to that science's method of grouping plants or animals according to a "family tree." This hierarchy descends from class to order to family to subfamily to genus and finally to species and even subspecies. Behind such divisions into subordinate groupings stands the idea of identifying meaningful elements, in order to enable our understanding more about the nature of things. All of the items being subdivided share the same fundamental characteristics as every other member of the overall (or highest) category. At the level of the largest class, the fundamental characteristics are very basic and general, for example, communication by vocal signs in language studies or warm-bloodedness in the study of animals. Various members then subdivide further into their own subordinate groupings according to shared differences, such as grammatical patterns or having four legs.

Dickason's paragraph also includes geographical divisions to provide further information about various language groupings. Half of Canada's 12 language families thrived in what is now British Columbia, a warm region. Families and languages in the north are less numerous, presumably because colder weather promoted nomadic patterns and restricted language diversification. This attention to one aspect of causality illustrates how rhetorical patterns complement or reinforce each other. It is rare that a paragraph or longer passage of text focuses exclusively on only one pattern or method of organization; it is equally rare to find a paragraph or section of text that does not organize itself around one of the six basic patterns we introduce under the heading "Exposition." The paragraph above emphasizes classification of languages and geography, with cause-effect insight applied to help complete important details.

In the preceding chapters of the *Rhetoric* you may have examined some examples of classification as a pattern already. Willard Dudley's reflective essay "Causes of Procrastination" in Chapter 4 identifies three causes of his problem. Classification-division goes further in "Life in the Stopwatch Lane," an analytical essay in Chapter 8, "The Summary," in which Amy Willard Cross discusses the numerous subdivisions of time among the perpetually busy (see "Identifying and Explaining an Excerpt," also in Chapter 8, p. 398). Pat Deiter-McArthur's "Saskatchewan's Indian People—Five Generations" (p. 87) provides another extended example of classification-division.

✒ PRACTICE

Review the *Reader* for examples of classification-division. Find at least three paragraphs, passages, or complete selections in which this pattern dominates. Describe the pattern in each as precisely as you can. *How* do the examples you have chosen apply this pattern? Share your findings with classmates and see whether you agree with their findings. Ask your instructor to clarify any uncertainties and differing interpretations.

Sample Thesis Statements Using Classification-Division

Many student essays may be successfully written according to exposition by classification-division. In Chapter 2, we recommend that you conclude your introductory paragraph with your thesis statement, giving both your point of view on the topic and your specific reasons for this view. Here are some sample thesis sentences that make various uses of classification-division:

Alberta presents a remarkable range and diversity of nature, with no less than five distinct ecological worlds existing in the one province.

[In this example, the division is spatial—different regions divided by ecology.]

Since contact with European settlers, Saskatchewan's five generations of Indian people have faced distinct challenges according to generation.

[The division is temporal—separate generations.]

Rabbi Cohen lived his life according to three principles from which he was never known to deviate: tolerance, compassion, and truth.

[The division is according to separate but related values.]

Members of the Busy Class are so insecure about a lack of time that they have divided personal time into five categories.

[The division is according to perceived function or application.]

Every food server knows the four classes of obnoxious customer: the commander, the mumbler, the sweet talker, and the raconteur.

[The division is according to behavioural attitude through a focus on speaking style.]

As you can see, classification-division leads to a very clear thesis and essay organization. The writer simply moves from subcategory to subcategory (subtopic to subtopic) according to spatial, temporal, or climactic order. In many cases, this is the simplest and surest approach to take in your expository essays. But to make this method work, you must be able to identify terms (values, functions, features) that truly share a qualitative common denominator.

Solving Three Common Problems in Classification-Division

Here are three common problems to try to avoid:
1. including too many terms
2. treating qualitatively different terms as equal, or identical terms as separate
3. forgetting that classification-division is a tool, not an end in itself

Let us now look at these three in more detail.

1. For a required paper three pages long, double-spaced, the following thesis statement is probably too ambitious:

   > Effective writing style should be coherent, concise, complete, correct, and consistent.

   By the time the writer illustrates and explains the first three values, he or she will have written three pages. The last two concepts, less central, may be left for another paper. Simply reaching beyond the limits of the assignment sometimes explains why too many classification-division terms are listed in the thesis. More commonly, using too many terms results from the following problem 2.

2. A common problem of classification-division is listing as equal subtopics terms that do not really share a proper common denominator.

   > Every food server knows the four classes of obnoxious customer: the commander, the mumbler, the sweet talker, and the vanisher.

   The error in this classification is that only the first three are distinguished by speaking style. Presumably the vanisher—who ducks out before paying the bill—could be any of the previous three. Following is a better way to word the introduction to this essay:

> Every food server knows the three obnoxious customer speaking styles and, of course, knows that worst of all customers, the one with no speaking style when it comes to paying the bill.

This error of failing to distinguish between accurate categories often underlies problem 1, above, of using too many terms.

> A good writer is aware of purpose, subject, audience, tone, and consistency.

The first three terms in this statement work together in a basic relationship: knowing his or her underlying purpose, the writer connects accordingly with the subject and audience. Tone comes about as an *effect* of the writer's assuming this stance through use of these three terms. Consistency, in turn, is a finer requirement of tone, as it should be maintained throughout. The writer of the above thesis statement would do well to remove "tone" and "consistency" from the thesis sentence entirely. These two terms can be worked into other, appropriate sections of the body. The old saying that "less is more" should guide you in writing essays based on classification-division. In short essays, try not to exceed four or five terms. Often you can consolidate two or more terms into one simple encompassing term. Try to correct the following thesis sentence:

> My father succeeded in life by following his heart, working hard, always having time to listen to another's problems, finishing every task he started, spending time with his wife and children, and keeping in shape.

In this case, the writer has equated examples and qualities, as well as failed to assign examples to the quality each illustrates. Having time for others' problems and spending time with the family exemplify following one's heart (exercising compassion). Finishing every task exemplifies perseverance. Keeping in shape exemplifies healthful living. Having reduced all of these terms into three qualities, you can now place them in an effective order. The following rewording, using climactic order, views compassion as most important quality of all and therefore places it last:

> My father succeeded in life by following three central values: hard work, health, and compassion.

The examples are reserved for the body of the essay where they elaborate whichever of the three terms they most relate to.

Along with confusing would-be partners with true equals (such as examples as values, effects as starting points), writers sometimes use two or more apparent divisions to say essentially the same thing.

Here's another example:

> Although the old house is charming inside, it is rundown outside, unevenly heated, unsightly, and misfitting among the neigbouring homes.

"Rundown outside" can be combined with "unsightly" and "misfitting among the neigbouring homes." "Unevenly heated" should be treated first, as part of the inside focus, not placed between two references to the outside. The better, revised thesis statement now reads:

Better

Although the old house is charming inside, it is unevenly heated; outside it is badly rundown.

3. Classification-division is a tool, not an end in itself. As with any pattern of organization, remember that you are using this method in the service of a higher purpose, demonstrating your thesis. Pat Deiter-McArthur describes the five generations of Indian people in order to orient her own and the reader's further thinking and action (p. 87).

Conclusion

Classification-division affects your writing any time you take pen in hand or turn on the computer to compose. Before you can explore and explain the meaning of things, you must recognize how things stand apart, yet relate to each other in groupings of common quality or function. As we have said, whether as tables of elements, orders of life, or some other schematic overview, classification-division underlies the basic content of most academic disciplines. It is, in a sense, the operating system you must have before going any further. How you explore basic content—whether through close and extended examples, comparisons, awareness of causes and/or effects, or complex definitions—leads us naturally to the remaining patterns of organization.

Example

Perhaps the most familiar comment instructors of writing place on first-year students' essays is "Good point, but now give an effective example." Examples are the bedrock of achieved, sound prose. Sometimes examples enter so significantly into an essay that they may be considered the dominant organizational pattern.

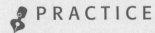 **PRACTICE**

Read George Orwell's essay "Politics and the English Language" (p. 227). Document its use of examples. What purpose do they serve?

As you will have noticed, Orwell runs examples through his essay. He wants to convince us that the language we use is full of "bad habits." His third paragraph, presenting five "representative samples" from published professors and other authors, drives home the point that bad habits *are* the norm.

Types of Supporting Detail

Supporting detail is discussed (in detail!) in Chapter 2, "Reviewing the Basics," under "Paragraphs." In a sense, all forms of supporting detail are examples (justifications, proofs) that help support your claims. As we mention elsewhere in this book, Albert Einstein once remarked that "God is in the details." Read our entire discussion of supporting details, paying special attention to the matters of "warm" and "cool" proofs, reliability, suitability, and balance.

The following essay by a student, Lorena Collins, further illustrates how a number of examples can be linked together to reinforce the writer's main point.

Sample Essay Use of Examples

Timone
Lorena Collins

1 I have had several pets share my home throughout my life, but one of the most enjoyable and most entertaining I have ever owned is a little white dog named Timone. Timone is a three-year-old Bichon Frisé I picked up from the city pound last May. As soon as I saw him, I was curious to meet him. Once I met him there was no way I could leave without him. He was so tiny, obviously undernourished, and afraid. When I asked the kennel technician if I could see him in the viewing room, the first thing he did when I squatted down to greet him was curl up between my legs and rest his head on my thigh. He wagged his tail and looked up at me as if to say, "Please take me home." After the paperwork was filled out and he was taken to the vet to get fixed, Timone was mine.

2 The first thing he did when I got him home was eat. It was like he had some sort of homing device built in because he knew where his food dish was even though he had never been in my house before. Once he had satisfied his hunger, he claimed a spot on the couch, and then another on my bed. He made himself at home almost instantly, as if he had always lived there.

3 Shortly after I brought him home, however, he developed a bit of an infection from licking his stitches. The vet supplied me with a cone-shaped collar. I waited until I got him home from the vet to put it on him. This cone came from his neck right to the tip of his nose. Once I finally managed to get it on him, he did the funniest thing I have ever seen a dog do. Timone slowly walked up to the kitchen wall and placed the top of the cone against the wall and just stood there, like a pouting child sent to the corner after being naughty. This went on for a few hours. He barely moved. For a while, I thought maybe he wasn't sure if he could move. He eventually accepted it, but it was even more humorous watching him sniff around the floor looking for scraps like a Hoover vacuum.

4   It didn't take long to realize that I would have to start from scratch when it came to training. The only thing he knew how to do was fetch. We started the house-training by keeping him in a medium-sized kennel when we couldn't watch him and allowing him in the kitchen and living room only when we could watch him. I was at wit's end when for weeks he would stand directly in front of me, look me straight in the eye, and proceed to do his business on my cream-coloured plush carpet. But after about four months, he seemed to catch on.

5   He was much quicker when it came to learning tricks. Within a few weeks he could sit, lie down, shake a paw, high-five and dance, all for a Milk Bone. In fact, he was so eager to get a treat that sometimes he would stand in front of me and proceed to do all the tricks in sequence over and over until I gave in and got him a Milk Bone.

6   Timone has proven to be quite an acrobat. When he is in a playful mood, he will sometimes run laps around the living room, leaping from one piece of furniture to the other with the agility and grace of a cat. Other times, if my six-year-old daughter is sitting on the floor watching television, he will run laps around her until she extends both her arms to her sides like an airplane. Timone will then run from one end of the room, jump over one arm, run to the other end of the room, turn around, run back and jump over the other arm. He will do this about three or four times. Sometimes he will even try to jump over her head, notwithstanding the occasional time he misjudges the distance and bounces off the top of her skull. He has the ability to jump straight up in the air to amazing heights from a standing position. Timone has kicked me in the back of the shoulder on occasion in an effort to grab my attention. Sometimes if I go outside without him, he will jump repeatedly at the door, kicking the latch in an attempt to open it. From outside it looks as if he is jumping on a trampoline. The neighbours have been known to remark, "That dog can get some pretty good air!"

7   Timone has proven to be a joy to live with. Whether he is flying around the house, trying to impress with his tricks, or being defiant, he is always loved and appreciated. His intelligence and abilities have often made me wonder what his life was like before he entered mine. He has a unique ability of warming up to anyone he comes in contact with, and I am sure he will continue to win over the hearts of anyone he meets.

PRACTICE

- Identify the various examples and the main point(s) they are demonstrating. Compare your answers with those of your classmates.
- Review our discussion of types of proofs (from cool to warm) in Chapter 4. Does Collins use one or more categories of proofs? How suited are her examples to her purpose? Now compare her examples to those Orwell uses in "Politics and the English Language" (p. 227), and to those Susan McClelland uses in "The Lure of the Body Image" (p. 83).

Balancing Examples with Logic

As discussed in Chapter 4, examples drawn from personal experience or observation can be more emotionally compelling than logically sound. Using examples can lead to the logical fallacy of overgeneralization. David Suzuki, for instance, uses his own example of a successful school visit to argue that high schools should teach sex education. One success by one person in anything is not enough, and even an essay patterned around several examples will probably still fail to offer conclusive evidence. On the other hand, in explaining why you believe something in a certain way, you will naturally give examples. These represent the inductive side of reasoning, an intrinsic and powerful tool when used with balance and care (see "Inductive and Deductive Forms of Reasoning" in Chapter 7).

Cause-Effect

What makes the world around us the way it is? What makes us the way we are? For centuries, religious practitioners, scholars, writers, artists, and seekers of many stripes have devoted themselves to humanity's eternal quest: a correct understanding of things as they really are. This pursuit of truth, so central to the mission of the university, involves careful examination of causes and effects.

Definition of Cause-Effect

In our pursuit of understanding, much of what we read and write focuses on causes, effects, or some combination of the two. **Cause-effect writing** simply refers to sections of text that are organized according to a concern with causes, effects, or both.

Here are two examples of cause-effect statements taken from "The Lure of the Body Image" by Susan McClelland (p. 83):

> Statistics on steroid use show an alarming number of male teenagers across the country are using the substance illegally simply to put on muscle.

> One of the sad consequences of the push towards a hyper-masculine image is that it can rarely be obtained without the use of potentially harmful drugs.

The first statement gives a *why*—the desire to look like a beefcake. The second statement gives a *what*—the harm for the steroid user. Now here are some more examples from selections in the *Reader*:

> "The 21st-century technologies—genetics, nanotechnology and robotics—are so powerful that they can spawn whole new classes of accidents and abuses," he writes.
>
> —John Markoff, "The Doomsday Machines"

The person quoted, Bill Joy, chief scientist at Sun Microsystems, emphasizes causes and effects.

For a growing number of middle-class youths graduating this spring, prostitution isn't seen as a shameful trap, but as a means of making it through the lean student years on the way to a respectable career.

—Sarah Schmidt, "College Girl to Call Girl"

The statement emphasizes the effects on today's youth of outrageous tuition hikes, but the article also asks is this "descent" into prostitution really necessary. Is the alleged cause real or putative?

All this changed when Canada's controversial Prime Minister, Pierre Trudeau, set the country on the road to "Multiculturalism within a Bilingual Framework" policy.

—Habeeb Salloum, "The Other Canadians and Canada's Future"

The article from which this statement is taken deals with the effects of government policies in countering prejudice and indifference.

 PRACTICE

- Find at least three cause-effect statements from each of the three sections of the *Reader*. Do you find cause-effect writing equally prevalent in personal, expository, and argumentative forms? In response to this question, discuss your impressions and ideas with classmates.
- Without referring to the table of contents for the *Rhetoric*, find at least one selection from the *Reader* that uses a cause-effect pattern as its primary method of organization. Compare your answer with those of classmates.
- Provide your class discussion group with one example of cause-effect writing taken from a source other than the *Reader* in this text.

Following are two further samples of cause-effect writing.

Scientific careers in Canada's universities and hospitals are heavily dependent upon a scientist's ability to attract and maintain industrial support. Thus, any scientist who acquires a reputation as a "trouble maker" knows that he or she may have to begin looking for a new career. The punishment for scientific "whistle-blowers" is usually swift and harsh. The desire by researchers to avoid such an unhappy fate can easily result in a conspiracy of silence among those who are not willing to embrace career jeopardy and personal martyrdom.

—Arthur Schafer, director, Centre for Professional and Applied Ethics, *Medicine, Morals, & Money* (chapbook) (Brandon, MB: University of Manitoba, 1999)

Poverty, on the other hand, is an issue that is easy for many of us to ignore. It is intentionally kept hidden away in dark corners, lest we recognize it for what it is, and have to deal with it. When we get into our car to go to the mall, dressed in our designer jeans, with hand-phone, Gucci accessories, etc., do we really give any thought to poverty or pollution? Probably not.

Well, maybe we should wake up. You and I are just as responsible for the abhorrent conditions of poverty in North America as anyone else. Our affluent lifestyles and preference for ignoring unpleasant things do little to help a very serious global problem. Our inclinations towards ignoring poverty are the result of centuries of unsavoury practices by our ancestors.

Poverty is a very destabilizing and often violent situation. Dr. James Gilligan observed the following about violence and poverty: "This form of violence, not covered by any of the majoritarian, corporate, ruling-class protected media, is invisible to us, and because of its invisibility, all the more insidious." How dangerous is it really? Gilligan notes: "[E]very fifteen years, on the average, as many people die because of relative poverty as would be killed in a nuclear war that caused 232 million deaths; and every single year, two to three times as many people die from poverty throughout the world as were killed by the Nazi genocide of the Jews over a six-year period. This is, in effect, the equivalent of an ongoing, unending, in fact, accelerating, thermonuclear war, or genocide, on the weak and poor every year of every decade, throughout the world." The implication is clear. Society chooses to sweep the problem of poverty under the rug; however, this does not erase the fact that there are millions dying yearly. Who is society? We are society, you and I.

—Thomas LaBrie, part-time student, from an online discussion group

Signal Words

Certain words help to signal an author's use of cause-effect structure. A complete list of words and phrasing used in this structure would fill many pages; the following is a small sample taken from the above examples. Please note that in many cases words used to signal causes may also be used or adapted to signal effects and vice versa.

Signal words and phrases showing causes

are using the substance illegally [in order] to put on muscle
they can spawn
set the country on the road to
The desire . . . can result in
It is . . . kept hidden
You and I are . . . responsible for
Our affluent lifestyles and preference for ignoring unpleasant things do little
Poverty is . . . very destabilizing
people die because of

Signal words and phrases showing effects

can rarely be obtained without
whole new classes of accidents and abuses
a means of making it through the lean student years
All this changed when
heavily dependent upon
acquires a reputation
The punishment for . . . is swift and harsh.
are the result of
because of its invisibility
This is, in effect,
this does not erase

PRACTICE

Look over the cause-effect passages and essays you have already identified as part of previous practice work in this chapter. Underline or highlight those words and phrases you feel signal the writers' rhetorical patterns and purposes. Discuss your answers with classmates and your instructor.

Striving for Sound Conclusions

Those of us with experience as parents or guardians of young children know only too well the child's questionable sense of causes and effects. "Take your sweater to the picnic," we say, knowing that the warm day will turn into a chilly evening. Unless the child is remarkably obedient, he will ignore our suggestion; six hours later we will be treated to his bemused observations about the cold. Yet in our writing, we too can neglect relevant cause-effect considerations. Under "Argumentation" in Chapter 7, review our discussion of "Logical Fallacies" and the problems of either/or false opposites, *ad hominem*, overgeneralization, oversimplification, false analogy, circular argument, *non sequitur*, *post hoc ergo propter hoc*, *ad populum*, bandwagon, slippery slope, and red herring. We humans take great pride in our ability to reason, in our supposed superiority as a species; yet careful analysis of our reasoning, of our tendency to ignore or warp major causal considerations, to bend even the most carefully collected empirical facts and statistics, should remind us that sound thinking—when it does occur—does so only with major effort.

Comparison-Contrast

We suggested that classification-division is the operating system beneath expository patterns, because it establishes items and catalogues of items organized in relation to each other. Comparison-contrast, in turn, is surely the tool we human beings use most commonly to make sense of the world around us, and specifically to make sense of those things that we recognize through division to be distinct from each other, yet through classification to share kinship in certain categories. Through comparison-contrast, one thing in a certain category is placed side by side with another in the same category. Suppose you wish to indicate how much your nephew has grown in the past year—you might say, "He comes up to my hip." Our equation of your nephew's new height to the level of your hip gives us a precise understanding. The extent to which we rely on comparison can be found at the heart of our language, specifically in our use of metaphor. Someone asks you how your hockey team did last night. You reply, "We were on fire." The degree of your performance has been compared to the intensity of a fire, even though the comparison was not directly stated by words such as "like" or "as."

Analogy

All of us use analogies as a natural method of expressing ourselves. This very common form of comparison is an extended illustration based on drawing a connection between two seemingly unlike things. Usually, one of the terms is complex or somehow unfamiliar to us, while the other is familiar. Through the familiar term we gain a clearer understanding of the more remote one. We might liken the growth of a creative project, such as a novel, to the stages of a butterfly. The caterpillar or larva emerges from a tiny egg, and eats and eats, growing to 100 times its original size. It then retreats into a cocoon, inactive to external observation for as long as two years. At last from the cocoon emerges the butterfly; it flies great distances and pollinates many plant species. Each stage of the insect portrays an aspect in the development of an essay. The original idea inspired from on high (larva born of a butterfly's egg) feeds upon lowly food as it crawls the earth; it then transforms in the unconscious (cocoon) and at last takes wing, through publishing and discussion, to spread far and wide and nourish further life.

 PRACTICE

1. List two or three examples of analogies public figures have used and that have been reported in the media. Study these examples: are they illuminating or misleading? Give what you believe is a useful, informing analogy and contrast it to an uninspired or false analogy. (See Chapter 7, "Logic and Logical Fallacies," which itemizes effective versus faulty analogies.)
2. In her English drama course, student Barbara Bower used a comic analogy to structure an essay evaluating the heroism of Oedipus, hero of Sophocles' tragedy *Oedipus Rex*, and Prince Hal, hero of Shakespeare's *Henry IV, Part One*. She compared the two dramatic characters to World Wrestling–style opponents in a Dramatis Personae Bout of Champions through the Nevada State Gaming Commission in association with Don King. You can read the full essay through the Introductory Composition cover page of Athabasca University's English 255 course at <**www.athabascau.ca/courses/engl/255/**>. Discuss the strengths of and possible problems with this choice of central analogy.
3. Read the "Allegory of the Cave" (p. 119) from Book VII of Plato's *The Republic*. Explain the extended comparison: what is being represented by each part of the description?

Comparison Defined

To **compare** means to place two things side by side in order to reach a better understanding of each, and usually, of some third thing. This could result in stressing similarity or difference. The two things being compared normally share some sort of generic category: two cars, two athletes, two friends, two cities, the country versus the city, etc. A dog is not generally compared to a computer, except for comic purposes. Some people feel that the phrase "compare with" signals the general act of comparing whereas the phrase "compare to" indicates that contrast will be emphasized. "His records are not so impressive compared to those of Gretzky." Reference books do not agree on this fine point of distinction.

Contrast Defined

Contrast deals with the difference between two things being compared. The study of difference could lead to upholding one thing over the other, or it could simply point out distinctions between them.

Remember, if you are asked to *compare* two things, you are free to decide whether to stress similarity or difference. If you are asked to *contrast* two things, you must attend to differences.

Widespread Uses of Compare and Contrast

As we said in our opening comments, comparison is the most common and funda-mental form of human reasoning. Consider that the binary code (a basic division of two) underlies the complex functions of the computer. The comparative tool is used to serve *all* writing purposes—evocative, analytical, and argumentative as well as expository (see Chapter 7 on the crucial importance of comparison in fair and effective debate). Comparison-contrast is also used across all academic disciplines. Students in literature might compare two characters in a play, or compare two novels or two poems. Students in political science might compare two political parties or systems. Students in mechanical engineering might contrast gasoline and electric car engines, concentrating on technical processes and specifications. Ecologists might compare these two, while concentrating on environmental effects.

Ways to Structure Comparisons

- point by point
- subject by subject
- combination of point by point and subject by subject
- similarities and differences
- advantages and disadvantages

PREPARATION

Read Mark Radford's essay "Different Worlds" (p. 43) and Pat Deiter-McArthur's essay "Saskatchewan's Indian People—Five Generations" (p. 87). Briefly describe each essay under the following headings:

- topic
- tone
- pattern
- conclusion

Here is how an essay comparing these two essays would be laid out according to the point-by-point method. "Points" are the four elements of prose you have already identified and described:

Point by Point

Topic, "Different Worlds"
Topic, "Five Generations"

Tone, "Different Worlds"
Tone, "Five Generations"

Pattern, "Different Worlds"
Pattern, "Five Generations"

Conclusion, "Different Worlds"
Conclusion, "Five Generations"

An essay using the subject-by-subject method, understanding "subjects" to denote the two essays, could be organized as follows:

Subject by Subject

"Different Worlds"
  Topic
  Tone
  Pattern
  Conclusion

"Five Generations"
  Topic
  Tone
  Pattern
  Conclusion

A combination of point-by-point and subject-by-subject organization could look like this:

Combination

Topic, "Different Worlds"
Topic, "Five Generations"

Tone, "Different Worlds"
Tone, "Five Generations"

"Different Worlds"
  Pattern
  Conclusion

"Five Generations"
    Pattern
    Conclusion

Following is a pattern using similarities and differences. For the sake of this illustration, let's agree that the topics of the two essays may be considered similar—both deal with generational change—and the tones are similar. Radford's tone contains an element of irony lacking in McArthur's, and there is somewhat more personal voice in his essay, since it is based on the first person. Nevertheless, Radford's primary tone, like McArthur's, is detached and observational. The patterns differ, largely as a result of Radford's use of the personal essay. He builds his discussion around three main examples, whereas MacArthur uses descriptive process to summarize how change occurred over five classifications. The conclusions might be variously interpreted as similar, different, or something of both. For the sake of the following example, let us say we interpret the conclusions as mostly different from each other.

Similarities and Differences

Similarities
    Topic, both essays
    Tone, both essays

Differences
    Pattern, both essays
    Conclusion, both essays

For other subjects such as comparing the country and the city, another common form is organization according to advantages and disadvantages. This pattern may be handled like the similarities-differences pattern above. No matter which pattern you find most suitable, analyze the two subjects according to three or four main points in your preliminary thinking. For example, you may wish to compare Business A and Business B. You make notes about each according to range and quality of products, prices, and customer service. Your essay might take shape something like this:

Advantages and Disadvantages

Advantages
    Range and quality of products, Business A
    Prices, Business A
    Customer service, Business B

Disadvantages
    Range and quality of products, Business B
    Prices, Business B
    Customer service, Business A

Avoiding Problems in Comparison

Comparison-contrast is one of the most challenging patterns to use effectively. Try to avoid these problems:

- failing to balance the discussion, so that one subject predominates
- creating a ping-pong effect by using point by point
- dwelling on one subject for so long that the reader begins to forget the essay's underlying comparative purpose
- following a structure that makes the material seem tedious and repetitious
- forgetting that comparison-contrast is a tool for focusing on a thesis, not an end in itself

The final problem is especially common. You may be tempted to cover all parts of your plan, noting, for example, similarities and differences, but then failing to conclude with any useful meaning or insight that flows from this comparison. Simply observing that subjects are equally weighted in their similarities and differences or advantages and disadvantages can lead to an essay that lacks any point or clear value. Your comparisons will have a stronger edge if your thesis sentences suggest strong subordination and emphasis, or assign specific value, like the following:

> While Big Bear and Louis Riel differed in many ways, including whether to choose conciliation or war, both were charismatic leaders doomed by the Europeanization of North America.
>
> —Adapted from Robert Fulford, "How the West Was Lost" (*Saturday Night*, 100. 7 (July 1985): 5–8)

> Life in the city and life in the country both have advantages and disadvantages: the former offers more to young people and seniors, the latter offers more to students and those beginning careers.

Sample Essay Comparison—Find the Structural Pattern(s)

Not Your Average Shopping Mall

1   We stare into computer screens. We work inside office towers with sealed windows and automatic circulation. We shop and entertain ourselves at indoor malls. How many of us even notice the great outdoors anymore? Let's pry ourselves free of the video arcade for a few minutes to visit the contrasting joys of summer and winter. It could be the best thing we have done in a long while.

2   Some might object that summer and winter, far from offering joys, really specialize in discomforts. It's true that cutting the grass exposes us to aches and irritations, while shovelling snow produces comparable aches and chills the flesh. But all this exercise benefits the health, and without the expense of club fees. We don't need that fancy gym bag or spiffy new outfit to work outside. As for the labour, where would we

be without a certain amount of effort to help us appreciate our time of relaxation? Those lost in video arcade stupor lose out on the satisfaction of completing the small outside chores necessary to daily living.

3   Yet all is not work. Summer and winter both provide ideal opportunities for outdoor recreation. In summer, it's boating, swimming, hiking, and canoeing, and games like soccer and tennis. In winter we can skate, ski, slide, or snowshoe. Winter games include hockey and curling. Summer offers peaceful joys such as berry-picking and tree-climbing; winter means ice sculpting and building that snow fort. Many activities, such as fishing and camping, can be enjoyed year round. For example, the summer fisher glides across a still lake in the early morning mist, your hand trails in cool water; the winter fisher kneels on a mirror of ice, peering into the dark mysteries of the fishing hole.

4   Appreciating summer and winter puts us in touch with the simpler pleasures. Can the virtual reality of computer space really compete with the real wonder of the great outdoors?

Focus Questions

1. Decide which of the five methods of organizing comparison has been used. Make a simple outline of the essay to match one of the five methods above.
2. Prepare outlines re-organizing the content of this essay according to as many of the other methods as you think would make sense.
3. Consider how you might outline a short essay if the video arcade mentioned in the introduction became one subject and the two seasons combined as the other subject.

Descriptive Analysis and Directional Process

Descriptive analysis and directional process tell us how something works. Both essentially provide information, so both are subcategories of exposition. Descriptive analysis enables us to understand some operation or process that we, the readers, are not expected to use or replicate. Directional process, on the other hand, is *how-to* writing; it describes certain steps that we are supposed to follow in order to make or do something. Both kinds of description often appear in technical writing.

Descriptive Analysis

Descriptive analysis explains how a particular process works, but does not expect the reader to perform that process. Process descriptions can be used in a wide variety of circumstances, whether describing how language develops in a child from gurgles to full sentences or explaining how a pulp-and-paper mill operates.

Process descriptions are especially common in scientific and technical writing, where they often describe mechanical or natural processes such as combustion, cell division, or oxidation. They can also be used to explain plans or strategies, from an emergency evacuation in a nuclear power plant to a politician's strategy for winning votes in the two months before an election. Many of your textbooks, including this one, contain descriptions of a variety of processes. Though most recognizable in technical writing, descriptive analysis reaches, through many fields and forms, from how historical events have unfolded to how the operative forces and relationships occur within an astrological chart.

Process descriptions are organized chronologically most often, moving in sequence from the first stage in a process to the last. We can organize cyclical processes, such as respiration or photosynthesis, in chronological steps, but we have to choose where to begin and to end our descriptions.

 PRACTICE

Find examples of descriptive process among the selections in the *Reader*. Compare your findings with those of classmates.

More Guidance for the Scientific Paper

Many first-year students feel themselves "at sea" when they are asked to write lab reports. Graduate student Tasha Ausman, an expert in this specialized form of descriptive-analysis writing, has prepared lab-report guidelines and samples; visit the Introductory Composition cover page of the Athabasca University's English 255 course at <www.athabascau.ca/courses/engl/255/>. See "Sample Essays" under "Supplementary Resources." Visit also <www.pearsoned.ca/brundage>.

Steps to Organizing Descriptive Analysis

Not every process description will be subjected to intense scrutiny, but imagine your readers will all be skeptics anyway, looking for holes in your methods. In describing a process, you should find the following organizational pattern works whether you are providing a brief description of a process within a longer paper or writing a lengthy report describing a more complex process:

1. Explain the purpose of the process by stating its main goal or its end result. You may want to give a general overview of the process by itemizing its main steps in the order you have written them. Besides defining the objec-

tive, consider defining how you will measure the results of stages in the process and how you will mark the passage of time in that process.

2. Divide the process into stages or steps, and explain them one at a time. In a process description of several paragraphs, begin each major step with a new paragraph. Steps are often—but not always—arranged in chronological order. A flow-chart diagram may help both you and your reader understand the overall process in its steps. For instance, if you are describing the writing process, the following flow chart may prove useful:

collage ➡ brainstorm ➡ topic sentence tree ➡ research ➡ revised topic sentence tree ➡ draft ➡ peer edit ➡ draft ➡ peer edit ➡ revision ➡ submission

3. Bring the steps back together. How do all the stages you have described work together? Is the whole as you have outlined it a cyclical process? Is it linear? Is there a predictable or variable end result? You may also want to restate the purpose of the process.

To describe a complex process, such as building a bridge or staging a play, you may have to divide the process into several subprocesses, each of which involves several steps. In these cases, the introduction and conclusion are especially important. You can use them to help the reader understand how you have broken down the major process into smaller processes, and how these processes work in combination with one another. If you are describing a process unfamiliar to your reader, you may find definitions, comparisons, and analogies helpful.

Process description is often used in combination with other rhetorical strategies (see "Mixed Modes"). For instance, your process description could be one part of a persuasive or analytical essay, report, or letter. To analyze a public relations campaign, write a critical paper on a theory of psychological development, or recommend environmentally-friendly changes for a production process, you might provide a brief description of the process before you go on to analyze it or argue for or against it.

Directional Analysis (How-to Writing)

Rarely do we come across a piece of writing that can move its readers to tears, rage, or profanity. Instructions have this power. Although they have a more direct impact on the reader than almost any other form of communication, instructions are often overlooked, underestimated, or poorly written.

Instructions are a form of process explanation that assumes that the reader will participate in the process. Instructions aim to teach the reader to replicate a process. Assembly instructions for furniture, operating manuals for cars, the Help function on a word processor, and a college registration pamphlet are all examples of instructive writing.

PRACTICE

1. Describe a process from your discipline or in an area of interest. Picture your audience as other students in your class who do not know the process. Break the process into steps before you begin. Here are some sample topics:

   - How an infant develops in the first year
   - How an engine works
   - How the heart pumps blood
   - How a musical instrument produces sound
   - How a corporation performs a hostile takeover
   - How a mountain gorilla finds a mate

2. Write a letter recommending changes or improvements to an unsuccessful or inefficient process. Describe the existing process, identify its weaknesses, and then recommend your improvements. Feel free to use your imagination to come up with an interesting illustration. Address your letter to a specific reader who makes sense within the context you have chosen. Here are some sample topics:

   - Write to a well-known politician who has been publicly exposed or compromised, telling her how she might have modified her plans to escape detection.
   - Write to a movie or TV villain to recommend improvements to one of his plans for defeating the hero (Help Dr. No outwit James Bond, Coyote finally trick Road Runner, Darth Vader defeat Luke Skywalker, or Dr. Zanis convince Charlton Heston that apes really are far superior at everything).
   - Write to the leader of an unsuccessful political campaign, recommending procedural changes (including speech topics) that would have made the campaign a success.
   - Write to the commander of an historic battle that was lost, recommending changes that would have resulted in victory.
   - Write a letter to your college administration recommending changes to the admissions, registration, or grade appeal process.
   - Write a letter to your employer, recommending improvements to a procedure you follow at your workplace.

In many ways, this form of writing is one of the world's most thankless. The writer is much less present than in a persuasive essay or a personal narrative. A good set of instructions simply allows the reader/doer to accomplish the task at hand effectively and to forget the author forever, whether assembling a bookshelf, setting up a VCR, or operating a piece of machinery. Well-written instructions tend not to call attention to themselves except through their absolute clarity, their transparency as pure, practical information. We could say that their aim is the opposite of what we would call establishing or asserting voice in other forms of writing. Although the art of writing instructions is often unappreciated, readers immediately notice poorly written instructions. Of course, poor instructions can cause the reader frustration, despair, or even injury.

Good instructions, like good process descriptions, guide the reader through a process one step at a time, leaving no room for confusion or misunderstanding. The only test of a set of instructions is that a reader can actually follow them. Writing good instructions, however, is not as easy as it may seem. Some instructors like to begin a class on the subject by asking students to write instructions for a seemingly simple task such as tying their shoelaces. Students soon see that this task that they perform automatically on a daily basis is much more complex than they would have thought. Writers find that they know the process so well that they omit important information and stages. Unfortunately, this is often the case with far more crucial instructions, which are usually written by people with expert knowledge of the process they describe. One of the greatest challenges in writing instructions is putting yourself in the place of the people who will need to follow the instructions, and trying to imagine what they need—and do not need—to know.

Steps to Writing Directional Process (How-to) Guidelines

Process instructions follow a pattern of organization very similar to a process description. The main difference is that instructions address the reader or user directly, usually in the form of short commands.

1. State the goal of the process, and its importance (if not obvious from the goal). List any equipment the reader will need to perform the procedure. Is any other preparation necessary or recommended? For complex procedures, you may want to provide an overview of the major steps or tasks involved. Include in your introduction the time, money, and effort that will be required of the reader (when relevant). Establish a tone that encourages your reader. Use of the second person—"you"—helps this friendly, assuring tone.
2. Break the process into ordered steps. You may want to begin with these steps laid out as a series of numbered statements or paragraphs with headings.

   For a complex process, divide the instructions into major tasks and subtasks, stating the overall goal as well as the goal of each major task.

Instructive writing can be more than a straightforward sequence of steps. Sometimes you will have to combine instructive and descriptive modes in order to explain a process clearly and effectively. For instance, if your purpose is to explain to a reader how to use a variety of internet search engines for different purposes, you might want to describe generally how each search engine works behind the scenes before you move to step-by-step instructions from a user's perspective.

Consider the following strategies in writing effective instructions:

- Address the reader directly in the form of a command. Avoid the passive voice. (See p. 578 of the *Handbook* on active and passive voices, "Fifteen Common Errors".)

  Poor: Once the coin is inserted, the knob should be turned.
  Better: Insert coin and turn knob.

- Use strong, precise verbs to describe the doer's actions: "grasp," "pull," "turn," "stab," "twist," etc. Stay away from vague terms such as "proper," "correct," "ready," and "right," etc. If your readers already know what you mean by "ready" or "correct," chances are they don't need your instructions.

Poor: Bake 30 mins, or until ready.
Better: Bake 30 mins, or until golden brown.

- Avoid ambiguous language that could lead to potential misunderstandings.

Poor: Place the bookshelf on the floor.
Better: Lay the bookshelf on the floor so that the back faces the ceiling.

- Do not over-instruct. Sometimes you will have to tell your reader exactly how to stand, or which finger to place where, but often this level of detail is unnecessary. Don't make your instructions a game of Twister for readers trying to follow them.

- State conditions before actions.

Poor: Press Ctrl-X if you have highlighted the text you want to delete.
Better: If you have highlighted the text you want to delete, press Ctrl-X.

- State the goal of a particular step before the action.

Poor: Rub the lens with three or four drops of solution for about 20 seconds to clean it.
Better: To clean the lens, rub it with three or four drops of solution for about 20 seconds.

- Place warnings and cautions *before* the step to which they apply. There's no use telling your readers the step they've just completely was actually quite dangerous, especially if they're already bruised or bleeding!

- Use illustrations to assist the text by identifying parts and equipment, or demonstrating what specific steps should look like.

Persuasion plays a role in many types of instructions. For instance, a pamphlet in a doctor's office instructing women how to examine themselves for breast cancer also aims to persuade its audience of the importance of catching breast cancer in its early stages. Self-help and how-to books not only teach their readers about a particular approach to weight loss, relationships, or sales, but also persuade them that the particular method or system described is better than others. Instructions on some commercial products are primarily intended to persuade. For example, one Australian shampoo bottle includes the following instructions under the heading "Salon Directions": "Saturate hair with water. Massage shampoo deeply into scalp and roots. Drench with water to rinse. Repeat." These instructions are clearly not intended to teach the novice user how to use the shampoo, but to persuade him or her to believe in that particular shampoo's luxurious or sensuous effect.

PRACTICE

1. Find a set of instructions in your house or school—the manual for programming your VCR, your school's instructions for requesting tuition refunds, your telephone company's instructions for setting up voice mail, etc. Evaluate the instructions. Could you follow them successfully? Why or why not? Identify specific strengths or weaknesses in them.

    In class, organize into groups. Pass around your sample instructions and discuss their relative strengths and weaknesses. Which set of instructions is the best of the lot, and which is the worst? Why? Based on these samples, try to come up with some general guidelines for writing effective instructions. Which writing strategies seem to work well, and which don't?

2. Write a set of instructions for a simple, everyday task such as brushing your teeth, putting on a pair of jeans, taking a shower, tying your shoes, or making a pot of coffee. Assume that your reader is an intelligent adult who for strange and obscure reasons has never performed the task before.

3. Write a set of instructions for a specialized process that other people in your class might not know how to perform. Here are some appropriate topics:

    - How to play a simple card game
    - How to change a bicycle tire
    - How to rescue a drowning person
    - How to stretch after running
    - How to make bread
    - How to edit a video
    - How to develop film

4. Write a letter persuading a friend or family member to perform a particular process or procedure. At least one paragraph should instruct your reader how to perform that procedure. Here are some possibilities:

    - Persuade your grandmother, who insists she can't work her VCR, to tape a show for you.
    - Persuade a friend to apply for a parking permit for you.
    - Persuade your friend that she should try a new way of styling her hair.
    - Persuade your technophobic brother to open an email account.
    - Persuade your parents to start a compost bin.

Now here is a sample directional process essay by part-time student Gisela Becker. Notice that while she does use first person to introduce her topic and engage interest, she then switches to the more typical second person ("you"), appropriate for speaking directly in a friendly, informal manner, to an involved reader. Note her use of MLA citation. See Chapter 12.

Sample Essay   The How-to Essay

Scuba Diving
Gisela Becker

1   It feels strange the first time. The mask. The awkward gear, a bit heavy. You ease into the water and your face slips below the surface. Inhale; the air comes with a reassuring hiss, and for the first time you breathe underwater. In moments, you forget the mask. The equipment transforms itself into something light and agile, and you're free as you've never been before. With that first underwater breath, the door opens to a different world. Not a world apart, but different nonetheless. Go through that door. Your life will never be the same. (IPADI 1)

The writer quotes from a suitable source, which uses present tense description and second person to draw us in

She suggests ways to become informed on the topic

2   I had decided that I wanted to learn how to scuba dive. First I read through *Open Water Diver Manual*, I watched several diving videos, and I received further useful information from my dive instructor. Then I went through several "confined water dives" in the pool. Finally I was ready and prepared for my first open water dive. I had it all in my head about buoyancy and pressure, volume and density under water, hand signals and emergency procedures. Yes, I was ready for the underwater excitement!

She summarizes what will be involved. This could include steps, materials, time, costs, and required attitude and skills

3   Before I could go for my very first sea dive under the watchful eye of my instructor, several preparatory steps had to be completed: finding the right diving location, reviewing and assembling the scuba equipment, gearing up, entering the water, and finally scuba diving.

Having previewed the steps, now she elaborates on each in order

4   Finding the right dive location is not as easy as it sounds, but do not worry. During your dive course your dive instructor will choose the dive site for you. As you gain more experience in scuba diving, you will also acquire confidence in deciding on an appropriate dive spot. Depths of water, water movement, low or high tide and easy accessibility are all considerations when choosing the right location. Do not forget about the weather, because changing weather conditions affect the water conditions.

5   Now that you have found a nice dive location, you need to get the scuba equipment ready for the dive. First let me say a sentence or two about whether it is better to buy or to rent scuba equipment. Scuba equipment is very expensive! It is probably best to rent your equipment for a starter, until you know how much diving you are going to do. Most dive centres rent the necessary equipment at a reasonable price.

6   Before assembling your scuba equipment, you need to gather all your gear to ensure that nothing is missing. If you thought that you could just jump into the water and enjoy the underwater world, you are wrong there!

7   First you need a mask that covers your eyes and nose, then a snorkel for surface swimming until you reach the dive site, and certainly you need scuba fins to increase your foot power. Your next piece of equipment is a weight belt. If you are like most people, you naturally float in the water. An extra weight system in the form of a belt will help you to sink.

Notice her use of effective transitional words ("now," "before," "first," "next," etc. to guide us from step to step

8   Finally your scuba unit consists of three basic components: the buoyancy control device (BCD), the scuba tank, and the regulator.

9   By now you probably think this is pretty complicated stuff, but I can reassure you that between now and a few dives you will have mastered the equipment with no problems at all. Until that mastery becomes second nature, you have your dive instructor at your side for assistance.

10   The BCD is most commonly a jacket style that you inflate or deflate to regulate your buoyancy. "You can do this orally, using air from your lungs, though most of the times you'll use a low pressure inflator, which inflates the BCD with air directly from your tank" (IPADI 38).

11   Your BCD integrates a backpack to hold the scuba tank on your back. The scuba tank itself is a metal container filled with high-pressure oxygen, which allows you to

breathe under water. With your regulator attached to the tank you are able to use the air from your scuba tank. The regulator has two main pieces, the first stage, which connects to the tank valve and the second stage, which integrates the mouthpiece. The two stages reduce high-pressure air from the scuba tank; this allows comfortable breathing under water. You may want to consider wearing a wetsuit depending on the water temperature and the climate you are diving in, but this is also a question of personal choice and preference.

12   You must be getting tired from all these explanations about scuba equipment! No? Maybe because you dream of that underwater world, where time seems endless and stress does not exist. You will not be that one inexperienced diver who is trying to remain neutrally buoyant, breathing frantically into his/her mouthpiece. Let me reassure you that with every moment you are getting closer to this extraordinary experience: your first underwater dive.

She remembers to reassure and motivate her reader

13   Now that you have had a chance to look at your gear, you want to get ready to assemble your scuba equipment. First you have to put together your tank, regulator, and BCD. You start with sliding the BCD over the standing scuba tank from the top. Then you secure the tank band tightly. You want to avoid a loose tank on your back while you are underwater. As a next step you attach the regulator on the tank valve and also connect the low-pressure hose from the regulator to the BCD low-pressure inflator. Finally turn on the air and confirm that the whole unit is working properly. Take a few breaths from the regulator. Your equipment is ready for your dive.

She maintains her "you" approach (thinking from the perspective of the reader)

14   Remember I told you that I was about to go for my first sea dive. Take a moment and picture me in all my gear: I put on my mask and snorkel. My instructor had to help me to put on the BCD jacket and the heavy scuba tank filled with air. I still remember wondering why air would be so heavy.

As in her opening, she appeals to the senses, to the imagination of her reader

15   I have a 12-pound heavy weight belt went around my hips and smaller weights around each of my ankles, because my feet kept floating on the surface during the training sessions in the pool. As a final step I put on my scuba fins.

16   In all my heavy gear I stand at the edge of the pier. My instructor asks me to enter the water with a giant stride entry. "Simply step out with one foot," I hear him say with an encouraging tone. When I finally decide that I have the courage to do it, I enter the water with one big "Splash." And there I am underwater, breathing and experiencing the freedom of "weightlessness" with the most beautiful sights of corals, ferns and underwater creatures.

She balances her opening description of the activity with a concluding image of the activity about to begin, rewarding the preparation she has guided us through

17   Now it is your turn to get ready for your first underwater adventure.

Her closing appeal reinforces that this is really about us, not her

Works Cited

International Professional Association of Diving Instructors, *Open Water Diver Manual*. Santa Margarita, CA: IPADI, 1999.

Definition

In the opening of her essay "Global Warming and Population" (p. 113), Brenda Platt announces two central questions: "Does population growth contribute to global warming? Should population control be a central strategy in stabilizing global environmental change?" Then she says, "In order to answer these questions it is necessary to introduce key concepts . . ."

Definition Used Widely in Introductions

Platt's opening represents a typical start to many academic papers dealing with complex issues: the need to establish the meaning of key terms. One of the terms she goes on to describe is global warming:

> Global warming is the increase in the mean average temperature of the earth's atmosphere. It occurs when the so-called greenhouse gases (carbon dioxide, methane, nitrous oxide, tropospheric ozone) absorb infrared radiation from the planet's surface that would otherwise escape into space. This absorbed radiation is converted to heat and the atmosphere becomes warmer. The predicted consequences include a decline in agricultural productivity, desertification, changes in forestation patterns, more and stronger storms, and flooding of low-lying coastal regions.

Drawing on Other Expository Patterns

Notice that Platt's explanation features descriptive-process writing, while this pattern serves the larger purpose of definition. What other patterns are used in the following definitions?

> Attributions are inferences that people draw about the cause of events, others' behavior, and their own behavior. If you conclude that a friend turned down your invitation because she's overworked, you've made an attribution about the cause of her behavior (and, implicitly, rejected other possible explanations). If you conclude that you're stuck at home with nothing to do because you failed to plan ahead, you've made an attribution about the cause of an event (being stuck at home). If you conclude that you failed to plan ahead because you're a procrastinator, you've made an attribution about the cause of your own behavior.
>
> —W. Weiten, *Psychology: Themes and Variations* (Pacific Grove, Calif.: Cole, 1992) 583–85

> Every language and its literature—written or oral—is also a world, linked to other worlds, of which the speakers of that language are often unaware. Every language and its literature form an intellectual bioregion, an ecosystem of ideas and perceptions, a watershed of thought. The several hundred oral literatures indigenous to North America—though constantly remade in the mouths of oral poets and new to every listener who comes from somewhere else—are parts of the old-growth forest of the human mind.
>
> —Robert Bringhurst, *A Story Sharp as a Knife* (Vancouver: Douglas and MacIntyre, 1999) 16

The image of the twentieth century as a time of progress for women, in stark contrast to the Victorian era, is based on a series of clichés. One forgets the massacres and world wars and remembers only the flapper of the Roaring Twenties, the liberated woman set free by "the pill," or the superwoman of the 1980s, that creature of feminism and consumer society, capable of juggling career, children, and lovers without missing a beat. In fact, the stereotypes of the flapper and the liberated female were more often invoked to denounce the collapse of the sex barrier and the double standard than to applaud the victories of the women's movement. And the superwoman image, which Betty Friedan criticized in *The Second Stage* (1981), is at the very least ambiguous: few women can live up to such an ideal and the tensions arising out of the contradictory demands it imposes are swept under the rug. Indeed, Rose-Marie Lagrave has argued that the social function of the superwoman ideal is to conceal growing inequality between the sexes.

—Françoise Thébaud, "Explorations of Gender" in *A History of Women*, eds. Georges Duby and Michelle Perrot, vol. V (London: Harvard, 1994) 2

The first definition uses examples to illustrate and clarify the essence and scope of a term. The second definition applies a number of vivid metaphors, making use of implicit comparison. The third definition begins by invoking contrast—a faulty definition of the meaning of the twentieth century for women—and then goes on through descriptive process to develop a critical response that opposes the clichéd definitions.

We have placed definition last in this list of expository patterns because it draws upon all the others to expound its concepts.

✑ PRACTICE

Read Wayne C. Booth's essay "The Rhetorical Stance" (p. 144), an extended attempt to define the ideal position for a writer in any writing occasion. How many different patterns does Booth call on to serve his central purpose in that essay?

ESSAY TOPICS

1. Discuss three or four different personality types.
2. Provide examples of a car, an animal, or a person that you know well. You may use the first person, but keep the emphasis on the subject (not yourself).
3. Discuss the causes of a social or medical disorder that concerns you.
4. Discuss the effects of music.
5. Compare two places that you know well.
6. Compare two different forms of education you have observed, researched, or experienced.
7. Describe the process of registration at a specific college or university.
8. Instruct your reader in how to write a successful text of a very specific type.
9. Instruct your reader in how to take a much-needed break from excess work, worry, and stress.
10. Define the university, considering what it sometimes is and what it should be.

Note: See the end of Chapter 4 for additional topics.

For more sample student essays using various expository patterns, visit the Introductory Composition cover page of the Athabasca University's English 255 course at <www.athabascau.ca/courses/engl/255/>. See "Sample Essays" under "Supplementary Resources."

Chapter 7

Argumentation

Argumentation is a subcategory in the large category of writing known as persuasion. All forms of persuasion attempt to sway an audience to behave a certain way or hold a certain opinion. For example, advertising tries to make people buy certain products or services. As we know, advertisers are not above *card-stacking* (lying, omitting or evading facts, underplaying or overemphasizing issues, and so on) in order to achieve their goal. Argumentation, in contrast, attempts to influence its audience through disinterested consideration.[20] Your command of argumentative methods is an important skill in scholarship, which seeks to solve difficult questions and to expose—rather than manipulate—truth.

FEATURES OF ARGUMENTATION

All writing is persuasive in the general sense of seeking to convince us of its reality or integrity; that is, a good personal essay persuades us that the writer really knows the place or experience being described. Formal assignments that call for argumentation, however, involve a more specialized sense of persuasion: they address *topics of strong debate*, for example, euthanasia, abortion, indigenous self-government, or some scientific controversy. Opinion on these topics tends to be intense and divided. You will be expected to know some portion of what has been recorded by other scholars, experts, and spokespeople on the topic; you will need to summarize some of the representative views and to give fair consideration to each. Thorough knowledge of the controversy in question should be demonstrated. In contrast to biased forms of persuasion—advertising, corporate or government propaganda, etc.—you do not attempt to sway your reader by ignoring difficult facts or opinions or by employing emotionally charged language. Your job is to confront challenges and explain how, despite other views, your position makes sense. In essence, a formal argument proceeds by comparing and contrasting, by showing your view as better than others on

---

[20] "Disinterested" means without personal bias. A disinterested conclusion is one that has been reached through open-minded research and reasoning based on all the gathered facts and opinions. A conclusion that accords with the views of an organization to which you belong may not be disinterested. The word is commonly confused with "uninterested."

the topic. The rhetorical strategy of **comparison-contrast** is therefore a major tool in most argumentation (we look at this structure below). Summing up, the *general* features of a formally structured academic argument are as follows:

- thorough awareness of other views, up-to-date research
- a moderate tone, respectful of other views
- consistent use of logic, the controlling value[21]
- appropriate appeals to ethics and emotion

✎ PRACTICE

- In this chapter we provide a sample academic essay of argumentation. Examine it carefully, then review Section 3 of the *Reader* and determine which selections there may be classified as formal arguments, as defined above.
- Choose one or two selections from Section 3 of the *Reader* that do not fit the formal definition. Discuss your observations of these informal arguments with your classmates.
- While many selections in Section 3 of the *Reader* do not represent formal argumentation, they do demonstrate persuasion. Discuss this distinction further, using one or two examples from the *Reader*.
- Make a list of the topics covered by Section 3 of the *Reader*. Do they meet the definition of "controversial" for today's Canadian readers?
- Make a list of some important argumentative topics that do not appear to be represented in Section 3 of the *Reader* (we could not include everything!). Outline a formal argument demonstrating why one of the omitted topics should have been included.

Structuring a Formal Argument—Comparison and Contrast

There are various legitimate ways to structure argumentative essays, but most often you will present your view balanced against the counter-arguments of other writers first, then go on to develop your own views. The specific pattern you select should, of course, be guided by the principles of all good essays: an **introduction** that engages the reader's interest, establishes the relevance of your topic, provides brief background; a **body** that develops the main points of your thesis; and a **conclusion** that reinforces your main claim while prompting further reflection or action by the reader. In deciding how to organize the specific points and supporting details of your discussion, however, you will find it useful to know classical patterns for argumentation.

Based on study of classic argumentative texts, here is a formal pattern as suggested by John Thompson, program coordinator, in Athabasca University's *English 255 Writing Skills Study Guide 1988*, page 32:

---

[21] See the section on cause/effect (p. 346) as well as the following discussion of logical fallacies, notably either/or, overgeneralization, oversimplification, circular argument, *non sequitur*, and *post hoc ergo propter hoc*. (p. 375)

Formal Pattern for Argumentation

1. My opponent says A is true (briefly allude to the reasons).
2. A is not true; B is true for these reasons (summarize them).
3. Elaborate on the reasons for believing A is not true.
4. Elaborate on the reasons for believing B is true.
5. State final implications and reflections.

Depending on the length of your essay, steps 1 and 2 above can be placed in the introductory paragraph, as we demonstrate in Chapters 3 and 4, "Reviewing the Basics" and "Thesis Statements." Step 2 is the thesis statement, and may be phrased, eventually, as one complete sentence. Steps 3 and 4 may break down into two or even three paragraphs each. Note that steps 3 and 4 as outlined above represent **block style** in comparison-contrast essays. Alternatively, you could handle steps 3 and 4 in **point-by-point style**, interweaving them into paragraphs focused on reasons rather than on which side of the argument is in question. If the reasons given by A and B are essentially opposite views of the same topics (French immersion places a person between two languages, which is a good thing, as opposed to French immersion places a person between two languages, which is a bad thing), then you might decide that point-by-point structure is the better choice. This choice would help you avoid repetition more effectively than the block approach would.

Essay Body Using Point-by-Point Structure

Reason 1	A's position
	B's position
Reason 2	A's position
	B's position
Reason 3	A's position
	B's position

Find the comparative pattern that most avoids repetition, yet maintains equal consideration of the two sides. Remember to acknowledge the good points and reasoning on the side you are opposing; express a tone of fairness and respect even as you stress the reasons for your final position. Following is an essay that illustrates content, tone, and structure in the formal argumentative approach.

Sample Argumentative Essay

This essayist employs point-by-point style to argue against opposing views. The essay draws heavily on internet sources, a resource that your instructor may or may not encourage you to use.

Sample Essay Argumentation

Kyoto *Discord*—Let's Be Wise, if Not Right or Rich

The opening defines the Accord, updates its current terms, and places it in the midst of the controversy

3 main points or topics foreshadow the essay's structure

The basic issue is asked

The thesis statement addresses that main issue

1   When American President Bill Clinton signed the 1997 Kyoto Accord, joining 37 other industrialized countries in commitment to a protocol that now calls for a carbon-emissions reduction of 3.5 percent by 2012 (over 1990 levels), American business immediately objected (Duff). Even the American Energy Department questioned the President. Clinton's opponents cited three main reasons: the failure to include developing countries; unconvincing scientific evidence; and the serious threat to the American economy. Canada, one of the 38 signatories, initially accepted the opinion of United Nations scientists: continued carbon emissions could contribute to greenhouse climate change and severe planetary disruption. With strong opposition from the United States and now from Alberta, Canada's prime minister Jean Chrétien must decide if he should ratify the Accord. While it is admittedly hard for us to know which scientist, which economist, and which politician to believe, the wisest course for Canada is to seek national consensus in support of Kyoto.

This paragraph will focus on the first of the 3 topics previewed above. The opposition side on the first topic is reviewed first

Having outlined the opposition's arguments on this topic, the writer responds with counter-arguments to each of the opposition points

2   The objections to Kyoto were embraced by President George W. Bush who, upon succeeding Clinton, withdrew support for the Accord. On the first point, he argued that by exempting developing nations the Accord defeats its goals: emissions from non-participants will offset the sacrifices made by participants. In response, let us consider that notwithstanding lack of scientific agreement on this entire topic, it only follows that emissions reductions by 38 heavily industrialized nations will do some good, and it is better to have controls begin in the highly industrialized countries (where the levels of emissions are highest) than in the less industrialized ones. Western parties can build emissions controls into future industry agreements with non-Kyoto nations. A system of rewards can be implemented for those who join the Accord. Mr. Bush, however, also pleads unfairness: why should the developed countries be the ones hampered by new standards? But the President overlooks the massive advantages and influence of the West. Our standard of living is so much greater than that of the excluded countries that surely we can better sustain the challenge of adapting to Kyoto standards. This will even help others to catch up, an important consideration for political health. Given the vast lead that Western nations have over those in developing areas, the exemption of poorer nations from Kyoto standards simply represents awareness on our part of a need to pursue a higher level of political and economic equity. In the meantime, having 37 highly industrialized nations set an example is surely a formidable starting point, one that would be all the more powerful, of course, with the United States, the world's leading emitter of greenhouse gases.

Opposition arguments on the second topic are reviewed

3   On the second objection, lack of scientific assurance that carbon emissions harm the environment, President Bush presented a petition of 15 000 scientists opposed to Kyoto. Yet these scientists remain themselves opposed by colleagues whose opinions have been accepted by 37 other countries. Just 450 pro-Kyoto scientists in each of

the other 37 signatory nations would outnumber Bush's list. Winston Gereluk, co-ordinator of industrial relations at Alberta's Athabasca University, contends that the Kyoto "protocol is based on one of the most extensive scientific exercises in history," one that began well before the 1988 global climate-change meeting. With scientific opinion divided, to say the least, we might ask does the viewpoint of one nation encourage greater conviction than that of 37 nations? Certainly arguments from the pro-Kyoto side need to be more deeply considered.

Counter-arguments on this second topic are advanced

4   The David Suzuki Foundation has gathered together views and evidence from the vast scientific sector discounted by Mr. Bush. Noting today's widespread scientific acceptance that global warming is a reality (0.2 degrees Celsius rise in temperature per decade) and that carbon emissions do contribute to this trend, the Foundation lists numerous scientific studies exploring the harmful consequences of global warming in three broad categories: extreme weather, imperilled ecosystems, and human health.

On the second topic, counter-arguments are elaborated

Response on the second topic is now divided into 3 categories

5   Such far-reaching consequences have begun to emerge in Canada. On the subject of weather, let us consider the recent cases of drought, intense summer heat, and violent storms. Victoria, British Columbia, recorded half of its usual winter rainfall in 2000–01, its driest winter since 1900. As a result, the reservoirs of available water dropped by 30 percent (ESEM). In 2002, Edmonton experienced its driest and hottest summer on record; unprecedented forest fires north of the city soon exhausted the normal firefighting budget. Turning to imperilled ecosystems, two University of Toronto scientists estimate that by the end of this century, 45 percent of Canada's habitat could be lost, along with 20 percent of its wildlife species (Malcolm and Markham). The human health factor has also been widely considered by scientists, many of whom predict increased asthma and heart disease. In some cases, scientists offer these predictions despite political pressure to remain silent. In October 2002, Dr. David Swann, medical health officer for the southern Alberta Palliser Health Authority, was fired from his job after expressing support for the Kyoto Accord as a health benefit (*Edmonton Journal*). Political denial cannot erase the real threat to health, however. As temperatures rise, there is also the threat of tropical diseases. Cases of mosquito-borne illnesses have recently occurred in North America. There may not be incontestable proof that carbon emissions cause these problems, but over the past 15 or 20 years, increasing numbers of reputable scientists have been making public statements to the effect that consumption of fossil fuels and global warming could be agents of dire change. Canadians seem to be reading and accepting these opinions. Seventy-eight percent of Canadians, including 65.6 percent of Albertans, supported ratification of Kyoto in a March 2002 poll by Decima Research. We know that all the people are not right all of the time—but is the majority right in this case?

The writer pauses to appeal to ethics and emotion, using an analogy. Is this analogy ad populum?

6   Let us imagine that your mother became ill and one doctor said you must sacrifice personal income and suffer hardship to secure the right herbs to save her. Another doctor said there was no reason to be so worried, that we should go on mak-

The writer summarizes and reinforces the 3 counter-arguments on the second topic

The writer restores focus to logic, concluding the analogy with a "reasonable" suggestion that does not claim absolute certainty but urges caution

The preceding conclusion justifies countering the third point. However, the opposition's view is summarized before more is said against it

Detailed rebuttal to the opposition's third point now begins

ing our usual income and not bothering to seek herbs. What would we do? Certainly the earth is our mother: we depend entirely upon the planet for our well-being. The air we breathe, if polluted, can harm and even kill us. This has been demonstrated in numerous scientific investigations. The earth nourishes us and all living things, so it is only right that we care for her. If there is a 50 percent chance, or even a lower chance, that the United Nations scientists are right and the Bush scientists are wrong, then it only makes sense to take the prudent course. Ignoring the possible consequences of global warming could mean no turning back. So let us say that while we may never be able to claim that by supporting Kyoto we are right, we can, like a loving child, strive to be wise.

7   Although Mr. Bush disagrees, the potential benefits to planetary well-being more than outweigh any possible costs of implementing Kyoto. This is so even if the worst-case economic fears of Kyoto opponents are realized. In 1997, the National Energy Department predicted that Kyoto would lower the American GDP by 4.1 percent; there would be 2.4 million fewer jobs by 2010. Bad as that picture may be, it still looks better than the possible harm of greenhouse emissions. Opponents within Canada argue that unless the United States ratifies the Accord as well, Canada will be at an extreme economic disadvantage in competition with our already prodigious neighbour. On the other hand, pro-Kyoto advocates, such as the David Suzuki Foundation, argue that the consequences of global warming bring their own major economic problems. The costs of dealing with drought, floods, fires, water shortages, illnesses, and the like should be considered. The Suzuki Foundation contends that ratifying Kyoto will stimulate the high-tech sector, bringing more jobs and net benefits to Canada. Stepping back from both sides of this economic debate, one may decide that predictions that the American and Canadian economies will significantly suffer or benefit from the Kyoto Accord may be as overstated as predictions that were made about the economic repercussions of the Free Trade Agreement. In reality, after all the extreme predictions of economic gains or losses arising from that agreement, some people benefited by it while others had to find new work or adapt in their existing employment. Some sectors went up, others went down. There is still no consensus on whether the Free Trade Agreement overall helped or hurt our economies.

8   What does seem possible—and what the Suzuki Foundation does not seem to address specifically—is that the Alberta economy could pay a significant short-term cost in adapting to Kyoto. We should consider that since the 1960s, Alberta's major industry has been the exploitation of petroleum and other mineral resources. The tar sands of the Athabasca River are considered among the richest oil deposits in the world. Half of Canada's coal is mined in Alberta. Natural gas is another major resource. Despite diversification of its economy in Calgary and Edmonton, Alberta relies on these resources and feels deep psychological dependence on the energy sector. Resentment over the imposed National Energy Policy (NEP) of the 1980s remains

strong. An Albertan writing online to CBC's program "Your Space" on May 16, 2002, suggests that 40 000 Albertan jobs were lost due to the NEP, and that the same ramifications could follow with Kyoto. We might respond that Alberta, NEP notwithstanding, still has the highest standard of living on the planet, and that non-renewable resources cannot continue fuelling Alberta's economy forever—but regardless of the above-mentioned Albertan's facts or reasoning, his response signals how seriously that province feels both exploited and excluded from national decision-making. Alberta's premier, Ralph Klein, has threatened to boycott discussions of Kyoto unless his modified proposal on controlling carbon fuel emissions is accepted. So while supporting Kyoto is paramount, Ottawa, in response to Alberta's concerns about national alienation, should also show renewed interest in a Triple-E Senate, a long overdue measure that would extend more say to the regions.

9   In conclusion, with the United States dominating world affairs, Canada is certainly wise to ratify Kyoto. If our nation supports, however modestly and diplomatically, a global balance of power and tenders an important vote for protection of the life source on which we all depend, our actions will resonate globally, perhaps influencing other nations to make a greater environmental commitment. Yet Canada's continued contribution to global well-being will be measured first in large part by its ability to settle political imbalances, perceived and real, within its own nation.

> Consideration for the opposition is restored (Alberta is part of the opposition). This prepares us for the special provision of this writer's conclusion—that underlying the Kyoto discord is an unfair political process in Canada

Works Cited

Chambers, Allan. "Doctor's Firing Tarnishes Alberta Stand." *Edmonton Journal*, 8 October 2002, A6.

Duff, Anna Bray. "Kyoto Accord Divides Business." *Investor's Business Daily*, 13 November 1998.

Gereluk, Winston. "Climate Science Faces Alberta-style Inquisition." *Edmonton Journal* 14 October 2002, A15.

Mullan, Vince. Comment to CBC, 16 May 2002. <**http://cbc.ca/news/viewpoint/yourspace/ kyoto_protocol.html**>.

<**http://www.sepp.org/pressrel/petition.html**>. The Science and Environment Policy Project (SEPP) is a group of American scientists and businesspeople opposed to the 1997 Kyoto agreement on reducing levels of carbon emissions.

The David Suzuki Foundation <**www.davidsuzuki.org/Climate_Change/Impacts**>.

"Environmental Science and Engineering," Western Canada Water and Wastewater Association, January 2002. <**www.esemag.com**>.

Malcolm, Jay, and Adam Markham. *Speed Kills: Rates of Climate Change Are Threatening Biodiversity*. Toronto: University of Toronto, 2002. <**www.panda.org/climate/ spotlight/speedkills.cfm**>.

Focus Questions

1. Does this essay overlook possible counter-arguments? (*Hint:* Australia decided not to ratify the Accord unless the United States also ratified it. By not mentioning this fact, does the essayist oversimplify the situation as one rogue country against all the others? Also, since Victoria experienced temperatures in 1900 equal to those in 2001, what makes the writer so certain that greenhouse gases caused the heat wave of 2001? Should this question have been recognized and addressed? Finally, China and India, both heavy polluters, were left out of the Accord. Does the essayist oversimplify by implying that these countries are "non-industrial"?)

2. Can you cite phrases that violate the recommendation not to use emotionally laden language in argumentation? How would you characterize most of the language in this essay?

3. On the issue of economics, how valid is the comparison to the Free Trade Agreement?

4. Do the listed Works Cited reflect a fair balance of views pro and con, as well as more neutral, purely informational sources?

5. Did the essay to any extent change or challenge your own thinking on this topic? If so, how?

6. Look ahead to the discussion of logic and logical fallacies. Is the thrust of this essay suitably logical? Can you detect any of the 12 listed logical fallacies? If so, explain why you believe your example is a fallacy.

7. Find an analogy in the essay. How crucial is it to the essayist's purpose? Explain. How successful do you consider this analogy? Explain.

8. Comment on any strategies you find particularly effective in this essay.

9. Consider the objectivity of public opinion polls. The writer overlooks mentioning that the Decima Research poll was commissioned by Greenpeace, a group that strongly supports the Kyoto Accord. In the autumn of 2002, the Alberta government flooded the province with brochures attacking the Kyoto Accord. The Alberta government then commissioned another poll within the province, and found that attitudes had shifted to around 72 percent now opposed to ratification of Kyoto. Concerning poll results, comment on the importance of recognizing who commissioned particular polls and what sorts of public propaganda campaigns preceded them.

As you can see, analytical contrast is an important dominant pattern in formal argumentation, with the opposing position measured against yours throughout a piece of writing. You can also see that emphasis on *reasons* is very important. You are called upon to demonstrate *causes and effects* in order to show the shortcomings of other positions and the merits of your own. It is therefore a very good idea to review the sections in Chapter 6 dealing with comparison-contrast and cause-effect methods.

In summary, here are more *specific* points to keep in mind when writing argumentation.

Steps to Effective Argumentative Essays

- Know different sides of the controversy *in detail* (be current).
- Employ comparison-contrast and cause-effect.
- Maintain a moderate, respectful, and serious tone.
- Put the emphasis on logic, but consider emotions and ethics.
- As with all essays, narrow your topic sufficiently for the length of that essay.
- As with all essays, apply the principles of effective openings and conclusions.

 PRACTICE

- Read through some of the essays in Section 3 of the *Reader*. To what extent do they apply the above considerations? Choose at least one essay for special attention and assess the effectiveness and fairness of its arguments. Discuss your findings with your classmates and instructor.

- In Section 3 of the *Reader*, carefully go through the two student essays arguing for and against euthanasia. Answer the questions following each of those two essays.

LOGIC AND LOGICAL FALLACIES

Although appeals to emotion and ethics are common in argumentation, the form depends heavily on logic. Most of us pride ourselves on our command of reason, yet in daily life we frequently stray into illogical conclusions. Acknowledging our biases, seeing issues from unfamiliar points of view, and properly applying the tools of reason may be the greatest task we face in college or university as well as in life. To help open up the discussion of intellectual integrity, we offer the following discussion of basic tools and common errors.

Inductive and Deductive Forms of Reasoning

In the Middle Ages, scholarship, closely tied to the Catholic church, was dominated by a type of intellectual reasoning based on traditionally accepted general principles and doctrinal presumptions until the Renaissance in Europe, which flourished in the sixteenth century. The study and evolution of empiricism followed, the scientific method of setting up experiments and basing conclusions on rigorous analysis through observation of phenomena, and the collection and measurement of data. This "modern" method of reasoning emphasizes induction, the use of concrete particulars to derive some larger principles. The much older method of reasoning tends to emphasize deduction, which posits (theorizes) a large principle and then looks for supporting examples.

Induction

Inductive conclusions, as we have suggested, flow from experience and observation. (A good memory device here for **ind**uctive is an **ind**irect observation.) For example, a child touches a red-hot burner. The next time she sees a red-hot burner, she will probably not touch it, because she has formed a conclusion, based on experience, that red-hot burners hurt her when she touches them. Inductive reasoning moves outward from the individual experience; that is, it moves from particular instances to general conclusions.

Deduction

Deductive reasoning, in contrast, moves inward, moves from the concept to the cases. Deduction starts with general principles and applies analysis in order to reach specific conclusions. The popularity of the British literary character Sherlock Holmes also made the process of deduction famous. He would often listen to an account of events and after a survey of the scene suddenly deduce the crime's complete solution.

More practically, in our world, deductive conclusions most often follow from an abstract mental process called the **syllogism.** This construction consists of three steps: a major premise, a minor premise, and a conclusion. A "premise" may be defined as a statement of accepted truth, such as "lawyers work long hours" or "Cathy is a corporate lawyer." The first of these statements expresses a general principle about all lawyers, so this may be considered a major premise. The second statement offers an accepted truth concerning a specific case, so it may be considered a minor premise. Considering the minor premise in relation to the established major premise, we can derive a conclusion:

Major premise:	Lawyers work long hours.
Minor premise:	Cathy is a corporate lawyer.
Conclusion:	Cathy works long hours.

Be aware, however, that the formal reasoning behind a syllogism can sometimes lead to a faulty conclusion, as in the following example.

Major premise:	Serious study requires personal discipline.
Minor premise:	Andrew, a Dalhousie student, is disciplined.
Faulty conclusion:	Andrew studies seriously.

If Andrew is disciplined in other ways (in exercise, diet, money management, confidentiality, dental care, punctuality, etc.) but not in studying, the conclusion does not hold, though the formal logic in the syllogism is technically correct. So be prepared for the possibility that a syllogism may seem structurally sound, yet the conclusion may be wrong when tested against the reality of the specific case.

Here is a conclusion on the nature of theatre plays taken from a sermon by an English preacher in 1577, the time of Elizabeth I and Shakespeare: "The cause of plagues is sinne, if you look to it well; and the cause of sinne are playes: therefore the cause of plagues are playes."[22] The preacher's syllogism follows the pattern correctly, moving from a major premise to a minor premise on the same topic to a conclusion; however, both premises in themselves contain faulty logic (see "Oversimplification"). The preacher's conclusion, far from disinterested, is dictated by his unquestioned assumptions and, perhaps, intensified by the human urge in desperate times to find a simple solution for a dreadful disorder.[23] In short, we might infer that the preacher of this sermon was unconsciously seeking to identify a scapegoat. This kind of professional and personal bias lurking beneath a formal facade of reason seems easy to spot in arguments from times past; we all too often make that assumption, however, if we believe we live in enlightened times today and do not commit many of the logical and ethical errors that we ascribe to our ancestors. Your instructors will always encourage you to examine your own conclusions with as much objectivity as you attempt to apply to those of others.

An imperfect but successful syllogism

As long as you remember that use of the syllogism form does not ensure sound results, the method can still be highly serviceable. Here is an example of a successful deduction in the form of a syllogism from *The Maltese Falcon* (the 1940s film noir starring Humphrey Bogart). Early on in the film, Private Eye Sam Spade (Bogart's character) concludes, through deduction, that his investigative partner must have been killed by someone his partner knew, because his dead partner's overcoat was still buttoned up and his gun was in his holster.

Major premise (presumption)

An experienced detective assigned to shadow a suspect would not allow a stranger to approach in an alley late at night without quick access to a weapon for possible self-defence.

Minor premise (fact)

The detective's buttoned coat, preventing quick access to his weapon, indicated he did not feel threatened by the person approaching.

Conclusion

The dead detective knew and felt secure around the approaching person who turned out to be his killer.

In the film, Sam Spade's conclusion proved correct: the victim knew the killer. However, notice how his major premise is only an assumption, an informed guess. What if the killer *were* not known to the dead detective, but appeared unthreatening—

---

[22] Reported by Peter Ackroyd in *London: The Biography* (London: Vintage, 2001) 100.

[23] The plague of 1348 killed approximately 40 percent of London's population. Between 1563 and 1603 there were five severe outbreaks of plague.

say, a uniformed police officer, a minister in starched collar, an early-morning milk-man, or an elderly person anxiously requiring directions somewhere? These absolute strangers would likely be able to approach the detective without causing enough alarm for him to prepare to defend himself. Thus the major premise would be wrong and the syllogism's conclusion would be faulty: an unknown killer in a reassuring disguise could have approached the experienced detective. As well, the dead detective might have been ambushed by the killer and not have had opportunity to defend himself. Or the killer, a person not known to the detective, might have returned the detective's gun to its holster and rebuttoned his overcoat in an effort to suggest that the killer was, in fact, someone the detective did know.

Our point here is that deductions are often our best-informed conclusions under limited conditions, conditions that include presumptions. Question your own deductions, and be alert to presumptions that veil possible exceptions and alternatives.

Deductive Premises Formed by Induction

Most everyday thinking, as well as scholarly work, combines both forms of reasoning. Many empirical (inductive) studies, for example, turn to deductive thinking in their conclusions, speculating to some extent on possible broader implications of their specific findings, even setting forth new presumptions or premises to assist future deductions. While probing reality through ongoing observation, physics nevertheless relies on the abstract, deductive-type reasoning of mathematics to direct and confirm its processes.

In many cases, we initially form our general principles or presumptions of deduction by inductive observation. We say that all living things die not because we have actually observed every living thing through the course of its own life to death, but because we are generalizing from several observations. We have seen some living things die, have heard of many living things dying, and have not seen or heard of any exceptions to this general belief. Such conclusions are often valid but not always. For just this reason, the "laws" of physics or other sciences are considered right only until they are found (as they sometimes are) to be wrong.

In short, deduction often begins and operates on *partial induction*—a generalization derived from a limited range of observed occurrences—for its major premise. Thus, deduction is often an informed estimate rather than a beautifully reliable, self-contained, nearly mathematical derivation, despite what Sherlock Holmes, *Star Trek*'s Mr. Spock, and late-night television detectives would try to lead us to believe. Shakespeare's *Hamlet* and *Othello* both dramatize—through a ghost and a woman's handkerchief, respectively—the serious uncertainties around the process of deduction.

Fact or Opinion?

We gave an example above of the preacher who stated the following syllogism: "The cause of plagues is sinne, if you look to it well; and the cause of sinne are playes: therefore the cause of plagues are playes." In today's times, we would view both premise statements as opinion, not fact. Sometimes, the difference between opinions and facts is unclear, and sometimes writers wish to manipulate this confusion.

 PRACTICE

Without reading our commentary below, discuss with your classmates whether the following statements are facts or opinions:

1. Christopher Columbus was the first person to discover North America.
2. Women are physically weaker than men.
3. Alberta has refused to support the Kyoto agreement due to self-interest.
4. Canada's national sport is hockey.
5. The birthplace of hockey was Victoria Rink, Montreal, March 3, 1875.
6. In 1763, under terms of the Treaty of Paris, almost all of New France was ceded to Britain.

Of the six statements, only the last can be safely called a fact. The first was widely stated as a fact in history textbooks for years; however, history, as we are often reminded, is written by "the winners." How could a European be the first person to discover a place inhabited by a people whose distant ancestors had already migrated there? As well, recent evidence in Newfoundland indicates that the Vikings also made the trip before Columbus. Yet this so-called fact of Columbus's discovery was seldom questioned because the mainstream point of view considered the Natives less civilized than Europeans. So distinguishing genuine fact from entrenched opinion is heavily influenced by systems of beliefs, by cultural assumptions.

The second statement above is demonstrably untrue in certain cases, and with respect to certain muscle groups it is untrue in most cases. Women have very strong leg muscles, for instance, and have made greater gains in marathon running for their shorter history in the sport than men. There is no consensus on the third statement; in any case, in a recent poll 65.5 percent of Alberta citizens supported Kyoto, contradicting the official government position. The fourth statement is demonstrably incorrect; lacrosse remains Canada's official sport. As for the fifth statement, while an international ice hockey team of six writers and researchers recently published an 18-page report declaring the statement true, a highway sign on the way into Windsor, Nova Scotia, still announces the town's status as "Birthplace of Hockey." There remains a major debate over how to define "birth" in the case of hockey, which illustrates the limitation of analogies (see "False Analogy," below). There are even similar claims for Kingston, Ontario. Since the authors of this book originally hail respectively from Quebec and New Brunswick, we have decided that Montreal will be the official birthplace of hockey in even years and Saint John in odd years. We will discount Windsor and Kingston arbitrarily. So it is with the frequent cultural construction of facts.

We can see from this lighthearted example that controversies often boil down to different interpretations of fact and opinion. Even our suggestion that one of the above statements could be "safely" called a fact is called into question by ontological considerations. Quantum physics suggests that no reality is certain, only probable, possible, or unlikely. Albert Einstein demonstrated the relativity of time, a measurement sometimes explained as an illusion, merely a mathematical conceit that is of collective service to humans. Depending on your personal inclination, these metaphysical ideas may seem like nonsense or truth. Even the debate over the material world as fact or illusion is ancient. As far as your writing is concerned, our point is to remind you not to state opinions as facts, and to be careful to consider whether something you consider a fact may seem an opinion to certain readers. The advice to draw from our discussion is to support your claims, which you do best by carefully avoiding logical fallacies.

Logical Fallacies

In daily conversation many of us so easily stray into illogical statements that that we find the following instructions valuable. Whether you draw on a logical, ethical or emotional appeal, or some combination of these three, in your efforts at written persuasion, you need to understand logical fallacies in order to avoid them. As well as undermining your argument, logical fallacies provide skeptical or impatient readers with the quick means to dispose of your entire position. In other words, a mistake in reasoning in one part of your argument may mean your observations will be disregarded altogether.

Below, we discuss 12 common types of logical fallacies: either/or false opposites, *ad hominem*, overgeneralization, oversimplification, false analogy, circular argument, *non sequitur*, *post hoc ergo propter hoc*, *ad populum*, bandwagon appeal, slippery slope, and red herring. As you will see, many of these overlap to certain degrees, often employing elements of overgeneralization, oversimplification, and circular reasoning.

1. Either/Or False Opposites

There are many authentic either/or situations. These cases of contrasting choices and fairly certain outcomes are pressing and sometimes dramatic: "Either I stop using heavy drugs or I will lose control of my future." "Bill Gates either limited Microsoft as a monopolistic company or faced further legal penalties." But in many cases, so-called either/or situations are bogus, instances of oversimplification.

A bogus either/or situation tries to conjure up the urgency of a genuine either/or scenario, but fails to convince us that other real alternatives do not exist for further consideration. The logical fallacy consists of the essayist's offering the reader false opposites. The careful reader quickly realizes that the urgent demand for a specific action is not as restricted or pressing as the essayist claims: with untrue either/or situations, you indulge in poor reasoning by reducing the immediate future to two outcomes only. These outcomes supposedly exist as sole alternatives to each other. Try to think past either/or false opposites toward a range of available, workable alternatives more appropriate to our multi-layered world of complex situations and challenges. When you *cannot* find a range of alternatives, you may well be facing a genuine either/or choice.

✎ PRACTICE

Decide whether the following either/or statements are false opposites:

1. If Anil doesn't receive a new car for graduation, he won't be able to function as an adult.
2. Our hockey coach said that if we lose these high school playoffs, we'll never accomplish anything worthwhile in our lives.
3. If legal aid didn't exist, then there would be many more unfair convictions.
4. Michelle believed that William had to write her a series of hasty, inflated reference letters for overseas graduate programs or she would never be happy in life.

2. *Ad Hominem*

This term is Latin for "to the man." It includes name-calling, mudslinging, and innuendo. *Ad hominem* attacks the person rather than his or her argument or policy. Although Canadian politics are often described as more "civilized" than those of the United States, the 2000 Canadian federal election demonstrated a great deal of name-calling. Whether or not Jean Chrétien improperly influenced the granting of a bank loan does not logically determine the value of his proposed national budget. Whether or not Stockwell Day libelled the good name of an Alberta lawyer would not determine the value of *his* proposed budget.

Often *ad hominem* attacks serve as a form of *red herring* (deflecting attention from real issues), and sometimes they include the *straw-man* strategy of deliberately inflating a perceived threat from a certain opponent in order to focus on a supposedly justified counter-attack. Prime Minister Pierre Trudeau gained demonic status in Alberta in the late 1970s and 1980s as a supposed enemy of the west; newspaper lampoonists even drew him with devil's horns. Alberta's political leaders routinely avoided complex thoughts and questions by merely invoking the spectre of Trudeau and his federal government. American political leaders have often used foreign leaders as embodiments of various evils to deflect the American people's attention away from questioning their own government.

3. Overgeneralizations *and* Stereotyping

If you argue that all British people are understated or that all Canadians are deferential and friendly, you are making a hasty generalization that can be easily invalidated. All it takes is one counter-example—Mick Jagger is British *and* flamboyant, Margaret Atwood is Canadian *and* authoritative—to undermine your claim. In both cases, you are endorsing false cultural stereotypes. Generalizations (unless you are analyzing and/or debunking them) too often illuminate nothing in particular. In your essays, immediately state the parameters of your particular discussion or analysis. A reader will respect your directness and your eagerness to begin your discussion in earnest.

Careless generalizations often mistake the part for the whole. They apply the extremely limited truth of a subset to every instance in an entire field; since *some* or even *most* athletes lead healthy lives, they *all* do. As our discussion of induction and deduction illustrates, some generalizing is an inevitable part of your moving from specifics to presumptions, to exploring broader possibilities. But always do so with caution, knowing that your presumption is simply a device in the cause of experimentation, not an absolute certainty. An essayist writes to make a *particular* case about a topic in some defined scope. One renowned writer once said that "to speak generally is to say nothing at all." And, as we note in Chapter 6, Albert Einstein once said that "God is in the details."

Emotional response explains a fair amount of *stereotyping*. As we have suggested, stereotyping is a particularly noxious form of overgeneralization; it is a gross distortion, often based on no tested truth whatsoever. An opponent, or perceived opponent, is reduced to inferior status based on an unfounded generalization concerning all people of his or her race, sex, faith, culture, orientation, or national origins. Quebec separatist leader Jacques Parizeau made instant headlines after he declared that the "Yes" side had lost the 1995 Quebec referendum on separating from Canada because of the "ethnic and moneyed" vote. Large numbers of Yes voters expressed outrage with their leader. This technique of stereotyping has become so officially despised, in fact, that a preferred tactic of reductive debate today seems to be one of hoping for an opportunity to tarnish the opponent with accusations of this abuse (*ad hominem*). Propagandists routinely revert to various logical fallacies by accusing their opponents of using the very same propaganda tactics they themselves are using.

4. Oversimplification

This form of faulty reasoning reduces complex situations to easy descriptions and unidimensional conclusions. Oversimplification differs from generalization in that generalization misleadingly blurs many aspects into one, whereas oversimplification inaccurately restricts the parameters of an argument. We would be generalizing if we claimed that many professors are badly dressed, absent-minded children. We would be oversimplifying if we claimed that Alberta's Bill 11 (on privatized health care) will improve Canadian health-care delivery. In saying that all physicians are smart, we would again be overgeneralizing. Generalization is unconvincing and lazy. Oversimplification may misrepresent facts and thereby *seem*, at least temporarily, convincing and therefore dangerous. Generalization moves *outward* and throws a wide, ineffective net, and oversimplification moves *inward* and delimits a subject falsely.

A large number of self-help, self-improvement ads depend on grand oversimplifications to inspire vulnerable people to buy products against what might normally be their better judgment:

> Keep to your ab workout and the rest of life's challenges will also burn away.

Such ads obviously reduce life to a single aspect; their oversimplification is obvious. Other oversimplifications are more subtle and can masquerade as conclusions. Generalizations may offend or bore, but oversimplifications reduce with a serious cost. Generalizations are what your friends say about New York or Halifax after spending two days in those cities. Oversimplifications are what people declare about social problems such as the cycle of poverty, racism, abuse, or youth socialization.

This everyday but dangerously influential oversimplification is why we stress that critical reading, thinking and writing are important to your freedom, your sense of self, and your future power as a person, as well as for your improved college grades and steady employment prospects.

 PRACTICE

Bring to class some oversimplifications that concern you in the newspaper, the law, provincial or federal government policies. Do the examples of oversimplification you have selected merely reason naively or are some oversimplifications calculated to address an issue deliberately without commitment?

---

5. False Analogy

Analogies provide helpful, illuminating, thought-provoking, and often unexpected comparisons that illustrate key points. (See "Analogy" under "Comparison-Contrast" in Chapter 6 (p. 350).) They are not, however, proofs of fact in and of themselves. An analogy is a rhetorical device for strategic amplification. Analogies help make a vivid assertion of some underlying similarity:

> Mr. Cleghorn, our history teacher, talks to his high school students in the same way that Mr. Dress-Up used to talk to his pre-school TV audience.

> Susan has more attitude than Madonna and Kid Rock put together.

> As flies to wanton boys, are we to the gods; / They kill us for their sport. (*King Lear*, 4.1.36–37)

A sturdy, internally sound analogy immediately illustrates your point. The analogy can be brief (merely part of a sentence) or quite extended (several sentences or paragraphs). In either case, it helps to define or describe a point of similarity.

Remember, however, that *all* analogies eventually break down because you are comparing some discovered or asserted similarity in essentially dissimilar items, people, situations, or events. All analogies have limits. A *false analogy* is a comparison with such a faulty or shaky basis that its clunkiness or inappropriateness detracts from rather than contributes to your point. You are doing yourself a serious disservice if your argument holds together on its own without the shaky analogy. Consider these **false analogies**:

Accountants are artists: both are important observers of details.

Canada's international peacekeeping reputation makes us the busiest goalie in the ongoing hockey game of foreign affairs.

Here is a discussion of these analogies to show you that all analogies will have their critics. In the first analogy of accountants and artists, the essayist presumes that because both accountants and artists analyze diverse information, they are essentially the same. The essayist here overlooks the fundamental distinction that artists—by definition—must use their imaginative powers to create original works of art, whereas accountants use their analytical skills to interpret existing numbers. The analogy invites readers to consider the ways in which accountants are fundamentally unlike Vincent van Gogh, Guy Vanderhaeghe, or The Tragically Hip.

Concerning the second false analogy, ask yourself if peacekeeping is an entertaining game with a small outcome. Is an intervening nation comparable to a goalie who protects only his team's position? Are the common Canadian traditions of cautious peacekeeping and frenetic hockey-playing enough basis for the convincing comparison of these pursuits? Why or why not?

 **PRACTICE**

Are the following analogies workable or weak?

- A dedicated teacher is a lifeguard constantly alert to any students drowning in apathy or defeatism.
- His heart is a lump of coal.

- The bedroom can become a beautiful exhilarating garden for 2 people in love.
- Like an unsupervised frontier sheriff, the U.S. government talks of law and order, but seems agreeable to dubious tactics if convenient.

---

6. Circular Argument *and* Begging the Question

All circular arguments wrongly presume that a premise, speculation, or assertion—what has *yet* to be proven—can be treated as a self-evident fact or, more often, as a thoroughly settled, compelling conclusion. In circular argument, premise wrongly masquerades as conclusion. In its most obvious form, circular reasoning is not too hard to spot: "Soap operas are terrible because they are awful." As used here, the terms "terrible" and "awful" have the same sense, are redundant to a degree that qualifies them as tautology. This entirely circular statement begs the reader to accept a pseudo-explanation that really remains at an utter standstill. In less immediately obvious forms of circular reasoning, an initial premise may seem to include an explanation, but on closer inspection, this explanation is itself merely the premise again: "God wants you to give me all your money, because an angel told me so in my dream last night." Why should we have to accept that this dream was the word of God? The writer is really saying that God wants you to do something because God wants you to do something. Here are some further examples of circular arguments:

Travel invigorates and educates students because travel is enlightening.

The U.S. Watergate ordeal of the 1970s established that Nixon was the most dishonest president because of the infamous break-in and missing Oval Office tapes, which caused a huge scandal about his integrity.

Swimming is good exercise because it's an excellent workout.

The RCMP did not use excessive force with the University of British Columbia student demonstrators at the 1997 APEC conference because it used the appropriate means to maintain civic order.

The 1999 liquidation of Eaton's, a long-standing symbol of Canadian business history, should have been prevented because Eaton's represents an important part of our national entrepreneurial tradition.

In these examples, the writer makes hasty pre-judgments about the truth of the premises that he or she is supposed to be inquiring into with an open mind and some careful skepticism. Remember that critical reading and persuasive writing form the basis of your post-secondary writing experience and instruction. In this context, a vital, healthy skepticism of *all* premises, conditions, examples, and conclusions will continue to further your own development as independent thinker and engaging writer. So even if essayists believe in their claims wholeheartedly, they must demonstrate to their readers *why* each claim is worth the reader's consideration, let alone their full or partial acceptance. The statements above offer as their supposedly conclusive evidence merely debatable observations that are to be discussed and reasoned for or against.

In the first example, travel may indeed be invigorating, educational, and enlightening, but in what specific ways and for what clear reasons? The claim in the example is only that travel invigorates and teaches because it enlightens. This reasoning is straight out of the Redundancy Department, establishes nothing, and may hurt a reader's trust in your ability to develop your assertions openly, incrementally, and therefore convincingly. Since it is extremely easy to establish that travel *is* all the essayist would like to claim, the essayist's lack of effort to offer a reason or two to back up this easy claim would puzzle any reader.

In the second example, Richard Nixon may or may not have been the most dishonest American president, but the fact that many of his closest staff and advisors were successfully prosecuted because of the Watergate cover-up does not *by itself* establish the premise of his own relatively colossal dishonesty among all American presidents ("the *most* dishonest"). If the reader simply asks have other presidents lied, covered up facts, or crossed over into possible illegal activity, then our example's foregone conclusion about Nixon's spectacular villainy compared to other U.S. executives-in-chief will begin to wobble. The circular logic at work here is that Nixon is the most dishonest simply because he was the most thoroughly exposed for his misdeeds. This logical fallacy is similar to arguing that "Mr. X is the most successful thief and fraud in history." However, we will never know the identities of the most successful thieves and frauds *if* they were truly successful. The logical fallacy here—*since* Nixon was thoroughly caught, he *must* be the most dishonest among presidents—offers only a belief or opinion, not a proof or a persuasive effort.

Circular reasoning is sometimes referred to as *begging the question* (pleading to have a claim accepted even though you haven't proved it). Some authorities are more likely to use the term begging the question when premises pose as would-be conclusions without any sign of attempted explanation. An example of such an assertion would be "immoral books like Salinger's *The Catcher in the Rye* undermine our youth's faith in society." The writer here offers no pretense of an argument, uses no "because" to signal the intention of reasoning toward a conclusion. The writer suggests no evidence that this effect of wholesale disillusionment really occurs, and even if it does, no explanation of why that necessarily constitutes immorality. A complex term has been reduced to an easy description (see "Oversimplification"), based in part on the circular notion that our society (whatever exactly that is) is moral because it is our society and our society is moral (See "*Ad Populum*," p. 388). In a general sense, all logical fallacies "beg" readers to accept unsubstantiated claims, so this term is sometimes applied to various other forms of assumption as well.

 ## PRACTICE

- How do the remaining three statements about the RCMP's use of force at the Vancouver APEC conference, the benefits of swimming as exercise, and the liquidation of Eaton's demonstrate circular logic? (Hint: For the final example, see *Ad Populum*, p. 388.)
- Can you offer two or three more examples of circular logic in current affairs?

7. Non Sequitur

This expression comes from the Latin and means "does not follow." A statement that does not follow or evolve in any logical way from a previous statement is a *non sequitur*. While circular argument refers back to unproven premises, non sequitur jumps tracks to an entirely different, disassociated premise. "Since the price of eggs continues to decline, there's good reason to invest in textiles." There may be many reasons to invest in textiles, but how is the decision related in any way to the egg market in this assertion? There may indeed be logic here, but the writer has not revealed it to the reader.

Other, far less obvious non sequiturs pervade much public logic, as dramatized regularly by politicians, sensationalist journalists, and everyday alarmists. Here is a non sequitur that appears in newspapers more and more often: "After O'Driscoll was apprehended, neighbours and colleagues found it difficult to believe he was a cigarette smuggler. They say he was always friendly, hard-working and punctual. He also loved softball." But what do these personal inclinations really have to do with the illicit activity in question? How do these activities preclude the culprit's other interest in smuggling? In fact, isn't smuggling itself hard work? Wouldn't it *help* a smuggler to be punctual and friendly? Wouldn't softball keep a smuggler limber and alert? So O'Driscoll's inclinations, recalled fondly by the people this newspaper chose to interview, do not determine either his honesty or dishonesty and are irrelevant to the smuggling in question. The people and the newspaper reporter here seem to presume in a non sequitur that, given certain sociable appearances, only certain predictable activities will follow. Obvious non sequiturs—such as "I feel sad. I guess I'll go drinking" or "I wish I knew more people. I'll rent an uplifting movie"—are easy to spot in others. However, a great deal of our lives features logical fallacies of both stupendous and subtle non sequiturs. How would you evaluate the following statements?

I really need to start my overdue essay, so I'll read some extra background work.

My boyfriend left me for superficial reasons, so I need to jump into a fling soon.

My former boss underestimated me, so I'll show her with my new job.

If I could walk 10 miles to school uphill when I was a boy, then you can put the garbage out and mow the lawn on time around here.

Beware of non sequiturs in your essays, but, as importantly, beware of them in the "public logic" that justifies dubious official decisions made all around us: "If Ontario school teachers can take time to coach volleyball, cross-country, and lacrosse teams, then they can certainly handle a few more students per class next year." This statement (apparently reasonable if read quickly over breakfast or in the subway) functions as a non sequitur, and it establishes a contradiction too. The premise that the Ontario teachers have time to burn, as supposedly evidenced in their volunteering to coach teams, *attempts* to be the rationale for increasing their classroom size and therefore their marking loads. The non sequitur here is that it does not follow that they would have extra time because of their coaching duties.

8. *Post Hoc Ergo Propter Hoc*

This expression in full comes from the Latin, which translates literally as "after this, therefore because of this." The logical fallacy of *post hoc* is the mistaken presumption that because A precedes B, A must be the cause of B. If there is a rainstorm every afternoon that you decide to go for a long run, and you believe that your workout schedule influences the weather, you have fallen into a *post hoc* fallacy. Of course, most versions of this type of faulty logic are less obvious than the example we have just given, but they still take the form of "*after* A, therefore *because* of A." If you always have a headache after drinking coffee and conclude that caffeine (rather than, say, the heat or sugar) causes your ailment, you may also have wrongly concluded here according to a post hoc fallacy.

In their most spectacular expressions, post hoc fallacies are superstitions, the opposite of logic. For example, Wayne Gretzky, the hockey star, reputedly put on his socks, skates, and equipment in exactly the same order before every game of his sports career. If he prepared this way without giving it much notice, dressing in that sequence would have been habit. If, however, he always suited up in the same order because he believed the sequence affected his hockey performance, then his routine would be a small, personal superstition modelled on post hoc fallacy. Gretzky might have believed his dressing routine ensured what followed it, an excellent performance.

 PRACTICE

Summarize the plot of a detective story (film or book) you have recently enjoyed. Explain how a certain suspect is falsely accused because of the fallacy of *post hoc ergo propter hoc*.

---

9. *Ad Populum*

This term is Latin for "to the people." In *ad populum*, the writer or speaker manipulates expected emotional responses in the audience, based on an awareness of symbols, values, or ideas of particular importance to that group. "Albertans believe in family values, and so they don't follow the stampede to legalize gay rights." "Québécois remember their history, and so they vote to separate from Canada." In the first example, the appeal to safeguarding the family and traditional way of life, combined with an evident tone of warning, is intended to imply that gays will somehow threaten family and conventional life. No evidence is given; an assumption is intended to slip by on the wave of emotion aroused by the appeal. The same is true of the second example. The allusion to Quebec history is meant to summon up thoughts of the persecuted *Patriotes*, of perceived wrongs at the hands of the English overlords. The word "history" will not mean, in this case, an objective visit to the past, to complex aspects of Quebec problems caused at least in part by some French institutions, people, or actions. The possibility that separating from Canada will not solve all problems overnight is swept aside. In this sense, ad populum employs large doses of oversimplification.

In the second example above, ad populum also appeals to a sense of patriotism. "A margin of 51 percent will never be good enough to break up Canada," declares the staunch federalist Jean Chrétien. But why not, if 51 percent is accepted in all other decisions? The bulk of his argument rests on the emotional appeal of "Canada." Ad populum invites strategies such as "plain folks" whereby politicians dress and speak like the "ordinary" people they imagine will support them. Before certain audiences, Peter Lougheed, a former premier of Alberta, would alter his pronunciation of "and" to "an,'" to speak with a rural accent. American citizens have said they support George W. Bush simply because he seems "like one of us" (a questionable conclusion, given that his father is a millionaire, former CIA chief, and a past president), and Alberta Premier Ralph Klein has made political hay out of his perceived common touch. Ad populum makes liberal use of *glittering generalities*, words like "country," "family values," "prosperity," "decency," and "freedom" that have traditionally positive associations. These values are transferred to the speaker or writer, even if he or she offers no real definition of these generally complex terms, nor any hard evidence to offer for upholding them. Underlying *ad populum* is the circular argument that we should be (or remain) what we are because this is what we are.

10. Bandwagon Appeal

Bandwagon appeal is groupthink, which operates not only on inclusion but also on fears of exclusion. If we were all honest with ourselves, we might see that we ride various bandwagons at various times in our lives. Bandwagon appeal is the principle upon which so much designer clothing is sold: "Tilo has a pair of Nikes, Mom, so I have to have one, too." Here, preference is not really personal expression, only mindless conformity. According to this fallacy, a desire—often a selfish one for a questionable goal—is misrepresented as a need. Like ad populum, this fallacy preys on an aspect of our emotional nature, the urge to fit in, to join the crowd, to be accepted. At its worst, bandwagon appeal becomes mob mentality.

11. Slippery Slope

Most of us have had dreams that magnify minor situations into grotesque exaggerations: our car receives a chip in the parking lot; that night we dream that it is covered in rust. Emotion and imagination have conspired through *hyperbole* (extravagant overstatement) to remind us that we should coat the chipped area before it begins to rust. However, if we were to tell a friend that our car received a chip and as a result the entire vehicle will soon be covered in rust, we would be committing the fallacy of slippery slope: asserting that a certain event will lead to another event (often an extreme event), without explaining why. We particularly notice this fallacy in conclusions that make us think of Chicken Little, who believed the sky was falling. A mother finds some marijuana in her daughter's purse and concludes that the girl will soon be hooked on heroin. The mother has overlooked that a number of significant intervening events need to occur before the imagined dire outcome. Strong emotion often underlies this form of illogic. The term evokes a snowball careening downhill, gaining size as emotion intensifies the presumptions.

The words "slippery slope" also suggest the path or continuum between state A (for example, mild drug use) and state Z (for example, serious addiction). Various successive states, stages, or events intervene between A and Z. Clear boundaries between these progressions are "slippery": they are hard to define, their cause-effect connections uncertain. We have considered how this difficulty sometimes results in the assumption that, because A is on a continuum with Z, therefore A will reach or become Z. A slide in the opposite direction on the slippery slope and one may conclude that, because borders and transitions along the path are indeterminate, therefore essential differences between A and Z do not occur. The girl with a little marijuana in her purse is already a serious addict. As the example shows us, this form of slippery slope thinking is what causes false analogies. To give one more illustration, francophone workers, as depicted in novels and films such as *Mon Oncle Antoine*, were certainly exploited and looked down upon, but were they exactly the same as Black slaves in pre-Civil War America, as some protesters in the 1960s suggested?

Like either/or thinking, slippery slope is a specific form of oversimplification. Like bandwagon appeal, it can, at its worst, become mob mentality.

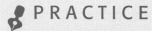 **PRACTICE**

Consider major events in current world affairs. Do you see any possible cases of the slippery slope fallacy op- erating on a collective basis? Discuss your responses with classmates and your instructor.

12. Red Herring

Red herring uses any number of other fallacies and distractions to divert attention from some issue the writer or speaker does not want examined: "Of course Native people were promised certain lands and payments, but wouldn't they like to stand on their own feet?" The writer intends to sweep aside a whole array of complex issues by this emotional appeal to self-reliance, irrelevant to the historical and legal matter in question. Another common form of the red herring is personal detraction of an op- ponent (see "*Ad hominem*").

The above 12 fallacies in writing may occur more commonly as a result of wobbly thinking than deliberate intent, but some—such as *ad hominem* and red herring—are usually deliberate. When used deliberately, logical fallacies are sometimes called *propaganda techniques*. The deliberate use of such techniques runs entirely counter to the spirit of genuine argumentation.

On the other hand, a fair-minded effort to think from an "opponent's" point of view can be a wonderfully enriching experience. Perhaps it is no coincidence that Shakespeare, widely admired for the balanced representation of multiple viewpoints and characters in his plays, was educated in the classical rhetorical tradition. From a young age, he was obliged by his education to construct arguments from both sides of a debate and to avoid the use of logical fallacies, regardless of which side he debated. In its best embodiments, argumentation encourages deeper under- standing and tolerance.

PRACTICE

Try to find at least one instance of each of the above 12 fallacies in various essays in Section 3 of the *Reader*. Compare your findings with those of your classmates and your instructor.

CULTURAL CONSIDERATIONS

Before leaving this topic, we should consider, again, the importance of cultural factors in how we relate respond to rhetorical traditions such as argumentation. Certain cul- tures neither engage in nor admire the oppositional, sometimes intensive adversarial ap- proach we discuss in this chapter, an approach vigorously taught in North American colleges and universities. For instance, the idea of challenging social traditions (*ad populum*) is considered generally unacceptable in many indigenous cultures.

Furthermore, some teachers and writers in mainstream Western culture also regret what they consider the unnecessarily combative spirit our society endorses in the activities of assertion and interpretation on the subject. In an essay entitled "Burying the Hatchet in Language," McGill University professor David Smith observes how frequently our culture uses military metaphors to discuss verbal engagements—metaphors such as "defend your claims" or be "right on target." He refers to linguistic research suggesting that the sort of language we accept can influence our perceptions and therefore our behaviour. He then offers a creative challenge: "Suppose instead of thinking about argument in terms of war, we were to think of argument as a pleasing, graceful dance."

Smith might suggest that our instruction on argumentation really is no less biased, after all, than the forms of biased persuasion we have discussed. The stressing of contrast—their view versus yours—could be seen as conducive to either/or thinking, promoting an unnecessary opposition of only two considerations. Although we have urged "fair play," we have implied that your goal is to "win" over someone else. Certainly the sample argumentative essay arguing for Canada's ratification of Kyoto could be accused of skimming over certain points and manipulating others. Smith's longing for a less confrontational approach in language corresponds with an apparently rising discontent with the adversarial political structures in our society.

 ## PRACTICE

Does argumentation, as discussed in this chapter, indeed offer an approach preferable to or even different from those of "biased persuasion"?

ESSAY TOPICS

1. What are the arguments for and against the participation of women in active combat? What is *your* position?

2. "The West must accept some responsibility for the terror attacks of last September," Prime Minister Jean Chrétien said while addressing the media on September 12, 2002. What are the arguments for and against this opinion? Explain your own position.

3. Read "The Case for Active Euthanasia" by Janice Procée (p. 188) and "Euthanasia Reconsidered" by Gail Deagle (p. 191). Develop a new idea or angle overlooked in both essays and write your own argumentative essay recommending a position on this controversial topic.

4. Mary Shelley's fictional Dr. Frankenstein undertook a career in science, full of ideals and optimism. However, his drive for progress—to overcome death—resulted in misery. Is applied science going too far today in a similar way? You may wish to read John Markoff's "The Doomsday Machines" (p. 135) for one discussion of this question. Develop your own answer using sources such as your field of work or study, forms of personal experience with the topic, and other research. You may wish to concentrate on one particular field, such as medicine, genetics, information technology.

5. Does our society place too much importance on appearance? Consider arguments from various sides of the question.

6. Is post-secondary education improving or declining? Interview older people who attended university or college in an earlier period. Also conduct other relevant research on this topic.

7. Is the gap between rich and poor in today's world as serious a problem as some people say?

Note: See the end of Chapter 4 for additional topics for argumentative essays.

Chapter 8
The Summary

The ability to write a summary confirms that you are a good reader. This ability is of considerable importance since reading skills contribute to writing skills in general. More specifically, you will often be called upon to apply the skills of summarization in your academic and vocational writing.

SUMMARIZATION AND ACADEMIC WORK

In any academic field you will be required to perform research. You will be expected to report to your instructor and classmates on the contents of various books, articles, studies, and so on. Since the goal of research is not simply to repeat what has already been said but to add to that work, you will need to identify the main points of existing work as briefly as you can, leaving time and space for your own critical response to it.

A **summary** concisely re-states the central ideas of a reading, using different words to express the writer's meaning accurately and without judgment. Most summaries also mention the kinds of rhetorical methods used in the material being summarized.

WRITING THE SUMMARY

The summary calls on you to exercise *two* main skills:

1. *First, separate the thesis, related ideas, and general rhetorical methods of the material to be summarized from the supporting details*.

    You may adapt this guideline somewhat on different occasions. Some instructors may want you to include supporting details, depending on the nature of the assignment. However, for the purposes of learning to separate ideas from details, it is a good practice for you to learn how to write summaries that omit any detail that is not crucial to expressing a central point.

    How long should a summary be? Again, you will want to satisfy different expectations for different assignments. Since good writing expresses one main idea per paragraph, follow the rule of thumb of trying to use no more than one sentence for each paragraph of the original. In most cases, your summary should be less than one-quarter the length of the original.

2. ***The second main skill required for a summary is to express ideas in your own words without altering the original meaning.***

Finding your own words to re-present the writer's ideas helps you to understand those ideas. It also develops your ability to avoid stating other people's words as your own, which is plagiarism.

You may quote one or two key words or phrases to convey the essence of an idea, but use quotation sparingly. Summarizing is almost always combined with analysis, critical response, and other types of writing. Yet the summary in itself should not express any of your own personal responses to what you are summarizing. Whether you strongly approve or reject what a writer is saying, your summary should simply convey the writer's ideas accurately and impartially. Using the third-person voice for your summaries helps to keep you from stating your own response.

FINDING THE THESIS AND CENTRAL IDEAS

Here are six tips to help you identify the thesis and related ideas in a reading:

1. Determine where the reading was published and who the author is. (This need not be your first step.)
2. Turn the title of the essay into a question, and read the text seeking an answer to that question.[24]
3. Scan the opening and closing paragraphs to see what main points are made. Concentrate on the opening and closing sentences of the paragraphs.
4. Scan the opening and closing sentences of the other (body) paragraphs, looking for new ideas related to the thesis.
5. Take special note of subtitles and any terms in bold or italics.
6. Look for rhetorical methods, a purposeful structure that helps you understand the relationship between ideas and sections of the reading.

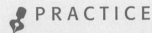

PRACTICE

Read David Suzuki's essay "The Right Stuff" (p. 181). Use a combination of highlighting or underlining along with marginal notes to apply the above tips. Then, with this preparation, write a short summary of no more than 10 sentences. Then look on the next page of this chapter, which provides our suggested highlights and marginal notes, our nine-sentence summary, and our commentary on how we applied the above reading tips to construct our summary.

---

[24] Use this tip with caution when summarizing from a newspaper. Titles of newspaper articles are usually decided upon by an editor (headline writer) working hastily and sometimes from the "Entertainer's Stance." (See "The Rhetorical Stance," *Reader*, p. 144.)

Sample Essay Finding the Thesis and Central Ideas

The Right Stuff

David Suzuki

What is meant by "The Right Stuff"?

1   Years ago I read a marvellous book entitled *Is There Life After High School?* In spite of the title, it was a serious comparison of human relationships at different stages in life. The study revealed that <u>impressions formed in high school are</u> more <u>vivid</u> and indelible than those formed at any other time in life. The author described how people in their seventies and eighties who had difficulty remembering most of their associates in university and at work would instantly recall most of their classmates by name while leafing through their high school yearbooks. In the analysis of the author, high school society is divided into two broad categories, the innies and the outies. The innies were football and basketball players and cheerleaders who set the whole social climate of the school. The outies were all the rest, the majority of the student body, most of whom lusted to be innies. I sure hope it's different today because that description fits my recollection of high school and it was awful. <u>But I'm getting off the point.</u>

How is this connected to "the right stuff"?

Is this information about "innies" and "outies" really important? He suggests himself that it is off the point. But he does seem to be saying that high school is a time of intense, memorable social experience

cause-effect relationship

cause-effect relationship

2   <u>Those high school memories are so intense because that is the time when puberty occurs.</u> The enormous <u>physiological changes</u> that take place in response to the surge of <u>new hormones</u> through the body completely <u>transform both anatomy and mind.</u> I always feel kids lose about half their intelligence for a few years in response to that blast of hormones. Relationships change radically. Suddenly parents change from protective, loving gods to dictatorial wardens incessantly imposing restrictions and criticizing everything. A pubescent teenager perceives adults and members of their own age group with totally new eyes. It's not surprising then that <u>attitudes</u> to school, courses and studying also <u>change dramatically.</u>

A personal anecdote/example begins. Narration

3   In the early 1970s, <u>I visited</u> a small northern town to judge a science fair. Back then, it was a tough town with a transient population of men working in the oil fields and a high proportion of Native people. The night I arrived, I dropped in to the bar of the motel and a man came over and said, "I hear you're going to talk to the students at the high school tomorrow." When I affirmed it, he shocked me by adding, "They'll kill you. I'm the science teacher there and I can tell you that all they think about is sex, drugs and cars. They'll tear you apart."

End of anecdote. The anecdote demonstrates the communication principle that you should know your audience. Is this the thesis (the Right Stuff)?

4   Well, he really scared me. I immediately formed images of a blackboard jungle, filled with switchblades and drug-crazed hoods. The next day when I walked into that auditorium, it was with great trepidation. There were 400 teenagers in the gym, about a third of them Indians. They looked pretty normal, but I had been warned and knew they were just biding their time before turning into raving animals.

5   So I began by saying, "I'm a geneticist. I know that you're basically walking gonads, so I'm going to talk about sex." That opener caught their attention. I started with the beginning of human life by describing eggs and sperm, talked about chromo-

somes and the X and Y basis for sex determination and went on from there. The kids were dead silent and attentive. I talked for about an hour and then opened it up for questions. I was astounded at the range of topics we covered. We discussed drugs and chromosomes, test-tube babies, amniocentesis and cloning. The principal finally had to step in to dismiss the group an hour and a half later.

6　Science education in high school should be designed around sex and human biology. It's a shock every time I hear that a school board has caved in to pressure and kept sex ed out of schools. I am sure opponents of sex education have no intention of providing that information to their own children. In a time of easy access to the most explicit films, videos, magazines and books, who can believe it's better to keep youngsters ignorant by denying them some accurate facts? They're going to get all kinds of anecdotal, apocryphal stuff about sex from their peer group, anyway.

7　By starting their instruction with human sexuality and reproduction, teachers will be able to go on to practically every other subject in science. It just takes a hard look from a different perspective. After all, we are not trying to train future scientists (only a small percentage of high school graduates will go on in science), yet all of them will be able to use information that science can provide for the rest of their lives. And you can bet they will remember those lessons vividly in their life after high school.

> Sounds like a major recommendation. Is this the thesis (the Right Stuff)?
>
> A reason given for the recommendation
>
> Another reason for the recommendation
>
> Another reason for the recommendation—closely tied to the previous one "By" signals cause-effect
>
> The first sentence of the last paragraph often restates the writer's thesis
>
> Another reason for the recommendation—closely tied to the above reason
>
> Using sex as a springboard to other subjects—is this claimed benefit part of the "right stuff"?
>
> Concluding sentence reminds us of the opening paragraph, which suggests that the lessons we learn in high school are the most vivid of our lives. This reinforces the general importance of improving high school education

The above underlining and margin notes reflect answers to most of the questions you should consider when developing a summary. Here, again, are the questions.

1. **Determine where the reading was published and who the author is.**
   You'll find this information in the *Reader*, as an introduction to the article. This essay, from a collection entitled *Inventing the Future*, first appeared as a newspaper column. David Suzuki, former host of the CBC radio program *Quirks and Quarks* and the CBC television program *The Nature of Things*, trained as a geneticist and has taught zoology at the University of British

Columbia. His David Suzuki Foundation enlists volunteer support for environmental causes. From this information, one can anticipate that Suzuki will be a supporter of change and what might be regarded as "liberal" reform.

2. ***Turn the title of the essay into a question, and read the text seeking an answer to that question.***

    The title does not directly convey the topic of the essay—sex education in high school—but it does imply that a recommendation is going to be made. Once we determine that the essay concerns high school education, what is being recommended—"the right stuff"—has to be the adoption of sex education. The marginal notes express some searching for a statement that best captures the writer's central idea. As stated in Chapter 2, "Reviewing the Basics," the best thesis statement is one that conveys the writer's attitude *and* reasons. Suzuki argues that sex education should be taught in high schools because the subject, unavoidable in today's media-charged society, is not properly covered elsewhere and, above all, because high school students will thereby develop an interest in science. This one sentence capturing the writer's main idea and reasons (the complete thesis) in effect summarizes the entire short essay.

3. ***Scan paragraph 1 (the opening) and paragraph 7 (the closing) to see what main points are made. Concentrate on the opening and closing sentences of the paragraphs.***

    i.   Impressions formed in high school are uniquely intense and vivid.
    ii. Teachers should start their science classes with human sexuality, a point of departure into other topics.

    Most students don't need more than a generalist's knowledge of science topics (but presumably they do need a good knowledge of human sexuality). What they learn at this time they will remember (which reinforces point i. above).

4. ***Scan the opening and closing sentences of the other (body) paragraphs, looking for new ideas related to the thesis.***

    High school memories are so strong because of hormonal transformations, which result in new and intense attitudes to everything. (para. 2)

    Suzuki visited a northern high school where a teacher warned him the students would be hostile. (para. 3)

    Concerned by the warning (para. 4), he began with the observation "I know you're basically walking gonads." (para. 5)

    The principal had to end the discussion of a vast range of topics. (para. 5)

    Science education in high school should be designed around sex and human biology. (para. 6)

    Teenagers will get this information, in any case, in corrupted forms. (para. 6)

Note that the only important points missed out by scanning the opening and closing of paragraphs are two in the middle of paragraph 6: (1) most parents won't teach sex education at home and (2) a proliferation of explicit material makes it impossible for parents to prevent their teenagers from learning about human sexuality.

5. ***Take special note of subtitles and any terms in bold or italics.***
   "The Right Stuff" is not subdivided by typographical indicators; other readings will be, however.

6. ***Look for rhetorical methods, a purposeful structure that helps you understand the relationship between ideas and sections of the reading.***
   The opening cites a book and elaborates on its point that the teenage years are intense and involve extreme (sometimes cruel) social awareness.

   Paragraph 2 goes into cause-effect relationships: hormones cause this intensity and result in a personal revolution of outlook.

   Paragraphs 3, 4, and 5 use narration to recount an anecdote offering the moral that you should know your audience in order to capture and hold their attention.

   Paragraph 6 states personal opinion and response ("I'm shocked when . . ."). Further opinion and some examples are offered to back up the main opinion that high schools should teach sex education.

   Paragraph 7 returns to cause-effect relationship, emphasizing the main educational benefit the author foresees for his recommendation.

Following is a summary constructed from the above reading analysis:

Summary of "The Right Stuff"

In his essay "The Right Stuff," David Suzuki argues that high school science courses should begin with sex education. He feels that human sexuality is unavoidable in today's society, yet poorly explained by parents, media, and peers. Most of all, Suzuki believes high school students will find human sexuality a relevant point of departure to other topics.

Suzuki introduces his discussion by emphasizing the intensity of the teenage years, an intensity caused by hormonal change. Using a personal anecdote, he demonstrates how teenage outlook can seem threatening to teachers faced by seemingly uninterested, even hostile students. The anecdote concludes by showing, however, that high school students *will* gain interest if the teacher begins with human sexuality.

Suzuki concludes his essay by briefly defending his thesis. He states that parents opposed to sex education in high school do not offer the necessary education at home. Students are then left to learn from sexually explicit media treatments and the distorted stories of classmates, both poor sources. Not many students, he points out, go on to careers in science, so high school science need not be in-depth. It is more important that high school science be relevant, interesting, and thus truly educational.

Note what has been omitted:

- any reference to the book *Is There Life After High School?*
- Suzuki's personal memories of high school and the innies and outies
- the various examples of different changes of attitude toward relationships, parents, and adults in general

- most of the narrative descriptive details concerning the trip to the northern high school (an extended example), such as how many students there were, what segments of society they represented, what topics they asked questions about
- the different forms of sexually explicit material (videos, films, magazines)

It is often difficult to understand the distinction between a point (an idea, an opinion, a claim), and a supporting detail. The above summary of "The Right Stuff" should help illustrate the difference. Supporting details can include any of the following:

- authorities cited or quoted
- research findings, data
- examples, whether brief or extended (including anecdotes)
- logical illustrations such as analogies (See "Logic and Logical Fallacies" in Chapter 7.)
- literary devices such as metaphors, imagery, etc.

Three paragraphs of "The Right Stuff" constitute one extended example, so almost all of this is omitted. We chose to include the bare bones of this example because Suzuki pins so much of his argument on it. In Chapter 10 on critical response, "Critical Analysis," we pursue the question of whether Suzuki bases too much on one specific example. But notice that none of this questioning is included in the summary. We have tried to be objective and impartial, and the wording is, as much as possible, our own. We have begun our summary by identifying the title and the author and giving the thesis (including the basic reasons supporting the thesis). Our opening sentence uses the verb "argues" to convey the purpose of the essay

Ten Steps to a Successful Summary

1. Begin by smoothly identifying the author and title of the reading.
2. In your first sentence or paragraph, re-state the complete thesis (including supporting reasons).
3. Include all significant points (ideas) and only inseparable details.
4. Re-present content in the same order that the author does.
5. Make each part of your summary directly proportional to the part it summarizes.
6. Use a neutral (impartial/objective) tone—third-person point of view.
7. Exclude any of your own critical response.
8. Be brief—try to summarize each paragraph in no more than a sentence.
9. Use almost entirely your own language—select only key words for quotation.
10. Enclose any of the author's words in quotation marks.

(argumentation). After that, we have summarized the central points in the same order they occur in the essay.

PRACTICE

Write as many summaries as you can until you have internalized these skills. The *Instructor's Manual* provided with this text gives a sample summary for selections in the *Reader*. Summary writing is not an absolute science; no two summaries will be exactly alike. As we have noted, different writing requirements affect the final form of any summary. Nevertheless, you and your instructor can review your summaries compared to those offered in the *Instructor's Manual* and according to the following checklist.

IDENTIFYING AND EXPLAINING AN EXCERPT

One of the most common examination questions asks you to identify an excerpt (a passage) and to identify how it relates to the reading from which it is taken. This process tests whether you have read and understood assigned readings. To do well with this particular assignment, you need to apply summarizing skills. Your answer must show that you recognize the important features and sections of the reading, including the thesis. Furthermore, you must explain how the excerpt relates to that thesis and to the other features of the reading.

PRACTICE

Read the following short essay, then the excerpt taken from it. In one paragraph of about 10 sentences, explain how the excerpt relates to the essay as a whole. Then read the sample summary provided by student Nancy Corscadden and our commentary on her answer.

For language support for the following essay, visit the online cover page for Athabasca University English 255 Introductory Composition at <**www.athabascau.ca/courses/engl/255/**>. Under "Supplementary Resources," see "Language Support for Selected Readings."

Practice Reading   Finding the Thesis and Central Ideas

Life in the Stopwatch Lane
Amy Willard Cross

1   If time is money, the rates have skyrocketed and you probably can't afford it. North Americans are suffering a dramatic time shortage since demand greatly exceeds supply. In fact, a recent survey revealed that people lost about 10 hours of leisure per week between 1973 and 1987. Maybe you were too busy to notice.

2   Losing that leisure leaves a piddling 16.6 hours to do whatever you want, free of work, dishwashing or car-pooling. In television time, that equals a season of 13 *thir-*

tysomething episodes, plus 3 ½ reruns. Hardly enough time to write an autobiography or carry on an affair.

3   How has replacing free time with more billable hours affected society? It has created a new demographic group: the Busy Class—who usurped the Leisure Class. Easy to recognize, members of the Busy Class constantly cry to anyone listening, "I'm *soooooo* busy." So busy they can't call their mother or find change for a panhandler. Masters of doing two things at once, they eke the most out of time. They dictate while driving, talk while calculating, entertain guests while nursing, watch the news while pumping iron. Even business melts into socializing—people earn their daily bread while they break it.

4   In fact, the Busies must make lots of bread to maintain themselves in the standard of busy-ness to which they've become accustomed. To do that, they need special, expensive stuff. Stuff like call waiting, which lets them talk to two people at once. Stuff like two-faced watches, so they can do business in two time zones at once. Neither frenzied executives nor hurried housewives dare leave the house without their "book"—leather-bound appointment calendars thick as bestsellers. Forget hi-fis or racing cars, the new talismans of overachievers also work: coffee-makers that brew by alarm; remote-controlled ignitions; or car faxes. Yet, despite all these time-efficient devices, few people have time to spare.

5   That scarcity has changed how we measure time. Now it's being scientifically dissected into smaller and smaller pieces. Thanks to digital clocks, we know when it's 5:30 (and calculate we'll be home in three hours, eight minutes). These days lawyers can reason in 1/10th of an hour increments; they bill every six minutes. This to-the-minute precision proves time's escalating value.

6   Time was, before the advent of car phones and digital clocks, we scheduled two kinds of time: time off and work hours. Not any more. Just as the Inuit label the infinite varieties of snow, the Busy Class has identified myriad subtleties of free time and named them. Here are some textbook examples of the new faces of time:

7   *Quality time*. For those working against the clock, the quality of time spent with loved ones supposedly compensates for quantity. This handy concept absolves guilt as quickly as rosary counting. So careerist couples dine à deux once a fortnight. Parents bond by reading kids a story after nanny fed and bathed them. When pressed for time, nobody wastes it by fighting about bad breath or unmade beds. People who spend quality time with each other view their relationships through rose-coloured glasses. And knowing they've created perfect personal lives lets the Busy Class work even harder—guilt-free.

8   *Travel time*. With an allowance of 16.6 hours of fun, the Busy Class watches time expenditures carefully. Just like businesses do while making bids, normal people calculate travel time for leisure activities. If two tram rides away, a friendly squash game loses out. One time-efficient woman even formulated a mathematical theorem: fun

per mile quotient. Before accepting any social invitation, she adds up travel costs, figures out the time spent laughing, drinking and eating. If the latter exceeds the former, she accepts. It doesn't matter who asks.

9   *Downtime*. Borrowed from the world of heavy equipment and sleek computers, downtime is a professional-sounding word meaning the damn thing broke, wait around until it's fixed. Translated into real life, downtime counts as neither work nor play, but a maddening no-man's land where *nothing* happens! Like lining up for the ski-lift, or commuting without a car phone, or waiting a while for the mechanic's diagnosis. Beware: people who keep track of their downtime probably indulge in less than 16 hours of leisure.

10   *Family time*. In addition to 60-hour weeks, aerobics and dinner parties, some people make time for their children. When asked to brunch, a young couple will reply, "We're sorry but that's our family time." A variant of quality time, it's Sunday afternoon between lunch and the Disney Hour when nannies frequent Filipino restaurants. In an effort to entertain their children without exposure to sex and violence, the family attends craft fairs, animated matinees or tree-tapping demonstrations. There, they converge with masses of family units spending time alone with the kids. After a noisy, sticky afternoon, parents gladly punch the clock come Monday.

11   *Quiet time*. Overwhelmed by their schedules, some people try to recapture the magic of childhood when they watched clouds for hours on end. Sophisticated grown-ups have rediscovered the quiet time of kindergarten days. They unplug the phone (not the answering machine), clutch a book and try not to think about work. But without teachers to enforce it, quiet doesn't last. The clock ticks too loudly. As a computer fanatic said, after being entertained at 16 megahertz, sitting still to watch a sunset pales by comparison.

12   As it continues to increase in value, time will surely divide into even smaller units. And people will share only the tiniest amounts with each other. Hey, brother, can you spare a minute? Got a second? A nanosecond?

♪ PRACTICE

Explain how the following excerpt relates to the essay as a whole: "Time was, before the advent of car phones and digital clocks, we scheduled two kinds of time: time off and work hours. Not any more."

Sample Answer   Explaining an Excerpt Relationship

Answer

Nancy Corscadden

In her wry classification essay, Amy Willard Cross identifies a new social group: the Busy Class. Members of the Busy Class are characterized by their complaint "I'm *soooo* busy," by their desire for expensive stuff, and by their penchant to divide time into smaller and smaller units. The excerpt given above ties these three features of the Busy Class into one bundle. Informal words and short, snappy phrasing relate to the short bursts of activity common to the Busy Class. Car phones and digital clocks represent the "expensive stuff" this class wishes to acquire. Willard Cross anticipates further divisions of time by identifying the crude, bygone classification of "time off and work hours." Her essay goes on to list six categories the Busy Class has invented to demonstrate its concern for the importance of time off. The excerpt, thus, is an excellent introduction to Willard Cross's thesis about ourselves in consumerist society: ironically, the more we invent intricate terms to describe our relationships apart from work, the less attention we pay to anything but making and spending money.

Commentary

Corscadden's answer draws from the elements of a good summary. She begins by observing that the tone of the essay is "wry" (ironic, tongue-in-cheek, playful). Willard Cross combines a playful approach to the academic's interest in categories. Behind the classification approach, she is really concerned with a cause-effect relationship: what motivates busy people to subdivide time, especially time off work? As Corscadden observes, the excerpt anticipates the answer to this question (the thesis) by implying that addiction to consumerism has divided and isolated the human psyche. The apt quotation "I'm soooo busy" speaks to the unease and posturing underlying our actual attitude to time off. We know that personal time is an endangered species; we aren't about to do anything truly significant to stop that trend.

This ability to identify the role of an excerpt in relation to the overall meaning of the reading to which it belongs draws primarily on summarization. As part of this process, you need to use analytical skills (see Chapter 10). Understanding what is said, especially in expressive and argumentative forms, requires drawing inferences from the figurative meanings of words and images, recognizing how tone contributes to meaning. This requires you to use your judgement about what the author is really saying—not the same thing as expressing your opinion about the reliability or merit of what the author is saying. In Chapter 10 we look at that step of critical thinking, a step that follows the summary: expressing your position.

Chapter 9
Essays in Exams

Courses in English, history, biology, philosophy, and psychology have exams that require essay writing. The exams are usually heavily weighted into your final grade. The challenge with writing these exam essays, unlike papers written at home, is that you must express a strong thesis, clear topic sentences, a satisfactory conclusion, and employ correct syntax all within a set time limit. Most essay exams are two hours long and require you to write two essays. This type of exam therefore requires strong organizational skills. The following test-taking tips ought to help you plan to write your essays in the allotted time.

PRE-EXAM PLANNING

1. All written exams require pre-reading. The reading may include short fiction, agricultural reports, case studies, historical information, novels, or textbook chapters. However, your exam essay will probably focus on only a few of the selections you have read all term. Therefore, instead of re-reading all of the items on your syllabus (you won't remember them all anyway), focus on reviewing those texts that apply best to the course objectives and main themes. By preparing fewer texts in more depth, you can write on them in more analytical detail. If your exam will emphasize wide course coverage, however, read more, perhaps all, texts on the syllabus. Broad coverage and concentrated knowledge are a difficult balance, so ask your instructors about *their* exam expectations to help you structure your pre-exam planning.
2. Identify possible topics. When studying at home, review the main topics covered on the syllabus. Focus on any prevailing themes or periods covered in detail during the course. Choose the main themes and issues around which you can focus most of your preparation.
3. Read your three or four selected texts with your chosen topics in mind. Set aside sheets of paper with the names of each of these texts as headings. As you read your selections, keep in mind the possible topics you identified in step 2 and jot down any passages from the work that may apply to your topics.

4. By the end of your studying, you will have a sheet of paper for each text outlining the passages you may use to address a variety of possible essay topics. Some texts will appear better than others for certain topics. Take some time now to identify some "if . . . then" strategies, that is, decide "*if* the question is on 'this' subject, *then* I will use 'this' text."

5. Generate possible theses for your different study essays. Using the notes you have made and the quotations or passages you pulled from each text, write out an essay plan, including topic sentences. Once you've done this preparation, you're usually more prepared than you were to write the test.

Mnemonic Devices: Memory Tricks

When you have large amounts of information to organize and remember, you may wish to "bundle" that information temporarily through mnemonic devices, or "memory tricks."These strategies are highly individual; some include anagrams (say, "FAN-BOYS" for the seven coordinate conjunctions: *for, and, nor, but, or, yet,* and *so*) or deliberately unusual expressions to encode larger, more serious blocks of information ("Portable Cross" to remember that Pierre La*Porte*, a Canadian politician, and James *Cross,* the British minister of trade, were kidnapped (illegally trans*port*ed) by the FLQ terrorists during the October Crisis in 1970 in Quebec).

Some mnemonic devices may rely on personal memory, silly expressions, puns and wordplay, or even irreverent constructions that are best kept private. In economics, for another example, a "bear market" is a strong market with rising stock values, while a "bull market" is a weakened market with declining stock values. People commonly think of a *bear* as *rising* on its hind feet to show dominance, while a *bull lowers* its head when threatened.

WRITING THE EXAM

Once you are in the exam, plan your time effectively so you can finish the entire test.

1. When you receive the exam, read all the possible topics and questions. Look for topics that are similar to those you considered when you were preparing your study notes. Don't panic if nothing matches exactly. Much of your prepared information may be flexible enough to work in part or in other combinations to satisfy the exam's essay questions.

2. Decide within the first five minutes of the test which one or two topics you will write on. If the examination has other components (multiple-choice, short-answer, definition, fill-in-the-blank), choose your essay topics *first* and your mind will "work on them" as you write the other sections.

3. When you begin the essay portion of the test, first note how much time you have to write each essay. If you have an hour, divide your time carefully, roughly according to this model:

- up to 10 minutes for planning by integrating ideas from the notes, topic sentences, and theses you generated at home
- up to 45 minutes for writing
- 5 remaining minutes for looking the paper over for correct syntax, grammar, and clarity

If you use your *planning* time correctly at the beginning of the exam, you should have no problems sticking to this schedule in the test.

Key Words in Essay Questions

Analyze: Discuss, interpret, and closely examine the many components of a single text, concept or situation. To analyze is to declare significance and implications, not merely to summarize.

Compare: Look at the similarities and, more important, the differences between two or more concepts, situations, or texts. Recognize both similarities and differences, but work toward a thesis emphasizing one or the other.

Contrast: Emphasize the differences between two concepts or texts. Set them in opposition in your discussion. One teacher of analytical writing once said, "A lot of things are like a lot of other things in this world, and that's why distinctions and contrasts are important."

Criticize: Analyze a given number of texts for comparative worth. Make judgments evaluating one against the other.

Define: Provide the meaning of crucial, often complex terms from the course. Be sure to state the exact limits of what is to be defined. Be brief, but articulate a precise meaning. Consider providing an example for pointed clarity.

Describe: Detail a given theme, genre, case, or set of circumstances. List the qualities and characteristics of the account you are rendering.

Discuss: This very broad term invites analysis, or cause-and-effect, or comparison and contrast to argue or debate an interpretation or a set of circumstances. Perhaps define, list pros and cons, contrasting qualities, unexpected conditions or effects, complexities, or examine meaning and effectiveness.

Explain: Clarify by describing logical development, use, effect. Give examples.

Illustrate: Use examples to explain a concept. Comparisons between works are effective here.

Interpret: Comment on a given text or situation by describing it and its issues first and then analyze it: what does it all mean? Describe comparisons and give examples.

Outline: Describe main themes, interpretations, characteristics, or events.

Relate: Show some broad and many specific connections between themes, ideas, or events. Establish a larger context in which to place your discussion.

Summarize: Briefly discuss or recount an event or discussion, including crucial ideas and facts and avoiding unnecessary details.

Chapter 10
Critical Analysis

Descriptive analysis, argumentation, and the summary, all covered in Chapters 6, 7, and 8, combine in critical analysis.

CRITICAL ANALYSIS DEFINED

The word "critical" here does not have the colloquial meaning of looking for faults. Rather, "critical" refers to seeking and expressing a properly informed understanding of a subject. An essayist employs appropriate academic tools and due impartiality in this pursuit. Whatever the exact nature of the subject or discipline of inquiry, the investigator will use analysis—the breaking down of a subject into meaningful constituent parts. The investigator examines those parts and how they function together, what causes them, what effects they may have, in what context they operate, and what relation we should have to them. Any or all of the expository patterns may be employed along with argumentation in the course of critical analysis.

In this section, we present three specific forms of critical analysis:

- critique of an essay
- comparative analysis
- literary analysis

Two other specialized forms—the case analysis in business and the film review of literature—are covered on the *Acting on Words* website at <**www.pearsoned.ca/brundage/**>. See the same material under "Supplementary Resources" on the English 255 website at <**www.athabascau.ca/courses/engl/255/**>.

Close attention to revealing relationships characterizes analytical writing. Following is an example, by student Lisa Lemieux, of the degree of scrutiny this form demands. Lemieux analyzed a photograph of two announcers sitting behind a news desk in a TV newsroom.

Sample Critical Analysis

Fact or Photo?

Lisa Lemieux

1   Television news programs have become a dominant source of information. In contrast to print media, broadcast journalism depends significantly on an engaging presentation, as television utilizes continuous visual and audio stimulus. In order to yield maximum impact, aspects of production, such as set design, choice of news anchors, and camera angles, are carefully controlled. The outcome of these production choices is suggested by a black-and-white photograph I have examined of a video camera filming two news anchors. Taken from over the shoulder of the person filming the broadcast, this photograph, from the *Edmonton Journal* archives, demonstrates and also questions the selective eye of a video camera. The image invites a critical evaluation of how information, or "fact," is presented and received, and what biases may result. The photograph's angle alters a typical perspective on news media, and illuminates the possibility that viewers' interpretation of news content is altered by aspects of production, thus undermining the objectivity of broadcast journalism.

2   The perspective captured in the photograph differs from that of the video camera filming the broadcast, as the photograph introduces areas of the set that would be excluded from view on television. Additionally, aspects of the set that would be seen on film are captured at a different angle. On television, the set would likely appear as a solid desk extending beyond the edge of the viewing frame, backed by a bold, centred logo. Yet from the angle of the photograph, the set is less impressive. The desk is actually quite flimsy and truncated, and stage lighting enhances the plain backdrop. Sets are constructed to create an impression for the viewer, as news is rendered credible in part by presentation. Therefore, the set is filmed at its most powerful angle to deliver the news with maximum impact. The image captured in this photograph illustrates the importance of set and camera angle in influencing the visual impression of a setting.

3   This news program is called *Fact*, which features contentious debate about news issues; however, in the context of this photograph, the irony of the title is augmented. Fact denotes truth and objectivity, yet stories presented on air are subject to interpretation based on what is said, or not said, and how it is said. The contrast between the angle of the video camera and the still camera illustrates an analogy between presentation and content. The video camera operator, like a journalist, presents one version of the set, and without further information, viewers are directed towards believing that version as "fact." However, the still camera presents a vastly different version of the same television studio. Though both cameras capture virtually the same information, slight changes in their angles alter the viewer's interpretation of the images. Similarly, slight alterations in approach to a news story can significantly modify the content of the story. These different approaches could be inevitable in journalism; however,

viewers should also be wary of purposeful biases introduced subtly into the news. This photograph illuminates that possibility, and undermines the use of the term "fact."

4   Broadcast journalism differs from print media in that people presenting information can be seen and heard, and their delivery can change the meaning of text. Therefore, part of the evaluation of a news program is an evaluation of the broadcasters. By capturing the scene without the distractions of sound, movement, or colour found in live television, this photograph draws attention to the anchors specifically. The employment of both male and female hosts for the program *Fact* could be a genuine and successful attempt to draw in viewers from both genders. However, pairs of men and women anchors, such as the pair displayed in the photograph, often include a young, attractive female and an older, if somewhat less attractive, male. This arrangement occurs so frequently that it cannot be considered merely coincidental. It reinforces certain societal stereotypes: the woman must look attractive and engaging to entice a larger audience, yet she will not be taken seriously unless she is coupled with an older and more serious-looking man. Since both anchors are dressed in conservative business suits, form is again attached to function. Theoretically, the news would be the same whether those reporting it were dressed in jeans and tank tops or in suits and ties, yet it would not be received in a similar manner. Viewers expect formality, as it makes the news appear more official, and what is more official seems more reliable and accurate.

5   This photograph deconstructs impressions of broadcast news as official reports by polished hosts and sturdy sets as seen on television. From this more vulnerable angle, a familiar broadcast scene becomes unfamiliar and open to reassessment. For example, the frontal image of the set would appear more imposing than the image shot from one side, thus changing the impact of information delivered. In addition, given the common occurrence of news anchors similar in appearance to the two in the photograph, it is unlikely that these hosts were selected solely for their ability to deliver the news; they represent a stereotypical combination of a serious man and an attractive female, presumably paired to maintain both credibility and ratings. Examination of nuances in broadcasting sheds doubt upon the prominent "Fact" logo in the background of the photograph, for if presentation of news contains biases revealed in this image, the information presented is also compromised.

Focus Questions

1. What is Lemieux's thesis?
2. What organizational patterns does she use to serve her purpose?

Since college and university training aims to raise the level of our awareness and insight, it relies heavily on the type of critical analysis conducted concisely in this student paper.

 PRACTICE

- Review the readings in Section 1 of the *Reader*. How many that we have placed in the personal reflective category, contain significant amounts of critical analysis?

- Inspect Sections 2 and 3 for types of critical analysis. Consider that since evaluation (judgment) is part of this form, critical analysis tends toward argumentation.

WRITING A CRITIQUE

In Chapter 8 we looked at six steps to help you write a good summary. A good summary does its best to express only the facts that an author intended to convey. You are urged *not* to interject your own opinions while creating a summary. By exercising this restraint, you keep your reader clearly and comprehensively informed about what the text under consideration says. This is not to say that your own opinion is unimportant.

Quite the contrary is true. Your own opinion *is* important. The goal of higher education is to help you contribute to a body of theory and practice in your chosen field of study. However, the difference between a hasty speaker who spouts off before proper consideration and a serious critical thinker is considerable. The first step in serious thinking is reading or listening attentively to what someone else is writing. In other words, you perform the work of a summary: apply an open, alert mind to identify the thesis and supporting points of what someone is saying on a topic. Only then are you ready to explore your own position and respond with support for that position.

In this section, we help you to direct your analytical skills toward writing a critique of an essay. Choose one of the readings from Section 3 of the *Reader* as the departure point for your response. In this chapter we give you guidelines on how to write that response. First, write a short summary of the reading, using the six steps outlined in Chapter 8. Then you will be ready to explore your own response to the reading.

Directions of Response

Here are several directions your thinking might take:

- The author offers solid support for the thesis, and the thesis is acceptable.
- Support for the thesis could be stronger, but still the thesis is relatively acceptable.
- Support for the thesis seems partly persuasive, but ultimately the thesis contains a serious flaw.

- Support for the thesis is insufficient, and wider consideration of the thesis reveals its serious shortcoming.

As you can see, these four positions reflect a spectrum of judgment ranging from nearly full approval to nearly full disapproval. You must base whatever position you take on solid knowledge of the subject under discussion as well as thoughtful analysis.

Steps to Writing a Critique

- Summarize the paper you are responding to. (See Chapter 8.)
- Note your initial personal responses and formulate questions.
- Do any necessary additional research and reading, to be sure your knowledge of the topic is accurate and complete (your knowledge covers crucial issues and is current).
- Reread the paper to consider the effectiveness of its methods of support: is it persuasive yet biased? Poorly argued yet soundly based? etc.
- Choose a stance that suits the occasion. (In most academic criticism, the writer chooses the third-person point of view.) Consult your instructor for his or her recommendation.
- Structure your response by summarizing the text you are evaluating, stating your thesis, then elaborating on your reasons.

Your critical response invariably requires a solid degree of analytical observation. The section "Descriptive Analysis" in Chapter 6 (p. 355) provides relevant advice. The topic you are responding to will determine the precise form of analysis required.

Another highly relevant chapter is 7, "Argumentation," (p. 367). Be aware of the persuasive techniques used to sway opinion. One of the roles of a critic is to point out manipulative persuasion and faulty logic. In particular, review the list of 12 logical fallacies beginning on page 380. If your position is strongly at odds with the paper you are critiquing, then you are essentially in the realm of argumentation. In that case, consider adapting the guidelines for structuring an effective argumentative essay. In Chapter 11, "The Research Paper" (p. 422), see relevant sections on conducting preliminary research, finding sources, evaluating sources, including web sources, incorporating those sources into your paper, and listing them properly at the end of your paper.

Here is a sample critical response to David Suzuki's essay "The Right Stuff" (p. 181). The writer could have assumed other, equally valid positions. This response reflects the sort of approach and concerns that apply to critical evaluation. Critical response is evaluated not only by *what* you say but by *how* effectively you say it.

Critique of Sample Essay

Critique of David Suzuki's "The Right Stuff"

1   David Suzuki's essay "The Right Stuff" features the gracious, entertaining, and informative style we have come to associate with this well-known host of "The Nature of Things." But does the essay successfully argue its thesis that high school science courses should begin with sex education? In support, Suzuki observes that human sexuality is unavoidable in today's society, yet poorly explained by parents, media, and peers. Most of all, he believes high school students will find human sexuality a relevant point of departure to other topics.

2   For such a controversial and complex subject, however, the essay is surprisingly brief—a mere seven paragraphs. This makes for quick, easy reading, but does not allow much room to expand on important points. Shortage of room to consider and explain all sides becomes a bigger limitation when we realize that almost half the essay is devoted to one personal anecdote. The author tells us of a visit he made to a certain high school in a "tough" northern town where he was to address 400 students in the school auditorium. Having dropped into the motel bar the night before his address, Suzuki was approached by the school science teacher, a prophet of doom, who predicted the sex-crazed students would "tear [Suzuki] apart." The next day, however, Suzuki greeted his young audience with the comment, "I'm a geneticist. I know that you're basically walking gonads, so I'm going to talk about sex." The audience was hooked. Only after one and a half hours of questioning on an "astounding" range of topics did the session end.

3   This is a highly entertaining anecdote, with an excellent point to make about the importance of knowing your audience, but one personal example, reported from one limited viewpoint, hardly supports an argument. The further weakness with this example is that Suzuki assumes he provoked all this interest entirely by his opening focus on sex. What about the appeal of his personality and celebrity? Can he so easily isolate one sole cause to explain his apparent success that day with the students? One can also imagine at least a few students, uncomfortable with his opening remarks, stayed and enjoyed his talk in spite of that beginning.

4   A tendency toward this sort of oversimplification mars other parts of the essay. In the first paragraph Suzuki leads us to his subject and the effects of puberty by mentioning a "marvellous" book on high school. The book asserts that memories from high school years are more intense than those from other stages of life. Suzuki neither questions this assumption nor explains why the book making this claim is marvellous. He uses its point in his conclusion, however, to argue that since the teenage years produce such vivid memories, high schools must not waste this opportunity to make their proper impact.

5   Another oversimplification is that the intensity of high school years—the associated vivid memories and changed attitudes toward parents and school—must be

caused solely by pubescent hormones. If biology is the single factor driving adolescent rebellion, what explains the vastly contrasting attitudes among teenagers in agrarian or hunting societies who remain shielded from Western popular culture and technology? In another essay, "Ancestors—the Genetic Source," Suzuki himself makes the point that "the overriding influence [on human behaviour] is environmental." The contrary assumption in "The Right Stuff" may well be the main weakness in its argument.

6   Only in the sixth paragraph does Suzuki consider counter-arguments. Here he tries to cram in the sort of debate that should inform the entire discussion. He quickly dismisses opponents of his view with an unsubstantiated generalization that such people are unlikely to educate their children about sex at home. The children, he says, will learn about sex only inappropriately, through films, videos, magazines, books, and peer comments. This reminds us, however, that environment also plays an important part in what teenagers experience and in how they behave. How much of adolescent obsession with sex is actually fuelled by the media, and is Suzuki's own recommendation merely bowing to a media-driven agenda? Surely more consideration of the relationship between our commercialized, sexually exploitative culture and teenage learning and behaviour is needed before we can assume that intense concentration on human sexuality in high school teaching is the best or only answer.

7   Even if we grant that some sex education in schools might be beneficial for the reasons Suzuki suggests, how should it be designed and taught? Great care would be required for such a sensitive topic. One needn't be a prude to question whether sexuality, a very complex, even disturbing, topic for many, could be capably handled by a teaching staff already staggering from budget cuts and increased workload. Suzuki gives no thought to the complicated practical challenges of implementation.

8   He implies that as nature kicks in, all young people want to talk about sex, and as customers in our consumerist society, they deserve to have this curiosity served by the school. For many high school students, never mind administrators, teachers, taxpayers and government bureaucrats, it may not be as simple as that. Yes, teenagers need accurate information and schools can help provide it—but perhaps not so simply as Suzuki supposes in this essay.

Works Cited

Suzuki, David. "Ancestors—the Genetic Source." In *Metamorphosis: Stages in a Life*. Toronto: Stoddart, 1987. 13–17.
_____. "The Right Stuff." In *Inventing the Future: Reflections on Science, Technology, and Nature*. Toronto: Stoddart, 1989.

Whether or not we agree with the viewpoint of this critique, note some of its features:

- a respectful view toward the source material, despite objections to its perceived weaknesses
- an introduction recognizing the value of the author and the importance of the topic
- a brief introductory summary of Suzuki's thesis and main supporting points
- a clear indication of the central concern of the critique (Does the essay acknowledge the complexities involved?)
- awareness of the author's work outside this reading as well as of related knowledge in the issues touched on here (the nature-versus-nurture debate, the relevance of current education policy and spending)
- attention to rhetorical methods, with an expectation that competing sides be given fair consideration
- insistence on sustained logical thinking

 PRACTICE

- Write your own critical response to "The Right Stuff," referring to the above evaluation as suits your purpose.
- Following is another essay for you to critique, followed by a critical response to it by Marni McNaughton, a student. You may wish to refer to her critique of John Gray's essay in developing your own.

Language support for Gray's essay is available at the website for Athabasca University's English 255 Introductory Composition at <**www.athabascau.ca/courses/ engl/255/**>. Under "Supplementary Resources, see "Language Support for Selected Readings."

Sample Essay Developing a Critical Response to this Essay

You're Thinking of Getting a What?

John Gray

1   Nothing evokes that superior shudder, that anal-retentive cluck of civilized disapproval, quite like a tattoo.

2   Find out for yourself: in casual conversation with a relative or colleague mention casually, as though an afterthought, "By the way, I'm thinking of acquiring a tattoo."

3   After the pause you will hear something like "What are you thinking of doing *that* for?" murmured with the inflection of "Why would you want to pull out all your teeth?"

4   Now switch to a neutral topic—a recent movie or the price of real estate. Note the lingering chill in the basement of the conversation, a vaguely sectarian distance, as though you had just declared yourself a Scientologist.

5   To complete the experiment you will need a point of comparison, a control. Try this: Under similar circumstances, turn to a family member or business associate and

declare, "I'm thinking of having a surgeon slice the pouches from under my eyes," or "I want to have bags of silicone sewn into my breasts."

6   Quite another response: concern about your self-esteem, perhaps; or reassurance as to the state of your pouches or bustline; be yourself, beauty only skin deep, etc. Even when laced with contempt (vanity, vanity), the reaction will not vibrate with that hum of theological alarm that accompanied the subject of tattooing.

7   While having animal tissue injected into one's lips with a needle the size of a bug sprayer, or artificial hairs poked into one's skull may not receive enthusiastic applause, these urges are treated as symptoms of a mild psychological crisis, endearing evidence of a vulnerable, insecure nature.

8   A tattoo, however, is a threat.

9   Unlike cosmetic-surgery enthusiasts, tattoos seek not to conform to a conventional standard of beauty, but to distance themselves from the rest of us, to join an alien opposition.

10   People either have tattoos or they do not. A tattoo does not win friends among the untattooed majority. A tattoo is no way to get ahead.

11   Tattooing has always emitted an unsavory aura in Western culture—a whiff of the criminal, the carnival sharp, the fallen woman, and the unhygienic lover.

12   "Tattooed Thracians are not well-born," sniffed Herodotus, the father of history, in the fifth century B.C. (According to Plutarch, Thracian women acquired tattoos as a souvenir of Orpheus, whom they tore to pieces in a fit of pique over his homosexual preferences.)

13   "Well-born" indeed! Today, tattoos are a common fetish of the shave-and-puncture subculture, to go with the radiation-victim haircuts and multiple rings of surgical steel in nostrils and nipples—visual codes, no doubt, for unseemly sexual enthusiasms.

14   According to the media, tattooing is about to go permanently mainstream. Don't believe it. Rumors of imminent respectability have been chasing the tattoo for a century. When respectable people acquire tattoos, and they do, it's not because the practice has become respectable, it's because the recipient wishes inwardly to be *not* respectable, seeking out acts of private outrage that won't adversely affect the career path.

15   It doesn't matter what the tattoo is—a dedication ("I Love Mom"), a motto ("Death Before Dishonor"), a vow ("Property of Vito"), a warning ("Fuck Off"), a death symbol, predatory or mythical animal, flower, patriotic gesture, cartoon character, pinup girl, automotive logo, or primitive tribal scrawl. It's not the subject but the *fact* of a tattoo that contains its stigma and appeal. The tattooee has chosen to have an image indelibly stamped on his or her hide for no apparent reason other than a desire to be different.

16   What's wrong with the rest of us? Who do they think they are?

17   For a quasi-medical practice that entails injecting a foreign substance into a wound, the tattoo parlor is a breathtakingly unregulated industry. Although the city health inspector may call now and then to update the crumbling certificate on the wall, only the tattooist's personal ethic prompts him or her to maintain sanitary premises, wear surgical gloves, use new needles, and learn the medical effects of the various pigments. (It is not unknown for amateurs and semiprofessional "bootleggers" to use house paint!)

18   Given the Darwinian, *laissez-faire* nature of the craft, it's a testament to human probity that there exist any standards at all: that most tattooists turn away clients who are drunk, stoned, warped, or underage; refuse to mark "public skin" (above the neck or below the waist); and usually refuse racist slogans, Nazi emblems, ill-advised vows, and obscenities. Such restraints are voluntary, however, and like most discretionary industrial standards of safety and cleanliness, apt to slip during an economic downturn.

19   In addition to medical qualms, there is every reason to fret about aesthetic standards, for nothing publicly or professionally identifies the impeccable craftsman or incompetent scratcher. Tattooists earn no degrees or fellowships; no magazine critics review their work. For the buyer there is no trial period, no guarantee, no five-year warranty on parts or labor.

20   Not that the average patron is fussy. Statistically, the majority of tattoos result from a momentary, possibly drunken, impulse (although the desire may have been present for some time), and tattoo parlors are chosen primarily on the basis of geographical convenience. As a rule, more thought goes into the purchase of a stereo than a tattoo.

21   With predictable results. Face it—most tattoos look dreadful. A few years after application, these ill-considered icons of crude personal symbolism have blurred into dirty blobs of ink with hairs growing from them, as meaningful and attractive as a large strawberry mole.

22   Despite these obvious drawbacks, approximately ten percent of the adult population choose to have themselves marked for life.

23   Why would they do that?

24   It's inadequate, though tempting, to dismiss them as mildly insane. Although psychiatrists usually view tattoos as symptoms of mental trouble, inmates of mental institutions have fewer tattoos than do the outside population. (On the other hand, it has been said that the three traits common to psychopathic serial killers are that they are male and white and they possess a tattoo.)

25   While it is no great challenge to understand why a person would not acquire a tattoo, the reasons why people *do* are interesting, contradictory, and elusive.

26   Like other persistent cultural practices just outside publicly acknowledged art, such as circuses, soap operas, and rock and roll, tattooing draws from deep wells in the collective and subjective consciousness. A cultural weed growing without encour-

agement, it is nourished by primitive needs. To frighten off an attacking enemy. To invoke magic or borrow power from another being. To ward off evil. To attract good fortune. To draw attention and sexual respect by means of an exaggerated plumage. To declare oneself different from, or part of, a tribe. To make permanent a decision or rite of passage. Tattooing is a complex act—social, sexual, mystical, and cosmetic.

27   The one fact about a tattoo that never varies is its permanence. There's no such thing as a temporary tattoo. Yes, tattoos can indeed be erased, but the resulting patch of scar tissue is as conspicuous as the mark it replaced.

28   People receive a tattoo *because* of its permanence. All tattoos represent a desire for a reality that endures despite our wrinkling skin and mutating identities. All tattoos, ugly or beautiful, Jesus Christ or Tweety Bird, represent the same urge: to transcend.

29   Subconsciously, in an absurd, naïve, slapstick fashion, people who receive tattoos are searching for God.

30   Think about it: a prominent 1930s tattooist named Jack Redcloud displayed a large bust of Jesus, complete with bleeding crown of thorns, *upon his bald head*.

Critique of Sample Essay

John Gray's "You're Thinking of Getting a What?" A Critical Response
Marni McNaughton

1 In the short time since 1995, when John Gray wrote his article "You're Thinking of Getting a What?" society's view of the tattoo has changed immensely. The older generations of the population, like Gray, still disagree with the idea of getting a tattoo; however, the younger generation's views and acceptance of the tattoo completely oppose these traditional views.

2   In the past, those people who had tattoos were viewed by most as criminals. They were the tough guys, thugs, dirty and vulgar, who donned leather jackets, grew their hair long and rode motorcycles. They were the ones rebelling against mainstream society, the ones who refused to follow the rules and weren't willing to conform. These people were seen as outcasts, making a bad reputation for themselves. From the older generation's point of view, that reputation has stayed intact.

3   But in today's world, tattoos are more acceptable. They are still looked upon as an act of rebellion by some. However, everyone is doing it now, not just the hoodlums. Tattoos, or Body Art as they are also referred to, are now categorized more as a form of fashion than rebellion, especially in the younger generations. A popular fashion at that! Gray stated that 10 percent of the population possess tattoos. Between the ages of 18 and 35, the number is currently closer to 30 percent, with at least another 30 percent of them considering getting one.

4   Today, with tattoos being so easily removable with lasers, and leaving very little scarring, you can change your mind in six months and be free of your tattoo forever, not stuck with it for the rest of your life.

5   Throughout history, tattoos have always been a trademark of belonging. Men in the military have had tattoos for hundreds of years and tattooing has been an acceptable ritual to all, young and old. As an example, Popeye the Sailor Man, bearing an anchor tattoo on his comic-book forearm, has been a popular cartoon character for many years. His tattoo was his trademark.

6   Street gangs, following the bad reputation from the past generations, are another group that is identified with tattoos. A tattoo identifies members of the same gang. It is used as a way of displaying a belonging to a certain group. They wear their tattoos with pride, silently seeking to challenge and intimidate those who don't belong.

7   So, depending on the age of the person asked, the opinion of the tattoo will vary. The older generations find them offensive, while the younger ones find them intriguing. One day, fashions will change, and opinions as well, but for now you're more of a minority if you don't have a tattoo than if you do.

Focus Questions

1. Which of the following statements is the more accurate expression of Gray's thesis
   a. Tattoos are silly.
   b. People are hypocrites and snobs.
2. Has McNaughton used argumentative and scholarly methods to their fullest? See Chapters 7 and 11, and explain.

WRITING A COMPARATIVE ANALYSIS

Under "Comparison-Contrast" in Chapter 6, "Exposition," we present five common structures used within this general pattern. Here we concentrate on examples of comparison-contrast that reflect an analytical purpose.

Philosophers and social critics tend to use this pattern to demonstrate perceived shortcomings in one system by contrasting it to another. The poet, linguist, and oral historian Robert Bringhurst illustrates this purpose in the following paragraph on Haida master storytellers:

> The Old World and the New are not two regions marked reliably on maps. The Old World is wherever indigenous traditions are permitted to exist and acknowledged to have meaning. The New World is wherever such traditions are denied and a vision of human triumph is allowed to take their place. The Old World is the self-sustaining

world—worldwide—to which we all owe our existence. The New World is the synthetic, self-absorbed and unsustainable one—now also worldwide—that we create.

—*A Story as Sharp as a Knife*, 16–17

In this one paragraph, Bringhurst simply states an opinion, using a point-by-point structure (see p. 351). The rest of his book, examining the old stories of Haida culture, develops analytical evidence in support of his view. Another writer expresses a compelling view on our cultural attitudes toward animals, again through comparison-contrast structure, in the following excerpt by Rupert Sheldrake, an ethologist:

[There are] split attitudes to animals expressed in our society as a whole. During work hours we commit ourselves to economic progress fueled by science and technology and based on the mechanistic view of life. This view, dating back to the scientific revolution of the seventeenth century, derives from René Descartes' theory of the universe as a machine. Though the metaphors have changed (from the brain as hydraulic machine in Descartes' time, to a telephone exchange a generation ago, to a computer today), life is still thought of in terms of machinery. Animals and plants are seen as genetically programmed automata, and the exploitation of animals is taken for granted.

Meanwhile, back at home, we have our pets. Pets are in a different category from other animals. Pet-keeping is confined to the private, or subjective realm. Experiences with pets have to be kept out of the real, or objective world. There is a huge gulf between companion animals, treated as members of our families, and animals in factory farms and research laboratories. Our relationships with our pets are based on I-thou relationships rather than the I-it approach encouraged by science.

—Rupert Sheldrake, *Dogs That Know When Their Owners Are Coming Home and Other Unexplained Powers of Animals*, 1

In these two paragraphs, organized subject by subject, Sheldrake develops his analytical evaluation and offers reasons to support it. Note how in the second paragraph he includes some point-by-point structure, in order to link his subject (the subjective reality of home) back to the preceding subject (objective attitudes of work). Like Bringhurst, Sheldrake analyzes many of the values and assumptions of our society, using a concise, point-by-point contrast to organize the part of the argument we feature here.

Murray Ross, an American writer and thinker, demonstrates yet another approach to social criticism employing comparison-contrast. Unlike Bringhurst and Sheldrake, who challenge aspects of the Euro-American tradition, Ross sets out to reveal the American psyche (Greek for "soul"). Here, in an opening paragraph from an essay on sports, he introduces the comparative analytical method he will be using:

It is my guess that sport spectating involves something more than the vicarious pleasure of identifying with athletic prowess. I suspect that each sport contains a fundamental myth which it elaborates for its fans, and our pleasure in watching such games derives in part from belonging briefly to the mythic world which the game and its players bring to life. I am especially interested in baseball and football because they are so popular and so uniquely American; they began here and unlike basketball they have not been widely exported. Thus whatever can be said, mythically, about these games would seem to apply directly and particularly to our own culture.

—Murray Ross, "Football Red and Baseball Green," *The Essayist*, Eds. Sheridan Baker and C. Jeriel Howard, 5th ed. (New York: Harper and Row, 1985) 185–97

In the following 25 paragraphs of his essay proper, Ross mixes point-by-point and subject-by-subject organization in a close, detailed study of both games. He compares and contrasts baseball and football according to their history, spatial organization, sense of time, uniforms, manners, personalities, relation to the crowd, intensity, and overall connection to mythic traditions such as the pastoral and the heroic. Here, in point-by-point structure, is the last paragraph of his essay, musing on final implications:

> It is interesting that the heroic and pastoral conventions which underlie our most popular sports are almost classically opposed. The contrasts are familiar: city vs. country, aspiration vs. contentment, activity vs. peace, and so on. Judging from the rise of professional football, we seem to be slowly relinquishing that unfettered rural vision of ourselves that baseball so beautifully mirrors, and we have come to cast ourselves in a genre more reflective of a nation confronted by constant and unavoidable challenges. Right now, like the Elizabethans, we seem to share both heroic and pastoral yearnings, and we reach out to both. Perhaps these divided needs account in part for the enormous attention we as a nation give to spectator sports. For sport provides one place, at least, where we can have our football and our baseball too.

—Murray Ross, "Football Red and Baseball Green," *The Essayist*, Eds. Sheridan Baker and C. Jeriel Howard, 5th ed. (New York: Harper and Row, 1985) 185–97

By choosing two activities he believes are central to, yet opposed within, his culture, Ross develops a comprehensive, complex method, while he maintains sharp focus on two specific subjects.

The following paragraphs come from a student essay with a less sweeping ambition. Rather than take on all of society, as the previous three authors do, Rhonda Nelson, a student, is interested in comparing traditional and distance forms of education:

> Traditional education institutions involve a slow administrative process and frequent complications on site. When accepted, students must wait for the new semester to begin, as long as twelve months in some cases. At registration, they must stand in line with hundreds of their peers. Next stop is a line at the finance office to pay fees. Lineups are usually long, especially at the bookstore, where students must go in a one-week crush to buy assigned textbooks and supplies. There is yet another line for a student identification card allowing students to take out library books. When classes start, parking becomes a major headache. The walk from student parking to class can take over 15 minutes. It can take even longer than that to cross some campuses from one class to the next, on a schedule that allows only 10 minutes between periods.
>
> Distance education, on the other hand, allows quick online or telephone registration. Once registered, students may begin their course within six weeks, a month, or sometimes even less. Since they have regular access to their instructor by email, phone, fax, and regular mail, there are no lineups, no parking problems, no cross-campus dashes to arrive late and receive an annoyed look from the professor. Visiting the crowded bookstore is eliminated by direct delivery of the course package, the cost of which is included in the all-in-one course fee.

—Rhonda Delorme, "University Education: Traditional or Distance?" unpublished, p. 3 (See "Sample Essays" under "Supplementary Resources" on the Athabasca University website at <www.athabascau.ca/courses/engl/255/>.)

Nelson's concluding reference to fees sets up her next paragraph, which shifts to point-by-point structure. She contrasts various types of fees in traditional and distance institutions. In her concluding two body paragraphs, she returns to subject-by-subject structure and contrasts the impact of opposite teaching methods.

As a university student, Nelson delivers an evaluation akin to a consumer report written by someone who has tested two products. Of course, a valid counter-argument could be developed in favour of traditional campus education.

 PRACTICE

- Read "I Am Half-Canadian" by Pamela Swanigan (p. 58). What comparative structures does she use? What would you say is the thesis of her analysis?

- Read "The Rhetorical Stance" by Wayne C. Booth (p. 144). How does he use comparative analysis to further his thesis in that essay?

WRITING A LITERARY ANALYSIS

Writing about literature is a special form of critical analysis; the literary text under study becomes your subject. You identify various techniques and aspects (elements) of the work and focus on one particular dynamic: for example, the symbolic importance of Lois's dress in Alice Munro's "Thanks for the Ride" (p. 62). Writing a literary analysis can be a rewarding way to gain a deeper appreciation for a particular work. To perform this type of analysis, however, you have to know the basic elements. (We provide a list of technical terms and explanations in the Selected Glossary of Literary Terms.) Most analyses will refer to the one or two of these elements of interest to you.

We have narrowed our advice to assist you with analysis of short stories in particular, such as those in the *Reader*. Analyzing poetry, plays, or films requires certain additional considerations. In the case of poetry, for example, you may need to explore metrical, rhythmical, and sound techniques that would take us beyond the scope of this particular book. With film, you need to recognize techniques such as lighting and camera focus that help shape characterization and theme. If you are interested in analyzing films, see "Writing a Film Review" under "Supplementary Resources" at the English 255 Introductory Composition website at <www.athabascau.ca/courses/engl/255/>. You can find the same material at the Pearson website at <www.pearsoned.ca/brundage/>. The following steps for writing a literary analysis of a short story will guide you equally well in analyzing subjects in other genres, including film, provided you learn the supplementary technical terms required for those other genres.

Before analyzing fiction as a genre, review our definitions of "poetry," "prose," "fiction," and "non-fiction" (including the "essay") given in the Selected Glossary of Literary Terms. There you will also find definitions and brief discussion of the main *elements of fiction* that should help you to read and write about short stories at a more rewarding level. These definitions will help you relate the stories to the broader world of writing as well as experience each story in more precise detail. All the elements of fiction discussed in the Glossary are revealed through the writer's distinctive vision and particular use of language, and all of the elements are essentially interconnected and mutually enriching.

Steps for Analyzing a Short Story

- Read the story for enjoyment and personal connections.
- Re-read the story, watching for the presence and interplay of the elements of fiction. (See definitions in the Selected Glossary of Literary Terms.)
- Decide which of the elements seem most engaging, important, or central.
- Try to express the theme of the story in your own words. Do so in a complete sentence.
- Begin to think about how the element or elements you find so important to the story contribute to a full expression of the theme.
- Develop your essay as an analysis of how one or two central elements contribute to theme. Check that the introduction in your essay clearly states the issue you intend to explore, and end your introduction with a firm statement of your thesis, explaining how and to what degree the elements under study contribute to theme.
- Find a logical organization for your discussion. One method is to begin the body of your essay with the element(s) that are most immediately noticeable, leaving the less obvious (but perhaps most complex and important) factors for the latter part of your discussion.
- Assume your reader already knows the story and its basic elements, but describe and reinforce these where necessary.
- Use the literary present; that is, refer to events in the story as occurring in the present tense ("When Lois invites Dick into her house, we sense some hidden motive").

Elements of Fiction

- setting
- characterization
- plot (see also "pace")
- point of view (see also "irony")
- image
- symbol and metaphor

Chapter 11
The Research Paper

Students commonly think of research papers as specialized forms of writing. As this section recognizes, research writing *does* involve certain considerations; however, all that really separates a research paper from other academic essays is the *extent* of the preliminary investigation required and your commitment to careful documentation. Your dominant research strategy may be to share first-hand observation, to organize secondary-source information, to analyze an issue, to argue a certain viewpoint, or to combine two or more of these purposes. First-year research papers typically aim to present reliable information as neutrally as possible (basic expository style), to weigh and decide upon varying opinions and conclusions (analysis), or to argue a perspective, often on a controversial topic (persuasive). Any combination of the types of writing previously described could be used. So as you proceed to learn and practise the techniques specific to this form of writing, continue to shape your work according to the general guidelines for all good writing.

What distinguishes research papers from other papers and leads to their separate categorization in reference books such as this one? As noted, it is the *extent* of the research that is required. In a true research paper, you need to find, organize, and evaluate a considerable body of existing knowledge. Sources may include academic writing, historical accounts, government reports, statistics, microfilm, interviews, and legal and medical opinions. Exploring all of this information without becoming lost or overwhelmed can be a challenge. This section of the text recommends you follow clear stages and provides details for the various formal techniques of integrating information. (The following chapter, 12, "Documentation," explains how to acknowledge your sources.)

If you proceed in a systematic way, you should attain a feeling of solid achievement as you complete your work. Be prepared to spend time on a research paper, remembering that this type of writing, based on a vigorous inquiry, is central to many professional activities. Research skills will take time to master, but they will serve you well.

As we said, a research paper requires several major steps from beginning to completion:

- You have to locate, select, organize, and synthesize your background sources.

- You have to arrange your paper as a cohesive body of research from these various sources and perspectives.
- As well, you probably have to present your own particular analysis or argument—emerge with a viewpoint that is your own.

Since a research paper requires your investigation and representation of other people's analyses, you need to consider some crucial factors that would not affect your non-research essays, such as *long-term scheduling* and careful *note-keeping* from your secondary sources.

GETTING STARTED

Break down the writing of a research paper into several steps. This is true for experienced research scholars or for first-year students. Each step requires some planning, from getting organized to narrowing your topic to proofreading the final draft. Some instructors may request a *proposal* and/or a *working thesis statement* and/or an *outline* and/or proposed *Works Cited page* to ensure that you observe the necessary stages and to start you moving in the right direction. More than anything, be aware as you begin that a good research paper can take you as long as a month or six weeks to prepare.

Scheduling

You cannot pull a research paper together in one night, though over history many students have tried. Since you have to locate and evaluate several credible sources, you will probably need at least three weeks of hard work for a serious effort. Students who do not thrive on stress may need more time. A weak research effort will be immediately obvious, so plan ahead. As instructors usually view a polished research paper as a measure of some academic commitment, you might think of this project as the consolidation of your previous efforts in a course or an opportunity to expand or reconsider an earlier essay or idea that arose in the course. Check with your instructor if you wish to expand on an earlier paper. Your research paper should differ significantly and be substantially deeper than the course paper you wish to build on. Writing is never a linear process, so the valuable experience of revisiting previous work to improve on it can develop your appreciation of the writing process, and even your sense of yourself as a writer.

What follows is a provisional model for a long-term research and writing schedule. We will explain specifics later, after this snapshot of an approach.

Step 1: *Settle on your topic*, even if only generally at first. What further angle or sub-category of your topic would you like to invest your time and effort in? Can you find sufficient background sources? Have you looked around? Are you genuinely interested in your topic? Why?

Step 2: Once you have found your specific area (say, masculinity in two recent African American novels, the return of social vision to Canadian politics, the influence of women in Canadian business, Kennedy's rationale for committing troops to Vietnam, or representations of love in three Tragically Hip songs), you need to **gather specific research material** on your topic. As you conduct your research, you will likely continue to adjust or redefine your selected topic, based on those research findings. Keep notes that thoroughly document all useful information and details from your source material (authors, titles, publishers, cities of publication, dates). Carefully record all exact quotations with their page numbers. Also write yourself little reminders for further possible areas of discussion in your paper. Try to outline a draft version, either in point form, in a topic-sentence tree, or in some provisional paragraphs.

Step 3: Now that you have read through both general sources and more specialized discussions on your topic, you will make some longer draft notes that contain quite a few quotations that can help your discussion. You can always delete or shorten some of these quotations later. Some quotations should be solid evidence, while some could be argumentative views that you may either support or challenge with other views on the subject. Some other references you may not use directly—verbatim, or word for word—but indirectly. With these, you want to offer a responsible, accurate paraphrase that you still attribute in the paper by citing the author's name and the page of his or her work where you found it. You probably have narrowed your topic sufficiently now to have a **working thesis**, a specific position on your topic that you can establish (expository) or argue (persuasive) confidently. Based on your reading and notes, you can now **develop your outline** into a fuller draft version of your paper: you will have provisional topic sentences in place by now to guide your paragraphs. You are probably ready to rewrite soon and refine this draft version into your research paper.

Step 4: **Rewrite your first draft**. Present your established thesis clearly and confidently in your introduction. In the paper's body paragraphs, present your supporting evidence and assert what you see as the implications of that thesis. You may wish to add footnotes or endnotes to include brief supporting or explanatory information.

Step 5: **Edit that draft for submission**. Check and recheck all quoted material for accuracy. Look at your topic sentences to check their relevance to and support of your thesis statement. Are your own voice and perspectives strong in the paper? What do you conclude at the discussion's end?

SELECTING YOUR TOPIC

For your research paper, your instructor may give you only one topic to research or provide you with choices or ask you to select your own topic. Whether you have been assigned choices (and therefore must provide an answer to a specific question) or an open topic (and must propose your own question and decide *when* you have answered it), select a subject that interests you. Select one for which you can find sufficient research material as well.

Settle on a topic you can research in no more than four weeks. Look for a topic that does not place you in a corner for available sources. You must always be prepared to find a compromise between your interests and the sources available to you. In part, this compromise may be further defined by your school's library and computer capabilities. If you are pressed for time, you are probably best advised to select a topic that you know has been widely written about, such as the influence of computing on education, or globalization and its consequences or the representation of childhood and youth in J.D. Salinger's fiction.

If you stay flexible at this stage, you should be able to pursue at least some aspects of your interests, while making a practical choice based on the available sources. Be true to your own curiosities; a research paper that bores you will also bore your reader. As well, a research paper that you half-heartedly write only to complete the course may end up reading like a barely connected string of quotations without any centre.

Here are some sample research essay topics that include a range of social, historical, literary, and business interests:

- Sept. 11, 2001, and the U.S. market
- diet and nourishment issues: meat, vegetables, junk food, vitamins, meal replacements
- male and female body images: size, health, media, fears, bodies and/as machines
- increased musical instruction and discussion in schools: from Mozart and Mahler to Muddy Waters, Bob Marley, and Metallica
- marketing to youth: strategies, ethics, social convergence
- Vimy Ridge in WWII: expendable Canadians in a global conflict?
- prenuptial agreements and support payments
- language use and family attitudes in Richler's story "The Summer My Grandmother Was Supposed to Die" (p. 14)
- sexual knowledge and social circumstance in Alice Munro's "Thanks for the Ride" (p. 62)
- men's and women's "lifestyle" magazines: content, presumptions, market, private and social fantasies
- Middle East conflict: history as ongoing negotiation
- the 1960s and 1970s: still going strong, but why?
- influenza, infection, antibiotics and super-bugs: the cure as the ailment?
- police brutality, pepper spray, freedom of speech, police helicopters, social control: the rise of the authoritarian state?
- "are we ourselves?": Canadian community values and private lives or regional and national self-perceptions
- intimacy and detachment in two films by Canadian director Atom Egoyan
- natural resource management: fish, forest soil, ozone, water, crops
- consumer protections, advertising frauds
- Vancouver: Canada's future city—now
- Canadian self-employment: benefits and perils

Many examples on this list are very broad topics. You would need to narrow those topics to a more specific issue within the general topic area. Remember that you will need to assert a **thesis statement** in your final draft, so develop a strong view on a particular angle of the topic.

After you have picked a subject for which you can locate some sources, you are on your way. Having a subject, however, does not mean you yet have a specific research topic. You need to narrow your interest to a particular angle. The Second World War itself is far too large to serve as a first-year research topic. However, a smaller category within that topic would lead to an interesting research project. How about the strategic effect of propaganda or counter-intelligence in one battle or stage of the conflict?

By narrowing your topic and investigating a specific area of inquiry within your general topic, you can move closer to several goals at once. You will eliminate extra reading that may be either too general or too specific in a direction that differs from yours. You will move toward a working thesis, a position on your topic. While narrowing your research topic from a large area of interest to a specific line of inquiry may seem difficult, this step only requires that you first ask yourself "What is my main concern?" and "What am I most interested in?" and "How would I prefer to spend my research time?" As you read some initial secondary sources, you will begin to develop a sense of what specific topic you would like to pursue.

Here are some further brief examples of how you might move quickly from general topic areas to working research topics, from a large category of interest to a research sub-category:

Violence in Sports

- NHL violence in the last two years
- soccer-crowd violence in last two World Cups
- women's hockey and football leagues
- boxing's future/changing gender roles
- criminal records of NBA and NFL athletes

Business Concerns in an International Economy

- controls of inventory in a multinational company
- the internet's impact on specific area of retail, manufacturing, and/or wholesale
- changes in specific business laws and recent effects
- Employment Insurance and proposals for revised cost-sharing between employees and employers
- cyber-commerce

EXPLORING SOURCES

The Information Age is an unrelenting blizzard of uneven and uncertain information. Finding the way to genuinely useful and accurate information is every researcher's challenge and goal. This brief guide will help you get started.

Your College or University Library

Your college or university library is usually the best place to start your search for good reliable sources. Take advantage of the resources available in your own library. Almost all libraries offer free assistance in the form of information sessions, classes, or individual consultation with reference librarians; these sessions can be extremely helpful to students new to college or university research. Most librarians are happy to help you as long as you are polite and patient. Saying "please" and "thank you" is often a productive strategy to ensure assistance with research questions and problems.

Library Catalogues

While library catalogues vary, you will find certain strategies applicable in most situations. You will want to try more than one way of accessing your topic, by various keywords, subject headings, words in titles, etc. If your searches are pulling up hundreds of sources, narrow your search. Use two keywords instead of one ("vampire and literature" or "vampire and film" instead of just "vampire") or identify a more specific topic ("Dracula" or "Bela Lugosi"). Conversely, if your searches on a topic are pulling up only one or two sources, try synonyms or related words ("pregnancy," "birthing," "midwife," "childbirth," "motherhood," "nursing") or broadening your topic term ("horror film" instead of only "John Carpenter's *Friday the 13th*" or scientific "entrepreneur" instead of only "marketing of lab mice").

Specialized Databases

To find a journal article, you will probably have to use one of your library's specialized electronic databases. Some specialized databases provide abstracts (summaries of the articles) or even full articles, while others simply give you a list of articles and their sources. Find out from your library or your instructor which databases are used in your subject area. Some examples are ERIC (for Education), MLA (for literature), Medline (for Medicine and Biosciences), and PsychINFO / PsychLIT (for psychology).

Encyclopedias and Dictionaries

Encyclopedias and dictionaries can help introduce you to your subject by defining terms, summarizing facts, and sometimes providing an overview of the main issues associated with your topic. Although these reference works are a good place to start a writing assignment, never stop there; reference books never provide enough depth for a college or university writing assignment. You must be more active in your research efforts.

Encyclopedias can be general or specialized. General encyclopedias cover numerous topics from a wide range of fields. Because of their broad scope, they do not cover subjects in the detail of specialized encyclopedias and dictionaries. Many of the most up-to-date general encyclopedias are now available in electronic form. *Encyclopedia Britannica*, *Britannica.com*, and *Encarta* are some examples.

You will find specialized encyclopedias and dictionaries useful when beginning your research on a topic. Some of these contain articles of several pages in length, written by experts in the field, while others contain shorter entries with highly specific information on specialized topics. Examples include the *Dictionary of Literary Biography*, *The Encyclopedia of Social Work*, *The International Dictionary of Films and Filmmakers*, and *The Gale Encyclopedia of Native American Tribes*.

Be sure to check the year of publication of any encyclopedia you are using. Some older college and university libraries have reference works dating back several decades. These sources may be extremely well researched and fascinating in their own right, but they can also be catastrophically out of date for your purposes. Research and representation of many subjects (such as mental illness, narrative techniques in fiction, Aboriginal cultures) have changed significantly over the decades, so make sure you examine the most recent sources available in your school library or online.

Books

Scholarly books form a solid basis for most college and university research papers. Often, you will need to read only two or three chapters of the books to gather valuable information. These chapters can provide serious, consistent, current, in-depth information on major ideas and research on your topic. They can help you to find and narrow your issue. Most college and university libraries specialize in scholarly or academic books appropriate for research papers, but not all books on your topic might be good sources for your particular paper. (Our discussion of "Evaluating Sources" later in this chapter will help you choose the right books.)

Journals

Articles in journals are usually your best source of information for a brief and highly specialized discussion of a topic. However, journal articles are sometimes written for experts in a particular academic field, so you may find some of the terms difficult to understand. You may have to decide whether you need to understand some of this terminology in order to write about your subject. Often, you can consult a special dictionary on theoretical terms or perhaps another article on the troubling term itself ("First-Person Confessional Narrative," "Diegesis," "Setting," "Autoeroticism," "Isothermic," "Historiography," "Hip Hop," "Tom Jones"). The authors of journal articles engage in specific arguments based on issues particular to their field.

Newspapers and Magazines

Articles in newspapers and magazines are both more superficial and more accessible than articles in academic journals because they address a wider audience. Sometimes you can use these general-interest articles as appropriate sources along with other more specialized sources for a research paper, especially if your topic is very recent and people have not had time to publish on it in longer books and scholarly journals. Reviews and interviews from newspapers and magazines, for instance, can be useful sources of beginning information. On the other hand, if your assignment requires that you draw on scholarly articles from academic journals in a proposed field, do not rely on newspapers or magazines. The journalists who write articles in newspapers and general-interest magazines such as *Maclean's* or *Cosmopolitan* are usually on assignments with no particular expertise in the areas they cover for those days; so they are not the most reliable sources when you are investigating serious developments in research or scholarly debates on a given subject. Some specialized magazines, however, such as *The Economist*, *Nature*, and *Scientific American*, are well researched and well respected by experts in the field and may be good places to begin your research.

Interviews and Personal Experiences

Interviews and personal experiences can add an interesting, surprising, and original dimension to your research paper. For example, one student may gain substantial insights for an essay on contemporary Jewish literature (Mordecai Richler, Philip Roth, Cynthia Ozick, Saul Bellow) by interviewing her grandparents, who may have survived Nazi internment camps, oppression, and/or migration. Another student may successfully incorporate his own Japanese-Canadian experiences in a study of some of the strengths and problems of Canadian multiculturalism.

A cautionary note: personal experiences are not always easy or appropriate to include in research papers, especially if you are very emotional about the experience. Before you include a personal experience in a research paper, ask yourself whether that experience contributes to the paper, provides an illuminating example or will distract your reader from your point. Also, some instructors may object to your including personal experiences, while others strongly encourage it. If you are not sure where your instructor stands on the politics of personal comments in a research paper, discuss your ideas with him or her.

The Internet

The World Wide Web can provide vast quantities of information on many subjects, particularly those that are current. Students who are comfortable with the internet (or who are starting their essays after conventional libraries are closed) may be tempted to use it as their only source of information, however. Usually this is not advisable. Certainly many websites provide stimulating discussions and well-researched, reliable information, but just as many are poorly researched, inaccurate, and otherwise misleading. There are very few occasions when it is appropriate for you to use the World Wide Web as your only source of information.

Research on the web works best for introducing you to recent topics, since the internet is the up-to-date international medium. The information it provides on history, complex topics or less popular subjects tends to be sketchier. When in doubt, consult recommended library sources before you turn to the internet, so you will have a better understanding of the credibility of the materials you find there.

Internet Search Engines

If you are looking for information on the World Wide Web, you will probably use an internet search engine. Most browsers have default search engine settings, with several other search options available as well. Each search engine works somewhat differently, so the same word or phrase may give you different results. Try out several search engines to see which one you like best. Your choice may also depend on your starting point. For example, if you have only a general idea of a subject for a research paper but not a precise topic, a search engine like Yahoo, which classifies information by subject heading, may be helpful. Conversely, if you have a very specific topic in mind, a search engine such as AltaVista, which scans websites for precise phrases or word combinations, will probably work best.

Note that some search engines, such as AltaVista and Hotbot, use a robot and an indexer to seek information and perform keyword searches. Others, such as Yahoo and Webcrawler, are directories with professional editors who index sites. These search engines allow you to search by subject as well. Experience and experimentation will show you which engines give you the best results for various assignments. Here are some URLs for search engines:

- www.yahoo.com
- www.altavista.com
- www.google.com
- www.excite.com
- www.webcrawler.com
- www.questia.com
- www.infoseek.com
- www.hotbot.com

Narrow your search by using options such as "all the words" or "the exact phrase." Although search engines vary in what they find and in the exact instructions for finding information, all of them have Help files to help you narrow your search to a manageable size. Note that some search engines can carry out Boolean searches as well, so that they can be more easily narrowed down using the following terms:

- By typing "music AND copyright," you search with both terms in that order.
- By typing "music OR copyright," you broaden your search by searching either term separately.
- By typing "music AND copyright NOT Napster," you now eliminate documents with the word "Napster" in them.

- By typing "music copyright," you confine your search to these two words grouped together.
- By typing "music NEAR copyright," you retrieve documents in which these terms are within 10 words of each other (on some engines, such as AltaVista).

Keep track of reference sites for writers. For no cost, you can find many guides and resource materials here (and in associated links). A good, academically credible source you might like to search further for general information is the Voice of the Shuttle, at **<http://vos.ucsb.edu>**.

Saving Material You Find on the Internet

It is often a good idea to download material from a website onto your computer or a disk. You can do this with a simple right click of your mouse. This step is important because websites may change from day to day, and the material you find today may not be accessible to you tomorrow. Keep a log to document when you referenced specific websites.

To avoid plagiarizing, take "notes" by cutting from a website you visit but pasting in another font, so that you can tell where your words stop and another's words begin. Record important websites among your "Bookmarks" or "Favorites" for easy reference.

 PRACTICE

1. Look up the same topic in three different encyclopedias or dictionaries, including at least one general and one specialized source. What are the strengths and weaknesses of each? Which source would be the best for getting you started on a research paper?
2. Choose a specific topic that interests you, such as the use of performance-enhancing drugs in sports, the medical use of marijuana, vampire films, or the Nuremberg trials. Try to find four articles on the subject: two from newspapers or magazines and two from academic journals. How helpful would these different sources be for writing a research paper on that topic?

Primary and Secondary Sources

Most areas of study make an important distinction between primary and secondary sources. **Primary sources** are the initial materials you are working with—a work of literature, a philosophical treatise, a historical document, or data you gather directly from an experience. Working directly with these sources allows you to come up with your own interpretation or analysis of them. The primary source or sources are *what* you are writing about, the topic of the paper.

Secondary sources are other writers' interpretations, analyses, or discussions of an event, an issue, or a primary source. Interpretations of literary or musical works, discussions of film, and political analyses of an international speech are all examples of secondary sources.

If you are writing a term paper on Alice Munro's story "Thanks for the Ride," for example, that text is your primary source. A scholarly discussion of that story, such as an article entitled "Summer Desires in Munro's 'Thanks for the Ride,'" would be a secondary source. If you were to analyze Canada's tax structure, the body of facts of our taxation system would be the primary source, whereas a piece of writing discussing an aspect of those facts, such as Erin Spronk's "GST and Other Irritating Taxation Techniques," would be your secondary source. If you were to conduct an interview with a retired taxation official from the Canada Customs and Revenue Agency on his or her view of certain flaws and possible improvements in the taxation system, then that interview would also be a secondary source.

Sometimes it can be a little tricky to identify the primary source. In fact, in some research situations what might usually be a secondary source can become your primary source, if you decide to write your paper on that secondary source! If you wish to write a paper or a review on attitudes in literary criticism toward female characters in recent Canadian short stories, for example, the pieces of literary criticism you examine would be your primary sources, since these articles are the texts that your research paper addresses. Similarly, a paper on the 1991 Gulf War would have to rely on a factual account of this event as the primary source, but a paper on *one* writer's interpretation of this war would use that writer's work as the primary source.

Primary Source	Secondary Source
Mavis Gallant's "My Heart Is Broken" (story)	"Romance and Self-Esteem in Mavis Gallant's 'My Heart Is Broken'" (scholarly article)
Travis Horncastle's "Gulf War Syndrome" (research article)	Other articles, other research on Gulf War Syndrome

EVALUATING SOURCES

You should always be careful about your sources. There is no need to take home every single book or other publication on your subject, or, on the other hand, to select randomly from the shelf. Good researchers look through a range of sources related to their topics, and use only some of these to write their papers. Evaluating your sources carefully before you use them will save you time on research and make your paper better.

When you assess a secondary source, you measure its relevance and usefulness to your project. Take into account the secondary source's *date of publication* (are its points and conclusions current or outdated?), its *scope* (is it too general or too specialized?), and its *Works Cited page* or *Bibliography* (is it a well-researched discussion or a one-sided "opinion" piece?). You might also be able to find other potential sources listed in one good secondary source's Works Cited page. Using such "cross-referencing" is an effective and common research technique.

When you first evaluate a source, "read" quickly—not as an involved reader, but as a research scanner—moving rapidly through the source's main argument to see if you can use it productively. Will it support your paper? Does it provide evidence and facts you can build on? Can you perhaps contend against the source's opinions and findings? Do you suspect errors, gaps, or bias in it?

Here are five steps to help you evaluate a source:

1. What is the source's main point, claim, or argument?
2. What is the author's perspective and/or tone (for/against/objective)?
3. Can you summarize the author's evidence?
4. Do you agree or disagree (or a little of both) with the author's point?
5. What questions does the source leave fully or partially unanswered or, equally important, completely unasked—in *your* opinion?

You should also look carefully at each source's table of contents and index (if a book), abstract (if an article and if available), introductory chapter or introductory paragraph, and Works Cited page. Sometimes these brief sections can help eliminate a useless source or generate new directions and new secondary sources in your research.

One advantage in using a college or university library is that some of the work in evaluating sources has already been done for you. Librarians, professors, and instructors who have a good idea of the sources their students need will have selected these books. If you use only a public library to do your research, you will have to be more careful; many sources there are intended primarily for high school students, hobbyists, or general-interest readers, and they may not be extensive enough for a college or university research paper.

Ask yourself these three questions to help you choose your sources well:

1. *Is the source written for researchers?* Does the book seem to be written for college or university students, or more advanced researchers in the field? Generally, your sources should be pitched just above your own current level of understanding, not a step or two below. You should be learning as you conduct your research. Many students are too easily put off by secondary sources that seem somewhat difficult. If you use a source that simplifies issues too much, you may not gain an understanding of the twists and turns of your subject, or the various debates within it. On the other hand, you need not struggle with a ferociously specialized source way beyond a first- or second-year student's level of comprehension, that is, a source that assumes a large body of knowledge you simply do not have yet. If you are writing a paper on the medical uses of marijuana, for instance, but you do not have a background in biology or medicine, expect to have to deal with some unfamiliar terminology, but don't waste valuable time agonizing over highly specialized scientific articles obviously intended for an audience of MDs and PhDs. Use such articles if you can, but if you feel lost, put them aside for more immediately useful material.

2. *Is the source relevant to my topic?* Always check the introduction, table of contents, and the index to make sure that the source really contains the information you need. If the source has only a couple of pages relevant to your topic, you can photocopy these for a mention in your paper or perhaps a footnote or an endnote, and keep looking.

3. *What is the secondary source's position?* Remember that many published articles are only interpretations of facts, and developments, rather than completely objective evaluations. The authors of secondary sources offer their expert opinions as persuasively as possible, but remember that the entire secondary source may be only that one person's view, not the whole truth. Be careful as a researcher to distinguish the facts from the perspectives. While using the facts of the primary source or the view of another secondary source, you may be able to argue against or to qualify the perspective presented in any one particular secondary source.

Reading as a Researcher

A great deal of published research (secondary sources) contains aspects of both explicit and implicit interpretation. By definition, all interpretations contain significant aspects of "subjective knowledge": personal experience, embedded perspectives, and professional attitudes toward what counts as evidence and toward what counts as a reasonable conclusion. You will come across many disputes between these different authors of secondary sources—all perhaps examining the same primary source—on the basis of the different interpretative strategies they employ. This tension is part of any research territory.

As a junior researcher reading the work of more experienced researchers, you need to be aware of the significant (and even sometimes trivial) ways your sources disagree with each other. Always be prepared to challenge these expert views. Sometimes the "experts" make mistakes in basic facts. Sometimes they draw arguably, or even blatantly, wrong conclusions from ambiguous premises. Sometimes they offer a wildly belligerent opinion or whimsical conclusion with which you have every right to disagree.

If you can "debunk"—that is, successfully challenge, expose, and overturn—a published or established view, you have performed one of the most important and respected functions of a researcher. The larger social function of all research is to locate a true account, a fair, just view.

Evaluating Sources on the Internet

Many of the strategies for evaluating printed sources apply equally to the World Wide Web: What is the source's authority? What is the source's background research? Does the source have a bias?

The web raises additional concerns:

- *Can you find out who is responsible for the site?* Do the individual organizations responsible for the site tell you anything about themselves? Are they established academics, teachers, or researchers? What if they are only Grade 11 students who harbour deep resentment over the cultural underestimation of Duran Duran? How can you compare the merits of one source and another on the internet?

- *Is the site connected to a university or college?* Some of the best research sites are based in academic institutions and are entirely sound sources for academic research. However, be cautious about using information posted by other students, who may be designing superficial websites or posting weak drafts of eventually mediocre papers for their own courses. If the document seems to be composed by someone who does not know anything about writing, evidence, essay structure, analysis, or documentation, then steer clear of the site.

- *Is the site trying to sell you something?* If it presents research on something that it also tries to sell, chances are the research is biased in its favour. For example, if a pharmaceutical company posts information about a drug they sell, they will predictably select information that presents the drug in a positive light. Although some of the research may be reliable, look at other sources as well to give you a sense of balance.

- *When was the site last updated?* If the site has not been updated for one or two years, its owner might have abandoned it. In any event, a site that has not been updated for some time is usually not a particularly good source of information.

- *Is the site just a cheap collection of flashy graphics?* Remember that you are looking for information in your research, not splashy nonsense. Evaluate the text or substance of the site. In some cases, the graphics may be exactly what you need for your research, yet often they have little or no bearing on the content or substance of the site.

 PRACTICE

1. Find four websites on a specific topic you would like to research. Evaluate the strengths and weaknesses of each. How are some sources appropriate and some not for a research paper?

2. In groups, compare notes on various websites. Talk about the best and worst sites. Can you tell which sites were written by knowledgeable people and which sites were written by charlatans? What do the best websites have in common?

3. In groups, discuss how some websites have bamboozled many people with needless or misleading information. Evaluate the internet's usefulness in your experience.

4. How do you define "information"? In groups, debate this definition and the ways it may differ from "fact," "knowledge," and "common sense."

NOTE-TAKING FOR RESEARCH PURPOSES

As you read into your topic area, you need to take exact notes of your findings. Many researchers first make their notes on regular paper and then later condense the most vital information to a small card: perhaps a useful quotation, a brief two- or three-sentence summary of an article or chapter, or a particular author's central argument. You can easily rearrange and add to these cards later to reflect changes in your outline—and your outline will certainly change, as you add and delete the information you collect and tighten your points and topic sentences to represent your revised thesis.

In this preliminary research stage, remember to record all source information precisely. The author's name, the source title, publisher, year, city of publication, and page numbers are crucial information. If there are errors in your research paper at this level, you will undermine your credibility as a researcher. All your quotations also need to be exact, so be careful when transcribing your initial notes, when condensing your longer notes to points on cards, when incorporating that information into various drafts, and when summarizing source material in paraphrases. Remember you will have to attribute all paraphrases to your source by the author's name and the page number, though you will not necessarily quote that author's very words.

Following is a hypothetical example of a handy research card that you might produce from some of your initial reading and note-taking, as you work toward shaping your thesis statement and an outline for your paper:

Sample Research Note Card

Tucker, Susan A. *The History of Boxing.* Toronto: McEwan Publishing, 1998.
- Chapter Five, "Mike Tyson's Presence," most relevant to my paper, especially the points about "social justification for bad behaviour," p. 134.
- Tucker asserts "only in professional boxing or crime could someone like Tyson flourish financially" (142).
- "Tyson himself seems genuinely confused about why his aggression is tremendously rewarded in the ring, but socially and legally denounced outside the ropes." (149)
- boxing a "circus or art" (151)?

The card contains all the necessary source information (author, title, city of publication, publisher, and date), as well as four exact quotations with their correct page numbers. You may later decide not to use all the quotations in your final draft, but these quotations may help you develop your thinking and initial draft for a research paper tentatively entitled, for example, "Sports Justifications for Bad Behaviour" or "Social Tolerance and Mike Tyson." This brief set of notes with page numbers on the research note card will save you from substantial rereading, since you will be able to relocate useful areas of discussion in the source quickly.

Photocopies from Secondary Sources

Some students photocopy significant articles and book chapters, in whole or part, when collecting their research materials. This may be useful later, as your outline and drafts are under way and expanding. You can later condense the photocopied information in the form of either direct quotations or attributed paraphrases on your note cards for integration into your drafts. Or you may draw in more detail from the photocopy, if you need to expand a certain part of your discussion at a later stage of revision.

Reflecting Critical Reading in Your Notes

We have already looked at the importance of evaluating your sources. We stressed that when you read your sources and take notes for a research paper, you should approach those sources actively and critically. Look for facts that back your argument, but do not disregard facts that challenge your view. Also try to develop your own ideas. Your notes should reflect 1) helpful information (facts, strong views on your selected subject, some useful quotations), 2) perhaps a couple of more provocative quotations (and whether you agree or disagree), and 3) your opinions and analysis. It is important to keep the facts, perspectives, and specific language of your sources separate from your own language and views. Note-keeping should be meticulous.

When reading and taking notes as a researcher, be conscious of your own responses to the sources you find and your impression or interpretations of the texts and facts at hand. These are important in pulling together your own thesis and overall research paper.

Here is a summary of the strategies we have discussed to assist you when reading and taking notes from research sources:

- Use the introduction, conclusion, and the table of contents to provide an overview of the secondary source's argument and to point you to the chapters and sections most relevant to your topic. The introduction or first chapter often states the author's thesis and goals, a preview of the argument, and sometimes even a summary of each chapter.
- Distinguish carefully between the author's interpretation and your own interpretation. You are gathering facts and evidence to support your own arguments, while you also assert your interpretation clearly and confidently. Remember that your view may or may not agree with your various sources' interpretations. (See "Fact or Opinion?" in Chapter 7, "Argumentation.")
- Keep track of disagreements among your sources. Whether your sources disagree with one another outright or differ only slightly in interpretation of the same events or texts, such discrepancies could lead you toward an interesting topic or thesis. You should also think about which argument you find more convincing and why.

- Keep track of your own impressions and reactions to what you read. Do you agree or disagree with the ideas? Do any facts or assertions seem strange, surprising, or completely wrong? Do you notice a bias in the writer's perspective? Do you object to any particular point or interpretation? Does the author seem to take certain points for granted or overlook certain possibilities?

- Note the source's critical or theoretical perspective. Some authors will acknowledge their critical perspective directly within the first few pages; others will leave you to work it out. An awareness of your source's theoretical assumptions or framework—textual, contextual, poststructuralist, environmental, feminist, conservative, as some examples—will help you understand the source's argument and possible limits. You do not have to agree with a source's theoretical perspective in order to use it as part of your paper. In fact, if you strongly disagree with its perspective, reading the source may give you important insight into the other side of the issue and help you sharpen your own argument. (See Chapter 10, "Critical Analysis.")

SHAPING YOUR WORK

Two important steps, as your note-taking proceeds, are *finding a working thesis* and *outlining a possible structure*.

Developing a Working Thesis

As you find new information or decide to emphasize a different angle or point in your analysis of a selected topic, your outline and your thesis will likely change, often only slightly but sometimes extensively. In either event, a working thesis will help you shape your early drafts.

If you have decided to work on the topic of a recent Canadian tuition increase, for example, you may have researched the public's changing attitudes toward education over the last three or four decades. You may decide to research the possibility that the idealistic approach of encouraging individual promise and identifying it through constant classroom dialogue, argument, student experience, and frequent teacher-student interactions has shifted to a new corporate model of processing students as customers at arm's length. There are recent studies, both in the form of books and articles in education journals, that even attempt to define what a college or university may be or should be. There are certainly plenty of newspaper and magazine articles on the social effects of tuition increases: on how financial obstacles to post-secondary education change the fabric of democracy, on how high tuition may be seen as gate-keeping on the dubious basis of socio-economic class, and how the increasing emphasis on money in exchange for knowledge can only perpetuate the generational cycles of "haves" and "have-nots." You might take the opposite view, however, based on your experience, and locate research sources to support your view.

Because the subject of post-secondary education has become one of Canada's most pressing concerns, your essay will have both academic and social implications. Here are some examples of how you might move from this general topic to a working thesis on it:

Tuition increases and their effects

1. Tuition increases change the social composition of the student body. Does tuition increase create unnecessary exclusion? And how might increases affect the future of Canadian society?
2. Is education vital to democracy and freedom? Could tuition increases threaten those ideals?
3. Tuition increases reflect the increasing financial responsibility young people and their families must accept in the pursuit of education. Is there a limit?
4. Do tuition increases threaten to turn education into just another luxury consumer product? Is education a right or a privilege?

You will develop your working thesis, whatever your perspective is, as you travel through your reading and form reactions to it. Keep asking yourself where you stand in relation to what you read. Question and challenge the perspectives of the authors you encounter in your research.

You can develop your outline—topic sentences, paragraph subjects, paragraph sequence, use of evidence, and quoted material from sources—after you have settled on your working thesis. Your outline, with this working thesis, will lead you into a draft, which will allow you to develop that working thesis further. Remember that as you develop your essay's content and form, you will adjust your thesis, topic sentences, and emphasis accordingly. (See Chapters 1 through 4 for more guidance on this formative stage of essay development.)

Outlining

Once you've chosen a working thesis for your paper, you can begin the outlining process to prepare for writing your first draft. First, take a look at the research you have already done and try to find further readings that focus on your own emerging perspective, whether they support or dispute your thesis. As you read, keep your working thesis in mind and how it compares or contrasts with other authors' perspectives and how those authors compare and contrast with each other.

You may now be able to construct the brief outline to represent the shape of your essay. Write down the main points from your different sources and state how they either support or refute the basis of your chief assertion. For each point try to represent a different source. You may wish to propose a topic sentence that asserts some point to be expanded into a paragraph later—your perspective in relation to the other researchers' conclusions and claims. Our example below shows hypothetical sources expanding upon a proposed thesis that you may derive from our tuition questions above.

Here are two examples of quotations that represent their authors' positions. The quotations are followed by responsible paraphrases that are attributed to the author with page numbers included to show how to handle potential paraphrasing.

Source

J. Tosako, 1999: "Some argue that tuition hikes are not offset by a slightly increasing number of scholarships and bursaries that offer limited sums" (113).

Paraphrase

Despite funds for post-secondary entrance students, some experts argue that these limited scholarships and bursaries are still insufficient to make up for tuition increases (Tosako 113).

Source

P. Murphy, 1998: "Statistics Canada surveyed three thousand individuals between the ages of 17 and 25, and determined that 42% of the population eligible for post-secondary entrance was forced to work nearly full-time to support full-time school costs or else not attend because of low funds" (7).

Paraphrase

Murphy's findings that nearly half of eligible post-secondary students must work full-time to cover costs (7) are supported by Tosako's recent findings on underfunding (113).

Once you have listed all your authors' central positions from your sources, you may find both similarities and differences in their perspectives. These will help you construct your argument. Group some sources together and support your claims about their similarities or differences by quoting or paraphrasing this research.

Now you can probably develop a series of provisional topic sentences. Use them to organize paragraphs of your essay draft, making sure to support the topic sentence with your chosen evidence. Be alert to any changes in your own perspective. You may revise not only the topic sentences, but also the way you position your argument and your supporting evidence. Through this work, you will produce your first complete draft.

DEVELOPING A MORE POLISHED DRAFT

With the first rough draft of your research paper, you are ready to begin writing a more polished draft using the techniques and considerations illustrated in Section 4 of the *Rhetoric*, Chapter 13, "Drafting and Revising an Analytical Essay." However, this is also the stage at which you should be careful about incorporating material from your various sources.

How to Avoid Quotation Overcrowding

Do not overcrowd your paper with quotations. Direct quotations are your most authentic, vital representation of another writer's words and thoughts, whether those quotations are incorporated into your own sentences—such as "Yun argues that the novel *The Postman Always Rings Twice* presents 'justice as only another random occurrence, a grim lottery'" (42)—or are much longer citations in block quotations. But be careful that you do not overcrowd your paper with a relentless string of direct quotations. By overcrowding, you avoid actually writing a paper and instead weakly cut and paste one, from various voices, none of which is your own.

"Quotation clustering" is a common student response and often the result of too much urgent reading as the deadline looms. Poor time management results in insufficient contemplation and synthesis of your materials into your own writing.

A research paper is first and foremost your work. It should always feature your writing voice strongly, whether you are weighing and evaluating your secondary sources, asserting your points or arguing against some published views.

Here is a hypothetical example of quotation overcrowding:

> Alice Munro's story "Thanks for the Ride" examines "the young male narrator's anxieties about romance while also showing how class differences can create the great distance between people" (Haggarty 41). According to Becky Cameron, "the main character is the young woman, not the male narrator, because she is the character for whom the most may be at stake" (183). Bill Sastri argues that since the male narrator has continued to think about this young, intelligent woman from years ago, "she has probably significantly changed him in some way" (30). Natalie Maharaj points out that the title suggests the middle-class narrator's sense of superiority has been "successfully undercut by the self-aware, sexually confident, articulate woman, especially by her parting words to him" (134). One critic also contends that the story is an "intersection of *her* sexual confidence fraught with class anxiety and *his* class confidence attempting to mask sexual anxiety (Jaster 42).

Although this paragraph would indicate that the essayist has ambitiously read several good secondary sources that analyze Alice Munro's story and has located several useful, specific quotations that make points about the story's intertwined sexual and socio-economic aspects, the student's own perspective on the text is completely absent from the paragraph. This weakness relates directly to the absence of any controlling point in the paragraph. Without this controlling point, which needs to be asserted in a topic sentence, the paragraph stalls as only a string of interesting quotations that neither work toward a larger interpretative point nor address each other's perspectives.

Apart from the need for a topic sentence, this essayist's paragraph needs to assert a sense of voice, an overall perspective on these various critics' points. A more assertive student voice here would balance the quotation overcrowding and enable the writer to synthesize the secondary sources *within* the essayist's own observations and claims. As well, these numerous quotations would serve the essayist better if they were spread through the paper to make their points as some kind of a progression within the student's discussion. Here they cluster together in uncertain connection.

When incorporating quotations, secondary sources, facts, and the opinions of others into your paper, you can use two respected techniques of representation besides direct quotation: the paraphrase and the summary.

The ability to paraphrase and to summarize a primary or secondary source accurately and confidently therefore presents you with two opportunities at once. You continue to incorporate attributed information from your sources into your research essay and you continue to express your voice in choosing your own words to articulate that information. Paraphrasing and summarizing can demonstrate both your accuracy in fair representation and your resourcefulness with language.

Paraphrasing

A paraphrase represents a specific point or expression drawn from another source. A paraphrase differs from a summary by representing a more concentrated section of a selected text. A paraphrase attempts to capture accurately a particular idea in a particular moment of the text, whether, for example, a poem, scholarly article, history book, or song. A paraphrase is a close, faithful representation of the original.

Original (excerpt from poem)

I should have been a pair of ragged claws/Scuttling across the floors of silent seas

—T.S. Eliot, "The Love Song of J. Alfred Prufrock," 1917

Inaccurate paraphrase

Prufrock wishes he had big claws so that he could run fast on the bottom of the ocean, feeling happy and alive.

This inaccurate paraphrase imposes invented facts and notions on these two quoted lines. First, the original lines state "ragged claws," not "big claws." This paraphrase error misconstrues the poem's language, representing the speaker as somehow feeling powerful ("big claws"), yet the original words "ragged claws" strongly imply bare survival, turbulent existence, and perhaps even a sense of future doom. The hasty paraphrase entirely erases the bleak aspects of a failing struggle conveyed within the poet's choice of words.

As well, the paraphrase's "run fast" completely misrepresents the action of "[s]cuttling" in the original line. "Scuttling" implies an intentional but highly inefficient movement: strenuous, makeshift, even frantic. "Run fast," as an inaccurate paraphrase, carelessly deletes such invoked "scuttling" connotations, arbitrarily replacing them with the student's projected image of athleticism, speed, efficiency, and joy.

Last, the paraphrase's closing description, stating that the poem's speaker would feel "happy and alive" in this ocean scene, is an entirely superimposed observation rather than a factually or contextually accurate re-statement of anything in the original lines. Be careful not to adjust paraphrases to "speak" your own view; instead the paraphrase must accurately reflect its original quoted text.

More accurate paraphrase (the two lines literally)

Prufrock here wishes to be nothing more than some kind of crustacean, scraping its way for its entire existence across the sea bottom. Prufrock also wishes for escape to the endless silence of the ocean floor.

More accurate paraphrase (within context of entire poem)

Rather than live in his pretentious, upper-class, paralyzing, and gossipy social world, Prufrock wishes he could become a simple creature of purely instinctive existence in a silent world of Nature, possibly even an undiscovered part of that world. Prufrock's wish indicates that he is prepared (or so he says) to trade a gracious but empty life of privilege and culture for an unthinking but uncomplicated anonymity. He would also trade all his human consciousness for the undisturbable peace of having no consciousness.

> **Tip:** A good paraphrase always carefully represents the telling details of the original quotation. Often, especially with compressed and literary language, the paraphrase may be longer than the original quoted lines.

 PRACTICE

Paraphrase the following two excerpts from a poem and a secondary source. These paraphrases can either be presented to your instructor for comment or discussed with classmates during group work or exchanged within the class as a whole, using multiple photocopies.

Poem Excerpt

She fears him, and will always ask
    What fated her to choose him;
She meets in his engaging mask
    All reasons to refuse him;

—E.A. Robinson, "Eros Turannos," 1916

Secondary Source Excerpt

In particular, compositional balance [in film noir] within the frame is often disruptive and unnerving. Those traditionally harmonious triangular three-shots and balanced two-shots, which are borrowed from the compositional principles of Renaissance paintings, are seldom seen in the better film noir. More common are bizarre, off-angle compositions of figures placed irregularly in the frame, which create a world that is never stable or safe, that is always threatening to change drastically and unexpectedly. . . . And objects seem to push their way into the foreground of the frame to assume more power than the people. (65)

—Janey Place and Lowell Peterson, "Some Visual Motifs of *Film Noir*," in *Film Noir Reader*, eds. A. Silver and J. Ursini, 1996.

There are two further areas of difficulty that complicate paraphrasing efforts:

Ambiguous Words and Phrasings

Ambiguous words and phrasings are everywhere and there are few places to hide from them. For example, if you were to paraphrase the line "an abundance of trout are suddenly biting off the coast of Vancouver," would you represent this occurrence as a happy opportunity for good fishing or as an unprecedented marine disaster? The slightly alarming phrase "biting off the coast" creates the ambiguity here.

Let us say this following sentence appeared in a year-end business report for a large corporation: "In the last year's busy and changing international economy, our company only faced two new lawsuits." Does this sentence mean that the only business this particular company engaged in was defending itself against lawsuits? Or does the sentence mean, despite all its other activities in the busy and changing international economy, only two lawsuits arose? Presumably the incorrect placement of the word "only" in the sentence creates this ambiguity.

Idiom

Imagine someone who does not speak English as a first language and is recently learning it trying to paraphrase this sentence:

> I <u>ran into Lisa</u> the other day and she asked me <u>to give her a hand</u>, but I said I was <u>wiped out</u> and wanted <u>to call it a day</u>.

The four idiomatic phrases here that most North American English speakers take for granted can pose serious comprehension, let alone paraphrasing, difficulties. Taken literally, the sentence makes little sense. Literature, music, political statements, and film dialogue from other cultures (even other cultures in the English language, such as Irish, Australian, British) can pose paraphrasing problems.

Summarizing

A summary is an extremely compressed representation of a longer text. Compared to a paraphrase, a summary is a far more sweeping re-statement. A paraphrase usually teases out the fuller meanings and implications, while a summary compacts one or two crucial points from the original texts as briefly as possible. We have discussed summarizing in Chapter 8, so here we will review only crucial points and offer examples for your consideration.

When summarizing, be prepared to capture the single point or points of a text that, in your view, summarize that text most fully. By necessity, summaries do not include many details. Thus, you need to be a bit bold in your willingness to compress and still be accurate.

> Shakespeare's *Macbeth* examines the political and psychological costs of sacrificing integrity for unrestrained ambition.

> Anne Murray's song "Snowbird" seems to express regret for the coming of winter, but really expresses the disillusionment of lost love.

Even in slightly longer summaries, most details, people, events, and characters involved, have been omitted. The point of the summary is to make one quick point that you will draw on or expand later in your essay.

Historical Summary
The late Pime Minister Trudeau, responding officially to the urgent requests of the premier of Quebec and the mayor of Montreal, invoked the War Measures Act in peacetime to contain the perceived threat of the FLQ against the elected government.

Literary Summary
Margaret Atwood's novel *The Handmaid's Tale* depicts a future post-nuclear world where radiation and environmental damage have resulted in mass infertility.

Militarized Christian fundamentalists have formed the government (now a "theocracy" rather than a democracy). Handmaids are the few young fertile women and must live in servitude for the purpose of attempted procreation with government and military officials.

 PRACTICE

Summarize a well-known movie in three or four sentences. Show your summary to a friend or classmate and see whether that person would agree or disagree that your summary accurately represents the main point or theme.

INTEGRATING QUOTATIONS

Any quotations you use must fit smoothly into the flow of your own sentences. You need to punctuate carefully when including quotations, as if the quoted words were a natural part of your own sentence. If you use a long quotation (more than four typed lines), try to precede the quotation with a complete sentence followed by a colon. This allows your reader some preparation—a breath—before plunging into the long quotation. Such longer quotations are always set off from the rest of the text by block indentation and do not require quotation marks.

Integrating a long quotation

Despite popular opinion, lemmings are a sturdy, independent species, as Cornelia Zahl observes:

> Investigators are interested in lemmings' seasonal movements, but of even more pressing interest to scientists are the little creatures' population explosions. These significant population increases occur every three or four years, sometimes astounding even the most experienced lemming experts. Lemmings, in fact, are among the most prolific of mammals. Sometimes the weasel population on the tundra starts to soar, since the lemmings, as small rodents, are staples of some carnivore diets. (41)

Note that the period appears before the page citation in parentheses at the end.

If, on the other hand, you want to use only a short part of a quotation, you might begin the sentence with a few words of your own and finish the sentence by incorporating the significant element from your source:

Integrating short quotations

Franklin is only one of several biochemists who claims that "working with Dr. Kostner was like being in daily contact with an unpredictable force of nature" (274).

Although Lisa-Marie Grierson maintains that society will eventually turn away from the computer, "coming to this point of anti-technological enlightenment will take decades and perhaps a century" (79).

In the second example above, the comma appears before the quotation simply because that is how the sentence would normally be punctuated. This comma separates the introductory dependent clause from the main or independent clause, which is your quotation here. Remember that you should not use any extra punctuation with a quotation when normal grammatical usage would not require that punctuation. In our first example above, no punctuation was required to work the quotation into your sentence's own language and syntax.

Watch for the extremely common mistake of creating a comma splice when introducing the quotation.

Comma splice

Some critics of Wong Kar-Wai's film *Chungking Express* find the camera technique purposefully distracting in order to complicate the representation of the characters, "the shifting and jarring camera work, which sometimes imitates a public area surveillance camera, tries to capture the rushing momentum in daily big city life, as well as the two main characters' emotional isolation" (Bugden 18).

The way to fix this punctuation error is to replace the comma directly before the quotation with a colon (:). This colon will set off your quotation, which is an independent clause, from your own preceding independent clause that introduces it.

Square Brackets

Square brackets appearing within a quotation indicate that a capital letter has been either added or removed or that a word or phrase has been added or changed.

Although Paul Hewson argues that "Big Rock [beer] tastes fresh and crisp . . . , [s]atisfying Canadian beer-drinkers is always a challenge" (30).

Here, the essayist has added the word "beer" in square brackets to clarify exactly what the brand name "Big Rock" indicates and has also used square brackets to indicate that a capital "S" has been changed to a lower-case "s," allowing the essayist to shape the quotation within the syntax of his or her own sentence.

Ellipses

The three periods after "crisp" in the above example are called **ellipses** and indicate that some words have been omitted. Three periods form ellipses within a quotation; however, an ellipsis that appears at the end of a sentence still requires the period.

Pamela J. Salzwedel argues that "Heathcliff in Emily Brontë's *Wuthering Heights* experiences a crisis as a boy because of sudden socioeconomic realization, but returns to the scene of his trauma as a wealthy and vengeful man . . ." (69).

Punctuation and Quotation

As prescribed by MLA or APA style (Chapter 12), the period follows the parentheses of the page reference. If there are no page references in parentheses, place commas and periods inside your quotation marks. Colons and semicolons should be placed outside your quotation marks, but only if they are not part of the quotation.

> E.L. Doctorow's 1971 novel *The Book of Daniel* is "a law-literature classic"; it explores the Rosenberg case during U.S. Cold War frenzy.

If your quotation runs into another sentence and the quotation does not need to be indented into a block note, the quotation marks straddle the two sentences.

> Fraser's book *Violence in the Arts* boldly contends that "our attitudes towards violence are deeply confused. The organized violence in the film *The Godfather* seems to have audience support" (19).

Fair Use

In general, small changes using square brackets and ellipses can be made within quotations from your sources, provided these changes do not alter or manipulate the quotation's original meaning. In a quotation, you must represent the author's view fairly.

Original quotation

"The U.S. trade embargo against Cuba stands as a colossal contradiction to the new principles of international free trade. A continuing embargo shows that rather than functioning as a fair and globally open economic plan, free trade is only what the U.S. government says it is at any given moment" (Kostyrenko, *Free Trade and Its Political Contradictions*, 232).

Unfair, misleading use

"The U.S. trade embargo against Cuba . . . function[s] as a fair and globally open economic plan . . ." (232).

Fair use

"The U.S. trade embargo against Cuba [reveals that] . . . free trade is only what the U.S. government says it is at any given moment" (232).

Use Only Significant Quotations

Remember to include only significant quotations in the final draft. A research paper is not supposed to be merely a smorgasbord of various quotations, quickly strung together until you have reached the required word limit. Be selective. Your voice and your perspective on the topic are supposed to be the most important dimensions in your college and university research paper. Your research source should be *integrated* into your own considered view of a text or topic rather than allowed to dominate the paper. Let your reader see clearly, in detail, and with articulated implications where you stand on the topic or text you are examining.

Weak integration of sources (sample paragraph)

Jim Simpson contends that the musical *The Sound of Music* "raises important questions about the fragile triumph of private happiness in the face of turbulent international events" (53). Mary Ciccione seems to disagree: "*The Sound of Music*, as pleasant as the singing is, addresses nothing of any substance, even more blatantly than *Willy Wonka and the Chocolate Factory*, a film musical about chocolate" (178). However, Julie Andrews' optimism, according to Burton Bachman, "allows viewers to believe in the healing-power of music, especially the singing voice as a sign of hope" (22). I guess I agree with some of these points, but not with all of them.

Better integration of sources with essayist's perspective

Critics continue to be divided on the thematic importance of the film musical *The Sound of Music*. Although Mary Ciccione argues that the film "addresses nothing of any substance" (178), Bachman's view is that Julie Andrews' optimism "allows viewers to believe in the healing-power of music, especially the singing voice as a sign of hope" (22). Simpson also agrees that the film has substance, since it raises "important questions of the fragile triumph of private happiness in . . . turbulent international events" (53).

Distinguishing between Source Material and Your Own Views

Here are hypothetical examples of two pieces of writing drawing from the same research note card. The first essayist falls into inadvertent plagiarism (see below) because he borrows language and points from the source without full acknowledgment. The second essayist shows care in separating the secondary source's argument and language from his own views and language.

Incorrect use of quotation (see also "Plagiarism," p. 451 below)

Ondaatje's poem "Letters and Other Worlds" explores how the turbulent, solitary father cannot communicate, at any level, with his diverse family, though, as Peters points out, he "could write so beautifully" (147).

Sample Note Card

Source: "The central question of Michael Ondaatje's poem 'Letters and Other Worlds' is why the turbulent, solitary father could not communicate, at any level, with his family, though he could write so beautifully." (Meghan T. Peters, "Ondaatje's Frightening Family View," *York Experiments*, Vol. 8, No. 2, page 147)

As you can see, most of the language of the secondary source ends up in the student's own sentence and most of it is not acknowledged. This is plagiarism and can lead to serious consequences.

Correct use of quotation

Although Meghan Peters correctly points out that Ondaatje's poem "Letters and Other Worlds" examines an unpredictable father who cannot communicate with his family, "though he could write so beautifully" (147), Peters overlooks the often complex, painful, and withdrawn relationship many creative people have with the world.

In the preceding example, Peters' language and point are attributed fully to her, and the student takes the opportunity to express his opinions of what Peters' perspective may overlook in an interpretation of Ondaatje's poem.

Such proper handling of your secondary sources—through accurate quotations, attributed paraphrases, sharp distinction between your ideas and those of others, fair use of context, square brackets, and ellipses, and smooth integration of quotations within your own writing—will contribute to an effective research paper.

✓ CHECKLIST of Steps to a Successful Research Paper

1. Make a realistic schedule that considers not only reading and rereading your sources, but also drafting and rewriting your paper.

2. Select, then narrow, your topic; define your point of interest, your specific research context.

3. Define crucial terms in your instructor's assignment, your selected research topic, and your subsequent research. You may have to research your terms to pursue your project.

4. Gather preliminary research and resume narrowing your topic and angle of inquiry.

5. Gather and evaluate secondary sources.

6. Take notes: ideas, issues, authors, titles, dates, summaries of arguments, quotations with page numbers.

7. Create your outline on paper: main points, your position, topic sentences, paragraphs.

8. Refine your working thesis then adjust topic sentences and parts of your paragraphs accordingly.

9. Combine your analysis and opinion with your material, solidifying your own position on the research. Keep your position distinct from those of your sources.

10. Draft, document, revise, proofread.

Chapter 12
Documentation

Why document sources? Documentation is taken very seriously in academic writing. When you document your sources, you credit other researchers' work that appears in some way in your own essays. Your readers need to distinguish between others' work and your own. Proper documentation informs your readers exactly what sources you decided to work with, what their positions are, and how these sources differ from your own ideas and language.

FORMS OF DOCUMENTATION

The preferred form for citations and bibliographic entries varies considerably among disciplines. Publications in the humanities and arts generally use the Modern Language Association (MLA) style or form of documentation. Editors in the social sciences prefer the American Psychological Association (APA) style. These two styles are regarded as the most widely used forms of documentation, but there are many others, including the University of Chicago style. Later in this section we present examples of MLA and APA style. We do not, however, represent the many other styles, nor provide complete information for all documentation scenarios concerning the two widely used styles that we have presented as illustrations. It is your responsibility to find out what form of documentation is used by the publication in which you intend to place your work. You should then supplement the information provided here by referring to a complete manual for the style required.

These manuals are available in most college or university bookstores, as well as the reference section of your college or university library. The most recent versions of APA and MLA documentation guidelines appear in the following publications (listed in MLA style, by the way):

- Gibaldi, Joseph. *MLA Handbook for Writers of Research Papers*. 6th ed. New York: Modern Language Association of America, 2003.
- *Publication Manual of the American Psychological Association*. 5th ed. Washington, D.C.: American Psychological Association, 2001.

MLA and APA forms are both based on the use of short parenthetical citations within the text. This basic technique is explained in more detail below.

Avoiding the Appearance of Plagiarism

Any loose or hasty attitude toward full and accurate documentation of your sources may lead to charges of plagiarism. When you plagiarize someone else's work, you are presenting his or her ideas or words in your own writing as though they were your own. Academic institutions consider plagiarism a serious offence, one that can result in academic failure or even expulsion. Many students plagiarize without intending to because they haven't learned when and how to document their sources, or because they have developed bad note-taking and composition habits that lead to plagiarism. In fact, some students claim to have gone through high school blissfully unaware that they were plagiarizing virtually in every essay and research assignment they ever wrote.

It is very important to learn the rules and expectations for documenting sources before you find yourself in the unpleasant situation of dealing with an accusation of plagiarism. Make yourself aware of your institution's definition of plagiarism. Treat that definition like a law.

WHEN TO DOCUMENT

Many students have the wrong impression. They believe they need to acknowledge their sources only when quoting directly from a text. This presumption is very misguided. Any time you use another person's idea or phrasing in an essay of yours, you have to acknowledge your source. This idea or phrasing is that of someone else's work and—because it is published—someone else's property. You must acknowledge sources when you quote directly, summarize, paraphrase, or otherwise use someone else's ideas. Sometimes you even have to acknowledge sources for factual information, not only opinions and interpretations.

You do not need to document sources for factual information that is considered common knowledge either to the public or in your field. Some examples of common public knowledge include Columbus' arrival in North America in 1492, Pierre Trudeau's service as a Canadian prime minister, Alice Walker's writing the novel *The Color Purple*, Newfoundland's joining Canada last among the provinces, and Leonard Cohen's writing sad songs. Sometimes it is difficult to know what would be considered common knowledge, but one indication would be that all the sources you have consulted agree on the facts. If you are doubtful about what counts as common knowledge, be safe and cite your source.

PARENTHETICAL CITATIONS WITHIN THE PAPER

MLA and APA styles of documentation work on the same principle: inserting short citations in the body of the essay within parentheses. These brief citations point to full ones listed at the end of your paper. Some of the most common types of citations are provided below.

MLA Parenthetical Citations Within the Paper

The MLA system requires that you provide your citation's page number in parentheses after the quotation. You must also provide the author's name if it is not already included in your sentence. If you refer to more than one work by the same author, you should also include in the parentheses a short version of the title, such as one key word.

> Winters argues unconvincingly that Hamlet "was written by Queen Elizabeth" (17). [Here there is no need to repeat the author's name in parentheses, so just include the number of the page on which this quotation can be found.]

> One critic even suggests that Hamlet was written by Queen Elizabeth (Winters 17). [Here the author's name is also supplied in parentheses because it does not appear in the sentence.]

> In her most recent article, however, Winters backs away from her earlier claims that Hamlet was written by Queen Elizabeth (<u>Reconsideration</u> 175–76). [Here a short

---

More Parenthetical Citation Tips for MLA Style

- Use "qtd. in" (for quoted in) for quotations taken from an indirect source:

  > James Bone wrote that London resides in "the appearance of great shadows where there can be no shadows, throwing blackness up and down" (qtd. in Ackroyd 110).

- Shorten publishers' names. Use "Pearson" rather than "Pearson Education."

- Use regular numerals to indicate act and scene in plays (Lear 2.2). Use Roman numerals (lowercase) only for pages from a preface, introduction, or table of contents.

- Use only the name of the first person listed when citing a source by more than three people:

  > Gold et al. suggest that Canada is more than the sum of its parts (27).

version of the article's title is given because now more works than one by Winters are listed in the Works Cited list for the essay.]

Contrary to popular belief, the first underground railroad between the U.S. and Canada existed to free slaves held on Canadian territory (Walker 19). [Here the citation is to little-known information.]

Tip: Note that in APA style, a *comma* separates author, publication date, and page number in the parentheses, while in MLA style *no comma* separates author and page number in the parentheses. Note also that APA uses the abbreviation "p." before the page number, while MLA does not.

APA Parenthetical Citations Within the Paper

The APA system requires that you provide not only the author's name and a page number or numbers, but also the date of the work in the body of your paper. Supply information in parentheses when it is not already part of your sentence. In the APA system these parentheses are placed within the sentence, right after the reference to the article or study:

In 1996, Hintz studied the intellect of mice. [There is no need for a page number here because there is no direct quotation, and the summary is very general.]

A recent study of the "previously underestimated intellect of mice" (Hintz, 1996, p. 56) proved that mice are smarter than seagulls. [Both author and date must be included in parentheses with the page number if the author and date do not appear in the sentence.]

Hintz (1996) argued that mice are not as large as they seem close up. [The author is part of the sentence, so only the date must be provided in parentheses. Note that this date appears right after the author's name.]

Several recent studies of the intellect of mice (Hintz, 1996; Lamb, 1994, 1997) have shown that mice have not yet discovered electricity or television. [Here is an example of how you would cite more than one study in parentheses. In this case, you are referring to one study by Hintz and to two studies by Lamb, conducted in different years.]

MLA FULL CITATION IN THE FINAL REFERENCES PAGE

Entries in a bibliography in MLA style are listed on a separate page under the heading "Works Cited" (see the sample research paper in MLA style that follows). All authors are listed alphabetically by surname. The author's last name appears first, followed by a comma, followed by his or her full first name, and then a period. Then the title of the work appears: a book title is italicized or underlined; an essay title in a scholarly journal appears in quotations, and the name of the journal, italicized or underlined, follows the essay title. With scholarly articles, volume and issue numbers follow the title of the journal, followed by the date in parentheses, a full colon, and the page spread (the article's first and last page). Here are some examples of common MLA citations:

Book

Axelrod, Alan. <u>Elizabeth I, CEO: Strategic Lessons from the Leader Who Built an Empire</u>. Englewood Cliffs, NJ: Prentice Hall, 2000.

Article in a journal or magazine

Kelly, Philip F. "The Geographies and Politics of Globalization." <u>Progress in Human Geography</u> 23 (1999): 379–400.

Article in an essay collection (including names of editors)

Partington, Angela. "The Designer Housewife in the 1950s." <u>A View from the Interior: Feminism, Women and Design</u>. Ed. Judy Attfield and Pat Kirkham. London: The Woman's Press, 1989. 206–14.

Article in a newspaper

Tibbetts, Janice, and Kate Jaimet. "Trudeau Dead at 80." <u>Edmonton Journal</u> (29 Sept. 2000): A1.

Book by a group or corporate author

American Psychological Association. <u>Publication Manual of the American Psychological Association</u>. 5th ed. Washington: APA, 2001.

Book or film review

Ebert, Roger. Rev. of <u>Jesus of Montreal</u>, dir. Denys Arcand. <u>Chicago Sun-Times</u> 18 July 1990: E4.

Website

Walker, Alice. "Letter from Alice Walker to President Clinton." 26 Oct. 2000. **<http://www.igc.apc.org/cubasoli/awalker.html>**.

Note that all lines subsequent to the first line of each entry are indented five spaces, a format known as a "hanging indent." Also double space both within and between your entries on the Works Cited page.

If your source is written or edited by two or three people, format the full citation as follows:

Gold, Eleanor, Eli Sky, and James Cedar. <u>Views of Canada</u>. Toronto: Maple Leaf, 2000.

If your source is written or edited by more than three people, give the name of the first-listed person followed by et al. (meaning "and others":

Gold, Eleanor, et al. <u>Views of Canada</u>. Toronto: Maple Leaf, 2000.

For more information on how to document online sources in MLA style, go to <www.bedfordstmartins.com/online/citex.html/>.

APA FULL CITATION IN THE FINAL REFERENCES LIST

Entries on the References page in APA style are listed on a separate page at the end of the essay under the heading "References." (See the sample research paper in APA style later in this section.) Like MLA style, APA uses the hanging indent format, with the first line of an entry flush left, but all subsequent lines of that entry indented five spaces. Again like MLA, double spacing is used between and within entries in APA. The author's last name appears first, followed by his or her initials, rather than the full first name. Then the date of publication follows in parentheses. The entries on this Reference page should appear in alphabetical order according to author surname. The APA style is a highly detailed format and requires the additional rules:

- Underline or italicize titles and subtitles of books and journals.
- Do not place titles of articles in quotation marks.
- Capitalize only the first word of a book or article title.
- List all authors' names rather than use "*et al.*"
- Separate two or more authors' names with an ampersand (&), not the word "and."
- Underline or italicize volume numbers of journals.
- Use the abbreviation "p." (or "pp." for plural) before page numbers of newspaper articles and works in anthologies, but not before page numbers of either scholarly journal articles or magazine articles.

Here are some common examples of APA style:

Book

Axelrod, A. (2000). *Elizabeth I, CEO: Strategic lessons from the leader who built an empire.* Eaglewood Cliffs, NJ: Prentice Hall.

You need to underline or italicize the title of the book, but capitalize only the title's first letter, the first letter after a colon, and any proper names. Next, list the city of your publication, followed by a colon. The publisher's name should appear after the colon. Close the citation with a period.

Article in a journal

Kelly, P. F. (1999). The geographies and politics of globalization. *Progress in Human Geography, 23,* 379–400.

Article titles appear in much the same form as a book title in APA style. Only the first letters, the first letter after a colon, and the proper nouns are capitalized. The title of the journal, however, shows each important word capitalized. Note that the page numbers of the article are listed from first to last page. No abbreviation for "page" or "pages" is included with journal articles. The volume number, as well as the title of the journal, is underlined or italicized in this style.

Article in an essay collection

Partington, A. (1989). The designer housewife in the 1950s. In J. Attfield & P. Kirkham (Eds.), *A view from the interior: Feminism, women and design* (pp. 206–14). London: The Women's Press.

APA style does not require quotation marks to enclose the titles of articles. Capitalize only the first words or proper nouns. List only the particular articles you referred to in your essay rather than the title of the entire collection, unless you use every essay in the collection, as we hypothesize in our example. To identify the book, supply the editors, the book title, and the publication information after the title of the article. Note that it is important to identify any editors as well as authors by including "(Ed.)" for "editor" and "(Eds.)" for "editors" after those editors' names. APA style requires the symbol "&" rather than "and" when the work has more than one author or editor. If the articles are contained in a book rather than in a journal, use the abbreviation "pp." for "pages" and place the listing of inclusive pages in parentheses after the book title, as in our title. Remember that the appropriate abbreviation for a single "page" is simply "p." For plural "pages" it is "pp."

Article in a newspaper

Tibbetts, J., & Jaimet, K. (2000, September 29). Trudeau dead at 80. *Edmonton Journal*, p. A1.

A newspaper article requires the year and the day of publication after the author's or authors' names. List the information in parentheses, with the year first. If you can find no author for the article, begin with its title, then give the date and other information. Note that the name of the newspaper is underlined or italicized to indicate that it is a publication. The page number follows after a comma with the abbreviation "p." for "page."

Website

Walker, A. (1996). Letter from Alice Walker to President Clinton. Retrieved October 26, 2000, from **http://www.igc.apc.org/cubasoli/awalker.html**

A website is cited in a manner similar to that for a book. Begin with the author's name, if available. Follow this by the date in parentheses, then the title. As with most items on the References page, separate each item with a period. After the title, provide the information to enable the reader to find the article online, including your date of retrieval (since the information might well have changed or even disappeared since that date).

Name the host if the document is in a large and complicated website, such as a university site:

Writing a research paper. Retrieved December 18, 2001, from University of Alberta Libraries website: **http://www.library.ualberta.ca/library_html/help/ pathfinders/respaper.html**

For more information on how to document online sources in APA style, go to <www.apastyle.org/elecref.html>. You will find updated information there on how to deal with electronic media in your essays.

FOOTNOTES AND ENDNOTES

A handy device for providing extra information briefly in your essays, especially research papers, is the footnote or endnote. *Footnotes* appear at the foot (or bottom) of the page essay, three line spaces below your last line of text. *Endnotes* appear at the end of the essay, on a separate page entitled "Notes" or "Endnotes." This page appears just before your last page, where you list your sources.

In an MLA-style essay, you can use either footnotes or endnotes, but not both. In APA-style research papers, you do not use footnotes, but list the endnotes on a separate page following the last page of the essay, before the References page.

In MLA style, the first line of each footnote is indented five spaces, and any remaining lines in the footnote are flush against the left-hand margin. The footnote is single-spaced but double-space between each footnote if you are including more than one on a single page. In both MLA and APA styles, the notes or endnotes (in contrast to the footnotes) are double-spaced.

Designate a footnote or endnote using a superscript number:

Elephant herds in Kenya are fluctuating because of uneven government protections and surges of poaching.[3]

The footnote related to this point then appears with its corresponding number at the bottom of the page or, if you are using endnotes, at the end of the essay—but before your Works Cited page, if you quoted sources.

Footnotes and endnotes usually function in three ways:

1. providing other references,
2. supplying further factual content, and
3. advancing related observations to bolster argument.

Footnotes and endnotes can supplement your discussion effectively and economically.

Footnote and Endnote Usage (hypothetical examples)

Britain's Royal Family continues to face damaging public exposure. The Duchess of York, Sarah Ferguson, seems prepared to become a spokesperson for almost anything to fend off her financial troubles,[1] while the young Royal Princes, William and Harry, continue to be ejected from London nightclubs for unruly behaviour. Furthermore, a former assistant to one of the chauffeurs for the late Diana, Princess of Wales, has recently given a controversial interview about Diana's alleged belief in intergalactic abductions.[2] Meanwhile, many senior members of British Parliament are raising legal questions about abolishing the Queen's traditional immunity to prosecution because of decades of unpaid parking tickets accrued by her carriage and horses during various royal processions.[3]

Footnote or endnote #1 (other references)

[1] For a detailed discussion of the Duchess of York's previous financial troubles, see Theodore E. Bear's "Sarah's Creditors in a New Royal Age," *Monarchy Quarterly* 3:2 (1998): 114–27 and Ja-Yoon Kim's *Duchess for Hire* (Toronto: Pentium Press, 2001).

Footnote or endnote #2 (further content)

[2] This account has been vigorously denied by spokespeople for Buckingham Palace. As well, the chauffeur's former assistant has recently told BBC News that he was misquoted, claiming that he said "ablutions," not "abductions."

Footnote or endnote #3 (further observations or argument)

[3] I believe, along with several constitutional law experts, that the Queen's complete legal immunity, as well as the Royal Family's blanket immunity from ever being called to testify in court, has no place in a modern England. Legal immunity actually damages their credibility rather than protecting it in the eyes of the public.

THE FINAL EDIT

Having produced a more polished draft, and carefully integrated quotations, proper citations, and bibliographic references, you should proof your work and perform any necessary final editing. See Section 4 ("Revising") for guidance in this last stage of your project. Here are two sample research papers that have passed through all steps to their final form.

Sample Essay Using MLA Documentation

Melanie Klingbeil's University of Alberta English 101 research essay on two poems by William Butler Yeats and two poems by Emily Dickinson offers an example of textual analysis drawing upon helpful secondary-source quotations. Also, note that a strong writer's voice marshals the research.

> **Format Note:** For submission to a journal or course instructor, this essay would be double-spaced, including every line under "Works Cited."

Sample Essay MLA Documentation

Beyond the Answers

1 Only without the universal questions of this world, without the mysteries that baffle great minds, and without the existence of contradictions, would the world be able to exist without philosophy. Mesmerized by their shared belief that there is more to understand than they already do, the poets Emily Dickinson (American) and W.B. Yeats (Irish) tried to walk through a door of understanding that could lead them into the

realm of philosophy. Their contemplation and their philosophies emerged as poetry. Examples of their poetry prove that they were both capable philosophers, that they both vigorously contemplated realities beyond the fundamental world of material reality. Consider some titles of their works: Dickinson's "I know that He exists" and "This world is not conclusion"; Yeats's "Byzantium" and "The Second Coming." Interpretations of these works can establish the differences between their two philosophies: where Dickinson questions religion, Yeats creates his own; where Dickinson considers the effects of the belief on the believer, Yeats puzzles over what shapes all human consciousness. What significance does this difference between the two poets truly bear? How does the distinction work? Interpreting these poems can lead to answers to these questions. I will consider what is at stake for both poets, and what, in their lives, accounts for their philosophical inclinations in order to explain what truly matters about the differences between Dickinson and Yeats.

1

2   The church was a part of Dickinson's early life. She understood the doctrines of Christianity and the practices of traditional religion. This understanding brought her to question, then reject the church. When the church claimed to have all the answers, Dickinson came up with new questions. How was Christianity an issue for Emily Dickinson? What would Christianity have taken from her were it not for her philosophy? Dickinson could not live as though she had the answers to the transcendental questions that troubled her; nor could she live as though she would ever attain them. Her poetry nourished her: with sanity, her contentment, her peace. "Dickinson lived with doubt without ever despairing" (Ferlazzo 31).

3   Dickinson's poem "I know that He exists" affirms not only her spiritual beliefs, but also the persistent disbeliefs that consume her. Her affirmation of her disbeliefs held her to an unconventional integrity—that all strong faith requires an ingredient of uncertainty in order for it to exist. Faith, by definition, must struggle with doubt. This uncertainty the church often ignores. The poem's first line, however, obviously makes a statement of faith. Dickinson acknowledges the separation God has from man by describing how He hides his "rare life/From our gross eyes." She thus affirms her belief in a supernatural being; she endorses a deity that seems no different than conventional Christianity's. Kimpel points out that other distinctions, however, between Dickinson's spiritual view and that of organized religion's eventually resulted in her social rejection:

2

> What she rejected, on the other hand, was their version of religion. . . . Her disparagement of their self-satisfied attitude about their own understanding of the nature of God was, consequently, their provocation for ostracizing her from the "converted" and the "saved." (209)

3

4   Dickinson's faith emerges in her poetry not from what she knows about God, but from what she does not know about Him. Once her faith is affirmed in her poetry,

Dickinson then suddenly expresses a profound perplexity over the possibility that this God plays a cruel game with his believers by offering salvation as nothing more than a joke: "Would not the fun / Look too expensive? / Would not the jest / Have crawled too far?" To deny this cosmic possibility would be to deny the spiritual uncertainties that engulf the human condition. For Dickinson, denying the uncertainties and anxieties of the human condition would be blasphemous, more so than questioning God's existence or God's intentions.

5   While Dickinson examines the personal uncertainties of spiritual beliefs, Yeats seeks broader answers to the metaphysical questions of the universe. Yeats pursues a life of fascination with metaphysics and the occult. Studying his philosophical poetry is much like taking a journey through a luminous spirit world. This is Yeats's non-institutional religion—a deep philosophy influenced by the realm of metaphysics. "Everywhere, he felt, was incontrovertible evidence of an invisible but eminently active spirit world" (Unterecker 19). But what was the value of this fascination to Yeats? Beckson, quoting Symons, one of Yeats's colleagues, points out that Yeats pursued the mysterious instinct to become an artist: "'he discovers immortal moods in mortal desires'" (128). These "mortal desires" underlie the purposes of Yeats's poetry. These desires reveal what was at stake for Yeats in his passion for metaphysics.

6   "Byzantium," for example, says more about the poet than most readers may realize. Yeats connects the flesh-and-blood reality of the twentieth century to the reality (that he believed) of the supernatural. The first stanza concludes with the clashing of two contradictions, but only through their clash do they truly become distinct. "A starlit or a moonlit dome disdains / All that man is, / All mere complexities, / The fury and the mire of human veins" (1150). Yeats describes one of his major symbols, the full moon, which represents full and complete consciousness: all that the mind can become. For the human mind to attain such a supernatural feat, it must escape the constraints of this material world—reality as we know it. This elevation was Yeats's aim, his ambition, his necessity to become a great metaphysician and poet. This ambition is what the poem tells us about the poet. The contradiction between this world and the one beyond, Yeats points out, clashes as the "moonlit dome disdains." Only when the potential transcendental consciousness looks down upon its current, lesser state does either become truly defined. This potential consciousness Yeats longed for. His belief that he could in fact attain it was what was at stake for Yeats. According to Unterecker, "[o]nly, Yeats believed, if he could discover the design of the world of spirit would the pattern of the world of matter in which he felt himself to be trapped make sense" (23). Yeats's only way to preserve the spirituality he felt at stake was to manifest his intellectual escape from the confines of material reality into his philosophy and his poetry.

7   Dickinson's unusually solitary life accounts for her deep introspection and her heightened state of self-awareness. Dickinson might have been considered a recluse, yet "she kept in vital touch throughout her life with all the people she loved and with

many who just interested her" (Sewall 521). This private, yet expressive life allowed Dickinson to think philosophically about the internalized world of faith. By ceaselessly pondering and challenging herself over the nature and existence of the supernatural, Dickinson explored the concept of the sublime. She considered such transcendental concepts with amazement, only because she realized her own minute existence relative to it. Her poem "This world is not conclusion" describes the struggle of a believer trying to reconcile daily experience with the conception of a higher, divine, more perfect reality. This is the human struggle of knowing of the existence of a spiritual world, but perhaps lacking the ability to absorb it: "A sequel stands beyond, / Invisible, as music" (lines 2–3). Dickinson by no means claims that the sublime is simple:

> The poet admirably characterizes the inaccessibility of this reality which is transcendent of the physical world and transcendent alike to the sensory experiences of which the human being is capable. It is, in other words, "invisible." (Kimpel 229)

8   Dickinson's words pose another dimension to this struggle. By comparing the "invisible" to music, she speculates that perhaps internalizing the sublime is no more difficult than engaging with the presence of invisible, yet real music. The poem continues with a firm statement that logic and faith are not to be confused. When it comes to believing in something that is invisible, "Sagacity must go" (line 8). This ambiguous statement could have two meanings. "Sagacity" is defined as shrewdness, or keen perception. One could interpret this the poet's statement as one of disdain for those who believe in something that is invisible. In this view, to have faith means to throw aside all rational thought. The opposing, but equally valid interpretation of this line would commend those who do not require logic in order to have faith—those people who can successfully internalize the sublime. Dickinson's poem strongly suggests that the human spirit does indeed possess the capacity to embrace more than a material world. The capacity to spiritually embrace the unknown, however, does not require keen perceptive skills. In fact, "sagacity" is irrelevant; it fails to offer human beings any guarantees about spirituality. The last two lines of the poem describe the irony of the nature of human existence: we have an immense ability to sense a connection between ourselves and a "divine" force but, at the same time, we have no sure means of defining that force: "Narcotics cannot still the Tooth / That nibbles at the soul" (lines 19–20). Neither timeless doctrines, intellectual theologies, nor structured religions (the "Narcotics") are capable of soothing or distracting us from the continual uncertainties (the "Tooth") that press upon the human soul. Narcotics are numbing; they induce sleep. Dickinson suggests that a rigid system of belief actually destroys and undermines, rather than nourishes, our spirituality and our philosophical sensibilities. Dickinson's introspective, yet socially aware life accounts for her philosophy that focuses on the hope for the human condition in reality. Her poetry offers a brief meditation on the effects of the possibilities of an unknown world, the sublime, on a soul that exists in a material world.

8   9   As Dickinson contemplates the Cosmos from her human standpoint, Yeats attempts to imagine the opposite. Yeats contemplates the fate of the human condition from the position of the Cosmos. Yeats's intricate poetry never directly
acknowledges the human soul—the soul of the individual. Instead, his poem "The
Second Coming" vividly and intensely describes the onset of the new millennium—
the chaotic onset of the second antithetical period. The entire poem penetrates into

9   the horror that Yeats prophesies. Where does this horror come from? The Spiritus
Mundi, a predominant concept of Yeats's philosophy, accounts for his fear. It releases the antithetical beast: "The Second Coming! Hardly are those words out /
When a vast image out of *Spiritus Mundi* / Troubles my sight" (lines 11–13). The
Spiritus Mundi represents the soul of the world, the spirit of all human consciousness. Yeats no longer separates the supernatural world from this one. The two realities become one. The soul of the world is, in fact, the source of the release of the
beast. Yeats's apocalyptic images in the beginning of the poem do not centre on
any physical details that appeal to our senses. Rather, the events he describes are
conceptual and abstract, suggesting that what the speaker "sees" is the product of a
mental world: "The ceremony of innocence is drowned; / The best lack all conviction, while the worst / Are full of passionate intensity" (lines 6–8). Although the
title of the poem alludes to the biblical prophesy of the return of the Saviour,
Yeats's vision emerges not from an all-powerful deity, but from a source that is embedded in the human mind. Yeats designates humans as the source of their own
chaos. Perhaps our minds and imagination have far more power than we are apt to
realize. Yeats obviously believed just that.

10   At this point, considering the meaning of Yeats's philosophy is meaningless without considering Yeats's life and work. What could possibly account for his complicated
and horrific vision? Yeats's world was full of political chaos and upheaval. An Irish nationalistic movement was taking place, but Yeats's class and personal beliefs prevented him from ever completely participating in it. Perhaps he never felt as though
he belonged to his own social reality because of this personal exclusion. MacGloin
criticizes Yeats for not being more accountable to the social conditions around him:

> William Butler Yeats's world was devastated, doomed, and unredeemable.
> His work is, in part, the marvel of a long personal anguish in its loss—a
> threnody—that by its obsessive and particularized nature allowed little com-
> passion for the living. (484)

10   11   MacGloin's argument falls apart, however, once one considers the reason for
Yeats's philosophy rather than only the philosophy itself. The existence of Yeats's poetry says something different than the poetry itself. It reflects a deep emotional awareness of his human condition, the conditions of his turbulent world. Yeats's poetry
allowed the little compassion he had to remain. Yeats's poetry is a demonstration of

his own conception of clashing contradictions. The clash of his reality with his philosophy signified the distinction he tried to make between them.

12   The beauty of philosophy lies in the combination of discipline and creativity it conceives. Logic, science, and even religion, in contrast, attempt to bear evidence for the separate proofs these areas of thought require to progress. Unfortunately, this sort of evidence might also terminate the seeking of spiritual development. Dickinson and Yeats, although very different, travelled this philosophical road through their poetry. While Dickinson expresses what spiritual change happens with her as a human being, Yeats theorizes about the effects that human consciousness has on the universe as a whole. Their philosophical searches exemplified how aspects of their lives accounted for their specific thoughts about their existence. Dickinson acknowledged in her poetry her belief that evidence for faith does not exist. In life, her refusal to join the church represented her refusal to diminish the concept of faith. For Yeats, his philosophy was his only means of coping with the politically unstable world around him. He was mesmerized by the possibilities of a spiritual world, simply because he was horrified by the material world around him. He does not look at the world of beyond from an individualistic point of view. It is almost as though Yeats tries to write to us from beyond that spirit world; his poetry gives him a place in that world—a claim to a part of it. Another beauty of philosophy.

11

Works Cited

Beckson, Karl. "'The Tumbler of Water and the Cup of Wine': Symons, Yeats and the Symbolist Movement." Victorian Poetry 28.1 (1990): 125–133.

Ferlazzo, Paul J. Emily Dickinson. Boston: Twayne Publishers, 1976.

Kimpel, Ben. Emily Dickinson as Philosopher. Lewston: The Edwin Mellen Press, 1994.

MacGloin, T.P. "Yeats's Faltering World." The Sewanee Review 95.1 (1996): 470–484.

Sewall, Richard B. "In Search of Emily Dickinson." The Michigan Quarterly Review 23.1 (1984): 514–527.

Unterecker, John. A Reader's Guide to William Butler Yeats. London: Billing & Sons, 1959.

We now offer a few suggestions and pose some questions about this sample student research paper.

1. It might be a good idea to identify the significance of the title "Byzantium" in a footnote here or to work a definition into the essay's introduction. The student does provide the biblical significance of the title later in the essay, but perhaps moving it closer to the beginning would help readers grasp Yeats's reference.

2. Would an explanatory footnote here help the reader understand the context of Dickinson's "social rejection" based on religious grounds? A brief footnote might provide some historical details to describe Dickinson's situation in her community.

3. Here, Melanie has decided to provide a longer quotation in block format. Altogether, she uses three block quotations through the paper, and this balance with shorter, incorporated quotations seems to work well for this length of essay. Be careful not to resort to an abundance of block quotations simply to eat up essay space.

4. The student might briefly mention here the source for this information on Yeats's "fascination with metaphysics and the occult." As well, a working definition of "metaphysics" would help the reader see how the essayist (and Yeats) understand this specific term. Remember to recognize opportunities for careful definitions of specific and crucial terms as important moments of communication and persuasion in your writing.

5. The student here correctly documents an important quotation (that of Symons) that she has discovered within another critic's work. Since Symons is not being dealt with directly as a secondary source, but appears in Beckson's article in *Victorian Poetry*, Symons does not appear in the student's Works Cited page.

6. This analysis of the full moon in Yeats's poetry is insightful and persuasive. In a footnote or additional sentence in the paragraph, Melanie might show either how the moon appears in another instance of Yeats's poetry (a brief reference to one other poem would be sufficient) or how she first became aware of this symbol's implication.

7. and 8. Note Melanie's effective use of topic sentences that serve two related purposes: to organize each paragraph of discussion and to keep the ideas in the essay moving forward energetically but cohesively.

9. A footnote further explaining these theological terms and notions would certainly help clarify these very specific references.

10. The student's counter-argument here of one of her secondary source's views is an important development in the paper. Melanie's disagreement with MacGloin's argument indicates that the student offers her own analysis and perspective rather than accept all "expert" observations at face value. Such dispute within a research paper also strengthens the necessary element of *student voice* in the project.

11. Melanie concludes her last paragraph with a deliberate sentence fragment. This stylistic choice, at the end of such a formal essay, has the effect of surprising the reader by making expression visceral as well as cerebral.

Sample Essay Using APA Documentation

Dr. Ella Haley, author of the following sample paper, is an assistant professor with the Centre for Global and Social Analysis at Athabasca University in Athabasca, Alberta. The essay, drawing on her PhD dissertation and subsequent research, adopts the stance of an undergraduate student asked to handle a topic on the sociology of environmental health:

Essay topic: using a variety of research sources, present the case study of a community that was affected by industrial pollution.

> **Tip:** Balance your sources rather than simply search for the first references you can find, for instance, on the internet. In marginal comments, we have noted the different sources used. Consider the value of first-hand sources, such as appropriate personal interviews, as well as legal transcripts and the like.

> **Format Note:** For submission to a journal or course instructor, this essay would be **double-spaced**, including *every* line under "References."

Sample Essay APA Documentation

The Toxic Legacy of the Phosphate Fertilizer Industry

1 Although most gardeners, farmers and lawn-lovers use some form of fertilizer, few probably think about the process involved in producing it. This research paper examines the 50-year history of a pollution controversy related to a phosphate-processing factory in a rural community in southern Ontario. In the 1950s, the area around Dunnville in southern Ontario was known for its mixed farming. The community included a number of post-war immigrants from Eastern Europe, Germany, and the Netherlands who developed a thriving market-garden industry. Farmers sold their produce to local canneries and markets, and dairy herds supplied the local dairy with milk (Haley, 2000, p. 84; Fieldnotes, June 14, 2002). *[margin: Unpublished PhD dissertation / Fieldnotes from community-based research]*

2   In the town of Dunnville, there were several knitting mills, which were known for their low wages. In the late 1950s a phosphate-processing factory set up seven miles outside of Dunnville, in Sherbrooke Township, the smallest township in Ontario (Haley, 2000, p. 84). Within a year, the Electrical Reduction Company (ERCO) purchased the plant and expanded its operations to produce triple superphosphate, bringing the phosphate rock in by train from Florida (Haley, 200, p. 85). Sherbrooke Metallurgical, a zinc reduction plant, was set up next to ERCO to provide it with sulphuric acid, which was used to break down the phosphate rock. *[margin: Unpublished PhD dissertation] [margin: Unpublished PhD dissertation]*

3   ERCO wielded considerable political and economic influence in the farming community and in the town of Dunnville. In an article titled "Death Fear in Dunnville," published in the Hamilton *Spectator* on October 21, 1967, G. McAuliffe reported that ERCO paid 75 percent of the tax base of Sherbrooke Township, and provided 300 high-paying jobs. The *Family Herald* reported that "It reached the stage where almost everyone in town [Dunnville] had either a relative or a friend working there" (Crew, 1967, p. 21). *[margin: Newspaper clipping] [margin: Newspaper clipping: Archival material, page # missing]*

4   Farmers noticed the effects of industrial emissions within a few weeks of ERCO's expansion. They notified local agricultural authorities that crops, trees, shrubs, and other plant life had become burnt and shrivelled. Farmers and local residents developed nosebleeds, itchy skin, and irritated eyes (Haley, 2000, p. 233). Local *[margin: Unpublished PhD dissertation]*

motorists recall driving through a fog-like dust that was difficult to see through. Joe Casina testified that

Transcript of official inquiry

> There were days when I drove to the market and I would pull out between half past one and two in the morning and there would be a span on my farm where you thought you were driving through a fog. (Committee of Inquiry, 1968, p. 491)

Unpublished PhD dissertation

Newspaper clipping: archival material, date missing

5   Behind the scenes, an official from the Department of Agriculture approached ERCO with concern about its fluoride emissions (Haley, 2000: 223). However, according to an article titled "Farmer's diary tells the story of six-year pollution fight" that was published on October 30, 1967, G. Dunford reported agricultural officials suggested to farmers that their problems lay in their farming techniques.

6   Local veterinarians were stumped by farmers' complaints of health problems in local livestock, such as painful swollen knees that made walking difficult, tooth and gum problems, and reproductive problems. "We had one calf born with two heads. We had quite a few abortions [in the cattle]. We had a big problem with insemination and this sort of thing. That was not unusual here" (T. Boorsma, personal communication, June 14, 2002). When the veterinarians finally diagnosed fluorosis (fluoride poisoning) in the local dairy cattle in 1965, the Department of Health arranged for ERCO to pay compensation for damage to crops and livestock. Although cows died and government officials advised farmers to get rid of their dairy herds, no cattle were officially condemned. According to one resident, such government policy protected both the government and ERCO from any lawsuit.

Interview

Interview

> That way nobody's guilty. You would never say condemn the animal, then you say why would you want to condemn this animal? Well it's been sick with fluoride pollution. You can't go there. You realize when you're government, that's like making big damage for a company. Because then in turn you could sue everybody. This way of course you keep everything closed. They say the milk is fine, the meat is fine. We were shipping milk and the cattle was going to the butcher. Oh no, you don't wanna condemn the animals; that would never fit in with the total picture. (Boorsma, 2002)

Transcript of official inquiry

7   Don Middleton, the farmers' negotiator, also said that the farmers continued to ship the milk from their dairy herds to local dairies for processing because they were assured that it was safe (Committee of Inquiry, 1968, p. 1568).

8   The two industries (ERCO and Sherbrooke Metallurgical) and the provincial Department of Health conducted extensive testing of the farmers' livestock, crops and soil, according to Middleton:

Transcript of official inquiry

> The farmers knew that everybody, but everybody, was wanting samples, everybody that came on the farm carried off branches, leaves, bags, boxes, urine and what-have-you, but nobody ever came back to tell you what they have taken away or what had happened to it. (Committee of Inquiry, 1968 , p. 1575)

9   According to Middleton, the provincial Department of Health initiated a secrecy pact between ERCO and the Ontario Federation of Agriculture (O.F.A.):

> In 1965 it was the decision by the O.F.A. executive and in fact in agreement with the company and with the Department of Health that there would be no publicity on the problem that we had at Dunnville . . . . It was a trust kept on all sides . . . . [T]he decision of the Federation of Agriculture having been through Strontium 90 in milk were [*sic*] not particularly in favour of having a go with fluoride. It was worried about the sale of dairy products. All we needed was a picture of one of these crippled cows and the milk industry could have been seriously hurt, not only for these farmers, but for all the farmers in Ontario, and that was a decision made in consultation with the milk industry in Ontario . . . . (Committee of Inquiry, 1968, p. 1568)

10   In its report, The Hall Commission, however, denied the "secrecy agreement," based on off-the-record statements by health and ERCO officials (Haley, 2000, p. 301; Hall, 1968, p. 289).

> The other parties to the alleged agreement, namely the Department of Health and ERCO, deny that any such agreement existed. The Committee rejects the evidence of Mr. Middleton. The Committee cannot understand why Mr. Middleton found it necessary or desirable to express the view that such a "secrecy agreement" existed. (Hall, 1968, p. 289)

11   When Middleton had been assured that the milk was safe, he broke the "secrecy pact" and sought media coverage from the CBC. In 1967, in a national television broadcast, the CBC aired *Air of Death*, a documentary film. The film documented the injured crops and livestock, and featured a fluoride expert who expressed concern that the fluoride emissions were causing health problems in some people in the area. Many members of the public were appalled at what they saw and expressed concern about pollution, and about the laissez-faire attitudes of both ERCO and the various levels of government. In reaction to the public concern, the Ontario government set up a Royal Commission (known as the Hall Commission) to investigate the health impact of the fluoride emissions (Haley, 2000, p. 185).

12   The Hall Inquiry was riddled with problems from the start, including conflicts of interest among the panel members of the inquiry and the use of various strategies that prevented the public from receiving a fair, thorough and sound scientific investigation. The hearing was not held in the affected community, nor was it held during the summer months when the pollution damage could be observed. The terms of reference were changed so that the focus shifted away from an investigation of health problems to that of "allegations" of fluoride related health problems. The study area was broadened, a strategy that worked to dilute the data on health problems and introduce testimony from people who were not in the pollution area: "The Commission may deviate from its preliminary plans as evidence and accumulated knowledge warrants..." (Hall, 1968, p. xvii).

Side annotations:

The ellipses in the quotation indicate where text has been left out. The brackets indicate that the capital "T" has been added by the researcher; in this case, in order to start a new sentence at a place where the original quotation uses a lower-case "t."

Sic (meaning "so thus it is") recognizes an error in something immediately preceding. The error is retained to remain faithful to the source

Transcript of official inquiry

Unpublished PhD; Report of official inquiry

Film

Unpublished PhD dissertation

Report of official inquiry

Unpublished PhD dissertation

13   People with health concerns were belittled, their testimonies blocked or side-tracked. Environment and health officials failed to provide adequate documentation and their testimonies were vague. None of the doctors who testified had any experience with human fluorosis (Haley, 2000, pp. 229, 307). Despite this, the Commissioners alluded to these doctors as qualified experts. In contrast, the CBC's

Transcript of official inquiry

key fluoride expert was not given a time slot in which to testify. In his absence, he was ridiculed, his research dismissed (Committee of Inquiry, 1968, pp. 397–398). The Inquiry officers conducted a limited literature review that minimized the health impact of fluoride exposure. No reference was made to the literature documenting chronic human fluorosis in people living near fluoride-emitting plants.

Transcript of official inquiry

14   None of the three "health experts" for the inquiry discussed any data related to ERCO's emissions. One witness testified that he was specifically instructed not to discuss the ERCO plant (Committee of Inquiry, 1968, p. 505). The Chair of the Inquiry allowed the testimony of the farmers' only expert witness on the grounds that he not discuss the ERCO factory.

Mr. Brooks: Would you be prepared to take a look at the Electric Reduction operation here and comment on it, Mr. Huffstutler, in comparison. . .

Transcript of official inquiry

"Emphasis added" indicates that the researcher deliberately added the italics to intensify a point.

Chairman Hall: I am sorry, I will have to interrupt here . . . the invitation [to testify] was extended to Mr. Huffstutler and approved by his supervisor . . . *on the basis that he would not become involved in anything other than telling the Committee about the operations in the State of Florida* . . . and it was under those circumstances and those only that he was permitted by his chief to come to us today. (Committee of Inquiry, 1968, p. 1171; emphasis added)

15 Furthermore, although one of the Commission's own experts explained that fluoride emissions from phosphate-processing plants are not very easy to control, and "ex-

Transcript of official inquiry

tremely irritating to breathe" (Committee of Inquiry, 1968, p. 513), his testimony does not appear in the final report.

Unpublished PhD dissertation

16   With such strategies, the Commissioners were able to concluded that there was "no evidence" presented in the inquiry to link local health problems and complaints to the emissions. They were able to draw this conclusion because none of the investigating doctors presented any documentation of their research, nor did they conduct the proper tests to investigate fluoride toxicity (Haley, 2000, pp. 291, 307).

Book, Unpublished PhD dissertation

17   Once complete, the conclusions of the Hall Report were broadly circulated in the media. Like the Thomas Panel, which investigated the health impact of the pollution from *Love Canal* (Levine, 1982), the findings of this prestigious panel were treated as "fact" (Haley, 2000, p. 312). Both reports enabled the parties responsible for the environmental health problem to use the power of government and access to the press to write their own version of what happened. Both perpetuated the status quo and helped their respective governments to repair a legitimation crisis.

18   The Hall Inquiry silenced the affected community near the phosphate-processing plant. Throughout the controversy, most of the workers remained silent and resentful of the farmers and the publicity that they received. For the most part, despite the dirty work conditions at the plant, ERCO's wages were the highest in the area, and some of the men feared that the publicity could shut down the plant (Haley, 2000, p. 86; Fieldnotes, August 5, 2002). Rumours circulated that the farmers were just being greedy and that they were being heavily compensated by ERCO.

Unpublished PhD dissertation, fieldnotes from community-based research

19   The result was a divided community, fearful of company sanctions. Meanwhile, over time, the workers began to notice their own health problems—premature heart attacks, "triple by-passes" in men in their forties, kidney problems, rare cancers (i.e., bladder, thyroid). Few of the men knew that the rock also contained uranium and that they were being exposed to radon in the processing of the rock. Even then, it is doubtful that many of the workers understood the health risks of exposure to radon.

20   The ERCO plant closed shortly after an article in the Hamilton *Spectator* on June 8, 1984, in which B. Stewart revealed that the plant's waste lagoons contained radioactive uranium.

21   Twenty years later, the men keep lists of the men who have died, and of what they died from. Only now are the various segments of the community—farmers, workers, widows and neighbours to the ERCO plant—coming together to hear each other's stories (Fieldnotes, August 12, 2002). Their individual stories form the pieces of a puzzle that is helping them to understand the impact of this industrial giant that dominated their community from 1960, and that will continue to leave a toxic legacy long after it has left Canada.

Fieldnotes from community-based research

References

Air of Death. (1967). Toronto: Canadian Broadcasting Corporation (CBC). [Documentary film].

Canadian Broadcasting Corporation. (1967). *Air of death*. Toronto. [Transcript of documentary film]. Unpublished.

Committee of Inquiry on Allegations Concerning Pollution in the Townships of Dunn, Moulton, and Sherbrooke. (1968). Ontario. Transcript of hearings prepared by Nethercut and Young Ltd.

Crew, J. S. (1967, October 26). Downwind from disaster. *Family Herald*, p. 21.

Dunford G. (1967, October 30). Farmer's diary tells the story of six-year pollution fight. *Toronto Star*. Retrieved from CBC archives, missing page number.

Haley, E. (2000). Methodology to deconstruct environmental inquiries using the Hall Commission as a case study. Unpublished doctoral dissertation, Department of Sociology, York University, Toronto.

Haley, E. (2002). [Fieldnotes from community-based research, Jue 14, August 5, August 12]. Unpublished fieldnotes.

Hall, G. E. Committee of Inquiry on Allegations Concerning Pollution in the Townships of Dunn, Moulton, and Sherbrooke. (1968). Ontario. Report. (Hall Commission)

Levine, A. (1982). *Love Canal: Science, politics and people*. Toronto: Lexington Books.

McAuliffe, G. (1967, October 21). Death Fear in Dunnville. Hamilton *Spectator*. Retrieved from CBC archives, missing page number.

Stewart, B. (1984, June 8). Radioactive uranium in lagoons. Hamilton *Spectator*, p. A10.

Waldbott, G. (1968, April 17). Letter to Matthew Dymond, Minister of Health and Brief to Hall Commission.

Related Web Resources

Connett, M. (1967). Partial transcript from the CBC film *Air of death*. Retrieved October 17, 2002, from **http://www.fluoridealert.org/cbc-transcript.htm**.

Fluoride Action Network. (2002). The phosphate fertilizer industry: An environmental Overview. Retrieved October 17, 2002, from **http://www.fluoridealert.org/phosphate/overview.htm**.

Related Reading

Waldbott, G.L., & Cecilioni, V. A. (1969). "Neighbourhood" fluorosis. *Clinical Toxicology*, 2(4), 387–396.

Focus Questions

1. How would you describe this essay? Is it persusasive? Expository? Explain your answer.
2. What rhetorical strategies does the writer use? Be as specific as you can.
3. The inserted editorial word "*sic*" means " so it is." *Sic* tells us that the researcher wishes to acknowledge an error or oddity in the spelling or grammar of a preceding word or phrase. Do you recognize an error before the word *sic*? (Review "Fifteen Common Errors" in the *Handbook* section for help in spotting the error.)
4. Look over the list of "Twelve Logical Fallacies." Are there any such flaws in reason in this essay?
5. Give some examples of vivid details in the essay. Do you feel the examples presented are sufficient to make the writer's case? Why or why not?

Section 4 Revising

Chapter 13
Drafting and Revising an Analytical Essay

All essayists work to make their writing strong, convincing, concise, and memorable. Your commitment to revising your drafts is crucial to achieving these goals. We will now turn to a detailed discussion of the revision process. Students revise in various ways according to their different writing and thinking habits, but all writers revise in some manner, and the best writers revise extensively.

What if you are interested in writing a brief analysis arguing, say, that World Wrestling Entertainment is a form of soap opera? Your paper will likely rely partly on *classification* (arguing that WWE is, surprisingly enough, part of a television genre widely known as the soap opera), partly on *definition* (defining what a soap opera is and how WWE displays some of these characteristics), and partly on *comparison and contrast* techniques to organize your paragraphs.

After you have worked through a point-form list, inkshedding, diagramming, or a topic-sentence tree in the pre-writing stages, you are ready to begin a draft of your discussion. Your topic-sentence tree for this analysis may look something like our diagram. The optional numbers attached to each topic sentence in the tree here would be added only later, as your draft takes shape and you make decisions about which topic sentences to use, which ones, possibly, to combine, and their order of appearance in your draft.

After constructing your topic sentence tree, you can write a first draft of your paper. The topic sentences in your tree diagram need not appear in the order you have thought of them; move them around as necessary and modify them in your draft. As you work on this draft, you may find your essay structure changes slightly with any new insights and developments. In fact, some of your tentative topic sentences from the topic-sentence tree may not even appear later as topic sentences, but become points in a paragraph organized by other topic sentences. Such flexibility and shape-shifting are skills you learn in the process of drafting and revising.

Your main aim in sketching a topic-sentence tree and in composing a first draft is to start developing your argument: (1) working thesis (the main claim or point), (2) the paragraph structure with provisional topic sentences, and (3) the significance of your observations. Your first draft of an analysis of the WWE as soap opera might unfold something like our example. The working thesis statement and topic sentences are underlined here to emphasize their presence as the frame—the backbone—of your essay.

Figure 13.1

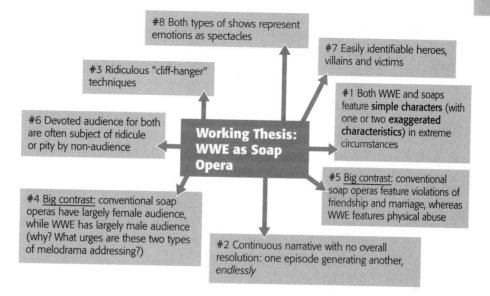

THE FIRST DRAFT

Sample Student Essay

World Wrestling Entertainment is really only a kind of soap opera. It is a big soap opera for a mostly male audience. WWE, like all soap operas, is about melodrama because of the exaggerated situations and extreme feelings. Although WWE is different in some ways from regular soap operas, there are lots of similarities.

Working thesis

Both WWE and daytime soap operas present lots of characters in painful, often exaggerated circumstances. The characters in both are always in some trouble, distress, or crisis. In both the wrestling world and the usual soap operas, there seems to be a whole lot of betrayal. The situations are the same over and over: someone lies or cheats on somebody in the daytime soaps and someone sneaks up on someone in the WWE and hits him with a chair. The situations are all pretty extreme, but also almost the same from week to week. It's all about simple characters with one or two exaggerated characteristics getting in trouble or causing trouble.

Topic sentence #1 from tree diagram

Another thing these two types of shows have in common is there's no overall conclusion or else the show would end as a series. Different problems get concluded, sure, but one thing spins into another and one big problem creates other ones for next week, next month, next year. When someone's marriage ends in the soaps, it often comes out that years of adultery are the reason. However, the cheating might be between a sultry corporate businesswoman and her shifty accountant, who would falsify all their expense accounts because he was obsessed with going to fancy spas in

Topic sentence #2 from tree diagram

a bikini with her, and now the company's stockholders are suddenly demanding an investigation that might also reveal that none of the company's new products meets safety standards. In WWE, a tag-team match turns bad when one of the partners is sucker-punched by a masked wrestler who is not even supposed to be in the ring. He climbs in because one of the other wrestler's brothers—also a wrestler—jumped on him last week from the top turnbuckle minutes before their match was supposed to start. There's lots of indiscriminate pushing in the ring until somebody gets hit with a garbage can while the ref was advising someone else about time restrictions for the bout. This cheap shot wins the match, but the revenge will probably come next week. In both soaps and wrestling, the episodes are cliff-hangers to deliberately set up lots of other related episodes, so the stories are continuous, unlike other television shows that usually resolve each episode before a new one next week.

Topic sentence #3 from tree diagram now incorporated into the paragraph

Despite similarities, there are some important contrasts between the wrestling and daytime soap opera worlds. Soap operas have largely female audiences, while WWE has mostly male audiences. Soap operas usually dramatize family problems and betrayals in friendships and relationships. But wrestling makes fun of physical aggression and bodily pain. The soaps look at emotions in the context of social and private life, while the WWE presents the pain of comic book make-believe physical abuse in male competition. These differences make the melodrama of soap operas seem more realistic, at least as far as their characters' problems relating in some way to the viewers' fears and perhaps hopes. So, while the women's soaps exaggerate and exploit a lot of genuine adult fears, the wrestling really only represents the immature boy's perspective of a schoolyard bullying tournament.

Topic sentences #4 and #5 from tree diagram now combined

With all these easily identifiable heroes, villains, and victims, the daytime soaps and WWE have a big devoted audience. Unfortunately, the people of these audiences are often ridiculed by people who are not fans. The fans are not necessarily silly, but perhaps are enjoying the simplistic characters in one crisis after another. The formulas please the viewers. This is because there are occasionally surprising variations in the same plots and themes. This requires real innovation. There are links between differences in the sex of the separate audiences and the differences in the types of fears and fantasies of the two types of melodrama. These differences in content reveal that the men and women who like melodrama seek different types in order to entertain themselves. However, both sexes seem to enjoy seeing emotions represented as spectacles.

Topic sentences #6 and #7 combined

Topic sentence #8 repositioned as concluding sentence

Suggested Revision of Draft

World Wrestling Entertainment is really ~~only a kind of~~ _{another} soap opera, ~~It is a big soap~~ _{except one}

~~opera~~ for a mostly male audience. WWE, like all soap operas, ~~is about~~ _{relies on} melo-

drama: ~~because of the~~ _{plot formulas that present} exaggerated situations and extreme feelings. Although the

WWE is different in ~~some~~ _{significant} ways from regular soap operas, ~~there are lots of~~ _{several} similarities

reveal that the different audiences seek the same experience in viewing emotional

displays.

Both WWE and daytime soap operas present ~~lots of~~ _{simplistic} characters in painful, ~~often~~

exaggerated, circumstances. These characters ~~in both~~ _{though predictably formulaic} are always in some ~~trouble~~, dis-

tress or crisis, ~~In both the wrestling world and the usual soap operas, there seems to~~ _{usually resulting from}

~~be a whole lots of~~ _a betrayal. The situations are the same over and over: someone lies

or cheats on someone in the daytime soaps and someone sneaks up on someone

in the WWE and hits him with a chair. _{Although} the situations are all pretty extreme, ~~but also al-~~ _{their repetition}

~~most the same~~ from week to week makes exaggeration a standard. ~~It's all about sim-~~

~~ple characters withone or two exaggerated characteristics getting in trouble or causing~~

~~trouble~~. Since both types of shows offer crisis as routine, viewers must enjoy watching

predictable emotional flare-ups.

~~Another thing~~ _{Both} ~~these two~~ types of shows ~~have in common is there's no~~ _{also depend on delaying any}

overall conclusion or else the show would end as a series. Different _{individual} problems

1. conciseness/ compression

2. verb choice/ specific diction

3. diction/concise-ness

4. precision/ significance/thesis statement

5. topic sentence

6. compression of point

7. subordination/ solid nouns

8. state implica-tions / avoid repetition

9. close paragraph with statement of implication

10. conciseness/ verb choice

11. diction/ formality

~~get~~ concluded~~, sure~~, but one ~~thing~~ spins into another, ~~and one big problem~~ creat[ing] [ordeal]

other ones for next week, next month, next year. When someone's marriage ends in

12. transitions within paragraphs

the soaps, for example, ~~it often comes out that~~ [often] years of adultery are the reason.

However, the cheating might [also] be between a sultry corporate businesswoman and ~~her~~ [the company]

13. diction/ verb tense

~~shifty~~ accountant, who ~~would~~ [has] falsif[ied] all their expense accounts because he was ob-

14. formality/ misplaced modifier

sessed with ~~going to~~ [visiting] fancy spas ~~in a bikini~~ with her, and now the company's stock-

holders are suddenly demanding an investigation that might also reveal that none of

15. transitions/ paragraph unity

the company's new products meets safety standards. [By comparison,] in WWE, a tag-team match turns

bad when one ~~of the~~ partners is sucker-punched by a masked wrestler who is not

~~even~~ supposed to be in the ring. He climbs in because one of the other wrestler's

brothers—also a wrestler—jumped on him last week from the top turnbuckle minutes

before their match was ~~supposed~~ to start. ~~There's~~ Lots of indiscriminate pushing in

16. conciseness/ verb choice

the ring ~~until~~ [results in] somebody ~~gets~~ ['s being] hit with a garbage can while the ref ~~was~~ advis[es] some-

one else about time restrictions for the bout. This cheap shot wins the match, but the

revenge will probably come next week. In both soaps and wrestling, the episodes are

cliff-hangers to ~~deliberately~~ set up ~~lots of~~ other related episodes, so the stories are

continuous, unlike other television shows that usually resolve each episode before a

new one next week.

Despite similarities, ~~there are some~~ important contrasts ~~between~~ _∧[characterize] the wrestling and

daytime soap opera ~~worlds~~[melodramas]. Soap operas have largely female audiences, while WWE

has mostly male audiences. Soap operas usually ~~dramatize~~[exploit the fears of] family problems and be-

trayals in friendships and relationships, ~~But~~[whereas] wrestling ~~makes fun of~~[parodies] physical aggression

and bodily pain. the soaps ~~look at~~[So, while] [dramatize the pain of] emotions in the context of social and private life,

~~while~~ the WWE presents ~~the pain of~~ [violence as] comic book ~~make believe physical abuse in~~ male

competition. These differences make the melodrama of soap operas seem more real-

istic, at least as far as ~~their~~[than that of the WWE] characters' problems ~~relating~~[and resolutions reflect] in some way ~~to~~ the viewers'

fears and ~~perhaps~~[Significantly] hopes. ~~So, while~~ the "women's" soaps exaggerate and exploit ~~a lot~~

~~of~~ genuine adult fears, errors and consequences, [while] the wrestling really represents only a

~~violent~~[sadistic] boy's ~~perspective~~[fantasy] of a schoolyard bullying tournament.

~~With all these~~[The] easily identifiable heroes, villains, and victims, [of both] the daytime

soaps and WWE have ~~a big~~[large and] devoted audiences. Unfortunately, ~~the people of~~

these audiences are often ridiculed by people who are not fans. The fans are not

necessarily silly, but perhaps ~~are~~ enjoy~~ing~~ ~~the~~[the repetition of] simplistic characters ~~in~~[working their way through] one crisis after

another. ~~The~~[Such] formulas [may] please the viewers[partly]. ~~This is~~ because there are occasionally

surprising variations in the same plots and themes. This requires real innovation.[element of surprise within formulaic episodes]

Margin annotations:

17. topic sentences / specific diction

18. diction/ compression

19. transition/ pointed contrast

20. clarity

21. emphasis/ detail/diction

22. topic sentence

23. conciseness

24. counter-argument/ strong diction

25. pronoun reference/ specific language

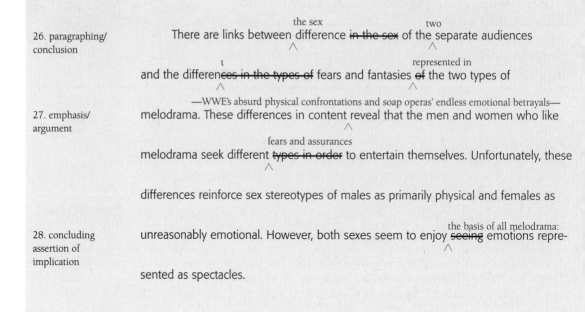

26. paragraphing/ conclusion

the sex   two
There are links between difference ~~in the sex~~ of the separate audiences

t   represented in
and the differen~~ces in the types of~~ fears and fantasies ~~of~~ the two types of

27. emphasis/ argument

—WWE's absurd physical confrontations and soap operas' endless emotional betrayals—
melodrama. These differences in content reveal that the men and women who like

fears and assurances
melodrama seek different ~~types in order~~ to entertain themselves. Unfortunately, these

differences reinforce sex stereotypes of males as primarily physical and females as

28. concluding assertion of implication

the basis of all melodrama:
unreasonably emotional. However, both sexes seem to enjoy ~~seeing~~ emotions repre-

sented as spectacles.

Discussion of Draft Revisions

We have numbered our revisions to assist with potential class discussions or individual student inquiries. Here we will discuss a sample of these revisions. Since our discussion is lengthy and detailed, you may wish to refer back to both the first draft sample (p. 473) and our revised version (p. 475) to check what we are changing and how we are doing it.

In the second draft, we have revised for *conciseness*, *compression* (two sentences becoming one), *active verb choice*, and *specific diction* for greater clarity of points. These changes appear throughout the revised draft.

We have also made structural changes to shape the paragraphs and draw out the significance of the observations in the analysis. We have strengthened the *thesis statement* by adding an *implication* to the initial observation that there are several similarities between WWE and soap operas. The revised thesis now articulates a point about that similarity.

Structurally, we have also revised the *topic sentences* with more pointed language to make their assertions more emphatic, punchier. In the topic sentence of the third paragraph, for instance, we have revised for the stronger phrasing of "depend on delaying any overall conclusion" in place of "have in common is there's no overall conclusion." "Depend" and "delaying" are more active and more specific word choices than "have" and "is," which describe states of being only, not actions. Similarly, the topic sentence in the fourth paragraph becomes more specific and analytically assertive with the active verb "characterize" (rather than the static "there are") and with the descriptive noun "melodramas" (rather than the general "worlds"). "Melodramas," as a crucial term in the discussion, keeps the analysis fully before the reader.

Another important revision strategy is to close your paragraphs strongly, especially in analytical writing. Your paragraph has developed a point, so articulate the implication of that point in the paragraph's last sentence or two. In our revised draft's second paragraph, for example, we eliminate the last sentence from the original draft because the sentence only repeats an earlier point without adding any new observation or analytical significance. In its place, we close the paragraph by adding a sentence that asserts an implication about both WWE's and conventional soap opera's reliance on crisis as a routine plot device. Importantly, this last sentence in our second paragraph is also directly linked to that paragraph's topic sentence, to the claim that both types of shows specialize in painful yet formulaic circumstances.

We have made the most extensive revisions in our second draft's conclusion. This new conclusion has been created by splitting apart a longer paragraph in the unrevised first draft. Such splitting and sometimes fusing or shuffling of paragraphs is part of the revision process. The conclusion's revised topic sentence now asserts that the largely male and female audiences of WWE and soap operas, respectively, enjoy different fears and fantasies in these two types of melodramatic shows. The conclusion wraps up—provocatively—by asserting that although the different melodramas reinforce sex stereotypes, both audiences share an enjoyment of spectacles of emotions.

The revised conclusion is now directly linked to the thesis statement and to the topic sentences. Such unity through the essay creates for readers a clear "line of argument," a focused and steadily developing analysis. The conclusion, then, should not merely end, but reinforce the line of argument.

Revisions for structural coherence are both crucial and demanding, and your care will always be a wise investment. A clear thesis, developed by chiselled topic sentences, wrapped up with a taut conclusion, will protect you from the downfall of a drifting discussion, the fuzziness of barely related points made in passing.

Whether or not you agree with the essay's points is less important here than the essayist's efforts to develop a thesis broken down into paragraphs with specific points that, taken together, cohere as a stance, as one position.

FIVE TYPES OF REVISION SKILLS

The ability to revise effectively is an extremely valuable skill that will help you in college, business, and private life. You must dedicate yourself to acquiring and to improving your revision skills. All writers constantly improve their ability to revise through continued writing and language experience. Here are five inescapable areas of writing where your sharpened skills in revision will help you articulate your ideas grammatically, methodically, and concisely—therefore powerfully. Your written ideas will have the clear and incisive form they need to inform and persuade your audience,

CLASSROOM DISCUSSION

1. How do the other revision suggestions in the second draft of our sample essay on the WWE as soap opera help the essay?
2. What changes improve *expression*: grammar, diction, active verbs, clarity?
3. What changes improve *structure*: thesis statements, topic sentences, transitions, paragraph closings?
4. How would you describe the function of the preceding structural elements?
5. In class, write a one-page analysis of an issue or current event. Exchange writing samples among the class for revision (peer editing). Upon receiving your revised work, discuss with classmates or your instructor your agreement or disagreement with the suggestions or changes.
6. Write a one-page analysis of an issue or current event in class. File that writing sample for one or two weeks, then edit your own work in another coloured pen or pencil. Submit the original and the revision to your instructor for possible class discussion or class examples.

whether you address teachers, classmates, employers, business colleagues, customers, disgruntled neighbours, or various appeal boards.

These five areas of revision skills, for your review and practice, are

1. Grammar
2. Introduction
3. Topic sentences
4. Conclusion
5. Conciseness

Rather than offer full essays in this section, we first present brief unrevised paragraphs to allow students and teachers to use for extended classroom discussion of possible strategies for revision. A revised version and detailed comment then follow each unrevised paragraph. As well, we offer several further examples of particular revisions in order to isolate the basic principles of our five selected areas. These brief paragraphs may also help instructors assign other sample paragraphs—generated either by students or instructors—for written revision as short assignments.

1. Revision of Grammar

Revising for grammatical errors requires a working command of grammatical principles. Build up a ready awareness of the common errors many writers commit so that you can steer clear of them. The *Handbook* defines, explains, and offers examples of the mechanics of writing and the common errors at length.

Here, also, is a brief revision exercise for frequent grammatical problems. In pencil, circle, identify, and correct the *15 errors* in the following paragraph before checking your answers against the corrected version. You may wish to photocopy this paragraph to work on it separate from the textbook. Remember to focus only on grammar, not stylistic changes, for this exercise.

Sample paragraph

Eighties music is not as bad or culturally frightening as many people say. Although its hard to defend Duran Duran. One band, Cameo had a great funk song entitled "Word Up" in the early Eighties. Two other band's styles from this decade have defined alot of modern music here and now; U2 and REM. Besides these two examples of writerly talent and innovative musicianship we need to really remember that some of Tom Petty's, AC/DC's, Bananarama's, and, of course Guns n' Roses' best work appeared in the Eighties. However the mysterious problem of all those one-hit or two-hit wonders are a concern to any true connoisseur of this decade's music, for instance: 'Til Tuesday's "Voices Carry," A-Ha's "Take On Me," Adam Ant's "Goodie Two Shoes," The Bangles' "Walk Like an Egyptian," Fine Young Cannibals' "Good Thing," and Glass Tiger's "Don't Forget Me [When I'm Gone]." Did these artists' managers suddenly run out of ideas, were they abducted by extra-terrestrials or by Lou Reed and Iggy Pop? Considering Elton John's recent work, is it better too burn out then fade away?

Corrected version

Eighties music is not as bad or culturally frightening as many people say. Although #1

it's hard to defend Duran Duran, one band, Cameo, had a great funk song entitled #2   #1   #3

"Word Up" in the early Eighties. Two other bands' styles from this decade have de- #4 bands'

fined allot of modern music here and now: U2 and REM. Besides these two examples #5   #6

of writerly talent and innovative musicianship, we need to really remember that #7   optional

some of Tom Petty's, AC/DC's, Bananarama's, and, of course, Guns N' Roses' best #8

work appeared in the Eighties. However, the mysterious problem of all those one-hit #9

or two-hit wonders are a concern to any true connoisseur of this decade's music, for is #10   optional :

instance, 'Til Tuesday's "Voices Carry," A-Ha's "Take On Me," Adam Ant's "Goodie , #11

Two Shoes," The Bangles' "Walk Like an Egyptian," Fine Young Cannibals' "Good

Thing," and Glass Tiger's "Don't Forget Me [When I'm Gone]." Did these artists' man-

agers suddenly run out of ideas, Were they abducted by extra-terrestrials or by Lou #12 ?   optional

Reed and Iggy Pop? Considering Elton John's recent work, is it better too burn out #13   we may ask if   is   #14 to

than fade away. #15 than

#1. This is a <u>sentence fragment</u> because it is only a <u>dependent clause</u>, not a full sentence. This fragment can be fixed if you make it an <u>introductory dependent clause</u> that introduces the independent clause following it. This correction requires only a comma to join the two: "Introductory dependent clause, independent clause." As another option, you could also attach the dependent clause to the preceding independent clause.

Another example:

> A flamboyant showcase of Rajasthani architecture, the Pink City of Jaipur in Northern India. Although many people think the city's single most striking feature, its pink colour, is as old as the buildings themselves. The buildings were in fact originally a sallow yellow. Pink is traditionally the colour of hospitality in Rajasthan, but this wash, now regularly reapplied, has only been compulsory only since the city was spruced up in preparation for the visit of Prince Albert from England in 1856.

Correction

The first two statements of the paragraph are <u>sentence fragments</u>. "A flamboyant showcase of Rajasthani architecture" is a phrase, so the sentence is incomplete without another independent clause or the addition of the verb "is" in place of the comma after "architecture." The second fragment can also be fixed with a second independent clause following it or the deletion of "Although."

#2. <u>It's/its confusion</u> is common in many first-year student papers. Remember that "it's" is a <u>contraction</u> and means "it is," whereas "its" (no apostrophe) is a <u>possessive pronoun</u> and stands in for a previous noun. Here we need the contraction "it's" or, more formally in a college essay, "it is."

Another example:

> The Great Wall of China can be easily detected from space by radar because it's smooth sides provide a good surface for reflection of the NASA radar beam.

Correction

The contraction "it's" is incorrect here because "it is smooth sides" makes no sense. We want the <u>possessive pronoun</u> "its" to stand for the Great Wall's smooth sides: "its smooth sides."

#3. Be careful not to forget the <u>second comma</u> on a <u>non-restrictive qualifier</u>. Non-restrictives provide extra, though not essential (or restrictive), information about the noun or noun phrase they modify. Non-restrictive qualifiers are set off by two commas. Here we have a special type of non-restrictive called an "appositive." Appositives name again what they qualify: "Our fire chief, Liam Gallagher, arrives tomorrow." In our unrevised paragraph, the band name 'Cameo' needs to be framed by commas to form the non-restrictive qualifier. In all non-restrictive qualifiers, appositives, and parenthetical expressions, the two commas function as parentheses, bracketing off the qualifier from the main elements of the sentence.

Another example:

> In 1884, Gabriel Dumont and three other Métis came to St. Peter's Mission to ask Louis Riel, the leader of the 1870 Red River Rebellion to become political leader of a Métis movement in Saskatchewan.

Correction
There should be a second comma after the non-restrictive qualifier "the leader of the 1870 Red River Rebellion."

#4. The sometimes confusing difference between the singular possessive and plural possessive hinges on a crucial distinction: look for the number possessing, not the number possessed. If you have "the two students' car," you have a plural possessive because there are *two* students possessing the car. In our featured error, we have a singular possessive ("band's"), but require a plural possessive ("bands'") because there is more than one band: "Two other bands' styles . . ."

Another example:

> Babies have poor vision at birth but can see faces at close range, even in the newborn nursery. At about six weeks, a babies' eyes should follow objects and by four months should work together.

Correction
The second sentence refers to the vision of a single baby, not many babies' eyes, so the sentence requires the singular possessive: "At about six weeks, a baby's eyes should follow objects . . ."

#5. "A lot" is always two words. There is no such fused word as "alot" in written English, though slang continues to insist that the necessary space between the two words is somehow wasted.

Another example:

> The University of Minnesota conducted a recent study on why North Americans are so unfit. Alot of meals are bought away from home on average, and even home cooked food often takes the form of pre-made frozen dinners.

Correction
The non-word "alot" should be changed to "a lot."

#6. Watch for incorrect use of the semicolon, whose main purpose is to join two independent clauses. A full colon, in contrast, needs to be *preceded* by an independent clause, but can be followed by almost anything—independent clause, dependent clause, phrase, list, or single word. In the sentence in our paragraph, we could correctly use the full colon, but not the semicolon, since "U2 and REM" do not form an independent clause.

Another example:

> Gustav Mahler used choral or solo voices in four symphonies; his Second, Third, Fourth, and Eighth. The Eighth symphony is known as the "Symphony of a Thousand" because of the enormous number of performers in its first performance; 1028.

Correction
Both <u>semicolons</u> are used incorrectly and should be changed to <u>colons</u>, commas, or dashes in these two sentences. The first semicolon is used incorrectly because it is followed by a list, while the second semicolon is incorrectly followed by a single word. Both lists and single words may follow full colons, commas, or dashes, but semicolons must have independent clauses on both sides (unless joining together items in a list where each item already features a comma or commas in it).

> **Reminder:**
> independent clause; independent clause
> independent clause: independent clause **or** dependent clause **or** list **or** phrase **or** single word

#7. You require a <u>comma</u> after a <u>long introductory phrase or clause</u>. If the introductory phrase or clause is <u>three words or more</u>, use a comma to set it off from the independent clause following it.
Another example:

> A border dispute that developed into international proportions the Iran-Iraq war was fought between 1980 and 1988.

Correction
You need a comma after "proportions" because this long introductory phrase introduces the independent clause beginning as "the Iran Iraq war . . ."

Optional
This <u>split infinitive</u> "to really remember" is still considered an error, but many instructors now accept it as a style choice. We advise against split infinitives, and here you can delete "really" for a better sentence.

#8. "Of course" here is a <u>parenthetical phrase</u>, which functions a bit like a non-restrictive qualifier; it requires two commas to set it off from the rest of the sentence. With non-restrictives and parentheticals, students most often incorrectly omit the <u>second comma</u>.
Another example:

> Pete Sampras, arguably the best tennis player of all time has won seven Wimbledon titles, the four U.S. Open championships, and the two Australian Opens, but, interestingly has never won the French Open title.

Correction
There are two missing commas, one after the <u>non-restrictive qualifier</u> ending "of all time" and one after the <u>parenthetical expression</u> "interestingly." These second commas correctly separate the qualifier from the rest of the sentence.

> **Reminder:** For parenthetical expressions, non-restrictive qualifiers, and apposi-tives, commas appearing <u>within</u>—not at the end of—your sentences are, as Professor John Fraser of Dalhousie University enjoyed pointing out, like tango dancers; there have to be two.

#9. "However" is a <u>conjunctive adverb</u>. It is set off by a comma or commas, de-pending on where it appears in your sentence. In our example, "however" be-gins the sentence, so it is followed by a comma. If "however" appeared later in this sentence, <u>two</u> commas would be necessary to set if off: "The mysterious problem, however, of all those one-hit or two-hit wonders . . ."

> Another example:

> > The perception of many small business owners is that "financing" means ac-cepting whatever money you can. However accepting money that comes from letting your brother, Sheldon Phillips, become a partner in your busi-ness might be far more costly than you could imagine.

Correction
Remember that "however" is always followed by a comma, whether it is preceded by a semicolon in the middle of a sentence or it begins a sentence.

> **Reminder:** "However" confuses many students. Although this word means the same as "but," it serves a different grammatical function. "However" is not one of the seven coordinate <u>conjunctions</u>, such as "but." "However" cannot join two in-dependent clauses with the help of a comma, as the coordinate conjunctions ("for," "and," "nor," "but," "or," "yet," "so") can. In fact, "however," improperly punc-tuated, probably creates a majority of <u>comma splices</u>.

#10. Subjects and verbs must always agree in <u>number</u>. Sometimes <u>subject-verb agreement</u> can be a little confusing if a <u>prepositional phrase</u> or a <u>non-restrictive qualifier</u> separates the subject and verb. In our example, "prob-lem" is the subject—and is <u>singular</u>—so the verb "are" must be changed to "is" for agreement (singular subject ➡ singular verb form). The <u>prepositional phrase</u> "of all those one-hit or two-hit wonders" qualifies the subject ("prob-lem"), but does not affect the subject-verb agreement.

> Another example:

> > Atherosclerosis is a disease of the arteries. Accumulation of fatty material, from high saturated fat and cholesterol in the vessel wall, eventually result in narrowing of the vessels and impairment of blood flow.

Correction
The plural verb form "result" should be the <u>singular verb form</u> "result<u>s</u>" because the subject ("accumulation") is singular.

Reminder: For subject-verb agreement, find the verb in your sentence, put your finger on it, and ask yourself, "who" or "what" *does* or *is* this word? The word you find—and it should be *one word*—is your subject. Watch out for any qualifiers of your subject (prepositional phrases and non-restrictive qualifiers) that may confuse you about subject-verb agreement.

Optional
An optional <u>full colon</u> after "music" here would nicely break up the syntax by separating the independent clause from the phrase, thereby setting up the second part of the sentence as a list. The original comma is grammatically correct, but will create a long sentence that may not effectively hold the attention of all readers.

#11. A <u>full colon</u> is an error here after "for instance"because "for instance" prevents the <u>preceding</u> word group from being an <u>independent clause</u>. Remember, an independent clause must precede a full colon. For your correction, you can either place the full colon <u>before</u> "for instance" or <u>follow</u> "for instance" with a comma.

Another example:

> On Dec. 7, 1941, while negotiations were conducted with Japanese representatives in Washington, Japanese carrier-based planes swept in without warning over Pearl Harbor and attacked the bulk of the U.S. Pacific fleet, including: nineteen naval vessels and eight battleships, all sunk or severely damaged, and 188 U.S. aircraft, all destroyed.

Correction
The full colon after "including" is incorrect because the statement before it is not an independent clause. This error can be corrected simply by deleting the colon.

#12. You create a <u>comma splice</u> by joining two <u>independent clauses</u> with a <u>comma</u>. In this case, you can correct this construction by placing a question mark after the first independent clause, since both of these independent clauses are questions. You could also fix the comma splice by keeping the comma after "ideas" and then adding an appropriate coordinate conjunction after the comma: in this case "or."

Another example:

> "Ao Dai," meaning "long dress," is the traditional attire worn by Vietnamese women, the designs of a bridal Ao Dai often display mythical figures, such as the dragon and phoenix.

Correction
This paragraph contains a comma splice, created by connecting two independent clauses with a comma. There should be a <u>period</u> or a <u>semicolon</u> after "Vietnamese women."

Optional
"They" here refers to "managers." If the writer wishes for "they" to refer to "artists," however, the sentence will have to be altered for clear <u>pronoun reference</u>. If "they" is to refer to "artists," the simplest solution would be to replace "they" with "the artists."

#13.   "Considering" is a <u>dangling participle</u>. We have no <u>appropriate subject</u> for "considering" to modify. Ask yourself who or what is "considering" Elton John's recent work. Fix this dangling participle by inserting a suitable subject, such as "we," after the phrase in which the participle appears.
   Another example:

   Looking at the recent genetic work on sheep, it is likely that choosing genes to clone the perfect human is not far behind.

Correction
There is no subject in the sentence for the participle phrase "looking at the recent work on sheep" to modify. An "it" cannot be "looking." "Looking" is therefore dangling here. An appropriate subject would be, for example, <u>scientists</u> claim that it is likely . . .".

#14.   Watch out for confusing "too" and "to." Here, you need "to" to form the infinitive "to burn." "Too" is an <u>adverb</u> that modifies an adjective: "<u>too</u> salty," "<u>too</u> expensive," "not <u>too</u> late for Wilson in Steven Soderbergh's film *The Limey* to find out the truth about the past." Remember that adverbs modify <u>verbs</u> ("he drank <u>quickly</u>"), as well as <u>adjectives</u> ("a <u>very</u> good plan"). In contrast to "too," "to" can be used not only as a <u>preposition</u> ("In *Beneath the Planet of the Apes*, the gorilla army points <u>to</u> the nuclear warheads"), but also as the <u>auxiliary verb</u> in an <u>infinitive</u> ("Nixon did not want Trudeau <u>to visit</u> China and pre-empt all the U.S. grandstanding about opening up international relations.")
   Another example:

   Rosemary Trainor thinks that Egypt's Mt. Sinai, or "Moses Mountain" as it's known locally, is to long a drive from Sharm El Sheikh. Almost all climbers tackle this mountain too see the sunrise.

Correction
Replace the incorrect "to" with the <u>adverb</u> "too" to amplify the adjective "long", and then replace the incorrect adverb "too" with "to" because we need the <u>auxiliary verb</u> here to form the <u>infinitive</u> ("to see").

#15. <u>Than/then confusion</u> is also common in first-year essays. Use "<u>than</u>" for <u>comparisons</u>: "Orange juice is more nutritious <u>than</u> beer." Use "<u>then</u>" for <u>sequence</u> or <u>cause-and-effect</u>: "We went to Montreal to visit Shauna, <u>then</u> to Prague to see Katka and Uta"; "If it rains any harder, <u>then</u> the hydrofoil service on the Danube River from Budapest to Vienna will be shut down for the day."

Another example:

> The bassoon is a double-reed woodwind instrument that plays in the bass and tenor registers and is lower then all the other woodwinds. When the orchestra, as we know it, developed in the 17th century, the bassoon was one of the original two woodwinds included, along with oboes. Flutes and clarinets were than added later.

Correction

In the first sentence, "then" should be changed to "<u>than</u>" because the bassoon is <u>compared</u> to the other woodwinds. In the third sentence, "than" should be "<u>then</u>," because the sentence refers to a <u>chronology</u>, a sequence (the addition of instruments to the orchestra throughout history).

2. Revision of the Introduction

A clear, terse introduction will go a long way to helping you organize your subsequent discussion and to gaining your reader's interest and confidence. Strive to achieve both compression in your language and pointed direction in your analysis for an effective introduction. Always revise and hone your thesis statement with care as the introduction's most important sentence.

Revise the following sample introduction for conciseness, clarity, and a more chiselled thesis statement. In our revision underneath this paragraph, we offer our suggestions. Over the course of this lengthy discussion, you may wish to refer back to this sample introduction to keep track of what we are changing and how.

Sample introduction

Video lottery terminals, available to the public, pose a danger for many of the vulnerable people who are playing them. They are often located in bars, where people tend to drink and lose some of their best judgment about how to spend their money and their time. They sometimes pay out money, but over a year, what would someone who likes to play them, spend annually? Probably a lot more than you would think. The government, bars, and casinos may make money from VLT machines, but not the players, especially those who start to become addicted. Does society have a duty to intervene with new laws and regulations when people's choices harm themselves only and not really anyone else? Should society ban video lottery terminals?

Revised introduction

Video lottery terminals, ~~available to the public,~~ pose a danger for many ~~of the~~ vul- [*(VLTs)* above "terminals"]   1. conciseness/ logic

nerable people. ~~who are playing them. They~~ are often located in bars, where [*The VLTs* above "who are"]   2. unclear pronouns/ strong nouns

some people tend to ~~drink and~~ lose ~~some of~~ their best judgment about how to spend

their money and ~~their~~ time. ~~They~~ sometimes pay out money, but over a year, what [*The machines* above "their"]

would ~~someone who likes to play them,~~ spend ~~annually?~~ probably a lot more than [*a frequent user* above; *The amount would* above; *be* above]   3. conciseness/ redundancy/ sentence fragment

~~you would think~~. The government, bars, and casinos ~~may~~ make money from VLT [*the winnings* above; *certainly* above]   4. facts/logic

machines, but not the players, especially those who ~~start to~~ become addicted. Does

society have a duty to intervene with new laws and regulations when people's

choices harm themselves only ~~and not really~~ anyone else? Government obligations in [*rather than* above "and not really"]   5. more assertive thesis statement

relation to video lottery terminals are still dangerously uncertain.

#1. The paragraph's first sentence is a good opening, but can be far more concise. Some of this conciseness will come from a stricter logic in expression. Since all video lottery terminals are "available to the public" (with restrictions only according to age), we can safely delete this qualifier as unnecessary. Similarly, the "vulnerable people" for whom VLTs pose a danger must be those "who are playing them," so we can delete this qualifier as redundant, too. Certainly, other people may financially suffer from the VLT user's habit, such as his or her children, but the "vulnerable people" in the paragraph are the gambling participants.

　　All redundancies are a form of illogic. More careful thinking about the nature of the object, person, scene, or concept you wish to describe will eliminate such "doubling" in your writing and, in the process, give you greater conciseness.

　　Here is another example for conciseness as logic:

　　　The rabid dog is <u>out of its mind</u>, as it hobbles <u>uncertainly</u> and menacingly toward the chicken coop <u>where the chickens go about their normal business</u>.

Better

　　The rabid dog hobbles menacingly toward the chicken coop.

　　Since, by definition, a rabid dog *is* "out of its mind" and hobbling *means* to move "uncertainly," and chicken coops are "where the chickens go about their normal business," why waste words explaining that? Avoid the Department of Redundancy Department. And even though "rabid" already indicates "menacingly," you might argue that this adverb emphasizes— without sacrificing conciseness—the defining quality of the situation: menace.

#2. The second sentence of this unrevised introduction begins with an <u>unclear pronoun reference</u>, since "they" can refer to either "video lottery termi-nals" or "vulnerable people." The third sentence in this sample introduc-tion also begins with an unclear pronoun reference, further muddying the attempt to communicate clearly: "they" here may refer to "people" or "ma-chines," or be alternating between the two. Whenever you offer an unclear pronoun reference, you weaken the clarity of your writing. When in doubt about the certainty of your pronoun references, use a <u>noun</u>. The noun will correct the grammatical error <u>and</u> make your sentence emphatic: "The VLTs . . . The machines . . ."

Another example for unclear pronouns:

> Many people consider Buddy Guy to be an innovator in Chicago blues, one of the most exciting contemporary blues guitarists, and a strong influence on Eric Clapton and Jeff Beck. <u>He</u> apprenticed as a young musician with Muddy Waters. <u>This</u> has been acknowledged by both Jimi Hendrix and the Rolling Stones.

Better

> Many people consider Buddy Guy to be an innovator in Chicago blues, one of the most exciting contemporary blues guitarists, and a strong influence on Eric Clapton and Jeff Beck. <u>Buddy Guy</u> also apprenticed as a young musician with Muddy Waters. <u>Guy's talent</u> has been acknowledged by both Jimi Hendrix and the Rolling Stones.

"He," beginning the second sentence, is an <u>unclear pronoun reference</u>: it could refer to Buddy Guy, Eric Clapton, or Jeff Beck. "This," beginning the third sentence, is an even more <u>unclear pronoun reference</u> because a reader can only guess at the smorgasbord of choices it ambiguously refers to: that someone apprenticed with Muddy Waters? That Buddy Guy is a strong in-fluence on Clapton? On Beck? That Buddy Guy is an exciting blues musi-cian? That he is a Chicago blues innovator? All of these options? Perhaps some? Only one? Replacing "this" with "Guy's talent" settles the dizzying <u>ambiguity</u>.

#3. Again, carefully edit for wordiness and repetitions: "someone who likes to play" the VLTs is, more <u>concisely</u>, "a frequent user," while "over a year" and "annually" are <u>redundant</u>, so eliminate one or the other. The fourth sentence in the unrevised introduction is a <u>sentence fragment</u>. You can build the fragment into an independent clause, as we have done here or, if the previous independent clause is not a question, select among the options of joining the fragment to the previous independent clause with a comma, a full colon, or a dash. After attending to this sentence fragment, you may want to revise that sudden shift to the <u>second-person pronoun</u>, "you"; it is probably too informal for a college or university essay.

Another example of wordiness, repetition, and sentence fragment:

> Many reports filed by journalists who are widely respected are now pointing to the questionable and dubious lobbying influence of lots of pharmaceutical companies. Especially on the health policy in Canada, university researchers, and the health of individuals.

Better

> Many respected journalists point to the dubious lobbying influence of pharmaceutical companies on Canadian health policy, university researchers, and individual health.

Conciseness and compression will come more naturally to you if you think your way through your expression. Once you know what you want to say, you can eliminate the unnecessary qualifiers and doublings (and even sentence fragments).

#4. Some essayists try to offer their <u>speculations or opinions as solid facts</u>: "the first step in the slow death of Canadian democracy is the banning of nudity in restaurants," or "everyone knows that all the worst disco became the best hip hop without the flared pant legs." Such tactics of pushing <u>opinions</u> as indisputable <u>facts</u> can seem like simple-minded bullying rather than fair argument. In the fifth sentence of our unrevised introduction, the opposite occurs: a solid fact is wrongly presented as a speculation. Governments, bars, and casinos <u>indisputably</u> make a great deal of money from VLTs—not only "may," possibly, if all goes well, make money. Keep your facts and speculations clearly identifiable, both to avoid confusing the reader and to assure the reader that *you* know the difference between the two.

Here is another example of a fact/opinion confusion and redundancy as illogic:

> People that we know, especially parents who raised us and teachers who taught us, may die, but we will remember their words, since they spoke them to us.

Better

> People we know, especially parents and teachers, will die, but we will remember their words.

#5. The unrevised introduction's <u>thesis statement</u> appears as a question, and in fact as a question that follows a previous question. Most instructors view a volley of questions in introductions suspiciously, and for good reason. As an essayist, you must assert a view, an argument. Asking rhetorical questions may well help you *think* your way into your discussion, through your draft revisions, but bombarding the reader with questions in the final paper usually reveals that your thinking is still in a preliminary stage. You may well be only writing until you can think of some point to assert: "What is the effect of Einstein's discoveries on world religions?" "What policy most represents Jean Chrétien's Canadian vision?" "Do hamburgers offer any health benefits?" "Can we define the basic elements of jazz?" A careful <u>assertion</u> far outweighs such loose-cannon rhetorical questions, especially those acting as <u>thesis statements</u> and <u>topic sentences</u>.

Here is another example of weak questions:

Do students pay attention to grammar lessons? What is the nature of education? Is freedom from all work always better than the vigour of commitment and discipline? Should I have worn this shirt?

Better

Students will likely pay attention to grammar lessons if an announced quiz or exam follows soon after.

3. Revision of Topic Sentences

We have said elsewhere, in Chapter 4, "Essay Structure," that effective topic sentences need to hit their pages running. A good topic sentence announces the subject of its paragraph, but a very good topic sentence asserts a rationale for its position that the paragraph then explores.

Good Topic Sentence

The Tragically Hip are an exceptional band.

Better

The Tragically Hip are an exceptional band because of poetic, often surprising lyrics, rich vocal power, and energetic musicianship.

Good Topic Sentence

Canada's most famous medical discovery is insulin.

Better

Insulin, Canada's most famous medical discovery, allowed Dr. Frederick Banting to bring diabetes patients back from the edge of death in 1922.

Good Topic Sentence

Prague isn't the only historically interesting part of the Czech Republic.

Better

Prague is only one of several dozen towns with carefully preserved medieval architecture in the Czech Republic.

These stronger topic sentences have "analytical spin": they articulate the significance of their own observations. This quality is a bit tricky and may take time to incorporate into your writing habits. You can successfully produce effective topic sentences through committed revision.

First-year composition student Caren I. Jameson has written a draft essay arguing a highly unusual, controversial view: "Euthanasia should be made legal and be decided by a hospital administrator's holding of a raffle after all those patients wishing for euthanasia put their names, to be drawn at random, into a hat." Your task is to go through Caren's draft essay revising the first few sentences of each paragraph in order to refine one effective topic sentence for each paragraph. Before this work, you wisely decide to revise her thesis statement for diction and conciseness. You express her thesis effectively as follows: "Euthanasia should be legalized and administered through a raffle for all declared candidates." Now you work with the opening of her draft paragraphs, which appear as follows:

Caren's Paragraph Openings

Paragraph #1

Euthanasia is serious. No one person should ever bear such bureaucratic responsibility for decisions such as these that affect such a large number of others. The wishes of the suffering patients need to be heard and respected, however.

Paragraph #2

Who can say what's morally right? So, what authority can decide a view, one way or the other? If the patient is dying painfully, beyond the help of medicine and the comfort of family, his or her view might be the most informed view.

Paragraph #3

Life is very random. We didn't choose our parents, our genetics, our talents and often our disposition. Let me tell you about that someday. Philosophically speaking, randomness is fair because it's a neutral quality. A raffle best represents this random quality of life.

Paragraph #4

A euthanasia raffle will thus satisfy the winners. It will alleviate guilt, indecision, and responsibility in the authorities. This will also be true for administrators. A raffle will imitate the quality of life itself, which is random.

Suggested Revisions for Caren's Topic Sentences

Paragraph #1

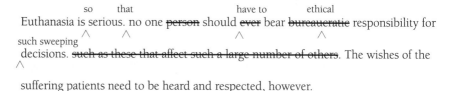

Euthanasia is serious. no one ~~person~~ should ~~ever~~ bear ~~bureaucratic~~ responsibility for such sweeping decisions. ~~such as these that affect such a large number of others.~~ The wishes of the

suffering patients need to be heard and respected, however.

Caren's unrevised topic sentence concisely states an indisputable fact, but in doing so states only the indisputably obvious, not any particular position on the topic. The revised topic sentence combines the original topic sentence and the paragraph's second sentence to assert a position *about* the seriousness of euthanasia: "so serious that . . ."

Paragraph #2

If nobody   make publicly convincing moral assertions about such a divisive topic in a pluralistic society, then

~~Who~~ can ~~say what's morally right? So,~~ what authority can ~~decide~~ a view, one way or assert   case by case,

the other? If the patient is dying painfully, beyond the help of medicine and the com-

fort of family, his or her view might be the most informed view.

Usually, offering rhetorical questions as topic sentences is a weak strategy, signalling to your reader that you are likely writing until you find something to say. If you feel, however, that your question is serious and genuinely opens up the issues in a debate, then use this technique, sparingly. Caren's revised topic sentence is still a question, and now one that names specifically some of the social implications of asserting morality as public policy.

Paragraph #3

almost entirely   since   do not

Life is ~~very~~ random, we ~~didn't~~ choose ~~our~~ parents, ~~our~~ genetics, ~~our~~ talents and often

the

~~our~~ disposition. ~~Let me tell you about that someday.~~ Philosophically speaking, ran-

of a euthanasia raffle   it is, by definition, absolutely   medical   would fairly   the essentially

domness is fair because ~~it's~~ neutral. ~~quality.~~ A raffle ~~best~~ represent ~~this~~ random qual-

ity of life.

Caren's unrevised topic sentence is too general to help further her thesis, her claim that euthanasia should be legalized and administered by a medical raffle. By the fourth sentence of her paragraph, however, Caren has written her way into an assertion that can be repositioned as a solid topic sentence. Such shuffling of sentences—a cut-and-paste reworking of your draft—is an important and sometimes surprising part of the revision process.

The other revisions to these sentences in paragraph #3 make the diction more specific and therefore the assertions clearer and stronger.

Paragraph #4

A euthanasia raffle will thus satisfy the winners. ~~It will alleviate guilt,~~ indecision~~, and~~ _{and solve} ~~responsibility~~ in the authorities. ~~This will also be true for administrators. A~~ raffle ~~will~~ _{The} imitate the quality of life itself~~, which is random.~~ _{'s accurately random}

Caren's fourth paragraph, which is her conclusion, can best be revised for conciseness and compression. The revised topic sentence can assert tersely the alleged benefits of a euthanasia raffle to both patients and administrators.

Since the essay's topic is extremely controversial—and Caren's argument for a medical raffle highly unusual, perhaps insupportable in a humane society—her conclusion should steer clear of whatever ethical dimensions the essay has not satisfactorily addressed. The euthanasia raffle will not "alleviate guilt," for example, because only those patients, families, doctors, and administrators already in favour of euthanasia would endorse such an idea as a medical raffle. So, logically, we can ask what guilt is alleviated? As well, medical and legal administrators will not be freed from "responsibility" merely because a raffle operates on a principle of randomness.

Remember to ensure that your conclusion doesn't attempt to take credit for more than you have argued. Also keep in mind that for all arguments, especially controversial ones, there will be opposing views. Many readers may be fully prepared to argue against your position, so argue as carefully and convincingly as you can. A further counter-argument to Caren's position on the administration of euthanasia through a raffle, which she justifies by citing the principle of randomness in life itself, might be the response that our public organizations and policies exist to alleviate the effects of randomness, not enforce them.

4. Revision of the Conclusion

We discuss conclusions on page 319 of the *Rhetoric*. Whether you or your instructor wishes your paper to end with a *suggestive* or *exhaustive* conclusion is an important point to discuss before you hand in the paper for grading. In either case, your conclusion needs to signal that the essay has come to an effective and satisfactory end. Presumably, you have built a case for your view and are ready to close the discussion.

Three tips can help you revise a draft conclusion:

A.   Try to avoid repeating your thesis in exactly the same words. Be more resourceful. Your reader will already know your thesis if you have stated it clearly in your introduction and have developed focused topic sentences to guide your body paragraphs.

If you have written an essay arguing that Don Cherry unfortunately functions in Canadian culture more as an entertaining buffoon than as a seasoned ex-player, experienced coach, sports historian, and respected strategist, then your thesis statement might appear as something like this: "Cherry's clownish presence and loud-mouth ranting degrade a sport that, to some people, is a form of culture."

Your conclusion should either pursue a final implication of this view of Don Cherry *or* completely rephrase this assertion, probably taking some of the essay's overall discussion into account. Here are sentences from possible conclusions.

Weak (repetitive)

Therefore, Cherry's clownish antics and loud rants do nothing but degrade a winter sport that some Canadians see as a form of culture.

Revised (exhaustive)

Cherry's self-presentation, though mildly entertaining, finally hurts the image of a world sport that has successfully outgrown a shouting bully.

Revised (suggestive)

A final implication of Cherry's regularly scheduled rants is that young players, especially children, may think that hockey continues to be a sport that embraces its lowest common denominator, dim-witted aggression, instead of its highest levels of controlled speed, masterful timing, passing and defensive skills, and shooting accuracy.

B.   Avoid adding such startling new information that you, in effect, set up a new body paragraph. New information, new implications, or new dimensions in your argument can be introduced, but only with care. The result will be a *suggestive* conclusion: it must still remember and clearly relate to the thesis of the essay.

Let us say you are completing an essay on the representation of romance in the music of Johnny Cash. Let us say you have argued that Cash, unlike many singers (except, for example, for Sinead O'Connor, The Eagles, and Barry White), contends that romance and love require great personal responsibility. Some possible conclusions might unfold as follows:

Weak conclusion (because of startling new information)

Johnny Cash also recorded a cover of Bob Dylan's "It Ain't Me, Babe." Cash's version, slower, vocally deeper, reveals more ethical and emotional dimensions within a failing relationship than even Dylan's original recording, which seems to skim along on lighter romantic and courtship differences.

Revised conclusion

Cash's work always presents romantic love as the serious endeavour of life, not escapism from it. He treats love as an ethical expression throughout his music. Cash's work, including [a song or songs you have mentioned in your essay], quietly reflects the multiple, demanding dimensions of deep love that most popular music often superficially misrepresents.

This revised conclusion economically addresses, though it may resourcefully restate, your essay's earlier discussion. The weaker conclusion does not attempt to resolve the issues of its discussion but instead acts as a brand new body paragraph. Though interesting, it does not signal and summarize any ending or implication. Remember that your conclusion must perform its primary function: to resolve the preceding discussion.

C. Avoid overstating the scope and significance of your earlier discussion. Many students panic as they conclude, and they offer sweeping claims when they could finish their essays nicely with controlled understated summaries. If your conclusion claims more than the arguments have, your writing—your evaluation and your sense of things—will appear unreliable or, worse, reveal that you think your reader is gullible.

Revise the following draft conclusion, keeping in mind some of the revision strategies we have discussed:

Sample conclusion

To conclude, self-employment is thus far more difficult and riskier than one would think sometimes. The problem of small resources makes competition with corporations tough. A new study claims governments do not take individual small business seriously until after five years. Making and maintaining business networks is also difficult, since most of your time is usually spent completing what work or contracts you have already. Even the problems of insurance and benefits are worrisome. Therefore, despite a self-employed person's being his or her own boss and taking lunch breaks whenever, there are reasons why 70 percent of first-year businesses fail and many people falsify tax claims and don't give much time or money to charities anymore.

Revised conclusion

Be concise

~~To conclude~~, Self-employment is thus far more difficult and riskier than one would think ~~sometimes~~. ~~The problem of~~ Small resources makes competition

Usually, avoid new, distracting information

with corporations ~~tough~~ [difficult]. ~~A new study claims governments do not take individual small business seriously until after five years.~~ Making and maintaining busi-

Compound subjects require plural verb forms

ness networks ~~is~~ [are] also difficult, since ~~most of your~~ [contacts] time is usually spent completing ~~what~~ work or contracts ~~you have already~~ [under way]. Even the problems of in-

Usually, use precise, summarizing diction rather than distracting description of an episode

surance and benefits are worrisome. Therefore, despite ~~a~~ self-employ~~ed person's~~ [the attractive independence of] [ment]

Avoid last-minute assertions not earned in your discussion

~~being his or her own boss and taking lunch breaks whenever~~, there are reasons why 70 percent of first-year businesses fail. ~~and~~ Many [of these failures are linked to the obstacles facing self-employment.] ~~people falsify tax claims and don't give much time or money to charities anymore.~~

5. Revision for Conciseness

Conciseness is a form of beauty, yet few people are spontaneously concise writers. Conciseness is sometimes even difficult to achieve in subsequent drafts of a paper. You can accomplish this conciseness after you return to your writing with a stronger sense of what you are trying to express; economy of expression will match clarity of concept. Conciseness also requires a little editorial perspiration, some sweat in the compression of your expression! Once you have your draft—have worked towards some observations, assertions, implications, paragraph form—you will be surprised to reread and see how much more economical you can be with words.

A. Revise the following passage for conciseness, spontaneously co-composed in a brief inkshedding session by two first-year students, Helen Allingham and Otto Graph:

Original paragraph

In terms of the very many persistent concerns about the question of our ongoing water safety after the frightening scare over health in the Canadian town of Walkerton, Ontario, many people, including all Canadians, need to start to consider the many facts about all this. The expectations that we have formed that our water will always be safe and hazard-free for us to drink are indicative of how we tend to rely far too much on the bureaucratic assurances that are given to us by people who work in the government agency. Like our other natural resources, water is a valuable resource that we cannot take for granted or fail to consider in the context of supply.

Revised version

~~In terms of the very many persistent concerns about the question of our ongo-~~

[crisis] ~~ing water safety~~ After the ~~frightening scare over~~ health in ~~the Canadian town of~~

Walkerton, Ontario, ~~many people, including~~ all Canadians~~,~~ need ~~to start~~ to con-

[ongoing water safety] [Our] sider the ~~many~~ facts about ~~all this~~. ~~The~~ expectations ~~that we have formed~~ that

~~our~~ water will always be safe ~~and hazard-free for us~~ to drink ~~are indicative of~~ [indicate]

how we ~~tend to~~ rely ~~far too much~~ on ~~the~~ bureaucratic, assurances. [dangerously] [not scientific,] ~~that are given~~

~~to us by people who work in the government agency.~~ [Water,] like our other natural re-

sources, ~~water is a valuable resource that we~~ cannot [be] taken for granted ~~or fail to~~

~~consider in the context of~~ [as an undepletable or self-sustaining] supply.

Conciseness requires your elimination of unnecessary words and phrases. Delete clunky phrases such as "in terms of," "about the question of," "are indicative of," and "to consider in the context of," which clutter up your sentences, your potentially terse and crisp expression.

Remember that much redundancy also results from a hasty disregard for logic. Slowly reread and reconsider your work, asking yourself simply and sternly, what "things" are, in and of themselves? Since "bureaucratic assurances" in our sample paragraph must be, by definition, "given to us by people who work in the government agency," you can easily eliminate this "doubling" of expression by recognizing that the term "bureaucratic assurances" conveys your meaning already. Similarly, if you say, as in our paragraph, that water is "a valuable resource," then, by definition "we cannot take for granted or fail to consider" its importance: calling water a "valuable resource" is fine by itself, and you can delete the unnecessary restatement of what that means.

B.   Revise the following interesting (but wordy) assertions appearing as part of a first draft by British exchange student Patsy Kensit-Murphy for a community affairs paper entitled "There's No McDonald's in Camden Town."

McDonald's is continuing to enjoy its great degree of success in fast-food products on a scale that could be accurately described as global. But why, given that more and more people are continuing to become vegetarians or at least are concerned to some extent about their nutrition, veggie intake, and cholesterol, why does such a company prosper? Firstly, to begin, a lot of their business success seems to be relying on the use of their slick, but merely image-driven advertisements: it's strange that there is little talk in these beautiful ads of factual nutritional wholesomeness, considering how McDonald's sells food for families and young people. Secondly, the price the company charges is always right. If a customer is worried about today's prices (like I am), McDonald's prices are appealing to customers. But what if the final outcome is that the deliberate lies of many promises in media join together with the appealing incentive of low price to make people forget their best interests?

Revised version

McDonald's ~~is~~ continu~~ing~~**es** to enjoy its ~~great degree of~~ success in fast-food. ~~products on a scale that could be accurately described as~~ **global**. But why, ~~given that~~ ~~more and more~~ **if** people ~~are~~ continu~~ing~~**e** to become vegetarians or ~~at least are~~ con-**to** cerned ~~to some extent about their~~ **themselves with** nutrition, veggie intake, and cholesterol, ~~why~~ does such a company prosper? First~~ly, to begin, a lot of their business~~ success **McDonald's** ~~seems to be~~ rel~~ying~~**ies** on ~~the use of their~~ slick, ~~but merely~~ image-driven advertise-ments: ~~it's strange that there is little talk in~~ **curiously,** these beautiful ads ~~of factual~~ **often neglect the facts of** nutrition~~al wholesomeness, considering how~~ **although** McDonald's sells food ~~and~~ **specifically** for families and young people. Secondly, the price ~~the company charges~~ **accounting for widespread success,** is always right. If a customer ~~is~~ worrie**d** about ~~today's prices (like I am)~~ **money,** McDonald's prices ~~are~~ appeal~~ing. to customers~~. But what if ~~the final outcome is that the deliberate lies~~ ~~of many~~ promises ~~in media~~ **misleading media** join ~~together~~ with the ~~appealing~~ incentive of low price to make people forget their ~~past experience~~ **best interests**?

In revising Patsy's draft for conciseness, we have <u>conjugated verbs</u> (so "is continuing" becomes "continues," "seems to be relying" becomes "relies," etc.).

We have also <u>eliminated redundancies</u> in phrasing ("Firstly, to begin" becomes "First," "joins together" becomes "join," and "appealing incentives" becomes "incentive," etc.).

With Special Attention to Fifteen Common Errors

When asked to argue for or against today's level of salaries for professional athletes, Stewart Thompson decided to hone his argumentative skills by writing two essays— one for and one against. As he reports, and as the following two essays demonstrate, this old-fashioned exercise in debating allowed him to appreciate the complexity of the issues, the worthiness of the views from various sides. His main focus in these two preliminary drafts was on organizing lines of reason. Like many students, he preferred to build his arguments first and leave matters of grammar and punctuation to subsequent revision. Included on the following drafts are comments an instructor or a peer editor might make to signal the sorts of mechanical issues that need attention now that Stewart has established the basic position. Numbers in the margins correspond to the "Fifteen Common Errors" checklist on the inside cover of this book. "LF" followed by a number signals an item from the list of "Twelve Logical Fallacies." You will see that the annotator also raises occasional matters in addition to the list of "Fifteen Common Errors" and covered in other sections of the *Handbook*. The annotations and the concluding summary comments are typical of those your instructor might use on your own essays. Such "nit-picking" observations are not meant to undermine the very good thinking, structuring, and style that have gone into the essays—these comments do, however, direct attention to mechanical considerations of utmost importance in the final revision stages. Words inserted by the editor are marked by a wave underscore.

Sample Student Essay   With Instructor's Revisions

<u>Sports Salaries: No Cap Needed</u> ——————— No underlining of
Stewart Thompson   your own title—see
                                                    MLA Style
A recent strike by professional baseball players and lockout of the professional basket- — CE: 3
ball players has have caused the issue of professional athletes and their salaries to   "of controversy" is
become a hot topic of controversy. The scope of professional sports has grown to an   redundant
                                                                                             mixed metaphor (a
enormous level, and the salary of sports players has sky rocketed. North America is   scope that grows/)
enjoying a state of prosperity, and the salary demands by pro athletes is are directly proportional to factors such as money invested in sports, attendance levels, and ticket   one word
prices. Professional sports have has become bigger and better in the twenty-first century,   CE: 3
but the salaries have come under fire by some of the very fans who attend the sport-   wordy
ing events. While some critics portray pro athletes as overpaid, spoiled men crying

Good thesis statement, but why first person

about not making enough money, I shall show in this essay that these people deserve the salaries they are asking for and there is enough money to meet their demands; thus, there should be no salary cap in professional sports.

LF 4

CE: 13

Professional athletes' demands for salary are reasonable for the services they provide. The abilities, talents, and physical attributes it takes to become a professional athlete are few and far between. The outstanding strength and skill of these men are utilized to perform daily for the enjoyment of the fans. These men's lives' are completely dictated by the sport they play. They are forced into a strict diet, hours of weight lifting, and endless nights of practice. This amount of commitment and the en-

CE: 3

tertainment brought about by these men's efforts demand demands the level of compensation for which these players have asked. If one were to compare these men to other celebrity figures of similar popularity, one would find a discrepancy. The average

CE: 3

LF: 4

Hollywood star makes more than any of these players, and the amount of work they put into their jobs pale pales in comparison. Oprah Winfrey has made more than $200 million a year and Tom Cruise over $80 million (Eskin). As one can see, people of such stature as pro athletes deserve the salaries they are requesting.

The money asked for by these players and limited by the salary cap is more available than one may know. The amount of money invested in sports by outside sponsors is on the rise yearly. Coca Cola and Nike have poured enormous amounts of money into professional sports. The owners reap this money along with ticket sales

CE:15

Wrong word— "rising"

and merchandise and then cut the cheques which pay the players' salaries. With ticket sales raising rising as quickly as endorsements, the pool of money the owners can draw from has grown again. Fans this year [i.e., 1998] were paying $60 for standing room only

"Standing-room": compound adjectives before a noun are hyphenated.

tickets at what could have been Michael Jordan's last game (Purist). Merchandising is another giant money-making machine for the owners. Between jackets, hats, T-shirts, book bags, and lunchboxes, the owners stand to make a great deal of money yearly off merchandise. The money for the salaries is there, and there is no cap on how

CE: 8 C

much the owners can make. It would be unfair to cap the players' salaries.

CE: 3/CE: 14: "solutions" is the subject

There has have been presented many solutions to the salary problems in professional sports. A merit system has been proposed wherein the players play on one-year contracts and at the end of the year are assessed, paid based on performance, and re-signed or

CE: 4

traded. This way each player is paid for what they are worth that year because of the level of play they exhibited the year before. Another solution that has been more readily implemented is the salary cap. This is the practice of limiting the amount an owner can pay a player, or the amount the owner can pay his team in general. There is a fixed amount assigned to each team stating the maximum amount of money one can spend on any certain player, and on the team after totalling all the salaries. This is intended to make the teams more evenly matched and the salary demands of players lower.

Hyphens for compound adjectives before a noun

The merit system is already in effect but not to the extent of a year to year re-evaluation. Players are, however, re-evaluated when their contracts run out and they are signed or traded due to their previous performance. The signing is the only form of job security ~~that exists~~ for these players. With the high risk involved in professional sports, multiple-year contracts are depended upon by these athletes. Yearly assessment of a player would be unfair because of slumps, injuries, and other unpredictable happenstance. The long-term contract is important to provide that sense of job security all but absent in professional sports.

> wordy
> hyphen: do you see why?

The salary cap is still the most widely used form of salary oppression of pro athletes. The cap ~~serves to stunt~~ stunts players' salaries and limits their ability to sign with a team that has many high-priced players. Such a cap does not exist for any other job but professional sports. The owners and commissioners have taken it upon themselves to decide the most a player could ever be worth. A salary should be something awarded to someone for their effort, not assigned by a limit set for all devoid of individual consideration. This system also limits the players, who will try harder and improve. When one has topped out his salary, what would be the incentive to continue to improve.? This hurts the sport now, for once a standard is set for the top salary, there will no longer be the need for such heated competition as displayed currently in pro sport.

> LF: 11
> wordy: "stunts"
> LF: 4
>
> CE: 4 (. . . to people for their . . .)
>
> Repetitious (however, a question mark is called for on "improve"

~~The dismay at the~~ The amount many professional sports players receive has ~~plagued~~ dismayed newspapers, magazines, and television. Most people agree that pro players should be compensated for their work, just the level of compensation has been an issue of much debate. These men do make more than the average twenty- to forty-year-old man, but the service they provide is way above average. Many of the critics of players salaries have called for the merit system or a strict salary cap. Were the tables turned, however, how many of these critics would want their salaries capped? The investment professional athletes have made in their job ~~call~~ calls for a higher level of compensation.

> Previously you have been using the plural
> Wordy
> Overstated
> CE: 2
>
> CE: 13 (players')
> LF: 12, LF: 2

The hard work and sacrifice of pro players ~~demands~~ demand a salary that will always draw attention. These salaries have been and will continue to be easily supplied by the abundant pool of money provided by sponsors, ticket sales, and T-shirts. A merit system or a salary cap is no way to reward these players after they have reached the top of their game. These are unmitigated forms of punishment for succeeding in their occupation. Therefore, such treatment is unfair and unprecedented, and the fans should agree that there should be no salary cap in professional sports.

> CE: 3
>
> LF: 11

Works Cited

Market Forces Determine Athletes' Salaries. 10 Aug. 1998. Jim Eskin. 12 Oct. 1998.
    <http://dallas.bizjournals.com/dallas/stories/1998/08/10/editorial2.html>.
Nonsense on Salaries. 24 Sep. 1998. The Purist. 12 Oct. 1998.<http://www.esportsmediagroup.com/
    e-sports/articles/1,1090,46—1326—1-2,00.html>.

> Incorrect MLA style; did you download this in case it disappears?
>
> Incorrect MLA style; author/editor?; description of source?; did you download this in case it disappears?

Essay comments

Your essay provides good context in the introduction (the recent baseball strike), and you conclude a well-written introduction with a solid thesis statement. You could be more concise, however. The paragraphs are clearly focused and effectively ordered, with the stronger arguments coming later. You conclude effectively. Be sure to explain and support your points a little more sufficiently. For instance, demonstrate why the service provided by athletes is above average. Consider valid counter-arguments, such as the merits of other members of society, those who are more than entertainers—what many consider athletes to be. Recurrent use of "men" to describe all athletes and owners in our society exhibits gender-biased language; it is a serious oversimplification (LF 4). Watch oversimplification in other places as well.

Writing mechanics need attention, as noted. The most common error is in subject-verb agreement. Other errors include shifts of number and person between pronoun and antecedent; a comma splice; misused apostrophe; ineffective use of passive voice; and wordy phrasing. Please note the use of hyphens for compound adjectives, as well as several formatting corrections required in the Works Cited. See MLA guidelines in Chapter 12 "Documentation," to make the necessary revisions to form and to complete your documentation.

Once you have had a chance to review the noted errors in conjunction with the list of "Fifteen Common Errors" in the *Handbook* and "Twelve Logical Fallacies" in Chapter 7, please ask any questions for clarification of the principles involved. This is a promising, well-structured argument using very good paragraph form; your correction of the numerous mechanical errors will result in solid work.

Sample Student Essay   With Instructor's Revisions

Sports Salaries: Enough Is Enough
Stewart Thompson

CE: 13 / CE: 13

Over the last century professional sport has become one of the most popular forms of entertainment. It's nickname "Americas Pastime" has become embedded in the hearts of the fans. In major league baseball alone more than sixty million fans attended games in 1997. Nonetheless, America's love affair with sports is not without controversy. One of the leading arguments is the salaries of these professional athletes, do athletes make too much money? There are numerous aspects to this question. Let's concentrate on whether the owners are paying the players what they are worth. Then you have to ask yourself, if the owners are overpaying players, are we the fans responsible for this action?

CE: 2 (. . . athletes. Do . . .)

Clear focus on your thesis through a rhetorical question. Good. But LF: 1?

These "demands" have not been referred to previously, so a specific allusion is not being made

The amount of money that many of these professional athletes receive has overwhelmed the media, and, most of all, the fans. Many people feel that professional athletes should be compensated for their hard work and sacrifices. After all, professional athletes are receiving a salary based on the market demands. Granted these individuals make more than the average twenty-to-forty-year-old individual, but the entertainment value they provide is far superior to that of the average person's abilities. Despite this, people are ~~screaming~~ calling for a salary cap or some type of merit system for salaries. Seriously, can one athlete spend $33 million dollars a year?

Whose fault is it that these athletes make ~~these~~ huge salaries? According to Chris Butterfield, it's the fans' fault. I agree that it's our fault. We the fans will go to these sporting events and shell out the $75 per ticket, $100 for the jacket, $20 for the hats of our favourite team. We support the professional teams and, in turn, the players. One reason for the rise in ticket prices is the constant demands for our favourite stars. Therefore owners must raise prices to bring the customers what they desire. If we stopped attending these games, buying the merchandise and ~~not~~ watching the television, salaries would begin to decline. The owners would have no choice. The skilled athletes are not going to be paid the multi million dollar contract if the money isn't there.

Since Michael Jordan is arguably the most famous and highest paid professional athlete in all of sports, we will concentrate on him. According to Marshall Burrow, Michael Jordan made an amazing 33 million dollars a year, not to mention ~~the~~ a lucrative 40 million a year in endorsements. Burrow even goes so far as to break this salary down to the day. Michael Jordan makes $170,000 a day! Is anyone, much less an athlete, worth $170,000 a day? Jordan's salary is not a true reflection of his value to society. The president of the United States only makes a modest $250,000 a year. Yet this athlete ~~nearly~~ brings nearly this amount home every day. Here are a few more quick facts on Jordan's salary for fun, he made $300,000 per game in his last season. Assuming he played about 30 minutes per game, this works out to $10,000 a minute. Jordan would make approximately $52,000 every night that he slept for seven hours.

It was only a matter of time before other athletes got in on the action of demanding unreal salaries. On December 12, 1998, Kevin Brown signed a seven year contract with the Los Angeles Dodgers baseball team worth $105 million dollars. As if this was not enough, the gifted pitcher will have use of the team's private plane to fly home from Los Angeles to Macon, Georgia 12 times per year according to ESPN.com. Peter Euler points out in his story ("Athletes Salaries Becoming Outrageous") that "Athletes should all take a look at the 1997 Pittsburgh Pirates. They were a bunch of average players whose salary was less than Albert Belle's personal salary; yet they were in the hunt for a playoff spot midway through the final week of the season, while Belle's White Sox were not."

This alone proves that you do not need to spend outrageous amounts of money to give the fans a competitive and successful team. Euler goes on to say that "greed destroys sports," and he is right.

In closing, not only are these athletes making too much money, but their greed is ruining ~~the nature of~~ sports. In a society in which salary and wages are traditionally

---

Margin annotations:

"Calling." "Screaming" has a pejorative connotation that works against your transition to the side you wish to support

The "not" is an element of mixed construction

Hyphenate compound adjective before a noun (multi-million-dollar)

You haven't referred to it before. "The" points to something specific and known

CE: 6 (makes only . . .)

CE: 2 A colon would work here

Hyphenate compound adjective before a noun (seven-year)

CE: 8 A

Write out numbers up to and including twelve

wordy

based on the value of one's work, we the fans must make an intelligent decision on what dollar value we should place on this type of entertainment. In my opinion these athletes are not working. They don't have routine nine-to-five day jobs, they don't make life and death decisions as a nurse or a paramedic has to. No one person is worth 15, 20, or 30 million dollars a year, much less an athlete. They are being paid these limitless amounts to play a game they love and treasure, and the salary they make is not reflective of their contributions to society. America's Pastime has become America's playground for the rich and famous.

Essay comments

Your essay demonstrates an effective introduction, body structure, and conclusion. The Michael Jordan example is particularly effective, thanks to the careful detail and use of vivid equivalents. This draft cannot be considered complete, however, until you include your sources, both as in-text citations and in the necessary Works Cited section at the end. See Chapter 12, "Documentation," for guidance in acknowledging and listing sources according to MLA style. You might also wish to consider whether Butterfield's thesis is something of LF: 1.

Once you have had a chance to review the noted errors in conjunction with the list of "Fifteen Common Errors" in the *Handbook* and the list of "Twelve Logical Fallacies" in Chapter 7, please ask any questions for clarification of the principles involved. Your style is clear and vivid, but work on correcting such glaring errors as comma splices. In the *Handbook* see "Articles (Determiners)" (p. 545), an aspect that raises questions for all of us, regardless of whether English is our first language. When the mechanics of this paper are revised to equal the quality of its argument and examples (and when the sources are included), you will have a strong essay.

PEER EDITING

You have probably experienced first-hand or heard that the best way to learn something is to try to teach it. Reviewing and commenting on the writing of your peers may not be exactly like teaching, but there are important similarities between the two tasks. As peer editor, you assume the role of encouraging and motivating someone's efforts, of acknowledging strong points and promise while constructively pointing out areas for improvement. You do not have to be a stronger writer than the person whose work you are editing: any professional writer will tell you that *all* writers need editorial review. Writers already know, or think they know, what they intend to say, so it is harder for them than for a detached reader/editor to recognize whether or not they have said it clearly. Good peer editing requires thoughtful reading, not always superlative writing skills. Your role in helping peer writers to assess and improve their work provides invaluable assistance to them, while also furthering your own appreciation of the art of composition.

Here are some tips to guide your comments as a peer editor:

- Begin with a sincere positive response to the work as a whole, concentrating on main features while at the same time recognizing its strong and weak notable details.
- While commenting on grammar, punctuation, and other aspects of language usage, concentrate mainly on the fundamentals of stance (clarity of purpose, intended audience, effectiveness of voice, structure, and supporting details).
- Consider relating your comments to three major areas: content, organization, and language style and mechanics. Move from content through organization to mechanics and style.
- Look for an effective thesis and topic sentences that assert a perspective, not only a fact.
- Look for effective transitions and modifiers within and between both the structure and the ideas of paragraphs.
- Look for effective introductions and conclusions (are they concise and pointed?).
- Consider the value of phrasing some of your suggestions as questions. Sometimes you may not be sure if a certain technique or new element of approach will work, but the writer might consider the idea worth trying.
- Offer comments about language usage and sentence mechanics after commenting on content and structure. Mention specific points of grammar if you can, such as comma splices, dangling participles, and subject-verb agreement.
- To help formulate your comments, refer to the "Checklist of Steps to a Successful Essay" on the inside back cover and to "Twelve Logical Fallacies" and "Fifteen Common Errors" on the inside front cover of this book. If the writing is a summary or a research paper, refer to Steps to a Successful Summary" in Chapter 8, "The Summary," (p. 398) or the "Checklist of Steps to a Successful Research Paper" in Chapter 11, "The Research Paper" (p. 449).
- Control your responses—too much feedback may swamp the writer. Four, five, or six precise sentences may be sufficient, depending on the length of the work under scrutiny. (In the first example, below, the peer editor "caught fire" and wrote two longish paragraphs, but notice that the tone of these suggested improvements remains constructive.)
- End by reinforcing the peer writer's attempts overall, despite the weaknesses.

Read the following first-draft, introductory paragraph by student Christina Angaran, who has underlined her provisional topic sentence. You don't want to overload the writer with too many comments; often it is best to find just one main area for recommended improvement. After you have done this, read the peer editor responses following the paragraph.

Sample Student Paragraph   Find One Area for Improvement

An Ideal Vacation Spot

When I was young I dreamt like every child did about far-away lands. Of course, children had their own ideal place, and I was no different. I would dream about a place that was warm all of the time, and when it rained, the water would feel like bath water on your skin. The place would be quiet with enough tourists to make it interesting. The people in this place would be warm and friendly. You would meet the local people and become friends, calling them by name as you would pass them on the street. There would be no crime, and the doors to people's houses would be open for all to come and visit. Staying out late would be welcomed because most people would sit on their porches, have lemonade and chat with their neighbours; meanwhile, their children would play ball on the street or play a game of hide-and-go-seek. Since the sea or ocean would back onto your hotel room or yard, you would wake up as early as possible every morning to take a dip in the water that would be waiting just for you. Then at the end of the day when dusk would fall, you would take another plunge into that warm, blue and inviting water. It wouldn't matter that you would wake up early and go to bed late, because in a place like this you would want to savour every day.

Sample peer editor comments (focus on organization)

Christina, I find this a very engaging, extremely well-written paragraph, developed around an imaginative topic with lots of universal appeal (we have all been children and have all had similar dreams). Your description is beautiful; this creates a strong dominant impression and elaborates your dream-place through good specific details. But could organization of these details be rearranged? I can see why you present the underlined sentence as your thesis sentence, because everything you have described is something great in this special place. When I go through the points in the paragraph, I find you have an order of aspects to savour: (1) warm, (2) quiet yet stimulating, (3) friendly, (4) safe, (5) beautifully inviting (with the sea to swim in, from dawn to dusk). Would it intensify the central impression of all this cool ocean beauty to begin with the morning swim, then cover the other features before moving on to the people (friendly, safe, available all day and evening), and then conclude with the evening swim? In other words, would a chronological scheme work here to develop a sense of place? I'm also wondering if your thesis sentence could become what our textbook calls a *direct list*. Also, maybe it's just me, but I feel some kind of really big idealized quality from this description. It so obviously contrasts with most people's "real life." Could you later add a sentence that makes that big feeling of contrast more explicit? What's up with this dream?

Some work is needed on mechanical improvements. The transition from first- to second-person seems a little distracting. I realize you probably use "you" to include the reader in this big, universal child's fantasy, so do you really want to start with the more personal "I"? What about "me"?? The reader wonders why the shift occurs, though you may have your own strategy here. Another questionable element is your use of conditional tense. While you reinforce the unreal aspect of the fantasy, I wonder if it compromises the writing's energy. Could your opening sentences be changed (to avoid too many "woulds")? How about this: "When I was young I dreamt, like every child, did about far-away ~~lands~~. (Of course, children ~~had~~ have their own ideal place, and I was no different.) In particular, I ~~would dream~~ dreamt about ~~a~~ this special place ~~that was~~ by the ocean, a place of permanent warmth and peace, of friendly people sharing their joy all day long. My special place is so warm that when it rains . . ." Maybe our instructor will disagree with my idea for shifting tense here (from "dreamt" to "is"), but I just wanted to raise the idea of playing with a move into the present tense, as if the writer and reader have become so caught up in the fantasy that it takes over, like childhood is immediate again. Would that add to a strong effect when we return to awareness that this is a temporary dream?

My only other question is about the word "vacation" in the title. I wasn't sure if this prepared me for a child's dream. Anyway, as you can tell, I think this work has a very strong evocative power. I'll be really interested to know how much these comments are of use to you.

Read the following first-draft paragraph by student writer Christina Angaran. You don't want to overload the writer with too many comments; often it is best to find just one main area for recommended improvement. After you have done this, read the peer editor responses following the paragraph.

Sample Student Paragraph   Find One Area for Improvement

Friendship

When we were young, anyone who was our age and played with us was considered a friend; however, as we age our definition of friendship becomes much more complicated. Personally, I am very demanding of a friend just as I would that he or she was demanding of me. I believe that the expression "mia casa è sua casa" explains it all; my house should be their house and vice versa. A friend is also a person that you can sit quietly with, because at times sitting silently together is worth more than talking to pass time or to fill an awkward moment. It's wonderful to know someone with whom you can share all of your thoughts, interests, and concerns with, without feeling that they're judging you because they respect you. A friend shouldn't be someone who is always polite; indeed, they should be able to tell you when you make mistakes and then be there for you without making you feel bad. Friends argue from time to time, but what separates them from everyone else is that they don't take everything personally. You work together to resolve your argument, because your friendship is much more important than a petty disagreement, whose cause isn't remembered in the end. My mother told me when I was young that friends are hard to come by, and I would be very fortunate to have only one friend in my life. Now that I'm older I realize that my mother was right.

Sample peer editor comments (focus on grammar and punctuation)

Christina, I think this is a very focused paragraph, offering a meaningful definition. The topic sentence works for me: it sets up the further explanations and examples that follow. Sentences seem to flow smoothly and logically. I really like your use of the Italian "my house is your house." I guess that's a good case of the writer's voice and experience enriching the general topic. The paragraph is cinched by an effective concluding sentence. All I can really nitpick in this one is English usage, so here goes:

> "Personally, I am very demanding of a friend just as I would that he or she was be demanding of me."

My mother tells me that the subjunctive mood is called for here. I looked this up in her old copy of the Prentice Hall Handbook for Writers. I'm not sure I can explain this yet, but it's also described on the Web if you search in Google.

> "It's wonderful to know ~~someone~~ people with whom you can share all of your thoughts, interests, and concerns with, without feeling that they're judging you, because they respect you."

I checked with Mr. Timms, and he says that without the comma before the concluding subordinate clause, it could seem like you are saying that they judge you because they respect you. You really mean the opposite, so if you use the comma, the clause refers more broadly to why you can share things with these people. I guess "someone" is considered singular, so you aren't supposed to go on and use "they" for someone. Mr. Timms suggested making "someone" into a plural, "people."

> "~~A friend~~ Friends shouldn't be ~~someone~~ people who ~~is~~ are always polite; indeed, they should . . . ."

Same thing again.

> ". . . they don't take everything personally. ~~You~~ They work together to resolve ~~your~~ their argument, because your friendship is much more important than . . . ."

Again, that thing about keeping pronoun person consistent.

That's it—I really wish my paragraphs were as smooth and coherent as this one.

Multiple Peer Editors

Professional writers may value one "pet" editor, but most of them also like to have their work reviewed by more than one reader. This is because multiple reviewers will help to separate genuine concerns from just one person's idea. If two, three, or more people make the same suggestion, chances are the writer should consider what they say. If only one person of several suggests a change, maybe the suggested change won't make a significant improvement for the majority of readers. Try to get as many thoughtful reviews of each piece of writing as you can.

THE
RHETORIC

Section 5

Oral Presentations

Chapter 14
The Oral Presentation

Many of us today face the task of writing and delivering oral presentations. These may take the form of student seminars, business meetings, or addresses at community, political or family gatherings.

Through this text you have many ideas for organizing your thoughts into essays that flow well and clearly communicate your intentions to a reading audience. In many ways, writing for public speaking is similar. You still need to know your audience and to structure your speech around a direct-list thesis statement containing a manageable number of points. You need an introduction, a conclusion, and smooth transitions. There are several important structural and rhetorical differences, however. One central difference in the writing of a speech, of course, is the physical aspect of preparation and presentation.

When you write a speech, always keep in mind that the audience will be listening to the **rhythms** and **enunciations of a voice**, not reading text. Your audience cannot go back and check words or ideas that they have trouble grasping. Although an oral presentation places special burdens on you as an author, you can help your listeners in a number of ways.

1. First, **use informal conversational language** that is appropriate to your purpose and to your audience. Use terminology that is familiar to that group. For instance, if you are addressing a group of horse owners, it would be appropriate to refer to centering the pommel of the saddle over the withers. A group of novice riders would be confused and eventually alienated by these terms if you continued your speech without explaining them. Use short sentences. Sentence fragments are acceptable in oral speech, and can be used to great effect.

2. **Emphasize colourful, concrete language.** Your audience will remember word pictures more easily than extended abstract ideas. Use your word pictures to give vitality to your concepts.

3. Use **repetition** and **internal summaries** to remind your audience of points you have made and those you are going to make. Make sure that you have included concise internal summaries sufficient for a *listening* audience to make the connections between your main points and between these main points and the overall thesis.

4. In most cases, you will want to **state your thesis clearly** in the introduction and again in the conclusion.
5. A speech has no footnotes so, for ethical reasons, **cite sources of information and quotations** as you speak. Vary the ways you introduce your quoted material: "One expert, Susan Smith, contends that . . . ," "As Peter Smith points out, . . ." and "According to Melanie Smith, . . ." Such variety will keep your listeners alert to the sometimes multiple voices in your presentation.

Simple, concrete language, internal summaries, and short, uncluttered sentences will help to give your points impact for the listening audience.

MODES OF ORAL PRESENTATION

The four modes of oral presentation are

- extemporaneous,
- manuscript,
- memorized, and
- impromptu.

Each of these modes is useful in certain situations, although the extemporaneous approach is generally the most effective.

Extemporaneous Presentations

In the extemporaneous mode, you speak with only key words and phrases written on file cards to remind you of your main points. This approach allows you to maintain eye contact with your audience and move freely as you speak, yet you have cues to keep you from losing your place. Extemporaneous speaking usually sounds the most natural. The section below, entitled "Developing the Oral Presentation," will look at ways you can prepare a speech to be presented extemporaneously.

Reading from Manuscript

In some circumstances, you may wish to read from a full-text manuscript. This mode of delivery is most often used when speeches are televised (usually read off a teleprompter) or in situations where exact wording is crucial. For example, Pierre Elliott Trudeau was known for his smoothly delivered, colourful extemporaneous speeches. But his address to the nation on October 16, 1970, when he announced his decision to invoke martial law in Montreal, was very different. He delivered this televised speech seated at a desk, reading from a carefully worded manuscript that he held in his hand. He used this delivery to signal to viewers that he was in control of the situation and that his plan, like his speech, had been carefully thought through.

This sense of careful planning is one of the strengths of using a manuscript when speaking. If you speak with authority, an oral presentation from a prepared manuscript can enhance both your perceived control of the situation and your material. This style does have weaknesses, however. One of these is the loss of eye contact. We have all seen local commercials featuring merchants who are not used to reading from teleprompters. Their eyes look glazed and move from side to side as they read. It takes practice to make yourself appear to be speaking to the viewer. Reading from a paper interferes with eye contact between speaker and audience even more. A class of public-speaking students who viewed the Trudeau speech said his quick glances away from the text and up to the camera made him look "shifty" and as if he were "hiding something." This effect can occur whether the speech is televised or delivered live. A second weakness, one regularly demonstrated by the local commercials mentioned above, is that most people sound stilted or monotonous when they read. Modulate your voice as naturally as possible during manuscript delivery and mark your text ahead of time for words you would like to pronounce more emphatically or more softly. You may also wish to mark the texts where natural pauses occur. Finally, if you lose your place it can be difficult to find it again. If you choose to deliver a speech with a manuscript, highlight or underline important points and rehearse the speech thoroughly so that you can maintain as much eye contact as possible.

Memorized Presentations

Some professional speakers present speeches from memory. This allows the speaker to maintain eye contact while retaining precise wording. For most people, however, this is a dangerous method. People who are not professional speakers or actors usually sound sing-songy when they speak material they have memorized. If you forget part of a memorized speech, you risk a long and embarrassing pause while you try to remember your chain of words. Either of these problems may cause your audience to remember the speech in a way you'd rather they didn't. (If you do go blank, improvise—rephrase your last idea and keep talking until your text comes back to you.)

You may wish to memorize parts of an extemporaneous speech. Speakers often like to memorize the introduction, the thesis statement, and the conclusion. This gives you the strengths of precise wording and eye contact, but is not so sustained a memory task as to allow problems to present themselves.

Impromptu Presentations

In business meetings or informal gatherings, you may be called upon to "say a few words" unexpectedly or to respond to a point that has been made. In such cases, you need to make an impromptu presentation. Even in these situations, you can and should structure your thoughts. Jot down a few notes if you have time. Decide what your objective is and state it as clearly as possible. That will serve as your thesis statement. Think of one or two points and evidence to support your thesis. Summarize your thesis and your main points as you conclude. Listeners will appreciate your ability to present your thoughts in a simple, concise, structured way.

If you are a member of a community business association, for example, and you are suddenly invited to respond to a concern about liquor laws during a brief meeting, you may be best advised to organize your thoughts around the implications of any changes to or violations of current liquor restrictions. Examples from the community's experience would help illustrate your points. In such an impromptu address, the audience would understand you are speaking provisionally: not offering shaped conclusions, but ideas to be discussed.

Each of these means of presenting an oral speech is useful in certain situations. One speech may use several modes: the body of the speech may be delivered extemporaneously while the introduction and conclusion are memorized, quotations and statistics read, and questions answered impromptu. As the extemporaneous mode is the most effective in most situations, the following section will focus on developing that form of speech.

DEVELOPING THE ORAL PRESENTATION

For many people, anxiety is the first obstacle to overcome for a good oral presentation. In fact, a survey conducted by *Psychology Today* (quoted by Lyle W. Mayer in *Fundamentals of Voice and Diction, 10th ed.*, 1994) found that many people are more afraid of public speaking than they are of death. So if you are nervous, recognize that most people share your feelings. Also realize that "nerves" can help you focus and energize your presentation as you control and channel them rather than allow them to control you. Remember that your preparation, your practice, and your focus are the essential elements in developing a good oral presentation. Whether you are a nervous speaker or not, these three elements are essential for a successful delivery of your carefully written speech, and your attention to them will see you through a case of nervous hesitation.

Preparation

Be absolutely sure you have done your homework, including all the research you would do for any good piece of writing. You may find the following steps helpful:

- Write out a full outline of your speech.
- Highlight the key words and phrases that the audience must hear in order to understand your message.
- Make up cue cards for yourself. Write just the key words and phrases. You may wish to write out the full text of your thesis statement and any quoted material and statistics, but keep this as brief as possible.

Practice

Perhaps the most valuable advice that can be given to a speaker is practise, practise, practise! Most oral presentations are not rehearsed enough. Speakers who go over their speeches too little in advance undermine their messages as well as themselves. Practise your speech until you can run through it smoothly, using only your cue cards for reference. Practise in front of a mirror to find the best hand gestures to emphasize your points while appearing natural and to eliminate excessive, distracting body language. If you will present while standing, practise standing, making sure your posture is straight but relaxed and that you don't fall into bad habits of fidgeting or shifting from side to side. If you will be seated when you speak, practise a good seated posture that helps you appear confident. Again, try to avoid excessive hand gestures or fidgeting that will advertise any discomfort.

You may wish to make a videotape of one of your practice runs. Or you may wish to round up a sympathetic audience of friends or family members. Even a child or a pet (other than a goldfish) can help you work at making eye contact and varying your voice to gain and hold attention.

As well as rehearsing the text of the speech and your presentation of it, prepare for questions the audience may ask you and practise your answers. Give special consideration to tough questions that may come up so that you will answer them confidently. Even if exact or even similar versions of the questions you have anticipated do *not* arise, you will usually be able to use parts of your prepared answers for other, unanticipated questions.

Focus

There are several techniques you can use to focus on the task at hand rather than on your butterflies as presentation day draws near. The most commonly used techniques are controlled breathing, stretching, simple kinetic exercises, and visualization. Whether you are nervous or not, these techniques can help you achieve peak performance.

Breathing

The beauty of breathing exercises is that you can do them lying on your back in a darkened room or seated at a boardroom table surrounded by others. The following is a simple progression that will help you to concentrate.

First, just notice your breath—is it fast and high in your chest? Begin to slow it down. Breathe deeply into your diaphragm (or belly). Feel your bottom ribs swing out and up slightly as you inhale. Once your breath is low and slow, count silently as you inhale and exhale. Start inhaling 1–2, hold 1–2, exhale 1–2–3. Work up to inhale 1–8, hold 1–8, exhale 1–10. The count should be slow enough to be relaxing, yet not so slow that you run out of air. If you feel lightheaded, return to normal breathing.

Kinetic Exercises

You can also use this technique while lying on the floor or discreetly while in a room full of people. Find a relaxed position, seated or lying down. If you are alone, close your eyes. Use the breathing exercises until your breath is relaxed. Starting with your toes and working up to your face, clench and release each muscle group in your body. Hold each set of muscles for a slow count of 10 before relaxing them. Let yourself feel the release for a moment before you move on to the next group of muscles, working your way slowly up your legs, trunk, arms and hands, to neck and head. Pay special attention to places where you hold tension; the shoulders and the jaw are the greatest tension points for many of us.

Visualization

Many professional and top-ranking athletes include visualization in their training. Visualization allows you to rehearse your "event" (in this case, your speech) in a relaxed, positive way that reinforces the correct techniques, making errors in your presentation less likely. It is good to run a visualization in the final day or two before you present. You can also do a mini-visualization on the spot if you find yourself losing confidence just before you are to speak. To practise visualization privately, find a relaxed position, seated or lying down. Close your eyes. Run through the breathing exercises and the kinetic sequence. When you feel relaxed, picture yourself in a favourite place where you feel safe and content, perhaps a sandy beach by the ocean. Enjoy the image for a moment, then picture yourself preparing to leave. See yourself packing everything you need for the presentation. You remember everything. You arrive at the space where you will present in plenty of time. You check it out and set everything up. It all goes smoothly. Watch your audience arriving. You are relaxed, they are friendly. It is your time to speak. You feel confident and prepared. Visualize yourself delivering your entire speech smoothly. (Do not check your notes or speak out loud—just watch the "movie" of your own polished presentation.) Watch the audience. They are clearly interested. As you finish, they applaud. You smoothly and constructively answer their questions. After you close, they compliment you on the effectiveness of your speech. Open your eyes and hold onto that happy, confident feeling.

If, in the moments before you speak, you start to feel anxious, guide yourself back to your positive visualization. Remember that few problems are beyond your ability to cope with in the context of your presentation. If you forget your speech, you have your cue cards. If you cannot answer a question, replying with an honest "I don't know" can be very effective in sustaining your audience's respect when you follow it with an assurance that you will find the information. Most important of all, see yourself succeeding.

Committed preparation, practice, and focus will help make your presentation an experience that is more pleasant for you and more effective for your listeners. In the longer term, there are many other ways to build your presentation skills.

PRESENTATION SKILLS: VOICE AND BODY

Voice

Your voice and body are tremendously important in communicating your presentation. You cannot escape them. They will affect the audience's perception of your message, so use them to fullest advantage. Develop vocal flexibility and physical expressiveness. You can incorporate the following exercises into your rehearsals of one important presentation, and you will find they become more effective if you do them over time. If your chosen career involves a lot of public speaking, you may want to consider joining an organization or speaking group where you can hone your skills continually with experienced speakers. If you have speech problems (nasal voice, soft consonants, etc.) or are very inhibited physically, classes in voice, yoga, tai chi, or even kick-boxing can make a big difference in the way your presentations are received.

Volume

Using volume, rate, pitch, and articulation appropriately is as important in public speaking as it is in singing. Speakers who know how to make these vocal qualities work for them deliver many otherwise questionable presentations convincingly. On the other hand, audiences overlook many thoughtful arguments in presentations when the speakers mumble in a monotone or hurriedly spit out their points. In oral presentations the speaker's voice will either contribute to or detract from the spoken content. There is no third alternative.

As for the volume of your voice, first of all you must be *audible*. Ask the audience if everyone can hear you, especially if you will be speaking without a microphone. Most people speak too softly when addressing a group. Unless you have been told you have a loud voice, always speak at a level that feels too loud without yelling. If you are soft-spoken, speak loudly every time you practise your speech.

A speaker who tries to be loud by straining the throat sounds shrill rather than confident. Learn to support your voice from the diaphragm. Start by breathing deeply. Use your diaphragm (just above your stomach) to push the air out slowly. After you have done this a few times silently, do the same on a hiss, then on an "ahhhh." As you build strength in the muscles between your ribs and your abdomen, start reading your text at a comfortable, fairly loud level. Each time you do the exercise, read farther on one breath, always stopping before you start to strain. If you are unsure where your diaphragm is or how to get started, consult a singing teacher or a voice coach.

Rate

The rate or pace of your speech is also very important. Second to insufficient volume, *racing*—speaking at a rushed rate—is the most common way speakers lose their audiences. If you race because you are nervous, use pauses to force yourself to slow down, even writing "pause here" on your cue cards. If your speech is running long, skip parts. **Do not race.** It is far better for the listeners to get some of your points than none. Talk slower than normally when you practise. Ask a friend to listen to you run through your speech and signal to you if you are going too fast.

Pitch

Another essential characteristic of speech is your pitch. Most people speak within a very narrow range, seldom using the upper and lower parts of their registers. So think of your presentation as a kind of performance, which it is. Think of pitch as a dramatic instrument that can help establish your presence and your content. Listen to a speaker you find interesting. You will likely notice that he uses a wider range of pitch than most of us do in day-to-day conversation. You too can develop this ability through practice.

Vary your volume, rate, and pitch when you practise your presentation at home. See what effect you create when you slow down and when you speak loudly or softly in making important points. Use the higher and lower parts of your range. Exaggerate. Move from deep down to high and squeaky. Race through some parts, slow to a crawl for others. Whisper a significant point or yell it like an old-time preacher.

Have fun with your whole presentation. After you have done this a few times, run through the speech in a normal speaking voice, holding onto the vocal variations that you found effective.

Articulation

Clear articulation is extremely important when an audience is relying on your oral delivery of information. You can confuse your listeners by phonetically substituting a "D" for a "T" when you are explaining unfamiliar terms. Over the long term, you will find tongue-twisters that feature consonants both enjoyable and useful for sharpening up overly casual articulation. Run each tongue-twister several times; the first time, run it slowly to exaggerate each sound, then increasingly speed it up, but don't lose the clear consonants. Follow up by running through your speech, exaggerating the consonants.

After you have practised bringing these examples of vocal variety into your speech, tape your presentation and check for crisp articulation and interesting, natural-sounding modulation. You will begin to recognize your speaking voice as a responsive instrument, a device valuable in expressing your prepared content and furthering your career.

Body Language

People take in far more information through their eyes than their ears. Body language is therefore an important tool for any presenter. Eye contact and facial expression, posture and gesture all send important signals to your audience.

Eye Contact

Novice speakers find making eye contact with audience members difficult, but such communication is essential to establishing rapport. Speakers who make eye contact appear friendly, confident, and candid about their messages (even if they are not). If you are nervous about eye contact, practise at home with someone you know. If you present to a small group, make eye contact at some point with each person. If you present to a group of more than 20 people, divide the audience mentally into four parts. If you make eye contact with at least one person in each quadrant, the entire audience will feel included. Choose a sympathetic-looking person to look at if you are nervous. If there is a bright light on you and the audience area is dim, make "eye contact" where you know someone will be.

Facial Expression

Facial expression also counts for a great deal in public speaking. Smile as soon as you begin your presentation. This will warm the audience to you and make you feel more confident. Smile where appropriate throughout the presentation. It will make a big difference in the listeners' perception of you and your message. In one study customers in a bank were asked to estimate the time they had spent waiting in line for a teller. Those whom the teller had greeted with a smile after their wait in line underestimated their total wait time; the other customers, who received no greeting smile, overestimated their time in line! If you tend not to smile when you are nervous, you may want to add "smile" on your cue cards at strategic spots.

Posture

A good, relaxed posture will also help you appear competent and confident. As you stand, picture your feet sinking into the floor and the crown of your head being gently pulled up by a string hanging from the ceiling above you. You want to avoid a stiff, military posture, while you avoid rounded shoulders, slouching, or hunching at the same time. You also want to keep track of what your feet are doing—imaginatively sinking them into the floor—comfortably—to anchor you and help you avoid aimless pacing. Note whether you are speaking at a podium that is open at its bottom and allows the audience a full view of your legs and feet. Speakers can often appear purposeful and strong above the podium, while their feet are fidgeting, twisting around each other, and even slipping their shoes on and off! On a raised platform, your busy feet and not your words will become the focal point of your presentation. Change your posture occasionally, of course, but exercise some physical self-discipline to create a minimum of distractions from your presentation.

Feel free to move away from the podium, however. A podium forms a barrier between you and the audience. Leaving it and crossing the stage or floor toward the audience can be a powerful way to emphasize a point, as well as to enact your sense of comfort with your material and the audience itself. By demonstrating this degree of comfort, you will put the audience at its ease, and they will be more likely to remember your particular presentation as both enjoyable and convincing.

Gestures

Gestures can greatly enhance a speech by making ideas visible. Keep them simple and natural, to amplify, not compete with, the points you are making in your presentation. For instance, an inclusive gesture on "all of us" visually underlines the meaning. Holding up fingers to count off your main points dramatizes the organization of your presentation. If you are not accustomed to "talking with your hands," decide on a few effective gestures and practise them as you run through your speech. Remember not to overdo gestures, however, since excessively "talking with your hands" can belie a lack of faith in the power of your words, your ability to inform and convince through language, logic, analysis, and argument.

Your hands are very influential as you speak. Trembling hands are one of the most common giveaways of nervousness, and one of the most upsetting to speakers. As you speak, your hands shake and the paper rattles. This makes you self-conscious, so the paper rattles more. You cannot stop the trembling, but you can make it irrelevant if you use large file cards rather than paper for your notes. Without the rattling paper, neither the audience nor you will be distracted from your message. Ideally, you will speak from a keyword outline, so all the notes you need should fit onto several cards. If you are speaking from a manuscript, place either the whole text or the bottom half flat on your desk or podium to anchor it and keep your hands from shaking. Contact with a steady surface will steady you.

Stretching, breathing, and relaxation exercises will all help you transform the stiffness of your nerves into the fluidity of effective movement, just as vocal exercises will make your voice more flexible and interesting to listen to. You can do these exercises as part of your preparation for a single speech; you will find them more effective if you make them part of your long-term routine.

PRESENTATION AIDS

As you move into final preparations, consider how you have incorporated presentation aids into your speech. These include all visual and audio aids, including PowerPoint, transparencies, objects, videotapes, or audio tapes and even your own appearance. Visual aids can be especially helpful in keeping your audience with you.

Computer-Generated Aids

Computer-generated aids are effective *if* you know how to use them. However, many presentations begin late or are delivered with distracting technical difficulties, be-

Ten Tips for Using Visual Presentation Aids

1. Limit the number of aids you use so that they enhance your presentation without overwhelming it.
2. Keep your visual aids simple and uncluttered.

   - Use bulleted lists rather than sentences, with no more than six bullets to a list.
   - Simplify maps so they show only the features relevant to your presentation.
   - Make graphs as simple as possible and use clearly contrasting colours.
   - Use charts that contain the minimum of information you need to get your point across.

3. Ensure all lettering is legible and can be seen from the back of the room.
4. Talk to the audience, not to the aid.
5. Avoid blocking your own aid.
6. Reveal points only as you make them in your speech, or the audience will stop listening to you as they read ahead.
7. Decide on your strategy for distributing a handout; unless you have set up this written material so that the audience uses it to follow you point by point, distribute it when you are finished talking (for the same reason given in #6). Reproduce photographs large enough that people at the back of the room can see them. Do not pass them around, as this will divide the audience into pockets of people concentrating on them rather than on what you are saying.
8. Do not try to speak over sound unless it is extremely soft.
9. Keep aids out of sight until you need them.
10. Be certain you have practised with and are in control of the aid. For example, always check that an overhead projector has a spare bulb. If possible, avoid using live animals unless you know you can focus audience attention back on you; a litter of kittens will make a much bigger impact than you do and can quickly get out of control, but a very well-trained adult dog may be helpful in a speech about seeing-eye dogs.

cause the speaker is unfamiliar with the program or the room (the outlet, the best place to project, or the best place to stand without blocking the audience's view). Nervous speakers sometimes fidget with a computer mouse, projecting a cursor that wanders distractingly over the image at the front of the room. If you are unfamiliar with the PowerPoint program but must use it, seek a knowledgeable assistant to run the program while you present—and be sure to practise with this person ahead of time!

Your Appearance

Consider your appearance a powerful presentation aid, too. Dress with your audience in mind. Your T-shirt and jeans would likely alienate a corporate board of directors, while a business suit could have the same effect on an audience of inner-city teens. If you are uncertain of the social atmosphere or your audience's expectations of dress code, seek middle ground: wear dress pants or a simple skirt, dress shoes, and plain shirt with a blazer you can easily remove or keep on for adding or reducing formality on the spot.

Nine Things to Do on the Day You Present

1.   Arrive in plenty of time. Check out the room if it is unfamiliar to you, to make sure it has all the resources you need. Arrange and set up your presentation aids, so you won't keep your audience waiting while you fiddle with them later.
2.   Keep your visualizations positive. Breathe.
3.   When you begin, smile at the audience, and establish eye contact with them individually. Stay in touch with them. If they look puzzled or bored, interact with them if possible: ask if there are any questions, or whether you need to explain anything again. Your honest interaction will keep the audience with you.
4.   Speak conversationally. Very few audiences actually want you to fail. In your position, they would be nervous, too. Speaking to them as if they were ordinary people (which they are) will relax both you and them.
5.   Find ways to make your presentation interesting as well as informative. Make jokes that illuminate the topic (generic jokes such as "ladies and germs" are rarely effective). Use natural gestures. Vary your voice. Use presentation aids as audio or visual components.
6.   Rephrase questions aloud as the audience asks them, since people at the back usually cannot hear the people at the front. Answer questions thoroughly, and do not be afraid of admitting you do not have the answer or that you may not have made up your mind on an issue. You may even use the question as an opportunity to strengthen your connection with your listeners by asking if there is anyone else in the audience who could answer.
7.   Respect your time limit out of consideration to the audience and any other speakers, and signal clearly when you are drawing to a close. The only thing worse than a speaker who goes on and on is one who repeatedly says "And in conclusion," and then goes on and on.
8.   Thank the audience and exit graciously. Save the introspective post-mortem for later!
9.   When you do your self-examining post-mortem, look for the strengths, especially if you are usually hard on yourself. Allow yourself to enjoy your strong points and build on them for next time. Audiences enjoy listening to speakers who enjoy speaking!

THE PRESENTATION

In summary, there are many naturally gifted speakers in the world. You may wish to improve your speaking style by emulating one of them, but you need not *be* one of them to be an effective speaker. Respect your audience as you prepare your oral presentations. Carefully word and structure your work to make it effective as spoken text, both in its information and its argumentation. Develop your ability to use your voice and body to enhance your message. Plan your presentations thoroughly, including your presentation aids. Your listeners will appreciate your respect for them and will receive your message as warmly as it deserves.

Sample Speech

In the speech below, Montreal theatre director Guy Sprung, addressing a conference in Calgary, asserts that Canada's insufficient commitment to theatre and the arts threatens the survival of the nation.

Note how he has crafted the speech to suit his audience of Alberta playwrights. He begins by speaking about theatre in Calgary, and then in Canada; finally he challenges his listeners to accept responsibility for the crucial role theatre plays in human society. Try to imagine that you are listening to the speech rather than reading it. Notice the many repetitions and internal summaries, and the use of colourful, concrete images. Would these help you to follow the speech if you were unable to glance up and down the page? Also note that Sprung cites his sources as he speaks. He leaves no doubt in listeners' minds that he has carefully selected and researched the material in his "Lagostina box."

Sample Speech   Oral Style and Technique

In Search of Wawa or Notes from my Lagostina Box
Guy Sprung

Transcript of the Keynote Speech delivered to the Theatre Alberta Annual Conference, Calgary, May 1, 1999

1   It's a pleasure being here, it is also a responsibility. I will presume upon your time by attempting a few sketches, ideas, perceptions on theatre past and present in our rapidly deteriorating country and also try to ask some questions as to what the implications of this present are for writers and for theatre as we look to the future.

. . .

2   I do have a certain neurotic association to Calgary. I was offered my first professional freelance-directing gig here. After a stint apprenticing in England I came home to Montreal and through a fortuitous unfolding of circumstances was offered the Premiere of W.O. Mitchell's *Back to Beulah* at Theatre Calgary. Harold Baldridge was the Artistic Director at the time and I think some wise soul at the Canada Council had

tried to explain to him that perhaps he should be programming something more adventurous than *Two for the See-Saw* and other American Summer Stock fare. He grudgingly included a new play by a local Calgary writer in his season.

. . .

3   Occasionally it is worth reminding ourselves how young our contemporary theatre tradition is. In 1976 the network of regional theatres across the country had only just been completed. Certain smaller alternative theatres, like ATP here, had only recently been founded with the specific mandate to produce our own plays. ATP, remember, was ghettoized out in the Canmore Opera House in a Heritage Village, doing "Ye olde Canadian Theatre." I am not talking about the work they did, but about how the general public inevitably perceived their work. Imagine asking to be taken seriously while performing in an artificial tourist attraction stuffed with artifacts from the Wild West. Today ATP has a wonderful home in this wonderful palace of culture, the Calgary Arts Centre. A ghetto of a different order of magnitude.

4   Anyhow, *Beulah* was the big box office success of the season and of many others. Not necessarily because it was great theatre, no, but because it caught the crest of a wave of Canadian plays that were big box office *a mare usque ad mare*. In fact, if you look individually at each theatre across the country you will probably find that the biggest single box office hit in the history of each company is a local play. With Theatre Calgary it is W.O.'s *The Black Bonspiel of Wullie MacCrimmon*. Three separate productions bankrolled the company's move into the Arts Centre.

5   I remember in the mid-Eighties the Playwrights' Union of Canada newsletter trumpeting the statistics: Over 80% of all plays being produced in Canada were our own! Sure, dismiss it if you like, newness sells and Canadian theatre was the flavour of the day. Nevertheless that was a phenomenal statistic. It was *Wawa*, man! *Wawa*? What is *Wawa*?

6   *Wawa* is an Algonquin/Huron word meaning the meeting place of the waters. If you were hitch-hiking across the country in the Sixties it was also the town on the North Shore of Lake Superior with the giant Canada Goose where, inevitably, you got stranded.

7   *Wawa* for me is the metaphor for the quintessential Canadian spirit. Not my term. Coined as such by Peter van Toorn, a Montreal English language poet. He used it first in a long poem called *In Guildenstern County*, written in 1973, the early Seventies, a time when, as Louis Dudek, the doyen of Montreal poets, liked to say ". . . it was the duty of Montreal to show the rest of the country what poetry really is.

8   Wawa,
    sound of wind:
    good grass out front, bad brush behind.
    Try feeling at home
    and the loon reminds you—smack in the gut
    boatmiles off
    of travelling way out alone.
    Wawa,
    . . . etc.

9   A poem of some seven pages and nine sections in length which this tiny excerpt cannot do justice to.

. . .

10   *Wawa* is the wordless. The unquantifiable. The unnameable.

. . .

11   *Wawa*, that indefinable essence that is Canada, that is Canada's moral responsibility to uphold in this confused and confusing universe. *Wawa*, blowing in the wind in the early Seventies. The energy that built a network of theatres across the country, that got writers writing and actors wanting to act and most importantly an audience wanting to catch where "it was at." Theatre was perceived as having an irresistible edge. The Doctors and the Dentists were buying out the preview subscriptions in their scramble for a hot bargain. Everyone wanted to be able to comment on the latest new play in town and talk about it around the office water cooler, pretend they were oh-so-knowledgeable. All over the country.

12   Between '71 and '81 over 500% increase in the number of Performing Arts Companies. Attendance up nearly 300%. Now statistics, as we all know, can be made to tell you any story you want. But attendance and energy probably reached a peak at the end of the Eighties. For me, a personal highpoint was during a matinee performance of David Fennario's *Balconville* at the Place des Arts in Montreal when I looked out at intermission and saw that the whole Montreal hockey team was there on an official outing. Lafleur, Shutt and Robinson passing around observations of our play instead of a puck!

13   Theatre had become a respected voice in Canadian society's dialogue with itself. As we know, in recent years theatre and the performing arts, however you try and quantify "it," have clearly lost that edge. Along with a good deal else, of course.

14   Statistics Canada figures, only one month old: In the two years between the '95 and '97 seasons, Not-for-profit Theatre lost 17% in attendance! Yet total revenues were up 4%! Fewer spectators paying more. Government grants down significantly, private donations up. We'll get to the reality of private donations in a moment. However you define your *Wawa*, it has been eroding big time in the last seven or eight years.

. . .

15   Is it Free Trade? Globalization? Ascendancy of Right Wing Politics? Loss of Canada's sense of identity? The lassitude of Canada's artists?

16   Here's a useful parable:

17   Easter Island was originally settled by Polynesian immigrants sometime after 400 A.D. An isolated island of fertile volcanic soil, with warm temperate climate, covered in palm trees, large variety of birds, edible fruits, crustaceans, the surrounding seas full of large edible fish, dolphins, breeding seal colonies. In short, it was paradise.

18   A few hundred years later, according to the Anthropologists—you know the guys and gals who dig up and analyze the garbage we leave behind—Easter Island is sup-

porting a civilization of as many as 20,000 inhabitants. This is the period of the creation and erection of the famous giant Easter Island statues. A mere two or three hundred years later and this civilization has already deteriorated.

19   What happened? Trees were all chopped down, for housing, for fuel and cooking, for vegetable gardens. Result, climate changes, birds, animals and all kinds of vegetation disappear because of lack of habitat. No trees, so the inhabitants can't build the large ocean-going canoes any more—they can't go and harpoon the large fish out in the deep sea.

20   Result: Starvation. Cannibalism. Internecine warfare. Inhabitants forced to live in caves for survival. By the time Europeans bump into the island in 1722, there are a few scraggly inhabitants left. Paradise destroyed.

21   Anybody here think that Western civilization which is controlling our planet is intrinsically wiser than Polynesian civilization which destroyed its island paradise? . . . So where are we today on the *Wawa* scale of things?

22   Since, by definition, *Wawa* is something you can't quantify, let's try a non-linear approach to grasp our current situation.

23   First Reality Check: Our legal status. For all the excitement and supposed relevance of the Seventies and Eighties, Not-for-profit Theatre never actually had an honest legal status. We exist on the sufferance of the bureaucrats. We achieve legal status by lying about the true nature of our work. How so?

24   If you want private funding you have to be able to give tax receipts, which means you have to be a registered charity. To qualify for charitable status your stated objectives in your Articles of Incorporation have to be: relief of poverty, advancement of education, religion or other purposes beneficial to the general public at large. Did Shakespeare write his plays for any of these purposes? Sure, he wrote and acted to alleviate poverty, his own.

25   But his theatre and all of Elizabethan Theatre never put the cart before the horse and never thought of themselves as doing socially "useful" work, in the same way a hospital or school does. No, most of the time they were banned, the theatres closed.

26   Theatre should be dangerous, it should be a discovery, it should be criticism, it should be provocative. We are the enemy. Plato was right when he wanted to keep the poets out of his perfect Republic. It is our responsibility to be uncontrollable, to be a voice of opposition.

27   A theatre that advocates changing a city by-law, even to build a new theatre, should, according to the law of the land, lose its charitable status. Advocacy is verboten! We really only exist because the tax authorities operate on the assumption that in some undefined way it is generally accepted by the public at large that theatres should be considered a charity. For the moment. It is sort of like smoking your own marijuana. As long as you don't flaunt it too much and don't traffic in it and don't smoke in public, the police will turn a blind eye.

28   As a consequence of this the legal reality, though we may not like to admit it, we tread the artistic ground we walk on with a beholden timidity. Consciously and unconsciously it seriously affects the strength, the conviction of our work.

29   But then this is Canada and no one is ever going to censure art for political reasons. Right? Never in Canada, right? So we don't need to worry.

30   Second Reality Check: Corporate generosity.

31   In recent years all levels of Government, to a greater and a lesser extent, have been cutting back on subsidy. (Except in Quebec, I must point out!) It is part of the universal drive towards eliminating the deficit and achieving greater fiscal responsibility. If anyone still believes these government cutbacks, with the rationale of eliminating the deficit, are not part of a political agenda, they should read Linda McQuaig's *Shooting the Hippo*.

32   In the Arts and theatre world the cutbacks have had cataclysmic consequences. Bottom line: Arts companies are forced to raise more and more of their financing privately and corporately. Our work is now, more than ever, at the mercy of private funding. How does this private funding system work?

33   You give money to a non-profit organization, in our enlightened society we reward this generosity with a tax break. Nice liberal idea? Supports the Arts, right? Wrong! The system of corporate philanthropy benefits not the arts but the corporations themselves. Money that should go to the people of this country in the form of taxes is being directed to promote corporations. Being used to benefit company CEOs.

34   Example: I was briefly on the Board of Directors of Toronto's Harbourfront. For reasons that have to do with history and real estate, Harbourfront gets the single biggest grant from the federal government of any arts organization in the country. In return the organization schedules an eclectic variety of activities on prime Toronto Waterfront. Harbourfront is able to negotiate some hefty corporate sponsorships for these activities. Chief among them are the so-called Site Sponsorships. You know, Ford Motor Company, in return for a major donation, is given the right to litter the Toronto waterfront with its vehicles. One of the other site sponsors was Molson's Brewery.

. . .

35   One not-so-funny moment in one of the Board meetings: The Canadian Baseball Hall of Fame was on the Harbourfront site and sponsored by Labatt's. Of course Labatt's wanted to put their name on the outside of the building. The Man from Molson's, the President of the Harbourfront Board, is outraged in the meeting. "They can't be allowed to put their name on our site!" I asked if he was speaking on behalf of Harbourfront or Molson's. A few Board members chortled, Mr. Molson included, but I never got a real answer to the question. It actually gets worse. The Director of Development at Harbourfront admitted to me in a private meeting that the corporations made the donations but, if requested, Harbourfront actually made the income tax receipt out in the name of the CEO!

36   Now all our arts organizations are scrambling for corporate donations and this has given the corporations more and more control on how their money is used, how their "partnership" is perceived by the world. They have turned us into marketing shills for them. Go to Stratford: The President of such and such a bank has a bigger photo in the program than Martha Henry. He gets to stand on opening night and gets a bigger round of applause than the actors.

37   Where does this donated money come from? It is all a pre-tax legitimate corporate expense. It means the individual corporations pay less in taxes. Have you checked the downward curve in corporate contribution to government finances recently? Decline in corporate taxes inevitably means that Canada Council gets less, then arts companies get less from the Canada Council and need to go after more private funding, thus the corporations get more control, etc., etc. It's a vicious circle.

38   Enough already. We are responsible for our own fate. We are doing it to the world, to ourselves. We have let corporations, the corporate conservative ethos take over our world. We are cutting down our trees both metaphorically and in reality, just like the Polynesians did in their Paradise.

39   When Arts organizations have to put more and more creative energy into scrambling for corporate cash instead of into the work, the real art is in the writing of grants. Any wonder why one by one all the Boards of theatres across the country are hiring General Managers to run their companies? That bureaucrats are running artistic organizations? The managers are the ones who are good at shmoozing the money out of the corporations, so naturally they should be running the organizations.

40   Needless to say it results in total re-orientation of the goals of the work itself.

41   Another Reality Check: The Public Image of the Artist.

42   Here is an article from my Lagostina Box. . . . Oh, yes, the Lagostina Box in the title of this little talk. . . . Well, A friend gave me an Eaton's gift certificate for Christmas— my friends know I won't buy at Walmarts, and I like cooking and I bought an Italian stainless steel frying pan at a going-out-of-business price with the gift certificate. The box then became the repository for any interesting clippings or notes to myself. So to prepare this talk all I had to do was to empty my Lagostina box and start writing. . . .

43   Here is a full page *National Post* article from the Comment page of Saturday, February 13, 1999. Headline: "The trouble with arts handouts." Subtitle: "Most Canada Council artists seek tenure, not challenge; their eyes are set on safety nets, not horizons." You don't even need to read it, you know the tendentious non-thinking it contains.

44   Anybody call the billions of dollars we throw at Oil corporations to underwrite exploration "charity"? In 1993, the dying days of the Mulroney misgovernment of this country, when the Canada Council was getting $100 million from the Federal government to dispense to us "welfare bum" artists who live off the taxes, the conservative government gave a total of over $300 million in export subsidies to arms manufacturers!

45   Compare this to an article on the same page in the same newspaper on Friday, July 9, 1999, "Making the case for business handouts." Apparently the $2.1 billion in

subsidies Ottawa hands out in formal subsidies is only a "fraction of government assistance to business." Who is the real "welfare bum" here?

. . .

46   How did we artists allow the perception of what we do to be so universally despised?

47   In Pakistan they have the Zinna laws. If a woman is raped, she can be sent to jail as the criminal. That's what it feels like to be an artist in this country; we are raped and then convicted for the crime.

48   Another little nugget from my Lagostina Box. A program from one of our regional theatres, this season. This could be a program from any theatre across the country. Opening the program, right off the top we find in the Director's notes: "I would like to thank (Name of Artistic Director) for his enormous insight, talent, generosity and support . . . and the wonderful (Name of theatre) staff." Every single program bio is riddled with this sycophantic drivel. This is a real measure of the status of the artist in this country. We have to kiss ass so bad just to get work. How humiliating for all theatre. Do you think anybody in the audience can have any respect left for us after reading such craven supplication?

49   We are doing it to ourselves. Remember Easter Island.

50   When was the last time you heard an actor or a writer or a director doing a radio interview actually talk about theatre itself, or Kosovo, or Canada for that manner? No, we are there to sell tickets, we get our 30 seconds of publicity air time and we have to repeat platitudes about how entertaining the play is . . . .

. . .

51   Here's an item reprinted in the Montreal *Gazette* from the magazine *Science*: "McGill scientists succeed in extending the life of Nematodes by 500%." Nematodes, that's round worms to you and me. Amazing! They found four genes that control the biological clock of the worms and they mutated them so that the clock runs five times slower than before, and now the worms live five times longer. Imagine when they can do this for human beings. It is only a matter of time. We'd have a life expectancy of 350 years. Sounds good, eh? Make your first million by the time you are 30, then retire for the next 320 years. There is a catch. The worms had no sex drive. They just lay around all day doing nothing. As we know, if you don't have a sex drive you probably don't have a few other things, like the drive to write plays or perform *Hamlet*.

52   So imagine the kind of choices we are going to be asked to make. "Ya, I'll have 200 years and 20% sex drive, no no no, make that 25% sex drive, I want to write a few plays. Actually, come to think of it, I really want to live only 40 years and be able to fuck like a rabbit."

. . .

53   The changes coming to human existence in the next ten years are going to be even greater than those of the previous 3 million, 100 years. We haven't even had the time to digest and understand the last hundred years and we are already going to be experiencing an even greater technological revolution in the next ten!

54   Human cloning? If it hasn't already happened it will any day. McGill Professor Margaret Summerville and others can argue eloquently about the ethics of cloning humans, but in reality it is already too late.

55   Nano-technology. Physicists can already move atoms and molecules around one by one with their Channeling Tunnelling microscopes. They are going to be able to build transistors and electronic circuits on a nano scale, that is on the scale of *one-billionth* of a metre! In theory they will be able to alter the molecular structure of matter with molecular actuators and change carbon into diamonds. Or grass into beef. That's right, they are designing little machines the size of a microwave oven that can reassemble molecules and permit you to insert a pound of grass and dial a switch and out will come a steak. Cooked to your taste. Dreaming? Maybe. Maybe not. At that point Quebec won't need Alberta beef anymore for our Montreal smoked meat. We can happily become independent.

56   Human organs? They are already growing fingers and skin and livers and kidneys in labs around the world. Take some human stem cells, insert kidney DNA, grow the cells in the shape of a kidney and hook the kidney up to a blood system and the kidney kicks in. You will be able to supply your own DNA for this process so it will be your kidney, and your body won't experience the trauma of trying to reject the implant as happens when a kidney is donated from another human. In theory, if you have the money, you can have a couple of kidneys waiting for you, most likely growing inside a pig in an organ farm. Apparently we share great genetic affinity to pigs, which allows them, short term, to carry human organs ready for transplanting. If you've got the money, have a bad night on a bender, need a new organ or two, Porky gets slaughtered, you get the fresh organs and have some fresh bacon for breakfast while you are at it.

. . .

57   But the question theatre has got to be asking is: What is this doing to our brains? How do we begin to see, to understand, what it is doing to our minds? To how we think? How we think of ourselves as human beings?

58   Another Reality Check: Our self-image as human beings. Michael McCauliff, the CBC radio reporter who exposed much of the whole scandal of the Airborne Regiment in Somalia, described a chance encounter with a group of Airborne soldiers in Petawawa. He was lost, wandering down a hallway in a barracks building, and accidentally opened the door on a TV room. Twenty to thirty Troopers were gathered around a VCR/TV watching a Vietnam War movie together. As a group they were mouthing all the lines and even miming some of the action in sync with the movie. You know, sort of like *Rocky Horror Picture Show* groupies at a Saturday night reunion.

59   Is it possible that our soldiers are going to war with the self-image of a Hollywood actor playing a GI in a Viet Nam war movie? No wonder the tragedy in Somalia happened!

60   How is technology altering our perception of reality? Surely this subject should be a thematic motherlode for theatre?

. . .

61   Joyce Nelson, a Canadian media commentator, writes some fascinating books trying to make *transparent* the nature of TV. In *Television: The Perfect Machine* she
tracks the evolution of our understanding of how the brain functions—you know, left
brain/right brain, rational verbal versus abstract thinking—and parallels this to the evolution of TV advertising.

62   She points out a very significant difference between theatre and TV. We watch
the two with different sides of our brain! The amount of information a TV throws at
our brain, the number of pixels and lines per second is too much for the rational side
of our brain to handle. So we actually watch TV with the same part of our brain that is
active when we are dreaming.

63   Theatre, on the other hand, we watch with the rational side of our brain—which in
most humans is on the side of the brain opposite to the hand with which you write.
The implications of this are fascinating and deserving of much greater analysis than I
have time for here.

64   Theatre is a Civic Forum. It is a collective experience. It is an activity we under-
take, for the most part with our waking minds. It encourages discussion. It validates
The Human Body, human sweat. We breathe together. We *conspire*. Theatre enhances the value of an individual human being per se. It conveys a sense of participation and responsibility. Theatre is the necessary element in the future investigation of
the human spirit.

65   The central question that the advances of technology have forced upon us is the
mind/body relationship. We know all about this in theatre. It is time that we stopped
hiding our light under the bushel. Theatre has a profound understanding of human
nature. Of course we do. That is how we pay the rent, for Christ's sake. Stanislavsky
and Chekhov understood subtext long before Freud did. Actors know, have to know
about the human body. And we know so much more about human nature and the
human body than we know we know.

66   Example: Every year David Smukler and his teaching team run a five-week intensive workshop for the voice: *The Actors' Equity Voice Intensive*. It is a workshop that
teaches a group of artists how the human voice functions. How an actor can reunite,
reconnect, integrate the Mind and the Voice with the Body to deepen a theatrical performance. It is a workshop that looks to understand the root of inspiration, in an effort
to expand and enrich the actor's voice. Consequently someone like David Smukler,
who has devoted his life to understanding the human voice, knows considerably more
than any scientist does about how the vocal cords really function.

67   One evening session we were visited by a nurse from a local hospital who
brought in videos, taken with a micro-camera, of a variety of human vocal chords. The
nurse was infatuated with a technologically captured *surface* image of what human
vocal chords *looked like*. Compared to what the teaching team knew about the reality
of vocal chords, how they functioned in relation to the rest of our being, how to make

them work more efficiently, how to access human inspiration to make the human body sing, the poor nurse was simply out of her league.

. . .

68   Where are the plays that analyze our future, that look at what our new media are doing to the human consciousness? It is our responsibility to confront these problems. And theatre is the only medium that has the ability to do just that. Look for the *Wawa*. Theatre is a significant portion of those trees we have to preserve on our metaphorical Easter Island.

69   A comparison to the Elizabethan Age uncovers certain similarities. Both eras are dominated by the discovery of a new world. In our case, Space; in their case, the Americas. Both eras are also dominated by the discovery of a new medium. In our case, movie and television; in their case, theatre. Certainly medieval church theatre had existed before, but Shakespeare, Jonson, Marlowe, they were basically *reinventing* theatre. Imagine being a shoemaker's apprentice and stumbling on the Globe Theatre or the Rose and seeing human beings being portrayed on the stage for the first time! The human self divided into watchers and performers. Imagine the profound split this had on the human mind. It *was* the invention of a new medium, a new technology. Like my generation experiencing television: *Bonanza, Danger Man, Hockey Night in Canada*.

70   What has this done to our sense of identity? Shakespeare wrote a play that tried to understand what his new medium was doing to the human consciousness. It is called *Hamlet*.

71   Three and a half hours trying to understand the difference between action, acting, performing an action, and doing an action and watching an action being performed. In one sense the play is a yearning for a return to the mythical Eden when the body and the mind were one again. It is an examination of the moral underpinning of action. It is also a major analysis of theatre and the craft of acting. "Words without thoughts will not to heaven go," says Claudius when he admits to himself in III, iii, he can't pray properly. This is a simple acting truism. If you can't get your thoughts behind the words you are saying, they won't reach the back of the house. In the Globe "The Heavens," as we know, were painted on the canopy that overhung the stage.

72   Today we theatre artists are the monks of the Middle Ages desperately and in secret trying to copy the great works of Antiquity before they get eradicated. We are the Christians hiding in caves daring to keep the Faith. We are the underground in Paris trying to keep the spirit of Resistance alive until the forces of Good can rally. We're the *Patriotes* of 1837 fighting the Oligarchy of privilege. Find whatever analogy you need to give your work a drive, to put the *Wawa* back in theatre.

73   Theatre has to dare to be dangerous. Creativity is sacred. Art should be discovery. Next time you have a radio interview, talk about important issues. Don't succumb to the vocabulary of business or we have already lost. Perhaps we should insist on being banned, banished outside city limits, like the playhouses in Elizabethan theatre.

74   Athens in the days of Aristotle or Artistophanes had no more than 25,000 citizens. It is not size that determines quality, it is application, focus, intellectual commitment. No reason Calgary or Alberta can't carry the playwrighting torch for our civilization.

75   Great Theatre starts with great scripts. If you want *Wawa*, it has to begin with the writers. So all I can say is, Playwrights of Alberta, the *Wawa* is up to you. . . . Thank you for your patience, your indulgence.

Focus Questions

1. What is the thesis of the speech? Is it stated in the introduction and the conclusion?
2. This is a manuscript speech, which Sprung read aloud to his audience. We can therefore assume the speech was delivered more or less exactly as written. What are the implications of its precise wording? How formal or informal is the language? Would it be easy for a listener to follow? (Should it be easy for a listener to follow?) What would the presentation gain or lose if it were delivered extemporaneously?
3. Would presentation aids be appropriate for this speech? If so, what would be effective and at what point or points?

Part 3

THE HANDBOOK

Section 1

Section 2

Section 3

INTRODUCTION

THE HANDBOOK covers the most common mechanical problems that arise in student writing. We realize many instructors will want to supplement this section with their own exercises and examples. Our immediate goal is to introduce students to the principles and terminology that will help them understand an instructor's advice and identify grammar errors. For ease of understanding, we have used the same terminology in the *Rhetoric*. Our long-term goal is to help students edit their own work more thoroughly and confidently.

While many classrooms do not take up explicit or sustained grammar instruction, our belief is that if students understand the logic of the mechanical principles of sentence construction, then not only their writing but also their clarity of thought will improve steadily. Students can then move on to polishing their sentences conceptually and stylistically after building them on firm foundations.

Better grammar skills will raise the quality of students' writing in all areas of their lives: in personal letters and emails, cover letters, college and employment applications, memos, future business writing and company reports, and, of course, letters of complaint and appeal.

The following three sections define principles that every writer works with daily.

1. Forms (Including the Nine Parts of Speech)
2. Punctuation Terms
3. Fifteen Common Errors

We explain the terms and provide examples for each grammar principle. With a little attention to the rationale of these principles and terms, students will find them fairly easy to grasp.

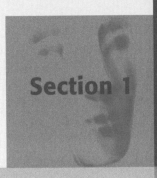

Section 1

Forms

(Including the Nine Parts of Speech)

The following types of words and word groups will be addressed in this section: nouns, verbs, adjectives, adverbs, pronouns, phrases, clauses, modifiers, conjunctions, articles, subjects, predicates, objects, participles, gerunds, infinitives, prepositions, subject and object complements, comparatives and superlatives, and interjections.

1. NOUNS

Nouns are naming words. They name persons, places, things, and concepts. Often nouns end in the suffixes *–ence, –ance, –ism,* or *–ity*. Nouns may be made possessive by adding an apostrophe and *–s*.

Plural or Singular

Many nouns may be either *plural* (more than one thing indicated) or *singular* (one thing indicated).

> **Examples**   bands, band

In the case of *collective* nouns, a single unit (treated as a singular subject) contains more than one thing.

> **Example**   The <u>team</u> prepares for the big game.

Some other collective nouns are *union, group, tribe, family,* and *herd.*

Count nouns name things that can be counted and therefore expressed in singular or plural form.

> **Example**   one woman, three women, twenty hamburgers, six trees

Non-count or *mass nouns* name things that cannot be counted and seldom have plural forms. These are often abstract nouns, grouped items, food and drink, or natural elements.

> **Examples**   hopelessness, traffic, flour, air

Articles (or Determiners) and Nouns

The article (also called a *determiner*) *a* is used before a singular count noun when your reader or you do not know its specific identity, and when no other noun marker, such as a possessive pronoun, precedes the noun. The article (also a determiner) *the* is used before a noun when your reader knows its specific identity, except for plural or non-count nouns meaning "in general" or "all" or proper nouns.

> **Examples**   The shopkeeper spoke to <u>a</u> customer on the telephone.
>
> Fires can result from <u>the</u> smallest of sparks.

noun

Four Main Types of Nouns

Nouns can be classified as four types: *proper, common, concrete,* and *abstract.*

A) *Proper nouns,* unlike all other nouns, are indicated by an initial capital letter. These "capital letter" nouns are the names of people or places.

Examples   Katrina, John, Ottawa, Salmon Arm

B) *Common nouns* name general groups, places, people, or things.

Examples   vegetables, cities, witness, instrument

King Arthur was an early <u>king</u> of England.

C) *Concrete nouns* name things perceived by the five senses.

Examples   muffin, sandpaper, perfume, sky, thunder

D) *Abstract nouns* refer to intangible concepts or values (things not perceived by the five senses).

Examples   love, truth, indecisiveness, pity

There is some overlap between categories: persons and proper nouns (John), places and proper nouns (Cape Breton), and concrete and abstract words (tomorrow).

2. VERBS

Verbs are action words (*jump, realize, write*). Verbs also express states of being (Peter Gabriel *is* here). A transitive verb is followed by an object that completes its meaning (They *found* the keys). Intransitive verbs do not require objects (We *listened*).

Verb Tense

Verbs have different tenses: present, past, future. Each of these categories has subcategories. *Uninflected* verbs (the infinitive) are expressed this way: to think, to feel, to understand. In order to express the time of action (tense) as well as to connect with the subject, verbs take on various regular or irregular endings and, in some forms of tense, helping or auxiliary words.

Examples   I <u>think</u>.

She <u>thinks</u>.

I <u>thought</u>. [irregular verb form to express past tense]

She <u>calls</u> the meeting to order. [regular verb ending]

She <u>called</u> the meeting to order. [regular verb ending to express past tense]

verb

Present tense	They <u>run</u>. [simple present—a conjugated verb expressing actions or conditions happening now]
	Helen <u>has decided to exercise</u> better judgment. [present perfect—actions or conditions began in the past but which continue in the present]
	Lisa <u>is rowing</u>. [present progressive—an auxiliary verb and participle expressing ongoing actions or conditions]
Past tense	Anthony <u>fell</u> on the sidewalk. [simple past—actions or conditions that occurred in the past]
	We <u>had left</u> the movie theatre before Melanie and Kirsten realized they had forgotten to call Mr. Salinger. [past perfect—actions or conditions that occurred in the past but were completed before some other past actions or conditions occurred.]
	The happy couple <u>were dancing</u> to swing music. [past progressive—ongoing actions or conditions that occurred in the past]
Future tense	Jim and Tammy <u>will sell</u> their Nashville house. [simple future—actions or conditions that have yet to occur]
	Céline Dion <u>will have sung</u> a lot of Las Vegas shows in the next two years. [future perfect—current actions or conditions that will be completed by some definite time in the future]
	Batman and Robin <u>will be waiting</u> for the Riddler to send another clue by next week. [future progressive—actions or conditions that will occur in the future]

For more detailed information on verbs, see the appendixes at the end of this section, "Appendix A: Twelve Verb Tenses" and "Appendix B: Irregular Verbs."

Active and Passive Voice

Strong verbs significantly control the sense of "voice" in your writing. Conjugated verbs create *active voice*, but active voice does not require only the present tense. Active voice depends on verbs that show the subject acting rather than being acted upon.

Active voice	The new candidate <u>hopes</u> to learn more about Canada as he grows older. [subject is acting]
Passive voice	The Montreal band <u>were cheered</u> when they opened for Avril Lavigne. [subject is acted upon]

3. ADJECTIVES

Adjectives modify nouns or pronouns. Adjectives tell the reader *what kind* and *what quantity*. Adjectives may be identified by various suffixes, including –*able*, –*ible*, –*ile*, –*ive*, –*ous*, –*ar*, –*ic*, –*ent*, –*ant*, –*ful*, etc.

adj

Example   The <u>busy</u> accountant checked her <u>various</u> forms to determine which of the <u>five corporate</u> files needed <u>careful</u> review in the <u>busy</u> days <u>ahead</u>.

In the *positive*, *comparative*, and *superlative*, adjectives change.

Example	**Positive**	**Comparative**	**Superlative**
	hot stove	hotter stove	hottest stove
	reasonable idea	more reasonable idea	most reasonable idea
	good student	better student	best student

> **Tip:** Most academic and business writers use adjectives only sparingly to maintain a formal tone. Personal and creative writers of fiction and non-fiction may use adjectives more frequently to intensify expression and effects. Advertising overuses adjectives to the point of meaninglessness: "colossal blowout bonanza sale."

4. ADVERBS

Adverbs modify verbs, adjectives, other adverbs, and entire clauses. Adverbs tell the reader *how* and *in what way*. Adverbs may be identified by the suffix *–ly*, though not all adverbs end in *–ly*, and not all words ending in *–ly* are adverbs.

Example   <u>Unexpectedly</u>, the musician <u>resourcefully</u> sampled some Sly and the Family Stone <u>subtly</u>, but <u>insistently</u>, into her new song in a <u>very</u> bold way.

Like adjectives, many adverbs change form from the *positive* degree to express the *comparative* and *superlative* degrees.

Example   intelligently, more intelligently, most intelligently

> **Tip:** As with adjectives, adverbs should be used sparingly in formal writing (academic and business composition), and can appear more frequently in personal and creative writing.

5. PRONOUNS

Pronouns take the place of nouns. When the pronoun stands in for a noun, that noun is then called the *antecedent* or *referent*.

There are nine categories of pronouns: personal, possessive, demonstrative, relative, reflexive, intensive, interrogative, indefinite, and reciprocal. We cover only personal and relative pronouns here.

A) *Personal pronouns* refer to specific persons or things. They agree in number and gender with the nouns they represent. Personal pronouns can be divided into two categories, called *pronoun case*: subjective and objective.

prn

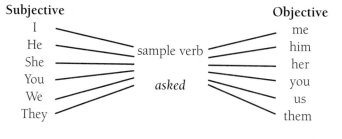

Pronoun case is determined by whether the pronoun functions as a subject or an object. Decide this according to the pronoun's relation to a verb or a preposition.

Example   subj verb   obj   infin   obj
(verb)   I *asked* <u>them</u> *to visit* <u>her</u> at her new job.

               subj   verb   obj
               <u>They</u> *drove* <u>him</u> to Vancouver for $50.

                               prep obj
Example   The sale of the car will be left up *to* <u>her</u>.
(preposition)

                     prep   obj
               The study group consisted *of* Dionna, Xiu and <u>me</u>.

B) *Relative pronouns* (*who, which, whose, whom, that*) introduce adjective clauses. They refer to the noun or pronoun that the clause modifies.

Examples   The runner, <u>who</u> had an early burst, has dropped back in the last two kilometres.

            The physics principle <u>that</u> we reviewed last week will be on the exam.

> **Tip:** *That* and *which* differ in that *that* introduces restrictive clauses while *which* introduces non-restrictive clauses.

Example   The Clint Eastwood movie <u>that</u> needs more scholarly attention is 1971's *Dirty Harry*. This film, <u>which</u> is set in San Francisco, explores violence and urban alienation.

Some writers, however, do use "which" with restrictive clauses.

6. PHRASES

There are gerund phrases, infinitive phrases, participial phrases, appositive phrases, and prepositional phrases.

Phrases can be nouns, verbs, modifiers. They differ from clauses in that they do not have conjugated verbs. Phrases do not have either *subjects* or *predicates*. (see "Verbs" and "Subjects"

phrase

modifier

As a noun	<u>Becoming a lifeguard</u> takes many hours in the pool. [This is a gerund-phrase: the present participle here (verb ending in *–ing* or *–ed*) functions as noun when accompanied by a modifier, object, or complement.]
As a noun	<u>To err</u> is human. [This is an infinitive phrase, as the infinitive here functions as the sentence's subject.]
As a modifier	<u>Linked by prison handcuffs</u>, Sydney Poitier and Tony Curtis were fugitives in the film *The Defiant Ones*. [In this participial phrase, "linked" is the participle. Participial phrases always function as adjectives.]
As a modifier	Emily Brontë's novel, <u>known as *Wuthering Heights*</u>, was her only published work. [This is an appositive phrase, which names the noun preceding it.]
As a modifier	The bowl <u>of fresh kiwi and grapes</u> looks refreshing. [This is a prepositional phrase, which modifies the noun "bowl" (a bowl of what?). A prepositional phrase begins with a preposition and ends with a noun or pronoun. The subject of the sentence is "bowl," not the prepositional phrase that modifies it.]

7. CLAUSES

A clause is a group of words containing a subject and a predicate. There are two types of clauses: *independent* (which have subjects and predicates and can stand alone as sentences) and *dependent* (which have subjects and predicates but cannot stand alone as sentences). Dependent clauses function as adverbs, adjectives, or nouns.

Independent clause	A <u>cigar smells</u>. [subject + conjugated verb]. ^{subj verb}
	The blues <u>singer</u>, an experienced Chicago musician, <u>looked</u> above the crowd while she performed a famous Lightning Hopkins song. [subject + conjugated verb].
Dependent clause	The teachers, <u>although they were undecided about the strike action</u>, asked for more information.

8. MODIFIERS

A modifier qualifies other words, providing extra information. Modifiers may be adjectives (tall, inexpensive, startled), adverbs (very, quickly, tightly), articles (the, a), phrases (of the valley), or clauses (which frightens Uncle Jim).

Example   <u>Soaked in rain</u>, <u>the young postal</u> worker walked <u>steadily</u> toward the <u>tall</u> building, <u>which was built in 1965</u>.

conj

> **Tip:** Watch out for misplaced modifiers, which do not clearly refer to the words they seek to modify. You will produce meanings you do not intend!

Examples   Last year, Sigourney only smoked two packs of cigarettes. [Is that *all* she did all year? Or, more likely, did she smoke *only* two packs last year?]

Tasha presumed in Seattle that everyone liked playing Crazy Eights.

[Did "Tasha presume *in Seattle*" or did she presume that "everyone *in Seattle*" liked this card game?]

9. CONJUNCTIONS

Conjunctions are joining words. They link words or word groups, expressing the relations between these elements. There are three types of conjunctions: coordinate, subordinate, and correlative.

A)   There are seven *coordinate conjunctions (for, and, nor, but, or, yet, so)*. They can be remembered as the acronym "FANBOYS."

Examples   Moby is an interesting musician, <u>but</u> not as interesting as Miles Davis.

The gifted photographer Yousuf Karsh created portraits of many famous people, <u>yet</u> not of Pat Benatar.

B)   *Subordinate conjunctions* introduce dependent clauses and express relations between dependent clauses and independent clauses.

Examples   <u>Although</u> we thought we knew a lot about Elvis Presley, we didn't realize he was a truck driver before he became a recording artist.

The air-conditioning doesn't work <u>because</u> of the tornado.

Some subordinate conjunctions include *after, although, as, because, before, even though, if, once, rather, than, since, that, though, unless, when, whenever, where, whereas,* and *while*.

C)   *Correlative conjunctions* appear as pairs of conjunctions that join word groups. Some correlative conjunctions include *both . . . and, either . . . or, neither . . . nor, not . . . but, not only . . . but also, whether . . . or.*

Example   <u>Both</u> porpoises <u>and</u> chimpanzees are very intelligent creatures.

> **Tip:** The words or word groups joined by correlative conjunctions must be grammatically parallel.

10. ARTICLES (DETERMINERS)

An article is a modifier appearing before a noun, adjective, or adverb. The three articles are *a*, *an*, and *the*. *A* and *an* are general, while *the* is specific.

Examples   <u>An</u> enzyme may be <u>the</u> source of this scientific mystery. [general (*an*) and specific (*the*)]

    <u>The</u> old piano needs tuning. [specific]

> **Tip:** *An* should appear before words beginning with vowel sounds or a silent "h." *A* should appear before words beginning with consonant sounds or a sounded "h" (<u>a</u> history lesson, <u>an</u> hour).

Especially if English is not your first language, see "If English Is Not Your First Language," "Determiners," under "Supplementary Resources" on the English 255 website at <http://www.athabascau.ca/courses/engl/255/>.

11. SUBJECTS

subj

A subject is one of two main parts of a sentence, the other being the predicate. There are simple subjects, complete subjects, and compound subjects.

A) A *simple subject* is a noun or pronoun that performs an action or is acted upon.

    Examples   The <u>movie</u> *was filmed* in black and white. [subject acted upon]

        The <u>car</u> *turns* right on the red light. [subject performing action]

B) A *complete subject* includes the simple subject and any words that modify it.

    Example   The <u>tall mechanic with the beard</u> fixed the Volkswagen van.

C) A *compound subject* is two (or more) simple subjects joined by a coordinate conjunction or correlative conjunction.

    Example   <u>Alfred Hitchcock and Ridley Scott</u> have made interesting movies.

> **Tip:** In some sentence constructions, the subject may not appear at the beginning of your sentence, nor appear in subject-verb sequence.

                    verb

    Examples   Where *does* <u>Lionel</u> find all those novels? [question]

                    verb

              Don't *call* Patricia! [command—"you" is implied subject]

verb

Here *are* some <u>Torontonians</u>. ["there" and "here" reverse subject-verb order to verb-object]

verb

It *is* a rainy <u>day</u>.

Writers sometimes use the expletives *there* or *it* combined with forms of the verb *to be* in order to control pace and emphasis in certain sentences. In the last example above, the actual subject *day* comes at the end of the sentence. Avoid expletives unless they seem the natural choice.

12. PREDICATES

There are three types of predicates: *simple predicate* (which is the main verb), *complete predicate* (the main verb and its auxilliaries, including objects or complements and their modifiers), and *compound predicate* (two or more verbs that have the same subject and are linked by a coordinating conjunction or a correlative conjunction).

A) Simple predicate

Example   The runner <u>stumbles</u>.

B) Complete predicate

Example   Lydia <u>will have represented her client to the best of her limited ability</u>.

C) Compound predicate

Example   The Halifax driver <u>signalled a left turn</u>, <u>slowed the school bus</u>, and <u>turned on the flashing green traffic light</u>.

13. OBJECTS

There are two types of objects: *direct* and *indirect*.

A direct object (DO) is a word or word group that names the person or thing acted upon by the subject. A direct object can answer the questions *what?* or *whom?* about the verb.

Examples   Lisa laced <u>her figure skates</u>.

Russell Crowe pushed <u>another bar patron</u>.

An indirect object (IO) is a noun or pronoun that can answer the question *for whom? to whom? to what?* or *for what?* about the verb.

Examples   Stephanie helped her classmates <u>for her teacher's sake</u>.

Marc sold his drum set <u>to the highest bidder</u>.

obj

14. PARTICIPLES

A participle is a verb form with either *–ing* or *–ed* on the end. Participles function as adjectives and appear as either *present* particles or *past* participles.

Examples   The <u>oncoming</u> ocean liner parted the cold waves. [present participle]

Now <u>stalled,</u> the car slowed the traffic on Sherbrooke Street. [past participle]

15. GERUNDS

A gerund is a verbal form that ends in *-ing* and functions as a noun. A gerund can be a subject or an object.

Subject   <u>Napping</u> is sometimes necessary.

Object   We know <u>swimming</u> does not require a swimsuit.

> **Tip:** Gerunds appear in the same form as present particles, but present participles function as *adjectives* while gerunds operate as *nouns*.

Examples   <u>Hoping for more peace</u>, the neighbour went on a <u>fishing</u> trip. [participle phrase and present participle (adjectives)]

<u>Fishing</u> takes more skill than bingo. [gerund (noun)]

16. INFINITIVES

An infinitive consists of the form of the verb preceded by "to" (*to* lift, *to* photograph, *to* kiss). We conjugate infinitives to derive specific verb forms (I lift, she photographs, they kiss).

Infinitives may function as subjects or objects of verbs.

Examples   <u>To dream</u> is courageous. [subject]

The cook wants <u>to relax</u>. [object]

The doctors hope <u>to find</u> the problem soon. [object]

17. PREPOSITIONS

Prepositions are connectors that express relationships between nouns or pronouns and the other words in a sentence. Some prepositions include the following: *about, above, across, after, among, around, as, at, before, behind, below, beside, between, beyond, down, for, from, in, into, near, of, off, on, onto, over, toward, under,* and *within.*

prep

A prepositional phrase begins with a preposition and ends with a noun or pronoun.

Examples The agreement <u>between the accountants</u> has been signed.

The bowl <u>of fruit</u> sits on the kitchen table.

> **Tip:** Remember to make your verb agree with your subject (bowl), not any noun in the prepositional phrase.

subj   prep-phrase   verb

Example This *collection* <u>*of fishing rods, old comic books, and toys*</u> *has* sentimental value.

18. SUBJECT AND OBJECT COMPLEMENTS

A subject complement is a word or word group that follows a *linking verb* and identifies or describes the subject. Linking verbs are forms of being and include the verbs *seem*, *appear*, *stay*, *look*, *become*, *sound*, *taste*, *feel*, and *smell*.

linking verb   subj compl

Examples This flower *smells* <u>like a mixture of talcum powder and fresh rain</u>.

linking verb

This milk *seems* sour.

comp

An object complement is a word or word group that follows a *direct object* and identifies or describes that object.

DO   obj compl

Example The CBC reporter called the author's <u>work self-centred</u>.

19. COMPARATIVES AND SUPERLATIVES

Comparatives are forms of adjectives and adverbs that describe a relation between *two* items or concepts.

Example Irvine Welsh, who wrote *Trainspotting*, is a <u>better</u> writer than Jane Owen, who wrote *Camden Girls*, in describing the modern urban dance club in the United Kingdom.

A superlative is the form of an adjective or adverb that describes the relationship between *more* than two items or concepts.

Examples Muhammad Ali is still the <u>most</u> spiritual and influential of all heavyweight champion boxers.

Barbara Frum was the <u>best</u> of all CBC interviewers in the 1970s and 1980s.

Tip: Usually, the comparative of one-syllable adjectives is formed by adding *–er* (small, small*er*), while the superlative of many one-syllable adjectives can be formed by adding *–est* (kind, kind*est*). Adjectives with two or more syllables can often be handled by adding *more* for the comparative and *most* for the superlative (*more* frightening, *most* frightening).

Tip: Be alert that there are many irregular comparatives and superlatives (little, less, least).

20. INTERJECTIONS

Isolated words or phrases expressing emotion are interjections and, although they are not independent clauses, usually they are permitted to stand alone as complete utterances.

Examples   *Alas*, poor Yorick! (*Hamlet* 5.1. 172)

O, brave new world. . . . (*Tempest* 5.1. 183)

Holy hole in a doughnut, Batman!

inter

Appendix A
Twelve Verb Tenses

(This appendix was prepared by Veronica Baig and is reprinted with the permission of Athabasca University.)

There are 12 verb tenses in English. The verb action can take place in the past, the present, or the future. There are usually word clues that indicate when the verb action occurs. Within each of these times there are four different situations.

1. *Simple tenses* occur at a particular point in time, or on a repeated or habitual basis.
2. A *progressive* or *continuous tense* indicates that the action takes place over time, and these tenses always use part of the verb "be" as the first part of the verb phrase and end with the main verb + *ing*.
3. A *perfect tense* indicates an action that ends before another action, always uses part of "have" as the first part of the verb phrase, and ends with the past participle of the main verb.
4. A *perfect progressive tense* indicates an action that happened over time and ends before another action. A perfect progressive tense starts with the relevant part of the verb "have" followed by "been" and ends with the main verb + *ing*.

If you remember these basic rules, you can always identify the verb tense being used, or use the verb tense you need without having to continually refer to a textbook or a table. Meanwhile, a chart like the one shown here can provide a quick and easy reference until you feel comfortable using the various verb tenses.

Also pay attention to the time clues in the following chart; while some of them can be used with more than one verb tense, they do restrict the number of possibilities and help you to understand which verb tense is being used, or which verb tense you should use.

Some examples:

simple past	yesterday
simple present	every day
simple future	tomorrow
past progressive	while
present progressive	now

Active Verb Tenses

	Past	Present	Future
Simple	*An action that ended at a point in the past*	*An action that exists, is usual, or is repeated*	*A plan for future action*
	cooked	**cook/cooks**	**will cook**
(time clue)*	He cooked yesterday.	He cooks dinner every Friday.	He will cook tomorrow.
Progressive be + main verb + ing	*an action was happening (past progressive) when another action happened (simple past)*	*an action that is happening now*	*an action that will be happening over time, in the future, when something else happens*
	was/were cooking	**am/is/are cooking**	**will be cooking**
(time clue)*	He was cooking when the phone rang.	He is cooking now.	He will be cooking when you come.
Perfect have + main verb	*an action that ended before another action or time in the past*	*an action that happened at an unspecified time in the past*	*an action that will end before another action or time in the future*
	had cooked	**has/have cooked**	**will have cooked**
(time clue)*	He had cooked the dinner when the phone rang.	He has cooked many meals.	He will have cooked dinner by the time you come.
Perfect progressive have + be + main verb + ing	*an action that happened over time, in the past, before another time or action in the past*	*an action occurring over time that started in the past and continues into the present*	*an action occurring over time, in the future, before another action or time in the future*
	had been cooking	**has/have been cooking**	**will have been cooking**
(time clue)*	He had been cooking for a long time before he took lessons.	He has been cooking for over an hour.	He will have been cooking all day by the time she gets home.

12 tenses

*Time clues: these are words that give some information about when an action occurs. Many words are time clues; some can be used to indicate a number of tenses.

If you learn to recognize these time clues, you will find them very helpful. Note that some time clues can be used with more than one verb tense and also that this table is not a complete list of all the time clues that can be used with all of the tenses.

Time Clues and Verb Tenses

Simple	Simple past	Simple present	Simple future
	yesterday last year/month/etc. before for five weeks/days/etc. one year/month ago	every morning/day/etc. always usually frequently sometimes	tomorrow tonight next week/month/etc. soon in the future
Progressive	**Past progressive**	**Present progressive**	**Future progressive**
	while when	now right now this week/minute/etc.	when after as soon as before
Perfect	**Past perfect**	**Present perfect**	**Future perfect**

	before
	already
	by the time
	until then/last week/etc.
	after
		until now
		since
		ever
		never
		many times/weeks/years/etc.
		for three hours/minutes/etc.
			by the time you go
			  (somewhere)
			by the time you do
			  (something)
			already

Perfect progressive	**Past perfect progressive**	**Present perfect progressive**	**Future perfect progressive**
	before for one week/hour/etc. since	for the past year/month/etc. for the last two months/ weeks/etc. up to now for six weeks/hours/etc. since	by the time for 10 days/weeks/etc. by

Irregular Verbs

There are a number of irregular verbs in English; they are irregular in the simple past form and/or the past participle. Rather than learning each verb separately, you can put many of the verbs into a group of verbs that change their forms in similar ways. If you are in any doubt about a verb, whether it is irregular or not, or about the exact form that an irregular verb takes, refer to your dictionary as a good reference. Many dictionaries contain a supplement listing a large number of irregular verbs alphabetically; they all indicate in the main listing whether a verb is irregular and, if so, the form(s) it takes.

Group I Verbs
- The verb name, the simple past, and the past participle forms are all different.
- The past participle forms ends in **n**.
- The vowel changes in the simple past and the past participle.

Note: V = vowel, C = consonant

	Change	Verb name		Simple past		Past participle
IA	i ➠ a ➠ u	begin	➠	began	➠	begun
IB	o/a ➠ e	blow	➠	blew	➠	blown
IC	double vowel ➠ o	break	➠	broke	➠	broken
ID	vowel ➠ o (past)	drive	➠	drove	➠	driven
IE	a ➠ oo (past)	take	➠	took	➠	taken

Group I Verbs

IA	IB	IC	ID	IE
i ⟶ a ⟶ u	o/a ⟶ e	VV ⟶ o	V ⟶ o (past)	a ⟶ oo (past)
begin	blow	bear	arise	forsake
drink	draw	break	drive	mistake
forbid	grow	choose	ride*	shake
ring	know	freeze	rise	take/undertake
shrink	throw	speak	stride*	
sing		steal	tread*	
sink		swear	write*	
spring		tear		
stink		wear		
swim		weave		

irr verb

* The spelling of these past participle are, respectively, "ridden," "stridden," "trodden," and "written."

Other Group I Verbs

Verb name		Simple past		Past participle
be	⟶	was/were	⟶	been
bite	⟶	bit	⟶	bitten
do	⟶	did	⟶	done
eat	⟶	ate	⟶	eaten
fall	⟶	fell	⟶	fallen
fly	⟶	flew	⟶	flown
get/forget	⟶	got/forgot	⟶	gotten/forgotten
give/forgive	⟶	gave/forgave	⟶	given/forgiven

(continued)

Other Group I Verbs (continued)

Verb name		Simple past		Past participle
go	➡	went	➡	gone
hide	➡	hid	➡	hidden
lie	➡	lay	➡	lain
see	➡	saw	➡	seen
swell	➡	swelled	➡	swollen
wake	➡	woke	➡	woken

Group II Verbs

The simple past and past participle forms are the same.

	Change	Verb name		Simple past/past participle
II A	*ee/ea* ➡ *e/ea** + *d*	feed	➡	fed
II B	*e* ➡ *o* + *ld*	sell	➡	sold
	ay ➡ *ai* + *d*	say	➡	said
	i ➡ *ou* + *nd*	find	➡	found
II C	*ee/ea* ➡ *e* + (C) + *t*	keep	➡	kept
II D	*i/a* ➡ *u* + (*n*) + *g/k*	sting	➡	stung
II E	final *d* ➡ *t*	send	➡	sent

irr verb

* Spelling may not change but vowel sound does change.

(continued)

Group II Verbs

II A		II B			II C		II D	II E
ee/ea ➡ *e/ea** + d		*e* ➡ *o + ld*	*ay* ➡ *ai + d*	*i* ➡ *ou + nd*	*ee/ea* ➡ *e* + (C) + t		*i/a* ➡ *u* + (n) + g/k	final *d* ➡ *t*
flee		sell	lay	bind	creep		cling	bend
bleed		tell	pay	find	feel		dig	build
breed			say	grind	keep		fling	lend
feed				wind	kneel		hang**	send
hear					leave***		stick	spend
lead					meet		sting	
read*					sleep		strike	
speed					sweep		string	
					weep		swing	
							wring	

irr verb

* Spelling may not change but vowel sound does change.
** "Hang" means "to fasten or attach from above." In the other meaning of "hang," "to hang a person," it is a regular verb.
*** Spelling changes, "leave" to "left."

Other Group II Verbs

Verb name ➡VV + *ght*		Past/past participle*	Verb name ➡ *d*		Past/past participle	Verb name ➡*o/u*		Past/past participle
bring	➡	brought	have	➡	had	shine	➡	shone
buy	➡	bought	hold	➡	held	spin	➡	spun
catch	➡	caught	make	➡	made	win	➡	won
fight	➡	fought	prove	➡	proved**			
seek	➡	sought	slide	➡	slid			
teach	➡	taught	stand	➡	stood			
think	➡	thought						

(continued)

Other Group II Verbs (continued)

Other Verbs		
deal	⟶	dealt
light	⟶	lit
lose	⟶	lost
mean	⟶	meant
shoot	⟶	shot
sit	⟶	sat

* Spelling is *au/ou*, but pronunciation remains the same.
** "Proven" is also acceptable for the past participle.

Group III Verbs

The simple past is different from the other verb forms; the past participle is the same as the infinitive.

Verb name		Simple past		Past participle
become	⟶	became	⟶	become
come	⟶	came	⟶	come
run	⟶	ran	⟶	run

irr verbs

Group IV Verbs

The verb form stays the same in the infinitive, the simple past, and the past participle.

Verb name	Simple past	Past participle
bet	bet	bet

Other Group IV Verbs

bid	cut	let	set	split
burst	fit	put	shed	spread
cast	hit	quit	shut	thrust
cost	hurt	rid	slit	upset

Group V Verbs

The simple past is the same as the verb name; the past participle is different.

Verb name	Simple past	Past participle
beat	beat	beat**en**

Section 2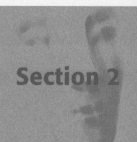

Punctuation Terms

There are very few punctuation marks available to writers. However, by varying your patterns of punctuation, you can keep your writing fresh and vital.

The forms of punctuation are the period, comma, semicolon, colon, apostrophe, quotation marks, parentheses, dash, slash, brackets, ellipses, question mark, and exclamation mark.

1. PERIOD [.]

The period provides the full stop at the end of sentences. A period brings order to writing, letting readers know when your sentence has ended. Pico Iyer, a travel writer, refers to the period as the dot that brought the world of writing to its senses. Correct use of the period shows that you recognize independent clauses.

Examples   Wayne Gretzky works on behalf of several charities. He is still a young, enthusiastic person.

Office flirting, a delicate matter, raises professional and ethical questions. Consequences and power relations must be considered.

2. COMMA [,]

The *comma* has many uses and may be considered the all-around utility player of punctuation. Commas can simply *separate* elements in your writing, or commas can also *set off* elements in your writing.

A)   Commas separate elements in a *list* (three or more items).

Examples   Pope John Paul II is the first pope to preach in a Lutheran church, visit England since before the time of King Henry VIII, address a Muslim audience of 80 000 people, re-establish diplomatic relations between Israel and the Vatican since 1948, and ask other religions and peoples to forgive the Catholic Church for its historical sins against them.

Pizza ingredients may include pepperoni, tomatoes, feta cheese, black olives, mushrooms or onions.

Tip: Some people place a comma before the *and* or *or* as the list draws to a close, and some people don't. Whether you do or not, be consistent through your paper or report.

However, here is a reason to use the comma before *and* or *or* in a list of items. Consider these:

Examples   The theatre conference invited well-known artists including Linda Griffiths, Ann-Marie MacDonald, and Mump and Smoot.

The theatre conference drew well-known artists including Linda Griffiths, Ann-Marie MacDonald, Tomson Highway, and Drew Hayden Taylor.

Explanation: Mump and Smoot are a team, and therefore may be considered as a single entity, such as Laurel and Hardy or Gilbert and Sullivan.

Highway and Taylor are individual artists, not a team. Placing the comma before the "and" allows the writer to clarify that the final item is not considered united with the one before it. Leaving out the comma clarifies that the last two items *are* considered part of one item in the list. This code will not work if you choose never to use the comma before the "and" or "or."

B) Commas separate *independent clauses* that are joined by *coordinate conjunctions* (for, and, nor, but, or, yet, so). The comma is placed before the coordinate conjunction.

Examples Some doctors and nutritionists claim vitamin supplements are necessary for a healthy diet, but other experts claim bottled vitamins enrich only manufacturers and urine.

Parenting deeply changes most people, so it is not surprising that watching our children grow compels parents to grow as well.

C) Commas separate *parts of dates and addresses*.

Example On March 10, 1978, a beagle named Barney ran away.

All fan mail for Donny Osmond for his Halifax and Toronto performances in *Joseph and the Amazing Technicolor Dreamcoat* may be sent to his Canadian agent at 2602 Agnes Street, Toronto, Ontario C2A R9A.

Tip: No comma appears before the postal code.

D) Commas set off a sentence's *introductory qualifier* (whether word, phrase, or clause). The comma separates this introductory element from the independent (or main) clause to help the reader recognize these two parts of the sentence.

Examples When the government clerk Igor Gouzenko defected from Russia to Canada in 1945, he brought with him 109 secret documents that revealed a highly developed spy ring operating effectively out of Canada.

Named the Gouzenko Affair, this unexpected international revelation forced Canada to confront Cold War espionage as both a global and a domestic activity.

E) Commas set off *non-restrictive qualifiers*. These are qualifiers that add extra, but not essential information to the sentence.

Examples Herb Alpert and the Tijuana Brass, a world-famous horn band, recorded the songs "A Taste of Honey" and "Tijuana Taxi" in the late 1960s.

Retro fashions, which have somehow managed to compress the forties, fifties, sixties, seventies, and eighties into one strangely layered moment of expression, present beautiful opportunities of expression and discovery through comparison and contrast.

F) Commas also set off *transitional expressions*, *parenthetical expressions*, *direct address*, and *interrogatives*.

Examples   Dr. Schaeffer is, thirdly, a fine poet. [transitional]

He was, of course, overlooked. [parenthetical]

Daphne, it's my round for beer, isn't it? [direct address *and* interrogative]

Tip: Watch out for mistaking *restrictive qualifiers* for non-restrictive qualifiers. You cannot remove a restrictive qualifier from a sentence without changing the meaning of the subject or noun being qualified.

Example   The car insurance that we discussed provides full coverage for our van.

3. SEMICOLON [;]

Semicolons join related independent clauses.

Example   In some parts of South Korea, spicy dog soup remains a popular delicacy; this is mostly among the older generations.

David Bowie issued his own investment bonds several years ago; they were financially backed by the future royalties on his music.

Sometimes, a semicolon can be used to separate items in a list where each item in that list already features commas for qualification. This is called internal qualification.

Example   The judges include Chief Justice Beverley McLachlin, who is from Pincher Creek, Alberta; Justice Claire L'Heureux-Dubé, who often sides with the state rather than the accused; and Justice Andrew MacKay, who used to be president of Dalhousie University in Halifax, Nova Scotia.

4. COLON [:]

A colon is used after an independent clause to introduce a list, clause, phrase, or single word. An independent clause must precede the full colon, however.

Examples   We worried about one thing all year: money.

The following cartoon characters will appear at the charity event: Tweety Bird, Sylvester the Cat, Space Ghost, Kamandi, Betty and Veronica, and Lex Luther.

Full colons are also used in memo headings, titles, bibliographical entries, and time notations.

Examples   The Vulnerable Self: State Power in Kafka's *The Trial* [essay title]

To: Jon Bon Jovi

From: Melanie Moustafa [memo]

5. APOSTROPHE [']

Apostrophes signal the possessive case and act as substitutes for letters in contractions. There are two types of possessive case: the singular ('s) and the plural (s').

Examples   The carjacker's attempt was thwarted by a passerby. [singular possessive]

The two biology teachers' attempts to coach the volleyball team were welcomed. [plural possessive]

They don't charge GST here. [contraction]

Tip: Joint possession requires one apostrophe.

Example   Sid and Nancy's party went late into the night.

6. QUOTATION MARKS [" "]

Quotation marks are used for direct speech, textual quotations and some titles (stories, newspaper articles and scholarly articles, songs, poems, speeches, chapters of books, radio programs). Sometimes quotation marks also set off certain words as ironic or as special terms.

Examples   Michael Ondaatje's poem "Letters and Other Worlds" examines emotional distances. [title]

Kofi Annan, the United Nations Secretary-General, said, "The use of child soldiers in Sierra Leone continues to concern all nations." [direct speech]

Faulkner wrote that "between grief and nothing, I'll take grief." [textual quotation]

Tip: Quotations of more than four lines require block quotation format, which is indented from the left margin and requires no quotation marks.

Tip: Punctuation with quotation marks can be a little tricky. Put commas and periods inside your closing quotation marks, unless you include a line or page reference after the quotation.

Examples "They paved Paradise," sang Joni Mitchell.

Some deep-water divers experience "shallow water blackout"; this is sudden unconsciousness in the final moments of ascent.

The "belief in life elsewhere in the universe is widely held" (173), according to Davis Marble and Mavis Darby in their article "Life Elsewhere."

7. PARENTHESES [( )]

Parentheses are the above rounded enclosing marks, sometimes mistakenly referred to as brackets, which are square and look like this: [ ]. Parentheses are sometimes used to enclose non-essential (non-restrictive) information.

Example Britney Spears (whose Web site is visited more than any other) champions virginity while taking sexually suggestive appearance to a new extreme.

Parentheses are also used to provide abbreviated terms for items.

Example We attended the fourteenth annual Canadian Information Technology Security Symposium (CITSS).

Terms to be replaced by abbreviations should be used in full the first time they occur in a piece of writing, followed as above by the abbreviation in parentheses. Thereafter the short form is used.

8. DASH [–]

The dash is the Evel Knievel of punctuation marks—a freewheeling, daredevil, expressive stretch. The dash can substitute for many other punctuation marks, but should be used sparingly in formal writing. The dash can set off non-restrictive and parenthetical elements (as commas can), can introduce a list, phrase, clause, or single word (as a colon can), can join two independent clauses (as a semicolon can) and can signal an interruption (usually in creative writing).

Examples The white T-shirt worn by itself—popularized initially by Marlon Brando and James Dean—has become widespread rather than a rebellious or anti-establishment statement. [setting off a non-restrictive]

Etiquette lessons can become quite detailed—when to bring a gift, when to write a thank-you card, how formal to be on a first date, what shoes are suitable for a wedding. [introducing a list]

The African famine continues—the G8 must take steps to avoid human catastrophe. [joining two independent clauses]

9. SLASH [/]

The slash or solidus is seldom used in formal writing. It usually separates lines of poetry and song lyrics in quotations, numbers in abbreviated dates, overlapping calendar years, and sometimes paired terms.

Example   Be shrewd my eyes / Least you shall reveal / The sadness of my nature /
And the truth of what I feel. [separating lines of poetry]

Every voter should be familiar with his/her candidate's political beliefs.
[paired terms: note that use of *his/her* is usually awkward]

10. BRACKETS [ ]

Brackets are not used often, but they are very important in research papers when you have to insert a word or phrase to help the quoted syntax, to identify people, events, or action, to make connections within quotations after you have omitted some elements for the sake of brevity, or to clarify references.

Examples   When he [Peter Parker] said he knows now that a radioactive spider
gave him unusual power, he realizes his life has changed forever.

"It [consumer culture] manipulatively forces children and youth to
make identity choices based on commodities before developing a full
sense of identity" (47), according to a recent report conducted at the
University of Western Ontario.

You may occasionally see the Latin word *sic* enclosed in editorial brackets within a quotation.

Example   "She was always so tired that she would just lay [*sic*] on the couch all
day."

[ ]

The speaker has confused the verbs "to lie" and "to lay" (meaning to place an object). Correct usage would be "she would just lie on the couch all day." The inserted word *sic*, Latin for "thus," indicates that the quoted wording remains faithful to the original source.

Brackets may occasionally also be used to enclose parenthetical elements that occur within parentheses.

Example   She told him that her mother (a mysterious woman with complex motives [some of which were even now under investigation] and boundless
energy) was returning from Europe that very evening.

Such awkward constructions are best avoided.

11. ELLIPSES [. . .]

When words are omitted from a quotation, three spaced ellipsis dots express this change—this gap—in the original material.

Original	"Doctors and nutritionists have cited the influence of the long Canadian winter, a geographical aspect, as a major contributing factor in the steady depletion that amounts to a shortage of vitamin D in Canadians."

Revised with Ellipses "Doctor and nutritionists . . . cit[e] . . . the long Canadian winter . . . as a major contributing factor in the . . . shortage of vitamin D . . . ."

Tip: If an ellipsis occurs at the end of a sentence, the three spaced dots are followed by the period to end the sentence, amounting to four dots.

12. QUESTION MARK [?]

The question mark appears after a question.

Examples   Who disagrees that golf knickers are foolish?

Why wasn't Rachel the academic valedictorian?

Sometimes a declarative statement can seem like a question, but it isn't.

Example   The controversy focuses on whether or not Christina Aguilera is a responsible female role model.

13. EXCLAMATION MARK [!]

Exclamation marks or points supposedly emphasize strong expression. The problem, however, is that so many young writers are tempted to use exclamation points to emphasize almost anything (!!) that this punctuation mark has been rendered meaningless!

Example   Some doctors claim that drinking eight glasses of water a day may not be enough!

Tip: Keep exclamation points to a bare minimum and try to express strength or urgency through your language and your ideas.

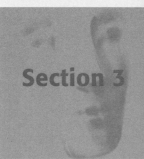

THE
HANDBOOK

Section 3

Fifteen Common Errors

Most usage errors in first-year essays fall into one of the following 15 common categories. Removing these 15 errors from your work will significantly improve your results in all forms of writing.

1. SENTENCE FRAGMENT

A *sentence fragment* is a group of words that is not a sentence. At its minimum, every sentence must form an independent clause; that is, it must have a subject and a predicate. Although most sentences will contain more than just a subject and verb, these two elements represent the simplest form of sentence. A sentence fragment is missing one or both of these two elements.

Example   Marissa misunderstands.

With a subject ("Marissa") and a conjugated verb ("misunderstands"), we have an independent clause, a complete sentence.

Sentence fragment (missing subject and verb) Not for a while.

Corrected   The *bus* <u>will</u> not <u>stop</u> for a while.

Sentence fragment (missing subject) Agrees, however, that some changes are necessary and soon.

Corrected   *Jennifer* agrees, however, that some changes are necessary and should be soon.

Sentence fragment (missing conjugated verb) John, hoping for a better job in the accounting field in either Nova Scotia or Ontario.

Corrected   John *hopes* for a better job in the accounting field in either Nova Scotia or Ontario.

Sentence fragment (dependent clause) Although U2 has often altered their musical style by introducing more futuristic technotronic sounds into some songs.

Corrected   U2 has often altered their musical style by introducing more futuristic technotronic sounds into some songs.

2. COMMA SPLICE

A comma splice is a major writing error committed by using a comma to join two independent clauses, "splicing" them together. The comma by itself is not considered a strong enough piece of punctuation to join or coordinate two independent clauses.

Comma splice   Cathy likes to read *People* magazine, Helen likes to read stock reports.

Corrected #1   *While* Cathy likes to read *People* magazine, Helen likes to read stock reports.

Corrected #2   Cathy likes to read *People* magazine, *but* Helen likes to read stock reports.

> **Tip:** Here are the four most common ways to correct a comma splice:
>
> 1. Add one of the seven coordinate conjunctions after the comma joining the two independent clauses;
> 2. Keep the comma but change one of the independent clauses into a dependent clause;
> 3. Delete the comma and separate the independent clauses with a semicolon instead; and
> 4. Delete the comma and use a period instead to make the two independent clauses into two sentences.

3. SUBJECT-VERB AGREEMENT PROBLEM

In English, subjects and their verbs agree in number. If your subject is singular, then your verb form should be singular. If your subject is plural, then your verb form should be plural.

Subject-verb error	The lawyer for the nurses, doctors, technicians, and medical students involved in the series of medical errors are prepared to admit guilt on behalf of his clients.
Corrected	The *lawyer* for the nurses, doctors, technicians and medical students involved in the series of medical errors <u>is</u> prepared to admit guilt on behalf of his clients.
Subject-verb error	The long Canadian winter, including snowstorms, ice storms, short days, nearly Arctic temperatures, and unpredictable windchills, require great endurance and patience.
Corrected	The long Canadian *winter*, including . . . , <u>requires</u> great endurance and patience.

> **Tip:** Watch out for collective nouns that function grammatically as singular nouns, but represent more than one person or unit.

sv agr

Subject-verb error	The group of electricians, welders, and carpenters vote tonight for a change in negotiations.
Corrected	The *group* of electricians, welders, and carpenters <u>votes</u> tonight for a change in negotiations.

Remember, since there is only *one* group here, "group" is a singular subject, although it may represent many people.

4. NOUN-PRONOUN AGREEMENT OR REFERENCE PROBLEM

Pronouns need to agree in number and gender with the nouns they represent, sometimes called their referents or antecedents.

Incorrect pronoun	Since the candles are not on sale, it is too expensive.
Corrected	Since the <u>candles</u> are not on sale, *they* are too expensive.

"They," a plural pronoun, refers correctly in number to the plural noun "candles."

The most typical pronoun-agreement error is misuse of *their*.

Incorrect pronoun	Everyone in the class used *their* textbook (to help a young sibling to reach the dinner table).
Corrected	All the students in the class used their textbook (to help a young sibling to reach the dinner table).
Corrected	Everyone in the class used *his or her* textbook (to help a young sibling to reach the dinner table).

> **Tip:** Indefinite pronouns such as *person, one, any, each, either, neither*, and words ending in *–one, -body, and –thing* require singular pronouns such as *she* or *he*. When possible, replace the indefinite singular pronoun with a plural noun, as illustrated above: *All the students* in the class . . . . instead of *everyone*. This avoids the exclusionist choice (of using *he* rather than *she* or *she* rather than *he*) as well as the clumsy choice of *he or she*. Use of *their* with indefinite pronouns is beginning to be sanctioned, but many readers still object to it. You are best to avoid this usage in your academic writing.

Pronouns should also refer clearly to their intended referents so that a reader has no confusion over what that particular pronoun represents. If you have more than one choice, consider that pronoun unclear or sometimes even incorrect.

Unclear pronoun reference	The difference between these corporate and government deductions in the three financial reports, prepared by rival accounting firms, raises a troubling question about the senator's travel expenses and a possibly illegal discount. This is very suspicious.

n/pn agr

You have several options in clarifying this unclear pronoun reference, "This," depending on your intended meaning.

Corrected #1	This <u>difference</u> is very suspicious.
Corrected #2	This <u>corporate and government discrepancy</u> is very suspicious.
Corrected #3	This <u>rivalry between accounting firms</u> is very suspicious.
Corrected #4	This <u>possible illegal discount</u> is very suspicious.

> **Tip:** "This" is a relative pronoun and may refer to a condition or state rather than specifically to a noun.

Example   It's raining today. This is good for the crops.

Unclear pronoun reference   Helen told Viola that *her* purse had gone missing.

Correction   Clarify whose purse has gone missing. Is it Helen's or Viola's?

Example   Helen told Viola that Viola's purse had gone missing.

It is better to repeat words, if necessary, than to allow serious ambiguity caused by unclear pronoun reference.

5. DANGLING PARTICIPLE

Dangling participles do not match the subjects or nouns they intend to qualify. A participle is a verb form ending in *–ing* or *–ed*. Participles and participle phrases modify nouns. When a participle or participle phrase appears at the beginning of a sentence, it functions as an introductory qualifier for the subject that should follow it directly.

Dangling participle   Skating hard, the open net loomed up ahead of the hockey player.

Corrected   Skating hard, *the hockey player* saw the open net loom up ahead.

Dangling participle   Flipping through the magazine, the recent articles on new bands seemed irrelevant to David Bowie.

Corrected   Flipping through the magazine, *David Bowie* thought the recent articles on new bands seemed irrelevant.

> **Tip:** Ask yourself who or what is performing or experiencing that participle and then check to see if an appropriate subject or noun directly follows the participle or participle phrase.

6. MISPLACED MODIFIER

mm

Be alert to what your modifiers are qualifying. Be sure they modify what you intend to qualify rather than modify any noun or concept haphazardly.

Misplaced modifier   The Diabetes Foundation, a quiet killer, needs donations for further research.

Corrected   The Diabetes Foundation needs donations to fight *their disease, a quiet killer*.

Misplaced modifier	If mowed regularly by highway crews, many more elk and deer might be visible from the Trans-Canada Highway through the field grass.
Corrected	Many more elk and deer might be visible from the Trans-Canada Highway if the field grass were mowed regularly.

7. PRONOUN CASE PROBLEM

Many people use the incorrect form of pronouns, especially when trying to sound formal. Pronouns have two forms: subjective and objective. These are called pronoun cases. Pronoun case depends on the pronoun's relation to either (a) the relevant verb or (b) the relevant preposition. The relevant verb determines whether the pronoun is a subject or an object, depending on how the pronoun functions with that verb. A subject pronoun takes the subjective form (I, she, he, they), while an object pronoun takes the objective form (me, her, him, them).

Pronoun Case with Verb

Examples   Ian <u>asked</u> Tim, Cliff and *me* for some fitness advice.

Tracy Q. <u>kissed</u> Tina and *him* on their cheeks.

"Me" is the objective form of the pronoun because it is the object of the verb "asked" in the first example. "Tina and him" are the objects of the verb "kissed" in the second example, so "him" appears as an objective pronoun. Pronoun case with a preposition follows a simple rule: the objective form of pronoun follows any preposition.

Pronoun Case with Preposition

Example   Stephen left a lot of the research up *to* Ravi, Tasha, and *me*.

"Me" takes the objective form because it follows the preposition "to." Often, you have to handle correct pronoun case in relation to both verbs and prepositions.

Example   She <u>told</u> him to <u>ask</u> *them* to leave the choice of gifts up *to* Steve Miller, Peter Frampton, and *me*.

"She" is the subject, performing the verb "told," and so appears in the subjective form of the pronoun. "Him" and "them" are objects of the verb "told" and of the infinitive "to ask," respectively, so appear as objective pronouns. "Me" appears as an objective pronoun because it follows the preposition "to" in a list.

pro

> **Tip:** The objective form of a pronoun appears after a preposition, despite an intervening list.

8. MISSING OR UNNECCESSARY COMMA

Comma errors are common in first-year, undergraduate, and even professional writing. Sometimes, bad advice circulates regarding the comma; this misinformation amounts to the claim that one should insert a comma wherever you would pause to draw breath if you were speaking. Unfortunately, this is overly loose, unreliable advice; it whimsically bases itself on fluctuating vocal patterns. Since people from New Jersey have speech rhythms that differ from those of people from Newfoundland, you need to rely on defined mechanical rules to sort out the proper locations of commas.

There are some distinct grammatical rules for use of the comma:

A)   Comma after introductory phrase or clause

Examples   Though usually disagreeing with Mike and Rebecca, Aimée finally conceded that Bryan Adams has an interesting voice.

Although beautiful, the long Canadian winter depletes our bodies of vitamin D.

B)   Two commas to set off a non-restrictive qualifier

Examples   The loonie, our dollar, still remains weak against the U.S. dollar.

Tommy Hunter, a Canadian musician, is considered the country music gentleman.

C)   Comma to separate independent clauses from dependent clauses

Examples   Legal decisions at the Appeal Court are seldom unanimous, partly because judges represent opposing legal, social, and philosophical views.

Mr. Simpson now likes golf and other sports, although he still enjoys *The London Times* and some of the quieter musicals.

D)   Comma before a qualifying phrase

Examples   Vancouver residents receive the best health care, according to recent surveys.

Tanya always liked to listen to the sounds of the New Brunswick night, especially ocean waves, crickets, freight trains, and wind in thick grass.

E)   Comma before a coordinating conjunction

Example   She trekked 20 miles from the disaster site to the heights, but still she had the stamina to scale the bluff and to build a large signal fire.

See B) under "2. Comma" of Section 2 of this *Handbook*, "Punctuation Terms."

9. MISUSED COLON OR SEMICOLON

These two pieces of punctuation are neither mystical nor inscrutable. The colon and semicolon are distinct units of punctuation and are governed by simple, definite rules.

The Colon

The colon allows several choices following it: on its right. However, the colon requires that an independent clause precede it: on its left side. The colon, sometimes called the full colon to distinguish it from the semicolon, can introduce a range of grammatical elements: a list, an independent or dependent clause, a phrase, or even a single word. Remember, however, that the colon must be preceded by an independent clause.

Incorrect use of colon	Some of the kind and interesting students from the SJHS Class of 1982 are: Tanya, Louise Mennier, Tzigane, Mike Moore, Peggy Grimmer, and Sue Logan.
Corrected #1	There are many kind and interesting students from the SJHS Class of 1982: Tanya, Louise Mennier, Tzigane, Mike Moore, Peggy Grimmer, and Sue Logan.
Corrected #2	Some kind and interesting students from the SJHS class of 1982 include the following: Tanya, Louise Mennier, Tzigane, Mike Moore, Peggy Grimmer, and Sue Logan.

Other uses of the colon include these options:

List	Many common household pets are quite small: poodles, cats, goldfish, and iguanas.
Phrase or dependent clause	Montreal has long been considered the Paris of North America: a city that offers francophone style and the second largest number of French speakers in the world.
Single word	One of the Atlantic provinces is not a Maritime province: Newfoundland and Labrador.

The Semicolon

The semicolon joins independent clauses. The semicolon, however, is often misused as a comma (perhaps a comma with a hat). To use the semicolon correctly, you must be able to recognize an independent clause (a subject with conjugated verb).

Incorrect use of semicolon	Yellow golf pants are silly; especially for Mr. and Mrs. Almond.
Corrected	Yellow golf pants are silly; this is especially true for Mr. and Mrs. Almond, who are usually as bland as anyone could imagine.

tense

10. TENSE PROBLEMS

Knowing when to use the various tenses in English can be a challenge; however, a number of tense errors occur simply because the writer is unfamiliar with the correct form of the verb called for in certain contexts.

Examples   Yesterday, he seen her skip class.

That evening she come back from the rock concert with a big poster and new T-shirt.

She was so tired today that she laid on the couch.

The correct form of the simple past of "see" is "saw," not "seen." "Seen" is a past participle, as in "She had seen the cougar in the ravine on several occasions before it was reported in the paper." In the second example, the correct word should be "came," the simple past of "come." The third example commits a common confusion between the verbs "to lie" and "to lay" (meaning to put down an object). The simple past of "lie" is "lay." The simple past of "lay" is "laid."

More detailed help with verb tenses is provided in the *Handbook*, Section 1, Appendix B, "Irregular Verbs," p. 553. See also the English 255 website, under "Supplementary Resources," for the following related information: "Passive Verb Tenses," "Conditional and Hypothetical Constructions," "Infinitives and Gerunds," and "Modals and Related Expressions."

11. MIXED CONSTRUCTION

Because English has alternative syntactical ways to express the same idea, writers sometimes find themselves stuck between two approaches.

Example   By endorsing the candidate at today's meeting means having to support him next month as well.

The writer has got caught between two possible statements:

Corrected   Endorsing the candidate at today's meeting means having to support him next month.

By endorsing the candidate at today's meeting, you [or possibly "we"] will have to support him next month.

Mixed constructions often involve clauses joined incorrectly by coordinating and subordinating conjunctions or conjunctive adverbs.

Example   Because you are such a good writer, so you should begin to outline a book.

Corrected   You are such a good writer that you should outline a book.

Because you are such a good writer, you should outline a book.

You are a remarkably good writer, so you should outline a book.

Be careful not to use subordinate adverbial clauses as subject complements.

Example   Another difficult situation in Scrabble is when your opponent has a blank and an "S."

Corrected   Another difficult situation arises when your opponent has a blank and an "S."

constr

Be careful not to use subordinate clauses beginning with "where" to describe conditions.

Example   Envy is where you wish you had someone else's possessions.

Envy, a quality or state of being, is not a place, so the modifying word "where" (normally used to refer to places) is inappropriate. Similarly, envy is not a unit of time, so you should not use "when" in place of "where" in the above example.

12. PARALLEL STRUCTURE REQUIRED

Some sentence structures require a writer to complete—by making parallel—a grammatical structure that he or she has already begun in the sentence. Parallelism requires this completion of a language pattern. This is really a matter of word order only, which is also called syntax. Your sentence construction will be parallel if it expresses equivalent elements in equivalent syntactical divisions.

Be alert to the need for parallelism in sentence structures with the following:

A) lists
B) verbs
C) prepositions
D) a "not only . . . but also" construction
E) an "either . . . or" construction

A) Lists

Faulty parallelism   Canada has become famous for its defence of human rights, democratic health care, for the interspace Canadarm, and when SCTV produced all those good comedians.

Corrected   Canada has become famous *for its* human rights, health care, Canadarm, and SCTV comedians.

After "for its," the list now runs parallel to a series of nouns.

B) Verbs

Faulty parallelism   Recent biotechnology developments *have sparked* fierce health debates, consumer rights, outcries, and <u>have raised</u> general concern about "Frankenfoods" in everyone's grocery order.

Corrected   Recent biotechnological developments *have sparked* fierce health debates, consumer rights outcries, and general concern about "Frankenfoods" in everyone's grocery order.

By deleting "have raised" we make the sentence parallel as a list whose different items all hang on "have sparked" (have sparked a, b, and c).

C) Prepositions

Faulty parallelism	We asked for more popcorn, extra chocolates, and <u>for more</u> peanuts.
Corrected #1	We asked *for* more popcorn, chocolates, and peanuts.
Corrected #2	We asked *for* more popcorn, *for* extra chocolates, and *for* more peanuts.

Though both versions are grammatically parallel, #1 is more concise.

D) "Not only . . . but also" Constructions

Faulty parallelism	John F. Kennedy cared not only for civil rights, but also cared about increased education.
Corrected #1	John F. Kennedy cared *not only* for civil rights *but also* for education.
Corrected #2	John F. Kennedy *not only* cared for civil rights *but also* cared for education.

Though both versions are parallel, #1 is more concise. In #1, "not only . . . but also . . ." are followed by nouns introduced by the same preposition. In #2, "not only . . . but also" are followed by the operative verb.

E) "Either . . . or" Constructions

Faulty parallelism	We either take the bus or a taxi.
Corrected #1	We *either* take the bus *or* call a taxi.
Corrected #2	We take *either* the bus *or* a taxi.

13. APOSTROPHE PROBLEM

The apostrophe signals possession or contraction.

Possession

The possessive case signals that one noun possesses another. "The hat that belongs to Samantha" becomes "Samantha's hat." "The trouble in Denmark" is "Denmark's trouble."

There are two types of the possessive case: singular and plural. You can determine which one you require by asking yourself what number (how many) is or are *possessing*, not how many *are possessed*.

Singular possessive   The International Space Station's problems are serious.

Since there is only *one* space station here, you use the *singular* possessive case ('s).

Plural possessive   These various students' concerns are serious.

Since there is *more than one* student here ("various"), you would use the *plural* possessive case (s's or s').

> **Tip:** Watch out for collective nouns, which usually operate as singular nouns, though they refer to more than one person or thing.

Example   The Navy's representatives asked for a meeting with the reporter.

Contraction

A contraction uses an apostrophe to note the omission of a character in a word. Do not confuse a contraction with the possessive case.

Example   The car wouldn't start this morning.

14. OVERUSE OF PASSIVE VOICE

"Voice" is conveyed partly by the form of the verb and its helpers (the predicate); however, be careful to distinguish between the concepts of *tense* (when a thing is taking place) and *voice* (whether the subject of the action is stated as the grammatical subject of the sentence). Passive voice can operate in *any* tense.

Examples   That bridge will be crossed by me when it is gotten to by me.

That bridge is crossed by me when it is gotten to by me.

That bridge was crossed by me when it was gotten to by me.

Passive voice adds unnecessary words and often results in awkward indirectness. Note that the person doing the action in the examples above is relegated to serving as the complement of the verb "will be crossed." It is even possible to express a complete sentence in the passive voice without including the doer of the action at all.

Example   That bridge will be crossed when it is gotten to.

Grammatically, this sentence is considered complete, because "bridge" functions as the subject. As you can see, passive voice tends to be wordy, indirect, and vague. Someone will cross the bridge, but who? In certain cases, you and your reader do not need to be concerned with the identity of the doer of the action; sometimes the passive voice is preferred as a way to deflect accountability. (Example: "A problem was introduced during the processing stage." The writer may well be attempting to cover up for the culprit: who caused the problem?) Sometimes the doers of the action are less important to the idea and purpose than what they have done or said ("Smoking is prohibited," "*Basic Instinct* will be shown at midnight"). For most occasions, however, active voice is the better choice: it gives more complete information and communicates energy.

Some handbooks and instructors consider all forms of "being" or "to be" to constitute passive voice, since a state of being may be thought of as inert.

Example   She was doubtful of her chances.

The same idea can be expressed more vigorously as "She doubted her chances." To constitute true passive voice as we are defining the concept, the above sentence would have to read, "Her chances were doubted [by her]." Regardless of the line between definitions, a good general rule is to try to make the doer of the action in any sentence you write the grammatical subject of your sentence—and when you can, try to add vigour by replacing verbs of being with more energetic alternatives.

15. CONFUSION OVER RESTRICTIVE AND NON-RESTRICTIVE QUALIFIERS

Some qualifiers require two commas to set them off from the rest of the sentence, while other qualifiers do not. Qualifiers that require commas are called non-essential or non-restrictive. They are not necessary for the sentence in which they appear to function. Qualifiers that do not require commas are called restrictive and are essential for meaning in their sentences.

Restrictive   No commas/qualifier is *essential* to meaning.

Non-restrictive   Two commas if appearing within a sentence
                     One comma if appearing at the beginning or end of a sentence
                     Qualifier that is *not* essential to meaning

Example (non-restrictive) Violence in the Middle East, an ongoing problem, has
            disrupted the lives of all citizens in the region.

The qualifier "an ongoing problem" is extra, not essential to this sentence. Since the sentence's grammatical structure and meaning can work without this qualifier, it is non-restrictive: this qualifier does not restrict the meaning of what it qualifies. By placing two commas around their qualifier, you show that it is non-restrictive.

> **Tip:** Often, students will forget the second comma, therefore forgetting to close off the non-restrictive qualifier from the rest of the sentence. If you open the qualifier, remember to close it: "our Irish friend, Ulton, likes funk music."

Example (restrictive) The Tragically Hip song "Cordelia" explores the attitude of a
            self-destructive man who takes the generous concern of others for granted.

Restrictive qualifiers are sometimes tricky. If you *cannot* "pop" the qualifier out of the sentence without changing or blocking the meaning of the sentence, then it is an essential or restrictive qualifier (and so requires no commas). In our example above, if you placed commas around "Cordelia," you would mistakenly turn it into a non-restrictive qualifier and just as mistakenly convey that it is optional, or non-essential, to the sentence's meaning. If "Cordelia" were not in the sentence as it is, what song would the sentence refer to? The sentence's meaning would be unclear, so "Cordelia" is necessary, essential, and restrictive—therefore without commas.

Example   People who live in glass houses should not throw rocks.

If you *can* "pop" the qualifier out of the sentence, then it is non-restrictive (or non-essential) and requires two framing commas. A non-restrictive qualifier provides extra, not essential information.

Example   Toronto and Vancouver, our largest cities, have high costs of living.

Selected Glossary of Literary Terms

Regarding many of the terms discussed below, we refer to Alice Munro's "Thanks for the Ride." See the Reader for this short story on page 62.

Characterization refers to the techniques that fiction writers use to show us the personalities and values of imaginary people in a work of fiction (and also non-fiction). In one of the earliest major books about writing fiction, *Aspects of the Novel* (1927), E.M. Forster introduces the terms "flat" and "round" characters to differentiate between caricatured (or one-dimensional) characters and more complex portrayals that suggest multi-faceted psychology.

We can also distinguish between melodramatic and dramatic characterization. The character in a melodrama, whether a protagonist (hero) or antagonist (a character opposed to the protagonist), does not change significantly in the course of the story. Dramatic characters, on the other hand, demonstrate an arc of experience through their hoping, suffering, and learning as the story progresses.

Stories generally feature a central character as well as two or more additional main characters, and often a number of secondary and even minor characters. Traditionally, we are introduced to the central and main characters through their motivations to achieve particular main goals, and we see them confronted by internal and/or external obstacles to achieving those goals. Be alert to *how* their authors develop these characters as you read: through narrative language, the particular characters' own words, the observations of other characters, and the characters' actions.

Writers and creative writing instructors often remark that character is action: a total of what the particular character does or does not do.

The **essay** takes its name from the French word *essai*, meaning an attempt or an effort toward something. This form of non-fiction writing therefore concentrates on a concerted movement toward meaning, through observation, memory, and reflection, by uniting ethics, emotion, and logic. The essay has about it a connotation of some serious purpose, even when it adopts a stance of humour or frivolity. (Think of Jonathan Swift's classic "A Modest Proposal" (1729)!) Characterized by this seriousness of purpose, the essay is otherwise a very broad-ranging form encompassing many variations of length, structure, and method.

The term "article" sometimes is used interchangeably with the term "essay." However, an "article" suggests a piece of writing more specific to a technical field, subject, or market, with less emphasis on any particular literary intention.

Fiction refers to narratives (stories) created through the reconstruction of reality, experience, and imagination. (See "Narration" in Chapter 5, "The Personal Essay," in the *Rhetoric* for a fuller definition and discussion.) In some cases, the story may closely resemble events and characters in the world of facts, what most people call "real life." But if alterations occur in the re-telling, we say the narrative is fictionalized.

Fiction subdivides into numerous types, such as comedy, gothic, satire, and the more commercially dictated groupings, such as "literature" (the writings of Thomas Hardy, Margaret Atwood, Alice Walker), and "popular," which includes mystery, eroticism, horror, speculative fiction, historical romance, etc. (John Grisham, Stephen King, Gene Roddenberry, Harlequin Romance). Not all fiction is expressed in written prose; think of Hollywood films or a community rumour, for example.

Image refers to any vivid detail that appeals to any of the five senses. Alice Munro's "Thanks for the Ride" abounds in rich, sharp, distinctive images, from the opening "fly-speckled" signs to the concluding experience of Lois in her outlandish party dress calling out in a voice described as "crude," "abusive," and "forlorn." Imagery contributes to atmosphere and tone; often it also acquires the power of symbol.

Irony also features as an important element in many stories. The simplest definition of irony is "distance." We describe a situation as ironic if what occurs or what is believed contrasts with what we think should happen, according to logic and our values. With irony, an apparent or superficial meaning differs sharply from (and often is the opposite of) a deeper meaning. For example, in "Thanks for the Ride" we recognize irony in the fact that a jaded young woman (Lois) lives in a town that claims to love its children.

Various forms of irony may be defined; broadly speaking, three common forms are *verbal*, *situational*, and *attitudinal*. We see verbal irony in someone's saying the opposite of what she means. Situational irony exists in something happening that opposes what common sense indicates it would be. We deduce attitudinal irony in one fictional character's thinking of or perceiving reality in a certain way when the reader and possibly other characters realize the opposite is true. Writers often use the naïveté of the central character, sometimes from whose point of view the story is told, as a form of attitudinal irony.

Metaphor is not easily separated from **symbol**. To stress the distinction, think of symbol as more imagistic and static; metaphor tends to apply to an entire action or situation, often one that carries on throughout a whole story. In Albert Camus's novel *The Plague* (originally published in French as *La Peste* in 1947), for example, rats begin dying in an Algerian city. Soon people begin to die, and both characters and the reader learn that bubonic plague has gripped the town. We can consider the disease, the quarantine it imposes, and its wake of destruction throughout the story a metaphor for a spiritual sickness in humanity. Writers often use blindness, illness, and physical de-

formity to convey metaphoric meaning in stories, symbolic references to underlying themes. Meaphors and symbols generate coded reference to concepts, events, or things.

Non-fiction encompasses the large realm of prose that is not fiction. The defining feature of non-fiction prose is its loyalty to actual facts, knowledge, and experience in the world outside the text, as opposed to those aspects invented or creatively amplified. Non-fiction subdivides into numerous categories such as biography, autobiography, the essay, and any number of works in specialized fields, such as history, psychology, and other disciplines and genres.

Despite its standard definition, students should never accept "non-fiction" at face value. The supposed clarity of non-fiction as a category of "pure fact" has come under increasing pressure recently through theoretical questions about the powerful influence of personal perspective (subjectivity) on the representation of raw events, cause-effect relations, and outcomes. Put another way, a rich person and a poor one would write very different books on any subject, though both works are non-fiction.

The pervasive influence of the writer's perspective on any set of facts—what is "actual"—is not as simple as determining whether those facts are "true" or "false." The impact of perspective can be as subtle as the *arrangement* of the facts and the presence or absence of *context* for the facts, or the *absence* or *omission* of certain facts. For example, Pierre Trudeau's views about the nature of Canadian society and identity were utterly opposed to those of the Quebec nationalists, though we could say that both were working with the same basic facts.

Pace refers to the rate at which storytellers reveal information and complications in the course of their writings. A writer who slows down the conveying of this information risks losing the reader, but slowing down also allows that writer to build suspense and intensity. Too fast a pace can also lose the reader: he or she will not have the time to develop sufficient interest in the characters and events. A knowledgeable writer grabs the reader's attention and feeds the reader just enough information to keep him or her turning the pages. While satisfying the reader's curiosity about one point, the writer raises his or her curiosity about another.

There are primarily four ways that fiction writers reveal information and engage their readers' interest while controlling pace: description, scene/action, exposition, and narrative summary.

From the storyteller's point of view, what would be the advantages and disadvantages of each? Here is an illustration of each method from "Thanks for the Ride":

Description

It was getting dark in there, and they had not turned the lights on, but you could still read the signs plastered against the mirror between the fly-speckled and slightly yellowed cutouts of strawberry sundaes and tomato sandwiches.

Scene/dialogue

Now I felt vengeful, and I said softly, "I had quite a talk with your mother."
"I can imagine," said Lois.
"She told me about that guy you went out with last summer."
"This summer."
"It's last summer now. He was engaged or something, wasn't he?"

[The scene continues in this manner for another page and a half.]

Exposition

I was just out of high-school at this time, and George had been working for three years in the Men's Shoes in a downtown department store, so there was that difference. But we had never bothered with each other back in the city. We were together now because we had met unexpectedly in a strange place and because I had a little money, while George was broke . . . .

[The passage of exposition continues for another two-and-one-half paragraphs, blending into a description of the town they are visiting, itself introduced through exposition.]

Narrative summary

We drove out of town to a farmhouse where a woman sold us a whisky bottle full of muddy-looking home-made liquor . . . .

Plot refers to a story's incidents and developments, to the pattern of causally linked events. E.M Forster points out that to say the king died and then the queen died is to tell a very brief story; to say that the king died and then the queen *died of a broken heart* is to tell a plot. The difference between story and plot is this link between cause and effect; in story, events may be said to transpire but, in plot, events specifically create, shape, and emerge from each other.

Bernard Grebanier is professor emeritus of English literature at Brooklyn College, a literary critic and writing instructor, and the author of *The Heart of Hamlet* and *Playwriting*. He has adapted the ideas of

William T. Price (1846–1920), likening plot to the syllogism of logic. (See "Deductive Reasoning" in Chapter 7 regarding syllogism.) He believes that plot, like syllogism, can be expressed in three steps. The first step of plot, the "condition" of the action, contains the roots of what follows. The middle step, the "cause," follows from the first step, of course, and raises the central question, which the rest of the story will answer. The third step of plot answers any main concerns posed by the major event of step 2.

What three steps would you offer to define the plot of "Thanks for the Ride"? Here is one suggested answer, in terms of the main character:

- Lois meets Dick. (Condition of action)
- She agrees to go with him for a ride. (Major action raising the story's main question)
- Will she find meaning in the experience? (Answer: The experience disappoints her.)

Are you surprised that we have suggested stating the plot in terms of Lois, our perceived main character? Dick narrates the story; he is the first character we get to know. Yet he is passive, more onlooker than actor. Lois, whose final words give the story its title, is the one who takes decisive action. The story could not occur if Lois did not agree to go along—and Adelaide makes it clear that Lois might say no to the boys' invitation to join them.

In literary fiction (fiction intended primarily to challenge the reader rather than to satisfy a more mainstream market), plot may often appear hard to isolate and identify. Many experimental writers choose to situate their plots far from easy view. William Faulkner's *The Sound and the Fury* (1929), Virginia Woolf's *To the Lighthouse* (1927), and James Joyce's *Finnegans Wake* (1939), for example, all reveal their plots through highly sophisticated and complicated structures that upset more familiar, linear developments of the action. Such non-chronological presentations force readers to delve deeply into individual characterizations: to try to understand *effects* (decisions, moods, attitudes, rationales, action) and put them into context without the benefit of explicit and immediate *causes*.

A final caution about plot: To think and write significantly about any story, you must identify its plot as precisely as you can. Unless your instructor requests a plot summary, however, you may assume your reader already knows the plot of the story. Your essay should explore and examine meaning within the story rather than merely summarize its plot. If you do refer to an element of the plot, ask yourself about the significance of that observation to your interpretation of the story. This question (sometimes called the "so what?" question) will help steer you clear of mere plot summary.

Poetry, it is often said, requires a lifetime to be defined and re-defined. Simply speaking, it offers thoughts, feelings, and insights through carefully crafted language that heightens the reader's awareness of sound and image. Lines of poetry do not run right across the page in the standard form of prose; they may be very short or they may vary in length. Like music, poetry specializes in intensity and compression of expression, so the average poem is much shorter than the average essay or article.

Many readers would say that poetry challenges the conventions of expression and communication far more than most prose does, since prose, by definition, works within a stricter—or, at least, more clearly definable—framework of language and rules. Certain creative works also deliberately cross the border between prose and poetry, such as Elizabeth Smart's *By Grand Central Station I Sat Down and Wept* (1945), Michael Ondaatje's *In the Skin of a Lion* (1987), Kristjana Gunnars's *The Substance of Forgetting* (1992), and Fred Wah's *Diamond Grill* (1996).

Point of view refers to the perspective of narrative observation. Is a character *in* the story telling that story through the *first-person* point of view? If so, the narrator will refer to himself or herself by the pronouns "I" and "me." How involved in the action is this first-person narrator? Does a first-person *observer* or a first-person *participant* tell the story? What is the narrator's emotional and social investment in the other characters, events, and outcomes?

If the narrator is not identified by name or pronoun and absent from events in the story, we deduce that the point of view is usually *third person*. The third-person narrator may be *omniscient* (all-knowing), a privileged party to the thoughts of all the characters, their feelings and experiences. Yet, he or she may be restricted to the thoughts, feelings, and experiences of only one specific character or more at any one time, not capable of understanding all the characters from within their own thoughts. This *limited third person* becomes clear as the narrator recounts parts of the story through the consciousness of one particular character at a time.

Within limited or selected third person, then, we can find varying degrees of this proximity between narrator and charater. A substantial mingling of the narrator's and any one character's language and out-

look is often referred to as *free indirect discourse*. In this narrative strategy, character experience and third-person points of view nearly overlap.

Both characters' and narrators' points of view may also follow a *stream of consciousness*, which presents the spontaneous mind of the focus character moment by moment. The text replicates the erratic and eccentric flow of a character's private thoughts and inner moods. This heightened psychological realism, which includes random associations and sudden memory fragments, unsettles narrative conventions of clear cause-effect in plot and the predictability we have come to expect in most characterization.

Fiction writers can also present their third-person narratives as objective or *detached* narrative points of view. In this case, the subject is seen only from the outside, as it would be by a camera: clinically, sociologically, coldly. Ernest Hemingway frequently practised this spare, disassociative, sometimes alienating technique. Another less common technique is that of addressing the reader directly, as "you" (*second person*), though, as Jay McInerney's 1984 novel *Bright Lights, Big City* proved, it can be very successful. Both detached and second-person techniques bring about new cause-effect associations, surprising narrative presentations, sudden intensities, and vital challenges to our presumptions and comfort as readers.

An ongoing issue concerning narrative point of view is the reliability of the narrator. Reliability involves more than accuracy; it also concerns psychology and ethics. What are the narrator's motives in telling a tale? Does the surface of the story differ from its undercurrents? To what purpose? Can we trust what we are being told? These questions go to the heart of narrative and representation itself. What clues do we find to help us address this issue of reliability? This is how fiction challenges all its readers—specifically through the various problems and challenges of narration.

Closely related to point of view are *voice* and *tone*. Through the writer's choice of words, we learn about the narrator's intellectual and emotional nature, level of formal education, class and cultural background, and idiosyncratic speech mannerisms. All of these elements contribute to voice. Tone refers to the more specific emotional response and attitude of the narrator toward the subject: for example, resigned, angry, depressed, etc. (See our discussions of tone and voice in Chapter 2, "Reviewing the Basics.")

Prose is a broad label for all speech or writing that is conversational (rather than patterned into lines or rhythms or verse, like poetry). Prose usually consists of complete sentences, and the lines of written prose run fully across the page. Orderly prose arranges its sentences into clearly unified paragraphs. Prose may be used for non-fiction or for fiction. Your letter or email to a friend is prose, as is the Canadian Charter of Rights and Freedoms or Lucy Maude Montgomery's *Anne of Green Gables*.

While some experimental prose flouts or plays with the grammar, word order (syntax), and visual presentation of orderly language, learn to control your prose before you depart from the rules and your reader's basic expectations.

Setting refers not only to where a story takes place; it covers the historical period and the span of time that runs from the beginning to the end of the narrative. Like all the elements of fiction, setting shapes and is shaped by the other elements. So, while the setting for a novel may definitely be Vancouver in the 1930s, the reader's impression of that setting will be shaped by the author's combined narration, characterization, plot, symbols, and theme.

The physical environment and our *sense* of the setting are certainly related, yet we can also try to distinguish between them in our reading and interpretation. Often, Canadian screenwriters hoping to sell their stories to Hollywood adopt generic American settings in the belief that American producers and audiences will be alienated by Canadian settings. Sometimes the use of a generic setting, such as a mid-America "anywhere," can be effective artistically, especially if the writer wishes to emphasize other elements of the story.

More often, however, removal of a story from its particular environment guts the narrative of its heart and soul. Novelists such as Charles Dickens, Flannery O'Connor, William Faulkner, and Margaret Laurence are rightly celebrated for an ability to imbue their works with intense representations of the places they know well. Setting in literature almost always expresses a psychological, moral, and even spiritual attitude rather than a mere collection of physical details. It is often said that stories, while universal in theme, can arise only from the particular places where they take place.

In Western culture we can trace the form of the **short story** in prose back to the Bible. As a formal genre, however, the short story emerged in the nineteenth century, through the works of writers such as Guy de Maupassant in France and Anton Chekhov in Russia.

In contrast to longer fictional form of the novel, the short story typically concentrates on one plot line or incident, within a contained time frame, concerning a limited number of characters. Since the form is so brief, all the elements in a short story resonate with particular meaning. The art of the story, therefore, is one of great clarity, but also one of impressions and suggestions.

Subject refers to the ostensible topic, to what the story is about. We can consider subject on two levels. First, we can identify the represented concrete or physical subject. Munro's "Thanks for the Ride" examines the subject of casual teenage sexuality, of two young men and two young women looking for a one-night fling. On a more abstract or general level, the story illuminates another aspect, the subject of romantic and social disillusion.

Theme may be the last element you define after several careful re-readings, but it is the most important one to keep in mind when you are writing about your selected story. Consider theme as similar to the thesis of an essay (see Chapter 3, "Thesis Statements"): it expresses, completely yet concisely, some essence of what the author wishes to say about the subject. We cannot isolate the theme in a story as quickly as we can, say, its setting or its individual characterizations; we must interpret the theme. In most works of fiction, we can find two or even more possible themes, sometimes standing in apparent opposition to one other!

For instance, "Thanks for the Ride" may seem to express an entirely cynical view of young male sexual behaviour (George and the summer "boy friend"), yet many years after his seemingly empty encounter with Lois, Dick remains sufficiently moved to write sympathetically about her—perhaps even with undertones of real affection. Munro's choice of narrator and point of view, telling the story years later, suggests that the incident was far from meaningless for Dick. Munro's choice further raises the question of whether it was, or could have been, more meaningful for Lois than she realized at the time. If Dick's involved narration represents, however faintly, an aspect of noble intention, then Lois's malaise adds a tragic note. We miss this point if we focus only on the theme of the rapacious males represented by George and, presumably, the summer boyfriend. When we find two or more themes contending in one story, we can respond in several ways: we can try to reconcile them into a new, perhaps deeper understanding of the subject, or we can assign one precedence over another in our argument, while we acknowledge that another theme also exists.

Literary Credits

Christina Angaran, "An Ideal Vacation Spot" and "Friendship." Reprinted by permission of the author.

Matthew Arnold, "Dover Beach." From *Arnold: Poetical Works,* edited by C.B. Tinker and H.F. Lowry. Oxford: Oxford University Press, 1950.

Margaret Atwood, "Canadians: What Do They Want?" Reprinted with permission from *Mother Jones* (January 1982), © 1982, Foundation for National Progress.

Gisela Becker, "Midwife in Rankin Inlet" and "Scuba Diving." Reprinted by permission of the author.

Wayne C. Booth, "The Rhetorical Stance." From *College Composition and Communication*, copyright © 1963 by the National Council of Teachers of English. Reprinted with permission.

Roch Carrier, "The Hockey Sweater." From *The Hockey Sweater and Other Stories*, copyright © 1979 by House of Anansi Press. Reprinted by permission.

Ellen Clark, "Quebec Separation: Anglophones Can Win at This Game, Too." Reprinted by permission of the author.

Lorena Collins, "Timone." Reprinted by permission of the author.

Nancy Corscadden, "Sample Critique of 'Life in the Stopwatch Lane.'" Reprinted by permission of the author.

Amy Willard Cross, "Life in the Stopwatch Lane." Originally published in *The Globe and Mail*, July 5, 1990. Reprinted by permission of the author.

Robertson Davies, "The Pleasures of Love." Originally published in *Saturday Night* Magazine, December 23, 1961. Used by permission of the Estate of Robertson Davies.

Gail Deagle, "Euthanasia Reconsidered." Reprinted by permission of the author.

Pat Deiter-McArthur, "Saskatchewan Indian People: Five Generations." From *Writing the Circle: Native Women of Western Canada*. Edited by Jeanne Perreault and Sylvia Vance. Edmonton: NeWest Publishers Limited, 1990. Reprinted by permission.

Rhonda Delorme, "University Education: Traditional or Distance?" Reprinted by permission of the author.

James Downey, "A Liberal Education Is Key to a Civil Society." From *Carleton University Magazine*, Spring 2000. Reprinted by permission of Carleton University Magazine.

Jane Farrow, "Diary Rock." From *Saturday Night* Magazine, December 1999/January 2000. Reprinted by permission of Jane Farrow, writer and broadcaster.

Roger Fouts, "Brownie." From *Next of Kin* by Roger Fouts and Stephen Tukel Mills. Copyright © 1997 by Roger Fouts. Reprinted by permission of HarperCollins Publishers Inc.

John Gray, "You're Thinking of Getting a What?" From *I Love Mom: An Irreverent History of the Tattoo* by John Gray (Toronto: Key Porter Books, 1994). Reprinted by permission of Key Porter Books.

Dr. Ella Haley, "The Toxic Legacy of the Phosphate Fertilizer Industry." Reprinted by permission of the author.

François Hébert, "Je Me Souviens." From *Saturday Night* Magazine, June 24, 2000. Reprinted by permission of the author.

Brian D. Johnson, "Atom's Journey." Excerpted from *Maclean's* Magazine, September 13, 1999. Reprinted by permission of Maclean's Magazine.

Carl Jung, "On Synchronicity." Originally published in *The Structure and Dynamics of the Psyche: Collected Works* (Vol. 8, par. 969-997) (New York: Bollingen Foundation, 1960). Copyright © 1969 by Princeton University Press. Reprinted by permission of Princeton University Press.

Susan M. Keaveney, "When MTV Goes CEO." Reprinted with permission from *Marketing Management*, published by the American Marketing Association, Fall 1997.

Melanie Klingbeil, "Beyond the Answers." Reprinted by permission of the author.

Thomas LaBrie, "Franken-Frogs and the Mushroom Bear." Reprinted by permission of the author.

Anita Lahey, "The Genome Generation." This article first appeared in *Canadian Business* Magazine, October 1999. Reprinted by permission of the author.

Lisa Lemieux, "Fact or Photo?" Reprinted by permission of the author.

Nicole Lombard, "Speaking South African English in Canada."

John Markoff, "The Doomsday Machines." From *The New York Times*, March 19, 2000. Copyright © 2000 by the New York Times Co. Reprinted with permission.

Susan McClelland, "The Lure of the Body Image." From *Maclean's* Magazine, February 22, 1999. Reprinted by permission of Maclean's Magazine.

Marni McNaughton, "Sample Critique of 'You're Thinking of Getting a What?'" Reprinted by permission of the author.

Joyce Miller, "Night Fades." Reprinted by permission of the author.

Diane Mooney, "Newfoundlandese, if You Please." Reprinted by permission of the author.

Bharati Mukherjee, "The Tenant." From *The Middleman and Other Stories* by Bharati Mukherjee. Copyright © Bharati Mukherjee, 1988. Reprinted by permission of Penguin Books Canada Limited.

Alice Munro, "Thanks for the Ride." From *Dance of the Happy Shades* (Toronto: Ryerson Press, 1968).

Reprinted by permission of McGraw-Hill Ryerson Ltd.

George Orwell, "Politics and the English Language." Copyright © George Orwell, 1946. By permission of Bill Hamilton as the Literary Executor of the Estate of the Late Sonia Brownell Orwell and Secker & Warburg Ltd.

Philip Kevin Paul, "Belly Button." From *Breathing Fire: Canada's New Poets*, edited by Patrick Lane and Lorna Crozier (Madeira Park, BC: Harbour Publishing, 1995). Reprinted by permission of the author.

Tamara Pelletier, "Suspended in Time." Reprinted by permission of the author.

Kim Pittaway, "Crystal Balls." Originally published in *Chatelaine* magazine, "herspective," January 2000.

Plato, "The Allegory of the Cave." From *The Republic*, Book VII. In *The Dialogues of Plato*, Vol. 11, trans. B. Jowett. Oxford: Clarendon Press.

Brenda Platt, "Global Warming and Population." Reprinted by permission of the author.

Janice Procée, "The Case for Active Euthanasia." Reprinted by permission of the author.

Mark Radford, "Different Worlds." Reprinted by permission of the author.

Daphne Read, "A Story to Pass On." This is a revised and shortened version of "Writing Trauma, History, Story: The Class(room) as Borderland," *JAC: A Journal of Composition Theory* 18.1 (1998): 105–21.

Howard Richler, "The Seven Deadly Sins Are 'In' and Proud of It." From *A Bawdy Language: How a Second-Rate Language Slept Its Way to the Top* by Howard Richler (Toronto: Stoddart, 1999). Reprinted by permission of the author.

Mordecai Richler, "The Summer My Grandmother Was Supposed to Die." From *The Street* by Mordecai Richler. Used by permission of McClelland & Stewart Ltd., *The Canadian Publishers*.

Murray Ross, "Football Red and Baseball Green." From *The Essayist*, Eds. Sheridan Baker and C. Jeriel Howard, 5th ed. (New York: Harper and Row, 1985). Reprinted by permission of the author.

Bertrand Russell, "What I Have Lived For." Prologue to *The Autobiography of Bertrand Russell*, 3 vols. (London: George Allen & Unwin, 1967, 1968, 1969). Reprinted by permission of The Bertrand Russell Peace Foundation and Taylor and Francis Book Ltd.

Leanna Rutherford, "An Anorexic's Recovery." First published in *Canadian Living* Magazine, October 1998 (vol. 23, no. 10). Reprinted by permission of the author.

Habeeb Salloum, "The Other Canadians and Canada's Future." From *Contemporary Review*, March 1997. Copyright Contemporary Review Company. Reprinted with permission.

Sarah Schmidt, "From College Girl to Call Girl." From *The Globe and Mail*, April 29, 2000. Reprinted by permission of the author. Sarah Schmidt is a senior writer (education) for CanWest News Service.

Rupert Sheldrake, *Dogs That Know When Their Owners Are Coming Home and Other Unexplained Powers of Animals*. (New York: Three Rivers Press, 2000). Reprinted by permission of Random House, Inc.

Guy Sprung, "In Search of Wawa, or Notes from My Lagostina Box." Reprinted by permission of the author.

David Suzuki, "The Right Stuff." From *Inventing the Future: Reflections on Science, Technology, and Nature* (Toronto: Stoddart, 1989). Reprinted by permission of David Suzuki, Professor Emeritus, University of British Columbia.

Pamela Swanigan, "I Am Half-Canadian." From *Saturday Night* Magazine, January 27, 2001. Reprinted by permission of the author.

Stewart Thompson, "Sports Salaries: No Cap Needed" and "Sports Salaries: Enough Is Enough." Reprinted by permission of the author.

Milena Tomol, "Equal Share of Miseries." Reprinted by permission of the author.

Michel Tremblay, "The King and I." Reprinted from *Bambi and Me* by Michel Tremblay, translated by Sheila Fischman, © 1988, Talon Books Ltd., Canada.

Pierre Elliott Trudeau, "The Ascetic in a Canoe." From *Against the Current: Selected Writings 1939–1996* by Pierre Elliott Trudeau. Used by permission, McClelland & Stewart Ltd., *The Canadian Publishers*.

Emma Lee Warrior, "White Breast Flats." From *A Gathering of Spirit: Writing and Art by North American Indian Women*, ed. by Beth Brant (Ann Arbor, MI: Firebrand Books, 2001). Reprinted by permission of Firebrand Books, Milford, Connecticut.

Corinne Wasylewich, "Marathon Journal." Reprinted by permission of the author.

Dorothy Williams, "The Quebec Experience: Slavery 1628–1834." Originally published in *Blacks in Montreal 1628–1986: An Urban Demography* by Les Éditions Yvon Blais Inc., 1989. This version abridged from *Boundaries of Identity: A Quebec Reader*, ed. William Dodge (Toronto: Lester Publishing, 1992). Reprinted by permission of the author.

William Butler Yeats, "The Second Coming." Reprinted from *The Poems of William Butler Yeats* (London: Macmillan, 1935).

Index